# Microsoft Visual C++ 6.0 Programmer's Guide

**Beck Zaratian**

PUBLISHED BY
Microsoft Press
A Division of Microsoft Corporation
One Microsoft Way
Redmond, Washington 98052-6399

Library of Congress Cataloging-in-Publication Data
Zaratian, Beck, 1952-
      Microsoft Visual C++ 6.0 Programmer's Guide / Beck Zaratian.
          p.   cm.
      Includes index.
      ISBN 1-57231-866-X
      1. C++  (Computer program language)   2. Microsoft Visual C++.
   I. Title.
   QA76.73.C153Z365   1998
   005.13'3--dc21                                        98-13997
                                                          CIP

Printed and bound in the United States of America.

1  2  3  4  5  6  7  8  9   WCWC   3 2 1 0 9 8

Distributed in Canada by ITP Nelson, a division of Thomson Canada Limited.

A CIP catalogue record for this book is available from the British Library.

Microsoft Press books are available through booksellers and distributors worldwide. For further information about international editions, contact your local Microsoft Corporation office or contact Microsoft Press International directly at fax (425) 936-7329. Visit our Web site at mspress.microsoft.com.

**Acquisitions Editor:** Eric Stroo
**Project Editor:** Saul Candib
**Manuscript and Technical Editing:**  Labrecque Publishing

*To Christine*

# CONTENTS *at a Glance*

# Acknowledgments

Second editions are easier to write than first editions, a writer's maxim that one begins to question half way through the second edition. But I enjoyed writing (or rather, expanding) this book, largely because I again had the help of dedicated people. Although the Microsoft Press team who handled the earlier edition have moved on to other tasks—a given in the fluid universe of book publishing—their contributions still live in the book, stamping it forever with their care and competence.

For the first edition, Lucinda Rowley served as project editor, devoting much time and a keen eye to reviewing manuscripts while handling a thousand other chores. (In that edition, titled *Microsoft Visual C++ Owner's Manual*, I dubbed Lucinda "the editor every writer dreams of." Still feel that way.) Manuscript editor Vicky Thulman pored over each sentence and technical editors Linda Ebenstein and Jim Johnson ensured that those sentences were accurate.

Saul Candib took over as project editor for this edition, while Jim Fuchs, Mary DeJong, and Michael Hochberg served as technical editors, carefully reviewing new material. Labrecque Publishing of San Francisco provided manuscript editing, page composition, proofreading, and production management; for these services, thanks go to Chrisa Hotchkiss, Curtis Philips, Lisa Bravo, Andrea Fox, and Lisa Labrecque.

Assistance of course came not only from the offices of Press and Labrecque, but also from the labyrinthine hallways of Building 42 on the Microsoft campus, home of the Visual C++ department. As before, Laura Hamilton generously acted as liaison—I'm glad I don't have to write a book like this without her help. Laura is a superb editor, and can claim credit for much of what is good both in this book and in the online *Visual C++ User's Guide*.

This edition builds on the help of the many people in the Visual C++ group (and elsewhere) who offered valuable suggestions and corrections for the first edition. Others reviewed new material for this edition, representing a collective effort that assures the book's continued accuracy and viability. My thanks go (in alphabetical order) to Dennis Andersen, Cathy Anderson, Chuck Bell, Diane Berkeley, Patricia Cornette, Stacey Doerr, Chris Flaat, Jocelyn Garner, Anita George, Eric Gunnerson, Karl Hilsmann, Mark Hopkins, Simon Koeman, Chris Koziarz, Louis Lafreniere, Martin Lovell, Michael Maio, Bruce McKinney, Diane Melde, Daryn Robbins, Steve Ross, David Schwartz, Scott Semyan, Terri Sharkey, George Shepherd, Kathy Shoesmith, Suzanne Sowinska, Yefim Sigal, Chuck Sphar, Yeong-Kah Tam, Donn Trenton, and Laura Wall. Some of these people are friends whom I've known for years. Others I've never met face-to-face, communicating only through the twin miracles of e-mail and Federal Express.

Barbara Ellsworth at Microsoft deserves special mention, since without her the book would not have been written. Thanks, Barb.

Formerly titled
*Microsoft Visual C++ Owner's Manual*

# Introduction

This book is about Microsoft Visual C++. Not the C++ language, not the MFC library, just Visual C++ itself.

True, Visual C++ already comes with a sort of programmer's guide—it's called online help. The vastness of the help system will probably inspire in you the confident belief that what you want to know is in there somewhere. But that's the problem with online help: it works best when you know what you're looking for. This book complements online help, but does not replace it. Purposes and styles of the help system and the written word are inherently too different for one to supplant the other. Where one dispenses information, the other teaches, if you see what I mean. Where one has breadth the other has depth. In presenting the cold facts as tersely as possible, online help can't afford to elaborate, giving you instead a list of steps to follow to accomplish some task but rarely taking the time to paint a larger view. You get the *how* that informs but not the *why* that teaches.

This book intends to make you a proficient user of Visual C++. It unfolds in a logical progression of material, demonstrates how parts of the whole interact, clarifies with sample code, and generally acts as a tutor. Moreover, you can curl up with it in your favorite chair. These are exactly the advantages that online help lacks. Help, on the other hand, offers immediacy and breadth. The many megabytes of help text can touch every obscure corner of Visual C++, while this book covers only the essentials. Start with this book to acquire a solid grounding in the art of Visual C++, then turn to online help as you become more experienced and your questions more arcane. Paradoxically, the more adept you are with the product the more online help will be of service to you.

The book is older than its title. The first edition appeared as *Microsoft Visual C++ Owner's Manual*, becoming Microsoft's official guide for Visual C++ version 5. But Microsoft has retitled this second edition to position it as part of a five-volume set of *Programmer's Guides* documenting the development tools of Visual Studio 98, including Visual Basic, Visual J++, Visual FoxPro, and Visual InterDev. The *Guides* function independently, however, so if your interest is confined to Visual C++, you've come to the right place. Any similarities between this *Guide* and the others stops at the cover, since the other books are printed copies of online help, exact reproductions of the online documentation that comes with each product. You will find this book very different from the other *Guides* in the set.

Microsoft has good reasons for renaming the book, but I regret losing the original title. I chose *Owner's Manual* to convey as clearly as possible the focus of the book to make sure that you, the reader, have an idea of what's covered and what isn't. A hundred years ago in an age more tolerant of lengthy titles I could have tacked on something like, *Being a Tutorial, Companion, and Reference Intending to Further Knowledge of and Familiarity with the Microsoft Visual C++ Compiler, Without Digressing into the Interesting Though Ancillary Subjects of the C++ Programming Language and the Microsoft Foundation Class Library*. Admittedly, that scholarly title wouldn't be entirely accurate. Visual C++ is so integrally tied to the C++ language and the MFC library that it's impossible to talk intelligently about Visual C++ while remaining mute on the other two subjects. The chapters that follow present many example fragments and programs, the purpose of which is to illustrate some aspect of Visual C++. Code must have commentary—it's useless otherwise—and descriptions of the example programs necessarily spill over into the topics of technique and MFC. But these occurrences are isolated and do not distract from the main focus of how to use the compiler. Other excellent books are available that explain C++ programming and the MFC library.

This book describes version 6 of Visual C++, but owners of earlier versions can also benefit from a reading. Some aspects of Visual C++ have changed considerably since previous versions, but many other areas have changed little or not at all. These days Visual C++ comes in a deceptively slim package containing a few flyers, some printed material, and a CD-ROM or two. But since you've read this far you probably realize an immense amount of material exists in Visual C++. I call it a "compiler" only for lack of a better name. Besides the compiler itself, Visual C++ provides a linker, a make utility, a debugger, a text editor, resource editors, a development environment, the Microsoft Foundation Class library (MFC), run-time libraries, many thousands of lines of source code, and a lot more. To repeat: this book does not examine everything. My aim is to help you master Visual C++, not bury you in minutiae.

## What You Should Already Know

A book of this type has to begin on the learning curve somewhere above point zero. Start too low and discussions become hopelessly muddled with preliminary explanations. Start too high and the author loses much of his audience (besides coming across as a pinhead). The trick is to speak in one voice to a readership made up of widely varied skills and interests, yet lose no one when speaking of esoterica and insult no one when presenting the fundamentals. The book makes no great demands. I assume you are already familiar with the C and C++ programming languages, have programmed before for Windows, and have at least a nodding acquaintance with MFC. You don't have to be an expert by any means, but you'll find the text and sample code easier to follow if you understand basic ideas such as pointers, classes, and messages. Fortunately, there's nothing abstract about a compiler. It's just software.

## A Brief History of Visual C++

One can make a case that the roots of Visual C++ began not with Microsoft but with Borland. Some readers may remember Turbo Pascal, which brought to DOS the idea of the integrated development environment or IDE. IDE is yet another abbreviation in a field already top-heavy with them. It just means the editor and the compiler work together, both accessible from the same place. You write your source code in the editor, hit the Compile button to launch the compiler, and when it finds an error the compiler sets the editor's cursor on the offending statement, ready for you to correct the problem. The idea is to provide an environment for program development that the programmer never has to leave.

The C language was catching on at this time (c. 1987), and Turbo Pascal led to Turbo C. Microsoft countered with a similar product named QuickC. I was contracted to do some programming work associated with QuickC and ended up writing a few chapters of a how-to book included in the package, titled *C for Yourself*. (The title wasn't my idea.) QuickC sold as a stand-alone product but was also included as part of Microsoft's C compiler, which we called Big C. At the time, Big C stood at version 5. Its competition included names from what now seems a misty past: Computer Innovations, Datalight, Lattice, Manx. Others of that era have survived, notably Borland and Watcom (now PowerSoft). Their fine products continue to provide healthy competition for Microsoft.

The purpose of pairing QuickC with Big C was so programmers could write code in QuickC's convenient IDE. QuickC offered fast compile times, mostly because it made only the faintest attempts at code optimization. (We'll talk about optimization later in this book and see how it can affect build times.) When it came to optimizing, QuickC was happy to enregister some variables, insert a few LEAVE instructions, and call it a day. The result was quick compiler turnaround. After a program was debugged and running in QuickC, the programmer could then create a release version with Big C, which was far more serious about code optimization. It wasn't unusual to shave 15 percent or more off the size of a program when compiled with Big C.

QuickC and Turbo C introduced many to C programming, but never earned the permanent affection of developers. For one thing, the editors of both products were not very good. (The QuickC editor was later incorporated into Microsoft QuickBasic and still exists today in Microsoft

Windows 95 as the DOS editor Edit.com.) Another problem with IDEs under DOS was that they took up a lot of memory, leaving little for executing the program under development. You often had to exit the IDE to run and debug your program. Many programmers who used QuickC in development work (myself included) relied only on its command line version.

But then Windows 3.0 came along.

Windows 3.0 and especially 3.1 ushered in the era of the serious IDE for the personal computer. The constraints of memory disappeared. And if you were going to program for Windows, a Windows environment seemed a natural place to be. It was clear that programming *for* Windows *in* Windows produces better products. Windows is a mindset, and working in it all day gives one better instincts about what a program should or should not do.

To the surprise of many, Microsoft concentrated its efforts in shoring up the internals of its C compiler rather than in upgrading its interface for the new age. When version 7 came out it was still a DOS-based product that ran either in a DOS box in Windows or with an extended memory manager (it came with Qualitas's 386Max right in the box). As a concession, version 7 offered a character-mode IDE named Programmer's Workbench that was cumbersome by today's standards. Nevertheless, the Workbench demonstrated a natural evolution from the days of QuickC. Many commands from its menus still seem modern, such as New, Open, Save As, Build, and Open Project.

The important contribution that version 7 made to the programming world was not its IDE but its support for C++. For the first time, Microsoft designated its compiler "C/C++" to emphasize its new dual nature. It was like watching a cell undergo mitosis. The support involved more than simply expanding the compiler to recognize new commands of the C++ superset. C/C++ version 7 also introduced version 1 of the Microsoft Foundation Class library, complete with source code. C++ would not be so popular a vehicle for Windows programming today without this competent set of prewritten classes, which Microsoft wisely gave away to developers.

With the next major release, Microsoft abandoned most of its product's ties to DOS. Microsoft C/C++ version 8, which sported a real Windows IDE, became known as Visual C++ version 1. The name capitalized on the success of the earlier Visual Basic but the two products never compared very well. Where Visual Basic allows the developer to build a working Windows program with lots of clicking and little coding, Visual C++ creates only starter source files through special dynamic link libraries called wizards. As we'll see in Chapter 2, wizards save much of the repetitive front-end work of development, the kind of work common to many Windows programs written with MFC.

After Visual C++ 1.5, Microsoft decided not to invest any more effort in supporting 16-bit programming. Visual C++ 2 still offered 16-bit support, but since then Visual C++ creates only 32-bit applications. There never was a Visual C++ 3. The release number skipped from 2 to 4 to synchronize Visual C++ and MFC, thus ending a small source of confusion. The consolidation was short-lived, however, since Visual C++ and MFC again use different version numbers.

The popularity of the Internet has clearly influenced the product's design, and in its fourth release Visual C++ introduced new library classes designed for Internet programming. Version 5 also added some new classes, but concentrated more on improving the product's interface to provide a better online help system, much superior macro capabilities, and support for sharing classes and other code within a team of developers. Version 5 also integrated the Active Template Library and significantly improved the compiler's ability to optimize code. As we will see in later chapters, version 6 extends these improvements even further.

## What's in this Book

The book is divided into six main sections, each covering a general subject about Visual C++ and its development environment. Discussions are intentionally kept basic up through Chapter 3, which covers the text editor. This helps ensure that every reader, whether novice or expert, is able to successfully navigate the Visual C++ development environment and write source code in the text editor. Beginning with Chapter 4, discussions gradually become more technical.

## Part 1—Basics

Much of what we call Visual C++ is actually its development environment, named Microsoft Developer Studio. Distinguishing between the two isn't important, and usually the terms are interchangeable. But you can't use Visual C++ effectively until you learn your way around Developer Studio. (Developer Studio sounds a lot like Visual Studio, but they have no relationship, so you can forget about Visual Studio throughout this book.)

Chapter 1 is an orientation session, introducing Developer Studio and describing the main windows you will encounter when working in the environment. The chapter also explains how to use Microsoft Developer Network (MSDN), which serves as the online help system for all Microsoft programming products, including Visual C++.

Chapter 2 introduces AppWizard, the Visual C++ wizard program that creates starter files for a typical Windows application using MFC. We'll use AppWizard throughout the book to create some of the example programs.

## Part 2—Editors

Visual C++ provides three different editors—one for creating text source code, another for menus and graphics files, and the third for dialog boxes. Each editor gets its own chapter, starting with the text editor in Chapter 3. This chapter examines important menu commands, shows shortcuts for opening text documents, and introduces macros.

Chapter 4 describes Visual C++'s multitalented graphics editor, used to create resource data including menus, bitmaps, icons, and toolbars. This chapter is lengthy, as befits the amount of material it needs to cover. An example program named DiskPie1 takes shape as the chapter progresses. Each main section first describes how to use the graphics editor to create a particular interface element such as a menu or toolbar, and then demonstrates by adding the element to the DiskPie1 program. By the end of the chapter, the program is a useful utility that displays disk and memory usage in the form of a pie chart.

Chapter 5 covers the dialog editor, showing how to use Visual C++ to design dialog boxes and create dialog-based applications like the Windows Character Map and Phone Dialer utilities. The chapter demonstrates with several examples, including one that creates a property sheet, also known as a tabbed dialog.

## Part 3—Programming Assistance

The chapters in Part 3 show how to use two essential tools in Visual C++ to speed program development. Chapter 6 introduces ClassWizard, which is hard to describe but easy to love. When developing MFC applications, you will find ClassWizard invaluable for creating and maintaining classes.

The Gallery, described in Chapter 7, offers a collection of add-in components that you can incorporate into your projects with just a few clicks of the mouse. Visual C++ comes with a number of ready-made components consisting of both class source code and ActiveX controls. Chapter 7 also demonstrates how to create your own components for the Gallery.

## Part 4—ActiveX Controls

Chapter 8 introduces ActiveX controls and shows how to use them in your applications. Chapters 9 and 10 take the opposite tack and explain how to write an ActiveX control using either MFC or the Active Template Library (ATL). Chapter 9 presents a well-documented example named Tower that takes you step by step through the creation and coding of an ActiveX control that relies on MFC. Chapter 10 then creates the same control using the Active Template Library, providing a clear illustration of the differences between the two approaches. The results can be embedded in any application that supports ActiveX controls.

## Part 5—Advanced Topics

Chapter 11 covers the essential subject of the debugger, one of Visual C++'s most perfect elements. The chapter examines the internals of debugging, describes the debugger windows and toolbars, then puts the debugger through its paces by fixing the hidden flaws of an example program.

After an application is debugged, you will want to turn on compiler optimizations to create a release version. Chapter 12 covers the often poorly understood subject of compiler optimization, showing you exactly what each of the many Visual C++ optimization switches do—and why.

By the time you get to Chapter 13 you will have spent a lot of time in the Developer Studio environment, enough to know what you like and what you would prefer to change. This chapter shows how to customize Visual C++ to suit your tastes. It also demonstrates through examples how to program macros and add-in utilities that integrate seamlessly into Developer Studio.

## Part 6—Appendixes

Appendix A presents standard tables that list ASCII and ANSI characters. You may find the ANSI table in Appendix A more useful than similar information in online help because the table shows octal numbers for the characters. There's a good reason for this. As we'll see in Chapter 5, including upper ANSI characters in dialog text requires the character's number in octal form. Armed with this information, you can add useful symbols such as © and ¼ to text strings displayed in a dialog.

Appendix B briefly describes the MFC classes that ClassWizard supports, serving as a quick reference designed to help you select the most appropriate base for your new class.

Appendix C provides an introduction to Microsoft Visual Basic Scripting Edition, better known as VBScript. Visual C++ incorporates VBScript as its macro language, so a primer is helpful if you have never before used VBScript or a similar Visual Basic dialect. Although recording macros in Visual C++ requires no knowledge of VBScript, you can create a general-purpose macro only by using VBScript programming.

# Example Code

Nearly every example program in this book is written in C++ and uses MFC. (The two exceptions are a cursor demonstration program in Chapter 4 and a small console-based utility presented in Chapter 13.) But I rely on C for some of the code fragments within the text. I find C++ isn't as good a medium as C for succinctly illustrating a programming idea, and besides the advantages of clarity and brevity, C serves as a sort of *lingua franca* among today's programmers. In theory, C++ programmers understand straight C but the reverse is not necessarily true. On the other hand, C has no place in demonstrating MFC applications. I occasionally present equivalent C and C++ code when I think the idea is important enough and the differences significant enough to warrant translations.

Many of the chapters in the book cover topics that are best demonstrated by example, and I've tried to include sample programs that are at once interesting, useful, and illustrative. Some of the programs are created with AppWizard and others are not, thus simulating as wide a range of programming practices as possible. Nearly every program is supplemented with a thorough discussion in the book text. The text also includes source code listings, so you needn't open a source file in the editor to follow a discussion. Program code strives for clarity over elegance, so you will no doubt see sections of code that you would handle differently in your own development work. For example, I've included very little error checking in the programs. The programs were created in Windows 95, but most have been tested under Microsoft Windows NT.

# The Companion CD

The project files for all sample programs are on the companion CD attached to the back cover of the book. To copy all the projects to your hard disk, run the Setup program by following these steps:

1. Click the Start button on the Windows taskbar and choose the Run command.

2. Type "*d*:\setup" in the Run dialog, where *d* represents the drive letter of your CD-ROM drive.

The Setup program copies more than 3 MB of files from the CD to your hard disk, placing them in a subfolder named Visual C++ Programmer's Guide (or whatever name you specify). Running Setup is entirely optional, and you can retrieve files manually from the CD if you prefer. You will find all files located in the Code subfolder.

Nested subfolders refer to the chapter number where the program is described and to the project name. The subfolder Chapter.05\MfcTree, for example, holds all the files required to build the MfcTree program presented in Chapter 5. Each project folder has a subfolder named Release that contains the program executable file, so you can try out a sample program without having to build it. If you want to follow a discussion in the text by building the sample program, start Visual C++ and choose the Open Workspace command from the File menu. Browse for the project folder on your hard disk and double-click the project's DSW file.

Project names for the example programs are kept to eight characters or less. This convention accommodates those readers who prefer to use an older text editor that may not recognize long filenames. Some older CD drives also have problems with long filenames.

The companion CD includes a program I wrote named Index. Index is not a sample program, so you won't find it described anywhere in the book chapters. Index supplements the book index, performing a full-text search through all the chapters and the appendixes. It ensures that if a subject is mentioned anywhere in this book, you can find it. The program is actually an electronic form of what bibliographers call a concordance—given one or more words, it tells you on what pages and in what paragraphs the words occur. To use the program, copy the files Index.exe, Index.hlp, and Index.key from the CD to your hard disk, making sure you place the three files in the same folder. Or you can run Index straight from the CD if you prefer. Here's what the program looks like:

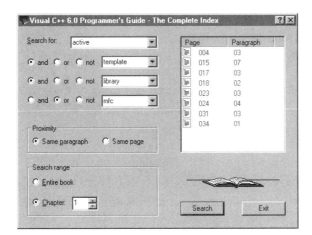

The four combo boxes in the Index dialog window each accept a single word. The words can form a phrase such as "Active Template Library" or simply specify unconnected words that occur together in the same paragraph or on the same page. The program also searches for plurals and word variations formed by *-ed* and *-ing*, and is intelligent enough to account for slight changes in spelling. Searching for the words *edit*, *handle*, and *debug*, for example, also locates occurrences of the words *edits*, *handling*, and *debugged*. Letter case of the search words does not matter, a simplification that on rare occasions may lead to an unexpected match, as when Index locates the word *guiding* when searching for the acronym GUID. To run a search, click either the Search button or the book icon.

The four combo boxes remember previous search words, so you do not have to retype an entry. To recall a word you entered previously, expose the box's list and select the word. Pop-up help messages explain other features of the program. Just click the small question mark button at the upper-right corner of the dialog and then click a control window or group box area. Users of Windows NT 3.51 must press the F1 key for help.

Index identifies each paragraph on a page by a number such as 2 or 7. As you scan a page to find a particular paragraph indicated by the program, keep in mind these rules that determine what the program considers a paragraph to be:

- The caption of a figure constitutes a separate paragraph, as does each row of a table.

- Each line of source code (except blank lines) represents a paragraph.

- A partial paragraph at the top of a page does not count as a separate paragraph because Index assumes the text belongs to the paragraph at the bottom of the preceding page.

The Index program recognizes the Boolean operators AND, OR, and NOT. If you are a little rusty on Boolean logic in full-text searches, Chapter 1 describes how to use the same operators when searching the MSDN online help system. See Table 1-1 on page 26 for examples.

# A Few Definitions

Before getting further into the book, a few terms should be defined, such as build, project, target, configuration, and application framework. Since I'll use these words in the chapters that follow, it's best to define them now.

Build means to compile and link, transforming a collection of source files into an executable application. You compile a source file; you link object files; you build a project. Project has two related meanings. It can mean the end-product—that is, the application you build—but the term more correctly refers to the collection of files that create the application, including source files, precompiled headers, resource scripts, graphics files, and whatever else is required to build the program. Visual C++ lets you open only one project at a time, which means you have ready access to all the project files and can edit, build, or debug. Each project can hold any number of nested subprojects, an arrangement that makes sense when you are developing a program consisting of more than one executable element. For example, you might develop an application as a main project while maintaining an auxiliary dynamic link library as a separate subproject.

When you build a project, the application you create is one of two types, either release or debug. Visual C++ sometimes uses the term *target* to refer to the build type. The project's release target is the executable program you give to your end-users. The debug target is the executable you work on during program development. The project settings, known as the configuration, determine the type of executable—release or debug—that Visual C++ creates when building the project.

The MFC library of general classes is designed to make Windows programming easier by representing the Win32 API as a set of class objects. A program using MFC takes advantage of tested code that serves as an application framework, handling many tasks the application would otherwise have to take care of itself. The only costs of these hidden services are a potentially larger executable size and a certain built-in rigidity common to most MFC programs. Through its classes, the framework dictates the structure of the application but not the details. However, MFC does not seriously constrain the programmer's creativity, as evidenced by the many diverse Windows applications written with MFC.

# Further Reading

Recommending books is an uncomfortable responsibility and I don't take it on lightly. Books are expensive, not just in terms of money but especially in terms of time. That said, here are a few works that I believe represent worthwhile investments for programmers using Visual C++. They all happen to be published by Microsoft Press, but that's only because I don't get out much.

- To begin learning about MFC, I believe you can't do better than Jeff Prosise's *Programming Windows 95 with MFC*. I like this book. It's well written, clear, and stays consistently with its subject without wandering off somewhere else.

- Another good work on MFC is David Kruglinski's *Inside Visual C++*. Don't let the title fool you—this book concentrates on MFC, covering topics that the Prosise book does not such as database management and OLE. The discussions and all the example programs assume the reader is using Visual C++.

- If you are new to Windows programming, want grounding in the basics, and prefer to program in the C language rather than C++, consider *Programming Windows 95* by Charles Petzold and Paul Yao. The latest of a series of editions that first appeared almost a decade ago, this book is justly famous for the clarity it brings to the subject of Windows programming. Note the caveats, though—except for the last chapter, the book makes no mention of C++ or MFC.

- For a good introduction to ActiveX, try David Chappell's *Understanding ActiveX and OLE*. Though it has nothing to say about Visual C++ and very little about programming, this readable book offers a good overview of a complex subject.

## Feedback

If you have any suggestions for future editions of this book, drop me a line. I will try to read every piece of e-mail I receive (I'm pretty diligent about these things), though I can't promise an answer. You can reach me via the Internet at *beckz@witzendsoft.com*.

# Basics

# The Environment

The Visual C++ package comprises many separate pieces such as editors, compiler, linker, make utility, a debugger, and various other tools designed for the task of developing C/C++ programs for Microsoft Windows. Fortunately, the package also includes a development environment named Developer Studio. Developer Studio ties all the other Visual C++ tools together into an integrated whole, letting you view and control the entire development process through a consistent system of windows, dialogs, menus, toolbars, shortcut keys, and macros. To use an analogy, the environment is like a control room with monitors, dials, and levers from which a single person can operate the machines of a sprawling factory. The environment is roughly everything you *see* in Visual C++. Everything else runs behind the scenes under its management.

Distinguishing between the product Visual C++ and its environment Developer Studio serves little purpose because the latter so completely represents the former. Rather than deal with yet another name, this book applies the term Visual C++ in a general sense that refers interchangeably to both the entire product and its development environment. Microsoft itself has adopted this course, and users of previous versions will notice that windows once labeled Developer Studio have been retitled Visual C++. We will resurrect the old name in the final chapter, however, when discussing how utility programs can integrate with the Developer Studio program to become part of the environment.

Let's begin this chapter with a summary of some of the many services provided by the Visual C++ environment that are designed to assist program development. Chapter numbers in parentheses indicate where in the book we will examine these services in detail:

- Windows that provide views of different aspects of the development process, from lists of classes and source files to compiler messages (this chapter).

- Menu access to an extensive system of online help (this chapter).

- A text editor for creating and maintaining source files (Chapter 3), an intelligent dialog editor for designing dialog boxes (Chapter 5), and a graphics editor for creating other interface elements such as bitmaps, icons, mouse cursors, and toolbars (Chapter 4).

- Wizards that create starter files for a program, giving you a head start on the mundane task of setting up a new project. Visual C++ provides wizards for various types of Windows programs, including standard applications with optional database and Automation support (Chapter 2), dynamic link libraries, dialog-based applications (Chapter 5), extensions for a Web server using the Internet Server API (ISAPI), and ActiveX controls (Chapters 9 and 10).

- ClassWizard, an assistant that helps create and maintain classes for MFC applications (Chapter 6).

- Drop-in executable components maintained by the Gallery (Chapter 7) that add instant features to your programs.

- An excellent debugger (Chapter 11).

- Logical and convenient access to commands through menus and toolbars. You can customize existing menus and toolbars in Visual C++ or create new ones (Chapter 13).

- The ability to add your own environment tools through macros and add-in dynamic link libraries (Chapter 13). You can develop these additions yourself or purchase them from various vendors.

Figure 1-1 shows a typical view of the Visual C++ main window. The environment's appearance has changed only slightly since the previous version, and its style and many of its commands remain unaltered. If you are familiar with the Developer Studio environment from previous versions of Visual C++ or other Microsoft products, you may want only to skim this chapter to touch on the new features, especially the revised online help system. If you have never used Visual C++ before, you will find that like any large Windows program it may take some getting used to. Don't underestimate its depth—just when you think you've discovered everything about Visual C++, another corridor opens up. But the interface is intelligent and so forgiving that it encourages experimentation, always the best teacher.

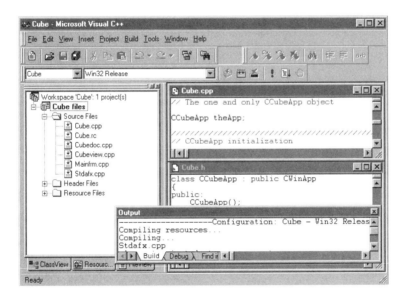

**Figure 1-1.**    *A typical view of Visual C++'s main window.*

This chapter is a start, introducing you to the Visual C++ environment shell and describing the interface and windows you will encounter when working on a development project. We won't worry about individual tools and menu commands at this stage, since every chapter that follows describes at least one menu and toolbar and the various commands they contain. At one time Developer Studio also served as host environment for

Visual J++ and Visual InterDev, but here we concentrate only on how the environment applies to Visual C++ and C/C++ projects.

# Toolbars and Menus

Visual C++ comes with an arsenal of predefined toolbars that provide one-click access to the most frequently used commands. And if you don't see what you need, you can augment the environment's collection of toolbars with custom toolbars of your own design. Each toolbar is identified by a name that appears in the bar's title strip:

As described in the next section, toolbars are often "docked" into position, in which case the title strip disappears. For example, Figure 1-1 shows what the Standard, Build, and Edit toolbars look like in their docked locations at the top of the Visual C++ main window. Toolbar arrangement is up to you. You can move toolbars around on the screen, adjust their rectangular shapes by dragging an edge, and make any set of toolbars visible or invisible. While you may prefer to have some toolbars such as Standard and Build visible at all times, other toolbars normally become visible only when you work in a window that requires them. The Debug toolbar, for instance, is visible by default only during a debugging session. The Colors and Graphics toolbars (described in Chapter 4, Resources) are visible only in the graphics editor, because that's the only place you need them. Figure 1-2 shows a list of toolbar names contained in the Customize dialog, in which you can toggle a toolbar's visibility on and off by clicking a check box. To open the dialog, click the Customize command on the Tools menu. (Chapter 13, Customizing Visual C++, has much more to say about the Customize dialog).

As the mouse cursor passes over a toolbar button, the button takes on a distinctive raised appearance. The status bar at the bottom of the main

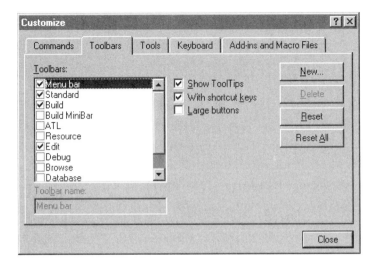

**Figure 1-2.**   *Turning toolbars on and off in the Customize dialog.*

window displays a brief description of the button and, if the cursor rests momentarily on the button, a small pop-up "tooltip" window appears containing the button name. On request, Visual C++ can even display enlarged versions of its toolbars:

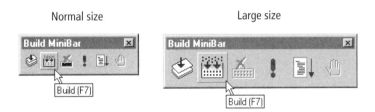

Both the tooltips and enlargement options are controlled in the Customize dialog box shown in Figure 1-2.

The Visual C++ menu bar is a special form of toolbar. Although you can hide the menu bar only in full-screen mode, it otherwise behaves much like a normal toolbar. Menu names on the Visual C++ menu bar take on the same raised appearance as toolbar buttons when the mouse cursor passes over them. When you click a menu name to pull down a menu, the name seems to recess into the screen. With a menu open, glide the cursor from one menu name to another to pull down other menus.

> ### Context Menus
>
> The Visual C++ environment almost always responds to clicks of the right mouse button, usually displaying a pop-up context menu with commands appropriate to the situation. Even when no windows are open in Visual C++, right-clicking the empty client area produces a menu with commands that make windows visible and toggle toolbars on and off. To expose the same menu, right-click anywhere on a toolbar except its title strip. Experiment with the right button as you work, and you will uncover a wealth of other convenient shortcuts.

You can drag toolbars and the menu bar into new positions on the screen by clicking and holding any area of the bar that is not a button or menu name. If the toolbar's title strip is not visible, the vertical separator bars that appear in many of the toolbars are a good place to "grab" a bar for dragging. Because of the docking feature, moving toolbars in Visual C++ is sometimes not as straightforward as you might expect. The next section delves into the secrets of repositioning windows and toolbars on the screen.

# Environment Windows

Besides its many dialog boxes, Visual C++ displays two types of windows, called document windows and dockable windows. Document windows are normal framed child windows that contain source code text and graphics documents. The Window menu lists commands that display document windows on the screen in a cascade or tiled arrangement. All other Visual C++ windows, including toolbars and even the menu bar, are dockable. The environment has two main dockable windows, called Workspace and Output, that are made visible through commands on the View menu. Other dockable windows, described in Chapter 11, The Debugger, appear during a debugging session. This section first looks at some of the characteristics common to all dockable windows, and then examines the Workspace and Output windows individually.

A dockable window can be attached to the top, bottom, or side edges of the Visual C++ client area, or disconnected to float free anywhere on the screen. Dockable windows, whether floating or docked, always appear on top of document windows. This ensures that floating toolbars remain visible as focus shifts from one window to another, but it also means that document windows can occasionally seem to get lost. This can be disconcerting the first few times it happens, but have faith that the document window is still there. If you are working on source code in the text editor, for instance, and then turn on a dockable window that occupies the entire Visual C++ client area, the source code document disappears, buried beneath the new window. If the overlaying window is docked into position, you cannot bring the source document window back to the top. The only solution is to either turn off the overlaying window or drag it out of the way. We'll see how to turn dockable windows on and off in a moment.

As you drag a dockable window, a moving outline appears that shows what the window's new location will be when you release the left mouse button. The outline is a fuzzy gray line until it comes in contact with an edge of the environment's client area or the edge of another docked window, at which point the outline changes to a thin black line. The change is a visual cue to notify you that dropping the window will cause it to dock into place against the nearest edge. A toolbar docks into a horizontal position against the top or bottom edge of the client area and into a vertical position when placed against the left or right side. You can reorient the toolbar's placement by pressing the Shift key while dragging the toolbar.

Getting a window to dock in the desired size and position sometimes takes several attempts. To dock a window so that it occupies the entire client area, drag it upward until the mouse cursor comes in contact with the top edge of the client area, and then release the mouse button. To coax the docked window back to a smaller size, drag the window until the cursor touches the left edge of the client area. This forces the window to undock, allowing you to drag the window by its title bar to a different location.

When you move a dockable window around on the screen, the window may seem to have a mind of its own, clinging tenaciously to an edge of the Visual C++ main window or to any other docked window it comes in contact with. You can prevent this in two ways. The first method is to press the Ctrl key while moving the window to temporarily suppress its docking feature. The second method works only for windows, not toolbars, disabling the window's docking ability until you enable it again. Right-click inside the window and choose the Docking View command from the window's context menu to turn off the command's check box icon. The Window menu also provides access to the Docking View command, as shown in Figure 1-3.

**Figure 1-3.**     *Toggling a window's docking mode with the Docking View command.*

Disabling a window's docking feature affects the window's behavior in several ways:

■ The window appears as a normal document window, with buttons in the title bar that minimize, maximize, and close the window.

■ The window's position is arranged along with any open document windows when you choose the Cascade or Tile command from the Window menu.

■ The window cannot be moved above the client area of the Visual C++ main window as it can when in docking mode.

■ Given input focus, the window can be closed with the Close command on the Window menu. The Close command otherwise does not affect a window in docking mode, even if it has focus.

When a window or toolbar is docked, distinctive raised knurls, sometimes called gripper bars, appear at the window's top or left edge, as shown in Figure 1-4. Double-clicking the gripper bars makes a window or toolbar float free; double-clicking the title bar of the floating window or toolbar

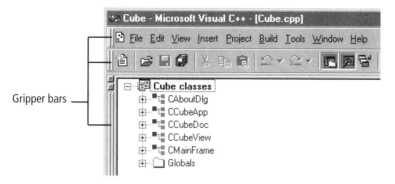

Gripper bars

**Figure 1-4.** *When docked, windows, toolbars, and the menu bar have raised gripper bars.*

returns it to its previous docked position. You can also drag a window by its gripper bars into another docked or free-floating location.

The window arrangement you create in Visual C++ lasts for the duration of the project or until you change it. The next time you open the project, windows appear as you left them. Windows belonging to utility programs executed within the environment are not subject to the environment's rules, however. Such windows are neither document nor docking windows, and their characteristics are determined by the utility program, not Visual C++.

## The Workspace and Output Windows

Visual C++ displays information about a project in the Workspace and Output dockable windows, shown in Figures 1-1 (page 5), 1-6 (page 13), and 1-7 (page 14). We'll encounter these important windows throughout the book, especially the Workspace window, so it's worthwhile spending some time examining how they work.

To make the Workspace or Output window visible, click its name on the View menu, as shown in Figure 1-5, on the next page. (The command is not a toggle, so clicking it again does not make the window invisible.) The windows are also activated by their own buttons on the Standard toolbar, which when clicked make the windows visible or invisible.

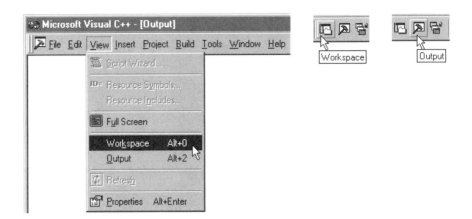

**Figure 1-5.** *Displaying the Workspace and Output windows. The tool buttons are on the Standard toolbar.*

In addition to using the toolbar buttons, you can hide the Workspace and Output windows in several other ways:

■ If the window is floating, click the Close button on the window's title bar.

■ If the window is docked, click the small X button located above or to the right of the window's gripper bars (see Figure 1-4).

■ Right-click anywhere in the window to display a context menu and choose the menu's Hide or Close command. Which command appears on the menu depends on whether the window's docking mode is on or off, but both commands have the same effect.

■ If the window's docking feature is disabled, click the window to give it focus and choose the Close command from the Window menu.

The Workspace window presents different perspectives of your project. Select a tab at the bottom of the window to display a list of the project's classes, resources, data sources, or files. Click the small plus (+) or minus (–) buttons in the window to expand or contract a list. Expanding the list of classes, for example, displays the names of member functions, as shown in the first screen of Figure 1-6. Double-clicking the text of a list heading adjacent to a folder or book icon has the same effect as clicking the heading's plus/minus button.

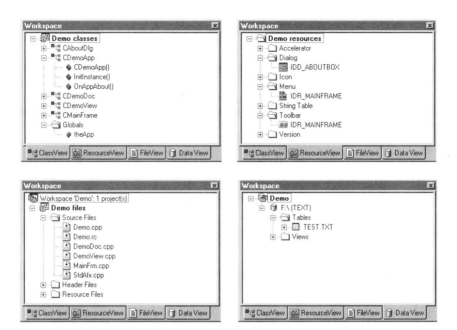

**Figure 1-6.**   *Four panes of the Workspace window.*

The Workspace window can display up to four panes of information, described here:

- **ClassView**—Lists classes and member functions in the project. To open the class source file in the Visual C++ text editor, double-click the desired class or function in the list.

- **ResourceView**—Lists project resource data such as dialog boxes and bitmaps. As with the ClassView pane, double-clicking a data item in the ResourceView list opens the appropriate editor and loads the resource.

- **FileView**—Lists the project's source files. Copying a source file to the project folder does not automatically add the file to the list in the FileView pane. You must specifically add new files to the project using the Add To Project command on the Project menu.

- **Data View**—Displays information about data sources for database projects. The Data View tab appears only in database projects hosted by the Visual C++ Enterprise Edition that are connected to a data source compliant with the Open Database Connectivity (ODBC) standard.

Right-clicking an item in the Workspace window displays a context menu containing frequently used commands. Commands on the menu depend on which item is clicked. Right-clicking a source file in the FileView pane, for example, displays a context menu that lets you quickly open or compile the file. You can also toggle individual Workspace panes on and off. Right-click any tab at the bottom of the Workspace window to display a context menu, and then choose the desired command from the menu list to make the pane visible or invisible.

The Output window (shown in Figure 1-7) has four tabs named Build, Debug, Find In Files 1, and Find In Files 2. The Build tab displays status messages from the compiler, linker, and other tools. The Debug tab is reserved for notifications from the debugger alerting you to conditions such as unhandled exceptions and memory violations. Any messages your application generates through the *OutputDebugString* API function or *afxDump* class library also appear in the Debug tab.

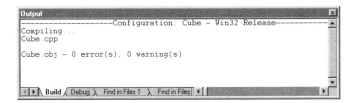

**Figure 1-7.**    *The Ouput window.*

The remaining two tabs of the Output window display the results of the Find In Files command chosen from the Edit menu. (This useful feature, similar to the UNIX *grep* command, is examined in more detail in Chapter 3, The Text Editor.) By default, the Find In Files search results appear in the Find In Files 1 tab of the Output window, but a check box in the Find In Files dialog allows you to divert output to the Find In Files 2 tab. The Output window can contain other tabs as well. We'll see in Chapter 13 how to add a custom tool to Visual C++ that can display messages in its own tab of the Output window.

# Online Help

Visual C++ provides three different sources of online help:

- Standard HLP files displayed with the WinHlp32 viewer
- Pop-up help messages in dialogs
- The Microsoft Developer Network Library, known as MSDN

The standard HLP files cover commands and windows of the environment, and are displayed only if you press the F1 key when the Help menu's Use Extension Help command is checked, or if Visual C++ can determine no specific context for a help topic. For example, consider this line in a typical source document opened in the text editor:

```
DECLARE_MESSAGE_MAP()      // MFC message map macro
```

The effect of pressing F1 in this case depends on the position of the flashing caret in the text editor window. If the caret rests within or at the beginning of the macro name and extension help is turned off, pressing F1 opens the MSDN Library window and displays information about the DECLARE_MESSAGE_MAP macro. If the caret instead rests on a blank line, there is no clear context for online help. In this case, pressing the F1 key produces information about the text editor window itself, displayed in the WinHlp32 viewer:

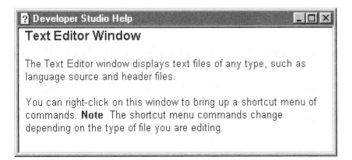

Pop-up messages—the second source of online help—are available in the many dialog boxes displayed in the environment. Labels and the occasional hint do their best to make clear the purpose of edit boxes and buttons in a dialog, but when labels are insufficient you can always query for more explanation about a particular control through any of these methods:

- Give the control focus and press the F1 key. Clicking a check box or radio button to give it focus may turn a switch on or off. If this is not what you want, remember to restore the switch to its former setting when you are finished reading the help message.

- Right-click the control to expose the What's This? pop-up button. If the control is an edit box, right-click the control's label text rather than the edit box itself. Clicking the What's This? button displays help text for the control.

- Click the question mark button at the upper right corner of the dialog box, and then click the control for which you want information.

These three methods all have the same effect, executing WinHlp32 to display a brief pop-up message like the one shown in Figure 1-8. The message disappears when you click a mouse button or press a key.

The third source for online help is the one you will probably use the most often while working in Visual C++. MSDN is generally logical and easy to use, but it is also immense. As we'll see in the next section, using the MSDN library to its full potential takes a little practice.

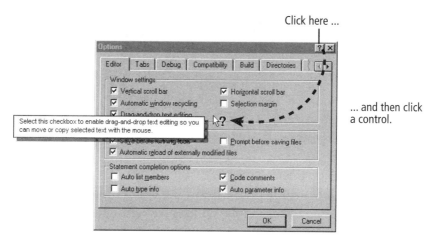

**Figure 1-8.**     *Getting help in a typical Developer Studio dialog.*

# MSDN Library

Once available only by subscription, the MSDN Library now serves as the online help system for the entire suite of Visual Studio development tools, including Visual C++. Because it is shared equally by all tools, MSDN runs as a separate application and is not tightly integrated into any single development environment. To access MSDN from within Visual C++, the Help menu's Use Extension Help command must be unchecked. Choosing the Contents, Search, or Index command from the Visual C++ Help menu causes the environment to run MSDN by executing the Windows\HH.exe program, which loads the MSDN table of contents from the file MSDNVS98.col, located in the MSDN98\98VS\1033 folder. (The name of the containing folder reflects system localization settings—1033 is a language code for United States English.)

The Library provides an immense trove of information touching almost every facet of Microsoft programming tools and Win32 programming. It comprises thousands of articles covering everything from Visual C++ to Visual J++, from MFC to ActiveX, and from the *abs* function to z-ordering. MSDN also includes the full text of several respected books published by Microsoft such as Bruce McKinney's *Hardcore Visual Basic* and Kraig Brockschmidt's *Inside Ole, 2$^{nd}$ Edition*. You can also find Knowledge Base articles, recent issues of *Microsoft Systems Journal*, full documentation of application and device driver development kits, conference papers, example source code, and a lot more. The interface is not perfectly conceived for this release, but MSDN's sheer volume of information is truly amazing.

The MSDN help system stores its text in a series of "chum" files recognizable by their CHM extension; the extension refers to the compiled HTML format in which the files are written. CHM files are like individual volumes of the MSDN encyclopedia, each containing articles devoted to a particular subject such as ActiveX or the complete Win32 API reference. Every file is paired with a separate index file that has the same name and a CHI extension. During installation of MSDN, the setup program writes all CHI index files to your hard disk but copies from the CD-ROM only those CHM files you specifically request. CHM files take up a lot of disk space, so you will probably prefer to install only those topics you are most likely to visit often. During execution MSDN has access to all CHM files, whether they are on your hard disk or left behind on the CDs. If the program cannot locate a required CHM file on your hard disk, it prompts for replacement of the correct CD. Which MSDN topics you should install on your system thus depends on how often you anticipate using MSDN, which subjects interest you most, and how willing you are to shuffle CDs.

The first time you call upon the MSDN Library to search for an article, it creates the MSDNVS98.chw keyword file, which contains a list of individual words used in all the articles along with pointers to where each word appears in the text. Compiling keyword references this way speeds up searches for particular words and phrases, as we'll see in a moment. Creating the keyword file is a one-time occurrence that may take several minutes, during which an animated message informs you of what is happening:

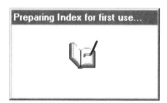

The process requires many megabytes of free disk space in the system's TEMP folder. If the TEMP environment variable currently points to a RAM disk of insufficient size, reset the variable in your AutoExec.bat file and reboot before searching the first time in MSDN. After MSDN creates the keyword file, you can restore the original TEMP setting.

Figure 1-9 shows a typical MSDN article displayed in the Library's two-paned window. The two panes are designed to work together, the left pane accepting input criteria for the article you want and the right pane displaying the located article itself.

Articles appear one at a time in the window's right pane, connected to other related articles through a web of hypertext links. Hypertext links, also known as hyperlinks, are special words or phrases within the article text. Links are underlined and appear in a distinctive color that makes them immediately recognizable. When the cursor passes over a hypertext

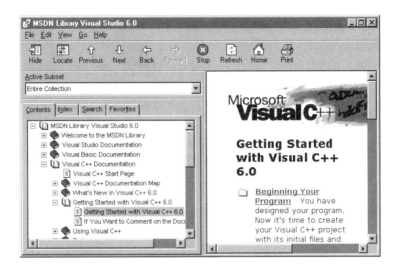

**Figure 1-9.** *Accessing online help through the MSDN Library application.*

link in the MSDN Library window, the cursor assumes the shape of a pointing hand (Figure 1-10). Clicking anywhere on a link removes the current article from the MSDN window and replaces it with the new article

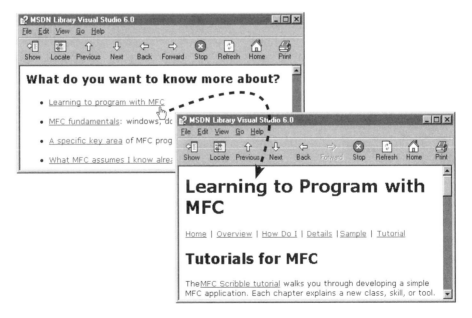

**Figure 1-10.** *Click a hyperlink to jump from one MSDN article to another.*

referenced by the hypertext link. The effect is very much like browsing Web pages on the Internet.

Interfacing with the right half of the MSDN window is extremely easy—you need do no more than scroll the window if necessary to read the help text and click any hypertext links that look interesting. Only one topic at a time appears in the window, so it is always clean and uncluttered. For more viewing area, you can turn off the window's left pane by clicking the Hide tool button, though unfortunately the entire window shrinks as a result instead of remaining a constant size. You may find it easier to collapse or expand the left pane by dragging the vertical splitter bar left or right, thus maintaining the overall size of the MSDN window.

The window's left pane holds four tabs labeled Contents, Index, Search, and Favorites. Each tab provides a different means of navigating the wide seas of online help.

## Contents Tab

MSDN groups topics according to subject matter under headings and subheadings, an arrangement that forms a table of contents. It's like the table of contents of a book, only interactive. You begin by searching for a general subject, then explore down paths of information that become increasingly specific to find topics that interest you. The table of contents serves best when you have in mind a general subject—the debugger, for instance, or programming with OpenGL—and you want to see what documents are available for that subject.

Choosing the Contents command from the Visual C++ Help menu opens the MSDN window and displays the table of contents. Expand the table until you find the title of the article you are searching for, either by double-clicking headings (identified by book icons) or by clicking the small plus sign (+) buttons shown in Figure 1-9. Article titles in the table of contents lie at the end of the hierarchical chain, each distinguished by an icon representing a sheet of paper with a dog-eared corner. Double-clicking a title in the list opens the article in the MSDN window's right pane.

By default, the table of contents summarizes the entire collection of MSDN articles. You can narrow the display by defining a branch of the table of contents hierarchy as an information subset. Subsets allow you to focus on topics of a particular category. As an example, here's how to create a subset of articles pertaining only to the MFC Reference:

1. Choose the Define Subset command from MSDN's View menu.

2. In the Define Subset dialog, expand the table of contents by double-clicking the multi-volume heading labeled "MSDN Library Visual Studio 6.0," and then do the same to the "Visual C++ Documentation" and "Reference" nested subheadings. Select the subheading named "Microsoft Foundation Class Library and Templates" and click the Add button to create the subset.

3. Type a name for the new subset in the edit box at the bottom of the Define Subsets dialog, and then click the Save and Close buttons.

To switch among subsets when using online help, select a subset from the drop-down list labeled Active Subset:

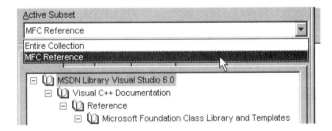

## Index Tab

The Index tab is generally where you should turn first to search online help, particularly when you have a reasonably clear idea of the subject you are looking for. The Index tab displays a comprehensive index of the entire MSDN file set, much like the index of a printed book. To locate an index entry, type a keyword in the edit box at the top of the dialog. As you type, the index in the list box automatically scrolls to the typed keyword. For example, the MSDN index includes the entries "exception handling," "handling exceptions," and "C++ exception handling," so typing any of these terms locates topics that pertain to the subject of exception handling. When you find the index entry you want, double-click it. If the entry targets only a single article, MSDN displays it immediately; otherwise the Topics Found dialog appears listing all the articles that the index entry refers to, as shown in Figure 1-11. Open an article in the dialog by double-clicking its title in the list or by selecting the title and clicking the Display button.

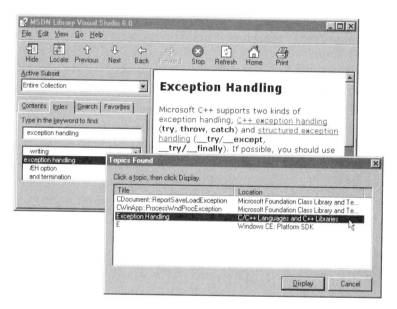

**Figure 1-11.**    *The Index tab provides a comprehensive index of MSDN articles.*

## Search Tab

MSDN is more than a passive set of help files. It also includes a search engine that scans the MSDNVS98.chw keyword file to determine which topic files contain a specific word or phrase, a process called full-text searching. Full-text searches are launched from MSDN's Search tab (Figure 1-12), allowing you to look for topics that contain a specified word or phrase. The MSDN search engine is intelligent, able to understand word variations, wildcards, Boolean associations, and the NEAR proximity operator. Although using these features efficiently requires more thought and planning on your part, they allow you to refine search parameters to increase the chances of finding only those topics that interest you most.

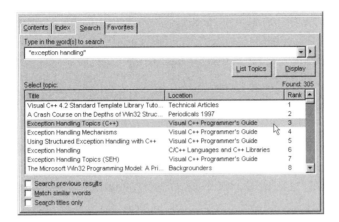

**Figure 1-12.** *The Search tab lets you search for topics that contain specific words or phrases.*

After examining the various options available from the Search tab, we'll focus on how to refine a search using wildcards and operators.

At the top of the tab, type the word or phrase you want to search for, enclosing phrases in double quotation marks to distinguish them from individual words. (Single quotation marks are ignored.) For instance, searching for the words displayed in Figure 1-12 finds only topics that contain the phrase "exception handling." Typing the same words without the quotation marks means that you want to search for topics that contain both the words "exception" and "handling," but not necessarily occurring together as a phrase. Searching for quotation marks is not possible.

Three check boxes in the Search tab govern switches through which you can further specify how and where to search. The Search Previous Results check box lets you confine searches to only those articles already listed in the Search tab. Turning on the Match Similar Words check box instructs MSDN to accept words that are grammatical variations of the search word (or words) you have typed in the first text box. The variations involve common word suffixes such as *s*, *ed*, and *ing*, forcing MSDN to recognize the words *edits* and *edited*, for instance, as matches for the keyword *edit*. Broadening the search criteria this way is of course apt to find more topics. The Match Similar Words switch applies to all search words typed in the edit box, so that searching for the phrase *handle exception* with the switch turned on also finds topics that contain close variations such as *handled exceptions.* MSDN recognizes even those variations that do not contain the full keyword, finding words such as *handler* and *handled* when searching for the keyword *handling.*

Turning on the Search Titles Only check box narrows the search considerably because it causes MSDN to scan only article titles, not the body of text within articles. Thus, searching for the phrase *exception handling* with the check box turned on finds titles such as "Exception Handling Topics (SEH)" and "Type-Safe Exception Handling," but not other related topics such as "Compiler Warning C4530," which mentions exception handling within its text.

When the search is completed, MSDN lists the titles of all articles that mention the given search string, and displays the number of located articles at the upper right corner of the list. The list is sorted in descending rank, determined by the number of times the requested search string occurs in the topic document. To sort the list by title or article location, click the button at the top of the appropriate list column. Double-clicking a list entry in the Search tab displays the article with all matched strings highlighted in the text, allowing you to quickly locate each occurrence of a string. Highlighted strings repeated often in the text may seem a little distracting, giving an article the aspect of a ransom note. To remove the highlights from the display, choose the Highlights command twice from the View menu or click the Previous and Next tool buttons to temporarily move to another article and then return. You can also use the Find In This Topic command on the Edit menu to find text within the displayed article.

Here are some basic rules and a few caveats for formulating search parameters in the Search tab:

- Searches are not case-sensitive, so you can type a search phrase in uppercase or lowercase letters.

- By default, MSDN finds only whole words. For instance, a search for *key* does not find "keyboard." Wildcards can override this default behavior, as explained shortly.

- You can search for any combination of letters and numbers, including single characters (*a, b, c, 1, 2, 3,* etc.), but not simple words such as *an*, *and*, *as*, *at*, *be*, *but*, *by*, *do*, *for*, *from*, *have*, *he*, *in*, *it*, *near*, *not*, *of*, *on*, *or*, *she*, *that*, *the*, *there*, *these*, *they*, *this*, *to*, *we*, *when*, *which*, *with*, and *you*. MSDN ignores these words when attempting to match text so that searching for *handle exceptions* can also find topics that contain the phrase "handle the exception" or "handle an exception."

■ MSDN accepts apostrophes in a search string but ignores other punctuation marks such as periods, commas, colons, semicolons, and hyphens. This ensures that strings will be found regardless of context, but it also opens opportunities for spurious matches. Searching for the phrase *exception handling*, for example, can conceivably locate an unrelated topic that contains text like this:

Messages are an exception. Handling a message...

### Wildcards and operators

A search string can be formed as a general expression using the standard question mark (?) and asterisk (*) wildcard characters, provided the characters are not inside double quotation marks. The question mark wildcard represents a single character in the expression so that searching for the string *80?86* can find "80286," "80386," and "80486" (but not "8086"). The asterisk wildcard represents any sequence of zero or more characters. Searching for *wnd*, for example, locates text such as "wnd," "CWnd," "HWND," and "wndproc." The asterisk wildcard ensures that MSDN finds all words related by a common root word. To locate words such as "keyboard," "keystroke," and "keypress," for instance, type *key** instead of *key* as the search string. Naturally, this approach may turn up unrelated search hits such as "keyword" and "key_type." Operators can further refine search criteria to minimize such unwanted side effects.

MSDN recognizes the Boolean operators AND, OR, and NOT, and the proximity operator NEAR. The best way to describe the effects of these operators is through the examples shown in Table 1-1, on the following page. The NEAR operator assumes strings are "near" each other when they are separated by no more than eight recognized words. MSDN provides no means of specifying a different criterion for determining proximity.

| Operator | Example | Result |
|----------|---------|--------|
| AND | `debug AND window` | Finds topics that contain both the strings *debug* and *window* anywhere within the text but not topics that contain only one of the strings. |
| OR | `mfc OR "founda-tion library"` | Finds topics that contain one or both of the strings. |
| NOT | `ellipse NOT cdc` | Finds topics that contain only the first of the given strings but not both. The example to the left specifies that topics containing the string *ellipse* should be skipped if they also contain the word *cdc*, thus ignoring topics about the *CDC::Ellipse* function. |
| NEAR | `handl* NEAR exception` | Finds topics in which the given strings are separated by no more than eight words. |

**Table 1-1.**     *The effects of string operators in MSDN's Search tab.*

To connect two words by an operator, type the operator between the words separated by spaces, as shown in Table 1-1; letter case does not matter. You can also click the arrow button (▶) adjacent to the combo box and select the desired operator from the small pop-up menu.

Operators have no implied order of precedence, and MSDN evaluates expressions in normal left-to-right order. Use parentheses if necessary to associate strings unambiguously with operators. MSDN ignores parentheses inside double quotation marks, so it is not possible to search the topic files for parenthetical remarks. The Search tab treats each white space in a search string as an AND operator, assuming AND in the absence of other operators, parentheses, or double quotation marks. Thus entering any of the following search strings in the Search tab has the same effect:

> *debug AND window AND breakpoint*
> *(debug AND window) breakpoint*
> *debug window AND breakpoint*
> *debug window breakpoint*

Previous versions of the InfoViewer help system allowed use of the C language equivalents of the Boolean operators, replacing AND, OR, and NOT with the ampersand (&), vertical bar ( | ), and exclamation mark (!) operators. MSDN ignores these characters, so they all have the effect of the AND operator.

### Search strategies

The method you should use to search online help depends not so much on what you are looking for but rather on how well you can describe what you are looking for. If you can associate one or two specific keywords with a subject, searching through the MSDN index is usually the most efficient way to find topics of interest. Like the index of a book, the MSDN index provides a connection between a keyword and a relatively small list of relevant articles, allowing you to quickly zero in on the information you need. A full-text search, on the other hand, casts a wider net, often presenting you with many more articles to select from than those referenced in the index. The results of your search depend on how carefully you phrase search strings and make use of search operators. After conducting a full-text search, it can be a tedious process to pore over each article in the search list looking only for the ones that best address your question.

If the subject area is new to you, you may prefer an overview and general background information. In this case, the MSDN table of contents might be your best recourse. Start by looking at the overall organization of the table of contents to see what is there. Sometimes a few index or full-text searches will help you locate a region of the table to focus on. After you have found an interesting topic this way, you can determine where the topic title occurs in the table of contents by clicking the Locate button on the MSDN toolbar. The Previous and Next buttons select the adjacent article listed in the table of contents, letting you browse through related articles in sequence. Many topics begin with a helpful row of standard hypertext links that take you to a home page, a subject overview, a list of frequently asked questions, and so on.

## Favorites Tab

When winding through corridors of help text by jumping from one article to another, you will inevitably want to go back to an article you passed earlier. The Favorites tab shown in Figure 1-13 helps out here, maintaining a list of bookmarks that flag selected articles so you can immediately return to them. The flags are like the list of favorite places or bookmarks maintained by a Web browser, and you will find them invaluable for retracing your steps when exploring online help. Titles added to the list remain permanently listed until removed, so the Favorites tab appears as you left it when you start the MSDN program.

The title of the current article—that is, the article displayed in the right pane—appears at the bottom of the Favorites tab. Click the Add button to add the title to the list; double-clicking a title in the list recalls the article.

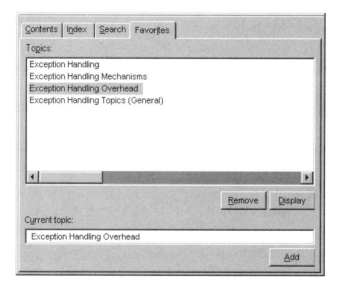

**Figure 1-13.** *The Favorites tab keeps a list of those articles you may want to revisit.*

## Accessing the World Wide Web

By embedding the Internet Explorer browser, MSDN can reach out to other information sources on the Web wherever they may be. An article can contain Internet addresses (universal resource locators or URLs) as hypertext links, so MSDN opens a Web page as seamlessly as any other article in the library.

To specify a target Web site, choose the URL command from the Go menu and enter the site's address. Figure 1-14 shows an example.

**Figure 1-14.**   *Accessing a Web site through MSDN.*

# Working Outside the Environment

Most Visual C++ tools are available to you only from inside the Developer Studio environment, but the compiler, linker, resource compiler, and make program are exceptions. These programs execute as 32-bit console-based utilities. When you build an application by compiling and linking, Visual C++ spawns the make program to execute the two compilers and the linker. Their output messages, which normally go to the system's standard output device, are captured and displayed in the environment's Output window. It is possible to build applications without the environment, executing the four programs from the command line as NMake.exe, CL.exe, Link.exe, and RC.exe.

But working outside Developer Studio is impractical. The list of features at the beginning of this chapter gives some idea of the wealth of assistance that the environment contributes to program development, especially (but not exclusively) for C++ development using the MFC library. Unless you have legacy source files in the C language and a workable make file that you do not want to disturb, you will almost certainly find development work easier and far more productive inside the environment. Chapter 3, The Text Editor, explains how to stay with your old text editor if you prefer, but Developer Studio is much more than just a text editor. Without it, Visual C++ is eviscerated. Every chapter of this book describes how to use some part of the environment to create and maintain C/C++ programs. This chapter is only the beginning.

# AppWizard

One of the most remarkable technologies of Visual C++ is its "wizards." Each wizard specializes in setting up a project for a particular type of program, giving you a head start in creating a new project so you don't have to start from scratch. Running as a dynamic link library under the Developer Studio environment, a wizard queries for the features you want in your new program, then generates starter source files in which much of the mundane coding for the requested features has been done for you. Visual C++ provides a variety of wizards for specialty projects such as ActiveX controls and Developer Studio add-in utilities. There's even a wizard that helps you create your own custom wizards. We'll encounter some of these types of projects in later chapters, but this chapter concentrates on Visual C++'s flagship wizard, called AppWizard. Except for differences in wording here and there, AppWizard has changed little in version 6 from previous versions. If you have used AppWizard before, you can safely skip this chapter.

## Advantages of AppWizard

AppWizard specializes in setting up a development project for a typical C++ Windows application that uses the Microsoft Foundation Class library.

If you want to write your program in C or prefer not to use MFC, forget AppWizard. Use the Win32 Application Wizard instead, as AppWizard will do nothing for you. Earlier versions of AppWizard were designed especially to create applications based on the document/view architecture, in which a program's data is maintained by document objects and presented to the user through view objects. MFC itself is heavily biased toward such a program structure. AppWizard has become more flexible in the latest version of Visual C++, able to prepare applications without built-in document support, an option suitable for many smaller programs that do not read or create files. You might call this compact type of logic "view-only architecture" instead of document/view, since the created application contains a view class that handles display, but does not provide a corresponding class for a document object. AppWizard can also create a dialog-based application that does not rely on document/view, interfacing with the user instead through a single dialog box. Chapter 5, Dialog Boxes and Controls, describes how to create dialog-based applications in Visual C++ with and without AppWizard.

Each class in the generated project gets its own implementation file and header file. The completeness of the source code in the files ranges from empty stub functions to fully formed program elements such as a toolbar and an About box that the user can invoke from the Help menu. AppWizard contributes code for a variety of program features, including:

- Single-document, multi-document, and dialog-based interfaces

- A docking toolbar, status bar, and printing support

- Menus with commands for typical operations such as Open, Save, Print, Cut, Copy, and Paste

- Starter files for context-sensitive help

- An About box that displays program information and the MFC icon

- Database support

- OLE/ActiveX support for compound documents, Automation, and ActiveX controls

- Support for Messaging API (MAPI) and Windows Sockets

In this chapter we'll look at how to use AppWizard to create a new project that comes preloaded with these and other features. To give you an idea of how much work AppWizard saves you, Figure 2-1 shows what a typical application looks like right out of the box, built from the project files that AppWizard generates. No other programming is needed.

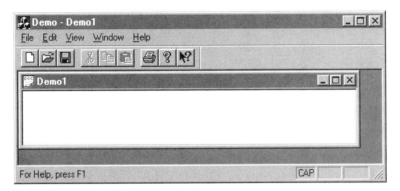

**Figure 2-1.** *A basic application created by AppWizard.*

AppWizard runs only once at the inception of a project, offering enough options to get you started but no more. You are not entirely cast adrift, however, because AppWizard sets up the project in a way that allows you to continue development using other Visual C++ tools such as Class-Wizard. For example, you will notice special comment statements when you look at the source files that AppWizard generates. As we'll see in Chapter 6, ClassWizard uses the comments to monitor the project's classes.

The number of source files that AppWizard generates for a project depends on the features you request; Table 2-1, on the following page, shows a typical list. Each implementation file in the list has a corresponding header file with the same name.

You might be tempted to dismiss AppWizard as training wheels for beginners, too confining for hard-core programmers. And if you regularly create the same types of projects, beginning a new project by copying and revising the source files from a previous project may have advantages over

| File | Description |
|------|-------------|
| *project*.cpp | Main application source file. |
| *project*View.cpp | Source code for the program's view class. |
| *project*Doc.cpp | Source code for the program's document class. |
| MainFrm.cpp | Source code for the class *CMainFrame*. Derived either from MFC's *CFrameWnd* or *CMDIFrameWnd*, this class controls the program's main window. |
| StdAfx.cpp | Used to build a precompiled header file named *project*.pch. The precompiled header contains a compiled form of the MFC include files used by the project, the names of which begin with the prefix "*Afx*." The resulting object data makes the precompiled header file large, often over 6 MB in size. But the header file significantly reduces build times by saving the compiler the work of recompiling the same unchanging code each time. |
| *project*.rc | Contains project resource data (described in Chapter 4, Resources). |
| Resource.h | Contains **#define** statements for the project's manifest constants. |

**Table 2-1.**    *Source files typically generated by AppWizard. The italicized word* project *represents the project name.*

enlisting AppWizard to create a new set of files for you. But wizard technology in Visual C++ has matured to the point where it's a mistake to avoid AppWizard because it somehow seems too easy. In less than 60 seconds you can step over the often tedious setup stages of a development project and immediately start production coding. And you can rely on the source code that AppWizard writes to be error-free, an assurance you do not have when cutting and pasting code between projects. If the type of program you have in mind is the type that AppWizard specializes in, don't hesitate. You can save a lot of time by setting the project up with AppWizard.

# Running AppWizard

An AppWizard project begins with the New command on the environment's File menu:

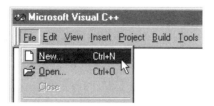

Clicking New displays the Projects tab of the New dialog box, which lists the Visual C++ wizards. To run the AppWizard that creates a project for a typical Windows application, select the icon labeled MFC AppWizard (exe), as shown in Figure 2-2. We'll concentrate on this AppWizard for now. A sister AppWizard invoked by the MFC AppWizard (dll) icon sets up your project for the development of a dynamic link library, as we'll see later in the chapter.

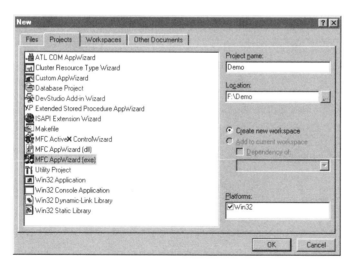

**Figure 2-2.** *To create a project for a typical Windows application, select the MFC AppWizard (exe) icon.*

Enter a name for the project. As mentioned earlier, AppWizard uses the project name to identify various files in the project, so keep the name reasonably short. Once a project is created, there is no practical way to change its name. By default, Visual C++ places AppWizard projects in the Common\MsDev98\MyProjects folder; if you prefer another location, specify a path in the Location text box. The OK button is not enabled until you select an icon in the list and enter a project name.

When you click OK, AppWizard presents a series of up to six steps in the form of dialog boxes. In each step, the left side of the dialog box displays a picture that gives a visual cue of the settings that the dialog is prompting for. Click the Finish button at any step to complete AppWizard and accept default settings in the remaining steps. To step forward or backward through the series of dialog boxes, click the Next button or the Back button.

## Step 1: Program Interface

In Step 1 of AppWizard, shown in Figure 2-3, specify the type of application you want, choosing either single-document interface (SDI), multiple-document interface (MDI), or dialog-based interface. To create a simple Windows application that does not require a document object to read data from a disk file, disable the check box labeled Document/View Architecture Support.

For an SDI application that handles only one document object at a time, turn on the Single Document radio button. This selection is also suitable

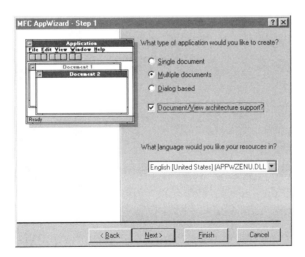

**Figure 2-3.**    *Select the application's interface in Step 1 of AppWizard.*

for an application that does not conform explicitly to the document/view architecture. An SDI application has less overhead than a comparable MDI application, so the SDI application's executable file is smaller.

An MDI application has the advantage of being able to handle any number of documents at once, displaying each document in a separate window. The user can work in different document windows and save each document as a separate file. As we'll see in the next two chapters, the Visual C++ environment is itself an example of an MDI application, able to display both text and nontext data in various editor windows.

The third interface option creates a dialog-based application. This selection is suitable for a small utility program that does not require a main window because the user interacts with the program through a single dialog box. A dialog-based interface isn't as limiting as it may sound, and Chapter 5, Dialog Boxes and Controls, demonstrates how to create a dialog-based application that displays a property sheet dialog box that can accept and display a large amount of information. The Phone Dialer utility that comes with Windows is an example of a dialog-based application.

Because Chapter 5 covers dialog-based applications in detail, the dialog-based interface option is not described here. However, much of the information in this chapter applies to dialog-based applications.

AppWizard's Step 1 also queries for the national language you want for your program's interface. The available languages depend on the AppWizard libraries you have installed on your system; click the arrow button adjacent to the text box to display the language options. Each language relies on its own dynamic link library installed by default in the folder Common\MsDev98\bin\ide. The name of a library file takes the form Appwz*xxx*.dll, where *xxx* represents a three-letter code for the language—for example, *enu* for United States English, *deu* for German, and *fra* for standard French. Figure 2-4, on the following page, shows what the File menu looks like in three different languages for an application generated by AppWizard.

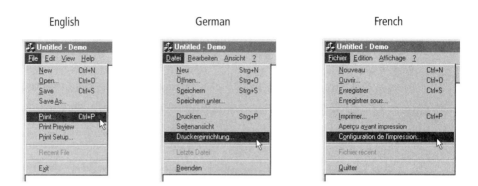

English          German          French

**Figure 2-4.**     *An application's File menu in three different languages.*

## Step 2: Database Support

AppWizard's Step 2 (shown in Figure 2-5) queries for the database support you want for your project. This step and the following steps assume that you selected either the Single Document or Multiple Documents option with document/view support in Step 1.

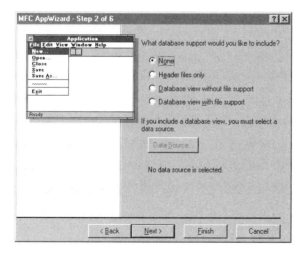

**Figure 2-5.**     *Select database support in AppWizard's Step 2.*

If your project does not use a database, click the Next button to skip this step and continue to Step 3. As shown in Figure 2-5, four radio buttons determine the extent of database support AppWizard adds to the project:

- **None**—Excludes the database support libraries from the project build. If your project does not use a database, select the None radio button to avoid adding unnecessary code to the project files. You can add database support to your project at a later time.

- **Header files only**—Includes database header files and libraries in the build, but AppWizard generates no source code for database classes. You must write all source code yourself. This option is appropriate for a project that does not initially use a database but to which you plan to add database support in the future.

- **Database view without file support**—Includes database header files and libraries, and also creates a record view and recordset. The resulting application supports documents but not serialization.

- **Database view with file support**—Same as the above setting, except that the resulting application has support for both database documents and serialization.

If you choose to include a database view using either of the last two options, you cannot continue to the next step until you define a source for the data.

### Data sources

To define a data source, click the Data Source button to display the Database Options dialog box shown in Figure 2-6, on the following page.

The Database Options dialog box prompts for a data source that conforms to the standards of either Open Database Connectivity (ODBC), Microsoft Data Access Objects (DAO), or OLE database (OLE DB). ODBC functions are implemented in drivers specific to a database management system such as Microsoft Access, Oracle, or dBase. Visual C++ provides a collection of ODBC drivers; others are available from various vendors. For a list of drivers included with Visual C++, see the article titled "ODBC Driver List" in online help.

When you select ODBC as the type of data source for your program, AppWizard generates code that calls the ODBC Driver Manager, which passes each call to the appropriate driver. The driver in turn interacts with the target database management system using Structured Query Language

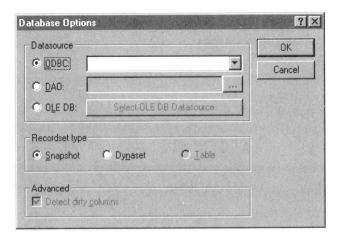

**Figure 2-6.**     *Identify a data source in the Database Options dialog box.*

(SQL). ODBC support ensures that an application can access data in different formats and configurations.

Selecting ODBC enables a drop-down list of all data sources registered with the ODBC Data Source Administrator. A data source includes both data and the information required to access the data. To register or unregister a data source, run the Administrator by double-clicking the 32-bit ODBC icon in Control Panel. Visual C++ normally sets up the Administrator during installation, but if you requested a custom installation of Visual C++, the Administrator might not exist on your system. If the 32-bit ODBC icon does not appear in Control Panel, run the Visual C++ Setup program again and install the necessary ODBC database support files.

DAO is the standard for Microsoft products such as Access and Visual Basic. Using the Microsoft Jet database engine, DAO provides a set of access objects including database objects, tabledef and querydef objects, and recordset objects. Though DAO works best with MDB files like those created by Microsoft Access, a DAO program can also access ODBC data sources through Microsoft Jet.

OLE DB is a new data access strategy that allows a client application, called a consumer, to retrieve data from any data source equipped with a data translator, called a provider. The provider, which appears to the consumer application as a set of Component Object Model (COM) objects, generally does not create the data, but instead serves as a go-between that accesses the data in its native format (whatever that might be) and passes it on to the consumer in a recognizable form. Figure 2-7 illustrates how the consumer communicates with the provider, not with the original creator of the data source.

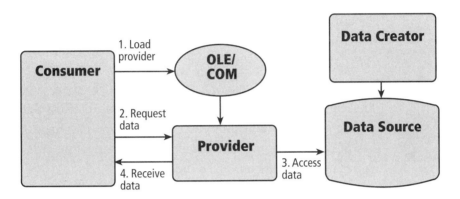

**Figure 2-7.**     *Typical interactions in OLE DB between data consumer and provider.*

An advantage of OLE DB is that there need not be any prior agreement between consumer and provider about the format of the data. At a minimum, the provider is responsible for translating the data into a form the consumer understands, usually in a tabular format. A provider can also add enhancements to the raw data, such as query processing or sorting by specified criteria. Selecting the OLE DB option in AppWizard's Database Options dialog is the first step to creating a data consumer application, not a data provider. The option generates code taken from a library of class templates, called the OLE DB Consumer Templates, which provide wrappers for OLE DB class objects such as *CDataSource* and *CSession*. Visual C++ provides another wizard, ATL COM AppWizard, that assists in writing provider applications. Chapter 10, Writing ActiveX Controls Using ATL, has more to say about ATL COM AppWizard and the Active Template Library, though from the perspective of writing ActiveX controls, not OLE DB providers.

### Recordset type

Specify the type of recordset your program will use by selecting one of the three radio buttons in the Recordset Type section of the Database Options dialog box. The radio buttons govern the three options described here:

- **Snapshot**—A snapshot recordset holds a view of data as the data existed at the time the snapshot was created. A snapshot is static, meaning that the recordset does not reflect changes to the original data until refreshed through a call to the *Requery* function of class *CRecordset* or *CDaoRecordset*.

- **Dynaset**—The contents of a dynaset recordset are dynamic, meaning that the recordset is automatically updated to reflect the most recent changes to the underlying records. However, a dynaset holds a fixed set of records. Once the dynaset is created, new records created by other users are not added to the set.

- **Table**—The Table option is enabled only when DAO is selected for the data source type. This option allows your program to use DAO objects to manipulate data in a base table. When you click OK to close the Database Options dialog box with the Table radio button selected, another dialog box appears in which you can choose the tables you want your program to use.

## Step 3: OLE and ActiveX Support

In AppWizard's Step 3 (Figure 2-8), set the desired type of OLE and ActiveX support for your program. The five radio buttons in the top half of the dialog box control the type of compound document support AppWizard adds to your program. Here are descriptions of the compound document support options:

- **None**—AppWizard does not generate any code for compound document support.

- **Container**—AppWizard creates a program that can contain linked and embedded objects.

- **Mini-server**—The program functions as a mini-server, able to create compound document objects that a container application can

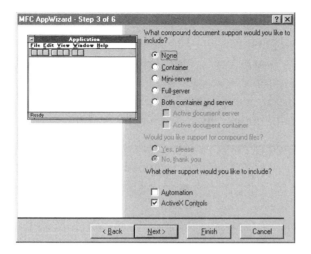

**Figure 2-8.**    *Specify OLE/ActiveX support in AppWizard's Step 3.*

incorporate into its own documents. The resulting document appears to the user as a single document, but in reality it is formed from different sources. A mini-server writes its data directly to a container's document, not a disk file, so mini-servers create objects that a container application can embed but not link. A mini-server application cannot run as a stand-alone program, but must be launched instead by a container. Microsoft Draw is an example of a mini-server.

■ **Full-server**—The program that AppWizard creates can function as a full-server application, possessing all the attributes of a mini-server plus additional capabilities. Like a mini-server, a full-server application can be launched by a container, but can also run as a stand-alone Windows application. AppWizard adds support for storing data to disk files, so a full-server application can support linking as well as embedding.

■ **Both container and server**—AppWizard generates code that enables your program to function as both a container application able to embed objects, and as a server application able to provide objects.

Selecting an option for compound documents, either for a container or server application, lets you choose additional support for Active

43

documents. Active documents provide a higher degree of integration between client and server than do normal embedded documents, allowing a document maintained by one application to appear inside the window of another application. Figure 2-9 shows an example of this type of integration, in which Internet Explorer—the container, in this case—has opened a document created by the server Microsoft Word.

If you want your container or server program to have the ability to serialize compound data—that is, save documents and objects to disk—turn on the radio button to request support for compound files. Though conceptually a single file, a compound file actually represents a consortium of different files, one file containing the document and other files containing the objects linked to the document. When a compound document is saved, the container is responsible for writing its own document object to disk. It then passes on to servers a request for them to save to the same "storage" their respective objects that the container is using.

Two check boxes at the bottom of the Step 3 dialog box query for Automation and ActiveX control support. By default, AppWizard activates the ActiveX Controls option; if your program will not embed ActiveX controls, clear the check box. This decision is not irrevocable, and you can easily add support for ActiveX controls to an MFC program later by including a single line of code. For an explanation of how to retrofit ActiveX control support to an existing MFC program, see page 343 in Chapter 8, Using ActiveX Controls.

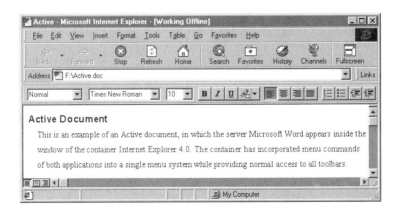

**Figure 2-9.**    *An example of an Active document container and server working together.*

## Step 4: User Interface Features

AppWizard's Step 4, shown in Figure 2-10, gives you control over which user interface elements AppWizard will create for your program.

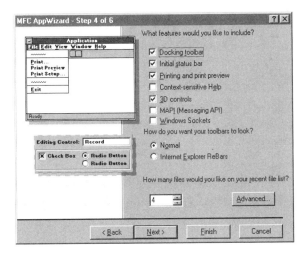

**Figure 2-10.**    *Select user interface features for your program in AppWizard's Step 4.*

AppWizard automatically generates code and data for a menu system, toolbar, and status bar for the program's main window. The toolbar contains buttons that mimic the menu commands, and the status bar displays descriptive help messages for commands and toolbar buttons. A help message appears in the status bar when the cursor rests momentarily on a menu command or toolbar button, as illustrated here:

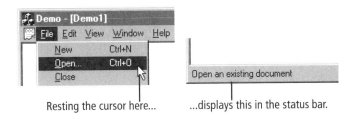

When no command is selected, the status bar displays a message such as "Ready" or "For Help, press F1" or any other message you wish. The status bar also includes indicators for the keyboard's Caps Lock, Num Lock, and Scroll Lock keys. The MFC framework updates the indicators automatically as your program runs, so you need add no other code to incorporate the feature.

The radio buttons labeled Normal and Internet Explorer ReBars offer two different styles for the application's toolbar. Selecting the ReBars option generates code for the toolbar using MFC's new *CReBar* class, resulting in the flat toolbar style found in Visual C++, Internet Explorer, and other applications. A flat toolbar is resizable—hence the shorthand term "rebar"—and displays flat buttons that become raised only when the mouse cursor passes over them. The subjects of menus, toolbars, and status bars are examined in more detail in Chapter 4, Resources.

## Printing support

By default, AppWizard activates the Printing And Print Preview check box. This option adds starter code to an application's view class that over-rides three virtual functions of MFC's *CView*:

```
/////////////////////////////////////////////////////////////////////////
// CDemoView printing

BOOL CDemoView::OnPreparePrinting(CPrintInfo* pInfo)
{
    // default preparation
    return DoPreparePrinting(pInfo);
}

void CDemoView::OnBeginPrinting(CDC* /*pDC*/, CPrintInfo* /*pInfo*/)
{
    // TODO: add extra initialization before printing
}

void CDemoView::OnEndPrinting(CDC* /*pDC*/, CPrintInfo* /*pInfo*/)
{
    // TODO: add cleanup after printing
}
```

The overrides provide skeleton functionality for printing in a document/ view program, but you have more work ahead of you before your program can intelligently print a document. For a good description of how to add printing capabilities to an MFC program, see Chapter 10, Printing and Print Preview, in Jeff Prosise's *Programming Windows 95 with MFC*. MSDN online help also provides information in a series of articles beginning with "Printing and Print Preview Topics." Locate the article by typing its title in the MSDN Search tab with the Search Titles Only check box set.

### Online help

Activating the check box labeled Context-Sensitive Help signals App-Wizard that you want your program to provide online help. AppWizard adds source code and a collection of files to the project that get you started on creating a complete help system. AppWizard takes care of documenting all the commands and toolbar buttons that it adds to your program, such as New, Open, Cut, and Paste. The descriptions are clear and well written, requiring no further work on your part. You need only enhance the help file by documenting those commands you add to the program yourself. This section first describes the help system that AppWizard creates, then briefly explains how to enhance it with your own help text.

When you request context-sensitive help for your program, AppWizard creates a subfolder named HLP in the project folder. Among the files in the HLP subfolder is a topic file named AfxCore.rtf. If you request printing support for your project, AppWizard adds another topic file named AfxPrint.rtf. Written in rich-text format, AfxCore.rtf and AfxPrint.rtf contain help text describing the features that AppWizard has contributed to the project. The HLP subfolder also contains a help project file that has the same name as the project and an HPJ extension. When you build your project, Visual C++ executes a batch file called MakeHelp.bat before launching the compiler. MakeHelp.bat runs the Makehm.exe Help Maintenance utility, which reads symbol definitions in the project's Resource.h file and creates a help map file, recognizable by its HM extension. The batch file then runs the Hcrtf.exe help compiler, which assembles information drawn from the help map, the project's HPJ file, and the text in the RTF files, to create an HLP file that the Windows WinHlp32 help file viewer can read.

AppWizard also writes source instructions that run WinHlp32 and load the project's HLP file in response to the user's requests for help. The entire help interface is accomplished through four entries added to the message map in the project's MainFrm.cpp file, as shown on the next page.

```
BEGIN_MESSAGE_MAP(CMainFrame, CFrameWnd)
    ⋮
    ON_COMMAND(ID_HELP_FINDER, CFrameWnd::OnHelpFinder)
    ON_COMMAND(ID_HELP, CFrameWnd::OnHelp)
    ON_COMMAND(ID_CONTEXT_HELP, CFrameWnd::OnContextHelp)
    ON_COMMAND(ID_DEFAULT_HELP, CFrameWnd::OnHelpFinder)
END_MESSAGE_MAP()
```

Each entry in the map points to one of three functions provided by the MFC framework. The functions are called in response to different events, each function invoking WinHlp32 and displaying appropriate text from the project's help file. The following table describes when the functions are called:

| This function is called . . . | When the user . . . |
| --- | --- |
| *OnHelpFinder* | Selects the Help Topics command from the Help menu. |
| *OnHelp* | Presses the F1 key to receive help on the current context. |
| *OnContextHelp* | Presses Shift+F1 or clicks the Help button on the toolbar. |

Selecting the Help Topics command from the Help menu displays a typical Help Topics dialog box in the WinHlp32 viewer, as shown in Figure 2-11.

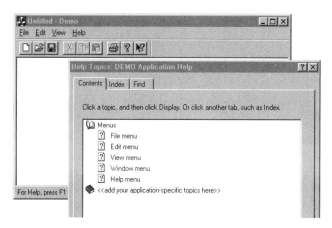

**Figure 2-11.**    *The Help Topics dialog box.*

The user can navigate the Help Topics dialog box to find help on the desired topic.

AppWizard also adds a Help button to your program's toolbar, similar to the small question mark button that appears in the upper-right corner of Developer Studio dialog boxes. Clicking the Help button changes the cursor image to an arrow with a question mark. The user can then click on any part of the program window, including menu commands, the status bar, and toolbar buttons:

Invoking the Help tool causes the program to execute WinHlp32, which displays a help window describing the clicked element. For example, requesting help by clicking the Save button as illustrated above displays the help window shown in Figure 2-12.

To enhance the help system with descriptions of other features that you program yourself, load AfxCore.rtf in a word processor that recognizes the rich-text format. Don't use the WordPad utility that comes with Windows for this chore. Although WordPad reads rich-text documents, it does not save information expected by the help compiler. Rich-text documents are in normal ASCII format, so in a pinch you can make small changes with a text editor.

The first step in creating your own help text is to search for the string "<<YourApp>>" and replace each occurrence with your application's name. Double angle brackets (<< >>) in the document enclose placeholder text that suggests the type of help text you should add. Replace both the suggestions and the brackets with new text. Remove any parts of the topics that do not apply to your application, taking your cue for the necessary formatting from the text placed in the file by AppWizard. Topics in the file must be separated with a hard page break.

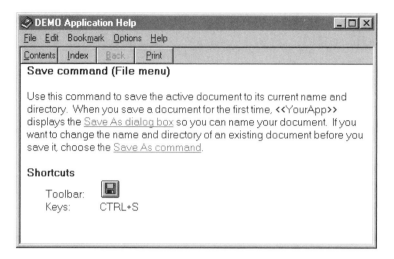

**Figure 2-12.**   *Help window for the program's Save command.*

Help authoring is a large subject, and a complete description is not possible here. Online help describes how to use the Help Workshop utility provided with Visual C++ to build on the help system that AppWizard creates.

### The Advanced button

In the lower right corner of AppWizard's Step 4 dialog box is an Advanced button that, when clicked, displays a two-tabbed dialog box titled Advanced Options. The first tab, labeled Document Template Strings, lets you rewrite certain character strings stored in the program's data that are used by Windows and the MFC framework. If you selected the Active Document Server check box in AppWizard's third step, you must specify in the Document Template Strings tab a file extension for your application's document files. Type the extension string in the tab's first edit box, as shown on the next page.

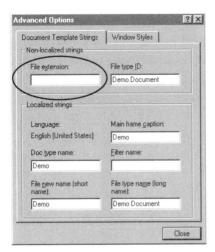

The system recognizes files with this extension as belonging to your server application in the same way it associates DOC files, for example, with Microsoft Word. AppWizard fills the remaining boxes with strings appropriate for your application, which you can accept or revise as you desire. We'll look at these strings in more detail in Chapter 4 in the section titled "The Document String," beginning on page 139.

The dialog's second tab, labeled Window Styles, lets you control both the appearance of your program's main window and, if you selected the Multiple Document option in Step 1, the appearance of your program's document windows. Selecting the Use Split Window check box at the top of the Window Styles tab adds this function to an SDI project's MainFrm.cpp file:

```
BOOL CMainFrame::OnCreateClient( LPCREATESTRUCT /*lpcs*/,
    CCreateContext* pContext)
{
    return m_wndSplitter.Create( this,
        2, 2,
        CSize( 10, 10 ),
        pContext );
}
```

An MDI project receives a similar *OnCreateClient* function in its Child-Frm.cpp file. For an SDI application, the *OnCreateClient* function enables splitter bars in your program's main window. A Split command in the program's View menu turns on the splitter bars, allowing your program to display data in one, two, or four different panes of the same window. For an MDI application, AppWizard places the Split command on the program's Window menu where it controls splitter bars for each child window. Figure 3-4 on page 71 shows an example of splitter bars used in the Visual C++ text editor.

## Step 5: Using the MFC Library

AppWizard's Step 5, shown in Figure 2-13, asks for the style of program you want to create, whether you want additional source code comments, and how you prefer your program to link to the MFC library.

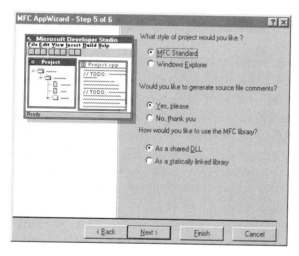

**Figure 2-13.**    *Selecting source file comments and MFC library options.*

### Project style

AppWizard offers two variations of program style determined by radio buttons at the top of the Step 5 dialog. The default radio button, labeled MFC Standard, is the correct choice for creating a normal Windows application with a view class derived from *CView*. Upcoming chapters in this book use the MFC Standard setting when employing AppWizard to create sample programs, so it's worthwhile to spend some time here examining the effects of the second radio button. The button is labeled Windows Explorer because the application that AppWizard creates has an appearance and user interface similar to the well-known Explorer utility that comes with Windows.

The main window of an Explorer-type application is split into two side-by-side panes, each pane showing a different display and each governed by its own class. The view class for the left pane derives from MFC's *CTreeView*, making the pane suitable for displaying a list of items related through a tree-like hierarchy, such as a company's personnel list, a genealogy chart, or the layout of files and folders on a hard disk. The view class corresponding to the right pane derives from *CListView*, designed to display a list of items that pertain in some way to the current selection in the left pane. Like Explorer, the program's toolbar contains four additional buttons that modify the pane's appearance, allowing the user to choose different display arrangements of large or small icons. Here's an idea of how a typical Explorer-type application might look:

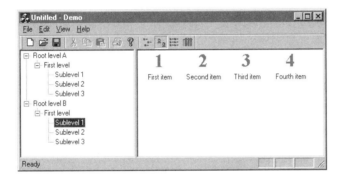

The items in the tree view control comprising the left pane have small plus and minus buttons that expand or collapse the list. The application adds the buttons and hierarchy lines by setting style flags in the window's CREATESTRUCT structure:

```
BOOL CLeftView::PreCreateWindow(CREATESTRUCT& cs)
{
    cs.style |= TVS_HASLINES | TVS_HASBUTTONS | TVS_LINESATROOT;
    return CTreeView::PreCreateWindow(cs);
}
```

We haven't yet talked about the Visual C++ editors with which you can examine and revise a program, but if you are interested in reviewing the source code for the simple application pictured above, you will find the project files on the companion CD in the folder Code\Chapter.02\Demo. The Demo project was created using AppWizard, choosing the Single

Document option in Step 1 and the Windows Explorer option in Step 5, and accepting AppWizard's defaults for the remaining selections. Demo is a rudimentary project, created only to suggest the type of code you should add to an Explorer-type application generated by AppWizard. Chapter 3, The Text Editor, and Chapter 4, Resources, describe in much more depth how to use the Visual C++ editors to access and view projects such as those found on the companion CD.

### Source file comments

Requesting source file comments causes AppWizard to add helpful "to do" notes to the generated source code. The notes appear as comments similar to the ones shown here, suggesting source instructions you should add to make a feature or function operable:

```
void CDemoDoc::Serialize(CArchive& ar)
{
    if (ar.IsStoring())
    {
        // TODO: add storing code here
    }
    else
    {
        // TODO: add loading code here
    }
}
```

Selecting the option to add source file comments also causes AppWizard to place a ReadMe.txt file in the project folder. The ReadMe file acts as a table of contents for the entire project, providing brief descriptions of all the files that AppWizard generates.

### Linking to the MFC library

The third query in Step 5 determines how your program links to MFC. By default, the As A Shared DLL radio button is selected, meaning that AppWizard sets up the application to link dynamically to the MFC library contained in a separate file. This type of link significantly reduces the application's executable size and typically results in a more efficient use of system resources.

However, linking dynamically to MFC requires the presence of the Mfc*nn*.dll library file, where *nn* in the filename represents the MFC version number. The file is usually located in the Windows System or System32 folder. If your application links dynamically to MFC and you distribute the application for general use on systems that might not have the Mfc*nn*.dll library, you should provide the file to users as part of your application package. If your application uses Unicode, provide the Mfc*nn*u.dll file instead. Microsoft allows you to freely distribute these library files with your application. Your application's installation program can search for the presence of the MFC library file on the user's hard disk and copy the file to the System folder if it is not already there. The Msvcrt.dll file must also be copied if it does not exist because MFC uses the shared version of the C run-time library. Libraries remain backward compatible with older applications, so your installation program need not copy the MFC and C run-time library files if the user's System folder already contains newer versions of the files.

There are additional considerations if your dynamically linked application is intended for overseas markets where it is likely to run on systems set up for a different language. The MFC library file contains string data such as dialog text and help messages that a program can access. You must ensure that your application does not access and display library strings written in a language other than the user's native language. There are two ways to solve this problem. The simplest solution is to write your application so that it uses its own string data exclusively without accessing text provided by the library. (Chapter 4, Resources, covers this subject in more detail.) You can then distribute Mfc*nn*.dll without regard to the user's regional settings.

The second solution involves writing your installation program so that it queries the host system for its local language, copies the redistributable file Mfc*nnxxx*.dll to the System folder, and renames the file Mfc*nn*loc.dll. (The *xxx* in the filename represents the three-letter code for the host language, such as *deu* for German and *fra* for standard French.) For more information on this topic, see Technical Notes 56 and 57 in online help, located through the "MFC components" entry in the MSDN index.

If you prefer to link your application statically to MFC, select the radio button labeled As A Statically Linked Library. Static linking means that your application does not depend on the presence of the MFC library file, though it still requires the Msvcrt.dll file. The cost of static linking is a larger executable size and potentially the inefficient use of memory. Linking statically to MFC is not possible with the Learning Edition of Visual C++.

The MFC linking option you choose in Step 5 is only the initial setting for the project, and you can select a different option at any time during development. Before building the project, choose the Settings command from the Project menu and, in the dialog box's General tab, choose either static or dynamic linking.

## Step 6: Classes and Filenames

AppWizard's sixth and last step itemizes the classes that AppWizard will create for the project. To change the name of a class, select it in the list and enter a new name in the Class Name text box. Other text boxes show the names of the files that AppWizard creates for the class source code. The names are only suggestions, and you can enter new filenames for all classes in the list except the application class (named *CDemoApp* in Figure 2-14). The source file containing the application class takes its name from the project, and so cannot be altered.

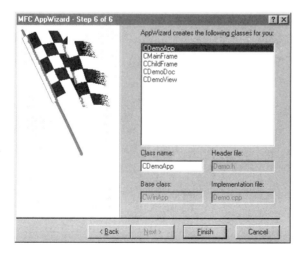

**Figure 2-14.**    *Specifying class names in AppWizard's Step 6.*

When you click the Finish button, AppWizard displays a summary sheet that lists the project features you have selected (Figure 2-15). The summary gives you one final chance to cancel the project. Clicking OK causes AppWizard to create the project at the location listed at the bottom of the summary sheet.

**Figure 2-15.**    *A summary of project features selected in AppWizard.*

## Creating a DLL with AppWizard

If you intend to develop a dynamic link library instead of a normal Windows application, select the MFC AppWizard (dll) icon in the New dialog box (see Figure 2-3 on page 36). This particular AppWizard displays only the single step shown in Figure 2-16 on the following page, which queries for information such as how your dynamic link library should link to MFC.

The wizard offers three different linking options, each with advantages and disadvantages. The first two options result in a dynamic link library that any Win32 program can access. The third option is more limiting because it creates a dynamic link library that can be used only by applications or other libraries that themselves use MFC. The linking options are described on the next page.

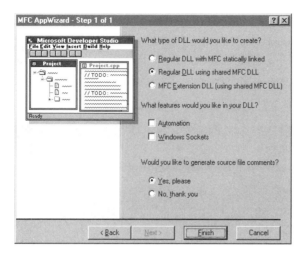

**Figure 2-16.**    *Setting up a DLL project with AppWizard.*

■ **Regular DLL with MFC statically linked**—Your dynamic link library links statically to MFC, enabling it to run on any Win32 system without relying on the presence of the MFC library file.

■ **Regular DLL using shared MFC DLL**—In order to run, your dynamic link library requires access to the correct version of the MFC library file. This reduces the size of the finished executable, but might require distribution of the MFC library file with your product as explained in the previous section. Consider this option especially if your dynamic link library is designed to operate with applications that dynamically link to the same version of MFC, since a single instance of MFC can then service both the calling applications and your library.

■ **MFC Extension DLL (using shared MFC DLL)**—This option is similar to the preceding option with the important difference that the calling process must also link dynamically to the correct version of the MFC library. An MFC Extension DLL provides classes that enhance or supplement the functionality of existing MFC classes. For more information about writing an MFC Extension DLL, refer to Technical Note 33, "DLL Version of MFC," in MSDN online help.

Check the Automation check box if you want to expose your dynamic link library to Automation clients such as Microsoft Excel and Visual Basic. Check the Windows Sockets check box to add support for communicating over the Internet or any network system that uses the TCP/IP protocol. Selecting Windows Sockets support causes AppWizard to add a call to MFC's *AfxSocketInit* function:

```
BOOL CDemoApp::InitInstance()
{
    if (!AfxSocketInit())
    {
        AfxMessageBox(IDP_SOCKETS_INIT_FAILED);
        return FALSE;
    }

    return TRUE;
}
```

You must of course write the actual communication code yourself.

## Managing the Module State

In keeping with the straightforward nature of dynamic link libraries, the code that AppWizard generates for a library project is austere compared to all the source code it writes for a normal application. A single CPP file named for the project contains a message map and the class constructor. The file also includes a comment block explaining that exported functions in the library may need to invoke MFC's AFX_MANAGE_STATE macro. It depends on whether your library links statically or dynamically to the MFC library DLL. Static linkage to MFC does not require AFX_MANAGE_STATE, but since linker settings for your project can easily change during development, it's best to assume at the outset that a dynamic link library using MFC services links dynamically to the MFC library. Exported functions that call MFC should therefore begin by invoking the AFX_MANAGE_STATE macro like this:

```
extern "C" __declspec( dllexport ) void WINAPI ExportedFunction()
{
    #ifdef _AFXDLL
        AFX_MANAGE_STATE( AfxGetStaticModuleState() );
```

```
#endif
    ⋮
}
```

Within each thread's local storage, MFC maintains a pointer to a structure called the module state, which contains information specific to the process module currently being serviced by the MFC library. When an application enters an exported function in your dynamic link library, the module state pertains to the calling application, not your library. Before passing execution on to MFC, the exported function should first alter the pointer to reference the DLL's own module state. This is the purpose of the AFX_MANAGE_STATE macro, which temporarily switches the module state pointer to reference the current module—that is, your dynamic link library—then restores the original pointer when the exported function goes out of scope and returns to the calling application. AFX_MANAGE_STATE is not necessary in exported functions called by the MFC library itself, such as *InitInstance* and handler functions listed in a message map, because MFC takes care of setting the correct module state before the call.

The AFX_MANAGE_STATE macro should appear near the beginning of a function, even before definitions of object variables, because their constructors may themselves include calls into the MFC library. The **#ifdef** condition block shown in the fragment ensures that the compiler includes the macro code only for a library that links dynamically to MFC. If linkage is static, the Visual C++ compiler does not predefine the _AFXDLL constant. For more detailed information about the AFX_MANAGE_STATE macro, refer to Technical Note 58, "MFC Module State Implementation," in MSDN online help.

# Editors

# The Text Editor

Visual C++ provides a true programming text editor that is designed specifically for the task of "cutting code." The editor integrates very well with other environment tools such as the debugger, and offers a wide range of sophisticated features including Undo/Redo, customizable keystroke commands, and instant access to Win32 and MFC references.

A text editor requires little in the way of preamble—as a programmer, you've already used at least one editor and probably several—so let's begin. This chapter covers the most important aspects of the Visual C++ text editor, describing useful and hidden features and showing you how to use the editor effectively. Even if you decide to remain with your current editor for most of your coding tasks, you should at least skim this chapter to get an idea of the Visual C++ editor's abilities. Sooner or later you will find it convenient to remain in the Developer Studio environment when editing text, if only to make quick revisions to fix compiler errors. There are also some tips at the end of the chapter you may find useful.

Because it is a Windows product, the Visual C++ text editor saves its text files in the ANSI file format. For a discussion of the ANSI standard and tables of both the ASCII and ANSI character sets, refer to Appendix A.

# Launching the Text Editor

When you first enter Visual C++, you don't see the text editor. Nor do you see a button that says "Start the text editor" or even the word "editor" mentioned in any of the menus. In the object-oriented environment of Visual C++, you worry only about the type of document you want, not about what tool you need to create it. The environment oversees several editors besides the text editor, so you need only indicate that you want to create or revise a text document rather than, say, a graphics document. Visual C++ infers from the document type which editor to start.

To begin a new document from scratch, pull down the File menu and choose the New command. On the Files tab of the New dialog shown in Figure 3-1, Visual C++ displays a list of document types you can create, arranging the list in alphabetical order.

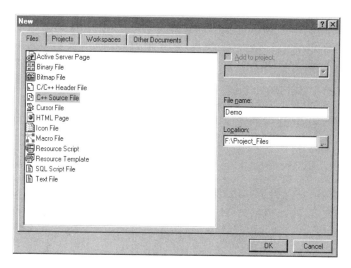

**Figure 3-1.**      *Selecting a document type in the New dialog.*

Enter a document name if you prefer, and then select from the list either Active Server Page, C/C++ Header File, C++ Source File, HTML Page, Macro File, SQL Script File, or Text File. Click the OK button to start the text editor, which appears in the form of a blank document window. There is little fanfare when this happens and the menus and toolbars hardly change. The continuity ensures a common appearance and behavior among the Visual C++ editors, making the entire product easier to learn and use. If the new document appears as a full-size window, only a few visual clues (besides the document itself) indicate that you are now in the text editor rather than the Visual C++ main window. One clue is a small page icon that appears at the left edge of the menu bar. Another visual indication is the appearance of the document name enclosed in brackets in the title bar at the top of the main window. If you do not enter a document name in the New dialog, the editor invents one for you, giving the new document a temporary name like Text1 or Cpp1. The name serves as a placeholder until you save the document and provide a more descriptive name for the file.

Beneath the surface, other changes occur within the menus. As we'll see in later chapters, the menus are common to all the Visual C++ editors, including the text editor. When the text editor starts, many of the menu commands that were disabled in the main window appear in normal text rather than gray text to indicate that the commands are now active. Visual C++ automatically enables appropriate menu commands for whichever editor has input focus. For example, because searching for text has meaning only in the text editor, the Find command on the Edit menu appears in normal text when the text editor is active but is gray when the graphics editor has focus. Figure 3-2, on the next page, briefly describes the menus available when the text editor is active.

Other commands are available as well. For example, if you delete text in the editor and then change your mind, the Edit menu offers the Undo and Redo commands. These commands remember a history of deletions starting with the most recent deletion. To restore text from earlier deletions, keep clicking Undo or press Ctrl+Z repeatedly until you work your way back through the history to the text you want restored. This has the side effect of restoring more recent deletions in reverse order, which may not be what you want. The Redo command on the Edit menu (also activated by pressing the Ctrl+Y key combination) reverses the most recent Undo command, letting you "undo an undo."

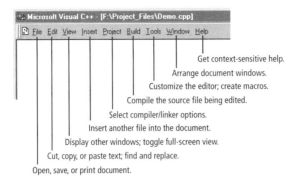

**Figure 3-2.** *Text editor menus.*

# Documents

This section is the longest of the chapter, describing how to create, open, view, save, and print a text document. As I mentioned in the Introduction at the beginning of the book, some of the material covered here will probably seem like a review if you have used a Windows-based text editor or word processor before. But even experienced Windows users may benefit from the topics on viewing and printing a document, since they cover material specific to the Visual C++ text editor.

For the record, the words "document" and "file" are commonly used interchangeably when referring to text editing. Opening a file and opening a document have the same meaning.

## Opening a Document

The Visual C++ text editor complies with MDI (multiple document interface), so you can have any number of documents open at the same time. Repeating the steps of opening a document with the New command creates a second empty document, this time with a default name like Text2 or Cpp2. If the window is full size, the name of the current document—that is, the document that has the input focus—appears in the title bar at the top of the screen. You can switch between open documents by pressing Ctrl+F6 or by selecting the desired document name from the Window menu.

A document is created only once during its life. When you save a new document to disk, it exists from that point on as a file and must be opened rather than created when you want to work on it again. Use one of the following methods to open an existing document:

- Click the Open button on the Standard toolbar.

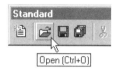

- Press Ctrl+O.

- Choose Open from the File menu.

- Choose the Recent Files command from the File menu and choose the desired filename.

The first three methods invoke the Open dialog, which allows you to browse through folders to find the file you want to open. The last method skips the Open dialog box altogether, presenting a list of most recently used files, called the MRU list, from which you can open a file directly.

### Most recently used files list

By default, the MRU list contains the last four files accessed through any of the Visual C++ editors, not just the text editor. To display the MRU list, pull down the File menu and rest the cursor momentarily on the Recent Files command. Selecting a filename in the list opens the document in the appropriate editor. The MRU list is a welcome convenience when you work on the same few files. For even a small programming project, however, you may find yourself continually editing more than four source files, so even recently accessed files can quickly disappear from the MRU list. Fortunately, Visual C++ lets you expand the list to hold more filenames. Click Options on the Tools menu, and then scroll right if necessary to select the Workspace tab. Enter a new value in the text box labeled Recent File List Contains, as shown on the next page.

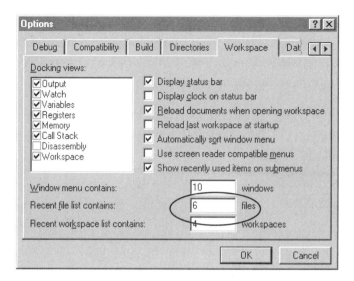

The Workspace tab provides another option that affects the appearance of the MRU list. If you prefer to see the list directly on the File menu instead of on a separate submenu, clear the check box labeled Show Recently Used Items On Submenus. The additional document and project names, however, can make the File menu seem overcrowded.

### The Open dialog

If the file you want does not appear in the most recently used files list, you must use the Open command and identify the file in the Open dialog. The dialog's default directory list displays files in the current project folder, so usually you won't have far to browse for the file.

Select a group of files to open in a single step by holding the Ctrl key down as you click the files in the directory listing. Each click adds a file to the group of selected files. To deselect a file from the group, click its file-name again with the Ctrl key pressed. When you click the Open button, the text editor opens all the selected files at once as separate documents. If the files you want to open appear sequentially in the directory list, there's an even faster way to select them. Click the first file to select it, then hold the Shift key down while clicking the last file of the group. All files in the list between the two you clicked are added to the selection group. To remove a file from the group, click it while pressing the Ctrl key.

**OTE** The file list in the Open dialog does not usually show all the files in a folder because of the filter setting in the Files Of Type combo box. A filter is a group of related file extensions; for example, the default C++ Files filter forces the Open dialog to include in the list only files with the extensions C, CPP, CXX, TLI, H, TLH, INL, and RC. To list other filenames—say, those with HPP or TXT extensions—select the appropriate filter in the Files Of Type box.

The Open dialog includes a check box labeled Open As Read-Only. This check box takes its job description seriously—when activated, it prevents you from making any changes to the open document. You can only scroll through the document, print it, and copy selected text to the Clipboard. Normally, you can remove the read-only lock by choosing Save As from the File menu and saving the document under a different name, thus ensuring that the original file is not altered. Visual C++ version 6 lets you prevent even this harmless circumvention of the read-only lock. On the Compatibility tab of the Options dialog (invoked through the Tools menu), set the check mark in the box labeled Protect Read-Only Files From Editing. When this option is in effect, a read-only document cannot be saved under a different name.

## Viewing a Document

Though the text editor uses the screen intelligently, space can sometimes get cramped in Visual C++ when several windows are visible. For the largest possible view of your source code, choose Full Screen from the View menu as shown in Figure 3-3, on the next page, or press Alt+V and then U. Title bar, menus, and toolbars disappear to provide maximum room. To switch back to normal view, press the Esc key or click the button on the floating Full Screen toolbar. You can access menus in full-screen view by pressing the Alt key followed by the first letter of the menu you want— Alt+F for the File menu, for example. (The Alt key activates the menu bar, so the two keys do not need to be pressed simultaneously.) Press the Right and Left arrow keys to move to adjacent menus. You cannot, however, use the mouse to glide to adjacent menus the way you can when the entire menu bar is visible.

If you find the Full Screen toolbar distracting, remove it by clicking the toolbar's close button. With the Full Screen toolbar disabled, your only

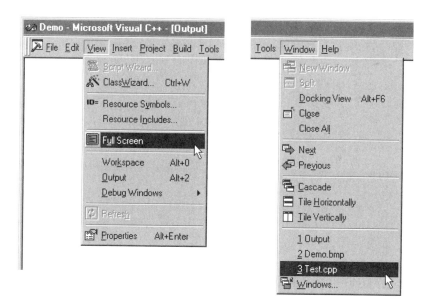

**Figure 3-3.**    *The View and Window menus.*

means of returning to normal viewing from full-screen mode is to press the Esc key. To re-enable the toolbar in full-screen view, press Alt+T to display the Tools menu, and then click the Customize command. On the Toolbars tab of the Customize dialog, activate the Full Screen check box in the list of toolbars. In the same way, you can make other toolbars or even the menu bar visible in full-screen mode.

The Window menu provides a list of all documents that are currently open, including those in other Visual C++ editors. The list in Figure 3-3, for example, contains a text document called Test.cpp and a bitmap open in the graphics editor (described in the next chapter). You can switch between the open documents by pulling down the Window menu and clicking the name of the document you want to work with. To see all document windows at once, choose either the Cascade, Tile Horizontally, or Tile Vertically commands.

Text editor document windows have multiple "splitter" panes, allowing you to view one, two, or four different parts of the same document at once. Figure 3-4 shows a four-pane view of a simple document.

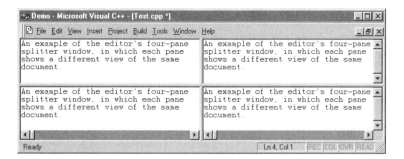

**Figure 3-4.** *A typical document window split into four panes.*

Visual C++ creates each text window using MFC's *CSplitterWnd* class, so splitter panes are enabled automatically when you create or open a document. The splitter bars that separate the panes initially appear as two small buttons, one button placed at the top of the vertical scroll bar and the other button tucked into the far left corner of the horizontal scroll bar. To position a splitter bar, drag its button into the window's client area and release. You can expose both bars in one step by choosing the Split command from the Window menu. The Split command centers an outline of the splitter bars in the window. Move the mouse to position the bars as desired, and then click to lock them into place.

Because splitter panes do not have their own independent scroll bars, the most useful split view employs only two panes, one on top of the other. To make a two-pane view, drag the vertical splitter bar to the far left or right of the window until the bar disappears. Jump from one pane to the other by clicking inside a pane or by pressing the F6 key.

A two-pane split view is very convenient for two horizontal views of a document, but is much less effective for vertical side-by-side views because each pane cannot scroll independently of the other. Fortunately, another command on the Window menu neatly provides two or more vertical views of a document. With a single document open in the text editor, click the New Window command to open another window containing the same document. This is not the same as opening the file again—the new window simply provides a second view of the original document in the editor workspace. Each window has its own scroll system and flashing cursor, so you can simultaneously view various parts of the document. To arrange the windows for side-by-side viewing, click the Tile Vertically command on the Window menu. Click inside a window or press Ctrl+F6 to jump between views.

You can create additional views by clicking New Window again. Although the view windows operate independently of each other, they all reflect the contents of a single document. Any change you make in one window immediately appears in all windows.

## Saving a Document

When you begin typing in a document window, an asterisk appears next to the document name both in the title bar and in the list of open documents on the Window menu. The asterisk lets you know that the document has changed in some way and that the contents of the document workspace in memory now differ from the file on disk. Unlike your word processor, the Visual C++ text editor does not automatically save your work-in-progress at regular intervals. As you type new source code, get in the habit of frequently saving your work to disk using any one of these methods:

■ Click the Save button on the Standard toolbar.

■ Press Ctrl+S.

■ Choose Save from the File menu.

When you save a document, the asterisk appended to the name in the title bar disappears. It reappears the moment you again alter the text. If you close a document when the asterisk is visible, the editor prompts you to first save the document.

In recommending that you save your work regularly, I'm speaking of when you edit a document for an extended period of time. As you type, ask yourself occasionally, "If the power went out right now, would I be disappointed?" If the answer is yes, press Ctrl+S. Saving the document is not important, however, during cycles of code correction when you make small changes to the source and then recompile it. Before relinquishing control to the compiler, the text editor automatically saves the document. It has to, because the compiler reads the file from disk, not from the editor's workspace in memory.

The first time you save an unnamed document, the Save As dialog opens. This is where you give the file a name and an extension. Give a source file an appropriate extension of CPP or C, because the compiler judges the contents of a file by its extension and compiles it as either a C++ or C program accordingly. If you do not specify an extension, Visual C++ adds one that is appropriate for the document type you selected from the New dialog (Figure 3-1 on page 64). For example, selecting C++ Source File from the dialog causes the editor to automatically add a CPP extension to the new filename.

Many programmers prefer an extension of HPP for header files specific to C++. It's hard to argue with the logic of this idea, but it carries a small burden of inconvenience in Visual C++. When you choose Open, the dialog at first displays only files with extensions of C, CPP, CXX, TLI, H, TLH, INL, and RC. To see a file with an HPP extension, you must change the file type filter either to C++ Include Files or to All Files. Otherwise, giving a header file an extension of HPP causes no confusion in Visual C++. Actually, you can name header files with any extension you want because Visual C++ scans source files for **#include** statements when creating a project. Any file referenced by an **#include** statement, regardless of its file extension, is also added to the project and appears in the list of header files in the FileView tab of the Workspace window.

When you save a new document and give it a name, that name replaces the default in the title bar and on the Window menu. Thereafter, whenever you save the file the editor overwrites the previous version on disk without prompting you with the Save As dialog. The editor does not first give the previous version a BAK extension or otherwise preserve it. Once you save a document, its former version on disk is gone forever. If you need several variations of your source, choose Save As from the File menu and give each source version a different filename.

## Printing a Document

To print the document that has input focus, click Print on the File menu or press Ctrl+P to open the Print dialog. If you want to print only a portion of a source listing—say, a single subroutine—first select the desired text. Doing so enables the Selection radio button in the Print dialog, shown in Figure 3-5.

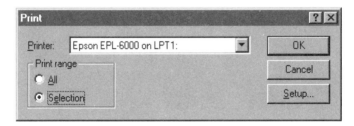

**Figure 3-5.**     *The Print dialog box.*

The Selection radio button indicates that only the selected text rather than the entire document will be printed. You can override the setting by clicking the All radio button.

The dialog shows the printer to which Windows will send the print job. To designate any other printer attached to your system, click the Printer combo box and choose from the list of available printers. Click OK to begin a print job. With print spooling enabled (which is likely), control returns almost immediately to the text editor, allowing you to continue working. You can print several jobs in rapid succession, though monitoring the progress of your print jobs requires an excursion to the Printers folder. Click the Start button on the taskbar, choose Settings, and then click Printers. Select the desired printer and click Open on the File menu to see the current queue of your print jobs.

When print spooling is active, your opportunity to cancel a print job from the editor lasts only a few moments. Once the system print spooler has control of the print job, the Cancel button disappears from the screen. After that, you can cancel a print job only from the Printers folder. If for some reason print spooling is disabled, the text editor must wait until the printer finishes before it returns control to you.

The Visual C++ text editor offers a limited amount of formatting for the printed page, letting you set margins and specify a header and footer to appear on each page. Choose Page Setup from the File menu, then type the desired text into the Header or Footer text box in the Page Setup dialog. Use the codes in Table 3-1 to include real-time information in the header or footer text.

| Print code | Meaning |
|---|---|
| &F | Filename of printed document |
| &P | Current page number |
| &T | System time in the format appropriate for the current language setting, such as 11:54:31 AM |
| &D | System date in the format appropriate for the current language setting, such as 12/16/98 |
| &L | Aligns header or footer text with left margin |
| &C | Centers header or footer text between margins |
| &R | Aligns header or footer text with right margin |

**Table 3-1.**    *Print codes for including information in headers and footers.*

There's no need to memorize these codes. Just click the arrow button adjacent to the text box in the Page Setup dialog to display a list of formatting options, and then click an option in the list to insert its code into your header or footer text. Print codes can be either uppercase or lowercase.

Combine print codes with normal text in any way you wish. For example, a header that identifies the name of the printed file and the date of the printing might look like this:

```
&RFile:  &F;  Date:  &D     page &P
```

The &R code at the start of the text forces the header against the page's right margin, a feature that word processors refer to as "flush right" or "align right." The &P code prints a page number, beginning with 1 for the first page. The page number is relative to the print job, not the document text. If you print text selected from the middle of the document, the &P code still marks the first printed page as page 1. No print code exists for the total page count, so it is not possible to number each page in the form "Page 1 of 20," for example. And because print codes in the header and footer apply to the entire print job, there is no option for specifying &R for odd-numbered pages and &L for even-numbered pages to alternate alignment from right to left.

A header or footer can occupy no more than 40 characters on a single line. Each print code counts as two characters. Tabs are not allowed in the text.

# Navigating Through a Document

Sure, you can move through a document by pressing arrow keys or sliding the scroll bar. But as we'll see, other methods can help you navigate the text editor more precisely and efficiently. First, we should agree on some terminology. The familiar cursor of DOS-based text editors has a different name in Windows. Windows calls the blinking indicator a "caret" because its function is similar to that of a proofreader's caret symbol ( ^ ) used to indicate where new text should be inserted. The word "cursor" is reserved in Windows for the arrow (or other image) that shows the current mouse position. Visual C++ online help calls the caret an "insertion point," but as a Windows programmer you should know the technical difference between cursor and caret. Then when you encounter API functions such as *ShowCaret* and *SetCaretPos*, they will hold no mysteries for you.

Keystrokes for moving the caret in the text editor should seem familiar to anyone who has used a Windows word processor. Table 3-2 describes the main text editor caret-movement keys.

## Moving in Virtual Space

There has never been a consensus among text editors about what to do when the caret reaches the end of a line. What should happen when the user presses the Right arrow key? Some (thankfully few) editors take no action at all, adamantly refusing to move the caret. Other editors see text as a continuous stream; pressing the Right arrow key at the end of a line simply wraps the caret to the beginning of the next line. If you hold down

| Keystroke | Caret movement |
|---|---|
| Left arrow, Right arrow | Moves backward or forward one character. If the caret rests at the beginning of a line, the Left arrow moves the caret to the end of the preceding line. If the caret rests at the end of a line, the effect of the Right arrow depends on the virtual space setting. |
| Up arrow, Down arrow | Moves up or down one line. If the target line is shorter than the current line, the position of the caret depends on the virtual space setting. |
| Ctrl+Left arrow, Ctrl+Right arrow | Moves backward or forward by one word. The editor treats many punctuation marks as separate words. For example, you must press Ctrl+Right arrow seven times to move through the phrase *can't/won't*. |
| Home, End | Moves to the beginning or end of a row. |
| Ctrl+Home, Ctrl+End | Moves to the beginning or end of the document. |
| Page Up, Page Down | Scrolls up or down by the number of lines visible in the window. The editor overlaps scrolls by one line, which means that as you press Page Down to scroll through a document, the line at the bottom of one view becomes the top line of the next view. There is no way to change the scroll overlap. |

**Table 3-2.**     *Text editor caret-movement keys.*

the Right arrow long enough, you eventually move the caret through the document all the way to the bottom. Still other editors allow the caret to drift off the edge of the line and continue to move right into blank (or virtual) space. The beauty of this approach is that it lets you treat the computer screen as a sheet of paper—just move the caret and type wherever you want. But virtual space has both advantages and disadvantages.

Consider what happens when the caret rests at the end of the first line of the following fragment and you want to move to the second line:

```
b   = SendMessage( hwnd, MY_MESSAGE, wParam, lParam );
b *= 2;
```

Without virtual space, pressing the Right arrow moves the caret immediately to the beginning of the second line. Pressing the Down arrow moves the caret to the end of the second line. A virtual-space editor, however, requires two keystrokes to move to either position. You must press the Down arrow, then either Home or End. On the other hand, a virtual-space editor facilitates adding a comment to the second line. Just move the caret down into the blank space and type:

```
b   = SendMessage( hwnd, MY_MESSAGE, wParam, lParam );
b *= 2;                                              // Double it
```

By the way, those other editors are correct: a document *is* a continuous stream of text. You can't have holes in it. So the Visual C++ editor intelligently "tabifies" the gap between existing text and any new text added to the line in virtual space. The editor fills the gap with tabs as much as possible, then adds spaces for the last few columns only if necessary.

Both schools have their adherents. Ever customizable, the Visual C++ text editor leaves the choice to you, letting you change the virtual space setting to your preference by following these steps:

1. From the Tools menu, choose Options.

2. Click the Compatibility tab.

3. Set or clear the Enable Virtual Space check box.

## Matching Delimiters

The text editor recognizes delimiter pairs that enclose blocks of C/C++ source code, letting you with a single keystroke move the caret from one delimiter to its matching counterpart. The editor can distinguish three different delimiters: parentheses ( ), curly braces { }, and square brackets [ ].

Delimiters occur in matching pairs that serve as bookends for blocks of source code. Each pair establishes a delimiter level and may enclose any number of nested sublevels. The following fragment shows a typical example in which levels are delimited by curly braces:

```
if (msg = WM_USER)
{                                              // Begin level A
    for (i=0; i < 5; i++)
    {                                          // Begin level B

        ⋮

    }                                          // End level B
}                                              // End level A
```

With the caret adjacent to any delimiter, press Ctrl+] to move to the matching delimiter. To select the text within a level, press Shift+Ctrl+].

Parentheses in C and C++ serve as delimiters for different code elements such as **if** statement expressions and function parameter lists. However, levels defined by parentheses do not depend on statement type, only on how they appear in the text. The following line illustrates the idea, showing three levels labeled A, B, and C:

```
if (HeapAlloc( GetProcessHeap( ), 0, sizeof (DEVMODE) ))
                                   C                  C
              B
    A
```

The two inmost groups have the same level (C), and both are contained in levels A and B. When the caret lies next to the first parenthesis (which begins level A), pressing Ctrl+] moves the caret to the last parenthesis at the end of level A, skipping over the intervening parentheses.

The editor determines to what level a delimiter belongs by using an old programmer's trick for checking source code: it counts the parentheses. There must be an equal number of open and closed parentheses within any level or the code is wrong. To move to the end of level A from the first parenthesis, the editor searches forward for a matching closed parenthesis while keeping a tally. For every open (right-facing) parenthesis it finds, it increments the tally by one. Every closed (left-facing) parenthesis decrements the tally. The tally becomes zero when the editor finds the delimiter at the end of the level at which it started.

The editor also recognizes the conditional compiler directives **#if**, **#ifdef**, **#else**, **#elif**, and **#endif** as delimiters, though it uses different keystrokes for navigating among them. When the caret is anywhere inside a block of conditional directives, you can move to the next directive by pressing

Ctrl+J to move backward or Ctrl+K to move forward. Adding the Shift key to the combination selects the text as the caret moves to the next conditional directive.

## Bookmarks

A text editor bookmark saves your place in a document, allowing you to quickly return to a marked line no matter where you are in the text. If you've relied in the past on your editor's Go To command to navigate back to an interesting area of your document, you will see the advantages of bookmarks. Go To aims for a line number, but as you add or delete text elsewhere in the document, a row of text can be pushed or pulled away from its original position. Go To drops you at whatever new line has moved into the slot. With a bookmark, you don't have to remember a line's number to get back to it, and the bookmark remains anchored to its line as the document grows or shrinks in size. The Visual C++ text editor offers two types of bookmarks, called named and unnamed.

### Named bookmarks

A named bookmark becomes a permanent fixture of your document until you remove it. It marks a precise position in the text, remaining in place between editing sessions. In fact, you can jump from one document to a named bookmark in another document even if the second document is not open. The text editor automatically opens the second document if necessary and drops the caret at the position that the bookmark points to.

To set a named bookmark, place the caret at the position you want to mark and click Bookmarks on the Edit menu to display the Bookmark dialog. Type a descriptive name if desired, and then click the Add button to add the new bookmark to the list. When you close the dialog, the new bookmark is set. You can return to a bookmark either indirectly or directly. The indirect method is most convenient if you don't have a lot of bookmarks in your document. Just press F2 to jump forward to the next bookmark or press Shift+F2 to jump backward. Or click one of the Next Bookmark buttons on the Edit toolbar for the same results:

The direct method for moving the caret to a named bookmark requires another visit to the Bookmark dialog. Either double-click the target bookmark in the list or select the bookmark and click the Go To button. You can also reach a named bookmark via the Go To command on the Edit menu, though it requires more work with the mouse.

Internally, a named bookmark is a 32-bit offset from the beginning of the document that marks a specific location in the text. When you add or delete a byte of text anywhere in front of a named bookmark, the editor increments or decrements the bookmark's value. The bookmark thus continues to point to its target, regardless of how the text changes around it. Unlike a word processor, the editor does not save named bookmarks inside the document file when you close the document because the extraneous characters would only confuse the compiler.

### Unnamed bookmarks

So persistent a bookmark may often seem like overkill. A named bookmark is inconvenient when you want only to mark a passage in your source code, refer back to it once or twice when editing other parts of the document, and then forget it. For quick marking, use an unnamed bookmark instead. An unnamed bookmark is temporary, lasting only until you remove it or close the document. It marks a line, not a precise caret position. When you jump to an unnamed bookmark, the caret lands at the beginning of the marked line. If you delete the line you also delete the unnamed bookmark.

The advantage of an unnamed bookmark is that it is easy to set and even easier to remove. To mark a line with an unnamed bookmark, press Ctrl+F2 with the caret anywhere on the line or click the toolbar button with the plain flag, shown on the next page.

If the selection margin is enabled (as described later in this chapter), a box icon appears in the margin to the left of the marked line. Otherwise, the editor marks the entire line with a distinctive color.

You can jump to an unnamed bookmark by clicking the toolbar buttons or by pressing the F2 or Shift+F2 keys. Each keypress moves the caret sequentially forward or backward through every bookmark in the document, both named and unnamed.

You have several choices for removing an unnamed bookmark:

- Place the caret on the line and press Ctrl+F2 again to toggle the bookmark off.
- Press Shift+Ctrl+F2. This removes all unnamed bookmarks in the document.
- Just ignore it. Unnamed bookmarks in a document disappear when you close the document.

# Searching for Text

The editor offers three variations on the familiar theme of searching for text. You can

- Search for text in an open document
- Replace text in an open document
- Search for text in disk files

The first two operations are practically universal among text editors. Searching for text in disk files may be a more unusual feature but is extremely useful, displaying a list of files that contain a particular word or phrase. Here's a detailed look at all three search operations.

## Searching for Text in an Open Document

Like most text editors, the Visual C++ editor can scan through a document and locate a given word or phrase, called a search string. There are two ways to specify a search string. The most convenient method makes use of the combo box located on the Standard toolbar:

Either type the string in the combo box or click the box's arrow button and select a previously entered string from the list. Press Enter to begin the search. When the editor locates the string, it highlights the string in the document window and places the caret at the first character of the highlighted text. As long as the combo box holds focus, you can continue to scan through the document for the next occurrence of the string by pressing the Enter key. To return to editing mode, press Esc or click anywhere in the document window. You can then continue to search for the same string by pressing F3 to search forward or Shift+F3 to search backward. Visual C++ provides toolbar buttons for these commands, though you must add them yourself to a toolbar. The section "Creating Toolbar Buttons for Commands" on page 98 explains how. Here's what the search buttons look like when placed on the Edit toolbar:

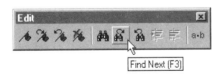

The second way to specify a search string involves the Find dialog. Although less direct than the first method, the Find dialog offers more alternatives. For instance, if an occurrence of the string you want to search for happens to be on the screen, you can borrow the string without having to retype it. For a single word, just click the word to set the caret on it; otherwise, select the text you want to search for by dragging the mouse cursor over it. Then open the Find dialog by pressing Ctrl+F or by choosing the Find command from the Edit menu. When the dialog appears, it is already initialized with the selected text.

You can refine the search with parameters that specify case sensitivity and whether or not the string should be matched only to a whole word. Click the Match Case check box to define a case-sensitive search in which the editor finds only text that matches the search string exactly. For example, a case-sensitive search for "abc" finds only that string, whereas a case-insensitive search for the same string may find *abc*, *ABC*, or *Abc*. Click the Match Whole Word Only check box to ignore occurrences of the search string contained in another word. A whole-word search for "any" finds only instances that appear as an entire word, ignoring words like *company*, *many*, and *anywhere*.

Click the Mark All button in the Find dialog to flag each search hit with an unnamed bookmark. This option lets you return to occurrences of a string throughout an editing session while continuing to use the Find command to search for other strings.

An interesting variation of the editor's search capabilities is a command called Incremental Search that begins searching as you type the search string. Press Ctrl+I in an open document and the prompt "Incremental Search:" appears in the status bar at the lower left corner of the window. As you type the search string, the editor immediately begins searching through the document, usually locating the string before you finish typing it. When the editor finds the word you are looking for, press Enter or an arrow key to return to edit mode. To search again for the same string, click the appropriate toolbar button or press the F3 key. The Shift+Ctrl+I key combination reverses Incremental Search so that the editor searches backward from the caret position instead of forward.

## Replacing Text

To search for text with the aim of replacing it with other text, choose Replace from the Edit menu. This presents you with a dialog similar to the Find dialog except that it queries for two strings instead of one. The first box takes a normal search string. In the second box, type the string with which you want to replace any occurrence of the found text. If you leave the second box empty, the editor replaces all search hits with nothing—that is, it deletes all occurrences of the search string from the document.

To selectively search and replace, click the Replace button when the editor finds the search string. It then automatically jumps to the next occurrence of the string. Clicking the Find Next button skips over the text without altering it. The Replace All button replaces all occurrences of the search string in one step. You can search and replace only in the forward direction and only in the current document, but not in multiple files.

If you select more than one line of text before invoking the Replace dialog, the Selection radio button is automatically turned on, indicating the editor will confine the search-and-replace operation to the selected section. Clicking the Whole File radio button overrides the setting. Although you can select a column of text in the editor by dragging the mouse cursor downward and right while pressing the Alt key, you cannot normally restrict replacements to a selected column. The Selection radio button is disabled if the selection is columnar. A macro can overcome this limitation, however, and Chapter 13 presents an example macro that lets you search and replace within a marked column.

## Searching for Text in Disk Files

UNIX users know this feature as *grep*. Given a search string, the editor can locate all files in a folder that contain the string. It can also "drill down" in its search, scanning through any nested subfolders. Click the Find In Files command on the Edit menu to open the dialog box shown in Figure 3-6. The dialog prompts for a search string, file type, and the folder in which you want the editor to begin searching.

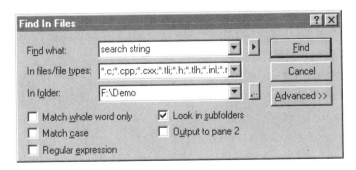

**Figure 3-6.** *The Find In Files dialog box, used for searching disk files.*

The default folder is the current project folder; if you want to search in another folder, enter the path in the In Folder box or click the adjacent button with the enigmatic three dots to browse for the new folder. The Look In Subfolders check box tells the editor whether to continue searching through any nested subfolders or to confine its search only to the indicated folder. By default, this check box is turned on. Click the Advanced button to specify any folders other than nested subfolders in which you want the editor to search. There are some handy check boxes for including subfolders that contain the project source and include files.

We saw in Chapter 1 that the Find In Files command normally displays its file list in the Find In Files 1 tab of the Output window (shown in Figure 1-7, on page 14). To direct the command's output instead to the Find In Files 2 tab, turn on the Output To Pane 2 check box, shown in Figure 3-6. Turning the check box on or off allows you to maintain two separate file lists so that the results of a search do not overwrite the results of a previous search.

Once you have set the search parameters, click the Find button. When Visual C++ finds a file that contains the given search string, it lists the filename and path in the Output window. Each entry in the list also includes a copy of the line in which the string first occurs in the file, so you can see how the string is used in context. Double-clicking a file in the list opens it in the text editor.

Before conducting a file search, Visual C++ first saves any unsaved documents open in the text editor, ensuring that the most up-to-date version of each file is searched. You can adjust this behavior in the Editor tab of the Options dialog through two check boxes labeled Save Before Running Tools and Prompt Before Saving Files. Clearing the first check box instructs Visual C++ not to save open documents before searching, thus restricting its searches to documents as they existed the last time you saved them. If you prefer that Visual C++ leaves the decision to you whether or not to save a document when you invoke the Find In Files command, set both check boxes. This causes the editor to first query for permission before saving each open document.

## Searching with Regular Expressions

The search dialogs we've seen so far contain a check box labeled Regular Expression. A regular expression is formed by one or more special characters that represent a string of text. We've already used something similar in the Open and Save As dialogs, in which a file type of, say, *.cpp* means "any file with a CPP extension." The asterisk wildcard acts as a regular expression that represents any text forming a valid filename.

Regular expressions for search strings are more sophisticated than wildcards, giving you precise control in refining a search string. Table 3-3 lists the default regular expression characters. The editor interprets these characters as regular expressions only when you check the Regular Expression check box in the dialog. If the box is not checked, the editor treats the characters literally and does not expand them into regular expressions.

| Character | Meaning | Example |
|---|---|---|
| . | Any single character | "..do" matches *redo* and *undo* but not *outdo* |
| [ ] | Any character or range of characters within the brackets | "sl[aou]g" matches *slag*, *slog*, and *slug* |
| [^] | Any character or range except those following the caret | "sl[^r-z]g" matches *slag* and *slog* but not *slug* |
| * | None or more of the preceding character or expression | "re*d" matches *rd*, *red*, and *reed* |
| + | One or more of the preceding character or expression | "re+d" matches *red* and *reed*, but not *rd* |
| ^ | Beginning of a line | "^word" matches *word* only if *word* begins a line |
| $ | End of a line | "word$" matches *word* only if *word* ends a line |
| \ | The next character is not a regular expression | "word\$" matches *word$* (without recognizing $ as an end-of-line character) |

**Table 3-3.**    *Regular expression characters.*

You don't have to memorize the table. All variations of the Find dialog provide an online version of Table 3-3 through a small button to the right of the combo box in which you type the search string. Click the button for a menu of regular expressions, and then select the ones you want.

The plus character (+) lets you designate a string. To get an idea of how this works, consider the regular expression [a-zA-Z]. It means any one character within the range of characters contained in the brackets—in other words, a single letter. Append a plus sign to the expression and the meaning changes. The plus sign means "one or more of these characters." The editor thus interprets [a-zA-Z]+ as any string of letters—that is, any word. Similarly, the regular expression [0-9] means a digit, but [0-9]+ expands to mean any positive integer, regardless of its size.

Regular expression searches are always case-sensitive. Even if you turn off the Match Case check box in the Find dialog, a search for the regular expression [0-9a-f]+ finds only hexadecimal numbers like 0x37ac but not 0x7A4B. To find the latter number, you must include uppercase letters in the regular expression like this: [0-9a-fA-F]+.

# Programming Aids

Coding for Windows and MFC forces even the most experienced developers to never stray far from massive reference books and online documentation when coding. Few of us ever commit to memory more than a tiny amount of the information necessary to write Windows programs, and we spend a lot of time looking up parameter lists and confirming the spelling of function and variable names. But the Visual C++ text editor has abilities designed to help free the developer from these endless interruptions. This section describes the newest and best of these features, a typing assistant called Statement Completion.

Statement Completion is a blanket term for a trio of programming tools named List Members, Parameter Info, and Type Info. In an almost literal sense, these tools put a condensed version of the Win32 and MFC reference material at your fingertips.

## List Members

Designed to speed code entry and minimize typographical errors, the editor's List Members feature remains continually close at hand as you type. Through a pop-up window, List Members provides a huge list of MFC class members, C run-time functions, manifest constants, structure names, Win32 API functions, and class members of the current project, allowing you to select from the list to complete the word you are currently typing. The List Members window appears automatically when you type the scope resolution operator (::), member-of operator (.), or pointer-member operator (->). As you continue to type a member name, the window's selection bar moves to the list entry that best completes the name. Figure 3-7 illustrates, showing how the List Members window zeroes in on the *CDC::SetMapMode* function even before you finish typing it.

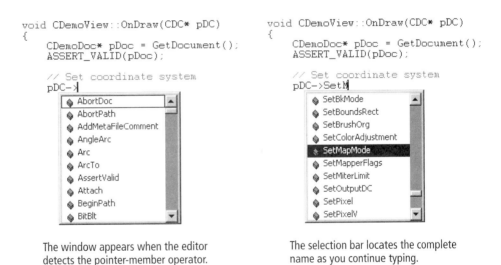

The window appears when the editor detects the pointer-member operator.

The selection bar locates the complete name as you continue typing.

**Figure 3-7.** *The List Members window displayed in the text editor.*

The text editor inserts the highlighted list entry into the document when you type a nonletter character such as a space or semicolon. The process is smoother than it sounds, especially after a little practice, because member names in source code are almost always followed by punctuation—a left parenthesis after a function name, or a semicolon or equals sign after a variable. The scenario illustrated in Figure 3-7, for example, is logically completed by typing a left parenthesis, producing this result:

```
// Set coordinate system
pDC->SetMapMode(
```

The editor dismisses the List Members window, inserts the highlighted entry *SetMapMode* at the caret position, and follows it with the left parenthesis, ready for you to continue typing the function's parameters. As we will see in the next section, Statement Completion does not abandon you at this point, and invokes the Parameter Info tool to assist you in finishing the parameter list. As the Members List window disappears, the next logical tool automatically takes its place.

Pressing the Tab key or Ctrl+Enter completes the word and dismisses the pop-up Members List window, but without adding a character. You can invoke the List Members pop-up window at any time in the text editor by pressing the Ctrl+Alt+T key combination. In positioning the selection bar in the List Members window, the editor takes its cue from the text immediately to the left of the caret. Invoking List Members after typing *cv*, for example, displays the window with the selection bar positioned at the *CView* entry:

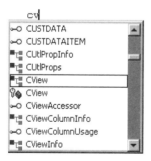

The list entry is outlined in this example rather than highlighted because of the difference in letter case between the typed word *cv* and the entry *CView*. List Members ignores letter case when positioning the selection bar, so you can type entirely in lowercase if you prefer, though you must then press Enter or Tab to make the selection. This can be helpful when dealing with inconsistent function names like *UnmapViewOfFile* and *UnMapAndLoad*, always difficult to remember.

Although the key combination remains the easiest means of displaying the window, you can also access the List Members command from the Edit menu or by right-clicking in a document window to bring up a context menu. The List Members pop-up window includes in its list only those symbol names that are valid for the current class or object. For example, the list contains the *PrevDlgCtrl* function when you are typing a member name for an object derived from *CDialog*, since *PrevDlgCtrl* is a member of that class. The same function does not appear in the list when you are adding a member to a class derived from, say, *CString*.

The Edit menu also contains a command called Complete Word, implying the existence of yet another Statement Completion tool. But Complete Word is not a new tool at all but merely a shortcut form of List Members. Rather than pressing Ctrl+Alt+T to invoke the List Members command, you will probably come to prefer the easier key combination of Ctrl+Space to execute Complete Word. Usually, both key combinations have exactly the same effect, displaying the List Members window with the selection bar positioned at the first entry that correctly completes the word you are typing. But should the list contain only one possibility that completes your word, interacting with the List Members window can seem an unnecessary distraction. In this case, the Ctrl+Spacebar combination streamlines the operation by completing your word without displaying the List Members window. Pressing Ctrl+Spacebar after typing *CreateMul*, for example, completes your typing in a single step because the text editor determines without ambiguity that you intend to type *CreateMultiProfileTransform* and not *CreateMutex*.

## Parameter Info

The Parameter Info feature works hand-in-glove with List Members, popping up as a discreet tooltip window when you type the first parenthesis after a function name. The tooltip window serves as an on-screen cue card, displaying the function's prototype and required parameters:

```
m_wndStatusBar.SetIndicators(|
```

BOOL SetIndicators (**const UINT \*lpIDArray**, int nIDCount)

The prototype remains on the screen as you continue filling in the function's parameter list, and then disappears when you type the closing parenthesis. If the function is overloaded to accept different sets of parameters, the Parameter Info window displays the prototypes one at a time. Numbers at the far left of the tooltip window indicate how many overloaded versions exist for the function. Cycle from one prototype view to the next by pressing Ctrl+PgUp or by clicking anywhere inside the tooltip window:

```
m_wndStatusBar.GetPaneText (|
```
◀ 1 of 2 ▶   CString GetPaneText (**int nIndex**)

```
m_wndStatusBar.GetPaneText (|
```
◀ 2 of 2 ▶   void GetPaneText (**int nIndex**, CString &rString)

The Parameter Info tooltip appears automatically when you need it, but can be invoked explicitly when the caret is positioned anywhere on or to the right of a recognized function name. Choose the command either from the Edit menu or by pressing the Ctrl+Shift+Spacebar key combination. Right-clicking a function name in a document also provides access to the command through the editor's context menu. As with any other command in Visual C++, you can assign a key combination of your own choosing to invoke Parameter Info. The section titled "Unbound Commands" later in this chapter explains how.

## Type Info

Type Info is similar to Parameter Info, appearing as a tooltip window that displays information about a variable or function. If Type Info recognizes the symbol name beneath the mouse cursor, the tooltip window appears automatically, disappearing when you move the cursor. You can also choose Type Info from the Edit menu or the context menu, or by pressing the Ctrl+T key combination. The latter method is convenient when you want information about a symbol you have just typed or pasted into the document from the List Members window. When the editor's caret lies within or adjacent to a function name, Type Info displays the same information as Parameter Info, listing the function prototype. When invoked for a defined type, Type Info displays the **typedef** statement that creates the alias:

```
OLECHAR
        typedef unsigned short OLECHAR ;
```

Type Info is perhaps most useful when called into service to display information about a variable. It shows the variable's declaration, so you no longer have to comb through source code or resort to the class's header file to confirm a variable's type. For example, the name of the *indicators* variable shown here gives no indication of its type, but the Type Info window immediately identifies the variable as an array of unsigned integers:

```
// Set status bar panes
statusbar.SetIndicators( indicators, 3 );
                         unsigned int indicators[] ;
```

The tendency of Type Info and other windows to pop up uninvited may seem distracting to you. If so, click the Options command on the Tools menu and clear the appropriate check boxes in the dialog's Editor tab (Figure 3-11 on page 102). You can still invoke Type Info, Parameter Info, and List Members at any time through their respective key combinations or menu commands.

# The Advanced Command

The Advanced command near the bottom of the Edit menu represents a collection of options that can be very useful when working on a text document. Rest the cursor briefly on the Advanced command to display the secondary menu shown on the next page.

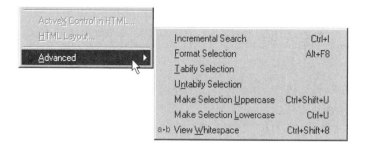

As you see, the menu provides access to the Incremental Search command described earlier, though pressing Ctrl+I is a more convenient way to invoke the command. The Format Selection command inserts tabs to set indentation levels in blocks of C/C++ code delimited by curly braces { }. The command can turn code like this:

```
if (msg = WM_USER)
{
for (i=0; i < 5; i++)
{
// Additional code
}
}
```

into this:

```
if (msg = WM_USER)
{
    for (i=0; i < 5; i++)
    {
        // Additional code
    }
}
```

The Format Selection command works by scanning selected text for curly braces to determine nested levels. Lines of text in the first level are indented one tab position, lines in the second level are indented two positions, and so forth.

The Tabify Selection command changes a selected series of space characters into an equivalent string of tabs. The Untabify Selection command reverses the process, expanding tabs into spaces. The effects of either command are best seen by turning on the View Whitespace toggle switch, which makes spaces and tabs visible in a document. When the switch is on, each space character in the text appears as a small dot ( · ) and each tab character as a guillemet (»).

The remaining two commands on the secondary menu act as their names suggest. The Make Selection Uppercase command changes all letters within a selection to uppercase, while the Make Selection Lowercase command does the reverse. Nonletter characters in the selection such as numbers and punctuation marks are not affected.

# Unbound Commands

Every Visual C++ command has a descriptive internal name. For instance, the Incremental Search and Tabify commands just described have internal names of SearchIncremental, SelectionTabify, and SelectionUntabify. Online help refers to many other commands you won't find on the menus—commands with names like GoToNextErrorTag, LineTranspose, and LineDeleteToStart. There are two reasons why help prefers to identify commands by internal name rather than by key combination such as F4 or Shift+Alt+T. First, you can change a key combination for a command to anything you like. Second, many commands do not have keystrokes already assigned to them. Such commands are said to be "unbound." To use an unbound command you must first assign it a key combination of your choice.

Beneath the surface of the Developer Studio environment lies an extensive set of commands—there are many more commands available than those that appear in menus and on toolbar buttons. Click Keyboard Map on the Help menu to see a list of command names, shown in Figure 3-8.

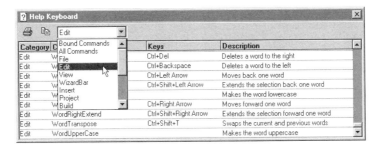

**Figure 3-8.**    *Select Keyboard Map from the Help menu to display a list of Visual C++ commands.*

The default list in the Help Keyboard window is called "Bound Commands," meaning that these are the commands that already have key combinations assigned to them. To see a list of both bound and unbound commands that pertain only to the text editor, select Edit from the combo box and click the Command button above the second column to sort the list alphabetically by command. As you scroll through the list, you will see in the Keys column that most commands already have assigned key combinations, but many do not. The set of unbound commands makes available a large selection of features that otherwise cannot be accessed through menus, toolbars, or the keyboard.

How you access a command is up to you. Visual C++ lets you add any bound or unbound command to a menu or toolbar, as described in Chapter 13, Customizing Visual C++. But since crowded menus and toolbars tend to be counterproductive, it's often best to enable an unbound command by assigning it a key combination. The only disadvantage is that you must then memorize the keystroke that invokes the command.

No one intends for you to enable all unbound commands at once. Choose only those you think will benefit you most, giving them key combinations that best suit your style and that will most likely jog your memory. As an example, let's add to the text editor two useful commands called WordUpperCase and WordLowerCase, which change the case of the word under the caret in the current document. By default, WordUpperCase and WordLowerCase have no key combinations assigned to them, nor are there toolbar buttons or menu options for invoking the commands. There is no way to use the commands until you specify key combinations for them.

Here's how to enable the commands. From the Tools menu, choose Customize to open the Customize dialog, and then click the Keyboard tab. Select Edit from the Category combo box and make sure that Text appears in the Editor box. These settings mean we're setting a keystroke for a command that applies only to the text editor. The commands listed in the Commands box are sorted alphabetically. Scroll down to the bottom of the list to find the WordUpperCase entry, and then click the entry to select it. A brief description of the command appears at the lower left corner of the dialog, but the Current Keys box remains blank, indicating that no command key is currently assigned to WordUpperCase. To assign a key, click the Press New Shortcut Key text box and press whatever key combination you want to invoke the command. If you press Ctrl+U, the dialog informs you that the key combination is currently assigned to the SelectionLowercase command. That doesn't mean you can't attach Ctrl+U to WordUpperCase if you want; it's only a reminder that if you do so, pressing Ctrl+U will no longer invoke SelectionLowercase, which would then become an unbound command. Alt+U is a better choice for Word-UpperCase, because Ctrl+U is already in use. When you press Alt+U, the dialog tells you that the keystroke is currently unassigned (see Figure 3-9). Click the Assign button and the keystroke is ready to use.

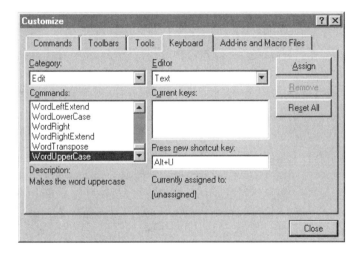

**Figure 3-9.**    *Assigning a key combination to a text editor command.*

Do the same for the WordLowerCase command, assigning it a keystroke of Alt+L. When you press Alt+L in the Press New Shortcut Key text box, a message informs you that the key combination is used to gain menu access. The message refers to the Layout menu, which is available only when the dialog editor is active. Because the Layout menu has nothing to do with the text editor, choosing Alt+L does not lead to a conflict of keystrokes. When the text editor is active, Alt+L invokes the WordLowerCase command; when the dialog editor is active, Alt+L pulls down the Layout menu as before.

To use the new WordUpperCase and WordLowerCase commands, open a text document and place the caret anywhere on a word. Pressing Alt+U or Alt+L invokes the commands, changing the case of all letters from the caret position to the end of the word. By coincidence, the new commands also duplicate the SelectionUppercase and SelectionLowercase commands because they act on any selected block of text, not on just a single word. The Selection commands are now superfluous, which isn't a tragedy. The new Alt+U and Alt+L keystrokes are easier to use and remember than the equivalent Shift+Ctrl+U (SelectionUppercase) and Ctrl+U (Selection-Lowercase) key combinations. The duplication applies only to selected text, however, because both SelectionUppercase and SelectionLowercase affect the character adjacent to the caret when there is no selected text.

## Creating Toolbar Buttons for Commands

If you are a fan of toolbars and find yourself frequently using commands like WordUpperCase and WordLowerCase that have no predefined toolbar buttons, you might want to create new buttons for the commands. You can place a button on any existing toolbar or even create a new toolbar. To demonstrate, here's how to create toolbar buttons for the new WordUpper-Case and WordLowerCase commands. In the Commands tab of the Customize dialog, select All Commands from the Category box to display an alphabetical list of Visual C++ commands. Scroll down the list to find WordUpperCase, and then drag the entry from the list and drop it onto one of the environment's toolbars, such as the Edit toolbar. If you prefer to create a new toolbar for the buttons instead of using an existing toolbar, simply drag the WordUpperCase entry out of the dialog and drop it onto an area of the screen not covered by a toolbar. Visual C++ automatically creates a new toolbar to hold the button. Drag the WordLowerCase command from the list to the same toolbar.

Because WordUpperCase and WordLowerCase have no predefined icons, the Button Appearance dialog opens (Figure 3-10), from which you can choose an icon for each new button. None of the available icon images reflect the unusual functions of WordUpperCase and WordLowerCase, but you can combine image and text to make a button's function unambiguous. Select an icon in the Button Appearance dialog, click the Image And

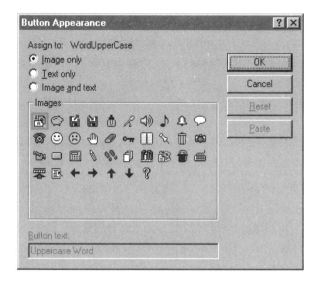

**Figure 3-10.**    *Visual C++ offers a choice of icons for a new toolbar button.*

Text radio button, and type the button text in the text box at the bottom of the dialog. Here's what a new toolbar might look like with buttons for both the WordUpperCase and WordLowerCase commands:

Unbound commands aren't just for the text editor. The next chapter describes how to use these same methods to implement useful commands for the graphics editor as keystrokes or toolbar buttons. Chapter 13 discusses in more detail the subject of creating toolbars in the Visual C++ environment, explaining how to rename and delete toolbars, how to copy buttons from one toolbar to another, and how to customize button images.

# An Introduction to Macros

You can think of a bound command as a predefined macro—that is, a set of instructions assigned to a keystroke. The environment also lets you create your own macros for the text editor by recording keystrokes and mouse clicks, combining them into a single reusable command that becomes part of the normal Visual C++ command set. You can execute a macro through a keystroke, menu command, or toolbar button just as you can any other command. In fact, macros are nearly indistinguishable from normal bound commands, making them a very elegant way to extend the environment's capabilities. This section is only an introduction to the subject of macros. Because macros apply to the entire Developer Studio environment, not just to the text editor, we defer a more detailed discussion until Chapter 13, Customizing Visual C++. For now, we can create a simple macro for the text editor just by turning on the command recorder.

To demonstrate, here's how to create a macro that builds on the Untabify Selection command described earlier. The macro expands the command to untabify an entire document, and not just selected text. First close all documents in the editor to prevent alterations to existing text, and then begin recording the new macro by pressing Ctrl+Shift+R or by choosing the Record Quick Macro command from the Tools menu. This exposes the Record toolbar and adds the image of a cassette tape to the mouse cursor, indicating that Visual C++ is now recording every keystroke and mouse click. The macro comprises four steps:

1. On the Edit menu, click the Select All command to select the entire document.

2. Choose Advanced from the Edit menu and click the Untabify Selection command.

3. Press Ctrl+Home to return the caret to the top of the document.

4. Click the Stop Recording button on the Record toolbar to end the recording.

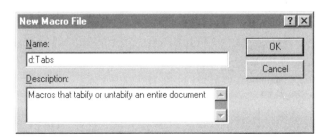

We now have a new macro. Visual C++ stores the macro in the Common\
MsDev98\Macros folder in a file named GlobalTemporary.dsm. (The file
extension stands for Developer Studio macro.) The file contains a single
Visual Basic subroutine containing instructions that invoke the three commands we just recorded:

```
Sub GlobalTemporary
    ActiveDocument.Selection.SelectAll
    ActiveDocument.Selection.Untabify
    ActiveDocument.Selection.StartOfDocument
End Sub
```

(Appendix C, A VBScript Primer, examines in much more detail the
macro source language, Visual Basic Scripting Edition.) To experiment
with the macro, open a representative document and turn on the View
Whitespace command in the Advanced submenu to make the macro's
effects visible. Now run the macro by pressing Ctrl+Shift+P or by clicking
the Play Quick Macro command on the Tools menu. The effect is the same
as retyping the recorded keystrokes manually.

The GlobalTemporary macro is unique in that it does not appear in the list
of Visual C++ commands shown in Figure 3-8 on page 95. It is reserved for
the "quick" macro created through the Record Quick Macro command.
Recording another macro through the same command overwrites the previous macro, so that only one quick macro exists at a time.

# Customizing the Editor

The Visual C++ text editor is willing to change many of its characteristics
to better accommodate your working style. We've already examined the
Customize command on the Tools menu, which lets you customize toolbars and assign custom keystrokes to commands. To change other characteristics of the editor's interface, choose Options from the Tools menu.

The Options command displays the dialog shown in Figure 3-11, on the
next page, letting you specify text editor characteristics such as:

- Appearance, saving documents, and Statement Completion options
- Tabs and indents

- Emulations

- Fonts

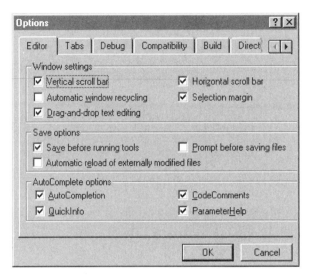

**Figure 3-11.** *The Editor tab of the Options dialog box.*

In the dialog's Editor tab, click your preferences for how and when the editor should save a document. (The check box labeled Automatic Reload Of Externally Modified Files is described in the next section.) You can also specify whether the editor saves altered files automatically before compiling and whether it prompts you before saving a document.

The Selection Margin check box in the same tab deserves special mention. The selection margin is a shaded column about one-half inch wide on the left side of a document window. The margin takes its name from the fact that by clicking in the column you can select the entire line adjacent to the click position. The margin also holds the icons for bookmarks and, as we'll see in Chapter 11, debugger breakpoints. If you prefer to recover that half-inch for document display, clear the check box to disable the selection margin.

To a limited extent, the Visual C++ text editor can emulate the behavior of the BRIEF or Epsilon programmer's editors. If you are accustomed to either of these products, you may prefer to turn on the appropriate emulation option. Click the Compatibility tab, and then choose either of the editors from the list or set the desired options by turning on individual check boxes.

The Format tab lets you specify font styles and colors for the editor windows. Click Source Windows from the Category list to see the current font. By default, the font is 10-point Courier, but you can change it to any style or size you prefer. The Colors area lets you adjust background and foreground colors for various markers and text in the editor, such as source comments and HTML tags. To change colors, select an entry from the list and choose the desired colors from the combo boxes.

# Editing Text Outside Developer Studio

Text editors share many characteristics with word processors, one of which is that users tend to be passionate about their favorites. Visual C++ gives you a very competent programming editor but if you currently use and enjoy another editor, I won't try to dissuade you. You may be more productive with a product you already know well. And if you never venture into the Developer Studio environment, you have no choice but to use another editor. The Visual C++ text editor is an integral part of Developer Studio, not a separate program. You can access the editor only from Developer Studio.

A big advantage of the Visual C++ text editor shows off what an integrated development environment is all about. When the compiler finds errors in your source code, it automatically sets the editor's caret at the first offending statement, ready for you to type in a correction. Double-click on the next error in the list and the caret moves to the correct location in your source. After editing, just click the Compile button on the Build toolbar to resubmit the revised text to the compiler. Visual C++ automatically saves the new source to disk for you. Working in an editor outside of the environment involves a bit more effort. You must switch to the editor, move the caret to the line number indicated for each compiler error, save the file after making corrections, and switch back to Visual C++ to recompile.

If you decide to use another text editor for composing and maintaining source code, you should make two small changes to the Visual C++ environment. First, if you use your other editor regularly, you may find it more convenient to run it from its own dedicated command on the Tools menu. By placing a new command on the Tools menu, you can launch your preferred editor from within the environment. If your editor accepts file-names from the command line, you can configure the command so that your editor automatically loads source files when it starts. The subject of adding a new Tools command to start a text editor (or any other external program) is thoroughly covered in Chapter 13.

The second change you should make is a small alteration to the default settings. When working on a file in another editor, you will often have the same file open in Visual C++. This happens during cycles of compiling and debugging the code, because the debugger loads the source file. When you alter and save the file in your editor and then switch back to Visual C++ to recompile, the environment recognizes its open copy is no longer current. By default, it displays the message box shown in Figure 3-12, which offers to reload the new file from disk. Your answer to the query will almost always be Yes or, at least, that you don't care. To prevent this polite but insistent message every time you pop back into Visual C++, click Options on the Tools menu. Place a check mark in the box labeled Automatic Reload Of Externally Modified Files in the Editor tab shown in Figure 3-11 to permit the editor to load altered files automatically without prompting you.

When you use another editor, you in effect make a pact with Visual C++ that you will not change a document simultaneously in both editors. However, the environment intelligently handles simultaneous changes to a document. Visual C++ recognizes external alterations because it checks the date and time signatures of all files open in the text editor whenever

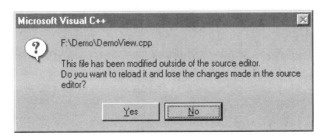

**Figure 3-12.**   *Resolving document versions when an outside editor has changed a file.*

the environment regains input focus. For the sake of safety, the environment reloads any file that has a more recent signature, but the Automatic Reload Of Externally Modified Files setting applies only while the editor's own copy of a document remains unchanged. If a document in the editor has been altered by even one character, Visual C++ displays the message box shown in Figure 3-12 regardless of the setting in the Automatic Reload Of Externally Modified Files check box. This gives you control over determining which version of the document is the correct one.

# Resources

Normally when we speak of a program's data, we mean the variables referenced in the source by names like *x* and *pString*. A typical Windows application also has another kind of data called resources, which contain text and graphics that determine the look and feel of the program's user interface. A program's resources define interface elements such as:

- Menus
- Accelerator keys
- Bitmaps, cursors, and icons
- Dialog boxes and controls
- Character strings
- Toolbars

When Windows loads a program, it reads code and values for initialized data from the program's executable file and copies them into allocated memory. With some exceptions, resource data are left behind in the program's executable file on disk. Resources are read at run-time rather than at load-time, extracted from the EXE or DLL file on an as-needed basis when the program creates a window, displays a dialog, or loads a bitmap.

Visual C++ provides several resource editors with which you can create and modify a project's resource data. In some respects this chapter is a continuation of the preceding chapter, which describes how to create and edit text documents with the Visual C++ text editor. Though the definition of the word "document" must be expanded here to include forms besides pure text, the principle of editing remains the same.

The subject of resources and resource editors is large, occupying both this chapter and the next. This chapter covers resource data for interface elements that the user generally first encounters in a program, including menus, toolbars, accelerators, icons, and mouse cursors. The important subject of dialog boxes and controls is left for Chapter 5.

# System Resources

Just so there is no confusion later, I should also mention system resources, which form a common pool of resource data that Windows makes available to applications. System resources are in effect loaned out to programs with the understanding they will be returned, either explicitly when the application frees a handle or implicitly when the application terminates. Some system resources such as mouse cursors are provided so that each program does not have to create its own. Although an application can display its own unique cursor (as we'll see later in the chapter), it's much easier to use the arrow, hourglass, and other bitmaps that the system provides. Besides being convenient for the programmer, this also ensures that the user is not presented with a bewildering variety of cursors when switching between programs.

Other system resources such as device contexts and the system caret cannot be duplicated by an application and have no real analogy to the program resources described in this chapter. Although it has no direct bearing on a program's appearance, memory is also commonly referred to as a system resource because it is doled out as heap allocations to programs that request it. Controls are another potential source of confusion when talking about resources. In its resource data, a program declares only the type of control it wants to use, the window coordinates, and perhaps an initial state. The display and operation of the control are handled by the system.

If the line between system resources and program resources seems indistinct at times, don't worry. As you learn more about resources in this chapter, the differences will become clear.

# The RC Resource Script File

A project defines its resources in a source file that has an RC extension and typically the same name as the project. The RC file contains only text much like a program source file, so you can view it with a text editor. Inside you will find tables that define character strings and the contents of menus but no graphics data containing bitmaps and icons. Graphics resources are stored in separate files, the names and locations of which are recorded in the RC file. The RC extension indicates that the file serves as source code for the resource compiler, a separate part of Visual C++ that compiles the text and graphics of the program's resources into object form, which the linker then binds to the EXE file. A project's RC file is often called a resource script or resource definition file.

A resource script file is optional. A Windows program that does not interact with the user does not require resources, and it's even possible for a program to create all its resources on-the-fly at run time. But as you will see in this chapter, resource scripts make life easier for the developer because the scripts separate the user interface elements from the source code. By working with the Visual C++ resource editors, the developer can design a program's interface, see what it looks like, and alter it with a few clicks of the mouse. And for programs intended for the international market, resource scripts are a necessity because they allow the translator to work on the user interface while leaving the program source code untouched.

Visual C++ recognizes only one main RC file per project. If you try to add an extra RC file using the Project menu's Add To Project command, the environment warns you that the file won't be compiled when building the project, as shown on the next page.

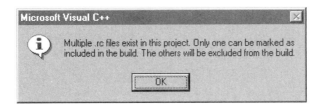

Nevertheless, a project can have any number of resource script files, though all second-level files can be added only through **#include** statements in the main RC file. For instance, AppWizard automatically creates a second resource file with the project's name and an extension of RC2, which provides a good place to put any resources you have previously developed and tested and that require no further modifications. To see how the RC2 file is included in a project created by AppWizard, open the project and choose Resource Includes from the View menu. Then scroll down in the Compile-Time Directives control to the following line (in which *project* represents the project name):

```
#include "res\project.rc2"  // non-Microsoft Visual C++ resources
```

Any resources included in supplemental files are compiled and linked to the project's executable file but are not accessible when you are working on the main RC file with one of the Visual C++ resource editors. That's why only complete and tested resources should go in the RC2 file. The resource compiler reads all script files and produces a compiled binary form with a RES extension that is analogous to an OBJ object file generated by the C/C++ compiler.

The Workspace window described in Chapter 1, The Environment, lists the project's resources defined in the main RC file. When the project is open, click the ResourceView tab and expand the list by clicking the plus signs adjacent to the folder icons. To open a resource in the appropriate editor (which we'll do shortly), double-click the resource in the list. Figure 4-1 shows resources displayed in the ResourceView pane of a typical AppWizard project named Demo.

The default RC file created by AppWizard is extensive, containing lengthy string tables, menu scripts, and code pertaining to cross-platform development. If you accept all of AppWizard's defaults when creating a new

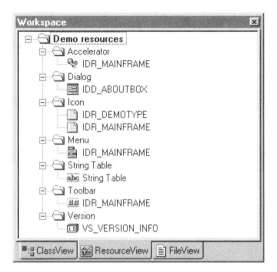

**Figure 4-1.**   *The ResourceView pane of the Workspace window.*

application, you can end up with an RC file of nearly 400 lines. You might be tempted to modify the RC file in a text editor, deleting the extraneous lines of code generated by AppWizard and reducing the file size to manageable proportions. But doing so means trouble later when you modify a resource with one of the Visual C++ resource editors. Although you may end up with a valid RC file, Visual C++ unfortunately no longer recognizes it as a product of AppWizard. You can still revise a resource with an editor, but when you save the revisions, Visual C++ overwrites your minimalist RC file with a new one containing many of the extraneous AppWizard additions you had previously removed. The only alternative is to save the modified resources under a different filename, then use the text editor to copy the lines you want from the new file and paste them into the original resource script. I recommend you learn to live with the large RC files that AppWizard generates and, except for small changes, revise resources only through the resource editors.

# The Resource.h Header File

Each resource in a project is identified in the RC file either by a constant identifier or, less frequently, by a name in the form of a character string. Resources in the fictitious Demo program of Figure 4-1, for example, are all identified by constant values: IDR_MAINFRAME for the menu and toolbar, IDR_DEMOTYPE for one of the program's icons, and IDD_ABOUTBOX for the About dialog. The constants that identify a project's resources are normally defined in a file named Resource.h, which serves as the main header file for the project's RC file. AppWizard creates Resource.h automatically as part of a project, assigning standard MFC prefixes to the resource identifiers. Table 4-1 lists some of the identifier prefixes that MFC uses.

| Prefix | Resource type |
| --- | --- |
| IDR_ | Main menu, toolbars, accelerator table, and the application icon |
| IDD_ | Dialog boxes |
| IDC_ | Controls and cursors |
| IDS_ | Strings |
| IDP_ | Prompt strings for message boxes |
| ID_ | Menu commands |

**Table 4-1.**    *Standard MFC identifier prefixes.*

Constant identifiers can be formed by letters (either uppercase or lowercase), numerals, and underscores, but cannot begin with a numeral.

C programmers know identifier numbers as manifest constants or "defines," but Visual C++ sometimes refers to them as symbols. Technically, a symbol is a name in the source code, such as a variable or a function name, that labels a memory address. We'll see in Chapter 11, The Debuger, how the compiler can generate a list of a program's symbols that the debugger reads to learn the names of variables and functions in the program. Don't confuse resource symbols with symbols in your source code. No doubt the Visual C++ designers chose the word symbol to promote the idea that the resource script is also a type of source code and that a resource identifier is analogous to a variable name in the program source.

You can change the name or numerical value of a resource identifier listed in the ResourceView pane of the Workspace window. First expose the identifier name by expanding the appropriate folder icon, as shown in Figure 4-1 on page 111. Then click the identifier in the list to select it, and click Properties on the View menu. You can also right-click an identifier and choose Properties from the pop-up context menu. Either way, change the identifier's name by retyping it in the ID control. At the same time, you can assign a new numerical integer value by adding it to the name like this:

```
IDD_ABOUTBOX_NEW = 3001
```

When you press the Enter key, an asterisk appears adjacent to the project line at the top of the ResourceView pane, indicating a change has been made but not yet saved. Choose the Save command from the File menu to have Visual C++ rewrite the Resource.h file, replacing the **#define** statement for the old identifier with the new identifier.

In theory, you can assign to a resource any identifier value from 1 through 65,535 (0xFFFF). However, Windows reserves values of 0xF000 and above for items on the system menu and MFC reserves values 0xE000 through 0xEFFF for internal use, so you should keep your own identifier values in the range 1 through 57,343 (0xDFFF). The value is limited to WORD size rather than DWORD size because WM_COMMAND messages pass the identifier value in the low word of the *wParam* message parameter.

You can also change, add, or delete identifier symbols in the Resource Symbols browser shown in Figure 4-2 on the next page, provided the RC file was created by AppWizard or one of the Visual C++ resource editors. To open the browser, click Resource Symbols on the View menu. The browser shows all the identifiers defined in the Resource.h file; to rename an identifier or change its value, select it from the list and click the Change button. The New button lets you add new identifiers to the Resource.h file and assign values to them. After you close the Resource Symbols dialog, right-click the project line in the ResourceView pane and choose the Save command to write the new values to the Resource.h file.

The symbol browser is designed to work best with RC files created either by AppWizard or by one of the Visual C++ resource editors. You can view the definitions of all identifiers referenced in a project's RC file, but the

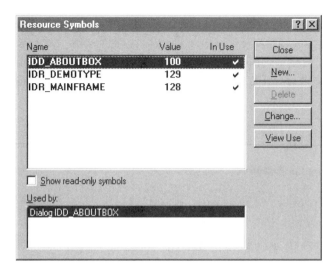

**Figure 4-2.**    *The Resource Symbols browser, invoked through the Resource Symbols command on the View menu.*

browser can modify only identifiers defined in the Resource.h header file. It treats identifiers defined in other included files as read-only and provides no means for changing their names or values. To see these identifiers, click the Show Read-Only Symbols check box in the browser dialog. For example, AppWizard adds to the RC file this line, which we will meet again later in the chapter:

```
#include "afxres.h"
```

When you enable the Show Read-Only Symbols check box, the browser includes in the list all the symbols defined in the Afxres.h file. You can distinguish read-only symbols in the list because modifiable symbols appear in boldface type.

A check mark in the In Use column indicates that a symbol identifies a resource in the RC file. As you develop a program you will probably change the names of identifiers occasionally. There is nothing wrong with this, but Visual C++ adds a definition for the new identifier name to Resource.h without deleting the old name. Consequently, some identifiers tend to end up as orphans, defined in Resource.h but not used anywhere in the RC file. The In Use column lets you easily spot any orphaned identifiers. To delete a symbol identifier—that is, remove its **#define** statement from the Resource.h file—select it from the list and click the Delete button. The deletion takes effect when you next click the Save command. Remember, though, that the browser is telling you only that an unchecked symbol does not appear in the RC file. That doesn't mean the symbol isn't used elsewhere in the source code or in another resource file.

# An Example of an AppWizard Resource

Before getting any more deeply immersed in descriptions, let's look at part of the resource script file that AppWizard generates for the fictitious Demo program. As we've seen, AppWizard automatically creates a resource script for an About dialog box, complete with an MFC icon. The dialog script in the generated Demo.rc file looks like this:

```
IDD_ABOUTBOX DIALOG DISCARDABLE  0, 0, 217, 55
STYLE DS_MODALFRAME | WS_POPUP | WS_CAPTION | WS_SYSMENU
CAPTION "About Demo"
FONT 8, "MS Sans Serif"
BEGIN
    ICON            IDR_MAINFRAME,IDC_STATIC,11,17,20,20
    LTEXT           "Demo Version 1.0",IDC_STATIC,40,10,119,8,SS_NOPREFIX
    LTEXT           "Copyright (C) 1998",IDC_STATIC,40,25,119,8
    DEFPUSHBUTTON   "OK",IDOK,178,7,32,14,WS_GROUP
END
```

The above instructions define the dialog box shown here, which is invoked by choosing About from Demo's Help menu:

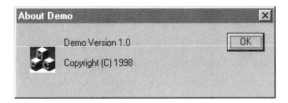

Not bad for having written zero lines of code. However, AppWizard isn't for every occasion. To show what life is like without AppWizard, the rest of the chapter develops a resource-laden program from scratch without AppWizard and discusses the pros and cons of this approach.

# Introducing the DiskPie1 Example Program

Here we begin a series of sections that develop step by step an example program called DiskPie1. Each section concentrates on a single resource type, beginning with menus and accelerators and following with status bars, bitmaps, and toolbars. A section begins with a general discussion of a resource type and ends by making a contribution to DiskPie1, demonstrating how to create or revise a resource with the appropriate Visual C++ editor. By the time we're finished, DiskPie1 will be a useful utility that shows at a glance current memory usage and available disk space.

In keeping with good development practice, we'll "spec" the program at the outset before writing any code. The specifications will give you an idea of the resources we will be adding to the program and make it easier to see how they work together to form a consistent interface. Here are DiskPie1's specifications in brief:

- **Description**—DiskPie1 is a small utility program written with MFC that displays a two-piece pie chart. Depending on menu or toolbar selections, the chart shows current space allocations for memory on a designated disk drive. One portion of the pie represents occupied space while the second portion, offset slightly from the first, shows free space. Labels clearly identify both portions.

- **Main window**—The program has four menus named File, Chart, View, and Help. The File menu contains only an Exit command, and the Help menu has an About command that displays program information. The View menu allows the user to show or hide the toolbar and status bar. The Chart menu at first contains only one command called Memory, which displays memory usage. At runtime, DiskPie1 searches for disk drives attached to the system, including RAM disks and remote network drives, and adds them to the Chart menu. The program ignores floppy disk drives, CD drives, and other removable media.

- **Toolbar and accelerators**—A dockable toolbar and keyboard commands supplement the program's menus, allowing the user to display a usage chart by clicking a button or by pressing a key to indicate a drive designation C through Z.

- **Status bar**—Identifies the current menu or toolbar selection.

- **Context menu**—DiskPie1 does not provide a context menu.

DiskPie1 could easily begin life as skeleton code generated by AppWizard, but I chose not to do this for two reasons. First, DiskPie1 isn't the kind of document/view application that AppWizard has in mind when it creates files, and removing extraneous resource scripts generated by AppWizard can be tedious and not very interesting. Second, we've already talked about AppWizard. It's time to see what it's like to create a project from the ground up in Visual C++. The sections that follow don't ignore App-Wizard by any means—they all describe AppWizard defaults so you can see what is gained or lost by using AppWizard to create a small project like DiskPie1.

The discussions assume that DiskPie1 begins as an empty project with no source files. If you would like to follow the steps outlined here and create the project from scratch, choose New from the File menu, and then click the Projects tab and the Win32 Application icon. Type the project name and click the OK button. The Win32 Application wizard displays only a single step, offering to set up a new project in three different degrees of readiness; click the Finish button to accept the default selection for an empty project:

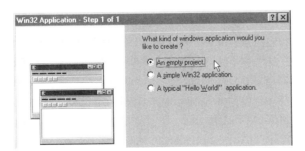

If you have already run the Setup program to copy the DiskPie1 project files from the companion CD to your hard disk, you may prefer to open the project and follow the discussions without creating the resources

---

## Opening an Existing Project

A new project, like a new file, begins with the New command, enlisting the services of one of the Visual C++ wizards (like AppWizard or Win32 Application) to set up the new project. Once the wizard finishes, the New command is not used again for that project. To open an existing project such as any of those installed from the companion CD, choose the Open Workspace command from the File menu and navigate to the project folder. For a project that you have worked on recently, the Recent Workspaces command on the same menu offers more convenience.

If you prefer, the Visual C++ environment can automatically open your most recent project at startup. This feature is very convenient for lengthy projects to which you devote most of your time. Click Options on the Tools menu and scroll to the right to find the Workspace tab, then activate the check box labeled Reload Last Workspace At Startup.

---

yourself. To open the finished project, choose Open Workspace from the File menu and browse for the DiskPie1 project folder on your hard disk. Double-click the DiskPie1.dsw file to open the project.

## Configuring the DiskPie1 Project

The Win32 Application wizard generates only a few files that form a bare project. The wizard also assumes the project does not use MFC—an incorrect assumption for DiskPie1. After selecting Win32 Application to create an MFC program like DiskPie1, you must configure the project to recognize the MFC library. As described in Chapter 2, AppWizard, this is done through a switch in the General tab of the Project Settings dialog. Invoke the dialog by choosing Settings from the Project menu, select All Configurations from the combo box in the dialog's upper left corner, and choose either static or dynamic linkage for the project. Figure 4-3 shows the latter choice.

Once the fledgling DiskPie1 project is open and properly configured, we can start creating resources for it and add the DiskPie1.rc and Resource.h

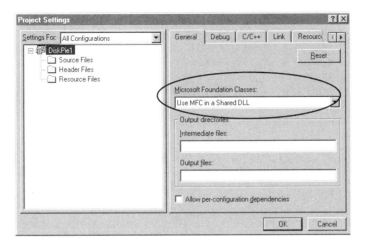

**Figure 4-3.** *Selecting dynamic linking to MFC in the Project Settings dialog.*

files. DiskPie1 is heavy with resources for such a small program, so most of the work involves creating the resource data. We'll write the actual code for the program last, after the resources are complete.

## Menus and Accelerator Keys

Figure 4-4 on the next page shows the menu system that AppWizard creates by default. You can see the correspondence between the menus in the figure and the menu script that AppWizard places in the RC file:

```
IDR_MAINFRAME MENU PRELOAD DISCARDABLE
BEGIN
    POPUP "&File"
    BEGIN
        MENUITEM "&New\tCtrl+N",              ID_FILE_NEW
        MENUITEM "&Open...\tCtrl+O",          ID_FILE_OPEN
        MENUITEM "&Save\tCtrl+S",             ID_FILE_SAVE
        MENUITEM "Save &As...",               ID_FILE_SAVE_AS
        MENUITEM SEPARATOR
        MENUITEM "&Print...\tCtrl+P",         ID_FILE_PRINT
        MENUITEM "Print Pre&view",            ID_FILE_PRINT_PREVIEW
        MENUITEM "P&rint Setup...",           ID_FILE_PRINT_SETUP
        MENUITEM SEPARATOR
        MENUITEM "Recent File",               ID_FILE_MRU_FILE1,GRAYED
        MENUITEM SEPARATOR
        MENUITEM "E&xit",                     ID_APP_EXIT
    END
    POPUP "&Edit"
```

```
           BEGIN
               MENUITEM "&Undo\tCtrl+Z",                    ID_EDIT_UNDO
               MENUITEM SEPARATOR
               MENUITEM "Cu&t\tCtrl+X",                     ID_EDIT_CUT
               MENUITEM "&Copy\tCtrl+C",                    ID_EDIT_COPY
               MENUITEM "&Paste\tCtrl+V",                   ID_EDIT_PASTE
           END
           POPUP "&View"
           BEGIN
               MENUITEM "&Toolbar",                         ID_VIEW_TOOLBAR
               MENUITEM "&Status Bar",                      ID_VIEW_STATUS_BAR
           END
           POPUP "&Help"
           BEGIN
               MENUITEM "&About Demo...",                   ID_APP_ABOUT
           END
       END
```

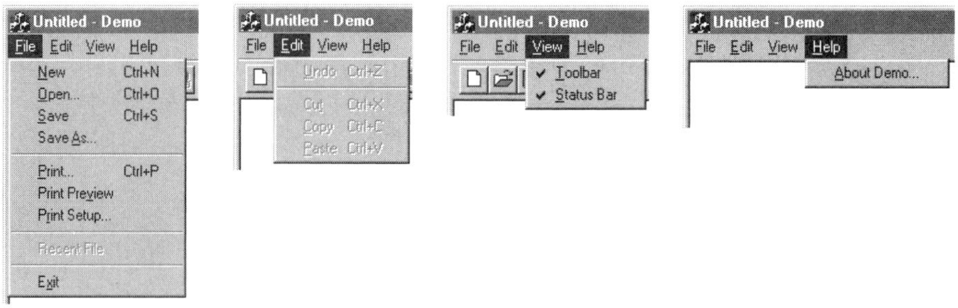

**Figure 4-4.**    *The menu system generated by AppWizard.*

The first line of the script gives the menu bar an identification number of IDR_MAINFRAME, which is defined in the Resource.h file that AppWizard adds to the project. Like all identifiers in the file, IDR_MAINFRAME is only AppWizard's default name; you can specify any name or value you want for a resource.

The PRELOAD and DISCARDABLE directives are not necessary in the script of a Win32 application. PRELOAD, which has meaning only for 16-bit applications, tells Windows to copy the menu resource data into memory when it first loads the program rather than later reopening the program's EXE file and reading the menu data when the program creates the main window. The DISCARDABLE directive is not required because in Win32 all resources are discardable. This means that the operating system can freely delete a program's resource data from physical memory to make the memory available to other processes. When the program again has focus and needs the deleted resource, the system rereads the data from the program's EXE file. This is possible because resources are static read-only data, and the copy in memory is the same as on disk. In contrast, removing dynamic data from memory involves the virtual memory manager, which must first save the data to the system swap file before the memory can be used for other purposes.

The indentations in the resource script show levels enclosed between BEGIN and END statements. The first level defines the complete menu resource including the menu bar, which is called a top-level menu. Secondary levels of BEGIN-END pairs specify the contents of each drop-down menu. Each POPUP statement is followed by a menu title that appears on the menu bar, and subsequent MENUITEM statements specify the commands listed on the menu. A line in a menu is called a command or menu item.

Some menu commands include keyboard combinations, such as Ctrl+N for New and Ctrl+O for Open. Known as accelerator keys, these key combinations serve as shortcuts that let the user choose a command without going through the menu system. For example, Ctrl+O immediately displays the Open dialog box—exactly the same effect as choosing Open from the File menu. The trouble with accelerator keys is that the user must memorize them; they appear on the menu only as a memory aid to remind the user that an easier way exists to choose a command. Accelerator keys require an additional table in the RC file, which we'll look at shortly.

The \t before the accelerator key combination is a tab character that aligns the accelerators neatly on the menu. You can also use \a instead of \t to right-justify the text on the menu, provided you are consistent. If you use \a to align an accelerator key combination on any line of a menu, you should not use \t on any of the other lines. Doing so confuses Windows and results in a ragged alignment of the menu text. The \a character gives you finer control over the menu width than does \t. If text on the menu seems too crowded, type a few spaces in front of the \a character to widen the menu and further separate the accelerator keys from the commands.

The ampersand (&) in each menu command prefaces the letter that serves as a mnemonic key for the command. As Figure 4-4 shows, a mnemonic letter appears underscored in the menus to identify it for the user. A mnemonic key should be unique to a menu or menu bar—a Format menu, for example, should have a mnemonic other than "F" to avoid conflicting with the File menu. But using unique mnemonics is a recommendation, not a rule; if a menu bar or drop-down menu contains the same mnemonic in two or more places, Windows highlights each command in turn as the user presses the mnemonic key, and only activates the chosen command when the Enter key is pressed. The menu editor, described in the next section, can check for duplicate mnemonics through a command on its pop-up context menu. Right-click anywhere in the editor work area to invoke the menu:

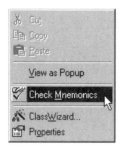

Mnemonics and accelerator keys aren't the same thing. An accelerator key activates a command without going through the menu system, whereas an underscored mnemonic key is available only when a menu is visible.

Each menu command has an associated identifier that begins with an ID_ prefix followed by a name that describes the command. The identifier name, including the ID_ prefix, is entirely up to you; the menu script on page 119 shows only what AppWizard comes up with. (As we'll see, however, there are advantages to using certain symbol names that MFC has already defined.) It's through the command identifiers that a program refers to menu events. When the user clicks a menu command or presses an accelerator key, Windows sends a WM_COMMAND message to the main window procedure with the command's identifier in the low word of *wParam*. If the command is in response to the user pressing an accelerator key, the high word of *wParam* has a value of TRUE; if in response to a menu selection, the high word is FALSE.

A C program traditionally handles menu commands by checking the *wParam* parameter of a WM_COMMAND message in a series of **switch-case** statements:

```
switch (msg)
{
    case WM_COMMAND:
        switch (LOWORD (wParam))
        {
            case ID_FILE_NEW:
                OnFileNew ();
                break;

            case ID_FILE_OPEN:
                OnFileOpen ();
                break;

                ⋮

        }
}
```

MFC programs accomplish the same thing with a message map:

```
BEGIN_MESSAGE_MAP(CMyFrame, CFrameWnd)
    ON_COMMAND(ID_FILE_NEW,  OnFileNew)
    ON_COMMAND(ID_FILE_OPEN, OnFileOpen)

    ⋮

END_MESSAGE_MAP ()
```

## Creating Menus for DiskPie1

When creating a menu resource from scratch as we'll be doing for DiskPie1, choose Resource from the Insert menu to display the list of resource types shown on the next page, and then double-click the list's Menu entry to invoke the menu editor.

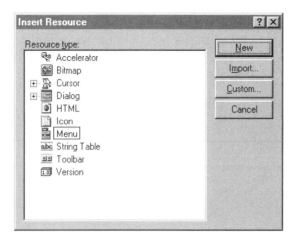

The project must be open and you might have to hide the Workspace or Output window to uncover the editor work area. When you design and save your menu, Visual C++ writes the menu script to the project's RC file and writes identifier **#define** statements to the Resource.h file. Thereafter, the environment automatically invokes the menu editor when you open a menu resource. To display a list of a project's menu identifiers, double-click the Menu entry in the ResourceView pane (see Figure 4-1 on page 111). Start the menu editor either by double-clicking the resource's identifier in the list or by right-clicking the identifier and choosing Open from the context menu.

Figure 4-5 shows what the menu editor looks like as we progressively add menus to the DiskPie1 project. The top-level menu—that is, the menu bar—contains a dotted rectangle called the new-item box that indicates the insertion point for menu caption text. When you type an entry on the menu bar and press Enter, a drop-down menu appears with its own new-item box. A fuzzy border indicates which new-item box is active, either

**Figure 4-5.**    *Creating DiskPie1's menus using the Visual C++ menu editor.*

the one in the menu bar or the one in the drop-down menu. If you want to type an entry in a new-item box that isn't active, click the box first to select it. Anything you type goes into the active new-item box and simultaneously into the Caption control of the Menu Item Properties dialog shown in Figure 4-6 on page 128. To go back and change a caption or menu item, either select the item and type the new text or double-click the item to invoke the Menu Item Properties dialog. The dialog's tendency to disappear is sometimes inconvenient when you are jumping between menu items. In such cases, click the push-pin button at the top left corner of the dialog, which forces the dialog to remain visible.

The File menu for DiskPie1 has only one command, called Exit. To create the menu, first type *&File* in the menu bar new-item box, press Enter, and then type *E&xit* as the menu item text. If you press Enter at this point, the menu editor helpfully gives the command an identifier called ID_FILE_ EXIT, which is an amalgam of the menu caption and menu item text. It also adds a **#define** statement for ID_FILE_EXIT to the Resource.h file.

Let's stop a minute and figure out why this might cause problems later. When you save the new menu resource, Visual C++ sees there is no RC file for the project and automatically creates one for you. It also adds these lines to the RC file:

```
#include "afxres.h"
#include "resource.h"
```

MFC provides the Afxres.h header to save you the trouble of having to define for every project the same common identifiers that appear in typical Windows programs. On the theory that most Windows programs have a File, Edit, View, and Help menu, Afxres.h defines a host of identifiers such as ID_FILE_OPEN, ID_EDIT_COPY, and ID_APP_ABOUT. This leaves Resource.h for the new resource identifiers you define yourself. By chance, Afxres.h has no definition for ID_FILE_EXIT, but what if it did? In that case, you would get an error when compiling the RC file because ID_FILE_EXIT would be defined twice, once in Afxres.h and once in Resource.h.

The resource scripts that AppWizard generates do not have this potential problem of name collision. All the menu items that AppWizard generates are defined in Afxres.h, so AppWizard does not add definitions for them to Resource.h. For a non-AppWizard project like DiskPie1, you have three choices for preventing duplicate definitions when using the resource editors:

- Open the RC file in the text editor and remove the **#include** statement for Afxres.h.

- Give resource identifiers your own names without accepting the editor's default names that may be in Afxres.h.

- Edit the Resource.h file and delete any identifiers already defined in Afxres.h.

The trouble with the first option is that it forces you to also remove from the file all other Visual C++ trappings that require definitions in Afxres.h. The second solution is more secure. When naming resource identifiers yourself, MFC Technical Note 20 recommends adding the prefix IDM_ to menu identifiers, since IDM_ is never used as an identifier prefix in Afxres.h. Specify the identifier name in the Menu Item Properties dialog, and optionally set a value for the identifier at the same time like this:

```
IDM_FILE_EXIT=1001
```

Make sure each menu identifier has a unique value, of course.

There are good reasons for adopting the third solution in the above list of options despite its inelegance. Consider what happens if you identify the Exit command in your program with a name like IDM_FILE_EXIT. For an MFC application like DiskPie1, you must then supply a handler function for the WM_COMMAND message that carries the identifier, and also add a line to the message map that points to the handler. The results might look like this:

```
ON_COMMAND (IDM_FILE_EXIT, OnFileExit)    // In the message map
    ⋮
void CMainFrame::OnFileExit()             // Handler for IDM_FILE_EXIT
{
    SendMessage( WM_CLOSE, 0, 0 );
}
```

Afxres.h contains several special identifier names for which MFC supplies its own handler functions, saving the application the trouble of doing so. One of these special identifiers is ID_APP_EXIT, which is automatically caught by an MFC function that closes the application. By assigning the value ID_APP_EXIT to the Exit menu command, DiskPie1 does not have to supply its own code to handle the Exit menu selection. For similar reasons, the two menu items on DiskPie1's View menu are assigned the values ID_VIEW_TOOLBAR and ID_VIEW_STATUS_BAR. MFC recognizes these special values and calls its own handler functions to display or hide the toolbar and status bar. DiskPie1 simply uses the identifiers in its menu script for the Toolbar and Status Bar commands, and the MFC framework takes care of everything else.

The disadvantage of giving commands special identifier names such as ID_APP_EXIT or ID_VIEW_TOOLBAR is that the menu editor writes definitions for the names in the Resource.h file, thus duplicating definitions already in Afxres.h. We have to use the text editor to delete the extraneous definitions in Resource.h after creating the resources.

The names of the identifiers for DiskPie1's menu items are specified by typing them into the Menu Item Properties dialog. Here's a summary of the results:

| Menu title | Item caption | Identifier |
| --- | --- | --- |
| &File | E&xit | ID_APP_EXIT |
| &Chart | &Memory\tCtrl+M | IDM_MEMORY |
| &View | &Toolbar | ID_VIEW_TOOLBAR |
| &View | &Status bar | ID_VIEW_STATUS_BAR |
| &Help | &About DiskPie1… | ID_APP_ABOUT |

The Menu Item Properties dialog shown in Figure 4-6 on the next page lets you refine the appearance of a menu item. For example, if a menu command is inactive when your program first begins, the text of the menu item should appear gray to cue the user that the command is currently disabled. Specify gray text for a menu item by clicking the Grayed check box in the dialog. To place a check mark adjacent to the menu command, click Checked. Specifying grayed text or check marks in the resource script isn't

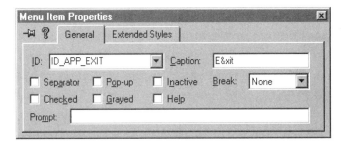

**Figure 4-6.**  *The Menu Item Properties dialog for a menu resource.*

necessary for an MFC program like DiskPie1, because the framework updates the menus automatically.

If you want a menu command to invoke a cascading pop-up menu, click the Pop-up check box in the Menu Item Properties dialog. The arrow symbol (▶) that appears next to the menu item tells the user that the command displays a nested pop-up menu. The editor displays another new-item box for the pop-up menu, in which you type commands as in any other menu. (The Recent Files command on the environment's File menu gives an example of a cascading pop-up menu.)

For programs like DiskPie1 that have a status bar, the Prompt text box in the dialog provides a convenient place to type a description that appears in the status bar when the user highlights the command on the menu. We'll add DiskPie1's menu descriptions in a later section using the Visual C++ string editor. When you see how repetitive the descriptions are, you'll agree the string editor is a better choice.

DiskPie1's menus are standard fare. The only interesting addition is the separator bar at the bottom of the Chart menu. Placing a separator bar last on a menu may seem odd at first glance, but DiskPie1 adds more commands to the Chart menu at run-time. The separator bar exists as a partition for two groups of menu commands: the Memory command at the top and Disk commands such as Disk C and Disk D at the bottom. To create a separator bar on a menu, click the Separator check box shown in Figure 4-6.

If you want to insert a new menu or menu command, drag the new-item box to the desired position. As you drag the box, a horizontal or vertical insertion line appears adjacent to the cursor. Release the mouse button to drop the new-item box, then type the new menu caption normally. You can also drag and drop individual menu items or entire menus to change the order in which they appear. To change the order of the Chart and View menus, for example, drag the View menu to the left until you see a vertical insertion line appear in the space between File and Chart. Release the mouse button and you're done.

When you create a new menu resource as we are doing here, the menu editor wants to name the new resource something like IDR_MENU1. The resource symbol name appears on the first line of the menu script in the RC file:

```
IDR_MENU1 MENU PRELOAD DISCARDABLE
```

A name like IDR_MENU1 is fine for the menu, but it may not be a good choice for an MFC program like DiskPie1. As a single-document interface (SDI) program, DiskPie1 can register templates for its resources with a single call to the *CSingleDocTemplate* constructor, provided the resources all have the same identifier value. It does not matter what the identifier value is or even if different identifier names are given to the resources, so long as the menu, toolbar, accelerator table, and status bar resources are all represented by the same constant number. If your program does not call *CSingleDocTemplate* or its MDI equivalent *CMultiDocTemplate*, you don't need to worry about identifying resources like menus and accelerators with the same symbol value.

By default, the resource editors give different names and values to all identifiers for the main window resources, so the Resource.h file might end up looking like this:

```
#define IDR_MENU1                    101
#define IDR_ACCELERATOR1             102
#define IDR_ICON1                    103
#define IDR_TOOLBAR1                 104
```

If you accept default names when creating resources, you must then edit the Resource.h file to give the identifiers a common value before using *CSingleDocTemplate*. We won't accept default names for DiskPie1; instead we'll assign to the menu and other resources the same generic symbol identifier used by AppWizard, IDR_MAINFRAME. This ensures that *CSingleDocTemplate* always gets a single value common to all resources. To change the menu's identifier, double-click the menu bar anywhere but on a menu name to call up the Menu Properties dialog, type in *IDR_MAINFRAME*, and press Enter.

At this point, the project's RC file does not yet exist. To save the first resource of a project, click either Save or Save As on the File menu and give the file the same name as the project, which in this case is DiskPie1. Visual C++ then creates the DiskPie1.rc file, writes the menu resource script to it, and creates the Resource.h file to hold the new definitions. Don't forget to edit the Resource.h file with the text editor at some point to delete the unwanted definitions for ID_APP_EXIT, ID_VIEW_TOOLBAR, ID_VIEW_STATUS_BAR, and ID_APP_ABOUT.

The next step is to add the DiskPie1.rc file to the project. Choose the Add To Project command from the Project menu, then click Files on the cascading menu as shown here:

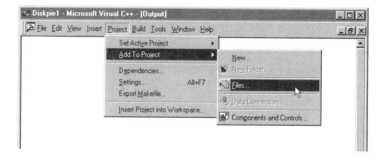

Double-click the new DiskPie1.rc file displayed in the file list to add it to the project. It isn't necessary to do the same for the Resource.h file because Visual C++ automatically recognizes header files as project dependencies. From this point on, DiskPie1 is an actual project. The next time we create a resource for DiskPie1, we'll save the resource with the Save command rather than Save As, since the DiskPie1.rc file now exists.

You can use the text editor to view the menu script that Visual C++ writes to the DiskPie1.rc file. Load the RC file as a text document by clicking Open on the File menu to display the Open dialog. Select Text from the

Open As combo box at the bottom of the dialog, then double-click DiskPie1.rc in the file list. Here's what the new menu script looks like in the file:

```
IDR_MAINFRAME MENU DISCARDABLE
BEGIN
    POPUP "&File"
    BEGIN
        MENUITEM "E&xit",                       ID_APP_EXIT
    END
    POPUP "&Chart"
    BEGIN
        MENUITEM "Memory\tCtrl+M",              IDM_MEMORY
        MENUITEM SEPARATOR
    END
    POPUP "&View"
    BEGIN
        MENUITEM "&Toolbar",                    ID_VIEW_TOOLBAR
        MENUITEM "&Status bar",                 ID_VIEW_STATUS_BAR
    END
    POPUP "&Help"
    BEGIN
        MENUITEM "&About DiskPie1...",          ID_APP_ABOUT
    END
END
```

Figure 4-7 shows what the finished menus look like for DiskPie1. The Disk C and Disk D commands on the Chart menu do not appear in the menu script above because these commands are added to the menu at run time. The icon on the title bar is created later in the chapter.

**Figure 4-7.**     *DiskPie1's menu system.*

If you want to dismiss the menu editor from the screen before continuing to the next section, choose the Close command from either the File menu or the Window menu. Make sure that the editor has input focus before applying the command.

## Creating Accelerator Keys for DiskPie1

Some future version of Visual C++ may scan for accelerator key combinations in the menu script and automatically generate a corresponding accelerator table. For now, we have to do it by hand. Since the above script has only one accelerator key—Ctrl+M for the Memory command—you might assume the table of accelerator keys in DiskPie1.rc will be short and simple. But in fact the table is fairly lengthy because we have to add keystrokes for items not yet on the menus but that may be added at run time. We'll do this with the Visual C++ accelerator editor.

For an existing accelerator table such as the one created by AppWizard, start the accelerator editor as you would any other resource editor, from the project's ResourceView pane. Double-click the entry in the Accelerator folder to launch the editor. To create a new table from scratch for a project like DiskPie1, start the accelerator editor by choosing Resource from the Insert menu and double-clicking Accelerator in the Resource Type list.

Figure 4-8 shows a partial list of DiskPie1's accelerator keys, which include Ctrl+M for the Memory command and 24 keys ranging from C through Z. These letter keys represent disk drives, serving as accelerators for the Disk commands that DiskPie1 adds to the Chart menu at run time. Because disk drives (including remote drives) can have any letter designation up to Z, DiskPie1.rc must include all possible accelerators in the

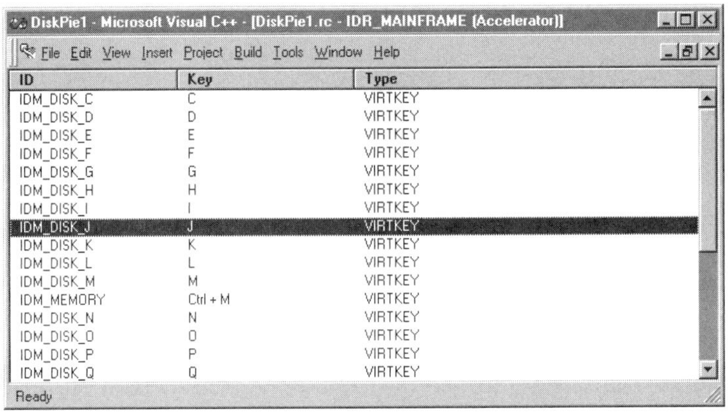

**Figure 4-8.**    *Creating DiskPie1's accelerator table with the Visual C++ accelerator editor.*

table. This won't cause any problems when the program runs because DiskPie1 ignores keypresses that don't correspond to an existing drive.

To add an accelerator key to the table, double-click the new-item box (which appears as a dotted rectangle) to invoke the Accel Properties dialog, then type the accelerator key and its identifier. For example, add the Ctrl+M accelerator key for DiskPie1's Memory command by typing *M* in the Key control and *IDM_MEMORY* in the ID control. By assigning to the Ctrl+M accelerator the same identifier given to the Memory command in the menu editor, we ensure that pressing Ctrl+M in DiskPie1 and choosing Memory from the Chart menu have the same effect. In either case, the same procedure gets called to display the pie chart for memory usage.

The accelerators for DiskPie1's Disk commands all have identifiers like IDM_DISK_C, IDM_DISK_D, and so on. Notice in Figure 4-8 that none of these accelerators are combined with other keys such as Ctrl or Shift, thus allowing the user to simply press a letter key such as C or D to display a usage chart for the C or D drive. To set or remove a combination key for an accelerator, check or uncheck the Ctrl, Alt, or Shift check box in the Modifiers area of the Accel Properties dialog.

Removing keys from the table is easy in the accelerator editor: just select the table entry and press the Delete key. To select a block of entries, click the first entry of the block, then hold down the Shift key and click the last entry of the block. Adding names to the table takes more work, especially if you have lots of keys. For symbol identifiers that have sequential names such as the ones in the DiskPie1 table, a text editor with macro capabilities is sometimes more convenient. If you create the accelerator table in the RC file using a text editor, remember to add appropriate definitions to the Resource.h file. If an accelerator key corresponds to a menu command, remember also to give the accelerator the same identifier as the menu item.

The Clipboard can be of service in the accelerator editor when adding a group of accelerators that have similar names such as IDM_DISK_C through IDM_DISK_Z. Type the first entry completely, select it in the list, and press Ctrl+C to copy it to the Windows Clipboard, then repeatedly press Ctrl+V to paste a series of duplicates into the accelerator editor. Next, double-click the first entry to invoke the Accel Properties dialog and click the pushpin button so the dialog remains on the screen. You can then move down the list to select entries and modify identifier names and keys as required.

Click Save on the File menu to save the new accelerator table. The editor gives the resource an identifier like IDR_ACCELERATOR1, which you can see in the ResourceView pane of the Workspace window. For DiskPie1, this isn't a desirable name for the same reason that IDR_MENU1 isn't a desirable name for the menu resource. Right-click the identifier in the ResourceView pane and click Properties on the context menu that pops up, then change the resource symbol name to IDR_MAINFRAME, as illustrated in Figure 4-9. This is the same name given to the menu resource earlier.

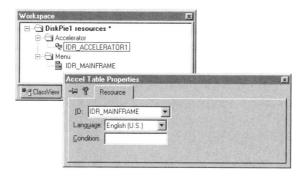

**Figure 4-9.**    *Changing the identifier name for the accelerator table.*

Choose the Save command again to set the new IDR_MAINFRAME identifier for the accelerator table. A fragment shows what the accelerator table now looks like in the updated DiskPie1.rc file:

```
IDR_MAINFRAME ACCELERATORS DISCARDABLE
BEGIN
    "C",            IDM_DISK_C,          VIRTKEY, NOINVERT
    "D",            IDM_DISK_D,          VIRTKEY, NOINVERT
    "E",            IDM_DISK_E,          VIRTKEY, NOINVERT
      ⋮
    "X",            IDM_DISK_X,          VIRTKEY, NOINVERT
    "Y",            IDM_DISK_Y,          VIRTKEY, NOINVERT
    "Z",            IDM_DISK_Z,          VIRTKEY, NOINVERT
END
```

DiskPie1's Resource.h file contains corresponding definitions for the identifiers:

```
#define IDM_MEMORY              130
#define IDM_DISK_C              131
#define IDM_DISK_D              132
#define IDM_DISK_E              133
    ⋮
#define IDM_DISK_X              152
#define IDM_DISK_Y              153
#define IDM_DISK_Z              154
```

The actual values you get for the IDM_DISK identifiers do not matter, but two good reasons exist for keeping the values sequential. First, sequential values for IDM_DISK_C through IDM_DISK_Z allow a single procedure in DiskPie1 to handle all menu commands or accelerator keys C through Z by using MFC's ON_COMMAND_RANGE macro. We'll iron out the details when we start adding code to DiskPie1. The second reason for using sequential identifier values has to do with how Windows loads strings contained in a program's resource data. That's next.

# String Resources and the Status Bar

When the user highlights a command on one of the menus, DiskPie1 displays a description of the command in the status bar at the lower left corner of the window. The same thing happens when the mouse cursor passes over a button on the toolbar. The descriptions are part of the program's data known as string resources, which are text strings stored in the resource area of the executable file. A Windows program can store any kind of read-only text as string resources; status bar descriptions are only one example.

This section begins with a general discussion of string resources, then narrows its view with a look at status bar descriptions. It finishes by composing DiskPie1's status bar descriptions using the Visual C++ string editor.

## String Resources

A string resource is no different from any other string in the program's data except that it must be read from the executable file into a buffer. A C program reads a string resource by calling the *LoadString* API function; an MFC program can call the *LoadString* member function of the *CString* class. And, at least in the case of status bar descriptions, an MFC program does not have to do even that. MFC provides default code that can load description strings automatically, as we'll see later.

A string resource is defined in the program's RC file in a string table, which is a list of strings identified by the STRINGTABLE keyword and bracketed either by BEGIN-END statements or by curly braces:

```
STRINGTABLE
{
    ID_STRING1   "Text for string resource #1"
    ID_STRING2   "Text for string resource #2"
}
```

A string resource in Win32 is limited to 4097 characters and can occupy no more than a single line in the resource script. An RC file can have multiple string tables, each with any number of strings.

String resources offer two main advantages over normal data strings. First, a string resource is not loaded into memory until it's needed, allowing a program to store "off-line" any text data it may never use. Consider a program that optionally displays helpful hints to the user, perhaps in a message box. Though many users may appreciate this feature, others will want no part of it and quickly turn the option off. By storing the hints as string resources, the program does not waste memory on the unused text every time it runs. The second advantage of string resources is that by organizing a program's string data as resources, the developer keeps the strings in one place rather than scattered throughout several source modules. Among other benefits, this allows a translator to create a foreign language version of the program by revising only the scripts in the RC file, after which the developer can recompile the file and relink. The source code is never touched.

You can add or modify string resources in the RC file using either a text editor or the Visual C++ string editor. If you change the name of a string identifier, the string editor offers the advantage of automatically adding to the Resource.h file a definition for the new identifier. The string editor does not, however, replace instances of the old identifier in your source code.

## Prompt Strings and Tooltips

Command descriptions in the status bar (a.k.a. prompt strings or flybys) have quickly become standard procedure in Windows applications. We've all been mystified at one time or another by a terse menu command or an inscrutable toolbar button covered with abstract art that offers little clue to its function. Discreetly tucked away in the status bar, prompt strings helpfully elaborate for the new user without intruding on the experienced user.

It's impressive how little programming effort prompt strings require. You tie a prompt string to a particular menu command and toolbar button by giving all three elements the same resource identifier. Then create a status bar and add the CBRS_FLYBY flag to the toolbar style. MFC takes care of the rest, displaying the correct string when a menu command is highlighted or the mouse cursor rests on a toolbar button.

Adding the CBRS_TOOLTIPS flag to the toolbar style enables a variation of prompt strings called tooltips. A tooltip is a small pop-up window that displays a brief description when the mouse cursor passes over a toolbar button. The Visual C++ environment uses tooltips to identify its own toolbar buttons, though the feature is optional. (To enable tooltips in Visual C++, turn on the Show ToolTips check box in the Toolbars tab of the Customize dialog, invoked by clicking Customize on the Tools menu.) Tooltip text is part of a prompt string, tacked onto the end with a \n newline character like this:

```
ID_PROMPT1     "Prompt string text in the status bar\nTooltip text"
```

Here's a simple example that illustrates the relationship between menus, toolbars, prompt strings, and tooltips. Although the code fragments that follow describe an MFC program that only opens and saves a document, the associated steps shown in boldface type apply to non-MFC programs as well.

137

## 1. Give the same identifier to corresponding menu items, toolbars, and prompt strings in the RC resource script file.

```
IDR_MAINFRAME MENU
BEGIN
    POPUP "&File"
    BEGIN
        MENUITEM "&Open",              ID_FILE_OPEN
        MENUITEM "&Save",              ID_FILE_SAVE
    END
END

IDR_MAINFRAME BITMAP                   "res\\Toolbar.bmp"
IDR_MAINFRAME TOOLBAR 16, 15
BEGIN
    BUTTON      ID_FILE_OPEN
    BUTTON      ID_FILE_SAVE
END

STRINGTABLE
BEGIN
    ID_FILE_OPEN            "Open an existing document\nOpen"
    ID_FILE_SAVE            "Save the active document\nSave"
END
```

## 2. Create the menu in the source code.

To create the main window and attach the menu in one step, call the *CFrameWnd::Create* member function:

```
Create( NULL, "Simple Demo", WS_OVERLAPPEDWINDOW, rectDefault,
        NULL, MAKEINTRESOURCE (IDR_MAINFRAME) );
```

Or use this code to load the menu separately after creating the main window:

```
CMenu     menu;
menu.LoadMenu( IDR_MAINFRAME );
SetMenu( &menu );
menu.Detach ();
```

## 3. Create the toolbar.

```
CToolBar toolbar;                              // In the header file

// Style defaults to WS_CHILD | WS_VISIBLE | CBRS_TOP
toolbar.Create( this );
toolbar.LoadToolBar( IDR_MAINFRAME );
```

```
// Add flyby and tooltip flags to style
toolbar.SetBarStyle( toolbar.GetBarStyle() |
                     CBRS_FLYBY | CBRS_TOOLTIPS );
```

### 4. Create and initialize the status bar.

```
CStatusBar      statusbar;                    // In the header file

UINT            nIndicator = ID_SEPARATOR;  // Single pane in status bar
statusbar.Create( this );
statusbar.SetIndicators( &nIndicator, 1 );
```

AppWizard generates similar code to do all this for you. You need only invoke the string editor and remove unneeded string resources, replacing them with strings that describe new commands in your program's menus. We'll get to the string editor in a moment, but first there's one more string resource to meet.

## The Document String

When we're finished with DiskPie1, it will have six program resources, each labeled with the identifier IDR_MAINFRAME:

- The application icon
- The menu for the main window
- The menu's accelerator table
- The toolbar window
- The toolbar bitmap
- A string resource that identifies the document

The last item in the list is called a document string, which consists of seven substrings separated by \n newline characters. When creating an SDI or MDI project in AppWizard, you can preview the seven substring components of the document string by clicking the Advanced button in AppWizard's fourth step. (The Advanced button is described in Chapter 2 on page 50.) Clicking the button displays the Advanced Options dialog, in which you can retype the default substrings for the project if you want to change them.

139

Had we used AppWizard to create DiskPie1, AppWizard would have defined a default document string like this in the DiskPie1.rc file:

```
STRINGTABLE PRELOAD DISCARDABLE
BEGIN
    IDR_MAINFRAME        "DiskPie1\n\nDiskPie1\n\n\n
                         DiskPie1.Document\nDiskPie1 Document"
END
```

(Like all string resources, the document string must appear as a single line in the RC file but for space reasons is shown above on two lines.) The substrings contain text and names that MFC assigns to the program and the documents it creates. In the order shown, the substrings specify:

- The program name that appears in the title bar of the main window

- The name assigned to new documents that the program creates

- A general document descriptor used in MDI applications that can open more than one type of document

- The document descriptor combined with a wildcard file specification, as it appears in the file-type lists of the Open and Save As dialogs

- The default extension given to documents that the program creates

- A name that identifies the document type in the system Registry

- A general descriptor for the type of document that the program creates

Since DiskPie1 does not create documents, we're interested in the document string only because of the second substring. When this substring is empty, MFC gives a default name of "Untitled" to new documents. You may have already noticed that programs created by AppWizard often have "Untitled" in their title bar along with the program name. For a program like DiskPie1 that doesn't save its data, calling its display "Untitled" can only confuse the user. One solution is to provide text for the second substring that describes the program, not the document—something like "Disk Usage." We'll do that in the next section.

## Creating String Resources for DiskPie1

For an AppWizard project that already has a string table in its RC script file, start the string editor by double-clicking String Table in the ResourceView pane of the Workspace window. To create a new string table for a project like DiskPie1, choose Resource from the Insert menu and double-click String Table in the Resource Type list.

The string editor is as prosaic as the strings themselves. The only interesting parts are the horizontal lines in the editor window, which you can see in Figure 4-10. These lines show divisions in the string table between groups of strings called segments, each of which holds a maximum of 16 strings. The value of the string identifier determines which string belongs to which segment. Strings with identifier values of 0 through 15 belong to the first segment, strings with values of 16 through 31 belong to the second segment, and so forth.

A segment acts something like a read-ahead buffer found on many disk drives, in which the disk controller reads not only a requested sector of the disk but a number of following sectors as well, storing them in a memory buffer for later use. Read-ahead buffers speed disk usage because one disk access is generally followed by more, which the controller can service by reading from the buffer instead of the disk. Following the same logic, the system reads string resources from the executable file one segment at a time. When a program calls the *LoadString* API function to read an individual string from its resource data, Windows reads the entire

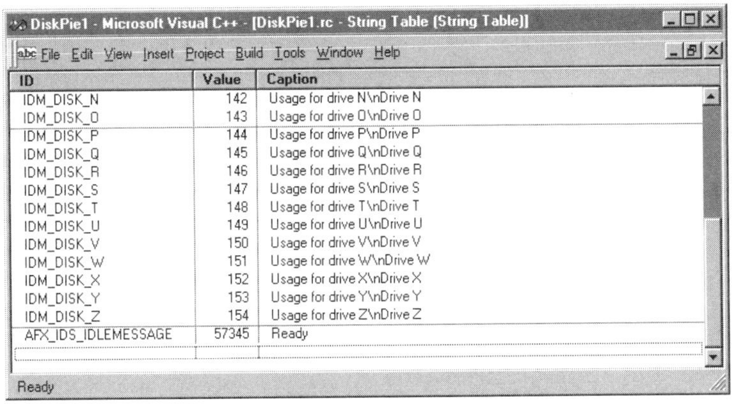

**Figure 4-10.** *The Visual C++ string editor.*

segment to which the string belongs on the assumption that if the program wants one string now, it will soon request the others. For this reason, you should try to group related strings by giving them sequential identifier values. You would probably do that anyway, but now you know why it's a good idea.

Like the other Visual C++ resource editors, the string editor indicates where the next string is placed in the table by displaying a new-item box as a dotted rectangle. To enter a new string, select the new-item box and start typing the string text. The String Properties dialog appears with a default symbol identifier. Rewrite the identifier name if you wish, or select a name from the drop-down list of the dialog's combo box. The list contains all identifiers defined for the project, including those in the Afxres.h file, allowing you to select a name such as IDM_MEMORY instead of typing it. The string editor automatically sorts the table entries by identifier value.

You can add special characters to a string by typing the escape sequences shown in Table 4-2. For a list of the ASCII and ANSI values mentioned in the table, refer to Appendix A.

| Escape sequence | Meaning |
| --- | --- |
| \n | New line (ASCII value #10) |
| \r | Carriage return (ASCII value #13) |
| \t | Tab character (ASCII value #9) |
| \a | Bell character (ASCII value #7) |
| \\ | Backslash ( \ ) |
| \ddd | Any ANSI character, where ddd is an octal number ranging from 001 through 377 (255 decimal) that identifies the character |

**Table 4-2.**    *Escape sequences for special characters in a string resource.*

The string table in the DiskPie1.rc file contains all the program's string resources:

```
STRINGTABLE DISCARDABLE
BEGIN
    IDR_MAINFRAME            "DiskPie1\nDisk Usage\n\n\n\n\n\n"
    IDM_MEMORY               "Memory usage\nMemory"
    IDM_DISK_C               "Usage for drive C\nDrive C"
    IDM_DISK_D               "Usage for drive D\nDrive D"
    IDM_DISK_E               "Usage for drive E\nDrive E"

       ⋮

    IDM_DISK_X               "Usage for drive X\nDrive X"
    IDM_DISK_Y               "Usage for drive Y\nDrive Y"
    IDM_DISK_Z               "Usage for drive Z\nDrive Z"
    AFX_IDS_IDLEMESSAGE      "Ready"
    AFX_IDS_SCSIZE           "Change the window size"
    AFX_IDS_SCMOVE           "Change the window position"
    AFX_IDS_SCMINIMIZE       "Reduce the window to an icon"
    AFX_IDS_SCMAXIMIZE       "Enlarge the window to full size"
    AFX_IDS_SCCLOSE          "Close the DiskPie1 application"
    AFX_IDS_SCRESTORE        "Restore the window to normal size"
END
```

The first string in the list is DiskPie1's document string, which has the same identifier as the program's other resources:

```
IDR_MAINFRAME            "DiskPie1\nDisk Usage\n\n\n\n\n\n"
```

This string specifies text that replaces the "Untitled" caption that MFC would otherwise write in the title bar. Take a look at DiskPie1's title bar in Figure 4-20 on page 167 and you will see how MFC takes the bar's text from the first two substrings of the document string. It's possible to remove "Disk Usage" entirely from the title bar, though this requires more than just deleting the second substring in the resource line. You must override the *CMainFrame::PreCreateWindow* virtual function, clearing the FWS_ADDTOTITLE flag that MFC adds by default to the window style:

```
BOOL CMainFrame::PreCreateWindow( CREATESTRUCT& cs )
{
    cs.style &= ~FWS_ADDTOTITLE;
    return CFrameWnd::PreCreateWindow( cs );
}
```

The last strings in the string table have special identifier symbols with an AFX_ prefix, indicating that the symbols are defined in the Afxres.h file. For example, MFC recognizes the identifier AFX_IDS_IDLEMESSAGE and displays the string assigned that value in the status bar when the program is waiting for user input. By convention, the string simply reads "Ready." The other AFX_ symbols identify prompt strings for DiskPie1's system menu, which is invoked by clicking the program's icon or by right-clicking in the title bar. The appropriate AFX_ string appears in the status bar when the user selects an item on the system menu. As we'll see when writing the DiskPie2 program at the end of the chapter, it's often not necessary to include these prompt strings at all.

# Bitmaps, Toolbars, Icons, and Cursors

The Visual C++ graphics editor is where you create and revise a program's graphics resources, which can consist of bitmaps, toolbars, icons, and cursors. Icons and cursors are bitmaps that have a narrow purpose—icons appear on taskbar buttons or in a directory listing, and cursors serve as designs for the mouse cursor when it's positioned inside the program client area. A toolbar is a window that contains several bitmap images overlaid on buttons in a horizontal row. Anything else, such as an image displayed in a window or an animated picture in a dialog, is called a bitmap.

The Visual C++ environment provides one graphics editor for all occasions, so you don't have to learn four different utilities. You may see references in online help to a "toolbar editor" or an "icon editor," but these are just shorthand terms that mean the Visual C++ graphics editor applied to a particular type of resource. The graphics editor can handle multiple documents of different resource types. Figure 4-11 on page 146 shows the editor with two different documents open, one a familiar 16-by-15 bitmap and the other a two-color 32-by-32 mouse cursor.

The editor's appearance differs only slightly for each resource type, indicating the kind of resource you are working on by an icon in the upper left corner of the document window. Table 4-3 shows the icon for each resource document and lists the extensions for the file types that the graphics editor reads and writes.

When you use the Open command to open an existing resource document with any of the extensions listed in the third column of Table 4-3, Visual C++ automatically starts the graphics editor adjusted for the proper resource type.

| Resource | Icon | Input file type | Output file type |
|----------|------|-----------------|------------------|
| Bitmap | | BMP, DIB, EPS, GIF, JPG | BMP |
| Toolbar | | BMP | BMP |
| Cursor | | CUR | CUR |
| Icon | | ICO | ICO |

**Table 4-3.**   *Graphics editor icons and file types.*

DiskPie1 has menus, accelerator keys, and string data, but no graphics resources yet. For a project under development like DiskPie1, there are two slightly different ways to create a new graphics resource. The method you choose depends on what you have in mind for the image file. If you have a project open and want to add a new graphics resource to the project, choose Resource from the Insert menu and double-click either Bitmap, Cursor, Icon, or Toolbar in the list. Visual C++ launches the graphics editor, displaying in the title bar an assigned identifier for the resource document. Depending on the resource type, the identifier is a generic name like IDB_BITMAP1, IDC_CURSOR1, IDI_ICON1, or IDR_TOOLBAR1. Subsequent resources opened in the editor receive similar identifiers that increment the digit, such as IDI_ICON2, IDI_ICON3, and so forth. When you save a graphics resource to a file, Visual C++ gives the file the same name as the identifier minus the prefix, and then defines the identifier in the project's Resource.h file. For example, saving a resource named IDB_BITMAP1 adds this line to the RC file:

```
IDB_BITMAP1          BITMAP  DISCARDABLE    "res\\bitmap1.bmp"
```

and adds a line like this to the Resource.h file:

```
#define IDB_BITMAP1    130
```

There's no need to accept these nondescript names, however. Before saving a resource, give it a descriptive identifier by clicking Properties on the View menu and typing a new identifier name. In the same Properties dialog, you can also specify a name for the graphics file.

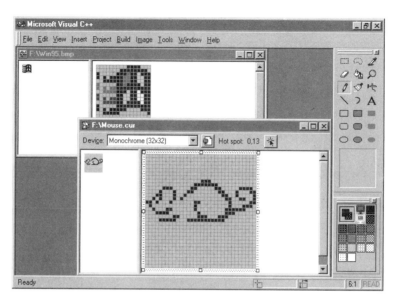

**Figure 4-11.**    *The Visual C++ graphics editor with two open documents.*

The second method for launching the graphics editor lets you create a new graphics resource without adding it to the list of project files. You may want to do this, for example, when creating a library of resources or designing bitmaps for toolbar buttons. This method does not require an open project; just click New on the File menu and in the Files tab choose the resource type you want from the list, either Bitmap File, Icon File, or Cursor File.

The work area of the graphics editor is split into two panes. By default the left pane shows the image in its actual size and the right pane shows an enlargement blown up approximately 36 (6 x 6) times. The enlarged image has an overlaying grid, each square of the grid representing a pixel in the actual-size image. If you have used a paint program before, such as the Paint utility that comes with Microsoft Windows, the Visual C++ graphics editor should seem familiar.

Select either image for painting by clicking anywhere in the left or right pane. For detailed work you will probably want to concentrate on the larger work area and observe the effects in the actual-size image. The splitter bar that separates the panes is moveable; just drag it left or right with the mouse. To begin drawing, select an appropriate tool by clicking a

Graphics toolbar     Colors palette     Transparency selector

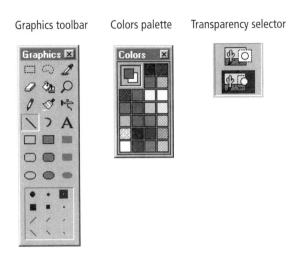

**Figure 4-12.**     *Tools in the Visual C++ graphics editor.*

button on the Graphics toolbar shown in Figure 4-12. As with any other toolbar in the Visual C++ environment, you can dock or undock the Graphics toolbar by dragging it into or out of position.

The graphics editor tools are intelligent and friendly enough to learn with a few minutes of experimentation. There are a few points, however, that may not seem intuitive and therefore warrant a brief discussion. First, the background color of the image depends on the graphics type. Icons and cursors have only a "transparent" background color, rendered blue-green in the editor window. When Windows draws an icon or cursor on the screen, it draws only the foreground colors; any pixels underlying the transparent background color are not erased. The background color of bitmaps, on the other hand, is opaque. A bitmap is drawn on the screen as a block that overwrites everything under it. Background transparency is probably the most important difference between the graphics resource types.

The transparency selector box appears at the bottom of the Graphics toolbar when you click the Rectangle Selection, Irregular Selection, or Text buttons, and is the toolbar version of the Draw Opaque command on the editor's Image menu. To understand the purpose of the selector box, think of an image in terms of two tiers, where one tier overlays the other. The upper tier is a floating image that you can move and set into position; the bottom tier, called the base image, is fixed. The selector box lets you set the background transparency of the upper tier, but does not affect the transparency of the base image itself. Selecting the top icon of the transparency selector box means that background pixels in the overlaying image tier should be treated as foreground colors, making the upper tier a solid rectangular block. The bottom icon of the selector box makes the upper tier transparent, in effect removing background pixels from the tier. For example, here's what the letter "A" might look like when typed on a base image with transparency on and off:

 Base image

 Transparency on

 Transparency off

The background color of the base bitmap image—white, in this case— remains opaque regardless of the transparency setting, so that displaying the bitmap on the screen overwrites any pixels covered by the bitmap's square area. A program can simulate transparent pixels when displaying a bitmap, however, by first masking out the bitmap's background color and replacing it with a copy of the screen area on which the bitmap will appear. If you are interested in this technique, you can find a good explanation complete with a derived class for transparent bitmaps in Jeff Prosise's *Programming Windows 95 with MFC*, in the chapter titled "Bitmaps, Palettes, and Regions." Often you just want to ensure that a bitmap has the same background color as the window it's displayed in, giving the illusion of transparency. There's an easy way to do that, which is explained in the next section.

Another hidden feature of the graphics editor is that the left and right mouse buttons generally correspond to the foreground and background colors, respectively. For example, clicking a color in the Colors palette with the left mouse button selects the foreground color; clicking with the right button selects the background color. You can draw on the image with either color by dragging or clicking the appropriate mouse button.

Table 4-4 summarizes the toolbar buttons found in the graphics editor. Buttons normally appear flat in the Graphics toolbar, as pictured in Figure 4-12. Table 4-4 shows the buttons in their raised form to help distinguish them from one another.

**Table 4-4.**    *Graphics toolbar buttons.*

| Button | Description |
|--------|-------------|
|  | The Rectangle Selection and Irregular Selection tools let you mark off a portion of the image to move, clear, or copy. Click the button, then drag the crosshairs or cursor point over the rectangle or region you want to mark. When you release the mouse button, a selection box appears around the marked area. You can move the selection by dragging it with the mouse, clear it by pressing Del, or copy it to the Clipboard by pressing Ctrl+C. |
|  | The Select Color tool lets you pick a drawing color from the image itself rather than from the Colors palette. Click the button on the toolbar, then click any square on the image that has the color you want. The left mouse button picks the foreground color and the right button picks the background color. |
|  | The Erase tool changes the cursor to a block that you drag over the image to erase pixels. Erased pixels are changed to the current background color, which depends on the resource type. As mentioned earlier, the background of icons and cursors is transparent. The background color of bitmaps is the opaque color shown in the upper left corner of the Colors palette. To change the size of the eraser block, click one of the size icons in the selector box at the bottom of the toolbar. |
|  | The Fill tool changes pixels of one color to the current foreground or background color. Click the Fill button, then click anywhere in the image on the color you want to change. Use the left mouse button to fill with the foreground color and the right button to fill with the background color. The editor changes all contiguous pixels of that color to the fill color. The pixels must touch either horizontally or vertically; pixels that touch diagonally are not considered contiguous. |

*(continued)*

149

**Table 4-4.** *continued*

| Button | Description |
|--------|-------------|
|  | To change the size of the selected image, execute the Magnify tool and select a value of 1, 2, 6, or 8. The magnification value specifies the number of horizontal screen pixels that correspond to one pixel in the actual-size image. If the enlarged image has a grid, the magnification value determines the width and height of each square of the grid. |
|  | Click one of the buttons pictured at left to execute a freehand drawing tool, then drag either mouse button to leave a trail of pixels of the foreground or background color. The Pencil tool draws only a thin line one pixel wide. Use the Brush to paint thicker lines, choosing the brush thickness from the selector box at the bottom of the toolbar. |
|  | The Air Brush paints a random pattern of color, simulating the effect of lightly spraying on paint. Choose the density and size of the spray in the toolbar's selector box. |
| 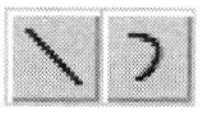 | The line-drawing tools draw straight or curved lines by "rubber-banding" from the initial click position. Click where you want the line to start, drag the cursor to the line's end point, and then release the mouse button to set the line. The Curve tool requires an extra step: after releasing the mouse button to set the end point, move the cursor to establish the line's curvature. When the line is shaped the way you want, double-click to set the line. (You must double-click the same mouse button used to drag the cursor.) If you change your mind while drawing a line, press the Esc key or click the other mouse button to start over. |
|  | The Text tool displays a small window for typing text that appears on the image in the current foreground color. Choose the text transparency in the transparency selector box as described earlier, then press Esc when finished to close the Text tool. |
| 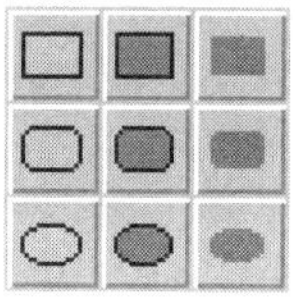 | These tools draw rectangles, round rectangles, and ellipses, either filled or unfilled. Select a tool, then draw the shape in either the foreground or background color by dragging the mouse cursor on the image from the upper left to the lower right of the area you want to cover. Holding down the Shift key constrains the shape, making a rectangle into a square or an ellipse into a circle. To cancel while dragging the cursor, press Esc or click the other mouse button. |

## Bitmaps

When you start the graphics editor for a new bitmap, it presents you with a clean work area 48 pixels square. Bitmaps don't have to be square, however—they can be rectangular of any size up through 2048 pixels on a side. To resize the work area, drag one of the resizing handles at the edge of the work area, noting the new size in the editor's status bar as you drag the handle. You can also type the desired size in the Bitmap Properties dialog, invoked by clicking Properties on the View menu.

Here's an example of how a C program might display a bitmap resource. The fragment assumes the bitmap is originally saved in the file Res\Bitmap.bmp and identified in the program's RC file by the name Bitmap-Demo, which is the same string given to the *LoadBitmap* function to load the resource:

```
// Resource declaration in the RC file
BitmapDemo      BITMAP       "res\\bitmap.bmp"

// In the C source file
HBITMAP         hbm;         // Declare a global handle for the bitmap
    ⋮
// Load the bitmap in WinMain or the InitInstance procedure
static char szAppName[] = "BitmapDemo";
hbm = LoadBitmap( hInstance, szAppName );
    ⋮
// Display the bitmap in the window procedure
case WM_PAINT:
    hdc = BeginPaint( hwnd, &ps );
    hdcMemory = CreateCompatibleDC( hdc );
    GetObject( hbm, sizeof (BITMAP), &bm );
    SelectObject( hdcMemory, hbm );
    BitBlt( hdc, x, y, bm.bmWidth, bm.bmHeight,
            hdcMemory, 0, 0, SRCCOPY );
    DeleteDC( hdcMemory );
    EndPaint( hwnd, &ps );
    break;
```

The steps are similar for displaying the bitmap in an MFC program. First, initialize a *CBitmap* object with the resource:

```
bitmap.LoadBitmap( szAppName );
```

Then display the image in the window's *OnDraw* function:

```
BITMAP   bm;
CDC      dcMemory;

bitmap.GetObject( sizeof (BITMAP), &bm );
dcMemory.CreateCompatibleDC( pDC );
dcMemory.SelectObject( &bitmap );
pDC->BitBlt( x, y, bm.bmWidth, bm.bmHeight, &dcMemory, 0, 0, SRCCOPY );
```

Before closing this section on bitmaps, let's revisit the subject of bitmap transparency one last time. We already know that a bitmap's background color is opaque, but if the image's background color is white and the bitmap is displayed in a window that is also white, the bitmap's square shape is hidden. Only the nonwhite foreground colors stand out, giving the illusion of a transparent background. But what if the window isn't white? In that case, the bitmap displayed in the preceding code fragments appears with its background color exposed as a square, which may not be what you want.

Application windows usually take on the system window color identified as COLOR_WINDOW, which by default is white. However, a program can change the system window color by calling *SetSysColors*, or the user can change the color in the Display section of the Windows Control Panel. (If you want to try it, select Window from the Item combo box in the Appearance tab of the Display Properties dialog, choose a new color from the Color drop-down list, and click OK.) A program can ensure the background color of a bitmap always matches the COLOR_WINDOW color by loading the bitmap using the *LoadImage* API function rather than *LoadBitmap*, specifying the LR_LOADTRANSPARENT flag like this:

```
hbm = LoadImage( hInstance, szAppName, IMAGE_BITMAP,
                 0, 0, LR_LOADTRANSPARENT );
```

This function looks at the color of the first pixel in the image, which lies in the upper left corner of the rectangular bitmap and presumably is part of the background. *LoadImage* then replaces the corresponding entry in the bitmap's color table with the current COLOR_WINDOW color. Thus all pixels in the image that make up the background are displayed in the default window color. The only caveat is that LR_LOADTRANSPARENT doesn't work if the bitmap has more than 256 colors.

We're not through with *LoadImage* yet. The function also loads icon images, as we'll see in a later section. But right now let's take a look at how a bitmap can become a toolbar.

## Toolbars

Creating a toolbar in Visual C++ is merely a matter of designing a bitmap that contains the images for the toolbar buttons. The bitmap is stored as a BMP file and referenced in the project's RC file with an identifier name:

```
IDR_TOOLBAR        BITMAP       "res\\toolbar.bmp"
```

Both the name of the identifier and the name of the file are up to you. DiskPie1 names its toolbar resource IDR_MAINFRAME to match the program's other resources, allowing a call to the *CSingleDocTemplate* constructor as explained earlier.

The toolbar bitmap is a series of images that overlay the toolbar buttons, one image for each button. By default, each image is 16 pixels wide and 15 pixels high, which is suitable for a toolbar button that has the standard size of 24 pixels wide by 22 pixels high. By dragging the edges of the editor workspace box in typical Windows fashion, you can set an image size that is larger or smaller, wider or thinner. The new size applies to all images in the toolbar, since you can't have buttons of different sizes in one toolbar. When you save your work, Visual C++ automatically specifies the new size of the toolbar buttons in the RC file.

If AppWizard generates the project for you, it creates a file called Toolbar.bmp in the project's Res folder. The file contains images for toolbar buttons that correspond to the commands New, Open, Save, Cut, Copy, Paste, Print, and Help. Figure 4-13 on the next page shows an enlargement of the bitmap in Toolbar.bmp and the resulting toolbar.

The following fragment shows the script that AppWizard writes to the program's RC file to create the toolbar. As you would expect, each button in the toolbar script has the same identifier as the corresponding menu command in the menu script listed on page 119.

Toolbar bitmap

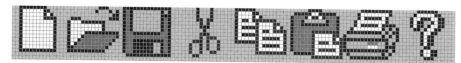

Resulting toolbar

**Figure 4-13.**    *The default toolbar generated by AppWizard.*

```
IDR_MAINFRAME              BITMAP  MOVEABLE PURE    "res\\Toolbar.bmp"

IDR_MAINFRAME TOOLBAR DISCARDABLE  16, 15
BEGIN
    BUTTON       ID_FILE_NEW
    BUTTON       ID_FILE_OPEN
    BUTTON       ID_FILE_SAVE
    SEPARATOR
    BUTTON       ID_EDIT_CUT
    BUTTON       ID_EDIT_COPY
    BUTTON       ID_EDIT_PASTE
    SEPARATOR
    BUTTON       ID_FILE_PRINT
    BUTTON       ID_APP_ABOUT
END
```

The BITMAP statement in the script points to the project's Toolbar.bmp file where the bitmap is stored. The TOOLBAR statement identifies the toolbar resource with the IDR_MAINFRAME value, and also specifies for each button an image size of 16 pixels by 15 pixels. A SEPARATOR statement forces a space between adjacent buttons, which are defined by BUTTON statements.

An MFC program creates a toolbar by calling *CToolBar::Create*. When the function returns, the toolbar it creates is merely an empty child window. The next step is to call *CToolBar::LoadToolBar* to read the toolbar button data, load the toolbar bitmap, and paint the buttons, all in one step. Windows provides an empty button for every BUTTON statement in the toolbar script and draws a corresponding section of the bitmap image over each button. For example, to load the toolbar defined in the above script, a program can declare a *CToolBar* object named *m_toolbar* and include these lines in the source:

```
m_toolbar.Create( this );              // Create the toolbar window
m_toolbar.LoadToolBar( IDR_MAINFRAME ); // Load the bitmap images
```

There are two approaches for creating a toolbar from scratch in Visual C++. The first will seem familiar by now: in an open project, click Resource on the Insert menu and double-click Toolbar in the Resource Types list. This launches the toolbar variation of the graphics editor, which displays the three split panes shown in Figure 4-14. The bottom two panes show actual-size and enlarged views of the current toolbar button you are working on, and the top pane shows a view of the entire toolbar. As you begin work on a button, the button image automatically appears in the toolbar view, changing in real-time as you edit. When finished with a button, click the blank new-item button in the top pane for a fresh work area for the next button. You can change the position of a button by dragging it within the toolbar, or delete a button by dragging it completely off the toolbar. To add a separator gap between buttons like the one in Figure 4-14, drag a button right or left approximately half the width of the button. You can close a gap the same way.

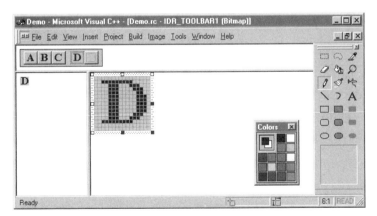

**Figure 4-14.** *Creating a toolbar in the Visual C++ graphics editor.*

Don't worry about the blank new-item button when you save the toolbar. It isn't included in the toolbar script that the editor writes to the RC file.

When working on the program's main toolbar, give each button the same identifier used for the corresponding menu items, such as ID_FILE_NEW or ID_FILE_PRINT. Enter the button's identifier in the Toolbar Button Properties dialog, displayed either by double-clicking anywhere in the work area or by choosing Properties from the View menu.

The second method for creating a toolbar calls for designing the bitmap images first, then converting the result to a toolbar. For DiskPie1, this method turns out to be more convenient.

## Creating a Toolbar for DiskPie1

DiskPie1 is unusual in that it determines at run-time the number of toolbar buttons required and their corresponding images. The toolbar script in DiskPie1.rc has only one entry:

```
IDR_MAINFRAME TOOLBAR 16, 15
BEGIN
    BUTTON        IDM_MEMORY
END
```

Buttons that display usage charts for disk drives are added when the program starts. For example, if DiskPie1 finds four disk drives with designations of C, D, P, and R, it specifies five buttons when it creates the toolbar—one button for the Memory command and the other four for the disk drives. Since there is no way to know beforehand what drive designations DiskPie1 will find for each system it runs on, the toolbar bitmap for DiskPie1 has button images for 24 different disk drives, labeled C through Z. As each of the 25 images is 16 pixels wide, DiskPie1's entire toolbar bitmap is 400 pixels wide and 15 pixels high. Figure 4-15 gives you a close-up view of some of the button images.

Enlargement of the first five images in the bitmap

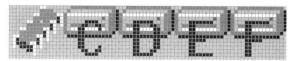

Entire bitmap shown actual size

**Figure 4-15.**    *DiskPie1's toolbar bitmap.*

The bitmap was not nearly as difficult to compose as you might think, taking only about 20 minutes. The secret is to tell the graphics editor you are creating a bitmap rather than a toolbar. The first step is the same in either case: start the graphics editor by clicking Resource on the Insert menu. For wide toolbar bitmaps with repeating images like the bitmap in Figure 4-15, choose Bitmap instead of Toolbar from the list of resource types. This lets you work on the button images in a continuous strip rather than as a collection of individual buttons. Converting an ordinary bitmap to a toolbar is easy in the graphics editor, which is designed to let you do just that.

Here are the steps for making a wide toolbar bitmap with repeating images. Double-click anywhere in the blank area of the editor workspace to invoke the Bitmap Properties dialog. Type in the toolbar identifier, which for DiskPie1 is IDR_MAINFRAME, and give a filename to the BMP file. Multiply the width of one toolbar button by the number of buttons and type this number as the bitmap width. The height of the bitmap is the height of a button. For DiskPie1, the dialog looks like this:

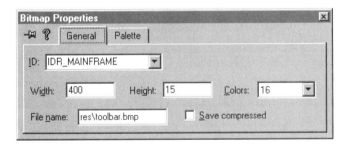

Press the Enter key to return to the work area, which now has the new dimensions. The next step paints the entire work area light gray so that each image blends with its button. Click the light gray color box in the Colors palette and select the ever-useful Fill tool in the Graphics toolbar.

Click anywhere inside the work area grid to paint the entire area light gray. Now draw the image of the first button in a 16-by-15 block (or whatever the button size) within the work area. Once you have drawn the first image, you can reproduce it by clicking the Rectangle Selection tool and dragging the cursor over the image's 16-by-15 block, as shown in Figure 4-16. Drag with either the left or right mouse button, depending on whether you intend to move the image or copy it. Use the left mouse button if you want to move the image elsewhere in the bitmap work area. When you release the button, a selection frame appears around the image, allowing you to reposition the selected area by dragging it. Dragging the frame with the Ctrl key pressed moves a copy of the selected image rather than the image itself, but there's a better way to duplicate an image.

To make a copy of an image, click the Rectangle Selection tool and select the image with the right mouse button pressed instead of the left button. When you release the mouse button, a copy of the selected image follows the cursor. Position the copy anywhere in the work area and click to drop it into place. Clicking the left button drops a copy of the image; clicking the right button drops a mask of the image in which foreground pixels are converted to the current background color and background pixels are treated as transparent holes in the image. You can make any number of copies this way. When finished, press the Esc key or select another tool to return to normal editing mode.

You will find alignment much easier if the image spans the entire 16-by-15 block like the disk drive image shown in Figure 4-16. If the image is narrower than the block, paint a temporary black line that spans the 16-pixel width along the top or bottom row of the block. You can then see exactly what you are dragging when copying the image. If you intend to label each button with text as was done in Figure 4-15 on page 156, add the labels last after all the images are in place. Click the Text tool, type the letter, and drag the letter image into position. Press Esc after each letter to cancel the Text tool.

When you are finished designing your bitmap, click Toolbar Editor on the Image menu to convert the bitmap to a toolbar. Accept the suggested

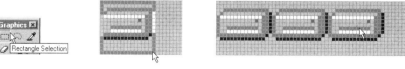

1. Click the Rectangle Selection tool.

2. Drag over the image with the right mouse button.

3. Position the duplication and click.

**Figure 4-16.**    *Duplicating a selected image.*

button size of 16-by-15 pixels in the New Toolbar Resource dialog. You can toggle back and forth between toolbar and bitmap with the same Toolbar Editor command. Click Save on the File menu to write the new toolbar script to the RC file and save the toolbar bitmap as the BMP file you named earlier in the Bitmap Properties dialog box. Visual C++ assigns default identifier values for the buttons in the new toolbar script, which now looks something like this in the DiskPie1.rc file:

```
IDR_MAINFRAME TOOLBAR DISCARDABLE   16, 15
BEGIN
    BUTTON      ID_BUTTON40030
    BUTTON      ID_BUTTON40031
    BUTTON      ID_BUTTON40032
    ⋮
END
```

The button identifiers must eventually be changed to the same values given to the corresponding menu commands—that is, IDM_MEMORY, IDM_DISK_C, IDM_DISK_D, and so forth. This ensures that clicking a toolbar button has the same effect as selecting the equivalent menu command. We could have specified the correct button identifiers in the graphics editor using the Toolbar Button Properties box, invoked by selecting a button and double-clicking anywhere in the work area. But that work isn't necessary. DiskPie1 assigns the correct values to the buttons when it determines at run time how many buttons must appear on the toolbar. We will edit the toolbar script later, replacing it with the stub script cited at the beginning of this section, and also remove from the Resource.h file the extraneous **#define** statements for the button identifiers.

## Icons

An icon is a special bitmap designed to visually represent a program or document. Usually the icon is assigned to a frame window so that the image appears in the window's title bar; when assigned to the program's main window, the icon resource is called the program icon or application icon. This section concentrates on how to create an application icon, which is the most common use of an icon resource. But an icon is an icon, and whether it represents the main window or another object on the screen, an icon is created the same way in the Visual C++ graphics editor.

An icon resource can contain more than one image, which often means different sizes of the same design. For example, Microsoft recommends that a Windows program provide three images of its icon resource, each image in a different size:

- A 16-color image 16 pixels square, which Windows displays in the program's title bar, on a taskbar button, and in a directory listing with small icons.

- A 16-color image 32 pixels square, used in dialog windows such as About boxes and to represent a program on the desktop or in a directory listing showing large icons.

- A 256-color image 48 pixels square, used in place of 32-by-32 icons in Windows 98 when the Use Large Icons option is checked in the Effects tab of the system's Display Properties dialog. (To open the dialog, right-click a blank area of the desktop and choose Properties. Windows 95 requires installation of the Microsoft Plus! pack, in which case the Use Large Icons option is located in the dialog's Plus! tab.)

You can see examples of large and small application icons in the Explorer window or by invoking the Save As or Open dialog in the Visual C++ environment. Right-click in the blank area of the directory list window and choose Large Icons from the View command of the context menu. The Small Icons command on the same menu shows 16-by-16 images.

An attractive and unique icon is considered good practice in Windows programming, but is not a requirement. If a program includes no icon at all in its resources, it can still use one of the standard system icons identified in the Winuser.h file as IDI_APPLICATION and IDI_WINLOGO. The system icons look like this in their 16-pixel size:

IDI_APPLICATION       IDI_WINLOGO

Three images encapsulated in a single icon resource can add almost 5,000 bytes to the size of an executable file. If this seems too much, you can create an icon with a single 16-by-16 or 32-by-32 image, which Windows scales appropriately when displaying icons of other sizes. You may be disappointed with the results, however, since scaled curves and diagonal lines are prone to ragged "pixelation" effects.

The next section shows how to create icons with the Visual C++ graphics editor, but first let's look at how a program loads an icon resource. A C program usually loads its application icon when creating the main program window. If the icon resource contains only one image size, the program can call the *LoadIcon* API function—the same approach used in older versions of Windows. But to load multiple images from the same icon resource, a program should use the *LoadImage* function instead. The program must also call *RegisterClassEx* with a pointer to a WNDCLASSEX structure to set both small and large icon images for the window class, since the old WNDCLASS structure used with the *RegisterClass* function accepts only one icon handle. Here's a code fragment that loads two icon images, one 16 pixels square and the other 32 pixels square:

```
// Declare the icon in the .RC file
IconDemo       ICON                  "res\\appicon.ico"


// In WinMain, initialize the WNDCLASSEX structure with image handles
static char    szAppName[] = "IconDemo";
WNDCLASSEX     wndclass;

wndclass.cbSize  = sizeof (wndclass);
wndclass.hIcon   = LoadImage( hInstance, szAppName, IMAGE_ICON,
                              32, 32, LR_DEFAULTCOLOR );
wndclass.hIconSm = LoadImage( hInstance, szAppName, IMAGE_ICON,
                              16, 16, LR_DEFAULTCOLOR );

    ⋮

RegisterClassEx( &wndclass );
```

An MFC program doesn't have to worry about any of this. AppWizard provides two icons for a project, one icon to serve as the application icon, and the other to represent documents that the application creates. The RC file identifies the icon resources as IDR_MAINFRAME and IDR_*project*-TYPE, where *project* represents the project name. AppWizard stores the icons, shown here, in the project's Res folder as the files *project*.ico and *project*Doc.ico:

*project*.ico          *project*Doc.ico

AppWizard automatically generates code that correctly loads the application icon along with the program's other resources. To replace a generic AppWizard icon with your own design, close the project workspace and choose New from the File menu. Double-click Icon File in the Files tab to launch the graphics editor, design the new icon, and save it in the project's Res folder, overwriting the existing *project*.ico or *project*Doc.ico file.

If you've written your MFC program without AppWizard's help, loading an application icon is still very easy. If the main window class is derived from *CFrameWnd*, identify the ICO file with the special AFX_IDI_STD_ FRAME value defined in MFC's Afxres.h header file. For example, an icon resource stored in a file named AppIcon.ico is identified in the project's RC file like this:

```
#include "afxres.h"
    ⋮
AFX_IDI_STD_FRAME          ICON  appicon.ico
```

If the window class is derived from *CMDIFrameWnd*, use this line instead:

```
AFX_IDI_STD_MDIFRAME       ICON  appicon.ico
```

If the icon file contains both a small and large image, MFC loads the images and correctly attaches them to the frame window, so that the small image appears in the title bar and the large image appears in the About box. If you look through the MFC source code to learn more about how allthis works, you will see that *CWinApp::LoadIcon* does not call *::LoadImage* as described earlier. Instead, it calls *::FindResource* with a value of RT_GROUP_ICON to load all images in the icon resource, and then searches the resource for the image that most closely matches the required size. *CWinApp::LoadIcon* retrieves the image by calling the API function *::LoadIcon* with the instance value returned by *::FindResource*.

## Creating an Icon for DiskPie1

DiskPie1's application icon is created in the open project by clicking the Resource command on Visual C++'s Insert menu, then double-clicking Icon in the Resource Type list. The graphics editor defaults to a 16-color work area 32 pixels square, which Windows calls the large or standard icon size. The editor displays the current size of Standard (32 x 32) in the Device combo box located just above the work area. The box's drop-down list contains only this one size, meaning the icon you are working on currently has one image, which is 32 pixels square.

The Visual C++ graphics editor can create an icon resource with any number of images, each with a different size or color capacity. To see the other sizes available, you have your choice of pressing the Insert key, choosing New Device Image from the Image menu, or clicking the New Device Image button:

All of these methods invoke the New Icon Image dialog shown in Figure 4-17, which lists the image sizes that are available but not yet attached to the icon. If you don't see the image size you want in the list, click the Custom button and specify a new image size.

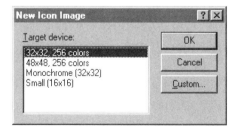

**Figure 4-17.**   *Selecting a new image size for an icon.*

The New Icon Image dialog provides the means for including multiple images in a single icon resource. After you have drawn the standard 32-by-32 image, select another size from the dialog and begin again. If you want to switch back to the original 32-by-32 image, click the drop-down arrow in the Device combo box and choose Standard (32 x 32) from the exposed list. When you select a new image size from the New Icon Image dialog, the entry disappears from the dialog's list and is transferred to the combo box list. In other words, the Device combo box lists the image sizes currently in the icon, while the New Icon Image dialog shows the available sizes you can add to the icon. To remove the current image from the icon, click Delete Device Image on the Image menu.

The DiskPie1 icon has three image sizes, ranging from 16 to 48 pixels square:

Small          Standard        Plus!
(16 x 16)      (32 x 32)       (48 x 48)

Normally, the images in a program's icon have the same picture, but different sizes. I gave the three images different designs to clearly show that Windows extracts the correct image from DiskPie1's resource data rather than just scale the 32-by-32 image. Double-click anywhere in the editor work area to open the Icon Properties dialog and assign the IDR_MAIN-FRAME identifier to the resource, and then save your work.

## Mouse Cursors

The specifications for DiskPie1 do not call for designing a custom mouse cursor, but let's take a moment here to see how it's done in Visual C++. A mouse cursor is a monochrome bitmap 32 pixels square with a transparent background and a "hot spot." The hot spot is the single pixel in the bitmap that Windows recognizes as the cursor coordinate. When a program receives a WM_MOUSEMOVE or WM_LBUTTONDOWN message, for example, the $x$ and $y$ cursor coordinates held in the message's *lParam* value represent the pixel under the cursor's hot spot:

```
case WM_LBUTTONDOWN:
    x = LOWORD( lParam );       // X-coordinate of mouse click
    y = HIWORD( lParam );       // Y-coordinate of mouse click
```

To create a mouse cursor, either choose New from the File menu and double-click Cursor File in the Files tab or, for an existing project, choose Resource from the Insert menu. Double-clicking Cursor in the list gives you a blank slate on which to design your new cursor. If you prefer to begin with a standard Windows cursor image, expand the Cursor heading and choose from IDC_NODROP, IDC_POINTER, or IDC_POINTER_COPY. The editor displays a work area 32 pixels square on which to draw the cursor. If you already have an image you want to use but it's in another form—say, a 32-by-32 bitmap—first open the bitmap in the graphics editor and press Ctrl+C to copy its image to the Clipboard. Then open the new cursor and press Ctrl+V to paste the bitmap image into the cursor work area. Colors in the bitmap are converted to black or transparent, depending on their intensity. If you don't like the results, press the Del key to delete the cursor image.

When the graphics editor loads a cursor image, a Set Hotspot button appears above the work area window. You can see the button in Figure 4-18 labeled with the coordinates (0,13), placing the hot spot at the nose of the rodent in the image. Click the Set Hotspot button, then click the point on the image grid where you want to set the cursor hot spot. Choose Save from the File menu when you are finished, and Visual C++ saves the

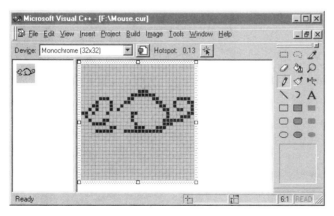

**Figure 4-18.**  *Creating a custom mouse cursor in the Visual C++ graphics editor.*

image as a CUR file, adding a resource definition to the project's RC file that looks like this:

```
IDC_CURSOR1              CURSOR  DISCARDABLE     "res\\cursor1.cur"
```

Setting the new cursor as a program's default cursor involves a call to the *LoadCursor* API function. In a C program, this is typically done when initializing the WNDCLASS or WNDCLASSEX structure for the window. Here's how to set up the new IDC_CURSOR1 resource:

```
WNDCLASSEX      wndclass;
wndclass.hCursor = LoadCursor( hInstance,
                                MAKEINTRESOURCE (IDC_CURSOR1) );

    ⋮

RegisterClassEx( &wndclass );
```

For a cursor resource identified by a string name rather than a value, the approach is nearly the same:

```
// Resource declaration in the RC file
MouseDemo       CURSOR                  "mouse.cur"

// Load and set resource during initialization in the C source file
static char     szAppName[] = "MouseDemo";
WNDCLASSEX      wndclass;

wndclass.hCursor = LoadCursor( hInstance, szAppName );
```

You can do the same thing in an MFC program with the *AfxRegisterWnd-Class* global function. The following example uses a generic icon for the last argument of *AfxRegisterWndClass*, but a real application should provide a handle to its own icon:

```
CString wndclass = AfxRegisterWndClass( CS_HREDRAW | CS_VREDRAW,
                    ::LoadCursor( hInstance, szAppName ),
                    (HBRUSH) (COLOR_WINDOW + 1),
                    theApp.LoadStandardIcon( IDI_APPLICATION ) );
```

These commands cause Windows to display the new cursor whenever the mouse pointer is positioned in the program's client area. Figure 4-19 shows what the cursor designed above looks like in a program. (You can find the source code for this tiny C program in the Code\Chapter.04\ Mouse subfolder on the companion CD.)

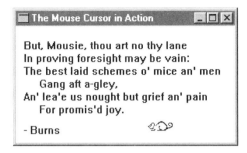

**Figure 4-19.**   *The new mouse cursor as it appears in a program.*

So much for cursors. Let's get back to the DiskPie1 program.

# Adding Code to DiskPie1

At this point DiskPie1 has a menu, accelerator keys, toolbar, status bar, icon—all the resource data it needs. Now it's time to add code to make it go. If you have followed the genesis of DiskPie1 in this chapter, you will recognize the user interface elements in Figure 4-20. The application icon, menu, toolbar, and status bar were designed in previous sections using the Visual C++ resource editors.

During creation of its main window, DiskPie1 finds all attached fixed disks, including remote drives and RAM disks, and for each one does the following:

■  Adds a command called Disk *x* to the Chart menu, where *x* is the drive designation letter

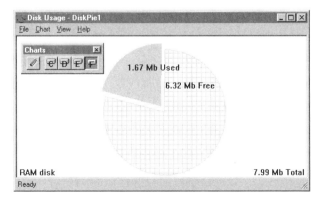

**Figure 4-20.**   *The DiskPie1 program, showing available space on an 8-MB RAM disk.*

■ Adds a button to the toolbar, selecting the button image from the 24 images in the toolbar bitmap that represent drives C through Z

Text at the lower left corner identifies the chart type as either memory, local fixed disk, RAM disk, or remote drive. Charts are composed of two pieces, one labeled "Used" and the other labeled "Free." The total amount of memory or disk capacity represented by the chart appears at the lower right corner.

Though a relatively small program, DiskPie1 complies with the common C++ practice of dividing classes into separate source files. The complete program listing follows, taken from the source files on the companion CD in the Code\Chapter.04\DiskPie1 subfolder. If you have created the resources for a new DiskPie1 project by following the steps in this chapter, you may wish to complete the project and build your own version of the program. In this case, copy the H and CPP source files to your project folder and add the four CPP files using the Add To Project command on the Project menu. The code expects an About box, so use the text editor to copy and paste the script from the DiskPie1.rc file on the CD to your own RC file. Remember to pare the toolbar script so that it looks like the one on page 159.

This table of contents describing the DiskPie1 source files will help you find your way around the code in Listing 4-1.

| Source File | Description |
| --- | --- |
| DiskPie | *InitInstance* function; displays the About dialog. |
| MainFrm1 | Creates the main window; determines the available drives and adds a menu command and toolbar button for each drive. |
| DiskDoc | Determines current memory and disk usage. |
| DiskView | Contains the *OnDraw* function, which displays the pie chart for the current usage data. |

**Listing 4-1.** *DiskPie1 source files.*

## Resource.h

```
// *************************************************************
//
// Resource.h
//
// *************************************************************

#define IDD_ABOUTBOX                    100
#define IDR_MAINFRAME                   101
#define IDM_MEMORY                      130
#define IDM_DISK_C                      131
#define IDM_DISK_D                      132
#define IDM_DISK_E                      133
#define IDM_DISK_F                      134
#define IDM_DISK_G                      135
#define IDM_DISK_H                      136
#define IDM_DISK_I                      137
#define IDM_DISK_J                      138
#define IDM_DISK_K                      139
#define IDM_DISK_L                      140
#define IDM_DISK_M                      141
#define IDM_DISK_N                      142
#define IDM_DISK_O                      143
#define IDM_DISK_P                      144
#define IDM_DISK_Q                      145
#define IDM_DISK_R                      146
#define IDM_DISK_S                      147
#define IDM_DISK_T                      148
#define IDM_DISK_U                      149
#define IDM_DISK_V                      150
#define IDM_DISK_W                      151
#define IDM_DISK_X                      152
#define IDM_DISK_Y                      153
#define IDM_DISK_Z                      154
```

## DiskPie1.rc

```
// *************************************************************
//
// DiskPie1.rc
//
// *************************************************************

#include "resource.h"
```

*(continued)*

**Listing 4-1.** *continued*

```
#include "afxres.h"

IDR_MAINFRAME        ICON         "res\\diskpie1.ico"
IDR_MAINFRAME        BITMAP       "res\\toolbar.bmp"

IDR_MAINFRAME MENU
BEGIN
    POPUP "&File"
    BEGIN
        MENUITEM "E&xit",                       ID_APP_EXIT
    END
    POPUP "&Chart"
    BEGIN
        MENUITEM "&Memory\tCtrl+M",             IDM_MEMORY
        MENUITEM SEPARATOR
    END
    POPUP "&View"
    BEGIN
        MENUITEM "&Toolbar",                    ID_VIEW_TOOLBAR
        MENUITEM "&Status Bar",                 ID_VIEW_STATUS_BAR
    END
    POPUP "&Help"
    BEGIN
        MENUITEM "&About DiskPie1...",          ID_APP_ABOUT
    END
END

IDR_MAINFRAME ACCELERATORS
BEGIN
    "M",            IDM_MEMORY,         VIRTKEY, CONTROL
    "C",            IDM_DISK_C,         VIRTKEY
    "D",            IDM_DISK_D,         VIRTKEY
    "E",            IDM_DISK_E,         VIRTKEY
    "F",            IDM_DISK_F,         VIRTKEY
    "G",            IDM_DISK_G,         VIRTKEY
    "H",            IDM_DISK_H,         VIRTKEY
    "I",            IDM_DISK_I,         VIRTKEY
    "J",            IDM_DISK_J,         VIRTKEY
    "K",            IDM_DISK_K,         VIRTKEY
    "L",            IDM_DISK_L,         VIRTKEY
    "M",            IDM_DISK_M,         VIRTKEY
    "N",            IDM_DISK_N,         VIRTKEY
    "O",            IDM_DISK_O,         VIRTKEY
    "P",            IDM_DISK_P,         VIRTKEY
    "Q",            IDM_DISK_Q,         VIRTKEY
    "R",            IDM_DISK_R,         VIRTKEY
    "S",            IDM_DISK_S,         VIRTKEY
```

```
    "T",              IDM_DISK_T,         VIRTKEY
    "U",              IDM_DISK_U,         VIRTKEY
    "V",              IDM_DISK_V,         VIRTKEY
    "W",              IDM_DISK_W,         VIRTKEY
    "X",              IDM_DISK_X,         VIRTKEY
    "Y",              IDM_DISK_Y,         VIRTKEY
    "Z",              IDM_DISK_Z,         VIRTKEY
END


IDR_MAINFRAME TOOLBAR 16, 15
BEGIN
    BUTTON          IDM_MEMORY
END


IDD_ABOUTBOX DIALOG DISCARDABLE  0, 0, 240, 65
STYLE DS_MODALFRAME | WS_POPUP | WS_CAPTION | WS_SYSMENU
CAPTION "About DiskPie1"
FONT 8, "MS Sans Serif"
BEGIN
    ICON            IDR_MAINFRAME,IDC_STATIC,10,22,20,20
    LTEXT           "DiskPie1 Version 1.0",IDC_STATIC,45,10,115,8
    LTEXT           """Microsoft Visual C++ Programmer's Guide""",
                    IDC_STATIC,45,26,140,8
    LTEXT           "Copyright \251 1998, Beck Zaratian",
                    IDC_STATIC,45,42,115,8
    DEFPUSHBUTTON   "OK",IDOK,195,10,35,40,WS_GROUP
END


STRINGTABLE
BEGIN
    IDR_MAINFRAME          "DiskPie1\nDisk Usage\n\n\n\n\n\n"
    IDM_MEMORY             "Memory usage\nMemory"
    IDM_DISK_C             "Usage for drive C\nDrive C"
    IDM_DISK_D             "Usage for drive D\nDrive D"
    IDM_DISK_E             "Usage for drive E\nDrive E"
    IDM_DISK_F             "Usage for drive F\nDrive F"
    IDM_DISK_G             "Usage for drive G\nDrive G"
    IDM_DISK_H             "Usage for drive H\nDrive H"
    IDM_DISK_I             "Usage for drive I\nDrive I"
    IDM_DISK_J             "Usage for drive J\nDrive J"
    IDM_DISK_K             "Usage for drive K\nDrive K"
    IDM_DISK_L             "Usage for drive L\nDrive L"
    IDM_DISK_M             "Usage for drive M\nDrive M"
    IDM_DISK_N             "Usage for drive N\nDrive N"
    IDM_DISK_O             "Usage for drive O\nDrive O"
    IDM_DISK_P             "Usage for drive P\nDrive P"
    IDM_DISK_Q             "Usage for drive Q\nDrive Q"
```

*(continued)*

**Listing 4-1.** *continued*

```
        IDM_DISK_R                "Usage for drive R\nDrive R"
        IDM_DISK_S                "Usage for drive S\nDrive S"
        IDM_DISK_T                "Usage for drive T\nDrive T"
        IDM_DISK_U                "Usage for drive U\nDrive U"
        IDM_DISK_V                "Usage for drive V\nDrive V"
        IDM_DISK_W                "Usage for drive W\nDrive W"
        IDM_DISK_X                "Usage for drive X\nDrive X"
        IDM_DISK_Y                "Usage for drive Y\nDrive Y"
        IDM_DISK_Z                "Usage for drive Z\nDrive Z"
        AFX_IDS_IDLEMESSAGE       "Ready"
        AFX_IDS_SCSIZE            "Change the window size"
        AFX_IDS_SCMOVE            "Change the window position"
        AFX_IDS_SCMINIMIZE        "Reduce the window to an icon"
        AFX_IDS_SCMAXIMIZE        "Enlarge the window to full size"
        AFX_IDS_SCCLOSE           "Close the DiskPie1 application"
        AFX_IDS_SCRESTORE         "Restore the window to normal size"
END
```

## DiskPie.h

```
// ***********************************************************
//
// DiskPie.h
//
// ***********************************************************

class CDiskPieApp : public CWinApp
{
public:
    virtual BOOL    InitInstance();
    afx_msg void    OnAppAbout();

    DECLARE_MESSAGE_MAP()
};
```

## DiskPie.cpp

```
// ***********************************************************
//
// DiskPie.cpp
//
// ***********************************************************

#define VC_EXTRALEAN

#include <afxwin.h>
```

```
#include <afxext.h>
#include "resource.h"
#include "DiskPie.h"
#include "DiskDoc.h"
#include "MainFrm1.h"
#include "DiskView.h"

CDiskPieApp theApp;

BEGIN_MESSAGE_MAP (CDiskPieApp, CWinApp)
    ON_COMMAND (ID_APP_ABOUT, OnAppAbout)
END_MESSAGE_MAP ()

BOOL CDiskPieApp::InitInstance()
{
    CSingleDocTemplate* pDocTemplate;
    pDocTemplate = new CSingleDocTemplate( IDR_MAINFRAME,
                                    RUNTIME_CLASS (CDiskDoc),
                                    RUNTIME_CLASS (CMainFrame),
                                    RUNTIME_CLASS (CDiskView));
    AddDocTemplate(pDocTemplate);

    CCommandLineInfo cmdInfo;
    if (!ProcessShellCommand(cmdInfo))
        return FALSE;

    return TRUE;
}

class CAboutDlg : public CDialog
{
public:
    CAboutDlg();
    enum { IDD = IDD_ABOUTBOX };
};

CAboutDlg::CAboutDlg() : CDialog(CAboutDlg::IDD)
{
}

void CDiskPieApp::OnAppAbout()
{
    CAboutDlg aboutDlg;
    aboutDlg.DoModal();
}
```

*(continued)*

173

**Listing 4-1.** *continued*

## DiskDoc.h

```
// ****************************************************************
//
// DiskDoc.h
//
// ****************************************************************

class CDiskDoc : public CDocument
{
    DECLARE_DYNCREATE (CDiskDoc)

public:
    static int      iDriveType[24];
    static DWORD    dwTotal, dwFree;
    static int      iChartType;
    static UINT     nCurrent;

    int             GetDriveCount();
    void            GetMemoryUsage();
    void            GetDiskUsage( UINT nID );
};
```

## DiskDoc.cpp

```
// ****************************************************************
//
// DiskDoc.cpp
//
// ****************************************************************

#define VC_EXTRALEAN

#include <afxwin.h>
#include "resource.h"
#include "DiskPie.h"
#include "DiskDoc.h"

#define  PIE_MEMORY     0;

IMPLEMENT_DYNCREATE (CDiskDoc, CDocument)

int     CDiskDoc::iDriveType[24]
int     CDiskDoc::iChartType = PIE_MEMORY;
UINT    CDiskDoc::nCurrent   = IDM_MEMORY;
DWORD   CDiskDoc::dwTotal, CDiskDoc::dwFree;
```

```
void CDiskDoc::GetMemoryUsage ()
{
    MEMORYSTATUS    ms;

    ::GlobalMemoryStatus( &ms );
    dwTotal    = ms.dwTotalPhys;
    dwFree     = ms.dwAvailPhys;
    iChartType = PIE_MEMORY;
    nCurrent   = IDM_MEMORY;
}

void CDiskDoc::GetDiskUsage( UINT nID )
{
    char      szDrive[] = "x:\\\0";
    DWORD     dwSectsPerClust, dwBytesPerSect, dwFreeClusts
    DWORD     dwTotalClusts, dwBytesPerClust;

    GetDriveCount();

    if (iDriveType[nID - IDM_DISK_C] == DRIVE_FIXED   ||
        iDriveType[nID - IDM_DISK_C] == DRIVE_REMOTE  ||
        iDriveType[nID - IDM_DISK_C] == DRIVE_RAMDISK)
    {
        szDrive[0] = (char) (nID - IDM_DISK_C) + 'C';
        if (::GetDiskFreeSpace( szDrive, &dwSectsPerClust,
            &dwBytesPerSect, &dwFreeClusts, &dwTotalClusts ))
        {
            dwBytesPerClust = dwSectsPerClust * dwBytesPerSect;
            dwTotal         = dwBytesPerClust * dwTotalClusts;
            dwFree          = dwBytesPerClust * dwFreeClusts;

            iChartType = iDriveType[nID - IDM_DISK_C];
            nCurrent   = nID;
        }
    }
}

int CDiskDoc::GetDriveCount()
{
    int  i, cDrives = 0;
    char szDrive[]  = "x:\\\0";

    for (szDrive[0]='C'; szDrive[0] <= 'Z'; szDrive[0]++)
    {
        i = (int) (szDrive[0] - 'C');
        iDriveType[i] = ::GetDriveType( szDrive );
```

*(continued)*

175

**Listing 4-1.** *continued*

```
        if (iDriveType[i] == DRIVE_FIXED   ||
            iDriveType[i] == DRIVE_REMOTE  ||
            iDriveType[i] == DRIVE_RAMDISK)
        {
            cDrives++;
        }
    }

    return cDrives;
}
```

## DiskView.h

```cpp
// *************************************************************
//
// DiskView.h
//
// *************************************************************

class CDiskView : public CView
{
    DECLARE_DYNCREATE (CDiskView)

private:
    static COLORREF rgbColor[2];
    static CString  strType[];

    void    GetLabel( CString* str, double e, PCSTR strTail );

protected:
    virtual void    OnDraw( CDC* pDC );
    afx_msg void    OnMemoryUpdate( CCmdUI* pCmdUI );
    afx_msg void    OnDiskUpdate( CCmdUI* pCmdUI );

    DECLARE_MESSAGE_MAP ()
};
```

## DiskView.cpp

```cpp
// *************************************************************
//
// DiskView.cpp
//
// *************************************************************

#define VC_EXTRALEAN
```

```
#include <afxwin.h>
#include "resource.h"
#include "DiskView.h"
#include "DiskDoc.h"
#include "math.h"


#define PI              3.141592654
#define RADIUS          900
#define SLICE_OFFSET    12
#define MEM_COLOR       RGB (0, 255, 255)   // Cyan
#define DISK_COLOR      RGB (0, 255, 0)     // Green

COLORREF CDiskView::rgbColor[2] = { MEM_COLOR, DISK_COLOR };
CString  CDiskView::strType[]  = { " Memory",
                                   " Fixed disk",
                                   " Remote drive",
                                   " RAM disk" };


IMPLEMENT_DYNCREATE (CDiskView, CView)

BEGIN_MESSAGE_MAP (CDiskView, CView)
    ON_UPDATE_COMMAND_UI (IDM_MEMORY, OnMemoryUpdate)
    ON_UPDATE_COMMAND_UI_RANGE (IDM_DISK_C, IDM_DISK_Z,
                                OnDiskUpdate)
END_MESSAGE_MAP()

/////////////////////////////////////////////////////////////////
// Paint the pie chart

void CDiskView::OnDraw( CDC* pDC )
{
    CPen        pen;
    CBrush      brush;
    CRect       rect;
    CString     str;
    int         x, y, i, iColor;
    double      dUseSweep, dFreeSweep;

    // Color is cyan for memory chart, green for drive charts

    iColor = (CDiskDoc::nCurrent == IDM_MEMORY) ? 0 : 1;

    // Set coord system so origin is at center of client area

    GetClientRect( rect );
    pDC->SetMapMode( MM_ISOTROPIC );
    pDC->SetWindowExt( RADIUS+100, RADIUS+100 );
```

*(continued)*

**Listing 4-1.** *continued*

```
pDC->SetViewportExt( rect.right/2, -rect.bottom/2 );
pDC->SetViewportOrg( rect.right/2, rect.bottom/2 );

// Create solid brush of current color for "Used" pie slice

pen.CreatePen( PS_SOLID, 1, rgbColor[iColor] );
brush.CreateSolidBrush( rgbColor[iColor] );
pDC->SelectObject( &pen );
pDC->SelectObject( &brush );

// Sweep angles in radians for "Free" and "Used" pie slices

dFreeSweep = (double) (PI*2 *
                       CDiskDoc::dwFree/CDiskDoc::dwTotal);
dUseSweep  = (double) PI*2 - dFreeSweep;

// For "Used" slice, sweep counterclockwise from due north

x = -(int) (sin( dUseSweep ) * RADIUS);
y =  (int) (cos( dUseSweep ) * RADIUS);
pDC->Pie( -RADIUS, RADIUS, RADIUS, -RADIUS, 0, RADIUS,x,y );

// Create hatched brush of current color for "Free" slice

pDC->SelectStockObject( WHITE_BRUSH );
pDC->SelectStockObject( BLACK_PEN );
brush.DeleteObject();
pen.DeleteObject();
pen.CreatePen( PS_SOLID, 1, rgbColor[iColor] );
brush.CreateHatchBrush( HS_CROSS, rgbColor[iColor] );
pDC->SelectObject( &pen );
pDC->SelectObject( &brush );

// Compute new center for "Free" slice, slightly offset
// from original center, then paint the "Free" slice

x =  (int) (sin( PI - dUseSweep/2 ) * SLICE_OFFSET);
y = -(int) (cos( PI - dUseSweep/2 ) * SLICE_OFFSET);
pDC->OffsetWindowOrg( x, y );
pDC->OffsetViewportOrg( x, y );

x = (int) (sin( dFreeSweep ) * RADIUS);
y = (int) (cos( dFreeSweep ) * RADIUS);
if (abs (x) > 4)
    pDC->Pie( -RADIUS, RADIUS, RADIUS, -RADIUS,
              x, y, 0, RADIUS );
```

```
pDC->SelectStockObject( BLACK_PEN );
pDC->SelectStockObject( WHITE_BRUSH );
pDC->SetBkMode( TRANSPARENT );
pen.DeleteObject();
brush.DeleteObject();

// Label "Free" slice

GetLabel( &str, CDiskDoc::dwFree, "Free" );
pDC->TextOut( 10, RADIUS/2, str );

// Ensure "Used" label doesn't occur near "Free" label

x = -(int) (sin( dUseSweep/2 ) * RADIUS);
y =  (int) (cos( dUseSweep/2 ) * RADIUS);
if ( y > 0  &&  (y - RADIUS/2) < 25)
{
    x = -(RADIUS - 10);
    y = 0;
}
GetLabel( &str,
          (CDiskDoc::dwTotal - CDiskDoc::dwFree), "Used" );
pDC->TextOut( x, y, str );

// Restore mapping mode so we can use DrawText function

pDC->SetMapMode( MM_TEXT );
pDC->SetWindowExt( rect.right, rect.bottom );
pDC->SetViewportExt( rect.right, rect.bottom );
pDC->SetViewportOrg( 0, 0 );
pDC->SetWindowOrg( 0, 0 );

// Write "Total" at bottom right corner of window

GetLabel( &str, CDiskDoc::dwTotal, "Total " );
pDC->DrawText( str, rect,
               DT_SINGLELINE | DT_BOTTOM | DT_RIGHT );

// Write device type at bottom left corner of window

i = 0;
if (CDiskDoc::iChartType == DRIVE_FIXED)
    i = 1;
if (CDiskDoc::iChartType == DRIVE_REMOTE)
    i = 2;
if (CDiskDoc::iChartType == DRIVE_RAMDISK)
    i = 3;
```

*(continued)*

**Listing 4-1.** *continued*

```
    pDC->DrawText( strType[i], rect,
                   DT_SINGLELINE | DT_BOTTOM | DT_LEFT );
}

void CDiskView::GetLabel( CString* str, double d, PCSTR strTail)
{
    char    ch = 'K';                   // 'K' for kilobytes

    d /= 1024;
    if (d > 1024)                       // If amount is greater than
    {                                   //   1024 kilobytes, divide
        d  /= 1024;                     //   again by 1024 to convert
        ch = 'M';                       //   to megabytes
    }
    str->Format( "%.2f %c%s%s", d, ch, "b ", strTail );
}

//////////////////////////////////////////////////////////////////
// Make sure menu check marks and toolbar buttons are in sync

void CDiskView::OnMemoryUpdate( CCmdUI* pCmdUI )
{
    pCmdUI->SetCheck( CDiskDoc::nCurrent == IDM_MEMORY );
}

void CDiskView::OnDiskUpdate( CCmdUI* pCmdUI )
{
    pCmdUI->SetCheck( CDiskDoc::nCurrent == pCmdUI->m_nID );
}
```

## MainFrm1.h

```
// ***************************************************************
//
// MainFrm1.h
//
// ***************************************************************

class CMainFrame : public CFrameWnd
{
    DECLARE_DYNCREATE (CMainFrame)

private:
    CToolBar        toolbar;
    CStatusBar      statusbar;
    CDiskDoc        diskdoc;
```

```
protected:
    afx_msg int     OnCreate( LPCREATESTRUCT lpCreateStruct );
    afx_msg void    OnMemory ();
    afx_msg void    OnDisk( UINT nID );
    afx_msg void    OnSetFocus( CWnd* );

    DECLARE_MESSAGE_MAP()
};
```

## MainFrm1.cpp

```
// **************************************************************
//
// MainFrm1.cpp
//
// **************************************************************

#define VC_EXTRALEAN

#include <afxwin.h>
#include <afxext.h>
#include <afxcmn.h>
#include "resource.h"
#include "DiskPie.h"
#include "DiskDoc.h"
#include "MainFrm1.h"
#include "DiskView.h"

IMPLEMENT_DYNCREATE (CMainFrame, CFrameWnd)

BEGIN_MESSAGE_MAP (CMainFrame, CFrameWnd)
    ON_WM_CREATE ()
    ON_WM_SETFOCUS ()
    ON_COMMAND (IDM_MEMORY, OnMemory)
    ON_COMMAND_RANGE (IDM_DISK_C, IDM_DISK_Z, OnDisk)
END_MESSAGE_MAP ()

////////////////////////////////////////////////////////////////
// Create main window, toolbar, and status bar

int CMainFrame::OnCreate( LPCREATESTRUCT lpCreateStruct )
{
    int         i, j;
    char        szMenu[] = "Disk &x\tx\0";
    CMenu*      pmenu;

    static const UINT indicator  = ID_SEPARATOR;
```

*(continued)*

**Listing 4-1.** *continued*

```
    static const UINT nButtons[] = { IDM_MEMORY, ID_SEPARATOR,
                IDM_DISK_C, IDM_DISK_D, IDM_DISK_E, IDM_DISK_F,
                IDM_DISK_G, IDM_DISK_H, IDM_DISK_I, IDM_DISK_J,
                IDM_DISK_K, IDM_DISK_L, IDM_DISK_M, IDM_DISK_N,
                IDM_DISK_O, IDM_DISK_P, IDM_DISK_Q, IDM_DISK_R,
                IDM_DISK_S, IDM_DISK_T, IDM_DISK_U, IDM_DISK_V,
                IDM_DISK_W, IDM_DISK_X, IDM_DISK_Y, IDM_DISK_Z };

    if (CFrameWnd::OnCreate( lpCreateStruct ) == -1)
        return -1;

    statusbar.Create( this );
    statusbar.SetIndicators( &indicator, 1 );

    toolbar.Create( this );
    toolbar.SetWindowText( "Charts" );
    toolbar.LoadToolBar( IDR_MAINFRAME );
    toolbar.SetBarStyle( toolbar.GetBarStyle() |
            CBRS_TOOLTIPS | CBRS_FLYBY | CBRS_SIZE_DYNAMIC );

    toolbar.SetButtons( nButtons, diskdoc.GetDriveCount() + 2 );
    toolbar.SetButtonStyle( 0, TBBS_CHECKGROUP );

    pmenu = GetMenu()->GetSubMenu( 1 );

    for (i=0, j=2; i < 24; i++)
    {
        if (CDiskDoc::iDriveType[i] == DRIVE_FIXED   ||
            CDiskDoc::iDriveType[i] == DRIVE_REMOTE  ||
            CDiskDoc::iDriveType[i] == DRIVE_RAMDISK)
        {
            szMenu[6] = 'C' + (char) i;
            szMenu[8] = 'C' + (char) i;
            pmenu->InsertMenu( 0xFFFF, MF_BYPOSITION,
                            IDM_DISK_C+i, szMenu);
            toolbar.SetButtonInfo( j++, IDM_DISK_C+i,
                            TBBS_CHECKGROUP, i+1);
        }
    }

    toolbar.EnableDocking( CBRS_ALIGN_ANY );
    EnableDocking( CBRS_ALIGN_ANY );
    DockControlBar( &toolbar );

    return 0;
}
```

```
/////////////////////////////////////////////////////////////////////
// Respond to menu/toolbar/accelerator commands

void CMainFrame::OnMemory ()
{
    diskdoc.GetMemoryUsage ();
    Invalidate ();
}

void CMainFrame::OnDisk( UINT nID )
{
    diskdoc.GetDiskUsage( nID );
    Invalidate ();
}

/////////////////////////////////////////////////////////////////////
// When focus regained, refresh display in case data has changed

void CMainFrame::OnSetFocus( CWnd* )
{
    if (CDiskDoc::nCurrent == IDM_MEMORY)
        diskdoc.GetMemoryUsage();
    else
        diskdoc.GetDiskUsage( CDiskDoc::nCurrent );
}
```

If you would like to follow the logic flow of the program, the important steps begin in the MainFrm1.cpp module. The *CMainFrame::OnSetFocus* function is called whenever Windows sends a WM_SETFOCUS message to inform the main window it is gaining input focus. This happens when DiskPie1 first starts and whenever the user switches back to DiskPie1 from another application. The function thus serves two purposes. It saves *CMainFrame::OnCreate* the trouble of calling *DiskDoc::GetMemoryUsage* to initialize data at program startup, and it also ensures that when the user runs another program or deletes a file, the current chart is automatically redrawn to reflect the new conditions when DiskPie1 regains focus.

Given a list of attached drives, the *CMainFrame::OnCreate* function inserts into the Chart menu commands such as Disk C and Disk D for each attached drive. It also adds toolbar buttons for the drives, selecting the appropriate section of the toolbar bitmap according to the drive designation letter. The button for drive D, for example, is painted with the bitmap's 16-by-15 section that contains the image of a disk drive and the letter D. (The complete toolbar bitmap with its 25 image sections appears in Figure 4-15 on page 156.)

The user can request a chart either for memory or a disk drive by

- Choosing a command from the Chart menu

- Clicking a toolbar button

- Pressing Ctrl+M for memory, or pressing any letter key C through Z for a disk drive

These events are handled by the *CMainFrame::OnMemory* and *CMain-Frame::OnDisk* functions, which receive control through the class's message map:

```
BEGIN_MESSAGE_MAP (CMainFrame, CFrameWnd)

    ⋮

    ON_COMMAND (IDM_MEMORY, OnMemory)
    ON_COMMAND_RANGE (IDM_DISK_C, IDM_DISK_Z, OnDisk)
END_MESSAGE_MAP ()
```

You may recall that when creating DiskPie1's accelerator keys earlier in the chapter, we made sure that the values of the identifiers IDM_DISK_C through IDM_DISK_Z were ordered sequentially. The above message map shows why. Because the identifiers have sequential values, the program can use MFC's ON_COMMAND_RANGE macro to route requests for any disk drive to the *OnDisk* function. From the drive identifier, which is passed as a parameter, *OnDisk* determines the drive for which the user has requested a chart. *OnMemory* does not require ON_COMMAND_RANGE because there is only one memory chart.

The mechanics of determining memory and disk usage is consigned to two functions in the DiskDoc.cpp module. The two functions, called *CDisk-Doc::GetMemoryUsage* and *CDiskDoc::GetDiskUsage*, employ similar logic. They retrieve the information they need from the system by calling the *GlobalMemoryStatus* and the *GetDiskFreeSpace* API functions, then use the information to determine values for the *dwTotal* and *dwFree* member variables, which contain the number of total and free bytes for the current chart. It makes no difference to the drawing function whether the data in the variables represents memory or disk space. After determining the current usage numbers, the *OnMemory* and *OnDisk* functions call *Invalidate* to force the display of a new chart.

The scene now shifts to the *CDiskView::OnDraw* function in the Disk-View.cpp file. This function uses the public *dwTotal* and *dwFree* values to determine sweep angles for the two pieces of the pie chart:

```
// Sweep angles in radians for "Free" and "Used" pie slices
dFreeSweep = (double) (PI*2 * CDiskDoc::dwFree/CDiskDoc::dwTotal);
dUseSweep  = (double) PI*2 - dFreeSweep;
```

*OnDraw* paints the "Used" slice first, sweeping the arc counterclockwise from the 12 o'clock position by the *dUseSweep* angle. The "Free" slice is offset slightly from the "Used" slice, drawn with a clockwise arc of *dFreeSweep* radians. *OnDraw* attaches labels to both sections and displays the chart. Requesting another chart starts the whole process over again.

A pie chart represents a snapshot of a current condition. The only convenient way to refresh a chart while DiskPie1 has focus is to press the accelerator key for the chart. Memory usage in a preemptive multitasking system like Windows is especially dynamic, changing every microsecond. If you continually press Ctrl+M while Visual C++ compiles a project in the background, you can see the effects of the rapid allocations and deallocations of physical memory. Adding an *OnTimer* function would update the display on a more regular basis.

More serious is DiskPie1's inability to account for the dynamics of drive attachments. We've seen how the *CMainFrame::OnCreate* function adds menu commands and toolbar buttons for disk drives attached to the system, including any remote drives provided through a network. The menu and toolbar then remain unchanged through the program's lifetime even though the user may subsequently add or detach a network drive, or an attachment may disappear because of problems on the server end. However, such an occurrence is not fatal—DiskPie1 still works correctly because *CDiskDoc::GetDiskUsage* always enumerates drives before displaying a chart. An enhancement to the program would add logic to recheck drive attachments when refreshing the display and add or remove menu commands and toolbar buttons accordingly.

# Unbound Commands (Revisited)

The previous chapter described how to bind commands named Word-UpperCase and WordLowerCase to the text editor command set by assigning key combinations and toolbar buttons to invoke the commands. The Visual C++ environment also provides many useful unbound commands designed for the graphics editor that you can implement using the same procedure described in Chapter 3, The Text Editor. To see a list of unbound and bound commands for the graphics editor, click Keyboard Map on the Help menu and select Image from the combo box in the Help Keyboard dialog. Figure 4-21 shows a sampling of the list.

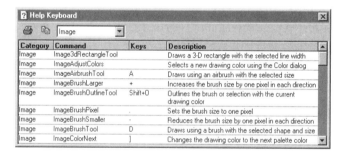

**Figure 4-21.**    *Commands for the graphics editor, displayed by selecting Keyboard Map from the Help menu.*

Many of the Image commands in the list already have keyboard assignments. Figure 4-21 shows that pressing the A key, for instance, invokes the Airbrush tool and pressing the plus (+) or minus (-) keys increases or decreases the brush size. But other commands are not available until you assign keystrokes or create toolbar buttons for them. To demonstrate, this section shows how to assign a keystroke combination for the first command in the list, called Image3dRectangleTool, which is a variation of the graphics editor's Rectangle tool.

From the Tools menu, choose Customize and click the Keyboard tab. Select Image from both the Category and Editor combo boxes, which tells Visual C++ to recognize the new keyboard command only in the graphics editor (also known as the image editor). Choose Image3dRectangleTool from the list of commands, click the Press New Shortcut Key text box, and type a key combination for the command, such as Shift+Ctrl+3. The dialog says that the key combination is currently unassigned, so we don't have to wonder whether we are taking Shift+Ctrl+3 away from some other command. Click the Assign button and then the Close button to dismiss the dialog.

The Image3dRectangleTool command is designed for bitmaps, so to see it in action start the graphics editor by choosing New from the File menu and double-clicking Bitmap File in the Files tab. When you press Shift+Ctrl+3 (or whatever key combination you assigned to the command), the image cursor changes to the same pixelated crosshairs used for the Rectangle tool. But the new cursor produces a slightly different effect when drawing a rectangle. As you drag the cursor from the upper left corner of the rectangle to the lower right, the top and left sides are painted in the current foreground color while the right and bottom sides appear in the background color. Dragging with the right button reverses the colors. With the right combination of colors, nested rectangles take on a three-dimensional look, letting you quickly create images like these:

Image3dRectangleTool is only one of many keyboard commands you might find useful when working in the graphics editor. The similar ImageWindowRectangleTool, for instance, quickly draws bitmap images of buttons in their normal, pressed, and inactive states—a time saver when designing owner-drawn buttons. Browse through the list and see what you like. If you want to create a toolbar button for a command, the procedure is explained in the "Unbound Commands" section in Chapter 3, beginning on page 95.

# Trimming Resource Data

Windows programs often carry around excess baggage in the form of unused or inefficient resource data, inflating the size of the program file and, worse still, wasting memory. Even resources that are never used can make their way into memory only to sit idle, tying up a piece of the virtual pool. With a little effort you can make sure your own programs do not have this problem. This section explores a few techniques for minimizing the size of a program's resource data and, by making some minor revisions to the DiskPie1 program, demonstrates how it is often possible to trim a significant amount of resource data from an application.

The first thing to remember is that you don't have to keep everything App-Wizard throws at you. Strings can be the worst offenders, as they are sometimes too verbose or even unnecessary. Win32 resource strings are stored in a program file as Unicode strings, which means every character you delete saves two bytes instead of one. If you remove a menu command from an RC file generated by AppWizard, be sure to remove the prompt string that goes with it. And don't forget the corresponding accelerator key.

AppWizard adds prompt strings to the RC file that describe the commands in a program's system menu:

```
STRINGTABLE
BEGIN
    AFX_IDS_SCSIZE          "Change the window size"
    AFX_IDS_SCMOVE          "Change the window position"
    AFX_IDS_SCMINIMIZE      "Reduce the window to an icon"
    AFX_IDS_SCMAXIMIZE      "Enlarge the window to full size"
    AFX_IDS_SCCLOSE         "Close the active window..."
    AFX_IDS_SCRESTORE       "Restore the window to normal size"
    ⋮
END
```

The MFC library file contains these same strings, so if your program links dynamically with MFC you can safely delete the strings from your RC file without changing the program's behavior. (However, if your program is destined for international markets where it may run on a system configured for a different spoken language, other factors may affect your decision whether to use strings supplied by the MFC library file. See the discussion about overseas markets and dynamic linking to MFC, beginning on page 55 in Chapter 2.) Besides freeing a few resource strings, dynamic linking to MFC rather than static linking dramatically reduces the size of an executable file because the MFC code is in the DLL, not in the calling application. The user benefits, of course, only if two or more programs running simultaneously use the MFC library.

I mentioned earlier in the chapter that if an application provides only one icon image 32 pixels square, Windows automatically scales the image to 16-by-16 or 48-by-48 pixels as necessary. If the icon image contains only straight lines and rectangles, scaling usually does not degrade the image. For icon images that are not affected by scaling, you might consider including only one 32-by-32 image instead of two or three images of different sizes.

You can further reduce the space requirements of icons and bitmaps by keeping their colors to a minimum. For example, by default the graphics editor's New Icon Image dialog (see Figure 4-17 on page 163) sets 256 colors for icon images that are 48 pixels square in size. But many icon images, like the DiskPie1 icon, contain only a few colors. Specifying 16 colors for an image uses only 4 bits per pixel rather than the 8 bits per pixel required by 256 colors. This simple step reduces by half the space occupied by the 48-by-48 image, a savings which, combined with the smaller color table contained in the icon, adds up to two kilobytes of resource data. To create a 16-color 48-by-48 icon image in the graphics editor, press the Insert key to invoke the New Icon Image dialog, click the Custom button in the dialog, and fill in the appropriate control boxes.

DiskPie1 devotes a lot of resource space to its large toolbar bitmap, as you can see in Figure 4-15 on page 156. Of the 25 images in the bitmap, 24 are duplicates, differing only in the letter that overlays the repeating image of the disk drive. In such cases, it's possible to provide one image and make it serve any number of toolbar buttons. At the cost of a little extra code, DiskPie1 can dispense with 23 of its toolbar images, resulting in significant savings in program size. Here's how it's done.

## The DiskPie2 Program

The release version of the DiskPie1.exe file is 24,576 bytes in size. By jettisoning much of its resource data, the new DiskPie2 program slims down to 17,920 bytes, decreasing the size by nearly a third without appreciably changing the program. DiskPie2 adopts four techniques to reduce the size of its resource data:

- With the exception of a "Ready" message, the program contains no prompt strings in its resource data. Relying instead on prompt strings provided by the MFC library file, DiskPie2 displays general descriptions in its status bar for all commands except those selected in the Chart menu.

- Without prompt strings, DiskPie2 must generate tooltip text on demand. The code to generate the tooltips occupies less space than would the tooltip strings themselves, resulting in an overall decrease in program size.

- The 48-by-48 icon image has a color table with 16 rather than 256 colors.

- The DiskPie2 toolbar bitmap has only two images instead of the 25 images required by DiskPie1.

Two views of the toolbar bitmap show the images used for DiskPie2's toolbar buttons:

Actual size    Enlargement

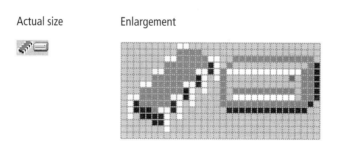

The images duplicate the first two images that DiskPie1 uses for its toolbar except that the second image is unlabeled, making it suitable for representing any disk drive. DiskPie2 adds drive designations such as "C:" and "D:" to the buttons at run time. You can see the results in Figure 4-22.

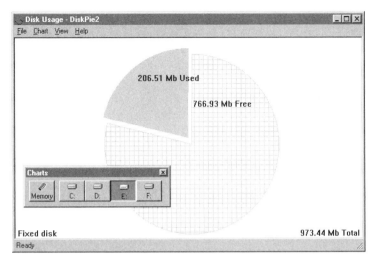

**Figure 4-22.** *The DiskPie2 program.*

The new DiskPie2 program requires changes to three of DiskPie1's source files to create updated versions named DiskPie2.rc, MainFrm2.h, and MainFrm2.cpp. Listing 4-2 shows the revised code, in which DiskPie2.rc sheds the unneeded prompt strings, and MainFrm2.cpp receives added instructions for labeling the toolbar buttons and constructing tooltip text.

**Listing 4-2.** *DiskPie2 source files.*

### DiskPie2.rc

```
// *************************************************************
//
// DiskPie2.rc
//
// *************************************************************

#include "resource.h"
#include "afxres.h"

IDR_MAINFRAME        ICON            "res\\DiskPie2.ico"
IDR_MAINFRAME        BITMAP          "res\\toolbar.bmp"

IDR_MAINFRAME MENU
BEGIN
    POPUP "&File"
```

*(continued)*

**Listing 4-2.** *continued*

```
    BEGIN
        MENUITEM "E&xit",                        ID_APP_EXIT
    END
    POPUP "&Chart"
    BEGIN
        MENUITEM "&Memory\tCtrl+M",              IDM_MEMORY
        MENUITEM SEPARATOR
    END
    POPUP "&View"
    BEGIN
        MENUITEM "&Toolbar",                     ID_VIEW_TOOLBAR
        MENUITEM "&Status Bar",                  ID_VIEW_STATUS_BAR
    END
    POPUP "&Help"
    BEGIN
        MENUITEM "&About DiskPie2...",           ID_APP_ABOUT
    END
END

IDR_MAINFRAME ACCELERATORS
BEGIN
    "M",            IDM_MEMORY,              VIRTKEY, CONTROL
    "C",            IDM_DISK_C,              VIRTKEY
    "D",            IDM_DISK_D,              VIRTKEY
    "E",            IDM_DISK_E,              VIRTKEY
    "F",            IDM_DISK_F,              VIRTKEY
    "G",            IDM_DISK_G,              VIRTKEY
    "H",            IDM_DISK_H,              VIRTKEY
    "I",            IDM_DISK_I,              VIRTKEY
    "J",            IDM_DISK_J,              VIRTKEY
    "K",            IDM_DISK_K,              VIRTKEY
    "L",            IDM_DISK_L,              VIRTKEY
    "M",            IDM_DISK_M,              VIRTKEY
    "N",            IDM_DISK_N,              VIRTKEY
    "O",            IDM_DISK_O,              VIRTKEY
    "P",            IDM_DISK_P,              VIRTKEY
    "Q",            IDM_DISK_Q,              VIRTKEY
    "R",            IDM_DISK_R,              VIRTKEY
    "S",            IDM_DISK_S,              VIRTKEY
    "T",            IDM_DISK_T,              VIRTKEY
    "U",            IDM_DISK_U,              VIRTKEY
    "V",            IDM_DISK_V,              VIRTKEY
    "W",            IDM_DISK_W,              VIRTKEY
    "X",            IDM_DISK_X,              VIRTKEY
    "Y",            IDM_DISK_Y,              VIRTKEY
    "Z",            IDM_DISK_Z,              VIRTKEY
END
```

```
IDR_MAINFRAME TOOLBAR 16, 15
BEGIN
    BUTTON              IDM_MEMORY
END


IDD_ABOUTBOX DIALOG 0, 0, 240, 65
STYLE DS_MODALFRAME | WS_POPUP | WS_CAPTION | WS_SYSMENU
CAPTION "About DiskPie2"
FONT 8, "MS Sans Serif"
BEGIN
    ICON            IDR_MAINFRAME,IDC_STATIC,10,22,20,20
    LTEXT           "DiskPie2 Version 1.0",IDC_STATIC,45,10,115,8
    LTEXT           """Microsoft Visual C++ Programmer's Guide""",
                    IDC_STATIC,45,26,140,8
    LTEXT           "Copyright \251 1997, Beck Zaratian",
                    IDC_STATIC,45,42,115,8
    DEFPUSHBUTTON   "OK",IDOK,195,10,35,40,WS_GROUP
END


STRINGTABLE
BEGIN
    IDR_MAINFRAME               "DiskPie2\nDisk Usage\n\n\n\n\n\n"
    AFX_IDS_IDLEMESSAGE         "Ready"
END
```

### MainFrm2.h

```
// ***************************************************************
//
// MainFrm2.h
//
// ***************************************************************

class CMainFrame : public CFrameWnd
{
    DECLARE_DYNCREATE (CMainFrame)

private:
    CToolBar        toolbar;
    CStatusBar      statusbar;
    CDiskDoc        diskdoc;

protected:
    afx_msg int     OnCreate( LPCREATESTRUCT lpCreateStruct );
    afx_msg void    OnNewChart( UINT nID );
    afx_msg void    OnSetFocus( CWnd* );
```

*(continued)*

**Listing 4-2.** *continued*

```
        afx_msg BOOL    OnTooltip( UINT id, NMHDR* pNMHDR, LRESULT*);

        DECLARE_MESSAGE_MAP()
};
```

## MainFrm2.cpp

```
// ***********************************************************
//
// MainFrm2.cpp
//
// ***********************************************************

#define VC_EXTRALEAN

#include <afxwin.h>
#include <afxext.h>
#include <afxcmn.h>
#include "resource.h"
#include "DiskPie.h"
#include "DiskDoc.h"
#include "MainFrm2.h"
#include "DiskView.h"


IMPLEMENT_DYNCREATE (CMainFrame, CFrameWnd)

BEGIN_MESSAGE_MAP (CMainFrame, CFrameWnd)
    ON_WM_CREATE ()
    ON_WM_SETFOCUS ()
    ON_COMMAND_RANGE (IDM_MEMORY, IDM_DISK_Z, OnNewChart)
    ON_NOTIFY_EX( TTN_NEEDTEXT, 0, OnTooltip )
END_MESSAGE_MAP ()


/////////////////////////////////////////////////////////////////
// Create main window, toolbar, and status bar

int CMainFrame::OnCreate( LPCREATESTRUCT lpCreateStruct )
{
    int       i, j;
    char      szDisk[] = "x:\0";
    char      szMenu[] = "Disk &x\tx\0";
    CMenu*    pmenu;

    static const UINT indicator = ID_SEPARATOR;

    if (CFrameWnd::OnCreate( lpCreateStruct ) == -1)
        return -1;
```

```
    statusbar.Create( this );
    statusbar.SetIndicators( &indicator, 1 );

    toolbar.Create( this );
    toolbar.SetWindowText( "Charts" );
    toolbar.LoadToolBar( IDR_MAINFRAME );
    toolbar.SetBarStyle( toolbar.GetBarStyle() |
            CBRS_TOOLTIPS | CBRS_FLYBY | CBRS_SIZE_DYNAMIC );

    toolbar.SetButtons( NULL, diskdoc.GetDriveCount() + 2 );
    toolbar.SetButtonInfo( 0, IDM_MEMORY, TBBS_CHECKGROUP, 0 );
    toolbar.SetButtonText( 0, "Memory" );

    // The second "button" is a separator
    toolbar.SetButtonInfo( 1, ID_SEPARATOR,
                        TBBS_SEPARATOR | TBBS_CHECKGROUP, 0 );
    pmenu = GetMenu()->GetSubMenu( 1 );

    for (i=0, j=2; i < 24; i++)
    {
        if (CDiskDoc::iDriveType[i] == DRIVE_FIXED    ||
            CDiskDoc::iDriveType[i] == DRIVE_REMOTE   ||
            CDiskDoc::iDriveType[i] == DRIVE_RAMDISK)
        {
            szDisk[0] = 'C' + (char) i;
            szMenu[6] = 'C' + (char) i;
            szMenu[8] = 'C' + (char) i;
            pmenu->InsertMenu( 0xFFFF, MF_BYPOSITION,
                            IDM_DISK_C+i, szMenu);
            toolbar.SetButtonInfo( j, IDM_DISK_C+i,
                                TBBS_CHECKGROUP, 1 );
            toolbar.SetButtonText( j++, szDisk );
        }
    }

    toolbar.SetSizes( CSize( 45, 40 ), CSize( 16, 15 ) );

    toolbar.EnableDocking( CBRS_ALIGN_ANY );
    EnableDocking( CBRS_ALIGN_ANY );
    DockControlBar( &toolbar );

    return 0;
}

/////////////////////////////////////////////////////////////////
// Respond to menu/toolbar/accelerator commands
```

*(continued)*

195

**Listing 4-2.** *continued*

```
void CMainFrame::OnNewChart( UINT nID )
{
    CDiskDoc::nCurrent = nID;
    OnSetFocus( NULL );
    Invalidate();
    toolbar.Invalidate();          // Necessary when bar is floating
}

/////////////////////////////////////////////////////////////////
// When focus regained, refresh display in case data has changed

void CMainFrame::OnSetFocus( CWnd* )
{
    if (CDiskDoc::nCurrent == IDM_MEMORY)
        diskdoc.GetMemoryUsage();
    else
        diskdoc.GetDiskUsage( CDiskDoc::nCurrent );
}

/////////////////////////////////////////////////////////////////
// When TTN_NEEDTEXT notification received, generate tooltip text

BOOL CMainFrame::OnTooltip( UINT id, NMHDR* pNMHDR, LRESULT* )
{
    static char   szMemTip[] = "Memory usage chart\0";
    static char   szDiskTip[] = "Usage chart for drive x\0";
    TOOLTIPTEXT* pTTT = (TOOLTIPTEXT*) pNMHDR;
    UINT          nID  = pNMHDR->idFrom;

    if (nID == IDM_MEMORY)
        pTTT->lpszText = szMemTip;
    else
    {
        szDiskTip[22] = (char) (nID - IDM_DISK_C) + 'C';
        pTTT->lpszText = szDiskTip;
    }

    return TRUE;
}
```

Besides their file sizes, the only obvious difference between DiskPie1 and DiskPie2 is the appearance of their toolbars. Because DiskPie2 makes use of a single disk drive image for its toolbar buttons, the program must label the buttons with text at run time. The *CMainFrame::OnCreate* function handles this task in a **for** loop that runs through every attached drive:

```
for (i=0, j=2; i < 24; i++)
{
    ⋮
    pmenu->InsertMenu( 0xFFFF, MF_BYPOSITION, IDM_DISK_C+i, szMenu);
    toolbar.SetButtonInfo( j, IDM_DISK_C+i, TBBS_CHECKGROUP, 1 );
    toolbar.SetButtonText( j++, szDisk );
}
toolbar.SetSizes( CSize( 45, 40 ), CSize( 16, 15 ) );
```

The call to *CToolBar::SetButtonInfo* duplicates the same instruction in DiskPie1 except for the last parameter, which is the zero-based index of the button's image in the toolbar bitmap. Where DiskPie1 used the loop counter to select the button image from among the 24 images available, DiskPie2 makes do with only one disk drive image. But rather than leaving each button looking like its neighbor, the code also calls *CToolBar::SetButtonText* to add a drive designation. The added text requires more room on each button, so the code finishes by calling *CToolBar::SetSizes* to enlarge the buttons to a size of 45-by-40 pixels, as opposed to DiskPie1's 24-by-22 pixels.

## Tooltips and Prompt Strings on Demand

Without prompt strings in its resource data, DiskPie2 must assemble its tooltip text as needed at run time. When the system is about to display a tooltip window, it notifies the program through a TTN_NEEDTEXT notification message, which DiskPie2 handles in its *CMainFrame::OnTooltip* function. The message provides a pointer to a TOOLTIPTEXT structure, which is an expanded form of NMHDR structure:

```
typedef struct
{
    NMHDR      hdr;
    LPTSTR     lpszText;
    char       szText[80];
    HINSTANCE  hinst;
    UINT       uFlags;
} TOOLTIPTEXT, FAR *LPTOOLTIPTEXT;
```

The *hdr.idFrom* value identifies the toolbar button over which the cursor has paused. From this value *OnTooltip* determines the appropriate tooltip text, points *lpszText* to the new text string, and returns a value of TRUE. The function maintains its tooltip text in two static strings:

```
static char  szMemTip[]  = "Memory usage chart\0";
static char  szDiskTip[] = "Usage chart for drive x\0";
```

A value of IDM_MEMORY in *hdr.idFrom* indicates tooltip text is required for the first toolbar button, in which case the code points the *lpszText* structure member to the string *szMemTip*. If *hdr.idFrom* identifies one of the disk usage buttons IDM_DISK_C through IDM_DISK_Z, *OnTooltip* points *lpszText* to the *szDiskTip* string after replacing the x placeholder character with the appropriate drive letter C through Z. DiskPie2's tooltips are thus easy to create because most of them differ only by a single character.

Through a somewhat similar technique, DiskPie2 could have been written to generate its missing status bar prompts on demand. Status bar prompts require a considerable amount of hit testing to determine over which toolbar button or menu command the cursor is positioned. The MFC framework takes care of this work automatically during idle time processing, continuously updating the status bar through the program's *CCmdUI* object. The secret to on-the-fly prompt messages is to provide only enough string resources to take advantage of the framework's hit testing, then build the full prompt string in an override of the *CStatusBar::OnSetText* function. DiskPie2, for example, could use drive designation letters as minimal prompt strings in the program's RC file:

```
STRINGTABLE
BEGIN
    IDM_MEMORY              "Memory usage"
    IDM_DISK_C              "C"
    IDM_DISK_D              "D"

      ⋮

    IDM_DISK_X              "X"
    IDM_DISK_Y              "Y"
    IDM_DISK_Z              "Z"
END
```

To hook the *OnSetText* function, declare a class derived from *CStatusBar* and use it to create the status bar in *CMainFrame*:

```
class CStatusHook : public CStatusBar
{
protected:
    afx_msg LRESULT OnSetText( WPARAM wParam, LPARAM lParam );
    DECLARE_MESSAGE_MAP()
};

class CMainFrame : public CFrameWnd
{
    DECLARE_DYNCREATE (CMainFrame)
private:
    CStatusHook        statusbar;
```

A message map and the *OnSetText* handler function trap the WM_SET-TEXT message that the system sends when about to display one of the abbreviated prompt strings in the status bar. The handler function forms a complete prompt string by inserting the single-character prompt into a more verbose text string, repoints *lParam* to the constructed string, and passes control on to the base's *OnSetText* function. Instead of writing only a single letter like "C" in the status bar, the system now displays the more meaningful string "Disk C usage chart." Here's how the handler function might construct such a prompt message:

```
BEGIN_MESSAGE_MAP (CStatusHook, CStatusBar)
    ON_MESSAGE( WM_SETTEXT, OnSetText )
END_MESSAGE_MAP ()

LRESULT CStatusHook::OnSetText( WPARAM wParam, LPARAM lParam )
{
    // Constructed string must be static
    static char szDisk[] = "Disk x usage chart\0";

    // If display is only 1 character, convert it to full string
    if (lstrlen( (LPCTSTR) lParam ) == 1)
    {
        szDisk[5] = *((LPCTSTR) lParam);  // Set drive letter
        lParam    = (LPARAM) szDisk;       // Repoint lParam
    }
    return CStatusBar::OnSetText( wParam, lParam );
}
```

Generating prompt strings at run time is usually worthwhile only if the implementing code takes less space than the resource data it replaces. The technique is sometimes useful, though, when prompt strings must reflect some dynamic program condition such as user input that cannot be anticipated as read-only string resources.

# Dialog Boxes and Controls

Dialog boxes and controls are usually mentioned in the same breath because it is rare to see one without the other. A control is a child window with a special talent—a button, for instance, or a check box or a progress indicator—and a dialog box is the parent window that contains one or more controls in its client area. The marriage of dialog boxes and controls is so well established that the whole collection is usually just called a "dialog."

While many dialogs such as About boxes do no more than convey information to the user, other dialogs query for input, providing a convenient place in which to type a filename or click a button to make a selection. If this reminds you of toolbars, you're right—a toolbar is a type of dialog. And like toolbars, most dialogs are part of the user interface elements that compose a program's resources.

Some dialogs, however, are not part of a program's resource data. Dialogs such as message boxes and the so-called common dialogs are provided by the system, invoked through API functions like *MessageBox* and *GetOpenFileName* or through MFC classes like *CFileDialog*. It's even possible for a program to design and create a dialog at run time using the *DialogBoxIndirect* API function, which takes a structure as input rather than data from the program's resource area. Such dialogs are strictly a programming problem, not a resource you create in Visual C++, so you won't find any discussions of them here.

This chapter forms the second half of our discussion of resource data begun in the preceding chapter. We'll start with a look at the resource script that defines a dialog in a project's RC file, and then get into the Visual C++ dialog editor, which makes dialog design as easy as point-and-click. The chapter demonstrates the editor's abilities with several example programs, one of which shows how to create a property sheet, also known as a tabbed dialog.

# The Dialog Script

Adding a dialog to a program is easy. Each dialog exists in the resource data area as a series of commands compiled from a script in the project's RC file. The commands specify such details as the size of the dialog window, the caption in the title bar, and the placement of controls. Revising a dialog is often only a matter of editing the script in the RC file.

To take a ready example, we saw in Chapter 4, Resources, that AppWizard generates a command on the Help menu and all necessary source code for an About box dialog, an extra feature that is becoming more common in Windows programs these days. AppWizard also writes a script in the project's RC file that defines what the dialog and its controls look like. Here's another look at the script:

```
IDD_ABOUTBOX DIALOG DISCARDABLE  0, 0, 217, 55
CAPTION "About Demo"
STYLE DS_MODALFRAME | WS_POPUP | WS_CAPTION | WS_SYSMENU
FONT 8, "MS Sans Serif"
BEGIN
    ICON            IDR_MAINFRAME,IDC_STATIC,11,17,20,20
    LTEXT           "Demo Version 1.0",
                    IDC_STATIC,40,10,119,8,SS_NOPREFIX
    LTEXT           "Copyright (C) 1998",IDC_STATIC,40,25,119,8
    DEFPUSHBUTTON   "OK",IDOK,178,7,32,14,WS_GROUP
END
```

The first line of the script identifies the resource with the symbol IDD_ ABOUTBOX, which is defined in the project's Resource.h file. The DISCARDABLE keyword is followed by four numbers that specify the size of the dialog. The first two numbers (0, 0) set the origin coordinates at the upper-left corner of the dialog window. All other coordinates in the script are relative to the origin, with positive $x$ toward the right and positive $y$ toward the bottom of the screen. The next two numbers determine the dimensions of the dialog window, in this case giving the window a width of 217 and height of 55 dialog units.

A dialog unit is not a pixel, and does not even represent the same distance in the $x$ and $y$ directions. The size of a dialog unit depends on the font used for the dialog text, which by default is the system font. (In the above script, the optional FONT directive specifies the dialog font as 8-point MS Sans Serif.) One dialog unit in the horizontal $x$ direction equals $\frac{1}{4}$ the average character width for the dialog's font. In the vertical $y$ direction, a dialog unit is $\frac{1}{8}$ the character height. Since Windows adopts a font measuring system in which character height serves as the font size, one vertical dialog unit for a dialog using an 8-point font is one point, or $\frac{1}{72}$ inch.

Although it makes placement of the controls more difficult to visualize, tying the dialog unit to the font size means that a dialog box remains the same size at different screen resolutions. It also ensures that controls stay in relative position to each other if the dialog font changes, since a larger or smaller font merely causes the dialog window and its contents to inflate or deflate in size. A program that places a control in a dialog window at run time should first determine the dialog's "base units" by calling the *GetDialogBaseUnits* API function. The base units define the relationship between dialog units and pixels for the current screen resolution. The *MapDialogRect* function performs the conversion automatically, translating a coordinate in dialog units to an equivalent number of screen pixels. MSDN online help describes both of these API functions in more detail.

The STYLE directive in the dialog script specifies various flags that affect the dialog's appearance, such as the WS_CAPTION flag that gives the dialog a title bar. The DS_MODALFRAME flag has nothing to do with the dialog's modal style, which depends solely on how the program creates the dialog. Modal style means that only windows belonging to other programs can receive input focus while the dialog is visible, so the user must close the dialog before continuing to run the program (or at least the thread) responsible for the dialog. About boxes, for example, are modal dialogs, blocking program execution until dismissed. Modeless dialogs are less insistent, allowing the user to switch to another window within the program without closing the dialog. The Find command of the Visual C++ text editor displays a good example of a modeless dialog. A sample program called Color presented later in the chapter demonstrates how to use Visual C++ to create a dialog with modeless style.

Despite its name, the WS_SYSMENU flag merely places a Close button at the far right side of the dialog's title bar, since child windows cannot have true system menus. The optional CAPTION directive specifies the text that appears in the title bar.

Control definition statements for the dialog are bracketed by BEGIN and END statements. Each definition contains the same type of four-number series as used in the script's first line, where the first two numbers give the $x$ and $y$ coordinates of the upper-left corner of the control relative to the dialog origin, and the next two numbers specify the width and height of the control window. Again, all coordinates and dimensions are in dialog units.

The dialog script gives the About box a push button labeled OK and three static controls, one of which contains a copy of the program icon. We'll meet these and other controls in sample code later in the chapter. For a complete list of controls including common controls, pay a visit to MSDN online help or consult one of the many available references such as *Programming Windows 95* by Charles Petzold.

The About dialog that AppWizard gives you can certainly stand some improvement—your name in the copyright line, if nothing else. Let's first take a look at the Visual C++ dialog editor, and then use the editor to add flair to the About dialog that AppWizard creates.

# The Dialog Editor

In the old days of Windows programming, developers had to design a dialog sight unseen by writing a script in the RC file, then compiling and running the program to see what the dialog actually looked like. This trial-and-error process usually required several iterations to get controls correctly positioned and working. But those days are over. It's the resource editors more than anything else that make Visual C++ "visual," and once you start designing dialogs with the dialog editor you will never go back to the old way. Not only can you put together a professional-quality dialog with a few mouse clicks, seeing it take form on the screen as you create it, you can also test a working model of the dialog right in the editor. A control doesn't look quite right? Change your mind about a mnemonic key? The editor makes revisions a pleasure, and when you have finished you know exactly how the dialog will behave and what it will look like in the running program. And as we'll see in the next chapter, the dialog editor also integrates well with ClassWizard, which can automatically generate code to initialize and retrieve data from the dialog's controls.

As with other resources, you may often find it easier to make small changes to an existing dialog script by editing the RC file with a text editor. Nothing wrong with that. But for most revisions and especially when creating a new dialog, the dialog editor is your best bet. Like the other Visual C++ resource editors, the dialog editor is launched in one of two ways, depending on whether you want to create a new dialog or continue working on one that already exists in the project's RC file. To create a new dialog from scratch, click Resource on the Insert menu to bring up the Insert Resource box, then select Dialog from the list:

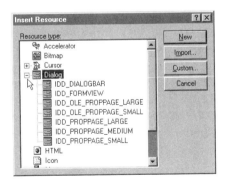

Expanding the Dialog entry in the Insert Resource box reveals identifiers for special dialog shapes such as IDD_DIALOGBAR, which has the dimensions of a toolbar. To create a normal dialog with default OK and Cancel buttons, double-click the Dialog entry without expanding it.

To continue working on an existing dialog, open the project and click the dialog's identifier listed in the ResourceView pane of the Workspace window. If you want to edit a dialog in a project other than the current project, click Open on the File menu and open the other project's RC file. This brings up a list of the other project's resources from which you can select the desired dialog. You cannot, however, save the resource into the current project because Visual C++ cannot merge a dialog script from one RC file into another. The text editor provides the most practical means of copying another project's dialog into the current project. Open the other project's RC file in the text editor as described in Chapter 4, select and copy the desired script, and paste it into the current RC file. Also define any necessary identifiers in the project's Resource.h file. You can then open the resource in the current project and edit it normally.

Figure 5-1 shows the Workspace window for a fictitious AppWizard project called Demo in which clicking the IDD_ABOUTBOX identifier starts the dialog editor and loads the program's About box dialog.

**Figure 5-1.** *Double-clicking a dialog identifier in the Workspace window launches the dialog editor.*

When you start the dialog editor for an existing dialog, the editor reads the script in the RC file and replicates the dialog in the editor work area. (If the Workspace or Output window is in docking mode, it may overlay the dialog editor window. If so, right-click each overlaying window and choose the Hide command from the context menu.) Figure 5-2 shows Demo's About dialog box loaded into the editor, ready for revision.

Though it looks real enough, the About box pictured in Figure 5-2 is only a nonworking representation, a canvas for you to paint on. Clicking a

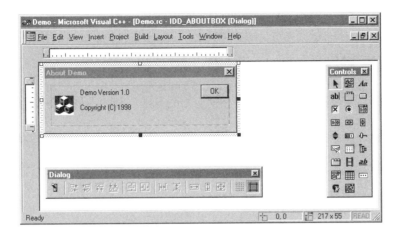

**Figure 5-2.** *The dialog editor.*

button or edit box in the dialog work area selects the control but does not activate it. The ruler guides shown in Figure 5-2 are optional, and you can turn them off by choosing Guide Settings from the Layout menu. The two toolbars, called Controls and Dialog, require a little more explanation.

## The Controls Toolbar

The Controls toolbar provides one-click access to controls that you can place in the dialog window. Click the toolbar button for the control you want and drag the control from the toolbar into position in the dialog box. A dotted rectangle shows an outline of the control window as you drag it, giving you an idea of the control's size and position before you release the mouse button to drop it into place. As an alternative to dragging and drop-ping, simply click anywhere in the dialog window after selecting a button from the Controls toolbar. The control window appears centered at the click location. Figure 5-3 on the next page identifies the control types available on the Controls toolbar.

Once you have dragged the controls you want from the Controls toolbar into the dialog work area, the next step is to arrange the controls in an eye-pleasing order. The Dialog toolbar helps out here, but first we have to talk about selecting control windows in the dialog.

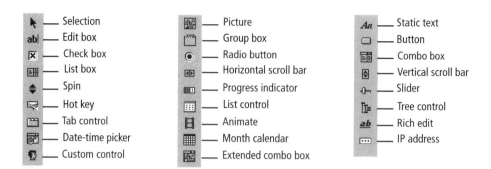

**Figure 5-3.**    *The Controls toolbar.*

## Selecting and Arranging Controls

When you drop a control window into the dialog box, a shaded rectangle surrounding the control indicates that the control is selected. The shaded selection rectangle has eight sizing handles, which are small squares placed at the corners and sides of the rectangle. As is typical in Windows, you can resize a selected control window by dragging one of the sizing handles with the mouse cursor or, for more precise work, by holding down the Shift key while pressing the arrow keys. Each keypress changes the size of the control by one dialog unit. You can also select and resize the dialog box itself by clicking anywhere in the work area other than on a control window.

It's not necessary to carefully position a control window when you drag it into the dialog because it's easy to move a control that's already in place. Click the control in the dialog work area to select the control window, and drag it using the mouse or move it using the arrow keys. To make alignment easier, turn on the grid by clicking the Toggle Grid button on the Dialog toolbar:

When the grid is visible in the dialog window, a control moves only from one grid line to another, a feature sometimes known as "snap-to-grid." By default, horizontal and vertical grid spacing is five dialog units, but you

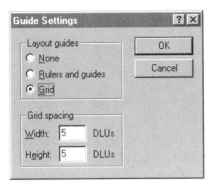

**Figure 5-4.** *The Guide Settings box.*

can change the spacing in the Guide Settings dialog shown in Figure 5-4. Click Guide Settings on the Layout menu to call up the dialog.

If the snap-to-grid feature prevents you from arranging the controls the way you want, just turn off the grid. If you turn it back on later, the editor does not disturb the placement of control windows already in the dialog. To temporarily suppress the snap-to-grid feature, press the Alt key as you drag a control.

It is often more convenient to move or resize controls as a group rather than one at a time. The dialog editor offers two methods for selecting several controls at once. The first method is to sequentially click the controls you want to select while holding down the Shift key. The second method works best for controls arranged as a group. Click the Selection tool on the Controls toolbar and drag a dotted rectangle over the controls to select them. Figure 5-5 on the next page illustrates the procedure.

If you want to deselect a control from a selected group, click the control while holding down the Shift key. You can add a control to the group the same way. When multiple controls are selected, the sizing handles of all but one control in the group appear hollow to show they are inactive. The remaining control with solid sizing handles is said to be the dominant control of the group, from which the editor determines how the group as a whole should be resized or aligned. For example, the Check1 control in Figure 5-5 is the dominant control of the three controls in the selected group because it's the only one with solid sizing handles. Clicking another

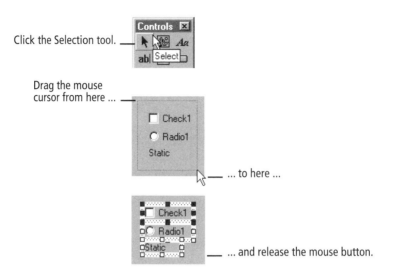

Click the Selection tool.

Drag the mouse cursor from here ...

... to here ...

... and release the mouse button.

**Figure 5-5.**   *Selecting several controls at once.*

control in the group with the Ctrl key pressed makes it the new dominant control.

Only solid sizing handles are active; if a sizing handle is hollow, the control cannot be resized in that direction. Combo box controls have active sizing handles on only two sides. This is because the drop-down area of the control, normally not visible, is also part of the control window and must be considered when establishing the window size. Figure 5-6 illustrates how to change the size of the drop-down area of combo box controls.

You can make a copy of a control and place it in the work area by dragging the control's window with the Ctrl key pressed, as illustrated in Figure 5-7. This creates a new window that is a clone of the original except that it has its own identifier value.

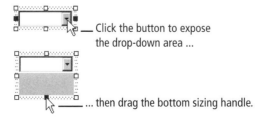

Click the button to expose the drop-down area ...

... then drag the bottom sizing handle.

**Figure 5-6.**   *Changing the size of a combo box.*

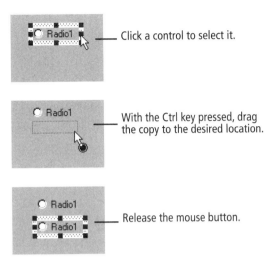

Click a control to select it.

With the Ctrl key pressed, drag
the copy to the desired location.

Release the mouse button.

**Figure 5-7.** *Duplicating a control window in the dialog editor.*

## The Dialog Toolbar

Now that you know how to select a group of controls, the Dialog toolbar
shown in Figure 5-8 will make more sense. Dragging controls around in
the dialog is fine for approximate positions, but for precise alignment of
the control windows you should use the tools on the Dialog toolbar. They
let you position control windows in neatly aligned rows and columns
within the dialog box, giving the dialog an orderly and professional
appearance. The toolbar also sports a test mode switch that lets you take
your new dialog for a test drive, so to speak, to see how it looks and
behaves in the real world.

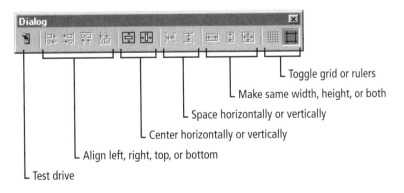

Toggle grid or rulers

Make same width, height, or both

Space horizontally or vertically

Center horizontally or vertically

Align left, right, top, or bottom

Test drive

**Figure 5-8.** *The Dialog toolbar.*

All the Dialog toolbar buttons have equivalent commands on the Layout menu, so you can turn the toolbar off if you prefer to work without it. To show or hide the toolbar, choose Customize from the Tools menu, click the Toolbars tab, and click the Dialog check box in the list.

As you see in Figure 5-8, the toolbar arranges the buttons in five logical groups for aligning, centering, spacing, and adjusting the size of controls, and for turning the grid and ruler guides on and off. The alignment, spacing, and size adjustment tools, which appear grayed in Figure 5-8, are enabled only when two or more controls are selected in the dialog.

The next few sections demonstrate some of the effects of the Dialog tools. It usually takes several tools to nudge a group of controls into the desired position, so you have to give some thought to the order in which you apply the tools. Nothing about control placement is written in stone, however, and if the effect of a tool is not what you expected, just click Undo on the Edit menu.

### Alignment tools

The alignment tools align the controls of a selected group with the dominant control. For example, clicking the Align Left button changes the $x$ coordinates of selected controls to match the $x$ coordinate of the dominant control without affecting the $y$ coordinates:

Click the Align Left tool ...

... to change this ...                    ... to this.

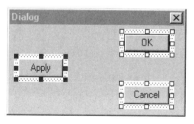                    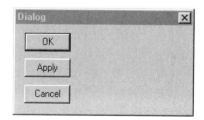

### Centering tools

The centering tools act on a single selected control or a group of controls, positioning the selection at the horizontal or vertical center of the dialog client area:

Click the Center Vertical tool ...

... to change this ...                                    ... to this.

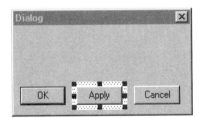                                    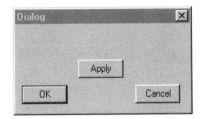

### Spacing tools

The spacing tools work only on a selected group of three or more controls. They are unique among the Dialog tools in that it makes no difference which of the selected controls is dominant. Horizontal spacing changes the $x$ coordinates of all controls in the group except the leftmost and rightmost controls, spacing the other controls of the group evenly in the horizontal direction. The vertical spacing tool does the same thing for the $y$ coordinates, spacing the controls evenly in the vertical direction. In the example shown on the next page, the vertical spacing tool—to which the editor gives the confusing name of Space Down—repositions only the Apply button; the OK and Cancel buttons remain in place.

Click the Space Down tool ...

... to change this ...                                                            ... to this.

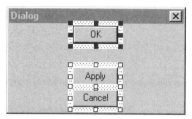                                                              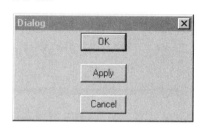

### Size-adjustment tools

The size-adjustment tools act on a selected group of two or more controls. Size adjustment does not move the control windows, but only changes the height and/or width of the selected controls to match the dimensions of the dominant control in the selection:

Click the Make Same Width tool ...

... to change this ...                                                            ... to this.

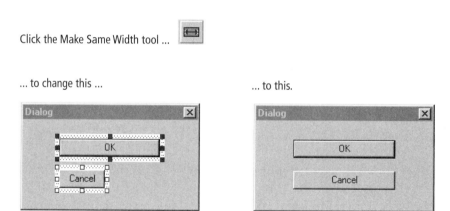

## Control Properties

Each control placed in the dialog work area has a Properties dialog box in which you can specify an identifier and value for the control, type in a label, and set style flags appropriate for the control window. To expose a control's Properties box, right-click the control window in the work area and choose Properties from the pop-up context menu. You can also select a control and click the Properties command on the View menu. The

Properties dialog differs slightly in appearance and content for each control type; Figure 5-9 shows what it looks like for a check box control.

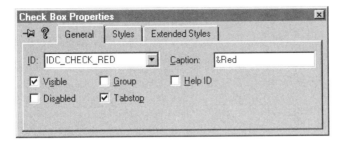

**Figure 5-9.** *The Properties dialog for a check box control.*

In Chapter 4 you may have become accustomed to double-clicking an item in the Visual C++ graphics editor to call up an appropriate Properties box, but the technique does not have the same effect in the dialog editor. Double-clicking a control window in the dialog work area can have one of three results, depending on the circumstances and the control type:

- If the control accepts user input, double-clicking the control window invokes a dialog titled Add Member Function that lets you quickly add a stub handler function for the control.

- Double-clicking a static control or the dialog window itself opens the dialog class source file in the text editor and positions the caret at the class constructor.

- If the project has no ClassWizard database CLW file (described in the next chapter), double-clicking a control other than a static control has no effect. This behavior differs from version 5, in which double-clicking without a CLW file displays the control's Properties box.

If the control accepts user input, such as a check box or slider control, assign a unique mnemonic key when you type the control caption. A mnemonic key enables the user to move input focus to the control by pressing a key on the keyboard. The previous chapter described mnemonic keys for menu commands, and mnemonics for control labels are no different. Just precede any character in the caption with an ampersand (&) to identify the character as the control's mnemonic. The check box in Figure 5-9, for example, has the caption "&Red," in which the mnemonic is the letter "R."

For a slider control or a text entry control such as an edit box, assign its mnemonic key in the static control label, as this simple example shows:

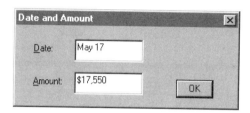

In this case, pressing Alt+D sets focus at the Date edit box, and pressing Alt+A sets focus at the Amount edit box. (The Alt key is optional when neither edit box has focus.) For the mnemonics to work, each edit box must follow its static control label in sequential tabbing order, which is discussed next.

## Tabbing Order

Mnemonics aren't the only way to give input focus to a particular control. The user can click the control with the mouse or tab to the control by repeatedly pressing the Tab key. Each time the system senses the Tab key, it moves input focus to the next control in a hierarchy called the tabbing order.

The tabbing order is implied by the sequence of control statements in the dialog script of the RC file. For instance, when the dialog defined in the script below first appears, the IDC_COMBO1 combo box control has the input focus. Pressing the Tab key moves input focus from the IDC_COMBO1 control to the other controls in the order shown. When the ID_CANCEL button has focus, pressing Tab again cycles the focus back to the beginning of the list to IDC_COMBO1:

```
IDD_DEMO_DLG DIALOG 0, 0, 247, 65
STYLE DS_MODALFRAME | DS_3DLOOK | WS_POPUP | WS_VISIBLE | WS_CAPTION
CAPTION "Demo Dialog"
FONT 8, "MS Sans Serif"
BEGIN
```

```
       COMBOBOX           IDC_COMBO1,15,15,159,80,WS_VSCROLL |
                          WS_TABSTOP | CBS_DROPDOWN | CBS_AUTOHSCROLL
       CONTROL            "and",IDC_RADIO1,"Button",BS_AUTORADIOBUTTON |
                          WS_GROUP | WS_TABSTOP,14,39,25,10
       CONTROL            "or",IDC_RADIO2,"Button",BS_AUTORADIOBUTTON |
                          WS_TABSTOP,44,39,20,10
       COMBOBOX           IDC_COMBO2,69,39,106,80,WS_VSCROLL | WS_GROUP |
                          WS_TABSTOP | CBS_DROPDOWN | CBS_AUTOHSCROLL
       DEFPUSHBUTTON      "OK",IDOK,196,12,44,17,WS_GROUP
       PUSHBUTTON         "Cancel",ID_CANCEL,196,34,44,17,WS_GROUP
END
```

The dialog editor insulates you from the details of what goes on in the RC file, but you still have to worry about tabbing order in a dialog that queries for user input. Checking the order is usually the last thing you do in the editor before hitting the test switch on the Dialog toolbar. Choose Tab Order from the Layout menu to display your dialog's current tabbing order, which appears as sequential numbers adjacent to the dialog controls. Here's what the work area looks like for the dialog defined in the preceding script:

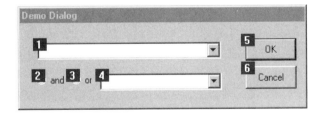

To revise the tabbing order, click each control in sequence beginning with the first control—that is, the control that you want to have input focus when the dialog first appears. If the existing order is correct only up to a certain point, you might find it easier to just change the part that's wrong. Press the Ctrl key while clicking the control window that has the highest correct tabbing order number, then release the Ctrl key and continue clicking controls in the desired sequence until the order is correct. For example, to change the order of controls 4 through 6, click control 3 with the Ctrl key pressed, then in sequential order click the controls you want to have tabbing numbers of 4, 5, and 6. Press the Enter key to set the order and return to editing mode.

Correct tabbing order is especially important for controls that appear in groups, such as radio buttons and check boxes. Chapter 6, ClassWizard, briefly returns to the subject of tabbing order and the role it plays in making a group of radio buttons mutually exclusive so that setting one button in the group automatically clears the others.

# Example 1: Revising an About Dialog

Here's an easy example that demonstrates some of the capabilities of the dialog editor. Say you want to revise the About box introduced earlier in the chapter for the fictitious Demo project. Figure 5-10 shows one possibility, a somewhat more elaborate About box for an equally fictitious program called SpiffyDemo.

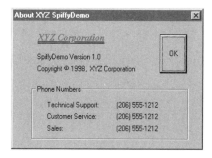

**Figure 5-10.**    *The revised About box.*

The bitmap logo was previously created in the Visual C++ graphics editor and saved to a file called XYZCorp.bmp. Other than that, the changes were made entirely in the dialog editor in only a few steps and about five minutes of work. If you would like to try revising the About box yourself, begin with a throw-away AppWizard project called Demo. Then follow the steps outlined here:

1. **Create the logo**—Click Resource on the Insert menu and choose Bitmap to launch the Visual C++ graphics editor. Design the logo bitmap and choose Properties from the View menu to give the new bitmap resource an identifier and optionally specify the filename. Click Save on the File menu when you are finished.

2. **Launch the dialog editor and load the About box**—In the ResourceView pane of the Workspace window, double-click IDD_ABOUTBOX to start the dialog editor.

3. **Resize the dialog**—Select the dialog window by clicking anywhere in the gray dialog work area that isn't occupied by a control and drag the bottom sizing handle to enlarge the window.

4. **Change the caption**—With the dialog window selected, click the Properties command on the View menu and rewrite the caption in the Dialog Properties box.

5. **Add the logo**—Select the MFC icon in the dialog work area and delete it by pressing the Del key, then replace it with the new bitmap created in Step 1 that represents the company logo. To add a bitmap to a dialog, click the Picture button on the Controls toolbar and drop the control anywhere in the dialog—the position need not be exact. With the picture control selected, use the Properties command to invoke the Picture Properties box for the new picture control. (To select hollow controls like pictures, click the frame that surrounds the control, because the editor does not recognize a click inside the frame as targeting the control.) Choose Bitmap from the list in the Type box and type the bitmap identifier in the Image box. Be sure to type the same identifier given to the bitmap in Step 1. You can add an icon to the dialog in the same way by selecting Icon rather than Bitmap in the Type box.

6. **Edit the dialog text**—Each of the two lines of text in the dialog is a static control. Invoke the Text Properties box for each static control and revise the text in the Caption box. In the above example, "Demo" was changed to *SpiffyDemo* and the copyright line expanded to include *XYZ Corporation*. Replace the "(C)" copyright symbol in the original text with \\*251*, which is the octal code for the © ANSI character. (For a list of other ANSI characters that you can add to a text control in the same manner, refer to Appendix A.)

Group Box

Static Text

7. **Add the phone numbers**—This step requires the Group Box tool and the Static Text tool from the Controls toolbar. First, click the Group Box button and drag its image into the lower blank area of the dialog. Enlarge it as required, then click the Properties command again to call up the Group Box Properties dialog and change the caption to "Phone Numbers." Next, click the Static Text button and drag it inside the group box in the dialog. With the static control window still selected, make two more copies of it by dragging the control a short distance with the Ctrl key pressed. Drop the copies onto separate lines, one slightly beneath the other. Alignment isn't important at this stage because it's easily taken care of later.

By default, a static control contains the single word "Static." Bring up the Text Properties dialog for each of the three static controls and in the Caption box, replace "Static" with the new text and telephone number. Clicking the pushpin button at the upper-left corner of the Properties dialog keeps it from disappearing between selections.

The \t tab character helps to space and align telephone numbers in the three static controls, as in "Sales:\t\t\t(206) 555-1212." However, typing the \t character in the Caption box extends the static control only a single space, so text following the \t character might not appear in the control window. To see the text, you must lengthen each static control manually by dragging the control's right sizing handle.

8. **Align the controls**—Turn on the grid and drag the controls into position using the mouse. The three text controls with telephone numbers should be aligned and evenly spaced. Set the first line where you want it, then select all three lines and click both the Align Left and Space Down buttons on the Dialog toolbar:

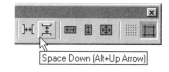

To add balance to the dialog, the above example also enlarges the OK button. Just click the button to select it and drag the sizing handles as desired.

9. **Test**—Click the test drive switch on the Dialog toolbar to see what the finished product looks like. To return to editing mode, click the dialog's OK button or press Esc.

When you save your work, the dialog editor overwrites the original script in the RC file with the new script for the revised About box:

```
IDD_ABOUTBOX DIALOG DISCARDABLE  0, 0, 217, 129
STYLE DS_MODALFRAME | WS_POPUP | WS_CAPTION | WS_SYSMENU
CAPTION "About XYZ SpiffyDemo"
FONT 8, "MS Sans Serif"
BEGIN
    CONTROL        IDB_XYZCORP,IDC_STATIC,"Static",
                   SS_BITMAP,17,16,85,10
    LTEXT          "SpiffyDemo Version 1.0",
                   IDC_STATIC,21,33,119,8,SS_NOPREFIX
    LTEXT          "Copyright \251 1998, XYZ Corporation",
                   IDC_STATIC,21,45,119,8
    DEFPUSHBUTTON  "OK",IDOK,166,15,32,40,WS_GROUP
    GROUPBOX       "Phone Numbers",IDC_STATIC,17,65,181,56
    LTEXT          "Technical Support:\t(206) 555-1212",
                   IDC_STATIC,33,82,140,8
    LTEXT          "Customer Service:\t(206) 555-1212",
                   IDC_STATIC,33,94,142,8
    LTEXT          "Sales:\t\t\t(206) 555-1212",
                   IDC_STATIC,33,106,141,8
END
```

The first CONTROL statement of the script refers to the IDB_XYZCORP bitmap, which contains the company logo created with the graphics editor in Step 1. The resource compiler knows where to find the IDB_XYZCORP bitmap because the graphics editor recorded the filename elsewhere in the RC file:

```
IDB_XYZCORP        BITMAP  MOVEABLE PURE   "res\\xyzcorp.bmp"
```

# Example 2: A Simple Modeless Dialog

An About box is a modal dialog, refusing to let the user continue working in the program until clicking OK to close the dialog. A modeless dialog, on the other hand, lets the user switch to another window in the same program and resume working. The dialog remains on the screen until dismissed.

Whether your dialog ultimately is modal or modeless depends solely on how your program creates the dialog at run time, not on how you design it in the dialog editor. You design modal and modeless dialogs the same way with one exception: a modeless dialog must have a style flag of WS_VISIBLE. Set the flag by right-clicking in the dialog work area and choosing Properties from the context menu to invoke the Dialog Properties box, then turn on the Visible check box in the More Styles tab:

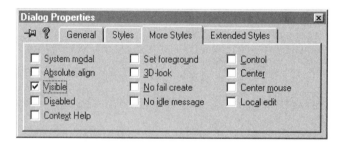

This adds the WS_VISIBLE flag to the dialog script's STYLE statement in the RC file.

A C program creates a modeless dialog by calling the *CreateDialog* API function or one of its variations, such as *CreateDialogIndirect*:

```
hDlg = CreateDialog( hInst, MAKEINTRESOURCE (IDD_DIALOG1),
                        hwnd, DlgProc );
```

In this example, *hInst* is the program's instance handle, IDD_DIALOG1 is the identifier for the dialog script in the RC file, *hwnd* is the handle of the dialog's owner, and *DlgProc* is a pointer to the procedure that runs the dialog and receives its messages.

A C++ program using MFC creates a modeless dialog with the *CDialog:: Create* function. The following lines assume the *CMyDlg* class is a derivative of MFC's *CDialog*:

```
CMyDlg* pDlg = new CMyDlg;
pDlg->Create( IDD_DIALOG1, this );
```

There is an important difference between *CDialog::Create* and *CDialog:: DoModal*. Because the latter function creates a modal dialog, it does not return until the dialog is closed. *Create* returns immediately, allowing the program to continue while the modeless dialog remains on the screen. The dialog exists until the program destroys it:

```
delete pDlg;
```

The Color program presented in this section displays a modeless dialog with three slider controls (also called trackbars) that adjust the red, green, and blue components of the main window's background color. As you move a slider "thumb" with the mouse or arrow keys, the main window changes color by taking on the new color component, which can vary in value from 0 through a high-intensity 255. With adequate video hardware, you can in theory display any of 16,777,216 ($256^3$) different colors by moving the slider bars. Figure 5-11 shows the program window with the modeless Color dialog displayed.

Color is an MFC program, but was not created with AppWizard. (The next section shows how to create a new dialog in an AppWizard application.) The Color project begins with the selection of the Win32 Application icon in the Projects tab of the New dialog. Type *Color* as the project name and

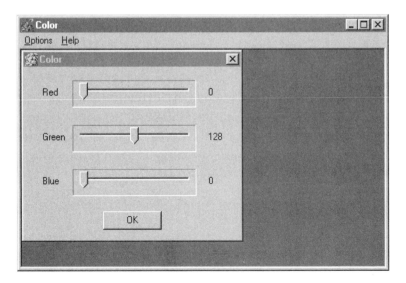

**Figure 5-11.**    *The Color program.*

click OK. Start the dialog editor by clicking Resource on the Insert menu and double-clicking Dialog in the list of resource types. The new dialog starts out with default OK and Cancel buttons; select the buttons in the work area and press the Del key to delete them.

Static Text

Button

Slider

Color's dialog contains only three different control types, created with the Static Text, Button, and Slider tools from the editor's Controls toolbar. The slider bars form three distinct lines in the dialog, labeled Red, Green, and Blue in Figure 5-11. The dialog design calls for creating the Red (top) line first by placing a slider control between two static text controls, all of which are then aligned and spaced. Initialize captions for the text controls to *Red* and *x* in the Text Properties dialog. The *x* serves as a placeholder that Color overwrites at run time with the current value of the slider thumb position. Give the slider control a static-edge border and a pointed thumb button. These styles are set in the Slider Properties dialog, invoked by right-clicking the slider control window in the dialog and choosing Properties:

1. In the Styles tab, select Bottom/Right in the Point box for the thumb style.

2. In the Extended Styles tab, click the Static Edge check box.

The Green and Blue lines are just clones of the Red line, copied by selecting the three controls of the Red line as a group, and then dragging the group with the Ctrl key pressed as explained earlier in the chapter.

At this point, the dialog editor work area looks like the one shown on the next page. Finishing the dialog requires only changing the second and third captions to *Green* and *Blue*, aligning the controls, and adding an OK push button at the bottom of the dialog window. Assign the button an identifier symbol of IDOK, and set the Default Button check box in the Styles tab of the button's Properties dialog.

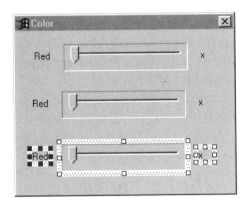

When you duplicate a selected control, the dialog editor automatically assigns the new control a different identifier symbol, ensuring that each control in the dialog is uniquely identified. The new symbol has the same name as the original with an added numeral. For example, the Red slider control in the first line was given an identifier of IDC_SLIDE_RED. When you create the Green and Blue lines by copying the Red line, the editor assigns identifiers named IDC_SLIDE_RED1 and IDC_SLIDE_RED2 to the new controls. (In the Color program, these identifiers were later changed to IDC_SLIDE_GREEN and IDC_SLIDE_BLUE in the Properties box for each control.) When you save the dialog, the editor writes **#define** statements for the new identifiers in the Resource.h file. The results are summarized here:

**Control Identifiers in the Color Dialog**

|  | Top line | Middle line | Bottom line |
| --- | --- | --- | --- |
| Color static control | IDC_STATIC | IDC_STATIC | IDC_STATIC |
| Slider control | IDC_SLIDE_ RED | IDC_SLIDE_ GREEN | IDC_SLIDE_ BLUE |
| x static control | IDC_STATIC_ RED | IDC_STATIC_ GREEN | IDC_STATIC_ BLUE |

The captions for the Color static controls (the leftmost controls) should be *Red*, *Green*, and *Blue*. The caption of the rightmost static control is *x* for all three lines.

Color's source code requires only one main file, two header files named Resource.h and Color.h, and a resource script file named Color.rc that defines the dialog. A brief synopsis of the program begins on page 232, following the source listing (Listing 5-1).

**Listing 5-1.** *Source files for the Color program.*

### Resource.h

```
// ****************************************************************
//
// Resource.h
//
// ****************************************************************

#define IDR_MAINFRAME                128

#define IDD_ABOUTBOX                 100
#define IDD_COLOR_DIALOG             101
#define IDC_STATIC_RED               102
#define IDC_STATIC_GREEN             103
#define IDC_STATIC_BLUE              104
#define IDC_SLIDE_RED                105
#define IDC_SLIDE_GREEN              106
#define IDC_SLIDE_BLUE               107
#define IDM_COLOR                    200
```

### Color.rc

```
// ****************************************************************
//
// Color.rc
//
// ****************************************************************

#include "resource.h"
#include "afxres.h"

AFX_IDI_STD_FRAME           ICON                "res\\Color.ico"

IDR_MAINFRAME MENU
BEGIN
    POPUP "&Options"
    BEGIN
        MENUITEM "&Color",                      IDM_COLOR
        MENUITEM SEPARATOR
```

```
            MENUITEM "E&xit",                        ID_APP_EXIT
        END
    POPUP "&Help"
    BEGIN
            MENUITEM "&About Color...",              ID_APP_ABOUT
        END
END


IDD_ABOUTBOX DIALOG 0, 0, 240, 65
STYLE DS_MODALFRAME | WS_POPUP | WS_CAPTION | WS_SYSMENU
CAPTION "About Color"
FONT 8, "MS Sans Serif"
BEGIN
    ICON            AFX_IDI_STD_FRAME,IDC_STATIC,10,22,20,20
    LTEXT           "Color Version 1.0",IDC_STATIC,45,10,115,8
    LTEXT           """Microsoft Visual C++ Programmer's Guide""",
                    IDC_STATIC,45,26,140,8
    LTEXT           "Copyright \251 1998, Beck Zaratian",
                    IDC_STATIC,45,42,115,8
    DEFPUSHBUTTON "OK",IDOK,195,10,35,40,WS_GROUP
END


IDD_COLOR_DIALOG DIALOGEX 0, 0, 186, 132
STYLE WS_POPUP | WS_VISIBLE | WS_CAPTION | WS_SYSMENU
CAPTION "Color"
FONT 8, "MS Sans Serif"
BEGIN
    LTEXT           "Red",IDC_STATIC,16,15,14,8
    LTEXT           "Green",IDC_STATIC,16,49,20,8
    LTEXT           "Blue",IDC_STATIC,16,83,14,8
    CONTROL         "Slider1",IDC_SLIDE_RED,"msctls_trackbar32",
                    TBS_NOTICKS | WS_TABSTOP,42,10,106,21,
                    WS_EX_STATICEDGE
    CONTROL         "Slider1",IDC_SLIDE_GREEN,"msctls_trackbar32",
                    TBS_NOTICKS | WS_TABSTOP,42,44,106,21,
                    WS_EX_STATICEDGE
    CONTROL         "Slider1",IDC_SLIDE_BLUE,"msctls_trackbar32",
                    TBS_NOTICKS | WS_TABSTOP,42,78,106,21,
                    WS_EX_STATICEDGE
    LTEXT           "x",IDC_STATIC_RED,158,15,12,8
    LTEXT           "x",IDC_STATIC_GREEN,158,49,12,8
    LTEXT           "x",IDC_STATIC_BLUE,158,83,12,8
    DEFPUSHBUTTON "OK",IDOK,68,111,50,14
END
```

*(continued)*

**Listing 5-1.** *continued*

## Color.h

```
// ****************************************************************
//
// Color.h
//
// ****************************************************************

#include "Resource.h"

class CColorApp : public CWinApp
{
public:
    virtual BOOL    InitInstance();
};


/////////////////////////////////////////////////////////////////
// CColorDlg dialog

class CColorDlg : public CDialog
{
public:
    int     nColor[3];
    BOOL    bCreate;

    CColorDlg ();

protected:
    virtual BOOL    OnInitDialog ();
    virtual void    OnOK ();
    afx_msg void    OnCancel ();
    afx_msg void    OnHScroll( UINT nCode, UINT nPos,
                               CScrollBar* pScroll );

    DECLARE_MESSAGE_MAP()
};

/////////////////////////////////////////////////////////////////
// CMainFrame

class CMainFrame : public CFrameWnd
{
public:
    CColorDlg*      pColorDlg;

    CMainFrame();
```

```
        ~CMainFrame();

protected:
    afx_msg void    OnAbout();
    afx_msg BOOL    OnEraseBkgnd( CDC* pDC );
    afx_msg void    OnColor();
    DECLARE_MESSAGE_MAP()
};

//////////////////////////////////////////////////////////////
// CAboutDlg dialog

class CAboutDlg : public CDialog
{
public:
    CAboutDlg();
};

CAboutDlg::CAboutDlg() : CDialog( IDD_ABOUTBOX )
{
}
```

## Color.cpp

```
// ************************************************************
//
// Color.cpp
//
// ************************************************************

#define VC_EXTRALEAN
#include <afxwin.h>
#include <afxcmn.h>
#include "Color.h"

CColorApp theApp;

BOOL CColorApp::InitInstance()
{
    m_pMainWnd = new CMainFrame;
    m_pMainWnd->ShowWindow( m_nCmdShow );
    m_pMainWnd->UpdateWindow ();

    return TRUE;
}

//////////////////////////////////////////////////////////////
```

*(continued)*

**Listing 5-1.** *continued*

```
// CMainFrame

BEGIN_MESSAGE_MAP (CMainFrame, CFrameWnd)
    ON_COMMAND (IDM_COLOR, OnColor)
    ON_COMMAND (ID_APP_ABOUT, OnAbout)
    ON_WM_ERASEBKGND ()
END_MESSAGE_MAP ()

CMainFrame::CMainFrame ()
{
    pColorDlg = new CColorDlg;

    Create( NULL, "Color", WS_OVERLAPPEDWINDOW, rectDefault,
            NULL, MAKEINTRESOURCE (IDR_MAINFRAME) );
}

CMainFrame::~CMainFrame ()
{
    delete pColorDlg;
}

void CMainFrame::OnColor()
{
    if (pColorDlg->bCreate)        // If the dialog already exists,
        pColorDlg->SetFocus();     // give it focus
    else                           // Otherwise, create it
    {
        if (pColorDlg->Create( IDD_COLOR_DIALOG, this ))
            pColorDlg->bCreate = TRUE;
    }
}

BOOL CMainFrame::OnEraseBkgnd( CDC* pDC )
{
    CBrush     brush;
    CRect      rect;
    COLORREF   rgbBackGnd = RGB ((BYTE) pColorDlg->nColor[0],
                                 (BYTE) pColorDlg->nColor[1],
                                 (BYTE) pColorDlg->nColor[2]);

    GetClientRect( &rect );
    brush.CreateSolidBrush( rgbBackGnd );
    pDC->FillRect( rect, &brush );

    return TRUE;
}
```

```
void CMainFrame::OnAbout()
{
    CAboutDlg aboutDlg;
    aboutDlg.DoModal();
}

///////////////////////////////////////////////////////////////
// CColorDlg dialog

BEGIN_MESSAGE_MAP (CColorDlg, CDialog)
    ON_WM_HSCROLL ()
END_MESSAGE_MAP ()

CColorDlg::CColorDlg ()
{
    nColor[0] = 0;            // Initial color is
    nColor[1] = 128;          //    medium-intensity green
    nColor[2] = 0;
    bCreate   = FALSE;        // Haven't created the dialog yet
}

BOOL CColorDlg::OnInitDialog ()
{
    CSliderCtrl*   pSlide[3];
    CString        szColorValue;
    int            i;

    for (i=0; i < 3; i++)
    {
        pSlide[i] = (CSliderCtrl*) GetDlgItem(IDC_SLIDE_RED + i);
        pSlide[i]->SetRange( 0, 255 );
        pSlide[i]->SetPos( nColor[i] );
        szColorValue.Format( "%d", nColor[i] );
        SetDlgItemText( i + IDC_STATIC_RED, szColorValue );
    }

    SetIcon( AfxGetApp()->LoadIcon( AFX_IDI_STD_FRAME ), FALSE );

    return TRUE;
}

void CColorDlg::OnHScroll( UINT nCode, UINT nPos,
                           CScrollBar* pScroll )
{
    CSliderCtrl*   pSlide = (CSliderCtrl*) pScroll;
    CString        szColorValue;
```

*(continued)*

**Listing 5-1.** *continued*

```
int            i = pSlide->GetDlgCtrlID () - IDC_SLIDE_RED;

nColor[i] = pSlide->GetPos ();          // Slider position is
szColorValue.Format( "%d", nColor[i] ); //   component 0-255

// Write current component value in the "x" static control
SetDlgItemText( i + IDC_STATIC_RED, szColorValue );

AfxGetMainWnd()->Invalidate ();
}

void CColorDlg::OnOK ()
{
    OnCancel ();               // Close dialog when OK clicked
}

// Close on OK, Esc, and dialog's Close command
void CColorDlg::OnCancel ()
{
    if (DestroyWindow ())
      ((CMainFrame*) AfxGetMainWnd())->pColorDlg->bCreate = FALSE;
}
```

All of the program's important work is performed by two classes, *CMain-Frame* for the main window and a *CDialog* derivative named *CColorDlg* that drives the modeless dialog. The *CColorDlg* constructor initializes an array of color values for the main window's background color, which begins as medium-intensity green. Since the red, green, and blue components of the window background color can vary in value from 0 through 255, the *OnInitDialog* function sets each slider scroll range from 0 through 255. This means that an integer number in that range represents the position of a thumb button at any moment, conveniently determining the current value of the color component.

When the user moves a slider thumb, the *CColorDlg::OnHScroll* function gets control and figures out which slider is being moved by calling *Get-DlgCtrlID*. The function then calls *GetPos* to get the new thumb position, writes that value to the *nColor* array and to the static text control in the dialog, and calls the *Invalidate* function.

The call to *Invalidate* causes the operating system to send the main window a WM_ERASEBKGND message to tell the window to repaint itself. This message gives an application like Color a chance to paint its own background. Most applications ignore the WM_ERASEBKGND message, in which case Windows paints the window with whatever default background color the program specified when it created the window (usually white). Color.cpp traps the WM_ERASEBKGND message in its *CMainFrame::OnEraseBkGnd* function, which declares a COLORREF object based on the current red, green, and blue color components stored in the *nColor* array:

```
COLORREF  rgbBackGnd = RGB ((BYTE) pColorDlg->nColor[0],
                            (BYTE) pColorDlg->nColor[1],
                            (BYTE) pColorDlg->nColor[2]);
```

*OnEraseBkGnd* then creates a brush from *rgbBackGnd*, paints the window with it, and returns a value of TRUE. The TRUE return value tells the operating system it should not clear the window with the default color because the application has already taken care of repainting the background.

All this explains why the program takes the unusual step of creating the modeless dialog object before the main window:

```
CMainFrame::CMainFrame ()
{
    pColorDlg = new CColorDlg;

    Create( NULL, "Color", WS_OVERLAPPEDWINDOW, rectDefault, NULL,
            MAKEINTRESOURCE (IDR_MAINFRAME) );
}
```

The operating system sends a WM_ERASEBKGND message immediately after the main window comes into existence, so creating the *CColorDlg* object first ensures that the *OnEraseBkGnd* function reads an *nColor* array with valid color values.

# Example 3: Adding a Dialog to an AppWizard Program

If you prefer to begin your projects with the help of AppWizard, the Color program presented in the previous section may not seem relevant at first glance. Actually, it is relevant—adding a new dialog to a program involves the same steps regardless of whether AppWizard created the program. But AppWizard produces code of a rigorous form that can be a little difficult to match against the compact style of Color.cpp. To show you exactly what is involved in adding a new dialog to an AppWizard program, this section demonstrates the necessary steps using an example AppWizard program called MfcTree.

The MfcTree dialog shown in Figure 5-12 is nothing fancy—just a tree view of some MFC classes and an OK button. But it serves well for the purposes of illustration and will be improved upon later in the chapter and again in Chapter 13.

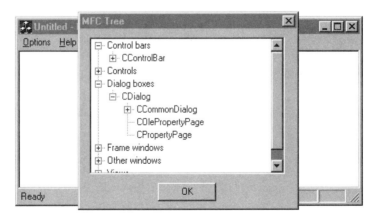

**Figure 5-12.**    *The MfcTree program.*

The program is created in five steps:

1.  Run AppWizard to create the MfcTree project.

2.  Create the dialog resource in the dialog editor.

3.  Add source files to the project for the new dialog class.

4. Revise the menu.

5. Add required source code to the project source files.

We'll take these steps one at a time.

## Step 1: Run AppWizard to Create the MfcTree Project

Click New on the File menu and select the Projects tab in the New dialog. Choose the MFC AppWizard (exe) icon, name the new project MfcTree, and then click the OK button to run AppWizard. Accept the AppWizard defaults with these exceptions: select the Single Document Interface in Step 1 and clear the check boxes for docking toolbar and print support in Step 4. To keep filenames short on the companion CD, the default MfcTreeDoc and MfcTreeView filenames were changed to MfcDoc and MfcView, but this step is entirely optional.

## Step 2: Create the MfcTree Dialog

Now that MfcTree is an open project, we can design its dialog resource. Launch the dialog editor by clicking Resource on the Insert menu and double-clicking Dialog in the list of resource types. Select the default Cancel button in the work area and press the Del key to remove the button. Right-click anywhere in the dialog work area and choose Properties from the context menu to invoke the Dialog Properties box. Change the dialog caption to MFC Tree and the dialog identifier to IDD_MFC_DIALOG.

Adding the tree view control is next. From the Controls toolbar, drag the Tree Control tool into the dialog work area and resize the dialog work area and control as desired. Click Properties on the View menu to invoke the Tree Control Properties box and change the identifier symbol to IDC_ MFC_TREE. In the Styles tab, click the Has Buttons, Has Lines, and Lines At Root check boxes, as shown here:

These style changes add small plus and minus icons to the list view which, when clicked, collapse or expand levels in the list hierarchy. Move the OK button to the bottom of the dialog and center both controls using the horizontal spacing tool described earlier in the chapter. The dialog now looks like this in the editor work area:

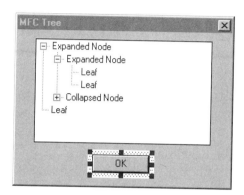

Choose Save from the File menu to save the new dialog script to the MfcTree.rc file. Visual C++ automatically adds **#define** statements for the new identifiers to the Resource.h file. Close the dialog editor by clicking the Close command on the File menu.

## Step 3: Add Source Files for the *CMfcDlg* Dialog Class

We now have a new dialog resource but it needs a class derived from *CDialog* to run it. In the next chapter we'll see how to use ClassWizard to generate a skeleton dialog class and automatically add its files to the project, but for now we can do the same thing using the text editor. Create source files named MfcDlg.h and MfcDlg.cpp to contain the new *CMfcDlg* dialog class (Listing 5-2). We need only these bare files at this point to add the *CMfcDlg* class to the project. We'll add source code to the files in Step 5.

To create new source files from scratch for an open project like MfcTree, rest the cursor on the Add To Project command on the Project menu, then click New on the secondary menu that appears. Select the type of file you want to create—either a header file or a source implementation file—and enter a filename. Click OK to launch the text editor, which presents a blank document window.

**Listing 5-2.**     *Skeleton source files for the* CMfcDlg *class.*

### MfcDlg.h

```
// *************************************************************
//
// MfcDlg.h
//
// *************************************************************

class CMfcDlg : public CDialog
{
public:
    CMfcDlg( CWnd* pParent = NULL );

protected:
    virtual BOOL OnInitDialog();
};
```

### MfcDlg.cpp

```
// *************************************************************
//
// MfcDlg.cpp
//
// *************************************************************

#include "stdafx.h"
#include "MfcTree.h"
#include "MfcDlg.h"

CMfcDlg::CMfcDlg( CWnd* pParent ) :
        CDialog( IDD_MFC_DIALOG, pParent )
{
}

BOOL CMfcDlg::OnInitDialog()
{
    return TRUE;
}
```

If you type the two source files in the text editor, save them to the project's folder when you are finished. As an alternative to typing, you can copy both files in their complete form from the Chapter.05\MfcTree folder on the companion CD. Copying the files requires you to add them manually to the project. Choose Add To Project and click Files on the pop-up secondary menu, then double-click the MfcDlg.cpp file in the list of files to add it to the project:

It isn't necessary to add the MfcDlg.h file in the same way, because Visual C++ recognizes the header file as a dependency of MfcDlg.cpp.

## Step 4: Modify the Menu

MfcTree requires a menu command to invoke the dialog but does not need all the other commands that AppWizard puts on the menus. Using the Visual C++ menu editor described in Chapter 4, revise MfcTree's menus to look like this:

Open the resource in the menu editor by double-clicking the IDR_MAIN-FRAME menu identifier in the ResourceView pane of the Workspace window. Double-click the MFC Tree menu item in the menu editor to display the Menu Item Properties box. Type in *IDM_OPTIONS_MFC* as the item's identifier and press the Enter key.

## Step 5: Add Required Source Code

If you typed the MfcDlg.cpp file as listed in Step 3, the file contains only a class constructor and a stub function called *OnInitDialog*. The *OnInitDialog* function needs to initialize the tree view control with the shaded code shown on the following pages. As you see, it can take a lot of instructions to initialize a tree view. If you are following these steps by building MfcTree yourself, there is no need to type in all the lines. Just type the first group or cut and paste the code from the MfcDlg.cpp source file in the Chapter.05\MfcTree folder of the companion CD.

The *OnInitDialog* function initializes a pointer named *pTree* that points to the dialog's tree view control, identified as IDC_MFC_TREE. The function then repeatedly calls the *CTreeCtrl:InsertItem* function to add to the control a hierarchical list containing some of the MFC classes derived from *CWnd*. The second parameter for *InsertItem* identifies the item's parent. An item is inserted into the list one level lower in the hierarchy than the parent. The second parameter is either the HTREEITEM value returned by a previous call to *InsertItem* for the parent level or, if there is no parent level, the value TVI_ROOT. The TVI_SORT flag instructs the tree view control to sort the root items in alphabetical order:

```
BOOL CMfcDlg::OnInitDialog()
{

    HTREEITEM   hRoot, hLevel1, hLevel2, hLevel3, hLevel4, hLevel5;
    CTreeCtrl*  pTree = (CTreeCtrl*) GetDlgItem( IDC_MFC_TREE );

    hRoot   = pTree->InsertItem( "Frame windows", TVI_ROOT, TVI_SORT );
    hLevel1 = pTree->InsertItem( "CFrameWnd", hRoot );
    hLevel2 = pTree->InsertItem( "CMDIChildWnd", hLevel1 );
    hLevel2 = pTree->InsertItem( "CMDIFrameWnd", hLevel1 );
    hLevel2 = pTree->InsertItem( "COlePFrameWnd", hLevel1 );

    hRoot   = pTree->InsertItem( "Control bars", TVI_ROOT, TVI_SORT );
    hLevel1 = pTree->InsertItem( "CControlBar", hRoot );
    hLevel2 = pTree->InsertItem( "CDialogBar", hLevel1 );
    hLevel2 = pTree->InsertItem( "COleResizeBar", hLevel1 );
    hLevel2 = pTree->InsertItem( "CStatusBar", hLevel1 );
    hLevel2 = pTree->InsertItem( "CToolBar", hLevel1 );

    hRoot   = pTree->InsertItem( "Other windows", TVI_ROOT, TVI_SORT );
    hLevel1 = pTree->InsertItem( "CPropertySheet", hRoot );
    hLevel1 = pTree->InsertItem( "CSplitterWnd", hRoot );

    hRoot   = pTree->InsertItem( "Dialog boxes", TVI_ROOT, TVI_SORT );
    hLevel1 = pTree->InsertItem( "CDialog", hRoot );
    hLevel2 = pTree->InsertItem( "CCommonDialog", hLevel1 );
    hLevel3 = pTree->InsertItem( "CColorDialog", hLevel2 );
    hLevel3 = pTree->InsertItem( "CFileDialog", hLevel2 );
    hLevel3 = pTree->InsertItem( "CFindReplaceDialog", hLevel2 );
    hLevel3 = pTree->InsertItem( "CFontDialog", hLevel2 );
    hLevel3 = pTree->InsertItem( "COleDialog", hLevel2 );
```

```
hLevel4 = pTree->InsertItem( "COleBusyDialog", hLevel3 );
hLevel4 = pTree->InsertItem( "COleChangeIconDialog", hLevel3 );
hLevel4 = pTree->InsertItem( "COleChangeSourceDialog", hLevel3 );
hLevel4 = pTree->InsertItem( "COleConvertDialog", hLevel3 );
hLevel4 = pTree->InsertItem( "COleInsertDialog", hLevel3 );
hLevel4 = pTree->InsertItem( "COleLinksDialog", hLevel3 );
hLevel5 = pTree->InsertItem( "COleUpdateDialog", hLevel4 );
hLevel4 = pTree->InsertItem( "COlepasteSpecialDialog", hLevel3 );
hLevel4 = pTree->InsertItem( "COlePropertiesDialog", hLevel3 );
hLevel3 = pTree->InsertItem( "CPageSetupDialog", hLevel2 );
hLevel3 = pTree->InsertItem( "CPrintDialog", hLevel2 );
hLevel2 = pTree->InsertItem( "COlePropertyPage", hLevel1 );
hLevel2 = pTree->InsertItem( "CPropertyPage", hLevel1 );

hRoot   = pTree->InsertItem( "Views", TVI_ROOT, TVI_SORT );
hLevel1 = pTree->InsertItem( "CView", hRoot );
hLevel2 = pTree->InsertItem( "CCtrlView", hLevel1 );
hLevel3 = pTree->InsertItem( "CEditView", hLevel2 );
hLevel3 = pTree->InsertItem( "CListView", hLevel2 );
hLevel3 = pTree->InsertItem( "CRichEditView", hLevel2 );
hLevel3 = pTree->InsertItem( "CTreeView", hLevel2 );
hLevel2 = pTree->InsertItem( "CScrollView", hLevel1 );
hLevel3 = pTree->InsertItem( "CFormView", hLevel2 );
hLevel4 = pTree->InsertItem( "CDaoRecordView", hLevel3 );
hLevel4 = pTree->InsertItem( "CRecordView", hLevel3 );

hRoot   = pTree->InsertItem( "Controls", TVI_ROOT, TVI_SORT );
hLevel1 = pTree->InsertItem( "CAnimateCtrl", hRoot );
hLevel1 = pTree->InsertItem( "CButton", hRoot );
hLevel2 = pTree->InsertItem( "CBitmapButton", hLevel1 );
hLevel1 = pTree->InsertItem( "CComboBox", hRoot );
hLevel1 = pTree->InsertItem( "CEdit", hRoot );
hLevel1 = pTree->InsertItem( "CHeaderCtrl", hRoot );
hLevel1 = pTree->InsertItem( "CHotKeyCtrl", hRoot );
hLevel1 = pTree->InsertItem( "CListBox", hRoot );
hLevel2 = pTree->InsertItem( "CCheckListBox", hLevel1 );
hLevel2 = pTree->InsertItem( "CDragListBox", hLevel1 );
hLevel1 = pTree->InsertItem( "CListCtrl", hRoot );
hLevel1 = pTree->InsertItem( "COleCtrl", hRoot );
hLevel1 = pTree->InsertItem( "CProgressCtrl", hRoot );
hLevel1 = pTree->InsertItem( "CRichEditCtrl", hRoot );
hLevel1 = pTree->InsertItem( "CScrollBar", hRoot );
hLevel1 = pTree->InsertItem( "CSliderCtrl", hRoot );
hLevel1 = pTree->InsertItem( "CSpinButtonCtrl", hRoot );
hLevel1 = pTree->InsertItem( "CStatic", hRoot );
hLevel1 = pTree->InsertItem( "CStatusBarCtrl", hRoot );
hLevel1 = pTree->InsertItem( "CTabCtrl", hRoot );
hLevel1 = pTree->InsertItem( "CToolbarCtrl", hRoot );
```

```
    hLevel1 = pTree->InsertItem( "CToolTipCtrl", hRoot );
    hLevel1 = pTree->InsertItem( "CTreeCtrl", hRoot );

    return TRUE;
}
```

Although the above code will do for now, it's not very efficient. The MfcTree3 program introduced in Chapter 13, Customizing Visual C++, shows a cleaner method for implementing a series of calls to *InsertItem*.

Next, edit the files MfcTree.cpp and MfcTree.h in the text editor to add a function called *OnMfcTree*. The *OnMfcTree* handler function gets control when the user clicks the MFC Tree command on the program's Options menu. To add *OnMfcTree*, open the MfcTree.cpp document by double-clicking its filename in the FileView pane of the Workspace window. Insert the following line somewhere near the beginning of the source code:

```
#include "MfcDlg.h"
```

Also, edit the message map in MfcTree.cpp so that it looks like this:

```
BEGIN_MESSAGE_MAP(CMfcTreeApp, CWinApp)
    //{{AFX_MSG_MAP(CMfcTreeApp)
    ON_COMMAND(ID_APP_ABOUT, OnAppAbout)
    ON_COMMAND(IDM_OPTIONS_MFC, OnMfcTree)
    //}}AFX_MSG_MAP
END_MESSAGE_MAP()
```

Add the *OnMfcTree* function to MfcTree.cpp:

```
/////////////////////////////////////////////////////////////////
// CMfcTreeApp message handlers

void CMfcTreeApp::OnMfcTree()
{
    CMfcDlg mfcDlg;
    mfcDlg.DoModal();
}
```

and declare it in the MfcTree.h file:

```
//Implementation
    //{{AFX_MSG(CMfcTreeApp)
    afx_msg void OnAppAbout();
    afx_msg void OnMfcTree();
```

```
//}}AFX_MSG
DECLARE_MESSAGE_MAP()
```

MfcTree is now ready for building. Click the Set Active Configuration command on the Build menu and select the Win32 Release target, then build and test the application.

# Dialog-Based Applications

All the action in MfcTree is in the dialog, not in the main window. The program would be more convenient to use if it dispensed with the main window entirely and just displayed the dialog, saving the user the trouble of clicking a menu command to invoke the dialog. You've seen such dialog-based applications before—the Character Map, Calculator, and Phone Dialer utilities that come with Windows are all examples of how a program can efficiently interact with the user through a single dialog that substitutes for the main window. In this section we'll look at how to write a dialog-based application in Visual C++ and build a couple of example programs to demonstrate the technique.

A dialog-based application written in C doesn't initialize a WNDCLASS or WNDCLASSEX structure, doesn't call *RegisterClass* to register the window class, and doesn't call *CreateWindow* to create a main window. It doesn't call *ShowWindow* and *UpdateWindow* and doesn't even have a message loop with calls to *GetMessage* and *DispatchMessage*. It doesn't need these things—all interaction with the user takes place in the dialog, and Windows handles that. The program need only create the dialog like this:

```
int WINAPI WinMain( HINSTANCE hInst, HINSTANCE hInstPrev,
                    LPSTR szCmdLine, int nCmdShow )
{
    DialogBox( hInst, MAKEINTRESOURCE (IDD_DIALOG),
               NULL, DlgProc );
    return( 0 );
}
```

In this code fragment, the IDD_DIALOG value identifies the dialog script in the program's RC file, and *DlgProc* is a pointer to the procedure that

receives the system messages such as WM_INITDIALOG and WM_
COMMAND.

An MFC program doesn't have a visible *WinMain* function or a message
pump anyway, so the amount of code saved with a dialog interface is less
dramatic. But MFC offers the advantage of AppWizard, which can generate boilerplate code for a dialog-based application.

## Example 4: A Dialog-Based Version of MfcTree

The code that AppWizard writes for a dialog-based application is cleaner
and easier to follow than the code it generates for a normal application.
Clicking the Dialog Based radio button in AppWizard's Step 1 (shown in
Figure 5-13) causes AppWizard to create source files for two classes, one
for the application and the other for the dialog object.

AppWizard generates a resource script for the dialog window that contains only an OK button, a Cancel button, and a static control with the
admonishment "Place dialog controls here." The dialog also includes a
Help button if you clicked the Context-Sensitive Help check box in App-
Wizard's Step 2. (For more information about this switch, see page 47 in
Chapter 2.) The idea is for you to run the dialog editor after creating the
project and add to the dialog whatever controls your application requires.

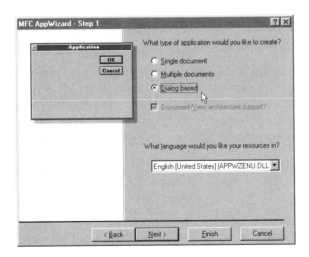

**Figure 5-13.**    *Creating a dialog-based application in AppWizard.*

In version 6 of Visual C++, the dialog editor starts automatically when AppWizard finishes. In earlier versions, you must start the editor yourself by double-clicking the dialog identifier in the ResourceView window.

Creating a dialog-based version of MfcTree with AppWizard involves only three steps, compared to the five steps outlined in the preceding section:

| Steps | Main-window version | Dialog-based version |
| --- | :---: | :---: |
| 1. Run AppWizard to create the project. | ✓ | ✓ |
| 2. Create or modify the dialog. | ✓ | ✓ |
| 3. Insert source files for the new dialog class. | ✓ | |
| 4. Revise the menu. | ✓ | |
| 5. Add required source code. | ✓ | ✓ |

Steps 3 and 4, which create a new class for the dialog and modify the main menu, are not required for the dialog-based version of MfcTree. AppWizard automatically generates skeleton source files for the dialog class, and eliminating the main window also eliminates the need for a menu. Even the source code that AppWizard produces is easier to modify because you need only edit the *CMfcDlg::OnInitDialog* function, adding the *InsertItem* calls after the function's "to do" line. As before, the gray shading in the fragment below indicates the new source lines, which are the same as those added to the original version of MfcTree introduced earlier:

```
BOOL CMfcDlg::OnInitDialog()
{
    CDialog::OnInitDialog();
    ⋮

    // TODO: Add extra initialization here
    HTREEITEM   hRoot, hLevel1, hLevel2, hLevel3, hLevel4, hLevel5;
    CTreeCtrl*  pTree = (CTreeCtrl*) GetDlgItem( IDC_MFC_TREE );

    hRoot   = pTree->InsertItem( "Frame windows", TVI_ROOT, TVI_SORT );
    hLevel1 = pTree->InsertItem( "CFrameWnd", hRoot );
```

```
    hLevel2 = pTree->InsertItem( "CMDIChildWnd", hLevel1 );
    ⋮
              // Add the rest of the source code here
}
```

Figure 5-14 shows what a dialog-based version of the MfcTree program looks like. In essence, it's the same program as the original version shown in Figure 5-12 on page 234 except that the main window has been eliminated, the dialog title bar now contains the application icon and system menu, and the program is easier to create and use. If you want to try out the new version yourself, you will find it in the Chapter.05\MfcTree2 folder on the companion CD.

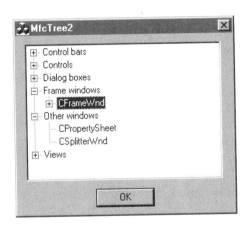

**Figure 5-14.** *The dialog-based version of the MfcTree program.*

## Example 5: A Dialog-Based Application Without AppWizard

AppWizard shines when writing dialog-based applications, probably because such applications are more uniform in their methods and App-Wizard is thus less likely to add code you don't want. Still, AppWizard may not be appropriate for your particular needs. If you are interested in writing a dialog-based application without using AppWizard, this section shows how. It illustrates with an example program called DirList1 that shows a directory listing in a dialog. But to make things a little more interesting, the dialog that DirList1 presents to the user is a property sheet, often called a tabbed dialog.

Property sheets can present a lot of information without overwhelming the user, neatly solving the problem of overcrowding in a dialog box. But in essence a property sheet is just a dialog—or rather a series of dialogs called pages, one overlaying the other. You design each page of a property sheet with the dialog editor as you would any other dialog. The dialog script for a page in the RC file looks the same as a normal dialog, except that all the pages of a property sheet have the same size. Windows displays the dialogs as property sheet pages when a program calls the *PropertySheet* API function or creates an MFC *CPropertySheet* object.

Tab Control

Incidentally, you may have already run across a tool called Tab Control on the dialog editor's Controls toolbar. This control displays a set of tabbed pages that can act as a property sheet within a dialog, but does not turn your dialog into a property sheet.

Figure 5-15 shows the first and second pages, labeled Location and Date, of the DirList1 property sheet dialog.

The Date tab makes use of the new Date-Time Picker control, allowing the user to select dates through a pop-up calendar. Although controls in the Date and Size pages function correctly, the pages exist only for demonstration purposes and have no effect in this version of the program. (The DirList2 project, introduced in Chapter 7, The Gallery, makes use of the Date and Size pages.) The important activity in DirList1 takes place in the Location page, which displays a directory listing in a list box control. DirList1 fills the list box with a directory listing by making a single call to the *CWnd::DlgDirList* function:

```
DlgDirList( pDir, IDC_LIST, IDC_DIRPATH, DDL_ALL );
```

The parameter *pDir* points to a null-terminated string containing the directory path. The constant IDC_LIST identifies the list box control that displays the directory listing, and IDC_DIRPATH identifies a static control to which *DlgDirList* writes the path string. DDL_ALL is a constant defined in the source code that combines the flags DDL_DRIVES, DDL_DIREC-TORY, and DDL_HIDDEN. These flags tell *DlgDirList* to include drives,

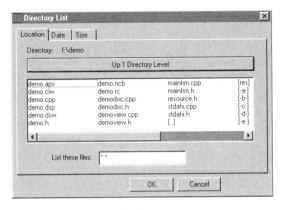

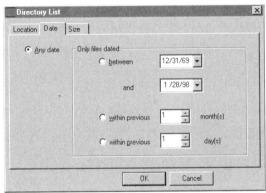

**Figure 5-15.**   *The Location and Date tabs of the DirList1 program.*

subdirectories, and hidden files in the directory list. Clicking on a drive or subdirectory in the list changes the path and refreshes the listing. The large button labeled Up 1 Directory Level in the Location tab allows the user to climb back up the path.

The property sheet dialog in DirList1 makes use of only five control types: push buttons, radio buttons, a list box, edit controls, and spin boxes. If you are interested in how the controls are assembled, open the DirList1.rc file and launch the dialog editor by double-clicking one of the dialog identifiers shown on the next page.

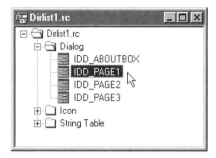

IDD_PAGE1, IDD_PAGE2, and IDD_PAGE3 identify the dialog's Location page, Date page, and Size page, respectively. Listing 5-3 shows the source code for the DirList1 project; commentary beginning on page 260 describes the code highlights.

**Listing 5-3.**   *Source files for the DirList1 program.*

### Resource.h

```
// ******************************************************************
//
// Resource.h
//
// ******************************************************************

#define IDD_ABOUTBOX      100
#define IDD_DIRLIST       101
#define IDI_DRIVE         102
#define IDI_FOLDER        103
#define IDI_FILE          104
#define IDI_APPICON       105
#define IDC_DIRPATH       110
#define IDC_LIST          111
#define IDC_BUTTON1       120
#define IDC_EDIT1         121
#define IDC_EDIT2         122
#define IDC_RADIO1        123
#define IDC_RADIO2        124
#define IDC_RADIO3        125
#define IDC_RADIO4        126
#define IDC_SPIN1         127
#define IDC_SPIN2         128
#define IDC_DATETIME1     130
#define IDC_DATETIME2     131
#define IDD_PAGE1         1001
```

```
#define IDD_PAGE2          1002
#define IDD_PAGE3          1003
```

## DirList1.rc

```
// ************************************************************
//
// DirList1.rc
//
// ************************************************************

#include "resource.h"
#include "afxres.h"

IDI_APPICON          ICON     "res\\dirlist.ico"

STRINGTABLE
BEGIN
    IDD_ABOUTBOX                 "&About DirList..."
END

IDD_ABOUTBOX DIALOG 0, 0, 240, 65
STYLE DS_MODALFRAME | WS_POPUP | WS_CAPTION | WS_SYSMENU
CAPTION "About Directory List"
FONT 8, "MS Sans Serif"
BEGIN
    ICON             IDI_APPICON,IDC_STATIC,10,22,20,20
    LTEXT            "Directory List Version 1.0",
                     IDC_STATIC,45,10,115,8
    LTEXT            """Microsoft Visual C++ Programmer's Guide""",
                     IDC_STATIC,45,26,140,8
    LTEXT            "Copyright \251 1998, Beck Zaratian",
                     IDC_STATIC,45,42,115,8
    DEFPUSHBUTTON    "OK",IDOK,195,10,35,40,WS_GROUP
END

/////////////////////////////////////////////////////////////
//
// Property page 1 - "Location"
//

IDD_PAGE1 DIALOG 0, 0, 282, 135
STYLE DS_MODALFRAME | DS_3DLOOK | WS_POPUP |
                     WS_VISIBLE | WS_CAPTION
CAPTION "Location"
FONT 8, "MS Sans Serif"
```

*(continued)*

**Listing 5-3.** *continued*

```
BEGIN
    LTEXT              "Directory:",IDC_STATIC,10,5,35,10
    LTEXT              "",IDC_DIRPATH,50,5,220,10
    PUSHBUTTON         "Up 1 Directory Level",IDC_BUTTON1,
                       10,17,260,15
    LISTBOX            IDC_LIST,9,38,260,73,
                       LBS_STANDARD | LBS_MULTICOLUMN | WS_HSCROLL
    LTEXT              "List these files:",IDC_STATIC,37,115,47,10
    EDITTEXT           IDC_EDIT1,91,113,100,15,ES_AUTOHSCROLL
END


///////////////////////////////////////////////////////////////
//
// Property page 2 - "Date"
//

IDD_PAGE2 DIALOG 0, 0, 282, 135
STYLE DS_MODALFRAME | DS_3DLOOK | WS_POPUP |
                   WS_VISIBLE | WS_CAPTION
CAPTION "Date"
FONT 8, "MS Sans Serif"
BEGIN
    CONTROL            "&Any date",IDC_RADIO1,"Button",
                       BS_AUTORADIOBUTTON | WS_GROUP | WS_TABSTOP,
                       15,10,40,10
    CONTROL            "&between",IDC_RADIO2,"Button",
                       BS_AUTORADIOBUTTON | WS_TABSTOP,
                       100,23,43,10
    CONTROL            "&within previous",IDC_RADIO3,"Button",
                       BS_AUTORADIOBUTTON | WS_TABSTOP,100,80,63,10
    CONTROL            "within &previous",IDC_RADIO4,"Button",
                       BS_AUTORADIOBUTTON | WS_TABSTOP,100,105,63,10
    GROUPBOX           "Only files dated:",IDC_STATIC,
                       70,10,200,115,WS_GROUP
    CONTROL            "DateTimePicker1",IDC_DATETIME1,
                       "SysDateTimePick32", DTS_RIGHTALIGN |
                       WS_TABSTOP,170,20,50,15
    LTEXT              "and",IDC_STATIC,128,50,13,8,NOT WS_GROUP
    CONTROL            "DateTimePicker1",IDC_DATETIME2,
                       "SysDateTimePick32", DTS_RIGHTALIGN |
                       WS_TABSTOP,170,45,50,15
    EDITTEXT           IDC_EDIT1,170,76,35,16,ES_NUMBER
    CONTROL            "Spin3",IDC_SPIN1,"msctls_updown32",
                       UDS_SETBUDDYINT | UDS_ALIGNRIGHT |
                       UDS_AUTOBUDDY | UDS_ARROWKEYS, 205,75,11,14
    LTEXT              "month(s)",IDC_STATIC,216,80,40,11,
                       NOT WS_GROUP
```

```
        EDITTEXT        IDC_EDIT2,170,101,35,16,ES_NUMBER
        CONTROL         "Spin3",IDC_SPIN2,"msctls_updown32",
                        UDS_SETBUDDYINT | UDS_ALIGNRIGHT |
                        UDS_AUTOBUDDY | UDS_ARROWKEYS,205,100,11,14
        LTEXT           "day(s)",IDC_STATIC,220,105,40,11,
                        NOT WS_GROUP
END


/////////////////////////////////////////////////////////////////
//
// Property page 3 - "Size"
//

IDD_PAGE3 DIALOG 0, 0, 282, 135
STYLE DS_MODALFRAME | DS_3DLOOK | WS_POPUP |
                     WS_VISIBLE | WS_CAPTION
CAPTION "Size"
FONT 8, "MS Sans Serif"
BEGIN
        CONTROL         "&Any size",IDC_RADIO1,"Button",
                        BS_AUTORADIOBUTTON | WS_GROUP | WS_TABSTOP,
                        15,20,42,10
        CONTROL         "&Only files between:",IDC_RADIO2,"Button",
                        BS_AUTORADIOBUTTON,15,40,75,10
        EDITTEXT        IDC_EDIT1,50,60,48,16,ES_NUMBER | WS_GROUP
        CONTROL         "Spin3",IDC_SPIN1,"msctls_updown32",
                        UDS_SETBUDDYINT | UDS_ALIGNRIGHT |
                        UDS_AUTOBUDDY | UDS_ARROWKEYS,98,62,11,14
        LTEXT           "and",IDC_STATIC,111,65,13,8,NOT WS_GROUP
        EDITTEXT        IDC_EDIT2,140,60,48,16,ES_NUMBER
        CONTROL         "Spin3",IDC_SPIN2,"msctls_updown32",
                        UDS_SETBUDDYINT | UDS_ALIGNRIGHT |
                        UDS_AUTOBUDDY | UDS_ARROWKEYS,188,61,11,14
        LTEXT           "kilobytes",IDC_STATIC,201,65,31,9,
                        NOT WS_GROUP
END
```

### DirList1.h

```
// ************************************************************
//
// DirList1.h
//
// ************************************************************


class CDirListApp : public CWinApp
```

*(continued)*

**Listing 5-3.** *continued*

```
{
public:
    BOOL    InitInstance ();
};

class CAboutDlg : public CDialog
{
public:
    CAboutDlg();
};


/////////////////////////////////////////////////////////////////
// CPage1 property page

class CPage1 : public CPropertyPage
{
private:
    BOOL            bEditFocus;
    CString         strDirectory, strFilter;
    void            GetCurrentDirectory ();
    void            ShowList ();

public:
    CPage1 () : CPropertyPage( IDD_PAGE1 ) {}

protected:
    virtual void    DoDataExchange( CDataExchange* pDX );
    virtual BOOL    OnInitDialog ();
    afx_msg void    OnEditGainFocus ();
    afx_msg void    OnEditLoseFocus ();
    afx_msg void    OnUp1Level ();
    afx_msg void    OnSelChange ();
    DECLARE_MESSAGE_MAP ()
};


/////////////////////////////////////////////////////////////////
// CPage2 property page

class CPage2 : public CPropertyPage
{
public:
    int     nAnyDate;
    CTime   timeMin, timeMax;
    int     PrevDays;
    int     PrevMonths;
```

```
        CPage2 () : CPropertyPage( IDD_PAGE2 ) {}

protected:
    virtual void     DoDataExchange( CDataExchange* pDX );
    virtual BOOL     OnInitDialog ();
};

//////////////////////////////////////////////////////////////////////
// CPage3 property page

class CPage3 : public CPropertyPage
{
public:
    int      nAnySize;
    DWORD    MinSize;
    DWORD    MaxSize;

    CPage3 () : CPropertyPage( IDD_PAGE3 ) {}

protected:
    virtual void     DoDataExchange( CDataExchange* pDX );
    virtual BOOL     OnInitDialog ();
};

//////////////////////////////////////////////////////////////////////
// CListSheet

class CListSheet : public CPropertySheet
{
public:
    CPage1   page1;
    CPage2   page2;
    CPage3   page3;
    CListSheet( LPCTSTR szCaption );

protected:
    virtual BOOL OnInitDialog();
    afx_msg void OnSysCommand( UINT nID, LPARAM lParam );
    DECLARE_MESSAGE_MAP()
};
```

*(continued)*

**Listing 5-3.** *continued*

## DirList1.cpp

```cpp
// ****************************************************************
//
// DirList1.cpp
//
// ****************************************************************

#include "afxwin.h"
#include "afxdlgs.h"
#include "afxcmn.h"
#include "resource.h"
#include "dirlist1.h"

#define  DDL_ALL        DDL_DIRECTORY | DDL_DRIVES | DDL_HIDDEN

CDirListApp DirListApp;

BOOL CDirListApp::InitInstance ()
{
    CListSheet sh( "Directory List" );  // Create property sheet
    sh.DoModal ();                       //    and display dialog

    return FALSE;                        // Return FALSE to exit
}

CAboutDlg::CAboutDlg() : CDialog( IDD_ABOUTBOX )
{
}


/////////////////////////////////////////////////////////////////
// CListSheet property sheet

CListSheet::CListSheet( LPCTSTR szCaption ) :
            CPropertySheet( szCaption )
{
    AddPage( &page1 );
    AddPage( &page2 );
    AddPage( &page3 );
}

BEGIN_MESSAGE_MAP (CListSheet, CPropertySheet)
    ON_WM_SYSCOMMAND()
END_MESSAGE_MAP()
```

```
BOOL CListSheet::OnInitDialog()
{
    CPropertySheet::OnInitDialog();

    // Add "About..." command to system menu
    CMenu* pSysMenu = GetSystemMenu( FALSE );
    CString str;
    str.LoadString( IDD_ABOUTBOX );
    pSysMenu->AppendMenu( MF_SEPARATOR );
    pSysMenu->AppendMenu( MF_STRING, IDD_ABOUTBOX, str );

    // Remove Apply button, since it's not needed
    CButton* button = (CButton *) GetDlgItem( ID_APPLY_NOW );
    button->DestroyWindow();

    // Set 16-by-16 and 32-by-32 icon images
    HICON hIcon = (HICON) ::LoadImage( DirListApp.m_hInstance,
                        MAKEINTRESOURCE( IDI_APPICON ),
                        IMAGE_ICON, 16, 16, LR_DEFAULTCOLOR );
    SetIcon( hIcon, FALSE );

    return TRUE;
}

void CListSheet::OnSysCommand( UINT nID, LPARAM lParam )
{
    if (nID == IDD_ABOUTBOX)
    {
        CAboutDlg dlgAbout;
        dlgAbout.DoModal();
    }
    else
    {
        CPropertySheet::OnSysCommand( nID, lParam );
    }
}

///////////////////////////////////////////////////////////
// CPage1 property page

BOOL CPage1::OnInitDialog ()
{
    bEditFocus = FALSE;
    strFilter  = "*.*";

    GetCurrentDirectory ();
    ShowList ();
```

*(continued)*

**Listing 5-3.** *continued*

```
        return CDialog::OnInitDialog ();
}

void CPage1::GetCurrentDirectory ()
{
    PTSTR pDir = new char[MAX_PATH];

    ::GetCurrentDirectory( MAX_PATH, pDir );
    strDirectory = pDir;

    if (strDirectory.Right( 1 ) != "\\")
        strDirectory += "\\";                    // Append backslash

    delete [] pDir;
}

void CPage1::ShowList ()
{
    PTSTR pDir = new char[MAX_PATH];

    lstrcpy( pDir, strDirectory );
    lstrcat( pDir, strFilter );
    DlgDirList( pDir, IDC_LIST, IDC_DIRPATH, DDL_ALL );

    delete [] pDir;
}

BEGIN_MESSAGE_MAP (CPage1, CPropertyPage)
    ON_EN_SETFOCUS   (IDC_EDIT1, OnEditGainFocus)
    ON_EN_KILLFOCUS  (IDC_EDIT1, OnEditLoseFocus)
    ON_BN_CLICKED    (IDC_BUTTON1, OnUp1Level)
    ON_LBN_SELCHANGE (IDC_LIST, OnSelChange)
END_MESSAGE_MAP ()

void CPage1::OnEditGainFocus ()
{
    bEditFocus = TRUE;
}

void CPage1::OnEditLoseFocus ()
{
    bEditFocus = FALSE;
    GetDlgItemText( IDC_EDIT1, strFilter );
    ShowList ();
}

void CPage1::OnUp1Level ()
```

```
{
    // If Enter pressed in edit control, refresh list

    if (bEditFocus)
    {
        GetDlgItemText( IDC_EDIT1, strFilter );
        ShowList ();
    }

    // Else go up one directory level

    else
    {
        // When strDirectory == "d:\", we're already at root
        if (strDirectory.Right( 2 ) != ":\\")
        {
            // Remove '\' at end of string
            strDirectory.GetBufferSetLength(
                        strDirectory.GetLength() - 1 );
            strDirectory.ReleaseBuffer ();

            // Find last '\' and truncate strDirectory string
            int cLastSlash = strDirectory.ReverseFind( '\\' );
            if (cLastSlash != -1)
            {
                strDirectory.GetBufferSetLength( cLastSlash+1 );
                strDirectory.ReleaseBuffer ();
                ShowList ();
            }
        }
    }
}

void CPage1::OnSelChange ()
{
    char    szItem[MAX_PATH];
    char    *pItem = szItem;
    int     i;

    i = SendDlgItemMessage( IDC_LIST, LB_GETCURSEL, 0, 0 );
    SendDlgItemMessage( IDC_LIST, LB_GETTEXT, i, (LPARAM)szItem);

    // We're interested only in drives [-d-] or subdirs [subdir]
    if (szItem[0] == '[')
    {
        if (lstrcmp( szItem, "[..]" ))  // Ignore parent "[..]"
        {
```

*(continued)*

**Listing 5-3.** *continued*

```
                pItem++;                        // Skip 1st bracket '['

                // If drive, change "[-d-]" to "d:"
                if (pItem[0] == '-'  &&  pItem[2] == '-')
                {
                    pItem++;                    // Skip 1st hyphen '-'
                    pItem[1] = ':';             // Overwrite 2nd '-'
                    pItem[2] = '\0';            // Truncate string
                    strDirectory = pItem;       // New directory
                }

                // If subdir, change "[subdir]" to "subdir"
                else
                {
                    i = lstrlen( szItem );
                    pItem[i-2] = '\0';          // Truncate with NULL
                    strDirectory += pItem;      // Append new subdir
                }

                strDirectory += "\\";           // Append backslash
                ShowList ();                    // Refresh list
            }
        }
}

void CPage1::DoDataExchange( CDataExchange* pDX )
{
    CPropertyPage::DoDataExchange( pDX );
    DDX_Text( pDX, IDC_EDIT1, strFilter );
    DDV_MaxChars( pDX, strFilter, 128 );
}


/////////////////////////////////////////////////////////////////////
// CPage2 property page

BOOL CPage2::OnInitDialog ()
{
    CSpinButtonCtrl* spin;

    // Initialize variables
    nAnyDate    = 0;
    PrevDays    = 1;
    PrevMonths  = 1;
    timeMin     = 0;
    timeMax     = CTime::GetCurrentTime();
```

```
    // Set limits of spin buttons
    spin = (CSpinButtonCtrl *) GetDlgItem( IDC_SPIN1 );
    spin->SetRange( 1, 100 );                      // Within x months
    spin = (CSpinButtonCtrl *) GetDlgItem( IDC_SPIN2 );
    spin->SetRange( 1, 365 );                      // Within x days

    return CDialog::OnInitDialog ();
}

void CPage2::DoDataExchange( CDataExchange* pDX )
{
    CPropertyPage::DoDataExchange( pDX );
    DDX_DateTimeCtrl( pDX, IDC_DATETIME1, timeMin);
    DDX_DateTimeCtrl( pDX, IDC_DATETIME2, timeMax);
    DDX_Radio( pDX, IDC_RADIO1, nAnyDate );
    DDX_Text(  pDX, IDC_EDIT1, PrevMonths );
    DDX_Text(  pDX, IDC_EDIT2, PrevDays );
}


/////////////////////////////////////////////////////////////////
// CPage3 property page

BOOL CPage3::OnInitDialog ()
{
    CSpinButtonCtrl* spin;

    // Initialize variables
    nAnySize = 0;
    MinSize  = 0;
    MaxSize  = 100;

    // Set limits of spin buttons
    spin = (CSpinButtonCtrl *) GetDlgItem( IDC_SPIN1 );
    spin->SetRange( 0, 9999 );                      // Min size
    spin = (CSpinButtonCtrl *) GetDlgItem( IDC_SPIN2 );
    spin->SetRange( 1, 9999 );                      // Max size

    return CDialog::OnInitDialog ();
}

void CPage3::DoDataExchange( CDataExchange* pDX )
{
    CPropertyPage::DoDataExchange( pDX );
    DDX_Radio( pDX, IDC_RADIO1, nAnySize );
    DDX_Text(  pDX, IDC_EDIT1, MinSize );
    DDX_Text(  pDX, IDC_EDIT2, MaxSize );
}
```

The program's *InitInstance* function first creates a *CListSheet* object, which derives from MFC's *CPropertySheet* class. The *DoModal* member function displays the property sheet:

```
CListSheet sh( "Directory List" );   // Make propsheet object
sh.DoModal ();                        // and display dialog
```

When the object's *OnInitDialog* function gets control, it adds a command to the system menu that invokes the program's About box, then removes the unneeded Apply button that the framework has placed in the dialog. The *OnInitDialog* function also demonstrates how a dialog-based application can set two icon images, a small image 16 pixels square that serves as the application icon on the dialog's title bar, and a large image 32 pixels square that appears in the About box. Both images are stored in the project's DirList.ico file. The MFC framework automatically extracts the large image when it creates the application window, so DirList1 must load the small image itself by calling the *LoadImage* API function introduced in Chapter 4:

```
// Set the 16-by-16 icon image
HICON hIcon = (HICON) ::LoadImage( DirListApp.m_hInstance,
                    MAKEINTRESOURCE( IDI_APPICON ),
                    IMAGE_ICON, 16, 16, LR_DEFAULTCOLOR );
SetIcon( hIcon, FALSE );
```

Calling *LoadImage* is necessary in this case because the *LoadIcon* function recognizes only a single 32-by-32 icon image—or more correctly, an image with dimensions that match the SM_CXICON and SM_CYICON system metric values. Passing a parameter value of FALSE to the *SetIcon* function sets the small 16-by-16 image as the application icon.

By itself, a *CListSheet* object is an empty dialog window. The *CListSheet* constructor adds the three property pages by calling the *AddPage* member function. *AddPage* takes a pointer to a *CPropertyPage* object, created by passing the dialog identifier to the *CPropertyPage* base initializer. For example, here's how DirList1.h declares the *CPropertyPage* object for the first page of the property sheet:

```
public:
    CPage1 () : CPropertyPage( IDD_PAGE1 ) {}
```

The *AddPage* function takes care of translating the dialog resource into a property page with a tab that contains the dialog caption, such as Location or Size.

When the first page is ready for display, its *CPage1::OnInitDialog* function calls the *GetCurrentDirectory* API function, appends a "*.*" filter to the current path, and calls *DlgDirList* to write the directory listing to the list box. The *strFilter* string contains the filter, which the user can change through an edit control. The most interesting part of the program takes place in the *CPage1::OnSelChange* function, which gets control when the user selects an item in the list box. If the user selects a filename, the function ignores the selection. If the selected item is a disk drive, the drive designation replaces the path in *strDirectory*, which then becomes the string *d*:\, where *d* is the selected drive letter. Selecting a subdirectory in the list box appends the subdirectory name to the path in *strDirectory*. When the path changes, *OnSelChange* calls *ShowList* to display the directory listing for the new path. *OnSelChange* distinguishes between filenames, drives, and subdirectories from the way that *CWnd::DlgDirList* writes them in the list box. Drive designations are contained in square brackets and hyphens, such as "[-a-]" or "[-c-]." Subdirectories are enclosed in square brackets without the hyphens. Filenames do not have brackets or hyphens.

While calling *DlgDirList* to add the directory listing is certainly convenient, the technique suffers from two serious defects. First, the directory listing is unattractive, not at all up to current Windows standards. And second, the *DlgDirList* function recognizes long filenames only in Windows NT. To address both concerns, we have to dispense with the list box entirely and try something else. We'll do that in Chapter 7 when we create a new class derived from MFC's *CListView* and add it to Visual C++'s collection of components, called the Gallery.

But there is another subject more pressing right now than the Gallery. Some of the work done in this chapter turns out to have been unnecessary—or at least, it could have been simplified. You may recall that in building the MfcTree project, we wrote stub functions for the MfcDlg.h and MfcDlg.cpp source files and also manually inserted entries into a message map. These tasks could have been more easily handled in Class-Wizard. ClassWizard is a natural partner to the dialog editor; use the editor to design a dialog and ClassWizard to generate source code to run the dialog. The next chapter shows how.

PART

3

# Programming Assistance

# ClassWizard

After creating a project with AppWizard, you have the option of working with a Visual C++ "programmer's assistant" called ClassWizard. In a broad sense, ClassWizard has the same relationship to classes that AppWizard has to applications. ClassWizard gets you started on writing a new class by generating an implementation CPP file and a header file with appropriate stub functions. Filling in the functions with actual code is your responsibility.

ClassWizard is designed to assist in four areas, generating code for:

■ New classes derived from one of the many MFC classes that receive messages or manage control windows

■ Member functions that handle messages

■ OLE/ActiveX methods, properties, and event firing

■ Exchange and validation functions for data entered into dialog controls

ClassWizard recognizes and supports MFC base classes that interface in some way with the user. With a few exceptions such as *CRecordSet* and *CHttpServer*, the base classes are derived from *CCmdTarget*, capable of responding to messages or managing controls in a dialog box. There are over 50 MFC classes from which you can create a derived class using ClassWizard; refer to Appendix B in this book for a complete list.

# Accessing ClassWizard

You cannot access ClassWizard from an empty project. The project must have at least an RC file attached to it, even if the RC file is empty. Once the RC file is attached to a project (AppWizard does this automatically), you can invoke the ClassWizard dialog by choosing the ClassWizard command from the View menu, as shown in Figure 6-1.

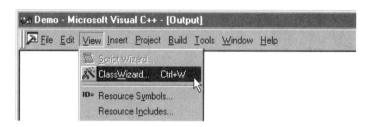

**Figure 6-1.**     *ClassWizard from the View menu.*

Two points about ClassWizard might not be obvious. First, its services are entirely optional. You can develop your project from start to finish without ever dealing with ClassWizard, if you prefer. Second, you can use ClassWizard to add new classes to an MFC project even if the project did not originate with AppWizard. ClassWizard compiles a database of the project's classes and stores it in a file that has the same name as the project with a CLW extension. If you always use ClassWizard to create new classes for the project, the CLW file remains up-to-date. However, Visual C++ does not lock you into an all-or-nothing relationship with ClassWizard, and you are free to write a new class on your own or to copy code from other source files outside the current project. In these cases where a class originates from a source other than ClassWizard, there is an easy way to update the CLW database. After you add the new class source files to the project using the Add To Project command on the Project menu, delete the CLW file and invoke ClassWizard again. Visual C++ detects that the database does not exist and offers to create it again:

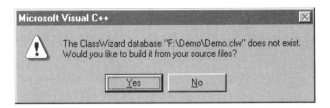

When you click Yes to accept the offer to build the new database, a dialog titled Select Source Files appears with a list of the implementation and header files that Visual C++ will read to build the class database. If you have inserted all the new source files into the project, the list should already be complete, so you need do nothing more than click OK. A progress indicator briefly indicates that Visual C++ is building the database file, after which the ClassWizard dialog appears.

# The ClassWizard Dialog

Figure 6-2 shows the main ClassWizard dialog. I call it the "main" dialog because ClassWizard can manifest itself in over 20 different dialogs, depending on circumstances. The dialog in Figure 6-2 acts as a sort of main entrance to ClassWizard, and is titled MFC ClassWizard to remind you that it deals only with MFC classes. ClassWizard won't help you create a class derived from anything other than one of the supported MFC

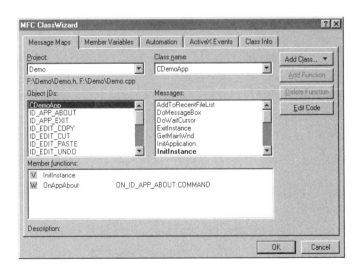

**Figure 6-2.**     *The MFC ClassWizard dialog.*

classes; for a class with any other base, you must write the code yourself from scratch using the text editor or the New Class command on the Insert menu. The New Class command is described in more detail later in the chapter.

The five tabs of the MFC ClassWizard dialog have very different purposes and are not all relevant to any one particular class. Table 6-1 can help you determine which tab (or tabs) you need, depending on what you want to do for your class.

| Tab | Purpose |
| --- | --- |
| Message Maps | Add or delete member functions that handle messages. |
| Member Variables | Add or delete member variables attached to classes that use controls. Generally, these are dialog classes derived from *CDialog*, *CPropertyPage*, *CRecordView*, or *CDaoRecordView*. |
| Automation | Add a property or method to a class that supports Automation, such as an ActiveX control class. |
| ActiveX Events | Add support for firing events, usually to a class that implements an ActiveX control. This tab is not used when developing a container application that receives a fired event. |
| Class Info | Miscellaneous information about the project's classes. |

**Table 6-1.**   *The five tabs of the MFC ClassWizard dialog box.*

The first two tabs of the ClassWizard dialog, labeled Message Maps and Member Variables, are described in the next two sections. Discussions of the Automation and ActiveX Events tabs are deferred until Chapters 8 and 9, which demonstrate how ClassWizard can help in the development of projects involving ActiveX controls.

## Message Maps Tab

The Message Maps tab is where you specify message-handling functions for your class. The two combo boxes and the first two list boxes in the tab are arranged so that each control displays a progressively higher level of detail—in other words, the contents of one control depend on the current selection in the preceding control. The Class Name combo box lists the classes of the project selected in the Project combo box; the Object IDs box shows the identifiers associated with the class selected in the Class Name box; and the Messages box displays messages and other information for the current selection in the Object IDs box. Table 6-2 shows the relationship between the item selected in the Object IDs box and the contents of the Messages box.

| Selection in Object IDs box | Contents of Messages box |
| --- | --- |
| Class name | WM_ messages and class virtual functions that handle messages. |
| Menu command identifier | ON_COMMAND and ON_UPDATE_COMMAND_UI macros for menu command messages. |
| Control identifier | Control notification messages. Reflected messages are marked with an equal sign (=) prefix. |

**Table 6-2.** *In the Message Maps tab, the selection in the Object IDs box determines the contents of the Messages box.*

When you select a message or virtual function in the Messages box, a terse description of the selected item appears at the bottom of the MFC Class-Wizard dialog. For more detailed information about the selected item, you switch to MSDN online help as described in Chapter 1, The Environment, and search the index. Unlike older versions of Visual C++, pressing the F1 key displays general information about the Messages box itself, not the selected item.

To add a message handler function to the selected class, double-click the message or virtual function in the Messages box. The Member Functions box contains a list of the current class functions, which in Figure 6-2 are *InitInstance* and *OnAppAbout*. The "W" identifies *OnAppAbout* as a function that handles a system message with a WM_ prefix, which in this case is WM_COMMAND containing the ID_APP_ABOUT menu value. The "V" identifies *InitInstance* as an overridden virtual function.

For each message handler function you add to a class, ClassWizard makes three changes to the class's source files:

- Adds a function declaration to the header file
- Adds a function definition with skeleton code to the CPP implementation file
- Adds an entry for the function to the class's message map

## Member Variables Tab

The Member Variables tab pertains to classes that use controls, which are almost always classes derived from either *CDialog*, *CPropertyPage*, *CFormView*, *CRecordView*, or *CDaoRecordView*. A class derived from one of these five MFC classes is called a dialog class because it requires an identifier for a dialog resource. The Member Variables tab is where you specify member variables that receive data from controls in the class's dialog.

To add a member variable to a dialog class, expose the Member Variables tab and select the class from the Class Name box. In the Control IDs box, select the identifier of the control to which you want to attach the new variable, then click the Add Variable button to open the Add Member Variable dialog shown in Figure 6-3.

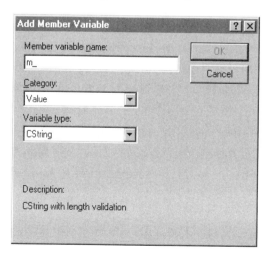

**Figure 6-3.**    *The Add Member Variable dialog box, invoked from the Member Variables tab.*

Type the variable name after the optional "m_" prefix and, depending on the control type, select either Value or Control in the Category box. The Value setting means that the variable contains the control's data, such as the text or numerical value that the user types into an edit box. The Control setting means that the variable represents the control itself. As an example, consider a member variable for a check box control. Selecting the Value category makes the member variable Boolean, able to contain a value of TRUE or FALSE that indicates the state of the check box. Selecting the Control category, however, makes the variable a *CButton* object that represents the check box control. If you want to use the variable to determine whether the user has turned the check box on or off, select the Value category. Select the Control category if you want to use the variable to alter the check box in some way at run time, such as changing its caption by calling *CButton::SetWindowText* or setting the check box state by calling *CButton::SetCheck*.

Table 6-3, on the next page, lists the available variable types for standard controls. Here are some points to keep in mind as you read the table:

■ Edit boxes are especially adept at passing data to variables of many different types. The "numerical" data type mentioned in the table is a catch-all term that includes BYTE, **short**, **int**, UINT, **long**, DWORD, **float**, and **double**.

■ ClassWizard does not list static controls identified by the generic IDC_STATIC value. To associate a static control with a variable, first assign the control an identifier other than IDC_STATIC.

■ Of a group of radio buttons, only the identifier for the group's first button appears in the Control IDs box. The reason why other buttons of the group are not included will become clear later in the chapter when we discuss how a single variable associated with the group's first button represents the entire group.

■ As indicated in the table, push button controls do not allow variables of the Value category, because these controls do not accept data from the user.

| Control | Data type | |
| | Value category | Control category |
| --- | --- | --- |
| Check box | BOOL | *CButton* |
| Check box (3-state) | **int** | *CButton* |
| Combo box | *CString* or **int** | *CComboBox* |
| Edit box | *CString*, BOOL, numerical, *COleDateTime* or *COleCurrency* | *CEdit* |
| List box | *CString* or **int** | *CListBox* |
| Push button | | *CButton* |
| Radio button | **int** | *CButton* |
| Scroll bar | **int** | *CScrollBar* |
| Static text | *CString* | *CStatic* |

**Table 6-3.**  *Variable types of the Value and Control categories for standard controls.*

By using ClassWizard to add member variables to a dialog class, you take advantage of a terrific labor-saving feature that ClassWizard provides free: automatic generation of source code for dialog data exchange and dialog data validation, better known as DDX/DDV. Data exchange and validation apply only to member variables for which the Value category is selected—that is, variables that have a type listed in the middle column of Table 6-3.

Dialog data exchange takes care of getting data into and out of a control. When the dialog first appears, each control window is automatically initialized with the value of the corresponding member variable. When the user closes the dialog by clicking the OK button or by pressing the Enter key, the flow is reversed, and whatever value or text a control contains is copied back to the variable. Dialog data validation makes sure that a value falls within prescribed limits. Both the exchange and validation mechanisms are provided by the MFC framework through a collection of functions listed in Tables 6-4 and 6-5. Each function has a prefix of *DDX_* or *DDV_* to identify it as a function for either data exchange or data validation.

| Exchange function | Gets/sets data of this type... | ...for a control of this type |
|---|---|---|
| DDX_CBIndex | int | Combo box |
| DDX_CBString | CString | Combo box |
| DDX_CBStringExact | CString | Combo box |
| DDX_Check | int | Check box |
| DDX_DateTimeCtrl | CTime | Date-time picker |
| DDX_LBIndex | int | List box |
| DDX_LBString | CString | List box |
| DDX_LBStringExact | CString | List box |
| DDX_MonthCalCtrl | CTime | Month calendar |
| DDX_Radio | int | Radio button |
| DDX_Scroll | int | Scroll bar |
| DDX_Text | CString or numerical (BYTE, **short**, **int**, UINT, **long**, etc.) | Edit control |

**Table 6-4.** *Common dialog data exchange functions.*

### Dialog data exchange (DDX)

MFC provides a variety of dialog data exchange functions that move data between controls and member variables in a dialog class. Along with the common functions listed in Table 6-4, there are specialized exchange functions for recordset data and data returned by ActiveX controls. The *DDX_Control* function transfers data for several different types of controls, such as Animate and IP Address. For detailed information about the data exchange functions, consult Visual C++ online help.

The *DDX_Radio* function listed in Table 6-4 warrants a little more discussion. This function is unique among the data exchange functions in that it applies to a group of controls rather than a single control. *DDX_Radio* returns an **int** value that indicates which radio button of a group the user has turned on—0 for the first button of the group, 1 for the second button, and so forth. A value of -1 means that all of the buttons in the group are clear. You can call *DDX_Radio* to determine the state of a single radio button provided it is the only button in the group. In this case, a returned value of 0 means the button is on, and a value of -1 means the button is off. Setting up a group of radio buttons is usually done in the dialog editor, as we'll see in a moment.

### Dialog data validation (DDV)

Table 6-5 lists the eight dialog data validation functions, which apply only to member variables for controls that accept data entered from the keyboard—namely, edit controls and combo boxes.

| Validation function | Verifies that... |
| --- | --- |
| *DDV_MinMaxByte* | A BYTE value is within specified limits. |
| *DDV_MinMaxInt* | An **int** value is within specified limits. |
| *DDV_MinMaxUInt* | A UINT value is within specified limits. |
| *DDV_MinMaxLong* | A **long** value is within specified limits. |
| *DDV_MinMaxDWord* | A DWORD value is within specified limits. |
| *DDV_MinMaxFloat* | A **float** value is within specified limits. |
| *DDV_MinMaxDouble* | A **double** value is within specified limits. |
| *DDV_MaxChars* | The length of a *CString* string does not exceed a specified maximum. |

**Table 6-5.**   *Dialog data validation functions.*

When you add a member variable for an edit control or combo box and then select the control in the Control IDs box in the Member Variables tab, one of two prompts appears at the bottom of the tab. The prompt depends on whether the variable holds numerical or text data; in either case, enter the variable's limiting values for validation:

Minimum/maximum limits of a number                Maximum string length

| Description: | int with validation |
| --- | --- |
| Minimum Value: | |
| Maximum Value: | |

| Description: | CString with length validation |
| --- | --- |
| Maximum Characters: | |

All but one of the dialog data validation functions monitor numerical data, ensuring that a value entered by the user falls between specified minimum and maximum limits. The exception is the *DDV_MaxChars* function, which verifies that the number of characters typed into an edit control or combo box does not exceed a given maximum. Unlike the exchange functions listed in Table 6-4, the validation functions take action only when the dialog is closed, not when it first appears. If a value entered in a control falls outside the specified limits, the validation function for the control displays a message box informing the user of the problem. When the message box is dismissed, the offending control has focus, signaling the user to re-enter the data. The user cannot close the dialog by clicking OK unless all the data validation functions are satisfied.

### The *DoDataExchange* function

ClassWizard adds a member function called *DoDataExchange* to the dialog class's CPP file. This function contains all the calls to the data exchange and validation functions that the dialog requires. For a single edit control that accepts an integer from 1 through 99, for example, ClassWizard writes a *DoDataExchange* function that looks like this:

```
void CDemoDlg::DoDataExchange(CDataExchange* pDX)
{
    CDialog::DoDataExchange(pDX);
    //{{AFX_DATA_MAP(CDemoDlg)
    DDX_Text(pDX, IDC_EDIT, m_nEditVal);
    DDV_MinMaxInt(pDX, m_nEditVal, 1, 99);
    //}}AFX_DATA_MAP
}
```

*DoDataExchange* is a complete function, not stub code to which you must make further additions. Since the framework calls *DoDataExchange* when the dialog both begins and ends, it is sometimes convenient to add initialization and clean-up code to it, but otherwise you can usually forget that the function exists. If you delete a variable in the Member Variables tab, ClassWizard removes any data exchange and validation calls for the variable in the *DoDataExchange* function.

ClassWizard and AppWizard write a *DoDataExchange* function for every dialog in a project, even dialogs that have no controls that accept user input. For instance, the About box class generated by AppWizard has a *DoDataExchange* function even though none of the dialog's controls—an icon, two lines of static text, and a push button—can receive data from the user. If you want a control to merely display data without allowing the user to change a value, you should delete any of the control's DDX/DDV function calls that ClassWizard adds to *DoDataExchange*. Another option is to remove the *DoDataExchange* function entirely, as we'll see in an example later in the chapter.

When creating a dialog, you should be thinking early in the design process about how the dialog's class will incorporate dialog data exchange and validation. As you may recall from Chapter 5, the dialog editor allows you to set properties of each control by turning appropriate check boxes on or off in the control's Properties box. When setting properties for a control that uses dialog data exchange and validation, keep these points in mind:

- For an edit control that accepts only simple integers of decimal base (rather than hexadecimal base), set the Number check box in the Styles tab of the Edit Properties dialog. This gives the control a style flag of ES_NUMBER, causing it to ignore any character that is not a digit from 0 through 9, including commas and periods.

- If a combo box or list box accepts only freeform numerical data, access the control's Properties dialog and turn off its sorting option. For a combo box and normal list box, clear the Sort property check box in the Styles tab; for a list control, make sure the Sort selection is *None* in the Styles tab. Because these controls sort numbers by the ASCII values of the digits, not numerical values, they sort a list of numbers correctly only when entries have a fixed number of digits and include leading zeros, such as 001 and 099.

- When you create a group of radio buttons, set the Auto property for each button in the group. This makes the radio buttons mutually exclusive so that clicking one button automatically clears all others in the group.

- Set the Group property only for the first radio button of a group and ensure all other buttons in the group follow the first in sequential tabbing order. Failure to do so disables the dialog's ability to move focus from one radio button to the next as the user presses the arrow keys. Also set the Group property for the control that immediately follows the last radio button of a group. This signals the end of the previous group and the beginning of another. Running the program in the debugger will tell you when a group of radio buttons is not properly delimited by Group properties, because when the dialog appears the debugger displays this message in the Output window:

*Warning: skipping non-radio button in group.*

## Adding a Class to a Project

All five of the MFC ClassWizard dialog tabs have an Add Class button, so you can start a new class from any tab in the dialog. After clicking the Add Class button, select one of these two options for the class's origin:

- **New**—Create a new CPP file and H file that contain the skeleton source code generated by ClassWizard.

- **From a type library**—Create source code for a class based on an OLE type library. The type library can be a stand-alone file, usually with a TLB extension, or it can be contained as resource data within a program such as a dynamic link library. The dynamic link library usually has an extension of OLB (object library), OCX (ActiveX control), or DLL. For example, choosing any of the ActiveX controls described in Chapter 8 adds class source code to your project generated from the type library information in the OCX file. After you locate and select the desired type library file, select a class from among the list of classes that ClassWizard garners from information in the library and displays in the Confirm Classes dialog. If you wish to rename the selected class for the current project, enter a new name in the Class Name control. You can also specify the names of the CPP and H files that ClassWizard creates.

Both options automatically update the CLW database for the new class. To create a new class by copying an existing class from another project, three different methods are available. The most direct way to borrow an existing class is to copy the source code to your project folder and add the CPP file to the project using the Add To Project command. Click Files in the pop-up secondary menu, then double-click the class's CPP file in the list of files. As mentioned in the previous chapter, it isn't necessary to add the header file the same way because Visual C++ recognizes the header file as a dependency. The second method requires inserting an existing project by choosing the Insert Project Into Workspace command from the Project menu. You can then freely borrow source files from the inserted project. The third method for importing an existing class is through the Gallery, which is discussed in Chapter 7.

Rather than adding an existing class from a type library, you will probably most often select the New option to have ClassWizard start a new derived class that you want to develop. Clicking New displays the New Class dialog shown in Figure 6-4, in which you enter a name for your class and select its base from among the MFC classes that ClassWizard supports.

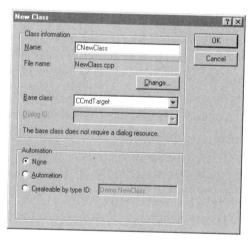

**Figure 6-4.**    *The New Class dialog invoked from ClassWizard.*

To name the class source files, ClassWizard adds CPP and H file extensions to the class name you specify, minus any "C" prefix. If you prefer another name for either file, click the Change button.

Whether the Dialog ID control is active in the New Class dialog depends on the selected base class. When you select as the base one of the five MFC dialog classes (*CDialog, CPropertyPage, CFormView, CRecordView,* or *CDaoRecordView*), the Dialog ID control becomes active, prompting for the resource identifier of the dialog associated with the new class. The best way to create a dialog-based class is to first design and save the dialog resource in the dialog editor and then, while the editor is still active and has input focus, access ClassWizard to create the new class for the dialog. We'll do exactly that for an example later in the chapter.

The appearance of the radio buttons in the Automation group box depends on whether the selected base class supports Automation. When you select a base class such as *CHttpFilter*, a discreet message informs you that Automation is not an option. For base classes that are Automation-aware, however, the Automation radio button is enabled. Turning on this button directs ClassWizard to write code to the generated source files that makes the new class a programmable object, visible to Automation client applications such as Microsoft Excel. Appendix B in this book identifies which MFC classes are Automation-aware. If you would like more information about Automation, *Inside Visual C++* by David Kruglinski devotes a lucid chapter to the subject, complete with references to ClassWizard.

Clicking the Createable By Type ID radio button generates code that allows other ActiveX applications to create an Automation object of your new class. ClassWizard automatically combines the names of the project and the class to form the type identifier shown in the edit control, a scheme that helps ensure the identifier is unique. The type identifier, also known as the programmatic identifier, can be used by an ActiveX client application to specify the object. An Excel macro, for example, can create an object of *CNewClass* like this:

```
Set DemoObj = CreateObject( "Demo.NewClass" )
```

### Adding a non-MFC class

The ClassWizard dialog is not your only means of adding a class to a project. Clicking the New Class command on the Insert menu displays the dialog shown in Figure 6-5 on the next page, which shares the same name as and looks very similar to the dialog pictured in Figure 6-4. The only difference is the addition of the Class Type box at the top of the dialog, indicating the dual nature of the New Class command.

The default selection for the class type is MFC Class, which causes the dialog to behave identically to the New Class dialog of Figure 6-4. Choose a base MFC class in the Base Class control and set the Automation radio buttons, just as before. To create a new form-based class, select Form Class in the Class Type box, and then choose a base class of either *CFormView*, *CDialog*, *CRecordView*, or *CDaoRecordView*. The third alternative for class type is Generic Class, which causes Visual C++ to generate stub code for a class not derived from MFC. Visual C++ is only borrowing technology from ClassWizard for this feat, and if you prefer to see the New Class command as just another part of ClassWizard, I won't disagree. But keep in mind that the variation of the New Class dialog pictured in Figure 6-4 is only for classes derived from MFC, to which you can always apply the full potential of ClassWizard, a tool designed from the ground up for MFC. Creating a generic, non-MFC class with the New Class command generates stub code, but otherwise orphans the class from the other features of ClassWizard.

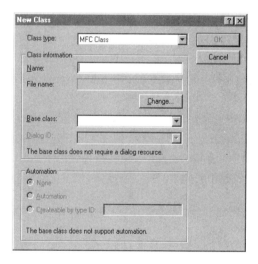

**Figure 6-5.**    *The New Class dialog, accessed by choosing the New Class command from the Insert menu.*

The Generic Class setting in the dialog enables a list box from which you can select a base for the new class. The generated source code consists of only stub functions for the class constructor and destructor, contained in a CPP file and H file named for the class. For example, here's the declaration that the New Class command writes to the header file for a class derived from the fictitious *CBaseClass*:

```
class CDerivedClass : public CBaseClass
{
public:
    CDerivedClass();
    virtual ~CDerivedClass();
};
```

Visual C++ offers other offshoots of ClassWizard besides the New Class command. As we'll see next, the WizardBar acts as a sort of side door to ClassWizard that is often more convenient than the main entrance.

# The WizardBar

The WizardBar is a dockable toolbar that tracks the caret position or current selection as you move around in the text and dialog editors. The bar continually adjusts its appearance and options to reflect whatever class you are currently dealing with. Opening the implementation file for the *CMainFrame* class, for example, automatically initializes the WizardBar for that class, offering a convenient means of quickly navigating to declarations and definitions of member functions. Turn the WizardBar on and off as you would any of the other Visual C++ toolbars, by clicking the Customize command on the Tools menu and selecting the appropriate check box in the Toolbars tab.

Figure 6-6 shows a typical view of the WizardBar.

**Figure 6-6.** *The WizardBar.*

The WizardBar's three combo boxes encapsulate information displayed in the Message Maps tab of the MFC ClassWizard dialog, and any changes made in ClassWizard are instantly reflected in the WizardBar. Table 6-6 on the next page describes the WizardBar's boxes and buttons.

The arrow button at the far right of the WizardBar displays the drop-down menu of options shown in Figure 6-7 on page 283.

| WizardBar control | Description |
|---|---|
| Classes | Displays the name of the class currently open in the editor and provides a drop-down list of all classes in the project. Entries in the box are grayed when neither the text editor nor the dialog editor has focus. |
| Identifiers | Lists symbol identifiers used by the current class. (The name of the current class appears in the WizardBar's Classes box.) |
| Functions | Contains the names of virtual functions and *CCmdTarget* procedures for the current class. |
| Default | Clicking the "wand" icon at the far right of the WizardBar executes the default command of the WizardBar menu. The default command depends on the current document and selections in the WizardBar. For example, if the class implementation file is open in the text editor and the caret is inside a function block, the default action is Go To Function Declaration, which opens the class header file and positions the caret at the function's prototype. The default action then changes to Go To Function Definition, sending the caret back to the implementation CPP file. The default action is always the first command listed on the WizardBar menu, shown in Figure 6-7. |
| Menu | Displays the WizardBar menu of available options, described in the bulleted list beginning on the next page. |

**Table 6-6.**    *Controls on the WizardBar.*

The contents of the menu reflect the document currently active, so commands such as Go To Next Function are available only when a source document is open in the text editor. In the following descriptions of the menu commands, the word "current" refers to settings in the WizardBar. The current class, for instance, is the class displayed in the WizardBar's Classes box, shown in Figure 6-6.

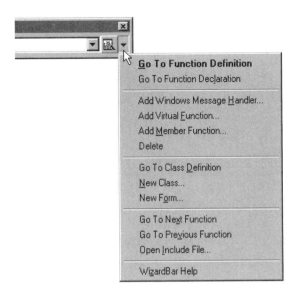

**Figure 6-7.** *The WizardBar menu, displayed by clicking the arrow button on the WizardBar.*

■ **Go To Function Definition**—Opens the source CPP file if necessary and places the caret at the first line of the current function, identified in the WizardBar's Functions box.

■ **Go To Function Declaration**—Places the caret at the prototype of the current function.

■ **Add Windows Message Handler**—Invokes the New Windows Message Handler dialog. This dialog lets you quickly add a stub message handler function to a window class descended from *CWnd*.

■ **Add Virtual Function**—Overrides a virtual function of the base class. This command displays two lists, one containing virtual functions that are available for overriding, and the other showing those functions already overridden by the current class. The lists provide the same information as the Messages box in the MFC ClassWizard dialog, but are easier to use and more convenient to navigate.

■ **Add Member Function**—Adds a stub member function to the current class. Enter the function's return type, declaration, and access label as shown on the next page.

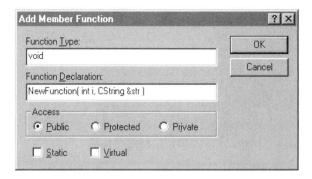

When you click the OK button, Visual C++ adds both declaration and definition code for the new function to the class source files:

```
// In the class header file
public:
    void NewFunction( int i, CString &str );

// In the class CPP implementation file
void CMainFrame::NewFunction( int i, CString &str )
{
}
```

- **Delete**—Removes the current function from the class's source. After querying for confirmation, Visual C++ deletes the function's declaration and comments out the implementation code. The editor's Undo command cannot restore a deleted function.

- **Go To Class Definition**—Places the caret at the implementation of the current class's constructor function.

- **New Class**—Equivalent to the New Class command on the Insert menu (described on page 279 in the section "Adding a non-MFC class").

- **New Form**—Displays the New Form dialog, which generates stub code for a new form-based class derived from *CFormView*, *CDialog*, *CRecordView*, or *CDaoRecordView*. This produces the same results as selecting the Form Class type in the New Class dialog.

- **Go To Next/Previous Function**—In an implementation file, sends the caret forward or backward to the next function definition. In a header file, sends the caret to the adjacent function declaration.

- **Open Include File**—Scans the current document for **#include** statements, then presents a list of all included files. To open a file in the text editor, double-click its filename in the list.

- **WizardBar Help**—Displays a topic titled "Overview: WizardBar" in the MSDN Help window. From there you can jump to other topics pertaining to the WizardBar.

The WizardBar provides quick access to ClassWizard and is a convenient alternative to the ClassWizard dialogs. Once you know the ins and outs of ClassWizard, the features of the WizardBar will seem familiar. Although this chapter concentrates on accessing ClassWizard through its various dialogs, the information applies equally to the WizardBar tools.

# How ClassWizard Recognizes Classes

The CLW database file is in ASCII text form, so you might be interested in reading through it, using the text editor. The database itemizes each class in the project, keeping a record of the class's base and source files. Resource data such as dialogs, menus, and accelerators are also itemized in the file along with their identifiers.

To construct the CLW database file, Visual C++ scans every source file attached to the project looking for special commented lines. You've seen these comments before in AppWizard programs; they begin either with //{{ or //}}, acting as brackets that mark declarations, message map entries, and other code pertaining to class members. The comments have no purpose other than identifying class information for inclusion in the CLW database. If you write a class without ClassWizard but later want to use ClassWizard to add other functions or data to the class, you must include the commented lines as described below. Otherwise, the comments are not necessary.

Each comment delimiter contains one of the thirteen keywords listed in Table 6-7 on the next page. Most of the keywords are used in pairs, one keyword marking a declaration in the class's header file while its counterpart, which has a _MAP suffix, marks a corresponding entry in a message map in the CPP file. For example, here's how Visual C++ recognizes a message handler function in a class named *CDemoApp*, derived from

| Keyword | File | Description |
|---|---|---|
| AFX_DATA | H | Member variable declaration for dialog data exchange |
| AFX_DATA_INIT | CPP | Initialization of a dialog data exchange member variable in a dialog class's constructor |
| AFX_DATA_MAP | CPP | Dialog data exchange call in a dialog class's *DoDataExchange* function |
| AFX_DISP | H | Automation declaration |
| AFX_DISP_MAP | CPP | Automation mapping |
| AFX_EVENT | H | ActiveX event declaration |
| AFX_EVENT_MAP | CPP | ActiveX event mapping |
| AFX_FIELD | H | Declaration of a member variable used for database record field exchange |
| AFX_FIELD_INIT | CPP | Initialization of a record field exchange member variable in a recordset class's constructor |
| AFX_FIELD_MAP | CPP | Record field exchange call in a recordset class's *DoFieldExchange* member function |
| AFX_MSG | H | Prototype for a function that appears in a message map |
| AFX_MSG_MAP | CPP | Message map entry |
| AFX_VIRTUAL | H | Declaration of a virtual function override |

**Table 6-7.** *Comment keywords required by ClassWizard.*

MFC's *CWinApp*. In the CPP implementation file, the special AFX_MSG_MAP comments bracket a message map entry for the handler function *CDemoApp::OnAppAbout*, making the entry recognizable to ClassWizard:

```
BEGIN_MESSAGE_MAP(CDemoApp, CWinApp)
    //{{AFX_MSG_MAP(CDemoApp)
    ON_COMMAND(ID_APP_ABOUT, OnAppAbout)
    //}}AFX_MSG_MAP
END_MESSAGE_MAP()
```

ClassWizard also needs to read the function's prototype, so the *OnAppAbout* declaration in the header file is marked with corresponding AFX_MSG comments:

```
public:
    //{{AFX_MSG(CDemoApp)
    afx_msg void OnAppAbout();
    //}}AFX_MSG
    DECLARE_MESSAGE_MAP()
```

With this information recorded in the CLW database, ClassWizard knows that the *CDemoApp* class contains a member function named *OnAppAbout* that is called when the program receives an ID_APP_ABOUT identifier contained in a WM_COMMAND message. The *afx_msg* prefix in the function prototype is included for the benefit of ClassWizard; otherwise, it is not required.

ClassWizard and AppWizard automatically add the correct delimiter comments when generating source code, insulating you from these details. But if you want to use ClassWizard in a project that did not originate with AppWizard, Table 6-7 shows how to convert existing class source files to make them recognizable to ClassWizard. The table describes the types of functions and declarations marked by the comment keywords and indicates in which source file a keyword is used.

# Creating a Dialog Class with ClassWizard

After designing a new dialog resource for an MFC program, you must also provide a class derived from *CDialog* (or one of the other dialog-based classes) to display the dialog and respond to its messages. Usually, ClassWizard is your next logical step after finishing with the dialog editor. We might well have used ClassWizard, for example, when writing the Mfc-Tree program in Chapter 5. Recall that MfcTree displays a simple dialog containing a tree list of some MFC classes. In Chapter 5 we wrote a class called *CMfcDlg* to run the dialog, first using the text editor to write skeleton implementation and header files named MfcDlg.cpp and MfcDlg.h, then adding the files to the project by choosing the Add To Project command from the Insert menu. ClassWizard can take care of both steps.

As a demonstration, let's back up and create the skeleton MfcDlg.cpp and MfcDlg.h files again, this time using ClassWizard instead of writing the files from scratch in the text editor. To get a clear idea of the work that ClassWizard automates, you might want to review the short section titled "Add Source Files for the *CMfcDlg* Dialog Class" beginning on page 239 in Chapter 5. That section describes the third of the five steps used to build MfcTree.exe.

In beginning this exercise, assume that MfcTree's dialog has just been created and saved in the dialog editor. With the IDD_MFC_DIALOG resource still open in the dialog editor, click ClassWizard on the View menu. Class-Wizard detects the new dialog resource and asks if you would like to create a new class for it:

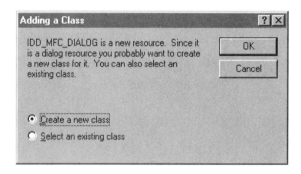

It's possible to add a class for which the source code already exists. For example, you might have already written the dialog class before you created and saved the resource in the dialog editor. In that case, you would click the Select An Existing Class radio button to attach the dialog to the class and prevent ClassWizard from generating new CPP and H source files. For this demonstration, however, the default Create A New Class radio button is the right choice since the *CMfcDlg* class doesn't exist yet.

Clicking the OK button opens the familiar New Class dialog. Enter *CMfc-Dlg* in the Name box to give a name to the new class. Skip the Change button to accept the default names of MfcDlg.cpp and MfcDlg.h that Class-Wizard proposes for the source files. Because it knows we are creating a class for the new dialog, ClassWizard has already selected *CDialog* as the base class. It has also filled in the Dialog ID box with the dialog identifier

IDD_MFC_DIALOG, which the dialog editor wrote to the MfcTree.rc file. Figure 6-8 shows what the New Class dialog should look like.

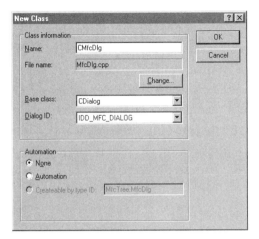

**Figure 6-8.** *Creating the new* CMfcDlg *class in ClassWizard's New Class dialog.*

Click the OK button to close the New Class dialog and uncover the MFC ClassWizard dialog shown in Figure 6-9. This is where you generate skeleton code for the new *CMfcDlg* class. *CMfcDlg* needs only an *OnInitDialog* function, which gets control just before the IDD_MFC_DIALOG dialog

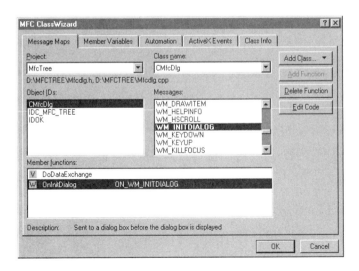

**Figure 6-9.** *Adding the* OnInitDialog *member function to the* CMfcDlg *class.*

appears. In the Object IDs box, select *CMfcDlg*, and then double-click WM_INITDIALOG in the Messages box to add the *OnInitDialog* function.

The names of the two member functions that ClassWizard creates appear in the Member Functions box at the bottom of the dialog. The selected item in the box indicates that the ON_WM_INITDIALOG message map macro is responsible for routing control to the *OnInitDialog* function when the program receives a WM_INITDIALOG message. The items in the *CMfcDlg* tree view do not change, so the *DoDataExchange* function is not needed. If you want to delete *DoDataExchange*, select it in the Member Functions box and click the Delete Function button. Doing so, however, removes only the function prototype from the MfcDlg.h header file:

```
//{{AFX_VIRTUAL(CMfcDlg)
protected:
virtual void DoDataExchange(CDataExchange* pDX);     // DDX/DDV support
//}}AFX_VIRTUAL
```

The *DoDataExchange* source code still exists untouched in the MfcDlg.cpp file, because ClassWizard deletes only code within comment delimiters, never implementation code. A message reminds you of this fact:

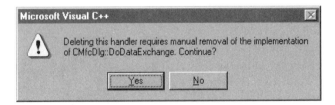

If you click the Yes button, you enter into an agreement with ClassWizard that you will delete the *DoDataExchange* source code yourself in the text editor. Otherwise, you run the risk of defining *DoDataExchange* twice if you later decide to add the function back to the MfcDlg.cpp file. When ClassWizard adds a new member function, it doesn't scan the file first to see if the function already exists—it just writes the new function shell:

```
void CMfcDlg::DoDataExchange(CDataExchange* pDX)
{
    CDialog::DoDataExchange(pDX);
}
```

Failure to delete the original implementation of *DoDataExchange* results in a compiler error, because the compiler won't accept two definitions of the same function.

When you exit the MFC ClassWizard dialog, ClassWizard adds the new MfcDlg.cpp and MfcDlg.h files to the project, both of which contain stub functions for the *CMfcDlg* class. Once you add code to the class's *OnInit-Dialog* function as described in Chapter 5, the new files are functionally equivalent to the ones written from scratch and are much easier to create. If you would like to compare the new source code with the old, you can find the original MfcDlg source files in the Chapter.05\MfcTree folder on the companion CD. The corresponding MfcDlg.cpp and MfcDlg.h files generated with the help of ClassWizard are in the Chapter.06\MfcTree folder.

# The Gallery

The Gallery is a sort of toolbox into which Microsoft has placed an assortment of "canned code" called components that you can add to your own projects. You can also use the Gallery to warehouse any of your own classes that you might want to later reuse. The Gallery holds three main types of components: source code, dialog resources, and ActiveX controls. Through the Gallery, you can browse your hard disk or network for a component, and then insert it into your project with a click of the mouse. Because a component can be stored anywhere, the Gallery serves as both a personal repository for code, storing components for your own private use, and a global code pool, allowing developers linked through a network to share a communal collection of components.

The prepackaged components that come with the Gallery are stored in two folders created by the Visual C++ installation program, one folder for source code components, the other folder for ActiveX controls. The Visual C++ Components folder contains shortcuts to dynamic link libraries that automatically add source code and resources to a project. The second folder, named Registered ActiveX Controls, contains shortcut links to all the ActiveX controls registered on your system. Some of the registered controls are provided license-free with Visual C++, so you can redistribute them with your own applications. There is a lot to say about ActiveX controls, most of it not directly pertaining to the Gallery, so the subject is deferred until Part 4 of this book. This chapter focuses on how to access the Gallery and build your own collection of reusable objects.

Visual C++ is not your only available source for prepackaged components. Many vendors offer component tools in both source code and binary form, advertising in trade journals and on the Internet. Prepackaged components tend to be flashier than the ones you create yourself because they can automate the entire process of adding a component to a project. Operating as executable libraries that the Visual C++ environment loads and runs, these professional packages can insert graphics resources and rewrite a project's existing files by adding functions and #**include** statements as necessary—usually to the point where there is little or no programming left for you to do. And prepackaged components often provide their own online help.

The Gallery displays its wares in the Components And Controls Gallery dialog pictured in Figure 7-1. When a C++ project is open in the environment, you can access the Gallery dialog by resting the cursor momentarily on the Add To Project command on the Project menu. This displays a secondary drop-down menu from which you choose the Components And Controls command. If the dialog's More Info button is enabled when you select a component from the list, the component can describe itself

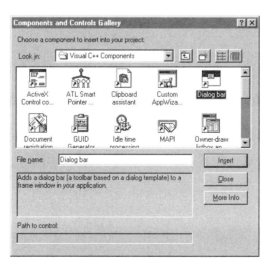

**Figure 7-1.**  *The Gallery's Visual C++ Components folder.*

through its own online help. To insert a Gallery component into your project, select its icon and click the Insert button.

In Visual C++ version 4, the Gallery (then known as Component Gallery) was apt to get crowded if you regularly created projects with AppWizard. Each time AppWizard executed, it automatically added a new category to Component Gallery and installed all project classes, such as *CMainFrame* and *CAboutDlg*, as source code components. By default, ClassWizard also added to the project category any new classes you created. The onus was on the user to occasionally clean out unwanted additions in Component Gallery, though many programmers simply ignored the expanding list of components or were unaware of what AppWizard and ClassWizard were doing behind the scenes. The entire Component Gallery database was stored in a single file called Gallery.dat, so there was no convenient way to share components with other developers.

Although the function of the Gallery in version 6 has not changed, its methods have been improved. Gallery.dat no longer exists, its database replaced by individual component files that can exist anywhere on a disk or network. And both AppWizard and ClassWizard no longer add classes to the Gallery. As we'll see in the next chapter, ActiveX controls can become part of the Gallery database without your expressed permission, but the same is not true for other component types. You must take specific steps to add a component to the Gallery, including any components you want to salvage from version 4 projects. A later section explains how to add a new component to the Gallery, but for now let's take a look at some of the prepackaged components that come with Visual C++.

# Example: Adding a Property Sheet

Chapter 5, Dialog Boxes and Controls, described how to use the dialog editor to create a property sheet dialog and incorporate it into a program. The Gallery comes with a component called Property Sheet that makes the job even easier. This section and the following section demonstrate Property Sheet and some of the other components that ship with Visual C++, first showing how to add a property sheet to a project called Gadgets, then dressing up the program even more with other code borrowed from the

Gallery. Gadgets starts out as a typical AppWizard project, then becomes more sophisticated as you add components to it. Here are the steps for setting up the project and adding the first component:

1. Choose New from the File menu to open the New dialog, and in the Projects tab choose the MFC AppWizard (exe) icon. Type *Gadgets* as the project name and click OK.

2. As AppWizard steps through its screens, select the Single Document radio button in the first step and deselect the status bar, docking toolbar, and printing support in the fourth step. Accept the default settings in the other steps.

3. When AppWizard finishes and Visual C++ opens the project, choose Add To Project from the Project menu and click the Components And Controls command on the secondary menu to display the Components And Controls Gallery dialog.

4. Open the Visual C++ Components folder in the dialog and double-click the Property Sheet component icon. (You may have to scroll through the list to find the icon.) The Gallery queries with a message box to confirm that you really want to insert the component.

5. Visual C++ loads and runs the component's executable library, which displays a dialog asking various questions about the type of property sheet you want to create. Just click the Next button to accept all the defaults. When finished, close the Gallery dialog.

You will find that the Property Sheet component has automatically placed in the Gadgets folder source files for the new property sheet class. The component has also modified four of the existing files in the Gadgets project: the Resource.h file now contains definitions required by the property sheet class; Gadgets.rc has been updated with dialog scripts for two property pages; and the MainFrm.h and MainFrm.cpp files contain new code for a function called *OnProperties*.

A "to do" comment in the *OnProperties* function explains that you must connect the function to a message handler so that the property sheet is displayed when the user clicks a menu command. This requires only two steps:

1. Add an entry for the function to the message map in MainFrm.cpp. The new map entry, shown here as a shaded line, must be inserted between the ClassWizard comment delimiters:

```
//{{AFX_MSG_MAP(CMainFrame)
ON_COMMAND (IDM_PROPSHEET, OnProperties)
//}}AFX_MSG_MAP
```

2. In the ResourceView pane of the Workspace window, expand the Menu folder and double-click the IDR_MAINFRAME menu resource to launch the menu editor. Edit the menu system so that it looks like this:

When you add the Property Sheet command to the Options menu, be sure to give it an identifier value of IDM_PROPSHEET in the Menu Item Properties dialog. This is the same identifier used in the shaded line added to the message map in the first step.

Using the Build toolbar, change the active project configuration to Win32 Release, build Gadgets.exe, and run it. Choosing the Property Sheet command from the program's Options menu displays the boilerplate property sheet dialog shown in Figure 7-2 on the next page. The two pages of the dialog are ready to be fleshed out with controls using the dialog editor. From start to finish, the whole operation takes only a few minutes. Property sheets have never been so painless.

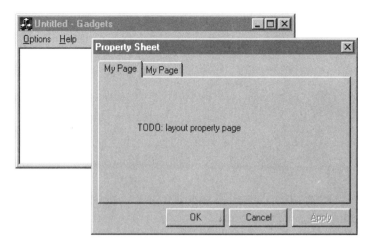

**Figure 7-2.** *The Gadgets program with its property sheet displayed.*

# Example: Adding a Splash Screen and Clock

A splash screen is a bitmap image that appears briefly at program startup. Large Windows programs (such as Visual C++ and even Windows itself) often put up a splash screen before displaying a main window while they load files and perform other initialization procedures. This not only gives the user something attractive to look at while the program is busy, it also conveys an impression of responsiveness. The Gadgets program is so small that it doesn't really need a splash screen, but that needn't stop us. Let's also add a status bar with a clock while we're at it. You won't believe how easy all this is.

The components we need, called Splash Screen and Status Bar, are identified with these large icons in the Visual C++ Components folder of the Gallery dialog:

Add each component to the open Gadgets project by double-clicking the component icon. The Status Bar component runs a dialog that lets you choose whether the new status bar displays the date and time. To include the time in the status bar, click the Use System Default radio button in the

second step. (Accept default settings for the other steps.) When you close
the Gallery, you will find code has been added to the MainFrm.cpp file
that creates a status bar with a small clock at the far right side. You need
only add this shaded line to the message map in MainFrm.cpp:

```
//{{AFX_MSG_MAP(CMainFrame)
ON_COMMAND (IDM_PROPSHEET, OnProperties)
ON_WM_CREATE ()
//}}AFX_MSG_MAP
```

The Splash Screen component provides a file named Splsh16.bmp that
contains a generic bitmap image. For a splash screen of your own design,
create a new 16-color image in the graphics editor and save it under the
same filename, overwriting the original Splsh16.bmp file. The default
duration of the splash screen display is ¾ second (750 milliseconds), but
you can change this by modifying the line

```
SetTimer(1, 750, NULL);
```

in the Splash.cpp file. To see the new components in action, rebuild the
Gadgets program and run it. Figure 7-3 shows what the new program
looks like.

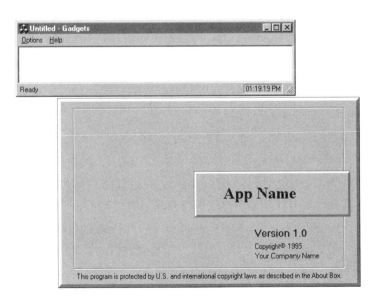

**Figure 7-3.**    *The Gadgets program with its new splash screen, status bar, and clock.*

# Creating a Custom Component

The Gallery is infinitely expandable. You can add to its collection by creating your own custom components—a dialog box, for example, or a new class. A custom component consists of source code for a class, usually a single CPP implementation file and an H header file. If the class is derived from one of the MFC dialog classes (*CDialog*, *CFormView*, *CPropertyPage*, *CRecordView*, or *CDaoRecordView*), the component also includes resource data for the dialog.

There are good reasons for saving your work as a new component. First, the Gallery serves as a convenient warehouse for reusable source code. When you develop a class for a project and save it as a component, you do not have to later pore through disk files looking for the source code to add the class to a new project. A second reason for creating new components is especially compelling for developers linked by a network, who can now add to and draw from a central data bank of components. Before developing a new class, you can check the Gallery to see whether someone has already done the work for you.

To add a component to the Gallery, right-click its class in the ClassView pane of the Workspace window and choose the Add To Gallery command from the context menu. Figure 7-4 illustrates the steps for a class named *CNewComponent*.

Clicking the Add To Gallery command creates a new subfolder if necessary in the Gallery's main folder. The subfolder has the same name as the project and contains the new component file, which has an OGX extension. The OGX component file is not a pointer to the original class source code; rather, it contains bound copies of the CPP and H text files that define the class. If the class is dialog-based, the OGX file also includes a copy of the dialog's resource script. Because the OGX file archives a complete copy of the code, a component can outlive its project. Even when project files are deleted or moved, the Gallery can always produce the original source code. This means that a component is a snapshot of code as it exists at the time you add it to the Gallery. A component is not automatically updated along with the source code; to update a component, you must add the class to the Gallery again.

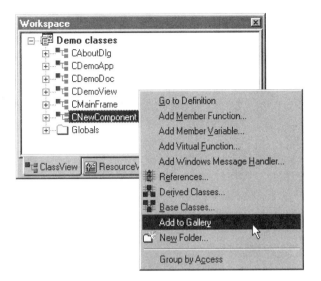

**Figure 7-4.** *Adding a class to the Gallery.*

The custom components you create have certain limitations. For one thing, the More Info button in the Gallery dialog is inactive for custom components because there is no direct way to add online help to explain how the component works. Nor can a custom component automatically modify existing source files in a project the way that the Property Sheet and Splash Screen components do. Creating professional-quality components suitable for the software market requires Microsoft's Component Builder's Kit, which lets you create executable components that can use the online help system. Microsoft does not charge for the kit, but currently it is available only to software companies, not to individuals. To request a copy of the Builder's Kit, send an inquiry on your company's letterhead to:

> Visual C++ Manager
> Microsoft Corporation
> One Microsoft Way
> Redmond, WA 98052-6399

## Example: A Custom Component for Directory Listings

This section demonstrates the process of creating a custom component, first outlining a new class named *CDirListCtrl* and then adding it to the

Gallery. Derived from MFC's *CListCtrl* class, *CDirListCtrl* displays a directory listing in a list view common control, attaching small icons that help the eye quickly distinguish between drives, folders, and files (Figure 7-5). Clicking a drive or folder in the list automatically changes the path and refreshes the list. And because *CDirListCtrl* does not use the *DlgDirList* API function, it correctly displays long filenames in Windows 95. If this seems like something we could have used in Chapter 5 for the DirList1 program, you're right. A later section shows how to add the *CDirListCtrl* custom component to create a new version of the program called DirList2.

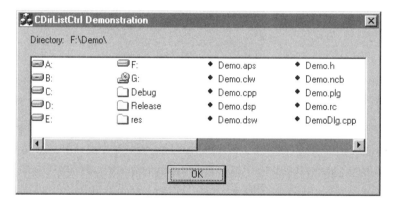

**Figure 7-5.** *The* CDirListCtrl *list view control in a typical dialog box.*

Listing 7-1 shows the source code for the *CDirListCtrl* class, contained in the DirCtrl.h and DirCtrl.cpp files located in the Code\Chapter.07\DirCtrl folder on the companion CD. *CDirListCtrl* contains five public member functions, three of which are declared inline in the DirCtrl.h header file. Of the other two public functions, *Create* sets up the list view control and *ShowList* refreshes the directory listing in the control. The path of the displayed directory is stored in the private *strDirectory* string. Changing the listing is a two-step procedure in which the creator of the *CDirListCtrl* object first calls the *SetPath* function to change the directory path, and then calls *ShowList* to display the new directory.

**Listing 7-1.** *Source files for the* CDirListCtrl *class.*

### DirCtrl.h

```
// **********************************************************
//
// DirCtrl.h
//
// **********************************************************

#define DL_DRIVE        1
#define DL_FOLDER       2
#define DL_FILE         4
#define DL_ALL          7

typedef BOOL (CALLBACK *PCALLBACK)( PWIN32_FIND_DATA );

class CDirListCtrl : public CListCtrl
{
private:
    int         iListFlags, idcPath;
    CString     strDirectory, strFilter;
    CListBox    listDummy;
    CImageList  imageList;
    CDialog*    pDialog;

    BOOL        FindFiles( DWORD dwFlags );
    void        GetCurrentDirectory ();
    PCALLBACK   pCallBack;

public:
    BOOL    ShowList( CString& Filter );
    void    GetPath( CString& strPath ) {strPath = strDirectory;}
    void    SetPath( CString& strPath ) {strDirectory = strPath;}
    void    SetCallBack( PCALLBACK pCB ) {pCallBack = pCB;}
    void    Create( CDialog* pDlg, LPRECT prect, int idcControl,
                int idcStatic, int iFlags=DL_ALL, int idiIcon=0 );

protected:
    BOOL        GetDirectoryList( int iType );
    afx_msg void OnSelChange( NMHDR* pnumhdr, LRESULT* pResult );

    DECLARE_MESSAGE_MAP ()
};
```

*(continued)*

**Listing 7-1.** *continued*

## DirCtrl.cpp

```cpp
// ****************************************************************
//
// DirCtrl.cpp
//
// ****************************************************************

#include "afxcmn.h"
#include "dirctrl.h"
#define IDC_DUMMY        48888

void CDirListCtrl::Create( CDialog* pDlg, LPRECT prect,
                           int idcControl, int idcStatic,
                           int iFlags, int idiIcon )
{
    pDialog   = pDlg;                 // Save ptr to dialog object
    idcPath   = idcStatic;            // Save ID of static control
    pCallBack = NULL;                 // Assume no call-back

    // Create DirListCtrl control
    if (!CreateEx( WS_EX_CLIENTEDGE, WC_LISTVIEW, NULL,
            LVS_LIST | LVS_SINGLESEL | LVS_ALIGNLEFT |
            WS_VISIBLE | WS_CHILD, prect->left, prect->top,
            prect->right, prect->bottom,
            pDialog->m_hWnd, (HMENU) idcControl ))
    {
        MessageBox( "Failed to create DirListCtrl" );
        return;
    }

    // Associate "file", "folder", and "drive" icons with control
    imageList.Create( 16, 16, TRUE, 1, 0 );
    if (idiIcon)
    {
        imageList.Add( AfxGetApp()->LoadIcon( idiIcon ) );
        imageList.Add( AfxGetApp()->LoadIcon( idiIcon + 1 ) );
        imageList.Add( AfxGetApp()->LoadIcon( idiIcon + 2 ) );
        imageList.Add( AfxGetApp()->LoadIcon( idiIcon + 3 ) );
        imageList.Add( AfxGetApp()->LoadIcon( idiIcon + 4 ) );
    }
    SetImageList( &imageList, LVSIL_SMALL );

    // Create dummy list box
    CRect rectDummy;
    rectDummy.SetRectEmpty ();
```

```
        listDummy.Create( WS_CHILD | LBS_SORT, rectDummy,
                           pDialog, IDC_DUMMY );

    // Start with current directory
    GetCurrentDirectory ();
    iListFlags = iFlags;
}

BOOL CDirListCtrl::ShowList( CString& Filter )
{
    static int  iType[3] = { DL_DRIVE, DL_FOLDER, DL_FILE };
    BOOL        bRetCode = FALSE;
    int         i, j, n, nIcon, nItem = 0;
    UINT        uType;
    PSTR        pItem   = new char[MAX_PATH];
    char        szRoot[] = {"x:\\\0"};

    if (Filter.IsEmpty ())
        strFilter = "*.*";
    else
    {
        strFilter = Filter;
        strFilter.TrimLeft ();                  // Remove leading
        if (strFilter.GetAt( 0 ) == '\\')       // white spaces or
        {                                       // backslash
            strFilter.SetAt( 0, ' ' );
            strFilter.TrimLeft ();
        }
    }

    // Update static control and empty the list

    pDialog->SetDlgItemText( idcPath, strDirectory );
    DeleteAllItems ();

    // Show directory list in this order:  drives, folders, files

    for (n=0, j=DL_DRIVE; n < 3; n++, j <<= 1)
    {
        if ((iListFlags & j))
        {
            if (GetDirectoryList( iType[n] ))
            {
                bRetCode = TRUE;

                // Copy list from dummy box to list view control
                i = 0;
```

*(continued)*

**Listing 7-1.** *continued*

```
            while (listDummy.SendMessage( LB_GETTEXT, i++,
                            (LPARAM) pItem ) != LB_ERR)
        {
            if (lstrcmp( pItem, "." )  &&
                lstrcmp( pItem, ".." ))
            {
                // Determine which icon the listed item
                // should have: floppy, hard disk, etc.

                switch (j)
                {
                    case DL_DRIVE:
                        szRoot[0] = *pItem;
                        nIcon = 1;
                        uType = ::GetDriveType( szRoot );
                        if (uType == DRIVE_REMOVABLE)
                            nIcon = 0;
                        if (uType == DRIVE_CDROM)
                            nIcon = 2;
                        break;

                    case DL_FOLDER:
                        nIcon = 3;
                        break;

                    default:
                        nIcon = 4;
                }

                InsertItem( nItem, pItem, nIcon );
                SetItemData( nItem++, iType[n] );
            }
        }
      }
    }
  }

  delete [] pItem;                              // Clean up
  return bRetCode;
}

BEGIN_MESSAGE_MAP (CDirListCtrl, CListCtrl)
    ON_NOTIFY_REFLECT (LVN_ITEMCHANGED, OnSelChange)
END_MESSAGE_MAP ()
```

```
void CDirListCtrl::OnSelChange( NMHDR* pnumhdr, LRESULT* pResult)
{
    NM_LISTVIEW* pnmlv = (NM_LISTVIEW*) pnumhdr;

    // Get item selected in list view
    if ((pnmlv->uNewState) & LVIS_FOCUSED)
    {
        // Is it a drive, folder, or file?
        int iType = GetItemData( pnmlv->iItem );

        if (iType != DL_FILE)                  // Ignore files
        {
            CString strItem = GetItemText( pnmlv->iItem, 0 );

            // If drive selected, replace directory
            if (iType == DL_DRIVE)
                strDirectory = strItem;        // Directory = "d:"

            // If folder selected, append it to current path
            else
                strDirectory += strItem;       // Append "subdir"

            strDirectory += "\\";              // Append '\'

            if (!ShowList( strFilter ))        // New dir listing
            {
                // If error, reset to current directory
                GetCurrentDirectory ();
                strFilter.Empty ();
                ShowList( strFilter );
            }
        }
    }

    *pResult = 0;
}

BOOL CDirListCtrl::GetDirectoryList( int iType )
{
    DWORD   dwDrives;
    char    szDrive[] = "A:";
    BOOL    bRet;

    // Empty the dummy list box
    listDummy.SendMessage( LB_RESETCONTENT, 0, 0 );

    switch (iType)
```

*(continued)*

**Listing 7-1.** *continued*

```
        {
          case DL_DRIVE:
              dwDrives = ::GetLogicalDrives ();
              for (; dwDrives && szDrive[0] <= 'Z'; ++szDrive[0])
              {
                  if (dwDrives & 1)
                      listDummy.SendMessage( LB_ADDSTRING, 0,
                                                 (LPARAM) szDrive );
                  dwDrives >>= 1;
              }
              bRet = TRUE;
              break;

          case DL_FOLDER:
              bRet = FindFiles( FILE_ATTRIBUTE_DIRECTORY );
              break;

          case DL_FILE:
              bRet = FindFiles( 0L );
              break;
        }

        return bRet;
}

BOOL CDirListCtrl::FindFiles( DWORD dwFlags )
{
    WIN32_FIND_DATA fd;
    HANDLE          hFind;
    CString         str = "*.*";
    BOOL            bOkay;

    if (dwFlags == 0)
        str = strFilter;

    hFind = ::FindFirstFile( strDirectory + str, &fd );
    if (hFind == INVALID_HANDLE_VALUE)
        return FALSE;

    while (TRUE)
    {
        if (dwFlags == (fd.dwFileAttributes &
                        FILE_ATTRIBUTE_DIRECTORY))
        {
            bOkay = (pCallBack) ? pCallBack( &fd ) : TRUE;
            if (bOkay)
                listDummy.SendMessage( LB_ADDSTRING, 0,
```

```
                                              (LPARAM) fd.cFileName );
        }
        if (!::FindNextFile( hFind, &fd ))
            break;
    }
    ::FindClose( hFind );

    return TRUE;
}

void CDirListCtrl::GetCurrentDirectory ()
{
    PTSTR pDir = new char[MAX_PATH];

    ::GetCurrentDirectory( MAX_PATH, pDir );
    strDirectory = pDir;

    if (strDirectory.Right( 1 ) != "\\")
        strDirectory += "\\";                    // Append backslash

    delete [] pDir;
}
```

The *Create* function, which is called only once to create the control, is prototyped like this in the DirCtrl.h header file:

```
void  Create( CDialog* pDlg, LPRECT prect, int idcControl,
              int idcStatic, int iFlags=DL_ALL, int idiIcon=0 );
```

Table 7-1 on the next page explains the function's six parameters.

The caller provides in its resource data up to five icon images, each 16 pixels square, that represent the various drive types and filenames displayed in the list view control. Figure 7-5 on page 302 illustrates possible icon images, which include a floppy disk drive, hard disk, CD-ROM drive, file folder, and a small diamond shape to represent files. *Create* attaches each icon to the control by calling the *CImageList::Add* function, beginning with the floppy disk drive icon identified by the *idiIcon* parameter. Identifiers for the other icon images follow in sequential order, so that *idiIcon+1* is the identifier for the hard disk image, *idiIcon+2* is the identifier for the CD-ROM drive image, and so forth. The icons are optional, and need not be present.

| Parameter | Description |
|-----------|-------------|
| *pDlg* | The **this** pointer for the containing dialog box. |
| *prect* | Pointer to a RECT structure that contains the dimensions of the list view control within the dialog window. |
| *idcControl* | Identifier of the list view control. |
| *idcStatic* | Identifier of a static control in the dialog. The *ShowList* function writes the current directory path to the *idcStatic* control. |
| *iFlags* | Bit flags defined in DirCtrl.h that determine the contents of the directory listing. Values can be any combination of DL_DRIVE, DL_FOLDER, and DL_FILE. The default DL_ALL value includes all three types in the listing. |
| *idiIcon* | Identifier value for the first of five possible icons displayed in the directory listing. |

**Table 7-1.**   *Parameters of the* Create *function.*

Before it exits, the *Create* function calls *CListBox::Create* to set up an invisible list box control called *listDummy*. The *listDummy* list box is never displayed, serving only as an intermediate storage bin for the filenames that make up the directory listing. The name of each file and folder that the *FindFiles* function locates in the directory is added to the *listDummy* list box. Since the list box is created with the LBS_SORT flag, it automatically sorts its collection of strings as it receives each file and folder name. When the *ShowList* function extracts the strings from the list box, the list box delivers the strings one by one in alphabetical order.

The *SetCallBack* inline function takes the address of an optional callback routine. If the *pCallBack* address is not null, the *FindFiles* function assumes the callback routine exists and calls it for each file before adding the filename to the *listDummy* list box:

```
bOkay = (pCallBack) ? pCallBack( &fd ) : TRUE;
if (bOkay)
    listDummy.SendMessage( LB_ADDSTRING, 0, (LPARAM) fd.cFileName );
```

By returning TRUE or FALSE from the callback routine, the creator of the *CDirListCtrl* object can accept or reject any file. We'll see later in the chapter how the DirList2 program takes advantage of this feature to winnow the files that appear in the directory list.

### Creating the *CDirListCtrl* class

Before we can add *CDirListCtrl* as a component, we need a temporary project to contain the source files. This is because the ClassView pane of the Workspace window is accessible only in an open project. Creating a temporary project is therefore necessary when the class you want to add to the Gallery exists as source code that does not belong to a project. Once the class is added to the Gallery, you can then delete the temporary project. The name of the project does not matter.

You can create a temporary project to contain an existing class in two ways. The first method relies on AppWizard. Click New on the File menu, select the MFC AppWizard (exe) icon in the Projects tab, and type a project name. (The steps outlined below assume the project name is DirCtrl.) Click the Finish button in AppWizard to accept all the defaults, which are not important because we will throw away all the generated files anyway.

The second method for creating a temporary project to contain a component class does not rely on AppWizard. Such a project needs only a stub RC file with the same name as the project—the RC file can even be empty. To create the project, select the Win32 Application icon (instead of the AppWizard icon) in the Projects tab of the New dialog, give the project a name such as DirCtrl, and click OK. At the wizard's next step, accept the default setting specifying an empty project and click the Finish button. Next, use the text editor to create an empty RC file and save it to the DirCtrl project folder. With the new project open, choose the Add To Project command from the Project menu and click Files on the secondary menu. In the Insert Files Into Project dialog, double-click the stub RC file to add it to the project. This is all that's required to enable ClassWizard, which is now accessible through the ClassWizard command on the View menu. When you invoke ClassWizard, Visual C++ detects that no CLW file yet exists for the project and offers to build a new file. You must click Yes at this offer and OK in the subsequent Select Source Files dialog to proceed to the MFC ClassWizard dialog.

Whichever method you use to create the new project, click the Add Class button in the MFC ClassWizard dialog, then choose New to invoke the New Class dialog pictured in Figure 6-4 on page 278. Type *CDirListCtrl* for the class name and select *CListCtrl* as the base class. Click the Change button and rename the generated source files to DirCtrl.h and DirCtrl.cpp. When you close the ClassWizard dialog, Visual C++ writes stub code for the new *CDirListCtrl* class and automatically adds the files to the project.

The next step is to provide source code for the new class. Copy to the DirCtrl project folder the DirCtrl.cpp and DirCtrl.h files from the Code\ Chapter.07\DirCtrl folder on the companion CD, overwriting the stub files that ClassWizard just created. Also copy the files DirCtrl.ico, Floppy.ico, HardDisk.ico, CD-ROM.ico, Folder.ico, and File.ico to the project folder; we will need these files later.

### Creating the *CDirListCtrl* component

*CDirListCtrl* is now a working class but not yet a finished and usable component. Expose the project's ClassView pane and right-click *CDirListCtrl* in the list of classes, then select the Add To Gallery command from the context menu, as shown in Figure 7-4 on page 301. Visual C++ combines both DirCtrl.cpp and DirCtrl.h into a single file named DirListCtrl.ogx and stores the OGX file in a new Gallery folder named DirCtrl. The paragraphs that follow have more to say about this new Gallery folder, so don't confuse it with the original DirCtrl project folder.

Open the DirCtrl folder in the Gallery to see the new component, which appears in large icon view like this:

Dir List Ctrl.ogx

It takes some extra work, but you can dress up the component's plain appearance. The first step is to move the OGX file out of the DirCtrl folder and replace it with a shortcut file. Right-click the new DirListCtrl.ogx icon and choose the Cut command from the context menu. Create a new sub-folder in the main folder of the Gallery dialog by right-clicking in any blank area of the large list box and choosing the New command. Give the new folder a generic name like OGX Files, then paste the DirListCtrl.ogx file into the new folder. Right-click the DirListCtrl.ogx icon, choose the Create Shortcut command from the context menu, then cut and paste the shortcut file back into the original DirCtrl folder.

Stay with me—we're almost finished. At this point, the original OGX file has been moved to a folder called OGX Files and replaced by a shortcut in the DirCtrl folder. Our final step is to improve the appearance of the short-cut icon in the DirCtrl folder. Give the shortcut icon a more descriptive name—Directory List, for example—by right-clicking the icon and choosing Rename. Component OGX files do not have their own icons, but short-cut links do. The main reason for substituting a shortcut for the original OGX file is so that we can attach an icon to distinguish the new Directory List component. Right-click the Directory List icon, choose Properties, and then click the Change Icon button in the Shortcut tab of the Properties dia-log. Enter (or browse for) the path to the DirCtrl.ico file you copied earlier from the companion CD. When you click OK to close the Properties dia-log, the component now looks like this in the DirCtrl folder:

Directory List

A little work, certainly, but the component looks better than what we started with. If you don't mind the effort, you can drop all your new com-ponent files into the OGX Files folder and replace them with shortcuts the same way.

Unfortunately, Visual C++ provides no easy way to attach a description to a new class component, neither in the OGX file nor in its shortcut. It's up to the filename to convey to other developers the essentials of your com-ponent's purpose. Creating a component that can describe itself requires the Component Builder's Kit cited earlier. Figure 7-1 on page 294 shows how such a description appears in the Gallery when the Dialog bar component is selected. Although beyond the scope of this chapter, building the Directory List component using the Builder's Kit would allow us to attach a similar description that appears when the DIR icon is selected in the dialog, something like:

```
Displays a sorted directory listing in a list view control,
complete with icons representing drives, folders, and files.
```

After exiting the Gallery, you can add the *CDirListCtrl* class to any open project by displaying the DirCtrl folder in the Gallery dialog and double-clicking the shortcut for the Directory List component. Now that the component has been installed in the Gallery, the DirCtrl project has served its purpose and is no longer needed. DirListCtrl.ogx contains the class source code, so you can safely close the project and delete the original DirCtrl.cpp and DirCtrl.h files along with the other files in the DirCtrl project folder. Don't delete the ICO files copied earlier from the CD, however. The Directory List shortcut link points to the DirCtrl.ico file, which contains the DIR icon that represents the component. And when you insert the new *CDirListCtrl* class into a project, it may require some or all of the remaining files such as HardDisk.ico and Folder.ico. The next section demonstrates the new Directory List component with an example program named DirList2.

## Example: The DirList2 Program

You may recall that the DirList1 program introduced in Chapter 5 uses the *DlgDirList* API function to display a directory listing in a list box control. The listing is not only plain in appearance and difficult to read, it displays long filenames only in Windows NT because *DlgDirList* does not recognize long filenames in Windows 95. The DirList2 program presented here fixes these shortcomings by incorporating the new Directory List component.

The DirList2 program pictured in Figure 7-6 is dialog-based like its predecessor DirList1, using a property sheet to interact with the user. Besides the more attractive directory listing provided by the Directory List control,

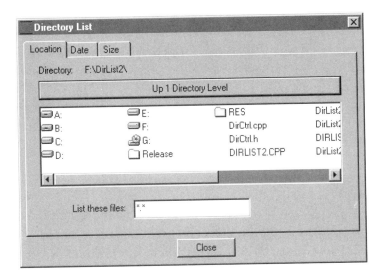

**Figure 7-6.** *The DirList2 program.*

DirList2 also makes use of the property sheet's Date and Size tabs, enabling the user to filter the list by file size or date. For example, the program can display only files created within the last month that are, say, between 5 and 10 KB in size. This additional filtering is accomplished using the *CDirListCtrl* callback feature described earlier.

With minor additions that we'll cover in a moment, the DirList2 program uses the same Resource.h file and the same RC file as the DirList1 program. The contents of these files are listed in Chapter 5, beginning on page 261. If you would like to build the DirList2 program yourself and have not executed the Setup program to install the sample projects from the companion CD, click New on the File menu and select the Projects tab. Because DirList2 is not an AppWizard program, click the Win32 Application icon to create the project. Enter the project name and accept the default settings when the wizard's dialog appears. After Visual C++ creates the empty project, click Settings on the Project menu. In the General tab of the Project Settings dialog, select the option Use MFC In A Shared DLL, as pictured on the next page.

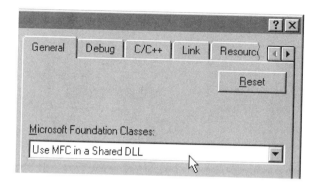

Copy to the project folder the files DirList2.cpp, DirList2.h, DirList2.rc, and Resource.h from the Code\Chapter.07\DirList2 folder on the companion CD. Also copy the DirList.ico file to the DirList2\Res subfolder so that DirList2 has an application icon. Attach the DirList2.cpp and DirList2.rc files to the project by choosing Add To Project from the Project menu and then choosing the Files command from the secondary menu.

Because the DirList2 program makes use of the new *CDirListCtrl* class, we still need a few more files. Of course this is the whole purpose of the exercise: adding the source files for *CDirListCtrl* is a snap now that the class has been installed in the Gallery. Open the Gallery dialog by choosing Add To Project again from the Project menu and clicking Components And Controls. In the DirCtrl folder of the Gallery, double-click the icon for the new Directory List component. The source files DirCtrl.cpp and DirCtrl.h are automatically extracted from the DirListCtrl.ogx component file and added to the project.

Unfortunately, the Gallery cannot also provide the ICO files that *CDirList-Ctrl* requires for the icons used in the directory listing. Except by building the component with Microsoft's Builder's Kit, there is no way to bundle the ICO files along with the source code in the OGX file, thus delivering all the necessary files to a project in one step. The user of the component must copy the ICO files manually. DirList2 requires only the drive and folder icons, which are contained in the Floppy.ico, HardDisk.ico, CD-ROM.ico, and Folder.ico files located in the DirCtrl project folder created earlier. Copy these four files to the DirList2\Res folder.

This is the kind of extra step that must be well documented for a custom component like Directory List. Since a custom component cannot provide online help in the Gallery dialog, the best way to document the component is by including a block of comments at the beginning of the CPP file. For Directory List, the comments should make clear four requirements for any project that uses the component:

- The ICO files must be copied to the project's Res folder.

- The RC file must include lines like these for each icon used in the control:

```
IDI_FLOPPY          ICON    "res\\Floppy.ico"
IDI_HARDDISK        ICON    "res\\HardDisk.ico"
IDI_CD_ROM          ICON    "res\\CD-ROM.ico"
IDI_FOLDER          ICON    "res\\Folder.ico"
IDI_FILE            ICON    "res\\File.ico"
```

- The identifiers IDI_FLOPPY, IDI_HARDDISK, IDI_CD_ROM, IDI_FOLDER, and IDI_FILE must be defined in the project's Resource.h file. IDI_FLOPPY can be any value; the remaining identifier values must be incremented by one in the order given.

- All source files that use the class must contain the line:

```
#include "dirctrl.h"
```

DirList2 operates in much the same way as DirList1, except that the *CPage1* class includes a new member function called *CheckDateSize*. *CheckDateSize* is a callback function registered with a call to *CDirList-Ctrl::SetCallBack*. As described in the source code commentary on page 309, *CDirListCtrl::FindFiles* calls the callback for each filename it proposes to add to the directory list, giving the callback a pointer to a WIN32_FIND_FILE structure that contains information about the file. *CheckDate-Size* determines whether the file conforms to filters that the user has set in the Size and Date pages, and returns a value of TRUE or FALSE to allow or disallow the file.

The revised source files are listed beginning on the next page. The DirList2.rc and Resource.h files are not included here because they differ only slightly from their counterparts in Chapter 5, incorporating

additional lines for the icon resources IDI_FLOPPY, IDI_HARDDISK, IDI_
CD_ROM, and IDI_FOLDER. Because the program elects to leave filenames
in the list unmarked by an icon, IDI_FILE is not defined. You can find all
files in the Code\Chapter.07\DirList2 subfolder on the companion CD.

**Listing 7-2.**  *Source files for the DirList2 program.*

### DirList2.h

```
// ************************************************************
//
// DirList2.h
//
// ************************************************************

class CDirListApp : public CWinApp
{
public:
    BOOL    InitInstance ();
};

class CAboutDlg : public CDialog
{
public:
    CAboutDlg();
};

class CPage2;                              // Forward reference
class CPage3;


////////////////////////////////////////////////////////////////////
// CPage1 property page

class CPage1 : public CPropertyPage
{
private:
    BOOL              bEditChange;
    CDirListCtrl      dirlist;
    CString           strFilter, strOldFilter;
    static CPage2*    pDate;
    static CPage3*    pSize;

    static BOOL CALLBACK  CheckDateSize( PWIN32_FIND_DATA pfd );

public:
    CPage1 () : CPropertyPage( IDD_PAGE1 ) {}
```

```
protected:
    virtual void    DoDataExchange( CDataExchange* pDX );
    virtual BOOL    OnInitDialog ();
    virtual BOOL    OnSetActive ();
    afx_msg void    OnUp1Level ();
    afx_msg void    OnEditGainFocus ();
    afx_msg void    OnEditChanging ();
    afx_msg void    OnEditLoseFocus ();
    DECLARE_MESSAGE_MAP ()
};


/////////////////////////////////////////////////////////////
// CPage2 property page

class CPage2 : public CPropertyPage
{
public:
    int     nAnyDate, PrevDays, PrevMonths;
    CTime   timeMin, timeMax;

    CPage2 () : CPropertyPage( IDD_PAGE2 ) {}

protected:
    virtual void    DoDataExchange( CDataExchange* pDX );
    virtual BOOL    OnInitDialog ();
};


/////////////////////////////////////////////////////////////
// CPage3 property page

class CPage3 : public CPropertyPage
{
public:
    int     nAnySize;
    DWORD   MinSize, MaxSize;

    CPage3 () : CPropertyPage( IDD_PAGE3 ) {}

protected:
    virtual void    DoDataExchange( CDataExchange* pDX );
    virtual BOOL    OnInitDialog ();
};


/////////////////////////////////////////////////////////////
// CListSheet
```

*(continued)*

319

**Listing 7-2.** *continued*

```
class CListSheet : public CPropertySheet
{
public:
    CPage1  page1;
    CPage2  page2;
    CPage3  page3;
    CListSheet( LPCTSTR szCaption );

protected:
    virtual BOOL OnInitDialog();
    afx_msg void OnSysCommand( UINT nID, LPARAM lParam );
    DECLARE_MESSAGE_MAP()
};
```

## DirList2.cpp

```
// ****************************************************************
//
// DirList2.cpp
//
// ****************************************************************

#include "afxwin.h"
#include "afxdlgs.h"
#include "afxcmn.h"
#include "resource.h"
#include "dirctrl.h"
#include "dirlist2.h"

CDirListApp DirListApp;

BOOL CDirListApp::InitInstance ()
{
    CListSheet sh( "Directory List" );     // Create object
    sh.DoModal ();                         // and display dialog

    return FALSE;                          // Exit DirList2
}

CAboutDlg::CAboutDlg() : CDialog( IDD_ABOUTBOX )
{
}


/////////////////////////////////////////////////////////////////
// CListSheet property sheet
```

```
CListSheet::CListSheet( LPCTSTR szCaption ) :
            CPropertySheet( szCaption )
{
    AddPage( &page1 );
    AddPage( &page2 );
    AddPage( &page3 );
}


BEGIN_MESSAGE_MAP (CListSheet, CPropertySheet)
    ON_WM_SYSCOMMAND()
END_MESSAGE_MAP()

BOOL CListSheet::OnInitDialog()
{
    CButton* button;

    CPropertySheet::OnInitDialog();

    // Add "About..." menu item to system menu
    CMenu*  pSysMenu = GetSystemMenu( FALSE );
    CString str;
    str.LoadString( IDD_ABOUTBOX );
    pSysMenu->AppendMenu( MF_SEPARATOR );
    pSysMenu->AppendMenu( MF_STRING, IDD_ABOUTBOX, str );

    // Remove Apply and Cancel buttons and rename OK button
    button = (CButton *) GetDlgItem( ID_APPLY_NOW );
    button->DestroyWindow();
    button = (CButton *) GetDlgItem( IDCANCEL );
    button->DestroyWindow();
    button = (CButton *) GetDlgItem( IDOK );
    button->SetWindowText( "Close" );

    // Set the 16-by-16 image (see closing remarks in Chapter 5)
    HICON hIcon = (HICON) ::LoadImage( DirListApp.m_hInstance,
                        MAKEINTRESOURCE( IDI_APPICON ),
                        IMAGE_ICON, 16, 16, LR_DEFAULTCOLOR );
    SetIcon( hIcon, FALSE );

    // Activate OnInitDialog for each page to init variables
    SetActivePage( 2 );
    SetActivePage( 1 );
    SetActivePage( 0 );

    return TRUE;
}
```

*(continued)*

**Listing 7-2.** *continued*

```
void CListSheet::OnSysCommand( UINT nID, LPARAM lParam )
{
    if (nID == IDD_ABOUTBOX)
    {
        CAboutDlg dlgAbout;
        dlgAbout.DoModal();
    }
    else
    {
        CPropertySheet::OnSysCommand( nID, lParam );
    }
}


//////////////////////////////////////////////////////////////
// CPage1 property page

CPage2* CPage1::pDate;                    // Static pointers to
CPage3* CPage1::pSize;                    //   Date and Size pages

BOOL CPage1::OnInitDialog ()
{
    RECT rect = { 15, 60, 390, 102 };    // DirCtrl dimensions

    strFilter   = "*.*";
    bEditChange = FALSE;
    pDate = (CPage2*) ((CListSheet*) GetParent())->GetPage( 1 );
    pSize = (CPage3*) ((CListSheet*) GetParent())->GetPage( 2 );

    dirlist.Create( this, &rect, IDC_DIRCTRL, IDC_DIRPATH,
                    DL_ALL, IDI_FLOPPY );
    dirlist.SetCallBack( &CheckDateSize );

    return CDialog::OnInitDialog ();
}

BOOL CPage1::OnSetActive ()
{
    dirlist.ShowList( strFilter );
    return CPropertyPage::OnSetActive ();
}

BEGIN_MESSAGE_MAP ( CPage1, CPropertyPage )
    ON_EN_SETFOCUS  ( IDC_EDIT1, OnEditGainFocus )
    ON_EN_CHANGE    ( IDC_EDIT1, OnEditChanging )
    ON_EN_KILLFOCUS ( IDC_EDIT1, OnEditLoseFocus )
    ON_BN_CLICKED   ( IDC_BUTTON1, OnUp1Level )
END_MESSAGE_MAP ()
```

```
// These three functions ensure that when the user types in
// another filter string (such as "*.txt"), the directory
// listing is automatically updated to reflect the change.
// -----------------------------------------------------------

void CPage1::OnEditGainFocus ()
{
    GetDlgItemText( IDC_EDIT1, strOldFilter );
}

void CPage1::OnEditChanging ()
{
    bEditChange = TRUE;
}

void CPage1::OnEditLoseFocus ()
{
    if (bEditChange)
    {
        bEditChange = FALSE;
        UpdateData( TRUE );

        // If user enters a new filter string, update the list
        if (strFilter != strOldFilter)
        {
            dirlist.ShowList( strFilter );
            strOldFilter = strFilter;
        }
    }
}

void CPage1::OnUp1Level ()
{
    CString strPath;

    // If Enter pressed in edit control, refresh list
    if (GetFocus() == GetDlgItem( IDC_EDIT1 ))
        OnEditLoseFocus ();

    // Else go up one directory level
    else
    {
        dirlist.GetPath( strPath );

        // When strPath == "d:\", we're already at root
        if (strPath.Right( 2 ) != ":\\")
```

*(continued)*

**Listing 7-2.** *continued*

```
        {
            // Remove '\' at end of string
            strPath.GetBufferSetLength( strPath.GetLength()-1 );
            strPath.ReleaseBuffer ();

            // Find last '\' and truncate strPath string
            int cLastSlash = strPath.ReverseFind( '\\' );
            if (cLastSlash != -1)
            {
                strPath.GetBufferSetLength( cLastSlash + 1 );
                strPath.ReleaseBuffer ();
                dirlist.SetPath( strPath );
                dirlist.ShowList( strFilter );
            }
        }
    }
}


// Each time it finds a file that is a candidate for inclusion in
// the directory list, CDirListCtrl::FindFiles calls this static
// callback function.
// ---------------------------------------------------------------

BOOL CPage1::CheckDateSize( PWIN32_FIND_DATA pfd )
{
    // Accept all subdirectories regardless of date/size criteria
    if (pfd->dwFileAttributes & FILE_ATTRIBUTE_DIRECTORY)
        return TRUE;

    // If options set in Date page, filter files by date criteria
    if (pDate->nAnyDate)
    {
        CTime  timeFile( pfd->ftLastWriteTime );

        if (pDate->nAnyDate == 1)
        {
            // Reject file not dated within min/max period
            if (timeFile <= pDate->timeMin ||
                timeFile > pDate->timeMax)
                return FALSE;
        }
        else
        {
            CTime     timeNow = CTime::GetCurrentTime();
            CTimeSpan timeAge( timeNow.GetTime() -
                               timeFile.GetTime() );
```

```
                    // Reject file older than specified number of months
                    if (pDate->nAnyDate == 2  && pDate->PrevMonths)
                        if (timeAge.GetDays()/30 >= pDate->PrevMonths)
                            return FALSE;

                    // Reject file older than specified number of days
                    if (pDate->nAnyDate == 3  && pDate->PrevDays)
                        if (timeAge.GetDays() >= pDate->PrevDays)
                            return FALSE;
            }
        }

        // If options set in Size page, filter files by size criteria
        if (pSize->nAnySize)
        {
            if (pSize->MinSize  &&
                pfd->nFileSizeLow < pSize->MinSize*1024)
                return FALSE;

            if (pSize->MaxSize  &&
                pfd->nFileSizeLow > pSize->MaxSize*1024)
                return FALSE;
        }

        return TRUE;
}

void CPage1::DoDataExchange( CDataExchange* pDX )
{
    CPropertyPage::DoDataExchange( pDX );
    DDX_Text( pDX, IDC_EDIT1, strFilter );
    DDV_MaxChars( pDX, strFilter, 128 );
}

///////////////////////////////////////////////////////////////////
// CPage2 property page

BOOL CPage2::OnInitDialog ()
{
    CSpinButtonCtrl* spin;

    // Initialize variables
    nAnyDate    = 0;
    PrevDays    = 1;
    PrevMonths  = 1;
    timeMin     = 0;
    timeMax     = CTime::GetCurrentTime();
```

*(continued)*

**Listing 7-2.** *continued*

```
    // Set limits of spin buttons
    spin = (CSpinButtonCtrl *) GetDlgItem( IDC_SPIN1 );
    spin->SetRange( 1, 100 );
    spin = (CSpinButtonCtrl *) GetDlgItem( IDC_SPIN2 );
    spin->SetRange( 1, 365 );

    return CDialog::OnInitDialog ();
}

void CPage2::DoDataExchange( CDataExchange* pDX )
{
    CPropertyPage::DoDataExchange( pDX );
    DDX_DateTimeCtrl( pDX, IDC_DATETIME1, timeMin);
    DDX_DateTimeCtrl( pDX, IDC_DATETIME2, timeMax);
    DDX_Radio( pDX, IDC_RADIO1, nAnyDate );
    DDX_Text(  pDX, IDC_EDIT1, PrevMonths );
    DDX_Text(  pDX, IDC_EDIT2, PrevDays );
}


///////////////////////////////////////////////////////////////
// CPage3 property page

BOOL CPage3::OnInitDialog ()
{
    CSpinButtonCtrl* spin;

    // Initialize variables
    nAnySize = 0;
    MinSize  = 0;
    MaxSize  = 100;

    // Set limits of spin buttons
    spin = (CSpinButtonCtrl *) GetDlgItem( IDC_SPIN1 );
    spin->SetRange( 0, 9999 );                          // Min size
    spin = (CSpinButtonCtrl *) GetDlgItem( IDC_SPIN2 );
    spin->SetRange( 1, 9999 );                          // Max size

    return CDialog::OnInitDialog ();
}

void CPage3::DoDataExchange( CDataExchange* pDX )
{
    CPropertyPage::DoDataExchange( pDX );
    DDX_Radio( pDX, IDC_RADIO1, nAnySize );
    DDX_Text(  pDX, IDC_EDIT1, MinSize );
    DDX_Text(  pDX, IDC_EDIT2, MaxSize );
}
```

# ActiveX Controls

Chapter

# Using ActiveX Controls

ActiveX controls are executable components designed to be dropped into a window or a Web page to perform some self-contained function. To the user, they seem very much like the normal Windows controls we've encountered in previous chapters, which are added to a program through the dialog editor or the Gallery. But unlike normal controls, ActiveX controls are equally at home on a Web page or in a dialog box, allowing developers to touch two distinct markets at once.

If you are interested in ActiveX controls—and as a developer, you should be—it's probably because you want either to use them or to write them. Visual C++ can help you do both. This chapter covers the first half of the subject, describing how to use ActiveX controls in a client application called a container. Chapters 9 and 10 deal with the second half, describing two different approaches to writing an ActiveX control. This chapter presents introductory information concerning ActiveX controls, so if you would like a primer on the subject, you should read this chapter first.

To keep discussions to a manageable length, the example programs in these chapters use MFC. The MFC framework takes care of the many hundreds of details of ActiveX programming, smoothing development to the point where writing a container or an ActiveX control is no more difficult than any other programming project in Windows. Writing an MFC container application that uses an existing ActiveX control often requires little or no knowledge of the underlying precepts. While there can be good arguments against using MFC when writing ActiveX controls—it's purely an issue of size, as we'll see in the next chapter—the arguments are less valid when applied to containers. So completely does MFC wrap the process of client/server interaction that it has become difficult to justify writing a container application without the help of the MFC class library or similar support. However, if you prefer not to use MFC, the Active Template Library (ATL) offers a viable alternative. Visual C++ includes an example project called AtlCon that demonstrates how to write a container application using ATL. The source files are located in the folder MSDN\Samples\VC98\ATL\AtlCon. Chapter 10 looks a little more closely at the type of support ATL offers for the development of container applications.

Although this chapter and the following two chapters delve into the requirements and internal operations of ActiveX controls, they are intended only as an introduction to what is a large subject, suitable for an entire book. The chapters concentrate on showing you some of the ways in which Visual C++ makes the programmer's life easier when dealing with ActiveX controls, whether you are writing a control or the container application that uses the control. For more detailed coverage of a field likely to become even more important to Internet programming, consult specialized references such as Kraig Brockschmidt's *Inside OLE, Second Edition*, the entire text for which you can find in MSDN online help.

# A Little Background

The name is new, but the technology is mature. ActiveX controls form only part of Microsoft's ActiveX technologies, which are based on Component Object Model (COM) and OLE. OLE used to stand for Object Linking and Embedding, but because object embedding has long since been only a minor part of OLE's abilities, Microsoft has gotten away from using the name as an acronym. Today, OLE has taken on new meaning and no longer has a version number. It has evolved from a technology created for a specific purpose to become a general architecture on which other specific technologies, ActiveX among them, are based. OLE defines a standard blueprint for creating and connecting diverse program components, including server modules called OLE custom controls. At least, they used to be called OLE controls—Microsoft now calls them ActiveX controls.

So what is an OLE/ActiveX control? The short answer is that an OLE/ActiveX control is a dynamic link library that operates as a COM-based server and can be embedded in a container host application. The long answer—well, in a way this chapter is the long answer. Let's start with some history to see exactly what an OLE control does before taking on the more involved subject of how it works.

Perhaps the first type of component software that caught the attention of Windows developers was the custom control of the Visual Basic Extension model. Custom controls were familiarly known as VBXs, named for the three-letter extension appended to the control filename. The VBX architecture allowed developers to create efficient and reusable additions to Visual Basic programs that could be placed as self-contained components in a window, called a form in Visual Basic. The advantages of VBX controls were three-fold:

- A VBX was capable of visual display and interaction with the user.

- The Visual Basic application could program a VBX through functions called methods exported by the VBX.

- As a dynamic link library, a VBX control was reusable in binary form instead of source code.

As we'll see, ActiveX controls offer these same advantages.

A VBX control also allowed programmers to compensate for some of the limitations inherent in Visual Basic. For example, since VBX controls were often written in C or assembly language, they could use pointers, which are not native to the BASIC language, to assist an application with pointer-intensive operations such as hashing and sorting. A problem with the VBX model is that it was not designed to gracefully make the transition to other languages and platforms. A C++ programmer, for instance, cannot easily create a VBX derivative because a VBX is not represented by a class. Further, the VBX model is a 16-bit standard tied to the segmented architecture of Intel processors. However, the active market in VBX controls proved that component software could play an integral (and marketable) role in Windows development.

The OLE control standard was designed to fill the next level, bringing the advantages of VBX-type components to all languages capable of Win32 programming. These languages include Visual Basic itself (since version 4.0), as well as its derivatives Access Basic, Visual Basic for Applications (VBA), WordBasic, and Visual Basic Scripting (VBScript).

Reflecting the way VBXs took their name, OLE controls are often called OCXs from the OCX extension usually added to the filename. There are other conventions common to OCXs and VBXs, indicative of how one evolved from the other. For example, Microsoft borrowed from VBX terminology the three interface types that define the communication between an OLE control and its client, the container application:

- **Methods**—Functions that the OLE control exposes to the container application, allowing the client to call into the control.

- **Properties**—Public data within the control and the container that serve to describe one party to the other. At startup, a control can read the container's properties and adjust its initialization procedures so that it matches the container's appearance and characteristics. While the control is active, the container can read the control's properties to learn its current status and, if the control allows, rewrite the properties to alter the control's behavior.

- **Events**—Notifications that the control sends to the container informing the container of occurrences within the control. As described in more detail later in the chapter, an event notification takes place by calling a function in the container, known as "firing" the event.

At about the time when people were noticing the limitations of 16-bit VBXs, OLE—called OLE 2 in those days—had matured to the point that it could spin off a logical successor to VBXs in the form of OLE controls, now called ActiveX controls.

# Control Containers

An ActiveX control is the server, and the container application is the client. ActiveX controls are best approached from the client's side of the equation, so this section begins a discussion of how a container can extend its abilities through an existing ActiveX control, demonstrating with a few examples and a little experimentation. Fortunately, there are a number of ready-made samples from which to choose. Visual C++ and Internet Explorer come with a collection of license-free ActiveX controls, some of which are listed in the Gallery dialog pictured in Figure 8-1. To bring up the Gallery dialog, choose the Add To Project command from the Project menu and click Components And Controls on the secondary menu. Then double-click the Registered ActiveX Controls folder to display the list of controls.

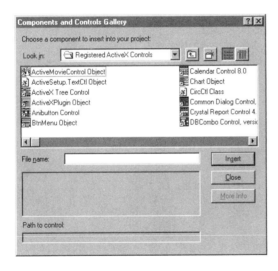

**Figure 8-1.**    *ActiveX controls in the Gallery.*

Table 8-1 on the next page lists some of the license-free ActiveX controls that Microsoft makes available. If the More Info button is enabled when you select a control's icon in the Gallery, it means that the control can describe itself through online help. Click the More Info button to view the control's documentation.

| Filename | Description |
| --- | --- |
| AniBtn32.ocx | **Animated button**—Uses a bitmap or metafile to create a button with changing images. |
| BtnMenu.ocx | **Menu**—Displays a button and a pop-up menu, as shown in Figure 8-2 on page 336. |
| DBGrid32.ocx | **Grid**—A spreadsheet control that displays cells in a standard grid pattern. The user can select cells and—unlike the older Grid32 control—enter data directly into a cell. Cells can also be filled programmatically by the container or tied to recordset data for automatic updating. |
| IELabel.ocx | **Label**—Displays text rotated at an angle or along a specified curve. |
| IEMenu.ocx | **Pop-up menu**—Displays a pop-up menu, as shown in Figure 8-2. |
| IEPopWnd.ocx | **Pop-up window**—Displays an HTML document in a pop-up window. |
| IEPrld.ocx | **Preloader**—Downloads the contents of a specified URL and stores it in a cache. The control fires an event after completing the download. |
| IEStock.ocx | **Stock ticker**—Downloads and displays the contents of a URL at a specified fixed interval. As its name suggests, this control is useful for displaying data that continually changes, like the stock ticker tape shown in Figure 8-2. |
| IETimer.ocx | **Timer**—An invisible control that fires an event at a specified interval. |
| KeySta32.ocx | **Key state**—Displays and optionally modifies states of the Caps Lock, Num Lock, Insert, and Scroll Lock keys. |
| Marquee.ocx | **Marquee**—Scrolls text in an HTML file in either the horizontal or vertical direction and can be configured to change the amount and delay of scrolling. |
| MCI32.ocx | **Multimedia**—Manages the recording and playback of multimedia files on Media Control Interface (MCI) devices. This control can display a set of push buttons that issue MCI commands to devices such as audio boards, MIDI sequencers, CD-ROM drives, audio CD players, video disc players, and video tape recorders and players. The control also supports the playback of Video for Windows AVI files. |

| Filename | Description |
|---|---|
| MSCal.ocx | **Calendar**—An on-screen calendar from which the user can select dates. |
| MSChart.ocx | **Chart**—A sophisticated charting control that accepts numerical data, and then displays one of several types of charts, including line, bar, and column charts. The control renders displays in either two or three dimensions, as shown in Figure 8-2 and Figure 8-3 on page 339. |
| MSComm32.ocx | **Comm**—Provides support for serial communications, handling data transmission to and from a serial port. |
| MSMask32.ocx | **Masked edit**—An enhanced edit control that ensures input conforms to a predefined format. For example, a mask of "##:## ??" restricts input to a time format, such as "11:18 AM." |
| PicClp32.ocx | **Picture clip**—Displays a clipped rectangular area of a bitmap, and can also divide a bitmap into a grid formed by a specified number of rows and columns. |

**Table 8-1.**    *Some of the ActiveX controls available from Microsoft.*

The "IE" prefix in some of the filenames in Table 8-1 stands for Internet Explorer, indicating the controls are included with that program. The OCX files can be anywhere on your system but are usually placed in the Windows\OCCache and Windows\System subfolders. If for some reason you do not have these files and want to follow the demonstrations in this chapter, copy the files from the OCX folder on the companion CD to your OCCache, System, or System32 folder. Don't assume this small sampling represents the latest word in ActiveX controls, however. New controls appear on the market every day, many of them demonstration versions that you can use in your own applications without charge. If you would like to browse the Internet for some of the controls available, these two addresses offer free downloads and provide links to other Web sites of interest to application developers:

*http://www.microsoft.com/com/*
*http://www.activex.com*

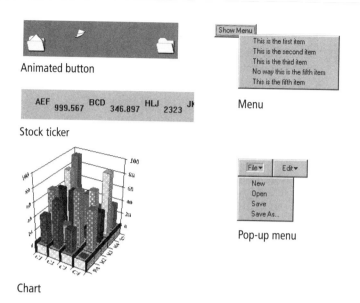

Animated button

Stock ticker

Menu

Chart

Pop-up menu

**Figure 8-2.** *A few of the Microsoft ActiveX controls as they might appear in a container.*

When you copy a control file to your hard disk from the companion CD or another source, register it using the RegSvr32.exe utility found in the VC98\Bin subfolder. RegSvr32 calls the control's self-registration function, which writes identifying information about the control to the system Registry. Until a control is registered, a container application normally has no way to locate it for embedding. Click the Start button and execute Reg-Svr32 from the Run dialog, specifying an OCX file in the command line:

```
regsvr32 \windows\occache\anibtn32.ocx
```

If your system PATH statement does not include the VC98\Bin folder, specify the correct path when typing *regsvr32*. To unregister an ActiveX control—that is, to remove its entry from the Registry—run RegSvr32 again the same way, but include the switch "/u" before the filename. Unregistering a control does not delete its OCX file from your disk.

You can also run RegSvr32 from within Visual C++ by clicking the Register Control command on the Tools menu. By default, however, the command assumes you want to register a control under construction and is therefore set up to register only the project target file. Chapter 13, Customizing Visual C++, explains how to modify tools like Register Control so that you can specify any file as a command line argument, not just a file in the current project.

## Adding an ActiveX Control to a Web Page

Before inserting an ActiveX control into your project, you may want to take a look at the control first. All you need are a text editor and a browser that supports ActiveX, one to create an HTML document and the other to view it. HTML stands for Hypertext Markup Language, which defines a simple convention for creating Web pages that is well-documented in various books and articles. You can learn most of what you need to know about HTML with only a few minutes of study. The Visual C++ text editor is HTML-aware to a limited extent, automatically color-coding tags and other document elements in the display window.

To use an ActiveX control in an HTML document, you must first locate the control's 32-digit class identifier number. We'll talk more about CLSIDs in the next chapter, but for now all you need to know is how to look up the number. The Registry editor provides a convenient way to find a control's CLSID. Click the Start button and type *regedit* or *regedit32* in the Run dialog, depending on whether your system is Windows 95 or Windows NT. Click the Find command on the Registry editor's Edit menu and type the control's filename.

For example, a search for *ietimer.ocx* in the Registry editor finds this hierarchy in the Registry:

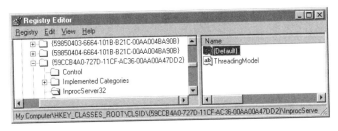

The 32-digit number at the bottom of the window is the CLSID for the Timer ActiveX control. Searching for *ielabel.ocx* in the same way turns up this CLSID for the Label ActiveX control:

99b42120-6ec7-11cf-a6c7-00aa00a47dd2

With these two numbers in hand, you can write a simple HTML document that uses the Timer and Label controls to display text that seems to tumble, endlessly bouncing off the bottom of a colored box:

To see the animation, use a Web browser such as Internet Explorer or any ActiveX-aware authoring tool to open the Tumble.htm document located in the Code\Chapter.08 folder on the companion CD. In Internet Explorer 3.0 and later versions, click the Open command and navigate to the document, then double-click to open it. Listing 8-1 shows the contents of the Tumble.htm document.

**Listing 8-1.**     *The Tumble.htm document.*

```
<OBJECT
     classid="clsid:59ccb4a0-727d-11cf-ac36-00aa00a47dd2"
     id=timer1
>
<PARAM NAME="Interval" value="100">
<PARAM NAME="Enabled" value="TRUE">
</OBJECT>

<OBJECT
     classid="clsid:99b42120-6ec7-11cf-a6c7-00aa00a47dd2"
     id=label
     width=150
     height=150
>
<PARAM NAME="Angle" value="0">
<PARAM NAME="Alignment" value="7">
<PARAM NAME="BackStyle" value="1">
<PARAM NAME="BackColor" value="255">
<PARAM NAME="FontItalic" value="-1">
<PARAM NAME="FontUnderline" value="-1">
```

```
<PARAM NAME="Caption" value="Tumbling text!">
<PARAM NAME="FontName" value="Times New Roman">
<PARAM NAME="FontSize" value="18">
</OBJECT>

<SCRIPT LANGUAGE="VBSCRIPT">
sub timer1_timer
    label.Angle = (label.Angle + 5) mod 360
end sub
</SCRIPT>
```

## The Test Container Utility

Visual C++ provides a tool named Test Container that does just what its name suggests, allowing you to load and experiment with registered ActiveX controls without having to create your own container application. Click the ActiveX Control Test Container command on the Tools menu to start the Test Container, which is pictured in Figure 8-3 with two typical ActiveX controls called Button Menu and Microsoft Chart, both provided on the companion CD. The program's executable file is TstCon32.exe, located in the Common\Tools subfolder on your hard disk.

To load a control in the Test Container, either choose the Insert New Control command from the Edit menu or click the New Control button on the toolbar, then choose the desired control from the list displayed in the Insert Control dialog. A control may first appear only as a small box in the Test Container window; if so, resize the control by dragging a corner. The

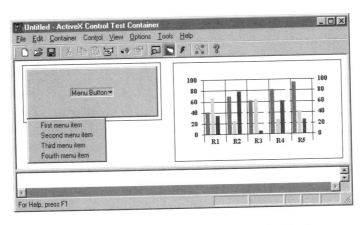

**Figure 8-3.** *The Test Container utility, invoked through the Tools menu.*

initial size of a control depends on the startup dimensions (if any) the control has requested from the container. An example project in the next chapter demonstrates how an ActiveX control written with MFC can call the *COleControl::SetInitialSize* function to establish its startup dimensions. As Figure 8-3 demonstrates, several controls can run at once in the Test Container; select from among the active controls by clicking just inside the rectangular border that frames each control window. When a control is selected, sizing handles appear on its border frame and the Invoke Methods and Properties tools become enabled on the Test Container toolbar.

Invoke Methods

The selected ActiveX control can be programmed throught its method functions. Click the Invoke Methods tool or choose the corresponding command from the Control menu to bring up the Invoke Methods dialog pictured in Figure 8-4. The drop-down list of the Method Name combo box itemizes all of the control's methods, which fall into two categories called normal methods and property methods. Normal methods are labeled Method in the drop-down list. Property methods are marked either PropGet or PropPut, depending on whether they correspond to a property's "get" method, which retrieves the property value, or "put" method, which writes the value. Figure 8-4, for instance, shows that the Button Menu control exports both types of methods, allowing a container to read

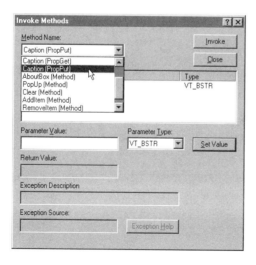

**Figure 8-4.** *Programming a control through the Test Container's Invoke Methods dialog.*

or write the control's *Caption* property—that is, the text that appears on the button—through get and put methods.

To add an item to the Button Menu control's pop-up menu, a container calls the *AddItem* method. We can do the same thing using the Invoke Methods dialog, adding a list of menu items like the ones shown in Figure 8-3 on page 339. Select *AddItem* in the Method Name box, then type the desired text in the edit box labeled Parameter Value. When you click the Invoke button, the Test Container calls the *AddItem* method to add the text to the control's list of menu commands. Close the Invoke Methods dialog and click the Button Menu control to see the new command.

When selecting a put method for a property of integer type, you must also make a selection such as VT_I4 in the Parameter Type box. Determine the correct parameter type by first invoking the corresponding get method and noting the return value, or choose VT_UNKNOWN in the Parameter Type box. If a put method takes more than one parameter, select each variable in turn in the Parameters list box and click the Set Value button after typing its value. When all values appear correctly in the Value column, click Invoke to pass the parameters to the method.

Color properties such as *BackColor* are 24-bit COLORREF values, which can be represented as VT_I4 integer types. The three bytes of a COLOR-REF value correspond to the red, green, and blue components of the whole color, as demonstrated by the Color example project of Chapter 5. Although a COLORREF value is most easily expressed as a hexadecimal number like 0xFF for bright red, the Invoke Methods dialog recognizes only values typed in decimal format. To enter a new color value in the dialog, type a number such as 16,711,680 for bright blue, 65,280 for bright green, or 255 for bright red. Selecting VT_COLOR in the Parameter Type box enables a button labeled Choose Color that displays an assortment of sample colors. However, this option currently does not correctly translate a selected color to a valid method parameter.

Many controls provide their own property sheet, which the Test Container makes accessible through the Properties tool button. Clicking the tool causes the Test Container to issue an OLEIVERB_PROPERTIES verb to the control, telling it to display its property sheet if it has one. Double-

Properties

clicking the border of a control's window also invokes the command, as does choosing Properties from the Test Container's Edit menu.

The Test Container window is divided by a movable splitter bar into two horizontal views. The bottom view normally displays a real-time record of events fired by the selected control. The record, called an event log, can be rerouted elsewhere by choosing the Logging command from the Test Container's Options menu. During development of an ActiveX control, the event log can save a lot of guesswork, letting you quickly test whether your control's events are firing correctly. We'll look at the event log feature again in the next chapter when testing an example ActiveX control.

## Adding an ActiveX Control to a Dialog Box

While any class derived from *CWnd* can embed an ActiveX control, MFC is optimized for dialog containers. This is fine, because ActiveX controls, like normal controls, commonly appear in dialog boxes. The optimization is reflected in Visual C++, which provides features that help you create a container application for ActiveX controls used by one of the dialog-based classes described in Chapter 6, ClassWizard—that is, *CDialog*, *CProperty-Page*, *CFormView*, *CRecordView*, or *CDaoRecordView*. Adding a registered ActiveX control to a dialog takes only a few clicks of the mouse, first in the Gallery, and then in the Visual C++ dialog editor.

The dialog editor in some ways makes a more convenient testing area for ActiveX controls than the Test Container utility. For one thing, the dialog editor displays a Properties box even if the control does not provide its own property sheet. For example, if you double-click the border of the Button Menu control in the Test Container window, a message box appears saying that "Property pages are not supported." But if you invoke the Properties command for the same control in the dialog editor, the editor adds to its normal Properties box an extra tab labeled All that lists the control's properties and allows you to edit them. The All tab provides more convenient access to the control's properties than the involved procedure of invoking methods in the Test Container utility.

Here's how to see an ActiveX control at work in a dialog box—no programming required. The dialog editor itself serves as the control client, as demonstrated here with the Animated Button ActiveX control. If you prefer to work with the complete project described in these steps, open Demo.dsw in the Code\Chapter.08\AniButtn folder on the companion CD. Run Demo.exe and click the About command on the Help menu.

### Step 1: Create a dummy project

Use AppWizard to create a throwaway project, giving it any name you like and accepting all defaults. By default, AppWizard makes every application an ActiveX control container by turning on the ActiveX Controls check box in Step 3:

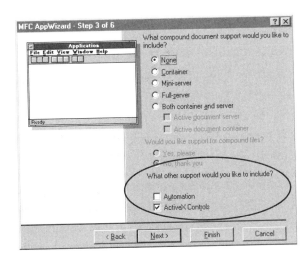

Selecting the ActiveX Controls option brings a lot of additional code into play to support control containment, but the framework takes care of everything. On the surface, the option merely adds this line to the application class *InitInstance* function:

```
AfxEnableControlContainer();
```

and this line to the StdAfx.h file:

```
#include <afxdisp.h>        // MFC OLE automation classes
```

If you have an existing MFC project that you want to turn into a control container, use the text editor to manually make the above changes to the code. To get the same results, you can also add to the project the ActiveX

Control Containment component located in the Visual C++ Components folder of the Gallery.

### Step 2: Insert the ActiveX control

When AppWizard finishes creating the project, choose the Add To Project command from the Project menu, then click Components And Controls on the secondary menu to display the Gallery dialog. Select the Anibutton Control icon in the Registered ActiveX Controls folder and click the Insert button. Accept the default settings in the Confirm Classes dialog, then exit the Gallery.

Going into the Gallery isn't strictly necessary because you can also add an ActiveX control to a project from the dialog editor. When the dialog editor's work area appears (as described in the next step), right-click anywhere in the work area and choose Insert ActiveX Control from the context menu. This brings up a list of the same registered controls shown in the Gallery dialog. Just double-click a control in the list to add it to the dialog.

### Step 3: Add the control to a dialog and initialize

Technically, a dialog container is not a parent window for the ActiveX control but only provides what COM calls a site, a word that should not be taken too literally. A site serves as a go-between for an embedded object and its container, in this case handling communication between the ActiveX control and the dialog window. Any dialog will do for demonstration purposes, even the project's About box. Better still, we don't even need to build the project to use the new control. All we need is a site, and the About box simulation in the dialog editor provides that.

Double-click the IDD_ABOUTBOX identifier in the ResourceView pane of the Workspace window to start the dialog editor and load the About box. When the editor's window appears, its Controls toolbar has a new button that represents the inserted Anibutton control:

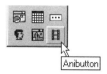

The tool isn't a permanent addition to the toolbar, existing only for this project. To add the Anibutton component to another project, you must go through Step 2 again to insert the control. As for getting the control into the dialog work area, there's no special treatment required. Just drag it into the dialog box as you would any of the other control tools, then right-click the selected control in the dialog and click Properties on the context menu to invoke the control's Properties dialog. Figure 8-5 shows the Control tab of the Anibutton Control Properties dialog, which is where we'll start initializing the control.

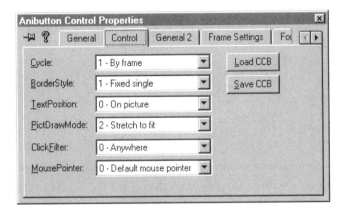

**Figure 8-5.**    *The Control tab of the Anibutton Control Properties dialog.*

OTE    If certain entries are missing from the Registry, Visual C++ displays a message that incorrectly states the Animated Button control requires a design-time license. If this message appears when you follow the steps outlined here, it indicates either that you have installed Visual C++ with only USER privileges or that the Registry is corrupted. Reinstalling Visual C++ seems to be the only solution. For more information about this potential problem and a list of other ActiveX controls known to be susceptible to it, visit this Knowledge Base site:

*http://support.microsoft.com/support/kb/articles/Q155/0/59.asp*

The following list walks you through the initialization settings required for this demonstration project. The settings are made in five of the Properties dialog's tabs.

- **Control tab**—Click the combo boxes in the Control tab and select the entries shown in Figure 8-5.

- **General 2 tab**—To specify text displayed in the control window, type *Click Here!* in the Caption box. Also set the check box labeled HideFocusBox, which prevents a dotted rectangle from appearing around the caption text when the control has focus.

- **Frame Settings tab**—The Anibutton control can hold a number of bitmaps that serve as the button images. For our demonstration, any bitmaps will do, including the system wallpaper image files in the Windows folder. Click the Load button and navigate to the Windows folder to display a list of BMP files, which have names such as Black Thatch, Blue Rivets, Sandstone, and Triangles. Select a file from the list and click the Insert button. Click the Load button again and repeat until you have added five or six different bitmaps to the control. When finished, you can check each bitmap entry by moving the scroll bar.

- **Fonts tab**—This is where you select the font for the caption that appears on the button. The font in Figure 8-6 is Times New Roman with an italic style and a point size of 32.

- **Colors tab**—Because the bitmap image stretches to fill the control window, the background color doesn't matter. Set the foreground color of the caption text by selecting *ForeColor* from the Property Name text box and clicking the white color patch.

An earlier section of this chapter noted that not all ActiveX controls provide their own property sheet, but it so happens that the Anibutton control does. The property pages listed above are resources contained in the AniBtn32.ocx executable file, which the dialog editor extracts and adds to its own General and All tabs to form the complete Properties dialog shown in Figure 8-5. This convenience means you don't have to interact with two dialogs, one provided by the control and the other by the dialog editor.

### Step 4: Test the control

Enlarge the control in the dialog work area by dragging its sizing handles, then reposition the control window in the center of the dialog box. Turn on the editor's test mode switch on the Dialog toolbar:

Click several times in the new ActiveX control window to cycle through the bitmap images, one of which is shown in Figure 8-6. Click the dialog's OK button to return to editing mode.

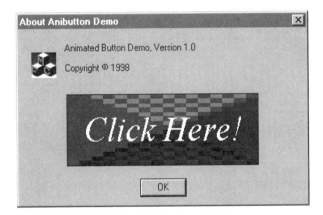

**Figure 8-6.** *The Anibutton ActiveX control in a typical dialog.*

Now that we have some idea of the many forms an ActiveX control can take, let's dissect one to see how it operates.

## Communication Between Container and ActiveX Control

An ActiveX control server attaches very efficiently to a client process. Although not strictly necessary, an ActiveX control usually operates as a dynamic link library, which means that the control executes in the address space of the client process. For this reason, an ActiveX control is often referred to as an in-process server. A container program does not load the ActiveX control by calling the *LoadLibrary* API function as it would to load a normal DLL. Instead it calls *CoCreateInstance* to request the run-time services of the Component Object Model framework to load the library and set up an initial communication point between the client and the control server. The communication point is called an interface. The container calls into an interface, traditionally represented in a diagram as a small circle like the one in Figure 8-7, and the call is routed to the correct function in the server. Notice in the diagram that once the initial interface is in place and all parties are talking to each other, COM drops out of the picture.

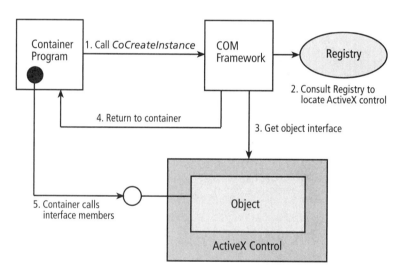

**Figure 8-7.**  *Connecting an ActiveX control to a container.*

Each interface is an array of pointers to functions that the ActiveX control exports. The array is often called a v-table because it is exactly analogous to a C++ table of pointers to virtual functions. Because only the interface's single step of indirection stands between the client and an in-process server, calls to an ActiveX control are practically as fast as calls to a normal dynamic link library.

Not all COM servers operate in-process. A server EXE application runs in its own address space, either on the same machine as the client or on another machine attached through a network. In either case, client and server are separated by process boundaries and cannot communicate directly. For out-of-process servers, COM loads two dynamic link libraries to handle communcation. The first library, called a proxy, is mapped to the client's address space; the other library, called a stub, is mapped to the server's space. When the client calls into the proxy's interface, the proxy bundles the function parameters into a packet and sends them to the stub via a remote procedure call (RPC). The stub converts the information in the packet back to a parameter list and calls the target function in the server. Any communication from the server winds its way back to the client through the same path. The process of connecting the client and server through the proxy and stub libraries is called marshaling. As you would expect, marshaling is slower than the more straightforward interaction between a client and an ActiveX control, since an in-process server does not rely on remote procedure calls for communicating with the client and does not require marshaling unless the communication is between threads. (Chapter 10, Writing ActiveX Controls Using ATL, discusses interthreaded marshaling in more detail.)

Communication runs in both directions between an ActiveX control and its container, so the container application must provide its own set of interfaces to receive calls from the control. Microsoft publishes guidelines specifying a minimum set of interfaces that a container should support. The guidelines are documented in online help, accessible through the Index tab of the MSDN Library window. Choose the Index command from Visual C++'s Help menu, then type *required interfaces* to locate the article of that title.

By supporting these interfaces, a container application ensures it can interoperate with any ActiveX control that also complies with the guidelines. Table 8-2 on the next page describes the eight interfaces your container should support to comply with the OLE/ActiveX specifications.

Providing only the first three interfaces in Table 8-2 gives you a compound document container but not a control container. Writing a container program with MFC frees you from having to worry about the details of interface support. As described earlier in this chapter, selecting ActiveX control support in AppWizard for a container project adds to the source code a call to the framework's *AfxEnableControlContainer* function. This function sets up all the interfaces listed in Table 8-2. Once the interfaces are in place, communication between an ActiveX control and its container takes place through events, methods, and properties.

## Events

Although an ActiveX control is self-contained, it can keep the container application informed of activity within the control by firing events. The

| Interface | Description |
|---|---|
| *IOleClientSite* | Used by an embedded object to query the container about the size of the client site and characteristics of the user interface. The *IOleClientSite* interface also provides services such as the *RequestNewObjectLayout* function through which the control can request a new size for its site. |
| *IAdviseSink* | Used by an object to inform the container of changes in the object's data. |
| *IOleInPlaceSite* | Manages interaction between the container and the object's site. |
| *IOleControlSite* | Provides various services for an embedded ActiveX control. For example, the *TranslateAccelerator* function asks the container to process a specified keypress, and the *OnFocus* function tells the control if it has input focus. |
| *IOleInPlaceFrame* | Used by an ActiveX control to govern the display of resources such as composite menus. |
| *IOleContainer* | Allows the control to force its container to remain in a running state or to query about other controls embedded in the same document or window. |
| *IErrorInfo* | Required for containers that support dual interfaces (described in Chapter 10). |
| *IDispatch* | Used by the control to access the container's ambient properties (described in the section titled "Properties," on page 354) and to call the container's event handler functions. The container implements a separate *IDispatch* interface for properties and events. |

**Table 8-2.** *Interfaces a container should support to comply with the OLE/ActiveX specifications.*

events fired by a particular control are whatever the control developer thinks the container application might want to know about. For example, the control can fire an event in response to a mouse click within the control window or to pass on to the container any keyboard input collected when the control has focus. A fired event might signal the completion of some task such as locating a URL, downloading data, or sorting a list. One can draw an analogy between event firing and the way a normal control sends notification messages such as CBN_DROPDOWN or BN_DOUBLE-CLICKED to its parent window, except that an ActiveX control fires an event by calling a function in the container, not by sending a message.

The function in the container that receives the fired event is a type of callback. If the container application wants to be notified of a particular control event, it must provide a function—known as an event handler or event implementation function—to receive the call. The container stores a list of pointers to its event handlers in an *IDispatch* v-table known as the event sink. The event sink connects each event with its own handler function. The container application does not have to provide a handler function for every event that a control fires, nor does every ActiveX control fire events.

The OLE/ActiveX standards predefine a number of stock events that inform a container about occurrences in the control window. For example, to notify the container when the mouse is clicked inside the control window, a control using MFC can set up the stock *Click* event through the EVENT_STOCK_ CLICK macro:

```
BEGIN_EVENT_MAP(CDemoCtrl, COleControl)
    //{{AFX_EVENT_MAP(CDemoCtrl)
    EVENT_STOCK_CLICK()
    //}}AFX_EVENT_MAP
END_EVENT_MAP()
```

The control requires no other code because the framework takes care of sensing the mouse click and firing the event. If the container wants to know when a mouse click occurs in the control's window, it provides a handler function for the *Click* event, which is referenced in a matching event sink map.

```
BEGIN_EVENTSINK_MAP(CDemoContainer, CDialog)
    //{{AFX_EVENTSINK_MAP(CDemoContainer)
    ON_EVENT(CDemoContainer, IDC_CTRL, DISPID_CLICK,
            OnClick, VTS_NONE)
    //}}AFX_EVENTSINK_MAP
END_EVENTSINK_MAP()
```

Parameters for the ON_EVENT macro in the above fragment may need some explanation. *CDemoContainer* is the container's class, which is derived from *CDialog*. The constant IDC_CTRL identifies the control in the class's dialog window. DISPID_CLICK is the *Click* event's dispatch identifier (dispid for short). Dispatch identifiers for stock events are defined in the OleCtl.h file, each with a DISPID_ prefix. Any event that is not stock is called a custom event to which OLE assigns a positive dispatch identifier, reserving negative identifiers for stock events. The macro's fourth parameter points to the container's member function that handles the event, named *OnClick* in this example. The VTS_NONE parameter specifies that the *Click* event has no parameters.

Table 8-3 lists function prototypes for the stock events defined by the OLE/ActiveX specifications. All stock events except *Error* can occur only while the ActiveX control has input focus. An event prototype may seem to imply the existence of a single function when in fact there are usually at least three functions involved, as idealized in Figure 8-8. At a low level,

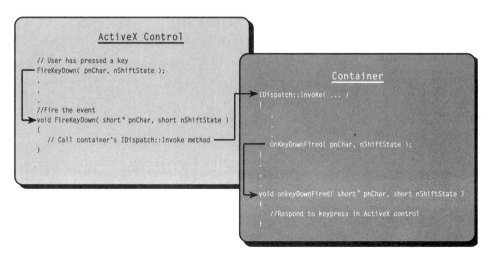

**Figure 8-8.**   *Firing a typical event.*

| Event prototype | Event fired when... |
|---|---|
| `void FireClick()` | Any mouse button (left, middle, or right) is clicked in the control window. The *Mouse-Down* and *MouseUp* stock events fire before *Click*. |
| `void FireDblClick()` | Any mouse button is double-clicked in the control window. |
| `void FireError( SCODE scode,`<br>`  LPCSTR lpszDescription,`<br>`  UINT nHelpID = 0 )` | The control detects an error. |
| `void FireKeyDown( short* pnChar,`<br>`  short nShiftState )` | The control receives a WM_SYSKEYDOWN or WM_KEYDOWN message. |
| `void FireKeyPress( short* pnChar )` | The control receives a WM_CHAR message. |
| `void FireKeyUp( short* pnChar,`<br>`  short nShiftState )` | The control receives a WM_SYSKEYUP or WM_KEYUP message. |
| `void FireMouseDown( short nButton,`<br>`  short nShiftState,`<br>`  float x, float y )` | Any mouse button (left, middle, or right) is pressed, generating a WM_*x*BUTTONDOWN message. |
| `void FireMouseMove( short nButton,`<br>`  short nShiftState, float x, float y )` | The control receives a WM_MOUSEMOVE message. |
| `void FireMouseUp( short nButton,`<br>`  short nShiftState, float x, float y )` | Any mouse button is released, generating a WM_*x*BUTTONUP message. |

**Table 8-3.**   *Stock events defined by OLE/ActiveX.*

a control fires an event by calling the container's *IDispatch::Invoke* method, passing it parameters appropriate for the event. But at a higher level two additional functions exist, one in the ActiveX control that wraps the call to *IDispatch::Invoke*, and the other in the container that ultimately handles the call. Both functions share the same parameter list and in effect behave as a single function, hiding the low-level *IDispatch* activity that occurs between them. Function names are arbitrary. MFC forms the names of firing functions by adding the prefix *Fire* to an event name—the *Fire-Click* function, for example, triggers the *Click* event.

## Methods

A method is the opposite of an event handler function. While event handler functions are located in the container and called by the control, methods are located in the control and called by the container. The container can call a method to learn a condition or to request the control to take some action.

OLE/ActiveX predefines three stock methods, called *DoClick*, *Refresh*, and *AboutBox*, none of which take a parameter or return a value. *DoClick* causes the control to fire its *Click* stock event (if it supports it), the *Refresh* method tells the control to invalidate its window and repaint itself, and *AboutBox* tells the control to display an informative dialog box. Any other method an ActiveX control exports is called a custom method, designed by the author of the control. To the container, a method appears as a normal function exported by a dynamic link library, with an optional parameter list of up to 15 parameters and a return value of any type.

## Properties

Properties are public data contained within both the container and control that each exposes to the other. OLE/ActiveX defines four categories of properties called stock, custom, ambient, and extended. Stock and custom properties belong to the control, and ambient and extended properties belong to the container.

### Stock and custom properties

Stock properties specify typical control characteristics defined by the ActiveX standards, such as the control's foreground and background colors, the text displayed in its window, and the font used for the text. Custom properties are any other data that the control designer wants to expose to the container. A container reads and writes a control's properties by calling functions known in MFC as Get and Set methods, which are exported by the control. These are the same get/put property methods we encountered when working with the Test Container's Invoke Methods dialog. The difference is strictly a matter of nomenclature—whereas MFC begins method names with the prefixes Get and Set, COM terminology prefers get and put (in lowercase). Typically, each property has a corresponding Get/Set method pair, but a control can prevent the container from changing a control property simply by not exporting a Set method for it. Chapter 9, Writing ActiveX Controls Using MFC, demonstrates how this is done.

Table 8-4 shows the link between stock properties in the control and the functions a container calls to read the properties. For each Get method listed in the table's third column, a corresponding Set method exists with a matching name. A Set method has no return value and takes a single parameter that is the same type as the Get method's return value. The prototypes for *GetAppearance* and *SetAppearance* illustrate the pattern for all Get/Set functions:

```
short GetAppearance( )        // Returns a property of type short
void  SetAppearance( short n )  // Passes a property of type short
```

| Property | Dispatch map entry in control | Get function called by container |
|----------|------------------------------|----------------------------------|
| *Appearance* | DISP_STOCKPROP_APPEARANCE | `short GetAppearance()` |
| *BackColor* | DISP_STOCKPROP_BACKCOLOR | `OLE_COLOR GetBackColor()` |
| *BorderStyle* | DISP_STOCKPROP_BORDERSTYLE | `short GetBorderStyle()` |
| *Caption* | DISP_STOCKPROP_CAPTION | `BSTR GetText()` |
| *Enabled* | DISP_STOCKPROP_ENABLED | `BOOL GetEnabled()` |
| *Font* | DISP_STOCKPROP_FONT | `LPFONTDISP GetFont()` |
| *ForeColor* | DISP_STOCKPROP_FORECOLOR | `OLE_COLOR GetForeColor()` |
| *hWnd* | DISP_STOCKPROP_HWND | `OLE_HANDLE GetHwnd()` |
| *Text* | DISP_STOCKPROP_TEXT | `BSTR GetText()` |
| *ReadyState* | DISP_STOCKPROP_READYSTATE | `long GetReadyState()` |

**Table 8-4.** *Stock control properties defined by OLE/ActiveX.*

### Ambient and extended properties

Ambient and extended properties belong to the client site and cannot be altered by the control. Extended properties are data that pertain to the embedded control but are implemented and managed by the container. Ambient properties describe the container itself, such as its current background color or font. By reading its container's ambient properties, a control can tailor its appearance and behavior to match the container. A control queries for an ambient property by calling the *COleControl:: GetAmbientProperty* function with a dispatch identifier for the desired property, like this:

```
LPFONTDISP fontdisp;
GetAmbientProperty( DISPID_AMBIENT_FONT, VT_FONT, &fontdisp );
```

For standard ambient properties predefined by the OLE/ActiveX speci-fications, a control can more conveniently call related helper functions provided by *COleControl* such as *AmbientFont*:

```
LPFONTDISP fontdisp = AmbientFont ();
```

Table 8-5 lists the standard ambient properties a container can support. An ActiveX control determines the value of an ambient property either by calling *GetAmbientProperty* using one of the dispatch identifiers listed in the table's second column, or by calling the equivalent helper function in the third column. If you use AppWizard to create your container applica-tion, support for standard ambient properties is built in and requires no special action. Calling *SetFont* or *SetTextColor* to set a font or foreground color in a container dialog automatically sets the *Font* and *ForeColor* ambient properties for sites in the dialog. When an ActiveX control calls the *AmbientFont* or *AmbientForeColor* functions, it receives the ambient data that are current for the dialog.

# Writing a Container Application

So how do you, the container developer, know in advance what events, methods, and properties an ActiveX control provides and what event han-dler functions your container application should include? The Gallery and ClassWizard take care of that for you. Using an existing control in your

| Property | Dispatch identifier | Function called by control |
|---|---|---|
| *BackColor* | DISPID_AMBIENT_ BACKCOLOR | `OLE_COLOR AmbientBackColor()` |
| *DisplayName* | DISPID_AMBIENT_ DISPLAYNAME | `CString AmbientDisplayName()` |
| *Font* | DISPID_AMBIENT_ FONT | `LPFONTDISP AmbientFont()` |
| *ForeColor* | DISPID_AMBIENT_ FORECOLOR | `OLE_COLOR AmbientForeColor()` |
| *LocaleID* | DISPID_AMBIENT_ LOCALEID | `LCID AmbientLocaleID()` |
| *ScaleUnits* | DISPID_AMBIENT_ SCALEUNITS | `CString AmbientScaleUnits()` |
| *ShowGrab-Handles* | DISPID_AMBIENT_ SHOWGRABHANDLES | `BOOL AmbientShowGrabHandles()` |
| *ShowHatching* | DISPID_AMBIENT_ SHOWHATCHING | `BOOL AmbientShowHatching()` |
| *TextAlign* | DISPID_AMBIENT_ TEXTALIGN | `short AmbientTextAlign()` |
| *UIDead* | DISPID_AMBIENT_ UIDEAD | `BOOL AmbientUIDead()` |
| *UserMode* | DISPID_AMBIENT_ USERMODE | `BOOL AmbientUserMode()` |

**Table 8-5.**  *Standard container ambient properties.*

container program depends on individual license arrangements—a subject covered in the next chapter—but once over that hurdle you select an ActiveX control from the Gallery and add it to your project as you would any other component. Visual C++ automatically scans the Registry to locate all controls registered with the system, so adding an ActiveX control to the Gallery is simply a matter of registering it.

When the Gallery places an ActiveX control in your container project, it examines the type library contained in the control's executable image for a list of the events, methods, and properties exported by the control. From this information, the Gallery creates a complete wrapper class that contains the Get/Set property functions and method calls through which the container gains access to the control's data. To get or set a property in the control—the background color, for instance—the container calls a function in the wrapper class:

```
OLE_COLOR CDemoCtrl::GetBackColor()
{
    OLE_COLOR result;
    GetProperty(DISPID_BACKCOLOR, VT_I4, (void*)&result);
    return result;
}

void CDemoCtrl::SetBackColor(OLE_COLOR propVal)
{
    SetProperty(DISPID_BACKCOLOR, VT_I4, propVal);
}
```

Since event handlers belong to the container's class, which is usually derived from a dialog-based class such as *CDialog*, the Gallery does not add source code for event handler functions. That job is left to Class-Wizard after the control is added to a dialog.

The procedure is best explained using an example. This section builds a simple container application called Hour that uses one of the license-free ActiveX controls included on the companion CD. The control is the same IETimer.ocx timer control used earlier in the Tumble.htm document. You can find the IETimer control listed under the name Timer Object in the Gallery's Registered ActiveX Controls folder. The list of controls in the folder may include another timer ActiveX control, created from an MFC sample project named Time Control. (The source files for Time Control are in the folder MSDN\Samples\VC98\MFC\Controls\Time.) Both timer controls export the same methods and perform the same function, so it does not matter which one you use for the Hour project.

Unlike other ActiveX controls such as Anibutton and Calendar, Timer Object is not a visible control. It does not display itself as a window within the container, but merely fires an event at a specified interval, serving as a timer mechanism for the containing program. The Hour program uses the timer events to manage the three progress indicators shown in

Figure 8-9. The progress controls display elapsed time in minutes, seconds, and tenths of a second. The Hour program takes its name from the fact that all three displays start over when the Minutes progress control fills up after the lapse of 60 minutes.

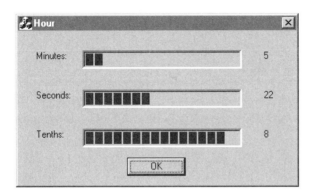

**Figure 8-9.**     *The Hour program.*

Building the Hour project takes only five steps from start to finish.

## Step 1: Create the Hour Project with AppWizard

Choose New from the environment's File menu, select the MFC AppWizard (exe) icon in the Projects tab, and type *Hour* as the project name. Hour is a dialog-based application, so click the Dialog Based radio button in AppWizard's Step 1 and make sure the ActiveX Controls check box is turned on in Step 2:

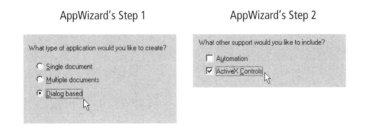

Click the Finish button to create the project.

## Step 2: Insert the Timer Object Control into the Project

This step should seem familiar by now. Use the Add To Project command on the Project menu to open the Gallery and display the list of ActiveX controls shown in Figure 8-1 on page 333. Scroll horizontally and select either the Timer Object or Time Control icon, then click the Insert button. This adds source files for either the *CIeTimer* or *CTimeCtrl* class to the Hour project, depending on the selected control. Click OK when the Confirm Classes dialog appears, and then close the Gallery dialog.

If Timer Object is not listed in the dialog's display, the control has not been registered yet. To register the Timer Object control, copy the IETimer.ocx file from the companion CD to the Windows\OCCache folder and run the RegSvr32 utility as described on page 336. When the control successfully registers itself, it appears in the Gallery list the next time you open the dialog.

## Step 3: Place the Timer Object Control in the Hour Dialog

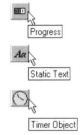

In earlier versions of Visual C++, you must double-click the IDD_HOUR_ DIALOG identifier in the ResourceView pane to start the dialog editor and load the main dialog. Delete the "to do" static text control and the Cancel button in the dialog work area by selecting them and pressing the Del key. Drag the Progress, Static Text, and Timer Object tools from the Controls toolbar onto the work area and arrange the controls to look something like this:

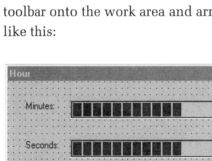

Because the Timer Object ActiveX control does not create its own window when the program runs, it doesn't matter where you place it in the dialog. Expose the Properties box for each control and type in the captions shown in the screen image above along with the identifiers listed in the second column of Table 8-6.

| Control | Identifier | Variable Name |
|---|---|---|
| Minutes progress indicator | IDC_PROGRESS_MIN | *progMin* |
| Seconds progress indicator | IDC_PROGRESS_SEC | *progSec* |
| Tenths progress indicator | IDC_PROGRESS_TEN | *progTen* |
| Top "x" static control | IDC_MINUTES | *strMin* |
| Middle "x" static control | IDC_SECONDS | *strSec* |
| Bottom "x" static control | IDC_TENTHS | *strTen* |
| Time control | IDC_TIMER1 | *time* |

**Table 8-6.**      *Control identifiers in the Hour program.*

The application class *CHourDlg* requires a member variable for each of the dialog's controls, which you can add through ClassWizard. With the dialog editor still active, click the ClassWizard command on the View menu to invoke the MFC ClassWizard dialog described in Chapter 6. In the Member Variables tab, select each new control in the Control IDs box and click the Add Variable button to display the Add Member Variable dialog. In the text box labeled Member Variable Name, type the control variable listed in the third column of Table 8-6. Figure 8-10 on the next page shows the final result.

We also need a function to handle the event fired by the Timer Object control. In ClassWizard's Message Maps tab, select IDC_TIMER1 from the Object IDs box and Timer from the Messages box, then click the Add Function button. ClassWizard adds stub code for an event handler function named *OnTimerTimer1*, shown on the next page.

The "E" prefix designates *OnTimerTimer1* as an event handler function. Click OK to close the ClassWizard dialog.

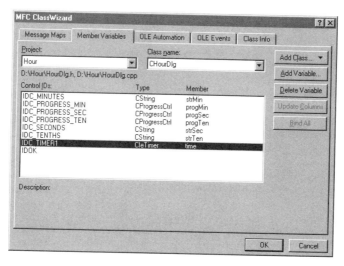

**Figure 8-10.** *Adding member variables to the* CHourDlg *class.*

## Step 4: Add Code to the Hour.cpp and Hour.h Files

To review the variable and function declarations that ClassWizard has added to the HourDlg.h header file, click the arrow button at the far right of the WizardBar:

and select Go To Class Definition from the drop-down menu. Visual C++ automatically opens HourDlg.h in the text editor and positions the caret at the start of the *CHourDlg* declaration, in which the new control variables have been added:

```
// Dialog Data
    //{{AFX_DATA(CHourDlg)
    enum { IDD = IDD_HOUR_DIALOG };
    CProgressCtrl    progTen;
    CProgressCtrl    progSec;
    CProgressCtrl    progMin;
    CString          strMin;
    CString          strSec;
    CString          strTen;
    CIeTimer         time;
    //}}AFX_DATA
```

ClassWizard has also added a prototype for the *OnTimerTimer1* event handler function:

```
    afx_msg void OnTimerTimer1();
    DECLARE_EVENTSINK_MAP()
```

We need add only two lines to the *CHourDlg* class declaration:

```
class CHourDlg : public CDialog
{
private:
    int        iMin, iSec;
```

As before, the shading indicates additions to the code that you must type yourself in the text editor.

The variables *iMin* and *iSec* keep tallies of elapsed minutes and seconds, which are written to the static controls adjacent to the progress indicators in the dialog. A similar tally isn't required for elapsed tenths of seconds, because the position of the IDC_PROGRESS_TEN progress indicator advances with every event fired by the Timer Object control. This will become clear in a moment when we add code to the event handler.

The final modifications to the source code are made in the *CHourDlg:: OnInitDialog* function. Click anywhere in the WizardBar's Members box to display a drop-down list of member functions and select *OnInitDialog* from the list shown on the next page.

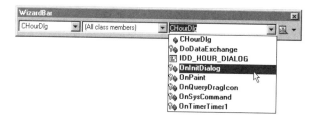

Visual C++ opens the HourDlg.cpp source file in the text editor and auto-matically places the caret at the beginning of the *OnInitDialog* definition. Add the shaded text after the function's "to do" line, as shown below:

```
// TODO: Add extra initialization here

time.SetInterval( 100 );        // Set timer interval to 1/10 second
progMin.SetRange( 0, 59 );      // Set ranges for progress indicators
progSec.SetRange( 0, 59 );      // Seconds: 1-60
progTen.SetRange( 0, 9 );       // Tenths:  1-10

progMin.SetStep( 1 );           // Set step intervals for prog indicators
progSec.SetStep( 1 );
progTen.SetStep( 1 );

iMin = iSec = 0;                // Initialize tallies
```

These instructions initialize the progress indicator controls. The instruction

```
time.SetInterval( 100 );          // Set timer interval to 1/10 second
```

calls a method in Timer Object to tell the control to start firing events every 100 milliseconds.

Use the WizardBar to navigate down to the *CHourDlg::OnTimerTimer1* function and add the following shaded lines:

```
void CHourDlg::OnTimerTimer1()
{
        // TODO: Add your control notification handler code here

        int i = progTen.StepIt ();

        if (++i == 10)
        {
            if (++iSec == 60)
            {
```

```
            if (++iMin == 60)
            {
                iMin = 0;
                progMin.SetPos( 0 );
            }
            else
                progMin.StepIt ();

            iSec = 0;
            progSec.SetPos( 0 );
            strMin.Format( "%d", iMin );
            SetDlgItemText( IDC_MINUTES, strMin );
        }
        else
            progSec.StepIt ();

        i = 0;
        progTen.SetPos( 0 );
        strSec.Format( "%d", iSec );
        SetDlgItemText( IDC_SECONDS, strSec );
    }

    strTen.Format( "%d", i );
    SetDlgItemText( IDC_TENTHS, strTen );
}
```

Every tenth of a second, the *OnTimerTimer1* implementation function receives the control's fired event and advances the IDC_PROGRESS_TEN progress indicator by one step. When the Tenths progress indicator reaches its maximum value, the indicator is reset to zero and the Seconds indicator increments by one. In the same way, the Seconds indicator is reset after 60 seconds have elapsed and the Minutes indicator increments. The entire procedure starts over when the program measures the lapse of one hour.

## Step 5: Build and Test the Project

Select the Win32 Release configuration on the Build toolbar, and then build a release version of the Hour.exe program. Click the Execute command on the Build menu to run the finished program. Note that Hour runs a bit slow, which is typical for a Win32 program that relies on a system timer resource. While you may be able to use it as an egg timer, the Timer Object control is not suitable for applications that require accurate timing.

The next chapter describes another container project called Game, which is similar to Hour. The difference is that Game uses a custom ActiveX control you write yourself, and not one that Microsoft provides.

# Working Without the Dialog Editor

The Visual C++ dialog editor makes it easy to add an ActiveX control to a dialog box, but there may be times when you want to place a control in a window other than a dialog. No technical obstacles bar your way—just as a normal control can appear in, say, a framed window, so can an ActiveX control—but you must forego the services of the dialog editor. This section explains how to add an ActiveX control to a non-dialog window, demonstrating by placing the Button Menu control into an application's client area.

The Button project introduced here requires only a little typing; otherwise you can find all source files on the companion CD. Notice that the project makes no use of the dialog editor, so the Button Menu control is never instantiated during development. The techniques described in this section can therefore overcome the creation error that some controls incorrectly exhibit at design time, as noted on page 345. Any ActiveX control can be placed in a window by following these steps, and the application will correctly compile. But true license protection is not circumvented because an unlicensed application cannot instantiate a protected control at run time. This will become clear in the next chapter, which discusses the ramifications of licensing.

## Step 1: Create the Button Project

Run AppWizard to begin the project, selecting the Single Document option at AppWizard's first screen. When AppWizard finishes, open the Registered ActiveX Controls folder in the Gallery and double-click the icon labeled BtnMenu Object. Accept the proposed class name *Cpmenu* for the new control and close the Gallery.

## Step 2: Add the Control to the *CButtonView* Class

Our intention is to place the Button Menu control inside the application's main window view, so coding begins in the ButtonView source files. First, add a *Cpmenu* object to the *CButtonView* class declaration located in the ButtonView.h header file:

```
#include "pmenu.h"
#define  IDC_BTNMENU    1001

class CButtonView : public CView
{
private:
    Cpmenu    btnmenu;

       ⋮

}
```

The next step involves writing code that initializes the *btnmenu* object. This is best done in the *CButtonView::OnInitialUpdate* function, ensuring that the application creates the control only once when the view first appears. ClassWizard can generate starter code for the function; just select *CButtonView* in the Class Name box of ClassWizard's Message Maps tab, then double-click *OnInitialUpdate* in the Messages box. Exit ClassWizard through the Edit Code button, which automatically opens the ButtonView.cpp source document in the text editor with the caret positioned at the new *OnInitialUpdate* function. Add to the function the initialization code shown here:

```
void CButtonView::OnInitialUpdate()
{
    CView::OnInitialUpdate();

    // TODO: Add your specialized code here and/or call the base class

    COleVariant v( 1L );
    CRect rect( 30, 30, 250, 120 );
    btnmenu.Create( NULL, WS_VISIBLE, rect, this, IDC_BTNMENU );
    btnmenu.SetCaption( "Click Here" );
    btnmenu.Invalidate();
    btnmenu.AddItem( "Menu item #1", v );
    v = 2L;
    btnmenu.AddItem( "Menu item #2", v );
    v = 3L;
    btnmenu.AddItem( "Menu item #3", v );
    v = 4L;
    btnmenu.AddItem( "Menu item #4", v );
}
```

*Cpmenu* is derived from *CWnd*, providing two versions of a *Create* function prototyped in the Pmenu.h file. For the sake of simplicity, the fragment shown here uses a *CRect* object to hard-code the control's size and position in the main window. The *Cpmenu::AddItem* function adds command strings to the button's pop-up menu, ordering the commands in the menu according to the VARIANT value given as the function's second parameter. The *OnInitialUpdate* function in this example merely creates a *COleVariant* object to hold the VARIANT values and calls *AddItem* four times to insert a representative list of menu commands.

If you compile and run the Button application at this point, it correctly displays the Button Menu control in the main window. Although clicking the control invokes its pop-up menu, the application itself does not respond when commands in the menu are selected and clicked. This is because we haven't yet added functions to handle the events that the Button Menu control fires during user interaction. That's next.

## Step 3: Handle Events

We still do not know what events the Button Menu control fires. That information is stored in the control's OCX file as part of its type library resource, but ClassWizard cannot read the data because it knows nothing about the control or the *Cpmenu* class. Visual C++ provides a utility that lets you explore a control's type library to learn what events the control fires and the required parameter list for handler functions. The program is named OleView.exe, and is invoked by clicking OLE/COM Object Viewer on the Tools menu. The View TypeLib command on the Object Viewer's File menu lets you open the BtnMenu.ocx file and display its type library. It turns out that the Button Menu control fires only two events, called *Click* and *Select*. The library script shows how a container application must declare handler functions to properly receive the event firings:

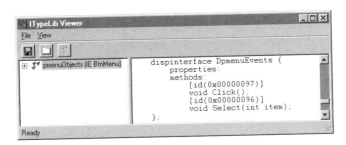

This is all the information we need to write handler functions for the events. But especially for a control that provides many different events, an easier alternative to poring through a type library is to simply inform ClassWizard about the control's existence. ClassWizard can then take on all the work of reading the type information from the control, generating code for stub handler functions, and adding their entries to the event sink map. All that's required is a little massaging of the project's class database and a small addition to the *CButtonView* class declaration. Here's how it's done.

First, open the Button.clw file in the text editor and add a new resource entry for a dialog box:

```
ResourceCount=3
Resource1=IDR_MAINFRAME
Resource2=IDD_ABOUTBOX
Resource3=IDD_FAKEDLG
```

Be sure to increase the resource count to 3 in the first line. At the bottom of the file add a description of the new dialog resource:

```
[DLG:IDD_FAKEDLG]
Type=1
Class=CButtonView
ControlCount=1
Control1=IDC_BTNMENU,{52dfae60-cebf-11cf-a3a9-00a0c9034920},1342177280
```

There is no such dialog in the project—hence the identifier name—but ClassWizard does not need to know that. The entry tells ClassWizard that a dialog resource identified as IDD_FAKEDLG belongs to the *CButtonView* class and contains the Button Menu control, which is identified by its CLSID number.

Next, return to the ButtonView.h file and emend the code we added earlier, adding a **#define** statement for the IDD_FAKEDLG identifier and declaring the value in the *CButtonView* class declaration. The new entry is marked by special AFX_DATA comment lines, making the dialog identifier recognizable to ClassWizard as explained in Chapter 6. The result looks like this:

```
#include "pmenu.h"
#define   IDC_BTNMENU      1001
#define   IDD_FAKEDLG      1002

class CButtonView : public CView
{
private:
    Cpmenu    btnmenu;
    //{{AFX_DATA(CButtonView)
    enum { IDD = IDD_FAKEDLG };
    //}}AFX_DATA
```

Save the file. Now when you invoke ClassWizard, the IDC_BTNMENU identifier shows up at the bottom of the objects list in the Message Maps tab when the *CButtonView* class is selected in the Class Name box. Select the IDC_BTNMENU entry to display the two events in the Messages box, then double-click the *Select* event to add a new handler function named *OnSelectBtnmenu*. The handler gains control whenever the user clicks a command in the control's pop-up menu.

With the new handler function selected in the Member Functions box, click the Edit Code button to reopen the ButtonView.cpp file. Add code to the *OnSelectBtnmenu* function that responds whenever the control fires its *Select* event:

```
void CButtonView::OnSelectBtnmenu( long item )
{
    // TODO: Add your control notification handler code here

    CString str;

    str.Format( "You selected item #%li\t", item );
    MessageBox( str, "Button application", MB_ICONINFORMATION );
}
```

Build the Button application and run it. You should see a message box each time you click an item in the control's menu, as illustrated in Figure 8-11.

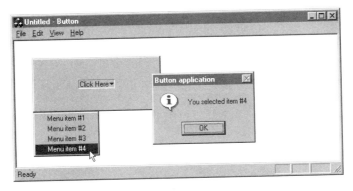

**Figure 8-11.**    *An ActiveX control placed in a framed window.*

# Writing ActiveX Controls Using MFC

Chapter 8 demonstrated that an understanding of the underlying structure of OLE and COM is not a requirement for creating an ActiveX container application, if you use MFC. Remarkably, the same is true when writing ActiveX controls. MFC handles so many of the details that you can write a control with little concern for its intricate underpinnings. If you decide to write your ActiveX control without MFC—and there can be good reasons for considering the idea—the project becomes more ambitious. Depending on your approach and the control's complexity, you may need a thorough grounding in the principles of ActiveX and Component Object Model.

This chapter picks up where the preceding chapter left off. It examines ActiveX controls from the perspective of the server rather than the client, describing the ways in which Visual C++ helps the developer who wants to write, not just use, an ActiveX control. Visual C++ makes available three different tools that help set up an ActiveX control project:

- MFC support for ActiveX controls
- The BaseCtl framework
- The Active Template Library

# Visual C++ Tools for Creating ActiveX Controls

MFC offers the easiest route to a working and stable ActiveX control. The Control Development Kit, formerly available on Microsoft Developer Network, has been incorporated into Visual C++ as a set of tools that includes the Test Container and ControlWizard, renamed MFC ActiveX Control-Wizard. As demonstrated with an example project later in the chapter, ControlWizard generates source files containing starter code that uses MFC to take care of nearly all the COM details. The generated source code handles serialization, displays a property sheet for the control, and provides many other conveniences for both the programmer and the user. You need only add any code required to draw the control, react to user input, and fire events.

Writing an ActiveX control using MFC can result in an OCX file of surprisingly small size, but the size is misleading because the control forever depends on the existence of two large files. Herein lies the disadvantage of MFC. Small executable size is especially important for controls intended for a Web page, since a user's browser program must first download a control to display it if the control's OCX file is not already available on the user's computer. An ActiveX control cannot statically link with MFC, which means that if the correct version of the MFC library DLL file does not exist on the user's hard disk, the file must also be transmitted along with the control. To make matters worse, MFC requires the C run-time library, so the Msvcrt.dll file may also need to be downloaded. Transmittal of the library files occurs automatically when the user first encounters a Web page that displays an ActiveX control dependent on MFC. While this may be a reasonable scenario for an internal Web site to which a user connects through a fast network, it is not realistic for the Internet. Since the MFC library is approximately a megabyte in size, downloading the file takes several minutes even over a fast modem.

The BaseCtl framework, also known as the ActiveX Controls framework, is a lightweight alternative to MFC. Though BaseCtl offers much less support for the developer, it also allows greater flexibility. An ActiveX control built from BaseCtl requires neither MFC nor the C run-time library. And because the framework provides only minimal code, the control has a smaller memory footprint than its MFC counterpart. But the advantages of BaseCtl carry a price—using BaseCtl takes more work on your part and a greater understanding of the principles of COM and ActiveX. For example, you must be reasonably comfortable with persistence interfaces such as *IStream*, *IPersistPropertyBag*, and *IPersistStream*. The framework provides core functionality through three main classes, named *CAutomationObject*, *COleControl*, and *CPropertyPage*.

BaseCtl used to require Visual Basic 4.0 to begin a project, but no longer. You now start a project by running the NMake utility provided with Visual C++, once to generate the library files and again to generate stub source files for the new control. The procedure is explained in a ReadMe.txt file provided with BaseCtl. If you requested the inclusion of sample code when you installed Visual C++, the ReadMe.txt file and source files for several sample BaseCtl projects are located in the folder MSDN\Samples\VC98\SDK\COM\ActiveXC\BaseCtl. For the most recent updates of BaseCtl, download the ActiveX development kit from this Internet address:

*http://www.microsoft.com/intdev/sdk*

BaseCtl is not often used today because the Active Template Library (ATL) provides a superior tool for the creation of small ActiveX controls. Although the resulting OCX file is apt to be larger than a similar control that relies on MFC, a control created through ATL usually occupies much less memory because it does not require the presence of other auxiliary files. Besides a library of intelligent template code that implements many standard interfaces for you, ATL provides a wizard that generates initial source files, greatly simplifying the early stages of an ActiveX control project. Creating an ActiveX control using ATL requires more work compared to building the same control with ControlWizard and MFC, but ATL is a good choice for creating lean ActiveX controls intended for use on the Internet. You may have heard that ATL is not suitable for writing ActiveX controls, but that's no longer true since the library's 2.0 release. ATL is not a simple subject, however, and a more detailed discussion is deferred until the next chapter.

This chapter covers the MFC approach to ActiveX controls. MFC offers the best way to try the waters of ActiveX programming, and by itself provides more than enough material for discussion. Besides saving you a great deal of coding, using MFC to write an ActiveX control makes available helpful Visual C++ features such as ClassWizard and ControlWizard. As we'll see next, ControlWizard provides an excellent starting point for an ActiveX control project.

# ControlWizard

In the same way that AppWizard creates a project for an MFC application, ControlWizard creates a project for an ActiveX control. A control created with the help of ControlWizard uses MFC, giving it the advantages and disadvantages described in the preceding section. ControlWizard is a customized form of AppWizard, and a ControlWizard project begins the same way as a normal AppWizard project. Choose the New command from the File menu to call up the New dialog, and in the Projects tab click the icon for the MFC ActiveX ControlWizard. Figure 9-1 illustrates the steps.

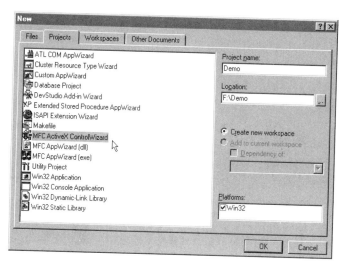

**Figure 9-1.**    *Beginning an ActiveX control project with ControlWizard.*

ControlWizard walks you through two steps before creating the project. This section examines options that the wizard offers and discusses when and why an option might be appropriate for your ActiveX control.

Figure 9-2 shows ControlWizard's opening screen, which first asks for the number of controls in the project. Like a VBX custom control, an OCX file can contain more than one ActiveX control component. Specify the number of controls you want in the text box at the top of the dialog. You can also add controls later during project development. The next option on the ControlWizard screen lets you restrict the control's use through a license. Although the license support option is turned off by default, many controls intended for general use should have the protection of a license, which is described shortly.

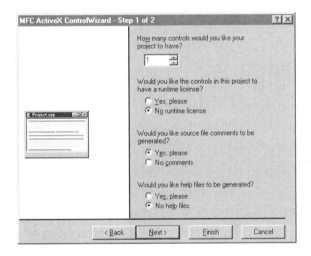

**Figure 9-2.**    *ControlWizard's Step1.*

The last option in Step 1 directs ControlWizard to generate help files for the control. A request for project help files adds the same sort of help support you receive from AppWizard. For a description of the generated help files, refer to the discussion in Chapter 2 beginning on page 47.

ControlWizard's second screen (Figure 9-3) presents you with options that determine how the control should interact with a container. The options in Step 2 require a little explanation, so the following list examines them in more detail.

■ **Activates When Visible**—Determines whether the container should automatically activate the control when it becomes visible. Immediate activation is often desirable for an ActiveX control, though

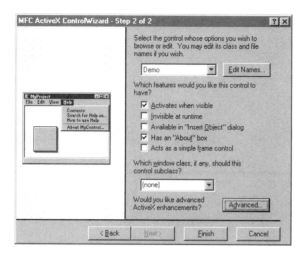

**Figure 9-3.**    *ControlWizard's Step 2.*

selecting the Activates When Visible option should be considered only a hint to the container application, which may ignore the request. A discussion below has more to say about this option.

- **Invisible At Run-Time**—If this option is checked, ControlWizard does not add an *OnDraw* function to the control class. Use this option for controls that do not require visual interaction with the user, such as the Timer Object control introduced in Chapter 8.

- **Available In Insert Object Dialog**—Pertains to the Insert Object dialog (or equivalent) offered by many container applications, from the Test Container tool to Microsoft Office applications. Leaving the box unchecked signals a container that it should not include the new control in the container's Insert Object dialog.

- **Has An About Box**—ControlWizard generates source code for an About method and resources for a generic About box.

- **Acts As A Simple Frame Control**—Adds support for the *ISimpleFrameSite* interface. This option sets up the control to act as a frame that encloses other ActiveX controls in the container window, grouping the controls visually and allowing them to be moved together. Not all containers support simple frames.

■ **Window Subclassing**—Sets up the control project by subclassing a normal Windows control such as an edit box or a progress indicator.

By default, ControlWizard turns on only two of the options listed above: Activates When Visible and Has An About Box. Deselecting the Activates When Visible check box clears the control's OLEMISC_ACTIVATEWHEN-VISIBLE status flag, which the control places in its Registry data through MFC's *AfxOleRegisterControlClass* global function. The container that embeds the control can determine the state of the flag by calling the control's *IOleObject::GetMiscStatus* method. A clear flag signals the container that the control should remain inactive when it becomes visible, thus postponing the creation of the control's window until the user requires it. For ActiveX controls that the user may never call into service, this can save the expensive operation of creating a window unnecessarily. Chapter 10 looks more closely at ActiveX control status flags such as OLEMISC_ACTIVATEWHENVISIBLE.

You may also want to consider turning off the About Box option because the added support for the About box increases the size of the finished ActiveX control. The standard About box that ControlWizard generates, for example, adds approximately 2 KB of extra code and resource data to the finished OCX file. Refer to the final section of Chapter 4 for a discussion on other means of minimizing resource data, which is especially important for ActiveX controls.

If the Available In Insert Object Dialog check box is selected, the control's self-registration procedure adds a Registry key named Insertable to the control's CLSID Registry hierarchy. The Insertable key informs a container that the ActiveX control can act as a passive embedded object. The container can thus create an object of the ActiveX control through the OLE Documents interfaces. These interfaces, identified by the *IOle* prefix, include *IOleCache*, *IOleClientSite*, *IOleContainer*, *IOleInPlaceObject*, and *IOleInPlaceSite*. Applications that can embed an object in a container document scan the Registry for objects that have the Insertable keyword and display a list of the objects in a standard Insert Object dialog. To see the list in Microsoft Word, for example, click the Object command on Word's Insert menu. An ActiveX control created using ControlWizard appears in the list only if the Available In Insert Object Dialog check box is turned on. Applications that do not support container documents ignore the Insertable keyword. For example, the New Control tool in the Test Container utility we encountered in Chapter 8 displays a list of all registered controls whether they are marked insertable or not.

If you want your ActiveX control to subclass a standard or common Windows control, click the box shown at the bottom of the screen in Figure 9-3. The drop-down window displays a list of 16 Windows controls ranging from buttons to tree views. Selecting an entry from the list causes ControlWizard to generate source code for the ActiveX control that subclasses the selected Windows control. Use this option to produce an ActiveX control that has the characteristics of a particular Windows control, but that you want to modify to add desired effects.

Click the Advanced button in ControlWizard's Step 2 to open the Advanced ActiveX Features dialog shown in Figure 9-4. The dialog provides options that set or clear bit flags defined by the *COleControl::ControlFlags* enumeration set, which describes characteristics of the control's behavior when activated. Setting any of the check boxes causes Control-Wizard to add code that overrides the *COleControl::GetControlFlags* method, which informs the container of the *ControlFlags* settings. To add the override yourself to an existing control project, set a specific bit flag such as *windowlessActivate* like this:

```
DWORD CDemoCtrl::GetControlFlags()
{
    return COleControl::GetControlFlags() | windowlessActivate;
}
```

The check box labels in the Advanced ActiveX Features dialog may seem a bit terse, but the options are easy to understand with a little explanation. The following list describes what the flags mean. For more information about the *ControlFlags* settings and how they affect a control's activation, consult the online help article entitled "ActiveX Controls: Optimization," located through the index entry *Optimizing ActiveX Controls*.

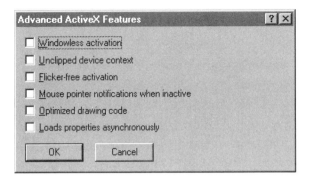

**Figure 9-4.** *Advanced ActiveX Features dialog, invoked by clicking ControlWizard's Advanced button.*

- **Windowless Activation**—Informs the container that the control does not create its own window when activated. A discussion below has more to say about windowless activation.

- **Unclipped Device Context**—Requests no clipping of the control's display, resulting in faster rendering. However, the control must make sure it does not display outside the site boundaries.

- **Flicker-Free Activation**—Requests the container not to invalidate the control window when the control switches states. This prevents the control from redrawing itself when it becomes active or inactive, thus eliminating the slight flicker that might otherwise occur. The option is suitable only for a control that draws itself the same way regardless of its state.

- **Mouse Pointer Notifications**—Requests the container to send mouse messages to the ActiveX control when the control is not in its active state. If the container complies with the request, the inactive control continues to receive WM_SETCURSOR and WM_MOUSEMOVE messages that pertain to mouse activity over the control window. Selecting this option enables the *IPointerInactive* interface, to which the container delegates those mouse messages that belong to the control. The *IPointerInactive* interface adjusts each message's mouse coordinates for the control window and dispatches the message through the control's message map. Through this capability, a control can function appropriately as a drag-and-drop target even when inactive.

- **Optimized Drawing**—Improves drawing speed by allowing the control's *OnDraw* method to return without restoring the original GDI objects for the device context. This option has effect only if the container supports optimized drawing, which the control determines by calling the *COleControl::IsOptimizedDraw* function. A return value of TRUE means that the control does not have to select the original GDI objects such as pens and brushes back into the device context when finished drawing.

- **Loads Properties Asynchronously**—This option can increase the responsiveness of an ActiveX control that requires a substantial amount of property data. Asynchronous loading enables the control to become active on a Web page as quickly as possible, even while the browser continues to download the control's data through the modem in the background. The control can thus immediately begin playing audio or video clips, for example, without waiting for the complete data set. However, the control must take no action that requires data that have not yet arrived. Asynchronous loading adds overhead to the control, so use the option only for controls that can benefit from it.

The Windowless Activation option is not the same thing as the Invisible At Run-Time flag described earlier. Windowless activation means only that the control does not provide its own window. By not creating a window, the control optimizes the speed at which it is created while slightly decreasing its executable size. The control is free to use the container's windowing services provided the container supports windowless objects. Support requires the *IOleInPlaceObjectWindowless* interface to reflect user input messages to the windowless control. By overwriting the container's window, a windowless control can appear with a true transparent background, an effect not possible for a normal ActiveX control that displays its own rectangular window. However, using the same idea of background transparency described in Chapter 4, a windowed control can often simulate a transparent background by matching the color of its own window with the container's ambient background color. As mentioned in the preceding chapter, a control can determine the container's current ambient color by calling *COleControl::AmbientBackColor*:

```
OLE_COLOR ContainerBkGrnd = AmbientBackColor ();
```

Incidentally, not all containers support the *Ambient* functions of *COleControl*. An ActiveX control should check for a valid return value after calling a function such as *AmbientBackColor*.

# Licensing

An ActiveX control placed on a popular Web page can soon end up on computers all over the world, viewed on thousands of browsers. This ability to easily reuse an ActiveX control is perhaps the technology's most compelling feature and greatest advantage. However, the wide distribution of a programmer's intellectual property also poses the potential problem of unauthorized use. To see the problem clearly, consider how an ActiveX control passes through three different parties identified as the Author, the Webmaster, and the User.

For a fee, the Author permits the Webmaster to install the ActiveX control on a Web page. The User visits the Webmaster's site through the Internet, and as a result the ActiveX control is copied from the Webmaster's computer to the User's computer where it appears in the User's browser program. So far, everything is as it should be and the control is being used as the Author intended. But without some sort of safeguard, nothing prevents other programmers who come into possession of the ActiveX control from using it in their own applications. Many developers might prefer that their creations are not reused in this way without authorization, especially in marketed applications that earn profit from a control without compensation for the control's author.

The most common safeguard against the unauthorized use of an ActiveX control involves a license. A license not only identifies the Author in our example as the owner of the control's copyright, but can also prevent subsequent reuse of the control by developers who have not received a license from the Author. The OLE/ActiveX control standard is designed with licensing in mind. The standard defines the *IClassFactory2* interface through which a container creates an instance of the control object and at the same time proves itself licensed to use the control. The creation of the control object is completed only if the container satisfies the control that a valid license exists.

Licensing is becoming a common practice for ActiveX controls, so it is worthwhile to examine the ControlWizard's licensing scheme in some detail. Another reason for spending time with the subject is that descriptions of licensing in the Visual C++ online documentation can be a little confusing, primarily because the documentation speaks of "the container" when there might be several containers involved. It's important to remember that any program is a container that can create an instance of an ActiveX control and provide a site for it. Chapter 8 demonstrated several different containers that can embed an ActiveX control under different circumstances:

- Internet Explorer or another ActiveX-aware browser, which locates a control through the class identifier specified by the OBJECT tag in an HTML document.

- The Visual C++ dialog editor, which creates an instance of a control when it is dropped into a dialog under development.

- A container application such as the Hour program that embeds an ActiveX control at run time.

A licensing scheme helps prevent a container application from making unauthorized use of a control, but which container? When the User in our scenario downloads the Author's control along with the HTML instructions that display it, the User's browser must be able to freely run the control without a license. Access should be restricted only for containers of the other two types in the list—that is, development programs (like Visual C++) and the container applications they create (like Hour).

Consider the chain of events when the Webmaster decides to develop an application that uses the Author's ActiveX control. To create the application, the Webmaster runs a Windows development program such as Visual C++ or Visual Basic. The program design calls for the application to display the control in a dialog box, so the Webmaster uses the dialog editor—itself a container—to create an instance of the control and display it in the dialog. At this point, called the design-time stage, licensing becomes an issue. In creating an instance of the control, the development program calls the control's *IClassFactory2::CreateInstanceLic* method with a NULL parameter, to which the control responds by returning a pointer to an interface only after confirming that the license exists. (We'll see how in a moment.)

Since the Webmaster is authorized to use the control in an application, the license verification succeeds and the dialog editor is able to create an instance of the control. The Webmaster completes development of the application and sells a copy of the executable to the User. As part of the package, the Webmaster supplies an installation program that places a copy of the Author's ActiveX control on the User's hard disk and registers it. Although the User has never entered into a licensing agreement with the Author, the new container application succeeds in creating an instance of the control object when it runs. (Again, the process is explained in a moment.) This is called the run-time stage of license verification.

Now consider what happens when the User (who also happens to be a programmer) tries to create another container application that embeds the Author's control. The User's development program calls the control's *IClassFactory2::CreateInstanceLic* method as before, but this time the control detects that the User does not possess a license and so disallows the creation attempt. The determined User can develop the application without the aid of the dialog editor, but the finished application is no more able to create an instance of the control than the development program. The licensing verification code in the control blocks unauthorized use both at design time and at run time.

The code that ControlWizard adds to a control project implements a licensing scheme like the one just described. The next section explains how the scheme works.

## ControlWizard Licensing Support

As shown in Figure 9-2 on page 377, ControlWizard's opening screen offers to add support for a simple licensing arrangement. If you request a run-time license for the new control, ControlWizard generates extra source code and a text file that together provide some assurance your control will be used only by authorized persons. The text file is a document with a LIC extension, containing the following text:

```
Copyright (c) 1998 author

Warning:  This product is licensed to you pursuant to the terms of the
license agreement included with the original software, and is
protected by copyright law and international treaties.  Unauthorized
reproduction or distribution may result in severe civil and criminal
penalties, and will be prosecuted to the maximum extent possible under
the law.
```

The word *author* in the first line of the license represents your user or company name. A file-based licensing scheme such as the one that ControlWizard implements requires that the LIC document exists in the same directory as the control OCX file when the container application adds the control at design time. For this reason, the Author must distribute the LIC text file to the Webmaster so that the Webmaster can create a container application that uses the control. But the terms of the license bar the Webmaster from redistributing the document to others. The User does not require the LIC file to run the Webmaster's application or to view the control in a browser.

ControlWizard places a master copy of the LIC file in the main project folder. When Visual C++ builds the OCX file, it copies the LIC file from the main folder to the Release or Debug folder where the OCX file resides, so a project may end up with two or three copies of the license file. Bear this in mind if you change the wording of the license. Make any alterations to the master copy of the LIC file before building the OCX file so that all copies remain up to date.

The source code that ControlWizard adds to the project consists of two functions, one named *GetLicenseKey*, which retrieves a unique password or key from the control's OCX file, and another named *VerifyUserLicense*, which checks a specified location of the user's disk for the existence of the license text file. A do-nothing project named License demonstrates how ControlWizard adds these two functions to the control's class source code. There is no need to create the License project yourself, because the control will not be developed here. It serves only to make the following discussions easier to follow and to illustrate ControlWizard's license scheme.

Here is the source listing for the two functions, taken from the project's LicenseCtl.cpp implementation file. (The _szLicString_ text on the third line will differ for your system.)

```
static const TCHAR BASED_CODE _szLicFileName[] = _T("License.lic");
static const WCHAR BASED_CODE _szLicString[] =
                L"Copyright (c) 1998 Witzend Software";


/////////////////////////////////////////////////////////////////////////
// CLicenseCtrl::CLicenseCtrlFactory::VerifyUserLicense -
// Checks for existence of a user license

BOOL CLicenseCtrl::CLicenseCtrlFactory::VerifyUserLicense()
{
    return AfxVerifyLicFile(AfxGetInstanceHandle(), _szLicFileName,
        _szLicString);
}


/////////////////////////////////////////////////////////////////////////
// CLicenseCtrl::CLicenseCtrlFactory::GetLicenseKey -
// Returns a runtime licensing key

BOOL CLicenseCtrl::CLicenseCtrlFactory::GetLicenseKey(DWORD dwReserved,
    BSTR FAR* pbstrKey)
{
    if (pbstrKey == NULL)
        return FALSE;

    *pbstrKey = SysAllocString(_szLicString);
    return (*pbstrKey != NULL);
}
```

Both the _VerifyUserLicense_ and _GetLicenseKey_ functions are called when a development program attempts to insert an ActiveX control into a container project at design time, as when the dialog editor adds the control to a dialog under development. When development is complete and the new container application is built and executed, its attempt at run time to create an instance of the control results in another call to the control's *GetLicenseKey* function. Let's examine both of these scenarios one at a time, looking first at how the control verifies at design time the existence of a license for the development program.

### Design-time license verification

By calling the control's *IClassFactory2::CreateInstanceLic* method, the development program says in effect, "If a valid license exists, create a new instance of the control and return a pointer to an interface on that instance." It's the control's job to verify the existence of a license. When *CreateInstanceLic* is called, the framework routes the call to the control's *VerifyUserLicense* function, which confirms that the LIC license file exists in the same directory as the control OCX file and that the first line of the file matches the contents of the *_szLicString* parameter. The *_szLicString* string is known as the license key.

If the LIC file exists and contains the correct license key, *VerifyUser-License* returns a value of TRUE, allowing the development program to create an instance of the ActiveX control for the container application under development. The development program next calls the control's *IClassFactory2::RequestLicKey* method. This call ends up in *GetLicense-Key*, the second of the two functions that ControlWizard added to the control source code. *GetLicenseKey* returns a copy of the control's *_szLic-String* license key, which the development program embeds in the container application executable file. We'll see why the container needs its own copy of the key when we talk about run-time license verification.

If the control does not find the LIC file in the same directory as the OCX file or if the first line of the license file has been altered, *VerifyUser-License* returns FALSE, in which case the development program displays an error message that explains the problem. For example, here's how Visual C++ handles the situation when the License.lic file has been altered or renamed. (If you try this experiment yourself, be sure to alter the License.lic file in the subfolder that contains the OCX file, because altering the master copy in the project folder has no effect after the control is built.) Assume that you are developing a container application called DemoContainer and wish to add the License ActiveX control to

DemoContainer's About box. Load the About box resource in the dialog editor and right-click in the work area to display the editor's context menu. Choose the Insert ActiveX Control command from the context menu, then select License Control from the list shown in Figure 9-5.

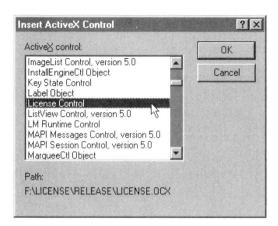

**Figure 9-5.** *Inserting the License control into a container project.*

The dialog editor attempts to create an instance of the License control, leading to a series of nested function calls. The editor calls the control's *IClassFactory2::CreateInstanceLic* method, which in turn calls the control's *VerifyUserLicense* function, which calls the framework's *AfxVerify-LicFile* function. This MFC function reads the file identified by the *_szLic-FileName* string—License.lic, in this case—and, if the file exists, compares the first line of the file with the license key contained in *_szLicString*. If the file does not exist or if its first line does not match the license key, *AfxVerifyLicFile* returns a value of FALSE to disallow the object creation. The result is an error message from Visual C++ that explains why the attempt failed:

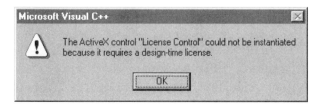

### Run-time license verification

If the license file is in order and the *VerifyUserLicense* function returns a value of TRUE, the development program succeeds in creating a control instance and inserts source files for the control's class into the container project. The next test for a valid license does not occur until after the container application is built and becomes an executable program.

When the container application runs and attempts to create an instance of the ActiveX control, it also calls the control's *IClassFactory2::CreateInstanceLic* method. But instead of passing a NULL value for the function's fourth parameter as the development program did at design time, the application provides a pointer to its copy of the license key. This is the same string that the development program obtained from the control's *GetLicenseKey* function and placed in the application's data. The call to *CreateInstanceLic* now says, "Create a new instance of the control and here is my proof that I am an authorized container." The control compares its own copy of the license key in *_szLicString* with the copy submitted by the container, verifies the match, and allows the create operation. The framework does not call the *VerifyUserLicense* function in this case, which is why the LIC file is not required when the application runs on the User's machine. Only the development program on the Webmaster's machine, not the finished container application, needs the license.

For more protection, alter the first line of the license LIC file to make the wording less generic. But make the same changes to the *_szLicString* character array in the source code, or *VerifyUserLicense* will fail to recognize the text file. You might also consider modifying the file-based licensing scheme described here to rely on a key in the system Registry rather than on a LIC text file. This would require a simple rewrite of the *VerifyUserLicense* function to search the Registry, and would also presume an installation program of some sort that registers the key for authorized licensees.

# Example 1: A Do-Nothing ActiveX Control

Before launching into the development of an ActiveX control, we should have a clear idea of the extent of ControlWizard's contribution to a project. The best way is simply to run ControlWizard and build a do-nothing control from the generated source files. As we will see in the next section, creating a useful ActiveX control requires a little work and a fair amount of discussion, all of which may obscure the fact that before we even start coding, ControlWizard has already generated source files for a working control with all the essentials. The remaining task for the developer is usually not so much to build an ActiveX control as to embellish one that already exists. Right from the start, a ControlWizard creation can run in a container, display its own window, react appropriately when its window is moved or resized, display an About box, and show a mock-up of its property sheet. The control performs no useful work, however, because it does not fire events, export custom methods, or contain properties.

Creating the ActiveX control pictured in Figure 9-6 requires no programming. If you would like to experiment, create a dummy project by running

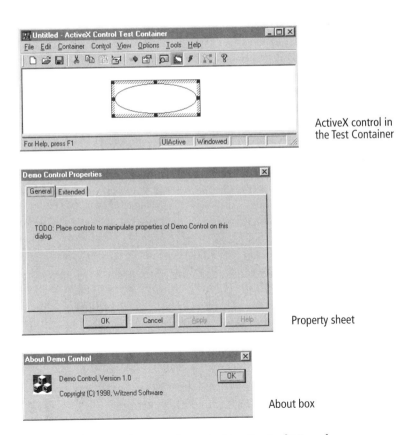

ActiveX control in the Test Container

Property sheet

About box

**Figure 9-6.**    *The default ActiveX control created by ControlWizard.*

New Control

the MFC ActiveX ControlWizard as explained earlier, change the project configuration to Win32 Release, and build the control from the generated source files. Like any ActiveX control, the result can be loaded only by an executing container such as the Test Container utility described in Chapter 8. Start the Test Container from the Tools menu, invoke its New Control tool, and search the list for the new do-nothing ActiveX control. The control has the same name as the project, appearing in the list as Demo Control or something similar. Insert the control into the Test Container, then call up the default property sheet shown in Figure 9-6 by double-clicking the control's window border or by clicking the Test Container's Properties button. To display the control's About box, select the Invoke Methods tool and click the Invoke button. When finished experimenting, exit Test Container and close the project. The control entry in the Registry can remain indefinitely without harm, but it's best to clean up the Registry before deleting an ActiveX control from your system. Run the RegSvr32 utility described in Chapter 8 and include the /u switch to unregister the control:

```
regsvr32 /u \demo\release\demo.ocx
```

The utility indicates success by displaying a message box:

When the control is successfully unregistered, you can delete the project files.

An overridden member function named *COleControl::OnDraw* paints the control window shown in Figure 9-6. As generated by ControlWizard, the *OnDraw* function displays an ellipse inside a white rectangle:

```
void CDemoCtrl::OnDraw(
            CDC* pdc, const CRect& rcBounds, const CRect& rcInvalid)
{
    pdc->FillRect(rcBounds,
```

```
        CBrush::FromHandle((HBRUSH)GetStockObject(WHITE_BRUSH)));
    pdc->Ellipse(rcBounds);
}
```

This function is one of the first places you will start when developing an ActiveX control created using ControlWizard. An example project demonstrates how to rewrite *OnDraw* to display a more meaningful control window.

# Example 2: The Tower ActiveX Control

This section expands on the preceding section, presenting a simple project that illustrates how to develop a useful ActiveX control that begins with ControlWizard. I've named the project Tower because it's a variation of a puzzle called Tower of Hanoi, credited to the nineteenth-century French mathematician Edouard Lucas. Figure 9-7 shows the Tower control as it appears in a dialog, displayed as a rectangular window divided into three panels. The object of the game is to drag the seven colored blocks one by one from the first panel and reassemble the stack in the third panel. You can move a single colored block from any panel to another, but you cannot place a block on top of a smaller block.

Although only a game, the Tower control demonstrates all the trappings of a typical ActiveX control. Tower contains stock and custom properties, exports methods, and fires events to let the container application know about the current status of the game. Later in the chapter we'll use the Test Container utility to monitor the control's events as they occur.

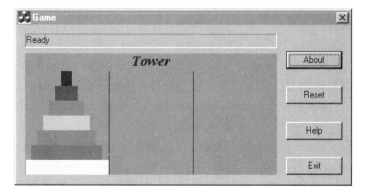

**Figure 9-7.** *The Tower ActiveX control embedded in a typical dialog.*

If you would like to build the Tower ActiveX control yourself, the following eight steps explain how. The discussions are not specific to the Tower project, however, and explore some of the alternative paths you might want to consider when setting up your own ActiveX control project. The first step runs ControlWizard to create the project, and the next four steps use ClassWizard to add properties, methods, events, and message handler functions to the Tower project. The sixth step creates a simple property page for the control. With ClassWizard's stub code in place, the seventh step shows how to flesh out the program with additional code to run the control, which is built and tested in the eighth step.

The Game program pictured in Figure 9-7 is a simple container written expressly to demonstrate Tower. It is a dialog-based application created with AppWizard's help, similar to the Hour program described in the previous chapter. Because we've already studied this type of program, Game is mentioned only briefly in the sections that follow. You will find source code for both Tower and the Game container program in the Code\Chapter.09 folder on the companion CD.

## Step 1: Create the Tower Project

The Tower project begins life through the ActiveX ControlWizard. Activate ControlWizard by clicking the New command on the File menu, then click the Projects tab and select the MFC ActiveX ControlWizard icon shown in Figure 9-1 on page 376. Type *Tower* as the project name and accept the defaults in ControlWizard's two steps.

## Step 2: Add Properties

The Tower control has five properties, named *Caption*, *Font*, *ForeColor*, *BackColor*, and *CurrentBlock*. The first four are stock properties that determine the content and appearance of the title text displayed at the top of Tower's window. At startup, the control initializes the title text to "Tower," but a container can specify new text in the *Caption* property if desired. *CurrentBlock* is a custom property containing an integer that represents the block being dragged. The integer value in *CurrentBlock* ranges from 0 for the smallest block to 6 for the largest block. Because the container has no reason to change this value, Tower keeps *CurrentBlock* a read-only property, as explained shortly.

Specifying properties in an MFC ActiveX control project like Tower requires precise placement and wording of various macros, so the job is best left to ClassWizard. In ClassWizard's Automation tab, click the Add Property button to call up the Add Property dialog (Figure 9-8), then click the arrow in the External Name box to display a list of stock properties. Add a stock property to the project by selecting it from the list. To specify a custom property, type any external name that is not in the list of stock names.

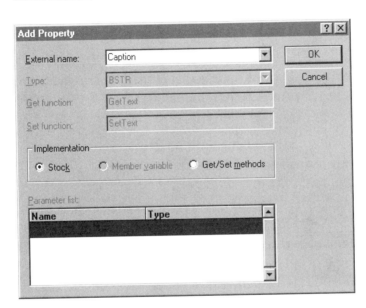

**Figure 9-8.**  *ClassWizard's Add Property dialog, invoked from the Automation tab.*

The Stock radio button in the Implementation group box lets you specify unambiguously whether a property is stock or custom, but the button is set by default when you select a stock property. The radio buttons labeled Member Variable and Get/Set Methods are commonly used only for custom properties, giving you two choices in how your control exposes a custom property to a container application. If you want to grant the client unrestricted access to the property, leave the setting at the Member Variable radio button. ClassWizard creates a variable for the property that the client can change through a property page and also generates a simple notification routine that lets the control know when the container has changed the property. If your control does not require the notification, clear the text box to prevent the function from being generated, thus saving a small amount of overhead.

For maximum control over how (or when) the container can read or write a custom property, click the Get/Set Methods radio button instead. This instructs ClassWizard to generate source code for a pair of methods that the container can call to read or write the property, as described in Chapter 8. To retrieve the property's current value, the container calls the corresponding Get method; to set a new value, the container calls the Set method. You can make a property read-only by omitting the Set method or write-only by omitting the Get method. However, turning on the Get/Set Methods radio button requires that at least one method is defined to make the property visible to the container.

We can accept ClassWizard's defaults for Tower's stock properties. As Figure 9-8 shows, selecting the *Caption* stock property automatically turns on the Stock radio button and exports the functions *GetText* and *SetText* to allow the container to read and write Tower's current caption. Here's one of the many ways that MFC helps make programming painless for ActiveX controls—the *GetText* and *SetText* methods are members of the framework's *COleControl* object, so we need only click and forget. The framework takes on all the work of maintaining the *Caption* property and exposing it to the container through the *GetText* and *SetText* functions. (The two functions take their names from the *Text* stock property, of which *Caption* is only an alias.) Click the OK button to add the *Caption* property to the Tower control, then repeat the same steps to add the *Font*, *ForeColor*, and *BackColor* stock properties.

To add Tower's only custom property, enter the Add Property dialog a fifth time and type *CurrentBlock* as the external name, giving it a type of **short**. Instead of accepting the proposed notification function *OnCurrentBlockChanged*, click the Get/Set Methods radio button. ClassWizard automatically assigns functions named *GetCurrentBlock* and *SetCurrentBlock*, but since the *CurrentBlock* custom property should appear read-only to the container, clear the Set Function box so that *SetCurrentBlock* is not added to the control's class. A container application that embeds Tower now has no means of altering *CurrentBlock*, though it can call *GetCurrentBlock* at any time to query the control for the property's current value.

Clicking the OK button in the Add Property dialog causes ClassWizard to write stub code for the *GetCurrentBlock* function in the TowerCtl.cpp file. Figure 9-9 shows what the ClassWizard dialog looks like after the five properties have been specified. The "S" and "C" codes adjacent to the external names indicate whether a property is stock or custom.

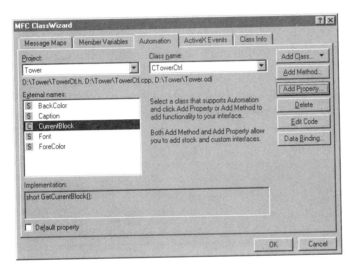

**Figure 9-9.** *Adding properties to the Tower ActiveX control.*

## Step 3: Add Methods

Technically, we have already added a method to the Tower project. The *GetCurrentBlock* function generated in the previous section is a method—that is, an exported function that the container can call through an interface. Here we'll add another method named *Reset*. The *Reset* function provides a way for the container to instruct the control to start the game over. The Game program pictured in Figure 9-7 on page 393 demonstrates how an application can use this feature, calling Tower's *Reset* method when the user clicks the dialog's Reset button.

While still in ClassWizard's Automation tab, click the Add Method button and type *Reset* as the external name. Select a return type of **void**, since *Reset* does not return a value. *Reset* has no parameters either, but if it did, they could be specified by double-clicking in the Name column of the box labeled Parameter List and typing the function parameters, one per line. We will do something similar when adding Tower's events in the next section.

Click OK to return to the ClassWizard dialog, which now lists the *Reset* method in the list of external names. An "M" prefix identifies *Reset* as a method.

## Step 4: Add Events

Move to the ActiveX Events tab of the ClassWizard dialog and click the Add Event button to call up the Add Event dialog shown in Figure 9-10. We'll add one stock event to the Tower control and four custom events, which collectively keep the container application informed about what is happening in the Tower control. The stock event is *Click*, selected from the drop-down list in the External Name box of the Add Event dialog. The *Click* event informs the container when and where a mouse click occurs in Tower's window. Click the OK button, then bring up the Add Event dialog a second time and type the external name *FromPanel* for the control's first custom event. Whenever the user selects a block in a panel, the Tower control fires the *FromPanel* event by calling the *FireFromPanel* function. *FireFromPanel* calls the event handler function in the client, passing it a single parameter 0 through 2 that identifies the panel from which the block is being dragged. Specify the function's parameter by double-clicking the blue area in the list box labeled Parameter List to expose the new-entry box. In the new-entry box, type *nPanel* for the parameter name and accept the default type of **short**, as shown in Figure 9-10.

The next custom event is called *ToPanel* which, like *FromPanel*, has a single parameter named *nPanel* of type **short**. Tower fires the *ToPanel* event when the user drops a block, indicating through the *nPanel* parameter which of the three panels has received the drop. The third custom event is named *Error*, which Tower fires to notify the container of an invalid move when the user attempts to drop a block on top of a smaller block. *Error* has no parameter list, so simply type it in the External Name box and click OK to return to the main ClassWizard dialog.

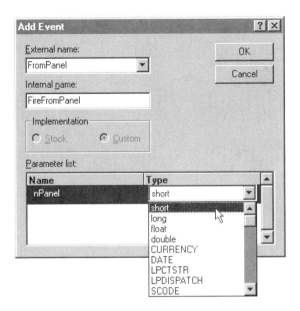

**Figure 9-10.** *Specifying a custom event and its parameter for the Tower ActiveX control.*

*Error* is also the name of a stock event included in the drop-down list of external names. Typing it in the External Name box rather than selecting it from the list indicates that ClassWizard should treat the event as custom. This demonstrates how it is possible to use a stock name and its dispatch identifier for a custom event. Because the *Error* stock event requires no less than seven parameters, code for both the control and its container is simplified in this case by using a custom event instead of a stock event.

The fourth and last custom event is *Winner*, which informs the container that the user has successfully moved the last block into the control's third panel, winning the game. Like the custom *Error* event, *Winner* has no parameter list. Figure 9-11 on the next page shows what the ActiveX Events tab of the dialog looks like after adding Tower's five events.

As mentioned in the preceding chapter, a container need not provide handler functions for all events that an ActiveX control fires. For example, the Game container program ignores Tower's *Click* stock event and processes only the custom events to update a status window when the events occur. The control designer must anticipate the type of information a container

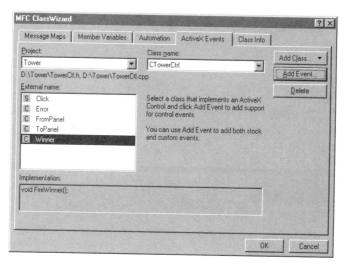

**Figure 9-11**    *Adding events to the Tower ActiveX control*

might need and provide events to convey that information while allowing for the likelihood that some containers will ignore certain events.

## Step 5: Add Message Handler Functions

Tower employs a sort of poor man's version of drag-and-drop to allow the user to move blocks between panels. When the user presses the left mouse button, the cursor changes to a crosshairs shape, providing visual feedback that indicates the drag operation is in effect. When the mouse button is released, the system restores the cursor to its former arrow shape. We'll examine the details of the process when writing code in Step 6 of this exercise, but for now we need only use ClassWizard to create stub handler functions for the mouse messages.

In ClassWizard's Message Maps tab, select the WM_LBUTTONDOWN message from the Messages box and click the Add Function button to create the *OnLButtonDown* handler function. Do the same for the WM_LBUTTONUP message, accepting the default function name of *OnLButtonUp*. For the third message handler function, select *PreCreate-Window* from the Messages box and click the Add Function button. This generates a stub override of a *CWnd* virtual function, providing a convenient place for Tower to do some last-minute initialization.

Figure 9-12 shows the appearance of ClassWizard's Message Maps tab after adding the three required functions. (Other member functions of the *CTowerCtrl* class, such as *OnDraw* and *OnResetState*, were previously generated by ControlWizard.) When you are finished, click the OK button to exit ClassWizard. We have yet to write code to fill in all the stub functions that ControlWizard and ClassWizard have added to the project, but one more task remains that requires the services of the Visual C++ dialog editor.

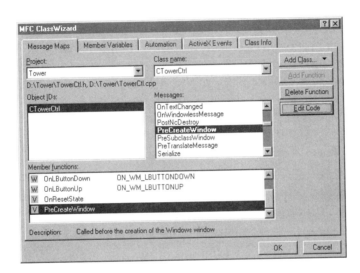

**Figure 9-12.** *Adding message handlers to the Tower ActiveX control.*

## Step 6: Create a Property Sheet

We saw earlier that ControlWizard adds a generic property page resource to a project (see Figure 9-6 on page 391). This section explains how to revise the resource, which will eventually expand into a usable property sheet that allows the user to view and change Tower's properties at design time. The first step is to modify the generic property page in the dialog editor. Load the resource by double-clicking the IDD_PROPPAGE_TOWER identifier in the ResourceView pane of the Workspace window. Select the "to do" static text control in the dialog work area and delete it, replacing it with a static label and edit box, as shown on the next page.

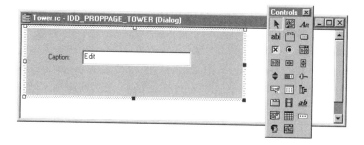

Select the edit box in the dialog work area, click Properties on the View menu, and give the box an identifier value of IDC_EDIT_CAPTION. The size of the property page itself does not matter. As we will see in a moment, MFC supplies property pages for the color and font stock properties that govern the finished size of the property sheet dialog.

Text entered in the edit box becomes the new value of the *Caption* property, which is stored in a string variable. Create the string variable by entering ClassWizard one last time and clicking ClassWizard's Member Variables tab. In the Class Name box, make sure that *CTowerPropPage* is the current class and that IDC_EDIT_CAPTION is selected in the Control IDs box. Click the Add Variable button and name the new member variable *strCaption*. The category should be "Value" and the variable type is "CString." Click the OK button to exit the Add Member Variable dialog. It's a good idea to limit the length of a text-based property such as *strCaption* through dialog data validation (described in Chapter 6, ClassWizard). Set the string limit by typing a value in the text box at the bottom of the Member Variables tab:

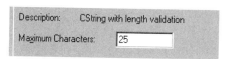

Click the OK button to exit ClassWizard. The user now has a way to change Tower's caption by invoking the property page at design time and typing a new string. We'll see how that's done in the next section.

## Step 7: Add Source Code

Between them, ControlWizard and ClassWizard have generated more than 500 lines of source code from some mouse clicks and a little typing. But if we built the Tower control at this point, it would still look and behave like the do-nothing Demo control described earlier. This seventh step of the exercise adds source code to the TowerCtl.cpp and TowerCtl.h files, filling out the stub functions added in the previous steps. The section ends with small revisions to the TowerPpg.cpp file and Tower.rc script file.

### TowerCtl.h

The TowerCtl.h header file requires only a few changes. Load the file in the text editor and revise it as shown here, adding the shaded lines:

```
// TowerCtl.h : Declaration of the CTowerCtrl ActiveX Control class.

#define    NUM_BLOCKS  7
#define    EMPTY       NUM_BLOCKS
#define    BLACK       RGB(   0,   0,   0 )
#define    BLUE        RGB(   0,   0, 255 )
#define    CYAN        RGB(   0, 255, 255 )
#define    GREEN       RGB(   0, 255,   0 )
#define    MAGENTA     RGB( 255,   0, 255 )
#define    RED         RGB( 255,   0,   0 )
#define    YELLOW      RGB( 255, 255,   0 )


///////////////////////////////////////////////////////////////////
// CTowerCtrl : See TowerCtl.cpp for implementation.

class CTowerCtrl : public COleControl
{

DECLARE_DYNCREATE(CTowerCtrl)

private:
    short       nPanel[3][NUM_BLOCKS];   // Panel contents
    short       nBlockNdx, nFromPanel;   // nPanel index of moved block
    BOOL        bMoving;                 // Flag is set when dragging
    COLORREF    color[NUM_BLOCKS];       // Block colors
    HCURSOR     hCrossHairs;             // Dragging cursor

public:
    short       GetPanel( int i );
```

```
// Constructor
public:
    CTowerCtrl();
    ⋮
```

We will encounter the six member variables of the *CTowerCtrl* class later when discussing the implementation code. Table 9-1 provides a brief description of the variables.

| Variable | Description |
|----------|-------------|
| *nPanel* | A 3-by-7 array that reflects the contents of the three panels at any moment. A value of 0 through 6 in an array element means that the position is occupied by one of the colored blocks, which are numbered from 0 for the smallest block to 6 for the largest. An element value of 7 means that the position is vacant. For example, when the blocks are neatly stacked in the first panel, the *nPanel* array looks like this:<br><br>`nPanel[0][ ] = {0, 1, 2, 3, 4, 5, 6}; // Panel 1`<br>`nPanel[1][ ] = {7, 7, 7, 7, 7, 7, 7}; // Panel 2`<br>`nPanel[2][ ] = {7, 7, 7, 7, 7, 7, 7}; // Panel 3` |
| *nBlockNdx* | The minor array index of the block being dragged. |
| *nFromPanel* | The major array index of the block being dragged. |
| *bMoving* | A Boolean value set to TRUE when the user drags a block. |
| *color* | An array of COLORREF values that contains the blocks' colors. Colors are arranged in order of increasing block size, placing the color of the smallest block in the first value of the array. |
| *hCrossHairs* | A handle to the system crosshairs cursor. The cursor changes to a crosshairs shape when the user drags a block. |

**Table 9-1.**     *Member variables of the* CTowerCtrl *class.*

### TowerCtl.cpp

The TowerCtl.cpp class implementation file is next. Open the file by clicking the wand icon on the WizardBar and scroll to the property page map shown here. Make the changes indicated by the shaded lines to add property pages supplied by the MFC framework for the color and font properties:

```
/////////////////////////////////////////////////////////////////////////
// Property pages

BEGIN_PROPPAGEIDS(CTowerCtrl, 3)
    PROPPAGEID(CTowerPropPage::guid)
    PROPPAGEID( CLSID_CColorPropPage )
    PROPPAGEID( CLSID_CFontPropPage )
END_PROPPAGEIDS(CTowerCtrl)
```

It's important to set the correct page count to 3 in the BEGIN_PROPPAGE-IDS macro of the map's first line. If you later add or delete pages in the property sheet, adjust the page count to reflect the change. It's possible to add more customized pages to a control's property sheet by creating additional resources using the dialog editor and inserting a new entry for each page into the property page map. The procedure is a little involved, so a discussion of additional property pages is deferred until the final section of this chapter.

Figure 9-13 on page 417 shows what Tower's finished property sheet looks like. The order of the sheet's first three pages—labeled Caption, Colors, and Fonts—corresponds to the order of the three entries in the property page map. The remaining modifications affect the last half of the TowerCtl.cpp implementation file, listed here beginning with the class constructor. The listing is divided into sections, each of which is followed by paragraphs of commentary that explain the purpose of the added code shown in shaded lines.

```
/////////////////////////////////////////////////////////////////////////
// CTowerCtrl::CTowerCtrl - Constructor

CTowerCtrl::CTowerCtrl()
{
    InitializeIIDs(&IID_DTower, &IID_DTowerEvents);

    color[0] = BLACK;                      // Initialize block colors
    color[1] = BLUE;
    color[2] = CYAN;
    color[3] = GREEN;
    color[4] = MAGENTA;
    color[5] = RED;
```

```
    color[6] = YELLOW;

    Reset();                              // Initialize panels
    SetInitialSize( 200, 75 );            // Control window size
}

/////////////////////////////////////////////////////////////////////
// CTowerCtrl::~CTowerCtrl - Destructor

CTowerCtrl::~CTowerCtrl()
{
}
```

The class constructor initializes the *color* array with the block colors and calls the *Reset* method to initialize the *nPanel* array. A call to the *COleControl::SetInitialSize* function gives the Tower control a default window size of 200-by-75 pixels. Many container programs override a control's initial size when creating a site, so calling *SetInitialSize* is often wasted effort for an ActiveX control. The function's purpose becomes evident when you open the control in the Test Container utility, which accepts whatever initial size a control establishes for itself. As we saw in Chapter 8, some ActiveX controls such as the Button Menu control appear in the Test Container as a small square block that the user must resize to expose the control window. That does not happen to Tower because it sets default window dimensions for itself through *SetInitialSize*.

```
/////////////////////////////////////////////////////////////////////
// CTowerCtrl::OnDraw - Drawing function

void CTowerCtrl::OnDraw(
          CDC* pdc, const CRect& rcBounds, const CRect& rcInvalid)
{
    RECT        rect;
    TEXTMETRIC  tm;
    CPen        pen;
    CPen*       pOldPen;
    CBrush      brush;
    CBrush*     pOldBrush;
    COLORREF    colorBack = TranslateColor( GetBackColor() );
    int         i, j, k, yCaption, iPanelWidth, iPanelHeight;

    // Paint control background
    brush.CreateSolidBrush( colorBack );
    pdc->FillRect( rcBounds, &brush );
```

```
pdc->SetBkMode( TRANSPARENT );
pdc->SetTextColor( TranslateColor( GetForeColor() ) );
SelectStockFont( pdc );

// Display caption
::CopyRect( &rect, rcBounds );
pdc->DrawText( InternalGetText(), -1, &rect, DT_CENTER | DT_TOP );

pdc->GetTextMetrics( &tm );
yCaption     = tm.tmHeight + tm.tmExternalLeading;
iPanelWidth  = rcBounds.Width()/3;
iPanelHeight = rcBounds.Height() - yCaption;

// Draw column dividers
pen.CreatePen( PS_SOLID, 1, TranslateColor( GetForeColor() ) );
pOldPen = pdc->SelectObject( &pen );
pdc->MoveTo( rcBounds.left+iPanelWidth,   rcBounds.top+yCaption );
pdc->LineTo( rcBounds.left+iPanelWidth,   rcBounds.bottom );
pdc->MoveTo( rcBounds.left+iPanelWidth*2, rcBounds.top+yCaption );
pdc->LineTo( rcBounds.left+iPanelWidth*2, rcBounds.bottom );

// Save current brush
pOldBrush = (CBrush*) pdc->SelectStockObject( NULL_BRUSH );

// Outer loop: for each panel...
for (i=0; i < 3; i++)
{
    rect.top    = rcBounds.top + yCaption;
    rect.bottom = rect.top + iPanelHeight/NUM_BLOCKS;

    // Inner loop: for each colored block in panel...
    for (j=0; j < NUM_BLOCKS; j++)
    {
        if (nPanel[i][j] != EMPTY)
        {
            // Determine left and right edges of colored block
            k = NUM_BLOCKS - 1 - nPanel[i][j];
            rect.left  = rcBounds.left + iPanelWidth*i +
                    (iPanelWidth*k)/(2*NUM_BLOCKS) + 1;
            rect.right = rect.left +
                    iPanelWidth*(nPanel[i][j]+1)/NUM_BLOCKS - 1;

            // Fill rectangle with block's color
            brush.CreateSolidBrush( color[nPanel[i][j]] );
            pdc->SelectObject( &brush );
            pdc->FillRect( &rect, &brush );
        }
```

```
        rect.top     = rect.bottom;
        rect.bottom += iPanelHeight/NUM_BLOCKS;
    }
  }

  pdc->SelectObject( pOldPen );
  pdc->SelectObject( pOldBrush );
}
```

The next major revision to the source code occurs in the class's *OnDraw* function, which executes whenever Tower's window is invalidated. We saw earlier that ControlWizard writes a simple version of *OnDraw* that displays a generic ellipse in a white rectangle. Here we revise the function to paint the current arrangement of colored blocks in Tower's three panels. Whenever the user moves a block, the window redraws itself to reflect the change.

*OnDraw* first paints the window background with the current value of the control's *BackColor* property. The function retrieves the property from the *COleControl::GetBackColor* function, converts it to a COLORREF value through *COleControl::TranslateColor*, and creates a brush with which it fills the window rectangle. (The *rcBounds* argument provides the coordinates of Tower's window relative to the origin of the container window.) Similarly, the function uses the current value of the *ForeColor* property to set the device context's text color and uses the *Font* property to set the current font. *OnDraw* then writes the string contained in the *Caption* property, centering the text at the top of Tower's window:

```
pdc->DrawText( InternalGetText(), -1, &rect, DT_CENTER | DT_TOP );
```

Subtracting the height of the caption text from the height of Tower's window leaves the height of the panels, which is stored in *iPanelHeight*. The height (thickness) of each colored block is one-seventh of the panel height, so a stack of seven blocks reaches from the bottom to the top of a panel. The width of each panel is a third of the window width. With these dimensions, *OnDraw* is ready to display the colored blocks in the panels.

The current location of each block is stored in the 3-by-7 *nPanel* array described in Table 9-1 on page 404. With an outer loop that iterates for each panel and an inner loop that iterates for each block, the function steps through each of the 21 slots in which a block can appear, progressively reading an element of the *nPanel* array at each step. An element value of EMPTY means that the slot does not contain a block. If an element has a value of 0 through 6, *OnDraw* paints a block in the slot using the corresponding color in the *color* array. A RECT structure named *rect* holds the coordinates of the current block.

```
///////////////////////////////////////////////////////////////////
// CTowerCtrl::DoPropExchange - Persistence support

void CTowerCtrl::DoPropExchange(CPropExchange* pPX)
{
    ExchangeVersion(pPX, MAKELONG(_wVerMinor, _wVerMajor));
    COleControl::DoPropExchange(pPX);
}

///////////////////////////////////////////////////////////////////
// CTowerCtrl::OnResetState - Reset control to default state

void CTowerCtrl::OnResetState()
{
    COleControl::OnResetState();  // Resets defaults in DoPropExchange
}

///////////////////////////////////////////////////////////////////
// CTowerCtrl::AboutBox - Display an "About" box to the user

void CTowerCtrl::AboutBox()
{
    CDialog dlgAbout(IDD_ABOUTBOX_TOWER);
    dlgAbout.DoModal();
}
```

Although Tower does not alter the class's *DoPropExchange* function, it's worthwhile to examine the function briefly. Property exchange allows an ActiveX control to save custom properties between embeddings. For example, each time it starts, the Tower control initializes the game and assembles the stack of colored blocks in the first panel. Through property exchange, Tower could be enhanced to save an interrupted game at shutdown and recreate the same block positions the next time a container embeds the control. Saving and restoring properties between runs is called persistence.

Stock properties managed by the framework are automatically persistent. To make a custom property persistent, add an appropriate property exchange function to the *DoPropExchange* function, which executes when the control is loaded and again when it terminates. Property exchange functions are identified by a *PX_* prefix followed by the data type that the function serializes. For example, the *PX_Bool*, *PX_Font*, and *PX_String* functions make Boolean, font, and *CString* properties persistent. For a description of these and other property exchange functions, refer to online help.

```
//////////////////////////////////////////////////////////////////////
// CTowerCtrl message handlers

short CTowerCtrl::GetCurrentBlock()
{
   return nPanel[nFromPanel][nBlockNdx];
}
```

The *GetCurrentBlock* function is a method established in Step 2 that the container calls to learn which block is being moved. (*GetCurrentBlock* isn't a message handler, despite the banner that ClassWizard adds to the code.) The function can be called at any time, but if the container is interested in the information that *GetCurrentBlock* provides, it will probably call the function in response to a *FromPanel* event, which announces that a block is being moved. A return value of EMPTY from *GetCurrentBlock* means that the user is not currently dragging a block. As you probably recall from Step 2 of this exercise, Tower does not export a corresponding Set method for the *CurrentBlock* property because a container has no reason to change the property.

```
void CTowerCtrl::Reset()
{
    int i;

    for (i=0; i < NUM_BLOCKS; i++)        // Initialize panel array
    {
        nPanel[0][i] = i;                 // Panel 0 = 0,1,2,3,4,5,6
        nPanel[1][i] = EMPTY;             // Panel 1 = 7,7,7,7,7,7,7
        nPanel[2][i] = EMPTY;             // Panel 2 = 7,7,7,7,7,7,7
    }

    nBlockNdx  = 0;                       // Ndx of block being moved
```

```
    nFromPanel = 0;
    InvalidateControl();
}
```

The *Reset* method allows the container application to start a game over.
The Game program, for instance, calls *Reset* when the user clicks the Reset
button, pictured in Figure 9-7 on page 393. The *TowerCtrl* class constructor also calls *Reset* to initialize the *nPanel* array at startup, stacking the
seven blocks in the first panel and marking as empty all positions in the
other two panels. *Reset* calls the *COleControl::InvalidateControl* function
to trigger a call to *OnDraw*, refreshing the control window. To invalidate
itself, an ActiveX control based on *COleControl* should call *Invalidate-
Control*, not the *Invalidate* API function.

```
BOOL CTowerCtrl::PreCreateWindow(CREATESTRUCT& cs)
{
    SetText( "Tower" );                         // Default caption
    hCrossHairs = ::LoadCursor( NULL, IDC_CROSS );  // Dragging cursor
    return COleControl::PreCreateWindow(cs);
}
```

Tower simulates drag and drop by monitoring the left mouse button.
When the user presses the mouse button inside Tower's window, the con-
trol changes the cursor to the system crosshairs shape, providing simple
visual feedback to the user that the drag operation is in effect. The
*PreCreateWindow* function, called when the container first embeds the
Tower control, loads the crosshairs cursor and stores the handle in
*hCrossHairs*. The function also calls *COleControl::SetText* to initialize the
*Caption* property.

```
void CTowerCtrl::OnLButtonDown(UINT nFlags, CPoint point)
{
    short   i=0;

    nFromPanel = GetPanel( point.x );// Panel from which block is taken

    while (nPanel[nFromPanel][i] == EMPTY  &&  i < NUM_BLOCKS)
        i++;                         // i=ndx of panel's smallest block

    if (i < NUM_BLOCKS)                 // Does panel have a block in it?
    {
        bMoving    = TRUE;              // If so, block is now moving
        nBlockNdx = i;                  // Save ndx of the block
```

```
            ::SetCursor( hCrossHairs );  // Change cursor to indicate drag
            FireFromPanel( nFromPanel ); // Tell container the panel number
        }

        COleControl::OnLButtonDown(nFlags, point);
}

short CTowerCtrl::GetPanel( int x )
{
        short    i=0;
        RECT     rect;

        GetClientRect( &rect );            // Control window

        if (x > rect.right/3)              // Hit test:
            i = 1;                         // i = 0 for first panel
        if (x > rect.right*2/3)            //   = 1 for second panel
            i = 2;                         //   = 2 for third panel

        return i;                          // Return panel number
}
```

When the user presses the left mouse button somewhere in Tower's window, the *OnLButtonDown* function handles the resulting WM_LBUTTON-DOWN message. The function first examines the click coordinates in the *point* argument and determines in which panel the click occurs. If the panel is empty, the click is ignored. Otherwise, *OnLButtonDown* changes the cursor to a crosshairs shape and fires the *FromPanel* event to inform the container that a block is being dragged.

Because only the smallest block in a panel can be moved, *OnLButton-Down* need only determine in which panel the click occurs, not on which block. Though this greatly simplifies hit testing in the helper *GetPanel* function, it has the effect of starting a drag operation for a block even if the click does not land accurately on a block.

```
void CTowerCtrl::OnLButtonUp(UINT nFlags, CPoint point)
{
        short    i=0, nToPanel;

        nToPanel = GetPanel( point.x );   // Panel in which block is dropped

        if (bMoving  &&  nToPanel != nFromPanel)
        {
            while (nPanel[nToPanel][i] == EMPTY  &&  i < NUM_BLOCKS-1)
```

```
        i++;                              // i=ndx of panel's smallest block

    // Is dragged block smaller than smallest block in panel?
    if (nPanel[nFromPanel][nBlockNdx] < nPanel[nToPanel][i])
    {
        if (nPanel[nToPanel][i] != EMPTY)
            --i;
        nPanel[nToPanel][i] = nPanel[nFromPanel][nBlockNdx];
        nPanel[nFromPanel][nBlockNdx] = EMPTY;
        FireToPanel( nToPanel );                    // Tell container

        if (i == 0  &&  nToPanel == 2)              // If we've filled
        {                                           // the third panel,
            FireWinner ();                          // fire Winner event
            Reset ();                               // and reset game
        }

        InvalidateControl();
    }
    else                                            // If invalid drop,
        FireError ();                               // tell container
}

    bMoving = FALSE;                                // Not moving now

    COleControl::OnLButtonUp(nFlags, point);
}
```

The *OnLButtonUp* function receives control when the user releases the left mouse button to drop a block in a panel. This function has more work to do than its companion *OnLButtonDown*. Besides determining in which panel the drop occurs, *OnLButtonUp* must also confirm that the panel does not already contain a block smaller than the one being dropped. If so, *OnLButtonUp* fires the *Error* event to signal the container that the user has attempted an illegal drop. If the drop is legal, *OnLButtonUp* fires the *ToPanel* event to announce the end of the drag operation. If the block is being dropped into the top slot of the third panel, the game is over and *OnLButtonUp* fires the *Winner* event.

A convenient side effect of releasing the mouse button is that the cursor returns to its original arrow shape without *OnLButtonUp* taking any action. Because Tower does not process the WM_SETCURSOR message, the system automatically restores the original window cursor when the user releases the mouse button.

### TowerPpg.cpp

In Step 6 on page 401, we modified Tower's generic property page by adding a text box that allows the user to rewrite the *Caption* property. Tower stores the contents of the text box in the *strCaption* variable, which is a *CString* object created in ClassWizard. A link is needed between the *strCaption* string and the *Caption* stock property so that when the user changes *strCaption* in Tower's property sheet, the control forwards the change to the stock property buried in the framework.

This is the purpose of MFC's property data transfer functions, recognizable by the *DDP_* prefix. The function we need for Tower is the *DDP_Text* function, which copies text from a string variable (*strCaption*) to a string property (*Caption*). To add the *DDP_Text* call, open the TowerPpg.cpp implementation file in the text editor and insert the shaded line shown here:

```
void CTowerPropPage::DoDataExchange(CDataExchange* pDX)
{
    //{{AFX_DATA_MAP(CTowerPropPage)
    DDP_Text(pDX, IDC_EDIT_CAPTION, strCaption, _T("Caption") );
    DDX_Text(pDX, IDC_EDIT_CAPTION, strCaption);
    DDV_MaxChars(pDX, strCaption, 25);
    //}}AFX_DATA_MAP
    DDP_PostProcessing(pDX);
}
```

### Tower.rc

By default, ControlWizard labels the generic property page General, storing the label as a string resource in the Tower.rc script file. To change the tab label, open the Tower.rc file in the text editor and change "General" to "Caption" in the shaded line shown here:

```
STRINGTABLE DISCARDABLE
BEGIN
    IDS_TOWER              "Tower Control"
    IDS_TOWER_PPG          "Tower Property Page"
    IDS_TOWER_PPG_CAPTION  "Caption"
END
```

You can also make the same modification using the Visual C++ string editor, described in Chapter 4. Figure 9-13 on page 417 shows the result.

## Step 8: Build and Test the Tower ActiveX Control

If you are building the Tower control from the source code, first copy the files Tower.ico and TowerCtl.bmp from the Code\Chapter.09\Tower folder to the project folder. The first file provides a unique icon resource that appears in the control's About box. The second file contains a bitmap from which a container can create a personalized tool button when embedding the control. Visual C++ itself makes use of a control's bitmap, as we saw in the preceding chapter. When an ActiveX control is added to a project through the Gallery, the dialog editor extracts the bitmap from the control's resources and uses the image to paint a new tool button on the Controls toolbar, like this:

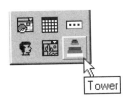

An icon is generally too large for this purpose, so ActiveX standards suggest the inclusion of a 16-by-16 bitmap image in a control's resource data. Controls that provide such a resource advertise it through the Toolbox-Bitmap32 key in the class's Registry data. We'll encounter this key again in the next chapter.

Set the project configuration to Win32 Release and choose the Build command from the Build menu. When the source code is successfully compiled and linked, Visual C++ automatically registers the control. If you want to experiment with Tower without building it as a project, you must register the control yourself before using it. To register Tower, first copy the Tower.ocx file to your hard disk if necessary, and then run the RegSvr32 utility:

```
regsvr32 path\tower.ocx
```

where *path* represents the location of the Tower.ocx file on your hard disk.

The Game program found on the companion CD provides the most convenient way to try out the new Tower control. Game has buttons to display

Tower's About box, reset a game, and list the game rules. The program also continually displays game status, which it learns by monitoring Tower's *FromPanel*, *ToPanel*, *Error*, and *Winner* events. The Test Container utility offers another way to experiment with the Tower control and is able to expose more of the control's inner workings than the Game program. With the control properly registered, run the Test Container, click the New Control button, and select the Tower control from the list shown here:

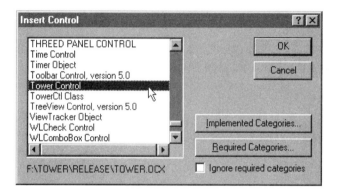

The Insert Control dialog responds to keyboard entries, letting you quickly scroll through the list by pressing the letter of a control name's first letter. Pressing T, for example, immediately sets the selection bar in the vicinity of the Tower control entry.

Try out Tower's property sheet by double-clicking the control's border. The MFC framework has added property pages in which you can modify both the control's colors and the font used to display the caption in Tower's window. Figure 9-13 shows the Fonts page exposed in the control's property sheet. Of the dialog's other three tabs, the one labeled Caption displays the property page modified back in Step 6. When you type new text for the caption, the change is reflected immediately in the control's window.

The Test Container displays a real-time record of Tower's events, an invaluable aid when you are debugging an ActiveX control. Move the splitter bar upward to expose additional space for the event log, then drag a block

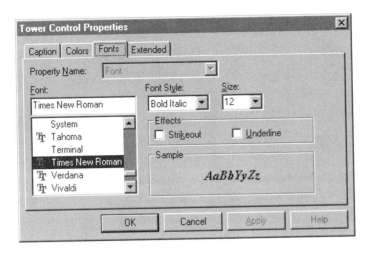

**Figure 9-13.**  *The Tower Control Properties property sheet.*

from Tower's first panel and drop it into another panel. In responding to the drag-and-drop operation, Tower fires the *Click*, *FromPanel*, and *ToPanel* events, which are recorded in the event log as they occur. As shown in Figure 9-14, each entry in the log begins with a label that indicates from which control the event originates. Since the Test Container can embed more than one control, the labels help keep the log entries straight when events arrive in clusters from controls that may not have focus.

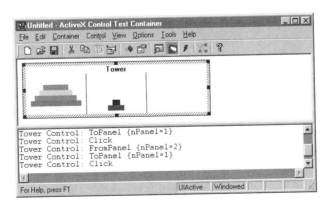

**Figure 9-14.**  *Monitoring events in the Test Container.*

# Adding Property Pages to an ActiveX Control Project

As we saw when developing the Tower control, ControlWizard generates a single property page for an ActiveX control to supplement the stock pages that MFC provides. For the Tower project, one page is sufficient because *Caption* is the only modifiable property that needs a customized property page. An ActiveX control with more property data, however, may need additional pages to present the data to the user. Each additional page requires its own dialog resource, class, and entry in the property page map. This final section lists the steps necessary to add a new property page to an ActiveX control project, using the Tower control as an example.

1. With the project open, click the Resource command on the Insert menu and double-click Dialog in the list to launch the dialog editor. You can also expand the list of dialog resources and select IDD_ OLE_PROPPAGE_LARGE. As before, the size of the new property page does not matter. Design the new property page as you wish, then select the dialog window in the work area and click the Properties command on the View menu to expose the Dialog Properties box. In the Styles tab, turn off the Titlebar check box, set the dialog style to Child, and disable borders. If you selected IDD_OLE_ PROPPAGE_LARGE to start the dialog editor, these settings have already been made for you. The Styles tab should look like this:

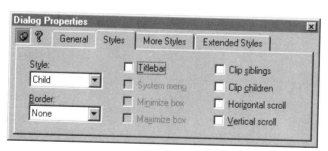

2. Press Ctrl+S to save the new dialog resource, then click the Class-Wizard command in the View menu. When asked if you would like to create a new class for the dialog resource, click the OK button to

accept. Type a name for the new class and select *COlePropertyPage* as the base class:

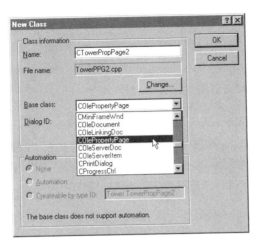

3. Add any member variables required for the new page, then exit ClassWizard. In the TowerCtl.cpp implementation file, add an **#include** statement for the property page class header file that Class-Wizard just created, as shown here:

```
#include "TowerPPG2.h"
```

The correct filename appears in the File Name box of the New Class dialog. Also add an entry for the new page to the property page map in the TowerCtl.cpp file. For the Tower control, the addition looks like this:

```
BEGIN_PROPPAGEIDS(CTowerCtrl, 4)
    PROPPAGEID(CTowerPropPage::guid)
    PROPPAGEID(CTowerPropPage2::guid)
    PROPPAGEID( CLSID_CColorPropPage )
    PROPPAGEID( CLSID_CFontPropPage )
END_PROPPAGEIDS(CTowerCtrl)
```

Remember to increment the page count in the BEGIN_PROPPAGE-IDS macro in the first line of the map. The new page count is now 4.

4. Open the project's RC file in either the text editor or the string editor and add two string resources. The first string identifies the registered

property page in the system Registry, and the second string holds the tab label that appears in the property sheet dialog:

```
STRINGTABLE DISCARDABLE
BEGIN
    IDS_TOWER                 "Tower Control"
    IDS_TOWER_PPG             "Tower Property Page"
    IDS_TOWER_PPG2            "Tower Property Page 2"
    IDS_TOWER_PPG_CAPTION     "Caption"
    IDS_TOWER_PPG_NEWPAGE     "New Page"
END
```

5. If you used the text editor in the preceding step to create the new string resources, add definitions to the Resource.h file for the IDS_TOWER_PPG2 and IDS_TOWER_PPG_NEWPAGE manifest constants:

```
#define  IDS_TOWER_PPG2       300
#define  IDS_TOWER_PPG_NEWPAGE   301
```

Adding these lines is not necessary if you used the string editor in the preceding step, because Visual C++ writes the definitions automatically when you save the string resource.

6. In the text editor, open the implementation CPP file that ClassWizard created for the new property page class. Search for the source code shown here, and in each of the shaded lines replace the 0 parameter with a string identifier:

```
BOOL CTowerPropPage2::CTowerPropPage2Factory
                    ::UpdateRegistry(BOOL bRegister)
{
    if (bRegister)
        return AfxOleRegisterPropertyPageClass(
            AfxGetInstanceHandle(),
            m_clsid, IDS_TOWER_PPG2);
    else
        return AfxOleUnregisterClass(m_clsid, NULL);
}
    ⋮

CTowerPropPage2::CTowerPropPage2() :
    COlePropertyPage(IDD, IDS_TOWER_PPG_NEWPAGE)
{
    ⋮
```

Rebuilding the Tower ActiveX control after having made these changes adds the new property page to the control's resources. Here's an example of what the new property page might look like, depending on the design you created in Step 1 of this exercise:

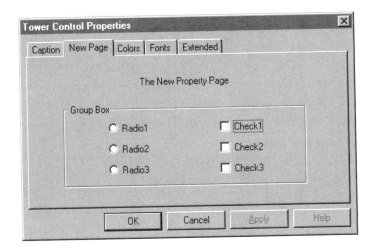

# Chapter 10

# Writing ActiveX Controls Using ATL

Chapter 9 demonstrated the ease with which you can write ActiveX controls using MFC, but also pointed out that the convenience comes at the cost of an unwieldy executable size. A small file image is a desirable quality for an ActiveX control, but is particularly important for those controls intended for service on the World Wide Web. Fortunately, Visual C++ offers other tools besides MFC for the development of component software. This chapter examines a popular alternative to MFC called the Active Template Library.

The Active Template Library, better known as ATL, provides an extensive set of C++ class templates[1] designed for the development of server objects that can be embedded in an application through the services of COM. Currently in its third release, ATL assists in programming various types of COM objects, and can even contribute to the creation of container programs; this chapter, however, focuses on how to use ATL to develop

---

1. A C++ class template, also known as a parameterized type, is a sophisticated form of macro that the compiler expands into a normal class definition based on parameters passed to the template. Unlike macros created with the **#define** statement, templates expand into normal types, making them type-safe. The compiler can oversee the program's use of a templatized class as it does a normal class and correctly recognize any type disparities.

ActiveX controls. The intent here is to give balance to the discussions of Chapter 9, demonstrating another avenue besides MFC open to the developer who wants to create ActiveX controls.

MFC simplifies the development of ActiveX controls, but the results are inseparably tied to the large MFC library DLL, generally disqualifying such controls for use on a Web page. In response to this problem, Microsoft has enhanced ATL by adding special support for ActiveX controls. Today, prevailing wisdom suggests these guidelines when choosing a development tool for ActiveX control projects:

- Consider MFC only to create controls intended for normal container applications like the Game program of Chapter 9. MFC takes on added appeal as a development tool when the container itself links dynamically to MFC, since the control is then not responsible for loading the library. The penalty has already been paid, so to speak.

- For ActiveX controls that might see service on the Internet, use ATL instead.

You will find that this chapter discusses COM matters in more detail than the two preceding chapters, but it also demonstrates how ATL lets you write sophisticated ActiveX controls without immersing yourself in COM. More so than MFC, ATL places the developer nearer to the surface of COM, but not necessarily under it.

# ATL and Container Applications

Though not the central theme of this chapter, ATL's support for container programming warrants a few words before we leave the subject entirely. ATL cuts a wide swath across COM programming, but leans heavily toward the development of servers, not clients. However, the library provides two class templates named *CComPtr* and *CComQIPtr* that often prove helpful when writing client-side code. These templates create smart interface pointers, designed to ensure that a client properly releases a control's interfaces even when an exception error interrupts the normal flow of execution.

Let's look first at the problem, then the solution. A container calls a control's *QueryInterface* method to request pointers to interfaces that the control provides. The only constraint is that when finished using an interface, the container must call the interface's *Release* method to inform the control that the interface is no longer needed. Failure to follow this fundamental rule of COM can leave the control object marooned in the system's memory pool even after the container terminates. A fragment demonstrates how a container requests a pointer to one of the control's interfaces, using *IOleObject* as an example:

```
void Function1( IUnknown* pUnk )
{
    IOleObject *pOleObj;
    pUnk->QueryInterface( IID_OleObject, (PVOID*) &pOleObj );
    ⋮                             // Use the IOleObject interface
    pOleObj->Release();           // When finished, release it
}
```

This code runs into trouble if the application terminates through an exception error before the final line can call *IOleObject::Release* to retire the interface. Casting *pOleObj* as a smart pointer solves the potential problem because the pointer's destructor, which calls the interface's *Release* method, executes even if the program abruptly terminates while *IOleObject* is in use:

```
void Function1( IUnknown* pUnk )
{
    CComPtr<IOleObject> pOleObj;
    pUnk->QueryInterface( &pOleObj );
    ⋮                             // Use the IOleObject interface
}                                 // Release called automatically
```

A noticeable difference between the two fragments is that the revised version does not explicitly call *IOleObject::Release* when finished using *IOleObject*. When *pOleObj* goes out of scope, either because *Function1* returns normally or because an error occurs, the pointer's destructor takes care of releasing the interface.

The function gains another advantage in casting *pOleObj* as a smart pointer. Retrieving the interface pointer *pUnk* is simpler now because

*CComPtr* provides its own *QueryInterface* function that infers the inter-face identifier from *pOleObj* itself. Besides the additional coding conve-nience, this also assures type safety by guaranteeing that both identifier (IID_OleObject) and object pointer (*pOleObj*) refer to the same interface (*IOleObject*). You are thus prevented from committing gaffes like this:

```
pUnk->QueryInterface( IID_ThisObject, (PVOID*) &pThatObject );
```

*CComPtr::QueryInterface* is able to cull the interface identifier from the pointer by applying the **__uuidof** operator. (The abbreviation UUID stands for universally unique identifier, another term for the GUID identifiers we encountered in Chapter 8.) In determining the identifier at compile time, **__uuidof** obviates the need to link additional code to the application that defines the identifier. The net effect is a reduction in executable size. We could have used **__uuidof**, for example, in the first version of *Function1* on the preceding page, replacing the call to *QueryInterface* with either of these lines:

```
pUnk->QueryInterface( __uuidof( IOleObject ), (PVOID*) &pOleObj );
pUnk->QueryInterface( __uuidof( pOleObj ), (PVOID*) &pOleObj );
```

*IUnknown* is rarely the interface that a client ultimately needs, but is the only interface the client can be sure an ActiveX control supports. Obtain-ing an interface is usually a two-step process in which the caller first obtains an *IUnknown* pointer—*pUnk* in the fragment code—then calls *IUnknown::QueryInterface* to retrieve the interface pointer actually needed. ATL provides another smart pointer that combines these two steps into one. The *CComQIPtr* template incorporates a call to *IUnknown:: QueryInterface* in one of its constructors. Here's a condensed listing of ATL's *CComQIPtr* template showing how the constructor obtains the desired interface pointer and how the destructor later retires it:

```
template <class T, const IID* piid = &__uuidof(T)>
class CComQIPtr
{
public:
    T* p;

    ⋮

    CComQIPtr( IUnknown* lp )
```

```
    {
        p = NULL;
        if (lp != NULL)
            lp->QueryInterface( *piid, (void **) &p );
    }
    ~CComQIPtr()
    {
        if (p)
            p->Release();
    }
      ⋮

}
```

The *CComQIPtr* template gives the caller a cleaner method of obtaining an interface pointer from the control. If the control does not support the requested interface, the pointer class's *p* member has a value of NULL:

```
CComQIPtr <IOleObject> pOleObj;
pOleObj = pUnk;
if (pOleObj.p)
{
    ⋮                            // Use the IOleObject interface
}
```

A caller can use *CComQIPtr* to create a pointer for any interface except *IUnknown*. To create a smart pointer for *IUnknown*, use *CComPtr* instead.

The *CComPtr* and *CComQIPtr* templates of ATL are inspired by the *auto_ptr* smart pointer class of the Standard Template Library, which ensures an object allocated through **new** is properly returned to the application's free store. Although the templates mainly benefit client applications that use ActiveX controls, they can just as easily serve controls themselves, and are particularly useful when a control aggregates or contains another control. An example project later in this chapter demonstrates how an ActiveX control can make use of smart pointers.

ATL's support for client programming is strictly passive, consisting only of source code files for inclusion in a project. The files, recognizable by their Atl prefix, reside in the VC98\ATL\Include folder. For an example container project that makes use of *CComPtr* and *CComQIPtr*, refer to the AtlCon project in the Samples\VC98\ATL folder of MSDN. ATL has much more to contribute to the development of COM servers like ActiveX controls, and for the rest of the chapter we will concentrate on this aspect of ATL.

# ATL and ActiveX Controls

Technically, the ActiveX standards make few demands on a control's abilities. To operate as an ActiveX control, a component needs only to implement *IUnknown*, be embeddable, and be able to self-register. Features such as properties, methods, and events are optional. But so minimal (and dormant) a COM object has little use outside of academic discussions. Realistically, an ActiveX control maintains a set of data, fires events, and supports enough interfaces that a client application can successfully interact with it. The ActiveX Test Container utility serves as a sort of litmus test for ActiveX controls. The two control projects developed in this chapter can successfully execute in the Test Container because they implement the interfaces described in Table 10-1. The listed interfaces represent the minimum support an ActiveX control must offer to comply with published Microsoft guidelines. Compare Table 10-1 with Table 8-2 on page 350, which lists the corresponding interfaces a container should support to embed an ActiveX control.

If you are expecting ATL to easily create minuscule ActiveX controls a few kilobytes in size, be prepared for a disappointment. The library incorporates a number of techniques that help reduce executable size, but implementing the interfaces listed in Table 10-1 brings a lot of code into play. The only way to produce smaller code is by using straight COM programming without the benefit of ATL or any other support library. (The Samples\VC98\ATL folder of Visual C++ contains a demonstration ATL project named Minimal that creates a small COM server only 5,600 bytes in size. The Minimal server, however, lacks several essential characteristics and does not purport to be a true ActiveX control.) As with MFC, the convenience of ATL comes inevitably at the cost of some extraneous code that finds its way into your finished product, never to be expunged. Expect a simple windowless ActiveX control, for example, to be about 40 KB in size—somewhat less if you are willing to do some extra work. A

| Interface | Description |
|---|---|
| *IOleObject* | Required for communication with a control's client site, except through events. Events are handled through the *IConnectionPointContainer* interface, described below. |
| *IOleInPlace-Object* | Implemented by controls that can be activated in place and that provide their own user interface. Requires support for *IOleObject*. |
| *IOleInPlace-ActiveObject* | Required only by controls that provide a user interface and that support *IOleInPlaceObject*. |
| *IDataObject* | Required by controls that transfer data to a container in some way, as through shared memory or a file. *IDataObject* provides the means for COM's Uniform Data Transfer, a protocol that sets the rules for the exchange of data of any type. |
| *IViewObject2* | Implemented by visible controls that display a window. |
| *IDispatch* | Required by controls with custom methods or properties that a client can access through *IDispatch::Invoke*. |
| *IConnection-PointContainer* | Required by controls that fire events. This interface enumerates for a client the events that a control object can fire. |
| *IConnection-Point* | Required by controls that support *IConnectionPoint-Container*. |
| *IProvideClass-Info* | Implemented by controls that contain type library information, which means most ActiveX controls. Through its *GetClassInfo* method, the interface provides a pointer to an *ITypeInfo* implementation from which a client can extract the control's type information. The similar *IProvideClassInfo2* interface is an extension that adds the *GetGUID* method, through which a client retrieves a pointer to an identifier for the control's default event. |
| *IPersistStorage* | Required by controls that can save to and load from an *IStorage* instance provided by the container. |
| *IClassFactory* | Instantiates a requested class object and returns a pointer to it. The object is identified by a class identifier registered in the system Registry. |
| *IClassFactory2* | Same as *IClassFactory*, but also adds support for licensing. (See "Licensing" in Chapter 9.) |

**Table 10-1.** *Interfaces that an ActiveX control must support to comply with guidelines.*

sample project later in the chapter demonstrates a few methods that help reduce the size of an ActiveX control created using ATL.

On the other hand, an ActiveX control written with ATL is much smaller than an equivalent control that uses MFC when you consider the weighty mass of the MFC library DLL that the control drags around with it. An ActiveX control built with the ATL library can use MFC, but this almost defeats the point of ATL. If you plan to write your control using MFC, you may prefer to stay with the MFC ControlWizard and draw on ATL only for its smart pointer classes *CComPtr* and *CComQIPtr*. The main benefit of ATL is that it can produce components that require neither MFC nor the C run-time library. Such components can be distributed over the Internet as stand-alone entities that do not rely on the availability of other support files on the user's machine.

Like MFC, ATL produces a single representative class for each object that the control contains. The class derives from all the interfaces that the object supports, a trick that MFC pulls off by nesting classes. ATL accomplishes the same result with more flexibility by using multiple inheritance in which the class derives from several base classes, inheriting member data and functions from each. The list of base classes, called an inheritance list, looks like this in the class declaration:

```
class CMyClass :
    public CClass1,
    public CClass2,
    public IInterface1,
    public IInterface2,
    ⋮
{
```

The most important service that ATL provides for the development of ActiveX controls is the library's implementation code for many COM interfaces that controls generally support. Taking the form of class templates, the library code saves you from having to write your own code to support common interfaces. ATL provides templatized implementation code for every interface listed in Table 10-1 (and a few others), giving each template the name of its interface followed by an *Impl* suffix. The *IQuick-ActivateImpl* template, for example, provides code for *IQuickActivate* methods such as *SetExtent* and *GetExtent*. As required by COM, all the methods of a supported interface are present, but not necessarily serviced. Many methods merely call the ATLTRACENOTIMPL macro, which writes a terse trace message to the Debug tab of Visual C++'s Output window and returns E_NOTIMPL to the caller. If you want your ActiveX control to service such methods, you must add the code yourself.

Along with its library of code, ATL also provides an AppWizard that gets you started on a server project, and another wizard that generates class code required by your ActiveX control. Once you get the feel of ATL you will find it no more difficult to use than MFC, but ATL expects you to watch over more project details than MFC and to deal with more COM issues. Before pressing on to build a demonstration project with ATL, let's pause here and acquire some background on three aspects of ATL that we will encounter later: interface maps, object maps, and threading models.

## Interface Maps

Interface maps arise from the common pattern typical to most implementations of the *QueryInterface* function. All interfaces of a COM object support this function, allowing a container application to call *QueryInterface* on any interface and receive a pointer to any other supported interface. If the control does not support the requested interface, it returns a value of E_NOINTERFACE. The fragment that follows illustrates what a typical *QueryInterface* function might look like when not using ATL. The parameter *riid* is a reference to the identifier of the interface that the caller is requesting, and the parameter *ppvObject* receives the interface pointer:

```
STDMETHODIMP CMyClass::QueryInterface( REFIID riid, PVOID *ppvObject )
{
    switch( riid )
    {
        case IID_UNKNOWN:
        case IID_IInterface1:
            *ppvObject = (IInterface1*) this;
            break;

        case IID_IInterface2:
            *ppvObject = (IInterface2*) this;
            break;
```

```
        case IID_IInterface3:
            *ppvObject = (IInterface3*) this;
            break;

        default:
            *ppvObject = 0;
            return E_NOINTERFACE;
    }
    (IUnknown*) *ppvObject->AddRef();
    return S_OK;
}
```

This sort of repetitious pattern readily lends itself to macros, a discussion of which will shortly make clear the physical layout of an interface map. When a client calls the class object's *QueryInterface* method, the interface map routes the call through the ATL function *CComObjectRootBase:: InternalQueryInterface*, prototyped in the AtlCom.h file like this:

```
static HRESULT WINAPI InternalQueryInterface( PVOID pThis,
    const _ATL_INTMAP_ENTRY *pEntries, REFIID riid, PVOID *ppvObject )
```

As before, *riid* identifies the interface and *ppvObject* receives its pointer. The function's second parameter *pEntries* points to the beginning of the interface map, which consists of an array of _ATL_INTMAP_ENTRY structures. Each structure in the array contains an interface identifier, a DWORD variable, and a function pointer:

```
struct _ATL_INTMAP_ENTRY
{
    const IID*          piid;       // Interface identifier
    DWORD               dw;         // Offset
    _ATL_CREATORARGFUNC* pFunc;     // Function pointer
};
```

The value of *pFunc* determines how *InternalQueryInterface* interprets the value of *dw*. If *pFunc* is ATL_SIMPLEMAPENTRY (defined as 1), *dw* contains an offset into the class object, allowing *InternalQueryInterface* to fulfill the call like this:

```
*ppvObject = pThis + pEntries->dw;
*ppvObject->AddRef();
```

where *pEntries* has been incremented to point to the interface's _ATL_
INTMAP_ENTRY structure in the array. If *pFunc* has a value greater than
1, *InternalQueryInterface* assumes that it points to a function. *Internal-
QueryInterface* calls the function, passing *dw* as a parameter:

```
pEntries->pFunc( pThis, riid, ppvObject, pEntries->dw );
```

The called function is responsible for writing the desired interface pointer
into *\*ppvObject*.

The *pFunc* member can also have a value of NULL. This special value is
reserved for the last _ATL_INTMAP_ENTRY structure of the array, serving
as a marker for the end of the interface map. You do not have to worry
about this, because ATL ensures the final structure is correct through a
special macro. Otherwise, there are no restraints on how you order the
_ATL_INTMAP_ENTRY structures in the map array. Here's what the interface map might look like for the fictitious *CMyClass* cited earlier. Notice
how an empty _ATL_INTMAP_ENTRY structure ends the array:

```
{ &IID_Interface1, 0, 1 },
{ &IID_Interface2, 4, 1 },
{ &IID_Interface3, 8, 1 },
{ 0, 0, 0 }
```

In code that uses ATL, an interface map is formed by a series of COM_
INTERFACE macros, each of which expands into an ATL_INTMAP_
ENTRY structure. ATL provides 17 different COM_INTERFACE macros
identified by suffixes such as _ENTRY and _TEAR_OFF that indicate the
type of interface the macro handles. The macro name is formed by joining
the suffix string to COM_INTERFACE, as in COM_INTERFACE_ENTRY.
Table 10-2 on the next page describes the COM_INTERFACE macros and
explains when to use them; to help keep the table uncluttered, the first
column lists only the macro suffix. For more information about the macros, see the article "COM_INTERFACE_ENTRY Macros" in online help.

ATL refers to the series of macros in the source code as a COM map, a
term often used interchangeably with the interface map that the macros
create. A COM map in ATL begins by invoking the BEGIN_COM_MAP

**Table 10-2.** *ATL's COM_INTERFACE macros.*

| COM_INTERFACE macro | Description |
| --- | --- |
| _ENTRY | Exposes an interface from which the class derives. |
| _ENTRY_IID | Same as COM_INTERFACE_ENTRY, but also specifies the interface's identifier. |
| _ENTRY2 | For a class derived from two or more dual interfaces, resolves the ambiguity of which interface should provide the pointer to the *IDispatch* interface. Dual interfaces are described later in this chapter. |
| _ENTRY2_IID | Same as COM_INTERFACE_ENTRY2, but also specifies the interface's identifier. |
| _ENTRY_IMPL | Alternative to COM_INTERFACE_ENTRY. |
| _ENTRY_IMPL_ IID | Same as COM_INTERFACE_ENTRY_IMPL, but also specifies the interface's identifier. This macro and COM_INTERFACE_ENTRY_IMPL are obsolete in ATL version 3; use COM_INTERFACE_ENTRY instead. |
| _ENTRY_FUNC | Specifies a hook function that gains control when ATL processes *QueryInterface*. The hook function can abort the process by returning E_NOINTERFACE, thus hiding the interface that ATL would otherwise return. |
| _ENTRY_FUNC_ BLIND | Same as COM_INTERFACE_ENTRY_FUNC, except that querying for any interface results in a call to the hook function. |
| _ENTRY_TEAR_ OFF | Declares a COM map entry for a tear-off interface, which is instantiated only when the client requests the interface through *QueryInterface*. The tear-off occupies no memory until needed, making it suitable for an interface such as *ISupportErrorInfo* that stands a good chance of not being used during the life of the control. A disadvantage of a tear-off interface is that it takes slightly more overhead to create than a normal interface.<br><br>The class implementing the tear-off must derive from *CComTearOffObjectBase* and have its own COM map. |

| COM_INTERFACE macro | Description |
|---|---|
| _ENTRY_ CACHED_ TEAR_OFF | Same as the COM_INTERFACE_ENTRY_TEAR_OFF macro, except that the interface data are saved (cached) after the first instance. If the tear-off interface is instantiated, caching effectively turns it into a normal interface. |
| _ENTRY_ AGGREGATE | Declares a COM map entry for an interface provided by an aggregated object. This macro queries for the interface identifier forwarded to the *IUnknown* interface of the aggregated object. Aggregation is discussed later in the chapter. |
| _ENTRY_ AGGREGATE_ BLIND | Same as COM_INTERFACE_ENTRY_AGGREGATE, except that all queries are forwarded to the specified *IUnknown* interface. |
| _ENTRY_AUTO- AGGREGATE | Same as COM_INTERFACE_ENTRY_AGGREGATE if the *IUnknown* pointer is provided. Otherwise the macro automatically creates the aggregate indicated by a given class identifier. |
| _ENTRY_AUTO- AGGREGATE_ BLIND | Same as COM_INTERFACE_ENTRY_AUTO-AGGREGATE unless the *IUnknown* pointer is provided, in which case all queries are forwarded to the *IUnknown* interface. If the *IUnknown* pointer is not provided, the macro creates the aggregate indicated by a given class identifier. |
| _ENTRY_CHAIN | Allows processing to continue in the COM map of a specified base class. The base class must appear in the current class's inheritance list—that is, it must be a base of the current class. The COM_INTERFACE_ENTRY_CHAIN cannot be the first entry in a COM map. |
| _ENTRY_BREAK | Calls *DebugBreak* when a specified interface is requested. Use this macro to trigger a debugger breakpoint (described in Chapter 11, The Debugger). |
| _ENTRY_ NOINTERFACE | Returns E_NOINTERFACE and ends COM map processing when a specified interface is queried. The macro thus disables the interface, preventing it from being processed by any COM_INTERFACE macros that follow in the COM map. |

macro and ends with the END_COM_MAP macro. Between them lies a series of COM_INTERFACE macros, one for each interface that the class supports:

```
BEGIN_COM_MAP(CMyClass)
    COM_INTERFACE_ENTRY(IMyClass)
    COM_INTERFACE_ENTRY(IDispatch)
    COM_INTERFACE_ENTRY2(IPersist, IPersistStreamInit)
    ⋮
END_COM_MAP()
```

The form of the map borrows heavily from the standard message map of MFC. (MFC provides its own macros for creating an interface map, though we did not encounter them in Chapter 9. An interface map in MFC begins and ends with the BEGIN_INTERFACE_MAP and END_INTERFACE_MAP macros.) The order of COM map structures is not important, but the first interface in the list must use a simple map entry—that is, COM_INTER-FACE_ENTRY or any other COM_INTERFACE macro that expands to an _ATL_INTMAP_ENTRY structure with a *pFunc* value of ATL_SIMPLE-MAPENTRY. This requirement stems from ATL's use of the first interface in the map to respond to requests for the object's *IUnknown* interface.

## Object Maps

An ActiveX control may contain several objects, each represented by a class and each providing its own interface map. Figure 10-1 shows the

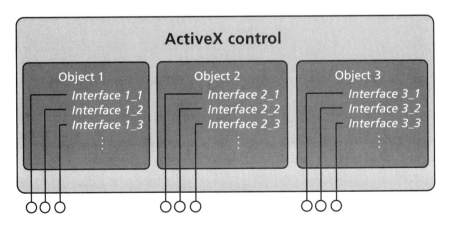

**Figure 10-1.** *Elements of an ActiveX control.*

hierarchical relationship between a control, the objects it contains, and the interfaces implemented by the objects. Similar in concept to an interface map, an object map tracks a control's objects, associating each object with its class identifier (CLSID). ATL arranges an object map as an array of _ATL_OBJMAP_ENTRY structures, each of which defines a series of helper functions. Here's an abbreviated form of the _ATL_OBJMAP_ ENTRY structure showing the function prototypes:

```
struct _ATL_OBJMAP_ENTRY
{
    HRESULT UpdateRegistry( BOOL bRegister );
    HRESULT GetClassObject( void* pv, REFIID riid, PVOID* ppv );
    HRESULT CreateInstance( void* pv, REFIID riid, PVOID* ppv );
    LPCTSTR GetObjectDescription();
    HRESULT RevokeClassObject();
    HRESULT RegisterClassObject( DWORD dwClsContext, DWORD dwFlags );
};
```

When a client first requests a class object, the *GetClassObject* function is called to create an instance of the object and provide the caller a pointer to the requested *IClassFactory* or *IClassFactory2* interface. The function stores the class factory pointer within the object map structure, making subsequent requests for a new instance of the object quicker to fulfill. Because the class object is instantiated on the stack or in the heap instead of in the control's static data, ActiveX controls constructed with ATL do not require linkage to the C run-time library. Avoiding C run-time functions and static constructors ensures that the finished control's executable size remains small, free of the extra initialization code that the C library otherwise links in.

## Threading Models

ATL supports four threading models named single, apartment, free, and both. A threading model describes the type and degree of thread safety a control implements, though any client application, regardless of its own threading arrangement, can safely access a control built from any threading model. If the client's threading is not compatible with that of the server, COM interposes itself between the two to assure thread-safe communication. Given this assurance, selecting a threading model for your control needn't be an agonizing decision. There are pros and cons for each choice, of course, generally pitting performance against code size, and efficiency against simplicity. The code that ATL adds to a project supports whatever threading model you select, so you need only make sure that the code you write yourself also complies with the requirements of the selected model. This section explains the differences between the four possible models, helping you decide which is best for your project.

It's easier to envision threading from the perspective of the client. Let's begin with a look at threading models as they apply to a container application, and then examine how each threading model affects the ActiveX control that the application embeds. Threading models are not difficult to understand, but the rules are sometimes a little convoluted. An example project later in this chapter applies some of the theory discussed here to illustrate how a control behaves under different threading models.

### Single threading

The single threading model is the simplest of the four because it does not require a control to guard against simultaneous use of its data, even its static data. The model allows a client to create any number of instances of a control's object, but confines to a single thread all client access to those instances. Single threading does not restrict the number of threads a client can run, and indeed an ActiveX control should assume that many of its clients are multithreaded. The model only dictates that all calls to an object's interfaces are made from the client's thread that first calls *CoInitializeEx* to initialize the COM framework. Because the ActiveX control does not need to expend additional effort in ensuring thread-safe access to its interfaces or other data, single threading leads to the smallest object size among the four threading models. Communication between client and server is direct and fast, as long as the client adheres to the model's restrictions.

But consider what happens when two threads in the client use the same ActiveX control. Thread A, which is not necessarily the client's main thread, initializes COM through *CoInitializeEx*, then calls *CoCreate-Instance* to create an instance of the control object. Thread B subsequently requires the control's services and, like Thread A, creates a new instance of the control. But this time COM does not return an interface pointer that points directly into the control's code as it did when Thread A called *CoCreateInstance.* Instead, the returned pointer references an invisible proxy object running on Thread B. When the client uses the pointer to call a method from Thread B, the proxy sends a message to a stub object that runs on Thread A. The stub in turn calls directly into the ActiveX control on the same thread, then passes the return value back to the proxy via another message. This exchange of messages switches threads, and ensures that the ActiveX control always executes within the context of Thread A, the thread that first initialized COM.

Rerouting a call from one thread and completing it on another is known as interthreaded marshaling, which is conceptually similar to the interprocess marshalling discussed in Chapter 8. The main difference is that the proxy and stub objects that carry out interthreaded marshaling are hidden windows set up by COM, not dynamic link libraries installed in separate processes. Messaging between the windows is analogous to the remote procedure calls that pass back and forth between a client's in-process proxy and its out-of-process stub. Marshaling between threads is usually faster than marshaling between processes, but exchanging messages and switching thread contexts still slows access to an object instance several hundredfold compared to directly calling the object. Each time the client calls one of the control's methods from Thread B, the same tortuous process repeats itself to marshal the call to Thread A. Worse yet, Thread A may be busy away from its message loop, in which case messages posted by the proxy must wait in the queue until extracted and routed to the stub. All method calls the client makes from Thread A go directly to the control and are not marshaled, giving Thread A special privileges not granted to other threads that use the control. The single threading model exacts a performance penalty only when the client calls the control from threads other than the first thread that registers itself with COM through *CoInitializeEx.*

### Apartment threading
The apartment threading model goes a long way towards eliminating the need for interthreaded marshaling. Under this arrangement all client threads enjoy equal privileges and are able to interact directly with an instance of an ActiveX control without first going through proxy and stub

services. In other words, every apartment thread is like Thread A of the previous discussion, and none are like Thread B. Each thread that requires the control's services first calls *CoInitializeEx* as before, then calls *Co-CreateInstance* to create a control instance. Under apartment threading, the returned interface pointer points directly into the interface's v-table in the instantiated object and not into a proxy. Each thread has its own object instance, and no marshaling takes place as long as a thread accesses only the instance it created.

Confusion sometimes arises because there exist two types of apartment threading. The model that ATL calls "apartment" is more correctly termed the single-threaded apartment model, often abbreviated STA. This is the model described in the preceding paragraph—one object instance per thread, each thread calling only its own instance. The multithreaded apartment model, or MTA, is what ATL calls the free model, described in a moment. An apartment is an abstract concept that has little correlation with the physical world the way processes and threads do, so don't waste a lot of time trying to visualize it. The idea arises from the analogy that a process is like a building in which threads represent separate rooms. An apartment comprises a single instance of an object along with the thread or threads that can safely call directly into that instance.

Although we often speak of STA or MTA client applications, the model designation more correctly applies to the threads within an application, because a process can contain both STA and MTA threads. When a client thread calls *CoInitializeEx*, it passes a value that specifies which apartment model the thread is designed for. A value of COINIT_APARTMENT-THREADED registers the thread under the STA model, sole occupant of a single-threaded apartment. A value of COINIT_MULTITHREADED registers the thread as part of a multithreaded apartment. A process can contain any number of single-threaded apartments but only one multithreaded apartment, to which any number of threads can belong. Interface pointers retrieved from the object are not marshaled when called on threads inside an apartment, but are always marshaled when used by threads in other apartments. When speaking of the single-threaded apartment model, the words apartment and thread are often used interchangeably without causing confusion, but the practice is wholly incorrect when applied to the multithreaded apartment model, described next.

### Free threading

Free threading is just another name for the multithreaded apartment model. Threads within a multithreaded apartment can safely share interface pointers supplied by a single instance of an object regardless of which thread created the instance. COM stays out of the way and does not marshal calls that occur within the confines of the apartment. As in the single-threaded apartment model, however, marshalling is required when a thread calls into an object instantiated in another apartment.

This sounds simple enough, but free threading places a heavier responsibility on you, the developer. Choosing to support the free threading model means writing code that can be safely accessed at any time by any number of threads. The next section looks at some of the requirements each threading model imposes on an ActiveX control.

### Choosing a threading model for your ActiveX control

Understanding threading models on the client side of COM enables you to choose the threading model best for your ActiveX control. Fortunately, threading in servers involves more coding and less theory. You need only select a threading model for your control and write the code accordingly, assured that COM will solve any mismatches through marshaling. A client thread conforms to either the STA or MTA model, but an ActiveX control adopts one of the four models listed earlier: single (nonthreaded), apartment (STA), free (MTA), or both. The both threading model means both STA and MTA—that is, the control must be written to accommodate either of the two possible models of a client thread without the need for COM to marshal the interactions.

We have seen how a client thread identifies its model to COM when calling *CoInitializeEx*, but the main thread of an ActiveX control, which is the thread that receives the client's calls, does not register itself. This makes sense because, after all, we are speaking of only one thread along which program logic flows from the client into the ActiveX control and back again, without passing through a marshaler. A control identifies its threading model through an entry in the system registry, either *apartment*, *free*, or *both*. If the entry is not present, COM assumes the control conforms to the single threading model. Projects later in the chapter demonstrate how an ActiveX control designates its threading model in the registry.

Having waded this far into the morass of threading models, we can at last tackle a very important question: how does an ActiveX control know in advance which threading model a client uses? The answer is beautifully simple: it does not know, nor does it need to know. The threading model you select for your control tells COM the kind of client thread your control is designed to handle without the need for marshalling. COM recognizes when any mismatches occur and transparently sets up marshaling only when required to resolve the differences. For example, an STA client thread that instantiates a control marked *apartment* interacts directly with the control instance. When an MTA thread instantiates the control, however, COM must marshal all calls to ensure both client and control run on the same thread. In registering the apartment threading model, the control has informed COM that each instance can accommodate only calls on a single thread; marshalling makes sure that's what happens. Table 10-3 summarizes under what conditions COM marshals calls between a client and its embedded control.

| When a client thread of this model . . . | . . . accesses an ActiveX control of this model . . . | . . . is marshaling required? |
|---|---|---|
| STA | single | No for the first thread to initialize COM; yes for all other threads |
| MTA | single | Yes |
| STA | apartment | No |
| MTA | apartment | Yes |
| STA | free | Yes |
| MTA | free | No |
| STA | both | No |
| MTA | both | No |

**Table 10-3.** *Conditions under which COM marshals calls between client and control.*

Which threading model is best for your control depends on the sort of client application you anticipate will use your control and on how much extra work you are willing to undertake to assure thread-safe access. The single nonthreaded model requires no extra coding at all to achieve thread safety, since only one client thread can directly access all instances of the control. Free threading, on the other hand, serves best only if you know in advance your control will be used exclusively by MTA applications. You rarely have this assurance, however, unless you write the clients yourself. Because the great majority of client applications today conform to STA threading, the apartment model generally represents the best choice for an ActiveX control designed to serve many different clients. Internet Explorer and Netscape Navigator are STA applications, as are container programs using MFC and those written in Visual Basic versions 5 and later. Microsoft Transaction Server also conforms to the rules of STA, so a control should use the apartment model if it supports MTS.

Thread safety is easily programmed under the apartment model, which requires only safeguarding against simultaneously writing static data, usually through critical sections or some similar mechanism. If you want to ensure fast access to your control regardless of the client's threading model, choose the both model. Accommodating STA and MTA access without marshaling requires extra work, especially for controls that run more than one thread. For a look into the intricacies of MTA threading, peruse the article by David Platt in *Microsoft Systems Journal*, volume 12, number 8. You can locate the article in MSDN online help under the Periodicals entry in the Contents tab.

# Example 1: The Pulse ActiveX Control

The Pulse control presented in this section illustrates how to use ATL to produce a simple ActiveX control. Pulse is selective in what it takes from the library. The goal here is not only to demonstrate ATL, but to show some of the ways you can reduce the size of a control short of modifying the ATL source code or resorting to straight COM instructions. The result should give you an idea of how small you can reasonably expect an ActiveX control to be when created using ATL.

Pulse is merely a timer control that fires an event at a programmable interval, thus behaving much like the IETimer control we used in Chapter 8 when building the Hour program. Like IETimer, Pulse is completely self-sufficient, using neither MFC nor the C run-time library. But at 37 KB, Pulse is less than half the size of IETimer.ocx, yet provides the same service. The main reason Pulse is so small is that it operates invisibly without displaying a window.

The Pulse control contains a single object governed by a class named *CPulseCtl*. Besides implementing the interfaces listed in Table 10-1 on page 429, the object provides these control elements:

- A property variable that contains the pulse interval in milliseconds

- Methods that allow the container to start and end event firing

- An event that notifies the container each time a pulse interval elapses

The ten steps described here illustrate how the Pulse project takes form. The discussions take a general approach to the subject of creating an ActiveX control project using ATL, and are not specific to invisible controls like Pulse. Don't let the digressions persuade you that what we are doing here is difficult. Creating a simple ActiveX control using ATL is amazingly easy.

## Step 1: Run ATL COM AppWizard

An ActiveX control project created with ATL always begins with the first of ATL's wizards, ATL COM AppWizard. Click the New command on the File menu, select ATL COM AppWizard as pictured in Figure 10-2, and type *Pulse* for the project name.

When the single dialog appears listing control options (Figure 10-3), click the Finish button to accept the default settings. These settings specify that the new control runs as a dynamic link library that does not use MFC. Leave clear the option labeled Allow Merging Of Proxy/Stub Code, which is available only for DLL server types. Selecting the option tells COM AppWizard to set up the project to link marshaling code into the control's executable image, producing a single DLL file that contains both the

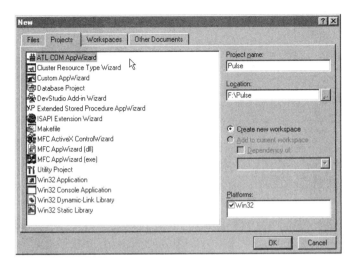

**Figure 10-2.** *Launching ATL COM AppWizard.*

control and its proxy/stub instructions. Clearing the option tells COM AppWizard to instead write marshaling code to a separate file named DllData.c, thus reducing the overall size of the finished executable. We'll talk more about a control's proxy/stub code in Step 5 of this exercise.

COM and ATL consistently refer to an in-process ActiveX control as a dynamic link library. As we saw in Chapter 9, an ActiveX control is indeed a dynamic link library, but of a specialized form. As you read

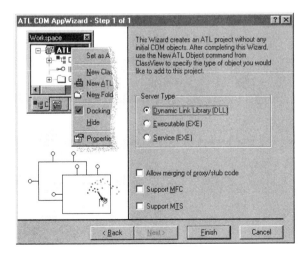

**Figure 10-3.** *Selecting a project type in COM AppWizard.*

through the source code in the steps that follow, keep in mind that "DLL" refers to the Pulse ActiveX control we are creating.

In setting up an ActiveX control project, COM AppWizard generates several source files containing necessary code. The Pulse.cpp file implements the *DllMain* function that the operating system calls when it first loads the library, along with four additional functions that serve COM. Since COM does not provide the functions, an in-process ActiveX control like Pulse must export them itself:

- **DllGetClassObject**—Called from *CoGetClassObject* when the client first requests COM to instantiate a control object in memory. The function services the call by creating an instance of the class factory and returning a pointer to the *IClassFactory* or *IClassFactory2* interface.

- **DllCanUnloadNow**—Called from *CoFreeUnusedLibraries* when the client is finished using the control server. The function informs the caller whether any objects managed by the ActiveX control are still in service, indicated by the control's internal reference count of outstanding objects. If the count is zero for all interfaces, the *DllCanUnloadNow* function returns S_OK to permit COM to unload the control from memory.

- **DllRegisterServer**—Inserts information about the ActiveX control into the system Registry. The most important of a control's Registry data is an entry under HKEY_CLASSES_ROOT\CLSID that specifies the location of the control's executable file. Given only the control's class identifier supplied by the container application, COM scans the CLSID folder to locate the control so it can load it into memory. This arrangement allows an ActiveX control to reside anywhere on a hard disk or network, in contrast to a normal DLL file that must usually be restricted to specific locations recognized by the operating system.

- **DllUnregisterServer**—Removes Registry data inserted by *DllRegisterServer* for each of the control's objects.

These four functions are short wrappers, only a single line each. They all call into an object named _Module_, which is an instance of ATL's _CComModule_ class. It is the _Module_ object that provides the main implementations for the functions.

COM AppWizard gives the finished control an extension of DLL instead of OCX, without offering an option for choosing the file extension. You may feel that the world is crowded enough with DLL files and that an ActiveX control should have an OCX extension to allow users to infer the file's purpose. If so, some editing is required at this point to change the file extension. Close the project workspace temporarily, open the Pulse.dsp file in the text editor, and use the Replace command to rename all occurrences of ".dll" to ".ocx." Then reopen the project and change the file extension in the Link tab of the Project Settings dialog. Don't try this, though, if your control runs in the Microsoft Transaction Server environment.

COM AppWizard creates a skeleton project, but does not add source code for the ActiveX class object itself. The next step after running COM AppWizard is to insert code for an object's class using the second of ATL's wizards, named ATL Object Wizard.

## Step 2: Run ATL Object Wizard

ATL's Object Wizard generates a class declaration and stub implementation functions for an object class, making it somewhat akin to MFC's ClassWizard. Run Object Wizard as shown in Figure 10-4 on the next page, either by choosing the New ATL Object command from the Insert menu, or by right-clicking the project name in the ClassView pane and choosing the command from the context menu. The WizardBar menu also provides access to the same command.

Object Wizard automatically adds ATL code to the project for any of 17 different object types, some of which are listed in Table 10-4 on the next page. The Full Control option is commonly selected when developing an ActiveX control project, but the option presumes the control will display a window and support such luxuries as a property sheet and a representative icon. For a small invisible control like Pulse, it is usually preferable to choose one of the simpler component types and build up from there,

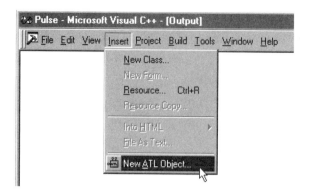

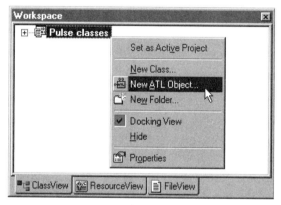

**Figure 10-4.**   *Two methods for invoking ATL Object Wizard.*

**Table 10-4.**   *Common object types that ATL Object Wizard supports.*

| Object type | Remarks |
| --- | --- |
| Simple Object | Creates a bare COM object. Interface support must be added manually. |
| Add-in Object | Creates a simple add-in object that connects to Developer Studio's *IApplication* interface. Chapter 13, Customizing Visual C++, explains Developer Studio add-ins in more detail. |
| Internet Explorer Object | Creates a COM object that supports the interfaces expected by Internet Explorer, but without additional support for a user interface. |
| ActiveX Server Component | Adds support for *OnStartPage* and *OnEndPage*, with pointers to ASP interfaces such as *IRequest*, *IResponse*, and *IServer*. |

| Object type | Remarks |
| --- | --- |
| Microsoft Transaction Server | Creates a skeleton implementation file that includes the Mtx.h header file required by a transaction server. |
| Component Registrar | Provides access to the system Registry through ATL's Registrar, implemented by the *IRegistrar* interface. |
| Lite Control | Creates a control with a user interface that can be embedded in Internet Explorer, but which does not support interfaces required by many other containers. Provides pointers to client's *IOleInPlaceSiteWindowless*, *IOleClientSite*, and *IAdviseSink* interfaces. |
| Full Control | Creates a control that can be embedded in all containers that comply with ActiveX guidelines. Provides the same pointers to site interfaces as Lite Control. |
| Composite Control | Creates a control similar to a dialog box that can contain other ActiveX controls and normal controls. |
| Property Page | Adds a property page object to the control project. Select this option once for each page of a property sheet. |
| Dialog | Adds a generic dialog resource to the project. |
| Provider | Creates an object that performs the data translating services of an OLE DB provider. |

rather than having to later remove unwanted code. The Pulse project does not require a lot of starter code, so select Objects in the lefthand pane of the wizard's dialog and double-click the icon labeled Simple Object, as shown in Figure 10-5 on the next page.

Object Wizard next displays the Properties dialog (Figure 10-6 on page 451), which queries for characteristics of the control. In the Names tab, type *PulseCtl* for the short name, from which Object Wizard fills in the other edit boxes with appropriate entries. The Class edit box contains the name of the *CPulseCtl* class that implements the control's only object. This class is important because it inherits from all the interfaces that the Pulse control supports.

Object Wizard writes the *CPulseCtl* class source code to the indicated H and CPP files. The CoClass edit box holds the name of the control's component class, which serves as the type library equivalent of the object

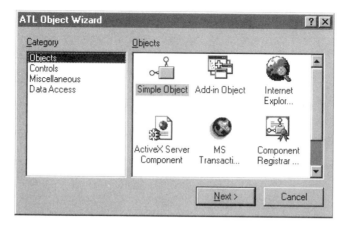

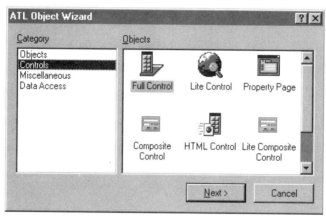

**Figure 10-5.** *The ATL Object Wizard dialog.*

class. The *CPulseCtl* class and the *PulseCtl* component class refer to the same object but distinguish between the two places where the object is defined. *CPulseCtl* refers to the C++ source code that implements the object, whereas the *PulseCtl* component class refers to the object's definition in the control's type library. The Interface box shows the name of the interface on which the control exposes to the world its custom methods and properties. The edit boxes labeled Type and ProgID hold strings that describe the *CPulseCtl* object and its programmatic identifier.

Some of the names shown in Figure 10-6 end up as entries in the system Registry, placed there by Pulse's *DllRegisterServer* function. The programmatic identifiers *PulseCtl.PulseCtl* and *PulseCtl.PulseCtl.1*, for instance,

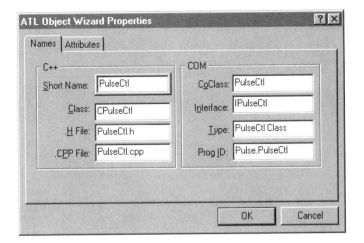

**Figure 10-6.** *Specifying names for an object in the ATL Object Wizard Properties dialog.*

become strings under Registry keys named VersionIndependentProgID and ProgID, respectively. The only difference between the two identifiers is that the latter contains the control's version number—1, in this case. Both strings act as human-readable alternatives to the control's class identifier, providing a means for a container application to request a control object without using the CLSID string. MFC's *CWnd::CreateControl* function, for example, accepts a programmatic identifier string like this:

```
CreateControl( "PulseCtl.PulseCtl.1", NULL, 0, &rect,
               pParentWnd, IDC_PULSECTL );
```

Similarly, a Visual Basic or VBA container passes the identifier to the *CreateObject* function:

```
Dim PulseCtl As Object
PulseCtl = CreateObject ("PulseCtl.PulseCtl.1")
```

A client possessing only a programmatic identifier for a control can determine the corresponding class identifier by calling the OLE function *CLSIDFromProgID*. The function *ProgIDFromCLSID* performs the opposite translation.

In the Attributes tab, select the check box labeled Support Connection Points, as shown on the next page in Figure 10-7. Connection points are necessary for ActiveX controls like Pulse that fire events. The same tab

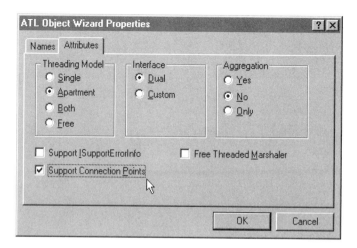

**Figure 10-7.**    *Object attributes in the ATL Object Wizard Properties dialog.*

displays radio buttons that determine the control's threading model, interface type, and whether it supports aggregation. We have already looked at the threading models that ATL supports, but dual interfaces and aggregation deserve more discussion.

- **Dual interface**—We saw in Chapter 8 that Microsoft extended the design of OLE to support custom controls, intending such components to act as 32-bit replacements for VBX components. Because of the way it passed function parameters, however, Visual Basic before version 4 could not call a control method directly. To solve this problem, Microsoft incorporated into OLE the *IDispatch* interface to provide the necessary link. The *IDispatch* interface today serves most often as a communication conduit for scripting clients such as VBScript and JavaScript, allowing them to call a control's methods through the services of the *IDispatch::Invoke* function, which converts parameters and return values to and from the client's native data type. Although a workable solution, the extra conversions and indirectness of calling *Invoke* slow the container's interactions with a control.

    For Web page scripts and older Visual Basic clients, *IDispatch* is a necessary compromise. Container applications written in languages such as C++, however, can directly access a control's methods by calling through pointers. *IDispatch::Invoke* and its time-consuming conversions are not required. To accommodate clients that support data types other than **Variant**, OLE supports the idea of dual interfaces. A method function of a dual interface can be accessed either indirectly through *IDispatch::Invoke* or directly by calling a pointer to the method, thus serving all container applications regardless of what language they are written in.

■ **Aggregation**—Through aggregation, another object can appear to its callers to have all of the abilities of the Pulse control plus whatever new services the second object provides. The aggregating object, often referred to as the containing or outer object, embeds the Pulse control the same way a container application would. The outer control then selectively filters *QueryInterface* requests from its client, passing on to Pulse any requests for the *IPulseCtl* interface. The outer object's client receives the desired pointer and calls into Pulse, unaware that now Pulse, not the object that has aggregated it, is providing the service.

The aggregation selection in the Object Wizard Properties dialog does not determine whether your control can aggregate another object, only whether your control can itself be aggregated.

If you do not intend your own control to serve older Visual Basic applications or to be scripted on a Web page or Active Server Page, select the Custom radio button in the dialog. This has the benefit of slightly reducing the size of the finished control because each implemented interface does not incorporate the four methods of *IDispatch*. Although a control with custom interfaces can appear in an HTML document, it cannot be programmed through a script. The script interpreter must find the *IDispatch* interface on the control object or it cannot access the control.

For the Pulse control, accept the default settings to enable apartment model threading and add support for dual interfaces, but not aggregation. After mulling it over a moment, let's make Pulse non-aggregatable by selecting the No radio button in the Aggregation group. This adds a single line to the *CPulseCtl* class definition, as shown on the next page.

```
DECLARE_NOT_AGGREGATABLE(CPulseCtl)
```

Although aggregation is usually a desirable characteristic for an ActiveX control, supporting aggregation adds about 2 kilobytes to the control's executable size. Since one of the goals of this project is to show how to minimize the size of a control created with ATL, forgoing aggregation seems a reasonable compromise.

The compromise is not as serious as it might first appear, because aggregation is not the only technique by which one ActiveX control can make use of another. Nothing prevents a control from acting as a client itself and embedding the Pulse control. In this technique, known as containment, the containing control provides its own method functions for running Pulse and advertises the methods through its type library. When a client application requests one of Pulse's services, the containing control—let's call it Outer—passes the call on to Pulse. When Pulse fires its event, control travels back to Outer's handler function, which in turn propagates the event by firing into its client application. As with aggregation, the client application is unaware that another control is providing the service. But unlike aggregation, containment slows communication between Pulse and the client application because the Outer control must serve as a middleman between the two.

Leave blank the check box labeled Free Threaded Marshaler. This option adds to the project an object known as the free-threaded marshaler, described in the sidebar.

---

## The Free-Threaded Marshaler

Selecting the Free Threaded Marshaler check box in ATL Object Wizard generates a call to COM's *CoCreateFreeThreadedMarshaler* function:

```
HRESULT FinalConstruct()
{
    return CoCreateFreeThreadedMarshaler(
        GetControllingUnknown(), &m_pUnkMarshaler.p );
}
```

The function creates an object called the free-threaded marshaler that aggregates to the control and oversees marshaling operations. Its primary purpose is to improve performance when a container application using the single-threaded apartment model embeds an ActiveX control using the both threading model. To see how the free-threaded marshaler can benefit such a control, it's necessary to peer into a typical client that runs two STA threads, where Thread B must call the object instance owned by Thread A. Thread A first calls *CoMarshalInterThreadInterfaceInStream*, receiving a pointer to a stream in return. (A stream is just a collection of data.) Thread A hands the stream pointer to Thread B, which uses it to call *CoGetInterfaceAndReleaseStream*, receiving a pointer to a proxy that represents the desired instance. Thread B can now safely call the proxy to access methods on the object's interfaces, even though the instance was created in a different apartment.

If an ActiveX control complying with the both threading model can safely handle direct calls from any apartment, even different STA apartments, routing calls from the client's Thread B through a marshaler is an unnecessary expenditure of time, because the client could just as correctly (and more efficiently) call the object's instance directly from Thread B. The client cannot safely assume this option exists, and so must request a proxy through *CoGetInterfaceAndReleaseStream*. But because the control is written to safely accommodate simultaneous access on different STA threads, it calls *CoCreateFreeThreadedMarshaler* to implement its own custom marshaling through the free-threaded marshaler. This object acts as a stub that copies to the stream a direct pointer to the interface that the client has requested through *CoGetInterfaceAndReleaseStream*. The result is that Thread B gets its interface pointer without having to switch threads or traverse the winding paths of the COM marshaler. The client cannot tell the difference, except that calls to the instance are much faster because they access methods directly and are not marshaled through proxy code. A control that adopts this technique, however, must ensure that the object can handle simultaneous usage.

Click the OK button to dismiss the ATL Object Wizard dialog, at which point the wizard generates three files:

- **PulseCtl.h and PulseCtl.cpp**—Definition and implementation code for the new *CPulseCtl* class.

- **PulseCtl.rgs**—Text file containing a script of the control's registration information. The registry script in the RGS file becomes part of the resource data contained in the control's executable file, which the *DllRegisterServer* function reads and installs in the Registry. Object Wizard adds a line to the project's RC file to reference the registry script:

```
IDR_PULSECTL    REGISTRY DISCARDABLE    "PulseCtl.rgs"
```

and inserts a **#define** statement in Resource.h for the IDR_PULSECTL constant.

Object Wizard also adds several **#include** statements to the StdAfx.cpp and StdAfx.h files. The statements bring into the project necessary ATL source files such AtlImpl.cpp, AtlCtl.cpp, and AtlWin.cpp. Although the names of the StdAfx files seem reminiscent of MFC projects, they reference MFC headers only if you select the MFC option in Step 1.

For each object that you add to a control, Object Wizard places an entry in the control's object map. Pulse contains only the *CPulseCtl* object, so its object map in the Pulse.cpp file looks like this when the wizard finishes:

```
BEGIN_OBJECT_MAP(ObjectMap)
    OBJECT_ENTRY(CLSID_PulseCtl, CPulseCtl)
END_OBJECT_MAP()
```

Finally, ATL Object Wizard makes necessary changes to the project's IDL file, from which the control's type library is generated. IDL stands for interface description language, and the IDL file serves as input for the Microsoft IDL compiler tool, MIDL. We will look at the project's IDL file in more detail when we add Pulse's event function.

## Step 3: Add the *nInterval* Property

Pulse exposes a single custom property named *nInterval* that contains the rate in milliseconds at which the control fires its event. To add the property to the interface, expand the list of Pulse classes in the ClassView window, right-click the entry for *IPulseCtl*, and choose the Add Property command:

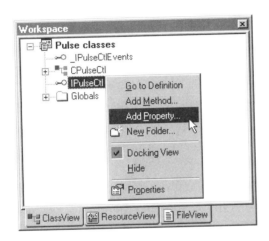

This invokes the Add Property To Interface dialog shown in Figure 10-8, which queries for the same information as ClassWizard's Add Property

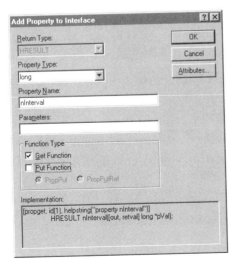

**Figure 10-8.** *Adding the* nInterval *custom property to the Pulse ActiveX control.*

dialog encountered in Chapter 9. Type *nInterval* for Pulse's property name, giving it a **long** property type. (The property could just as easily be **short**, but that would restrict the maximum tick interval to a little over a minute.) The default IDL prototypes for the property's get/put methods appear at the bottom of the dialog:

```
[propget, ...]
    HRESULT nInterval([out, retval] long *pVal);
[propput, ...]
    HRESULT nInterval([in] long newVal);
```

The get/put methods of COM are the low-level equivalent of MFC's Get/Set functions, providing the means for a container to read and write a control's property data. When the MIDL compiler compiles the project's IDL file, it defines the two methods in the interface by prepending *get_* and *put_* to the property name. The get function's *pVal* parameter points to the property's current value; the *newVal* parameter of the put function contains a new property value that replaces the old one. If your control's get/put methods require a more extensive parameter list, add the variables in the dialog's Parameters box. The dialog inserts any additions in front of the *pVal* and *newVal* parameters, and makes them common to both the get and put methods. If you do not want the same list for both functions, you must make the changes later by manually editing the IDL file using the text editor. Feel free to change the parameter order or names in the IDL file, but leave the *pVal* and *newVal* parameters last in the parameter list together with their **[out, retval]** and **[in]** attributes.

The Put Function check box is accompanied by two radio buttons labeled PropPut and PropPutRef. PropPutRef is similar to the default PropPut option, except that it tells the container that the property's put function accepts the *newVal* parameter by reference instead of by value. In this case, the container sets the property by calling *IDispatch::Invoke* with the DISPATCH_PROPERTYPUTREF flag instead of DISPATCH_PROPERTY-PUT. Visual Basic clients, for example, use the **Set** keyword to indicate a property assignment is by reference, not value:

```
Set PulseCtl.nInterval = x
```

Clear the Put Function check box as shown in Figure 10-8 to prevent the MIDL compiler from generating a put method entry for the *nInterval* property. A container should not be allowed to change *nInterval*, and clearing the Put Function check box in the dialog keeps the variable read-only. One of the control's other methods provides the client a more logical means of setting the *nInterval* property.

The dialog's Attributes button opens a dialog that allows selection of property characteristics such as its dispatch identifier, an optional description, and special flags. Selected attributes wind up in the IDL file and ultimately in the type library where they describe the property to prospective containers. Click the combo box shown in Figure 10-9 to display a list of available attribute settings described in Table 10-5 on the folowing page. Keep in mind that the attributes refer to the property's get/put functions rather than to the property variable itself. In COM, the word property is often used as a shorthand term for the get/put methods that provide a client access to the property.

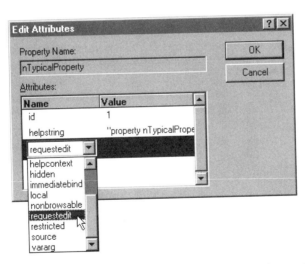

**Figure 10-9.** *Selecting property attributes in the Edit Attributes dialog.*

**Table 10-5.** *Property attributes.*

| Attribute | Description |
| --- | --- |
| **id** | Specifies a dispatch identifier (DISPID) for the property's get or put method. |
| **helpstring** | Specifies a short text string that describes the property. The container can retrieve the string through the control's *ITypeInfo::GetDocumentation* method. Although the help text is stored inside the control as part of its type information, deleting a **helpstring** entry in the Edit Attributes dialog does not reduce the size of the control's executable image. |
| **bindable** | Uses data binding to tie the property to a specific field in a database. This means that whenever the property changes in value, the control notifies the database and requests that the bound record field be updated to reflect the new value. For more information about this powerful concept, refer to the MSDN article titled "ActiveX Controls: Using Data Binding in an ActiveX Control." You can locate the article by searching for its title in MSDN's Search tab with the Search Titles Only check box set. |
| **call_as** | Enables a client to access the property's get/put functions via a different name. This is helpful for functions that have numerous "nonremotable" parameter types, such as **int** or **void**. A nonremotable variable does not appear exactly the same to operating systems on dissimilar machines. An **int** value, for example, is nonremotable because COM has no guarantee that each machine (or even each client) ascribes the same size to the variable. In contrast, **short** and **long** variables are remotable because every machine recognizes them as occupying two and four bytes. For this reason, lists of variable types in Object Wizard include **short** and **long** types but never **int**, which is too ambiguous for COM. <br><br> Individual nonremotable parameters can also be specified through the **represent_as** and **transmit_as** attributes. But for get/put functions that take several parameters of nonremotable types, **call_as** is more convenient and efficient than **represent_as** and **transmit_as**. Giving a property function a **call_as** attribute means that your control can make all necessary conversions in a single step, rather than several steps, one for each parameter. |

| Attribute | Description |
|---|---|
| | Using nonremotable function parameters is particularly inefficient for in-process servers like ActiveX controls, because it forces calls to **call_as** functions to be marshaled through proxy/stub code. You must provide a conversion routine to the container's proxy DLL that handles the nonremotable parameters and another conversion routine in the control's stub to receive the call. Using remotable types for all function parameters in an ActiveX control ensures that calls from the container directly access the control without marshaling. |
| **defaultbind** | Identifies the bindable property that best represents the control object. Only one of the control's properties can have the **defaultbind** attribute, and it must also have the **bindable** attribute. The **defaultbind** attribute allows a container to bind to the entire control object instead of to individual properties. |
| **defaultcollelem** | Allows clients written in Visual Basic for Applications to directly access the property's get/put functions. |
| **displaybind** | Indicates to the container that the property should be displayed to the user as bindable. The property must also have the **bindable** attribute. |
| **helpcontext** | Specifies a 32-bit number that identifies information in the control's help file pertaining to the property. |
| **hidden** | Requests that the container should not display the property to the user. |
| **immediatebind** | Requests that the database is notified immediately of any change to the property rather than waiting until the control loses input focus. The property must also have the **bindable** attribute. |
| **local** | Specifies that the MIDL compiler should generate only the interface header files, not the stub code. The **local** attribute is not relevant to in-process ActiveX controls like Pulse. |
| **nonbrowsable** | Requests the container not to include the property in the container's properties browser. |

*(continued)*

**Table 10-5.** *continued*

| Attribute | Description |
|-----------|-------------|
| **requestedit** | Indicates that the control will query the container for permission before changing the value of the property. Permission is requested through the *IPropertyNotifySink::OnRequestEdit* function, which notifies the container that the property is about to change and that the object is asking for permission to proceed. A return value of S_FALSE from *OnRequestEdit* denies the request; a return value of S_OK grants permission to change the property's value. Upon receiving S_OK, the control must then call *IPropertyNotifySink::OnChanged* if the property also has the **bindable** attribute. |
| **restricted** | Specifies that the property's get/put methods must not be called from a macro. |
| **source** | Indicates that the get/put functions return an object or **Variant** that is a source of events. The **source** attribute is rarely used for properties, but we will apply it shortly to Pulse's list of interfaces. |
| **vararg** | Indicates that the property's get/put methods can accept a variable number of arguments. The method's last argument must be a safe array of **Variant** type that contains default values for each unspecified argument. |

## Step 4: Add Methods

Closing the Add Property To Interface dialog writes the property information to the IDL file. The next step is to add three method functions named *StartPulse*, *EndPulse*, and *_OnTimer*. By calling the *StartPulse* method, the container tells Pulse to begin its metronomic event firing. The function's parameter specifies in milliseconds the timing interval at which the container wants to receive the event notifications. The container calls *EndPulse* to stop the event firing, after which the control becomes inactive, drawing no CPU time. The *_OnTimer* function is used by the *CTimer* class, described in Step 6. For each method, right-click the *IPulseCtl* interface in the ClassView pane as we did before, but this time choose the Add Method command:

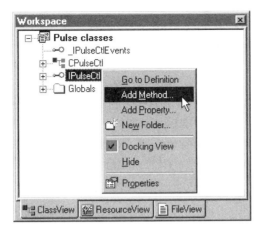

The *nRate* parameter of *StartPulse* becomes the new value for the *nInterval* property. This explains why in the previous step we decided a client does not need access to a *put_nInterval* function, because calling *StartPulse* serves the same purpose. Enter the function and parameter name in the Add Method To Interface dialog shown in Figure 10-10, then click OK to dismiss the dialog. Repeat the process to add the *EndPulse* and *_OnTimer* methods. Neither *EndPulse* nor *_OnTimer* takes a parameter, so leave the Parameters box blank. Close the Add Method To Interface dialog, at which point Visual C++ adds appropriate code for all three methods to the Pulse.idl file. It also writes stub functions for the methods to the Pulse.cpp file, which we will edit after adding an event function to the control.

**Figure 10-10.** *The Add Method to Interface dialog.*

## Step 5: Add the *Pulse* Event

The final addition to the project before we start coding is the *Pulse* event, which fires at every lapse of *nInterval* milliseconds. In previous versions of ATL, adding an event to a control required a little manual labor, involving the generation of a GUID identifier for the event interface, editing the IDL file, and running a tool called the ATL Proxy Generator. But with the library's third release, the procedure has become much smoother and more user friendly. Events are now almost as easy to add to a control project as methods and properties, requiring only a short detour to compile the project's IDL file.

Here's a list of the steps required to generate code for the new event, after which we will discuss what is happening behind the scenes. Figure 10-11 illustrates the four steps.

1. Right-click the *_IPulseCtlEvents* entry in the ClassView pane and choose the Add Method command from the context menu. In the Add Method To Interface dialog, select a return type of **void**, name the event function *Pulse*, and click OK to close the dialog.

2. Expose the FileView pane in the Workspace window, right-click the entry for Pulse.idl, and choose the Compile Pulse.idl command. This launches the MIDL compiler, which produces the type library file Pulse.tlb and adds it to the project.

3. When the MIDL compiler finishes, switch back to the ClassView pane and right-click the *CPulseCtl* entry. Choose the Implement Connection Point command from the menu to expose a dialog of the same name.

4. Set the check box labeled *_IPulseCtlEvents* and click OK to close the dialog.

The bottom half of the project's IDL file lists a **library** block titled PULSELib, which describes the new *Pulse* event to the MIDL compiler. Some container applications read only the **library** block when searching a type library for a control's methods and properties, so it's usually prudent to edit the IDL file to move the first two indented blocks of code into the **library** block. The first block, formed by square brackets [ ], contains

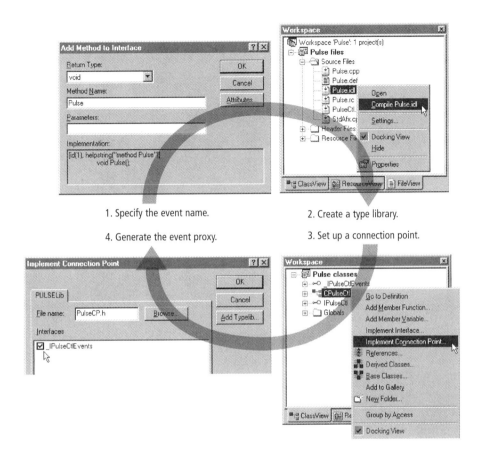

1. Specify the event name.

2. Create a type library.

4. Generate the event proxy.

3. Set up a connection point.

**Figure 10-11.** *Adding an event to an ATL ActiveX control project.*

attributes of the *IPulseCtl* interface; the second block encloses in curly braces {} a list of the interface's methods. Listing 10-1 on the next page shows what the result should look like after rearranging the code. If you are developing the Pulse project yourself by following these steps, the GUID numbers for your own IDL file will not match the ones shown in the Listing.

The **importlib** directive brings in precompiled type information from the OLE type libraries StdOle32.tlb and StdOle2.tlb, which are usually located in the Windows System or System32 directory. Although not required, the interface name *_IPulseCtlEvents* begins with an underscore. This convention serves as a notification to interface browsers that the _IPulseCtlEvents interface is private to the control, and that browsers

**Listing 10-1.**    *The revised Pulse.idl file.*

```
import "oaidl.idl";
import "ocidl.idl";

// **********************************************
// First two blocks have been moved from here...
// **********************************************

[
    uuid(3B365F9D-C3AE-11D1-BEC9-E0F4E352507A),
    version(1.0),
    helpstring("Pulse 1.0 Type Library")
]

library PULSELib
{
    importlib("stdole32.tlb");
    importlib("stdole2.tlb");

    // ********************************************************
    // ...to here:

    [
        object,
        uuid(3B365FA9-C3AE-11D1-BEC9-E0F4E352507A),
        dual,
        helpstring("IPulseCtl Interface"),
        pointer_default(unique)
    ]
    interface IPulseCtl : IDispatch
    {
        [propget, id(1)] HRESULT nInterval(
                                [out, retval] long *pVal);
        [id(2)] HRESULT StartPulse(long nRate);
        [id(3)] HRESULT EndPulse();
        [id(4)] HRESULT _OnTimer();
    };
    // ********************************************************

    [
        uuid(7C7E168F-C2F1-11D1-BEC9-E4F4ACA02373),
        helpstring("_IPulseCtlEvents Interface")
    ]
    dispinterface _IPulseCtlEvents
    {
        properties:
        methods:
```

```
        [id(1), helpstring("method Pulse")] void Pulse();
    };
    [
        uuid(8C9BABDD-BCE5-11D1-BEC9-D43CA8CB2F51),
        helpstring("PulseCtl Class")
    ]
    coclass PulseCtl
    {
        [default] interface IPulseCtl;
        [default, source] dispinterface _IPulseCtlEvents;
    };
};
```

should not display the interface to the user. Not all browsers comply with the convention, however. The lines

```
[default] interface IPulseCtl;
[default, source] dispinterface _IPulseCtlEvents;
```

identify *IPulseCtl* as the control's default dispatch interface and *_IPulse-CtlEvents* as the control's default source interface, through which the container receives the control's event notification. The **source** attribute tells the MIDL compiler that the container, not the control, is expected to provide an *IDispatch* implementation for *_IPulseCtlEvents*. The control is the source of calls into the *_IPulseCtlEvents* interface, and the container's event *IDispatch* is the event sink.

A single line identifies the control's event by its internal name, and associates the event with a unique dispatch identifier value specified by the **id** keyword:

```
[id(1), helpstring("method Pulse")] void Pulse();
```

The control does not call the *Pulse* function directly to fire events, but instead calls a wrapper function named *Fire_Pulse* that ATL adds to the project. The wrapper function, called a proxy, in turn calls the container's *IDispatch::Invoke* method, supplying the dispatch identifier number to identify the event being fired. That's how a proxy function gets its name. The *Fire_Pulse* function acts as a stand-in or proxy for the container's event handler function, serving as a place for the control to call when firing an event without having to worry about the details of how the call ultimately gets to the client. Proxy functions are members of a single proxy class that serves as one of the base classes from which *CPulseCtl* derives, allowing the control to fire its event anywhere within its *CPulseCtl* implementation. The role of the proxy class is different than that of a proxy object that COM sets up to marshal interthreaded calls. Both class and marshaling object are often called "proxy" for short, so it's sometimes easy to confuse them. But they are not the same thing.

In executing the Implement Connection Point command, we added to the project an implementation of the *IConnectionPoint* interface, through which the container determines which connection points the ActiveX control supports. The command examines the control's type library file from which it extracts the interface names *_IPulseCtlEvents* and *IPulseCtl* to create the proxy class. An ActiveX control usually includes its type library as resource data contained in the control's executable file, allowing type browsers such as ClassWizard to access the data. During the control's development stage, however, the type library exists as a separate file with a TLB extension.

ATL's *IConnectionPointImpl* template defines a base for the new *CProxy_ IPulseCtlEvents* proxy class. The code for this class, which resides in the file PulseCP.h, contains Pulse's single event proxy as a member function:

```
template <class T>
class CProxy_IPulseCtlEvents : public IConnectionPointImpl<T,
                                 &DIID__IPulseCtlEvents,
                                 CComDynamicUnkArray>
{
public:
    VOID Fire_Pulse()
    {
        T* pT = static_cast<T*>(this);
        int nConnectionIndex;
        int nConnections = m_vec.GetSize();

        for (nConnectionIndex = 0; nConnectionIndex < nConnections;
            nConnectionIndex++)
        {
            pT->Lock();
            CComPtr<IUnknown> sp = m_vec.GetAt(nConnectionIndex);
            pT->Unlock();
            IDispatch* pDispatch = reinterpret_cast<IDispatch*>(sp.p);
```

```
        if (pDispatch != NULL)
        {
            DISPPARAMS disp = { NULL, NULL, 0, 0 };
            pDispatch->Invoke(0x1, IID_NULL, LOCALE_USER_DEFAULT,
                        DISPATCH_METHOD, &disp, NULL, NULL, NULL);
        }
    }
}
};
```

Notice that the *Fire_Pulse* proxy function is of type **void**. Events, unlike methods, never return a value.

Through its base class, *CProxy_IPulseCtlEvents* implements the connection point for the interface identified by the second template parameter. In our case, the interface is *_IPulseCtlEvents* and its dispatch interface identifier is DIID__IPulseCtlEvents, defined in the Pulse_i.c file. The third template parameter specifies an ATL class that handles the connections. The default *CComDynamicUnkArray* class allows an unlimited number of connections; the alternative *CComUnkArray* class allows only a fixed number of connections.

## Step 6: Add the *CTimer* Class

Pulse could simply capture WM_TIMER messages to activate its event firing, but that would require creating a window to receive the messages. A window takes a toll in system resources, requiring a lot of time to set up and take down, and a streamlined ActiveX control like Pulse should avoid creating windows when possible. Fortunately, the AtlButton sample project included with Visual C++ contains a simple thread-safe *CTimer* class that does just what we need. Because the code is not generated by an ATL wizard, it appears on the next page in its entirety as Listing 10-2.

A glance through the listing shows *CTimer* taking several steps for which the reasons may not be immediately apparent. The class arms the timer through its *TimerOn* function, which creates a new thread that calls the *Sleep* function to sleep for the requested duration. When the thread wakes up, it calls the _OnTimer method we added in Step 4 to announce that the interval has elapsed. The thread then goes back to sleep again, a process that continually repeats in a loop until the *TimerOff* function is called. The class is interesting because it performs its own custom marshaling

**Listing 10-2.** *The Timer.h file.*

```
// Timer.h : Declaration of the CTimer class (borrowed from
//              Samples\VC98\ATL\AtlButto\AtlButto.h file)

template <class Derived, class T, const IID* piid>
class CTimer
{
public:
    CTimer() { m_bTimerOn = FALSE; }           // Timer is OFF

    HRESULT TimerOn( DWORD dwTimerInterval )  // Arm the timer
    {
        Derived* pDerived = ((Derived*) this);
        m_dwTimerInterval = dwTimerInterval;
        if (m_bTimerOn)    // If already on, just change interval
            return S_OK;

        m_bTimerOn        = TRUE;
        m_dwTimerInterval = dwTimerInterval;
        m_pStream         = NULL;

        HRESULT hRes = CoMarshalInterThreadInterfaceInStream(
                    *piid, (T*)pDerived, &m_pStream );

        // Create thread and pass the thread proc the this ptr
        m_hThread = CreateThread(NULL, 0, &_Apartment,
                    (PVOID) this, 0, &m_dwThreadID);
        return S_OK;
    }

    void TimerOff()                           // Disable the timer
    {
        if (m_bTimerOn)
        {
            m_bTimerOn = FALSE;
            AtlWaitWithMessageLoop( m_hThread );
        }
    }

// Implementation
private:
    static DWORD WINAPI _Apartment( PVOID pv )
    {
        CTimer<Derived, T, piid>* pThis =
                            (CTimer<Derived, T, piid>*) pv;
        pThis->Apartment();
        return 0;
```

```
    }

    DWORD Apartment()
    {
        CoInitialize(NULL);
        HRESULT hRes;
        m_spT.Release();

        if (m_pStream)
            hRes = CoGetInterfaceAndReleaseStream(
                m_pStream, *piid, (PVOID*) &m_spT );

        // Main timer loop that periodically calls _OnTimer
        while(m_bTimerOn)
        {
            Sleep( m_dwTimerInterval );
            if (!m_bTimerOn)
                break;
            m_spT->_OnTimer();
        }

        m_spT.Release();      // When TimerOff function sets
        CoUninitialize();     //   m_bTimerOn = FALSE, unregister
        return 0;             //   and quit
    }

public:
    DWORD       m_dwTimerInterval;
    BOOL        m_bTimerOn;

private:
    HANDLE      m_hThread;
    DWORD       m_dwThreadID;
    LPSTREAM    m_pStream;
    CComPtr<T> m_spT;
};
```

across threads, ensuring that the _OnTimer function receives the call not on the new thread, but on the original thread that started the timer. In our case this is the main thread of the Pulse control, from where _OnTimer can safely fire the Pulse event. Marshaling back to the main thread is a necessary step for an apartment-threaded control like Pulse, because the rules of COM dictate that an object must fire its events within the client's apartment—that is, on the same client STA thread that instantiated the object.

If you are creating Pulse as a new project, simply copy the file Timer.h from the companion CD to your own project folder. The file is a header, so there is no need to add it to the project using the Add To Project command.

## Step 7: Edit the PulseCtl.h File

The project began back in Step 2 with the selection of the simplest object type available from ATL Object Wizard, which set up the *CPulseCtl* class to inherit only three base classes and two interfaces. A real ActiveX control must implement more interfaces than these, so in this step we will expand the class's inheritance list to include additional interfaces that typical containers expect a control to implement.

Open the PulseCtl.h file in the text editor and add the two **#include** statements shown here in gray, one for the *CTimer* class we created in the preceding step, and the other to bring in additional interface implementations the project requires:

```
#include "resource.h"        // main symbols
#include "PulseCP.h"
#include "timer.h"
#include <atlctl.h>
```

Next, add the following lines to the *CPulseCtl* inheritance list. The actual order of the lines does not matter, but note that all entries in the list except the last end with a comma:

```
class ATL_NO_VTABLE CPulseCtl :
    public CComObjectRootEx<CComSingleThreadModel>,
    public CComCoClass<CPulseCtl, &CLSID_PulseCtl>,
    public IConnectionPointContainerImpl<CPulseCtl>,
    public IDispatchImpl<IPulseCtl, &IID_IPulseCtl, &LIBID_PULSELib>,
    public CTimer<CPulseCtl, IPulseCtl, &IID_IPulseCtl>,
    public IObjectWithSiteImpl<CPulseCtl>,
    public CComControl<CPulseCtl>,
    public IPersistStreamInitImpl<CPulseCtl>,
    public IOleControlImpl<CPulseCtl>,
    public IOleObjectImpl<CPulseCtl>,
    public IViewObjectExImpl<CPulseCtl>,
```

```
    public IOleInPlaceObjectWindowlessImpl<CPulseCtl>,
    public IPersistStorageImpl<CPulseCtl>,
    public IProvideClassInfo2Impl<&CLSID_PulseCtl,
                        &DIID__IPulseCtlEvents, &LIBID_PULSELib>,
    public CProxy_IPulseCtlEvents< CPulseCtl >
{
```

Although the Pulse control is invisible rather than windowless, the *CPulseCtl* class must nevertheless derive from *IOleInPlaceObject-WindowlessImpl*. (Recall from Chapter 9 that windowless controls rely on the client for display services.) This is an example of how ATL is not optimized for invisible controls like Pulse. Instead of offering a separate implementation of the *IOleInPlaceObject* interface that our control needs, ATL provides only *IOleInPlaceObjectWindowless*, which is an extension of *IOleInPlaceObject* that adds support for window messages and drag-and-drop operations. Pulse does not require these extra methods, but must include them nonetheless to obtain the implementation for *IOle-InPlaceObject*.

Following the class inheritance list, add a prototype for the *FinalRelease* member function, which ATL's *CComObject* calls when unloading the Pulse control:

```
public:
    HRESULT FinalRelease();
    CPulseCtl()
    {
    }
```

Notice that *CPulseCtl* does not declare a class destructor. This is because destructors are not virtual in the ATL base classes from which *CPulseCtl* derives, so the class cannot safely assume its destructor will ever be called. Instead, an ActiveX control class using ATL should perform any necessary clean-up duties in the *FinalRelease* function, which is called just before the object instance is destroyed. Its corollary is the *Final-Construct* function, to which a control should confine its initialization tasks. A second project later in this chapter demonstrates *FinalConstruct*.

To match the interface templates placed in the *CPulseCtl* inheritance list, we must add corresponding entries to the class's COM map as shown here:

```
BEGIN_COM_MAP(CPulseCtl)
    COM_INTERFACE_ENTRY_IMPL(IConnectionPointContainer)
    COM_INTERFACE_ENTRY(IPulseCtl)
    COM_INTERFACE_ENTRY(IDispatch)
    COM_INTERFACE_ENTRY(IConnectionPointContainer)
    COM_INTERFACE_ENTRY(IObjectWithSite)
    COM_INTERFACE_ENTRY(IViewObjectEx)
    COM_INTERFACE_ENTRY(IViewObject2)
    COM_INTERFACE_ENTRY(IViewObject)
    COM_INTERFACE_ENTRY(IOleInPlaceObjectWindowless)
    COM_INTERFACE_ENTRY(IOleInPlaceObject)
    COM_INTERFACE_ENTRY2(IOleWindow, IOleInPlaceObjectWindowless)
    COM_INTERFACE_ENTRY(IOleControl)
    COM_INTERFACE_ENTRY(IOleObject)
    COM_INTERFACE_ENTRY(IPersistStreamInit)
    COM_INTERFACE_ENTRY2(IPersist, IPersistStreamInit)
    COM_INTERFACE_ENTRY(IPersistStorage)
    COM_INTERFACE_ENTRY(IProvideClassInfo)
    COM_INTERFACE_ENTRY(IProvideClassInfo2)
END_COM_MAP()
```

*IProvideClassInfo2* is new among OLE interfaces, replacing the older *IProvideClassInfo*. Some containers do not recognize *IProvideClassInfo2*, so the map includes an entry for *IProvideClassInfo*. Because *IProvideClassInfo2* delegates to the older interface, the addition does not increase Pulse's code size. *IProvideClassInfo* and *IProvideClassInfo2* support Pulse's event firing. Both interfaces provide the *GetClassInfo* method, which supplies type information pertaining to the *PulseCtl* component class object. The type information, which comes from the control's type library, tells the client how to set up its handler function for the Pulse event.

Besides forming the core of Uniform Data Transfer, the *IDataObject* interface provides the means for data change notifications to the client. A client that implements the *IAdviseSink* interface calls the control's *IDataObject::Advise* method to begin receiving notifications when the control's data is altered. This does not apply to Pulse, and the control can operate normally without supporting *IDataObject*. However, some clients such as the Test Container utility require the interface to set up the advise connection.

Make sure the COM map includes an entry for *IConnectionPointContainer*:

```
COM_INTERFACE_ENTRY_IMPL(IConnectionPointContainer)
```

If you did not select the Support Connection Points option in Object Wizard back in Step 2, type the entry into the COM map and add *IConnectionPointContainerImpl* to the class inheritance list. A container queries the object through its *IConnectionPointContainer* interface to learn what outgoing interfaces the object supports, which in our case is the event interface *_IPulseCtlEvents*. Connecting and disconnecting the container's event sink to and from the object takes place through the object's *IConnectionPoint* interface. The COM map does not require a separate entry for *IConnectionPoint* because *IConnectionPointContainer* provides the *FindConnectionPoint* method, which returns a pointer to ATL's implementation of *IConnectionPoint* representing *_IPulseCtlEvents*. Figure 10-12 illustrates the steps in which a container hooks up its event sink to Pulse's event function.

*FindConnectionPoint* and its sister method *EnumConnectionPoints* read an array known as the connection point map, which contains a list of interface identifiers for every connection point the control offers. Pulse

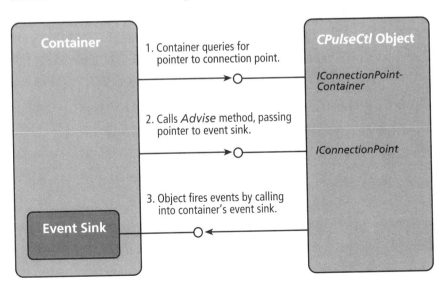

**Figure 10-12.** *How a container establishes connections to receive event firings.*

supports only one connection point for *_IPulseCtlEvents*, specified in the connection point map that follows the COM map:

```
BEGIN_CONNECTION_POINT_MAP( CPulseCtl )
    CONNECTION_POINT_ENTRY( DIID__IPulseCtlEvents )
END_CONNECTION_POINT_MAP()
```

Below the connection point map, add the property map shown here. The map is empty because Pulse does not support a property sheet, but some interface implementations we added to the *CPulseCtl* class expect the map to exist:

```
BEGIN_PROPERTY_MAP(CPulseCtl)
END_PROPERTY_MAP()
```

## Step 8: Edit the PulseCtl.cpp File

Add the instructions shown here in gray to complete the stub functions in the PulseCtl.cpp file:

```
///////////////////////////////////////////////////////////////
// CPulseCtl

#define   MIN_RATE  10           // Minimum firing rate

STDMETHODIMP CPulseCtl::get_nInterval( long *pVal )
{
    *pVal = m_dwTimerInterval;
    return S_OK;
}

STDMETHODIMP CPulseCtl::StartPulse( long nRate )
{
    if (!m_bTimerOn)
    {
        if (nRate < MIN_RATE)              // Ensure firing rate
            nRate = MIN_RATE;              //   is not too low

        TimerOn( nRate );                  // Start the timer
        m_dwTimerInterval = nRate;
        return S_OK;
    }
    return S_FALSE;
}

STDMETHODIMP CPulseCtl::EndPulse()
```

```
{
    TimerOff();
    m_dwTimerInterval = 0;
    return S_OK;
}

STDMETHODIMP CPulseCtl::_OnTimer()
{
    Fire_Pulse();
    return S_OK;
}

HRESULT CPulseCtl::FinalRelease()
{
    return EndPulse();
}
```

The *get_nInterval* method informs the caller of the current timer interval, which is stored in the *CTimer::m_dwTimerInterval* member variable. There is no matching put function because we specified the *nInterval* property as read-only back in Step 2. *StartPulse* and *EndPulse* implement the control's two methods, setting and stopping the timer. In case the container does not call *EndPulse* when finished with the control, the *FinalRelease* function calls *EndPulse* to ensure that the timer's worker thread exits properly before the control terminates.

## Step 9: Edit the Pulse.rgs File

We saw earlier that the project's RGS file contains scripted information that the control's *DllRegisterServer* function writes into the system Registry. Selecting the Simple Object option in Step 2 caused ATL Object Wizard to leave out some Registry information required by a normal ActiveX control, such as a list of OLEMISC flags. The sidebar on page 479 discusses the flags in detail, but for now we need only add a value to Pulse's registration data that specifies the required flags in the MiscStatus Registry key. Open the Pulse.rgs file in the text editor and add these lines:

```
ForceRemove {8C9BABDD-BCE5-11D1-BEC9-D43CA8CB2F51} = s 'PulseCtl Class'
{
    ProgID = s 'Pulse.PulseCtl.1'
    VersionIndependentProgID = s 'Pulse.PulseCtl'
    ForceRemove 'Programmable'
    InprocServer32 = s '%MODULE%'
```

```
    {
        val ThreadingModel = s 'Apartment'
    }
    ForceRemove 'Control'
    'MiscStatus' = s '0'
    {
        '1' = s '148624'
    }
    'TypeLib' = s '{7C7E1682-C2F1-11D1-BEC9-E4F4ACA02373}'
}
```

The Control entry advertises Pulse as an embeddable ActiveX control. The MiscStatus value 148,624 represents the combined value of five flags: OLEMISC_SETCLIENTSITEFIRST, OLEMISC_INSIDEOUT, OLEMISC_CANTLINKINSIDE, OLEMISC_INVISIBLEATRUNTIME, and OLEMISC_NOUIACTIVATE, all described in the sidebar.

Ordinarily, ATL Object Wizard adds a default bitmap to a control project, but not for simple object types like Pulse. If you would like to enhance the Pulse control by adding a small bitmap, here's how to do it. We've seen how some containers—the Visual C++ dialog editor, for instance—can display a bitmap on a tool button to represent a control to the user. The container extracts the bitmap image from the ActiveX control's own resource data, in which the image is identified by the control's ToolboxBitmap32 key in the system Registry. To insert the ToolboxBitmap32 key, include this line along with the others we added to the PulseCtl.rgs file:

```
ForceRemove 'ToolboxBitmap32' = s '%MODULE%, 1'
```

A control's bitmap is entirely optional, but adds a professional touch for those controls intended for the marketplace. The size of the bitmap is 16-by-15 pixels, so a 16-color image takes up 512 bytes of the control's resource data section. Choose the Resource command from the Insert menu, choose Bitmap, and press Alt+Enter to expose the Bitmap Properties dialog. Change the dimensions of the work area to 16-by-15 and assign the resource identifier the same value given in the **ForceRemove** statement for the ToolboxBitmap32 key. In our case, the value is 1:

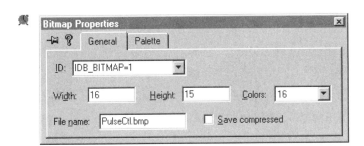

## OLEMISC Flags

An ActiveX control registers a set of OLEMISC bit flags stored as a 32-bit value in the system Registry. The flags publish information about a control, informing a container of the control's characteristics, operating preferences, and abilities. Making this information public in the Registry means that a prospective container need not first embed the control to determine its requirements and abilities. If a control needs services that the container cannot offer, the container determines the match is not suitable without having wasted time and resources in loading the control.

To determine a control's OLEMISC flag settings, a container can call the *IOleObject::GetMiscStatus* function. The call does not cause the control to be loaded because OLE provides a default implementation for the function that reads the control's OLEMISC flags from the Registry. As an alternative to involving the OLE run-time library, the container itself can read the control's flags directly from the Registry, accessing the \MiscStatus\1 folder under the control's CLSID entry.

ATL Object Wizard generates a MiscStatus value in the RGS file only for ActiveX controls, not for simple objects like Pulse. A normal visible ActiveX control, for example, receives a MiscStatus value of 131,473, representing these five OLEMISC bit flags:

- **OLEMISC_RECOMPOSEONRESIZE**—Indicates that when being resized, the control wants to recompose its display beyond merely

*(continued)*

**OLEMISC Flags**  *continued*

scaling it. Therefore, the container should activate the object when resizing it and call the control's *IOleObject::SetExtent* method with its new window size.

- **OLEMISC_CANTLINKINSIDE**—Indicates that if the object is copied to the Clipboard, the container must not allow the user to activate the object linked to the Clipboard.

- **OLEMISC_INSIDEOUT**—Required for ActiveX controls. The flag tells the container that the control object can be activated in place inside the container's window, without the container having to display any special user interface elements such as menus and toolbars to enable the user to interact with the control. In-place activation, also known as visual editing, requires the container to support the *IOleInPlaceSite* interface.

- **OLEMISC_ACTIVATEWHENVISIBLE**—Indicates that the object wants to be activated when it becomes visible.

- **OLEMISC_SETCLIENTSITEFIRST**—Used only with ActiveX controls, this flag indicates that the control prefers to use *IOleObject::SetClientSite* as its initialization function, even before a call to *IPersistStreamInit::InitNew* or *IPersistStorage::InitNew* to retrieve the control's property data from disk. This allows the control to access a container's ambient properties before loading information from persistent storage. Note that the current implementations of *OleCreate*, *OleCreateFromData*, *OleCreateFromFile*, *OleLoad*, and the default handler do not understand this value. Control containers that wish to honor the flag must currently implement their own versions of these functions in order to establish the correct initialization sequence for the control.

An invisible control like Pulse normally substitutes these two flags for OLEMISC_ACTIVATEWHENVISIBLE:

> - **OLEMISC_INVISIBLEATRUNTIME**—Informs the container that the control has no user interface and does not display to the screen.
>
> - **OLEMISC_NOUIACTIVATE**—Indicates that the control does not require shared user interface elements such as menus, and does not need input focus to operate.
>
> If your control has other run-time requirements not identified by the flags that Object Wizard sets, make the appropriate change to the MiscStatus value in the RGS file before building the project. For a complete list of the flags and their bit values, refer to the article "OLEMISC" in Visual C++ online help.

## Step 10: Build and Test the Pulse ActiveX Control

This final step oversees the completion of the Pulse project and presents a few ideas on how to exercise the new control. First we must select a build target. The ATL COM AppWizard sets up an ATL project with four release configurations:

| Configuration | Preprocessor definitions |
|---|---|
| Release MinSize | _ATL_DLL |
| Release MinDependency | _ATL_STATIC_REGISTRY |
| Unicode Release MinSize | _UNICODE, _ATL_DLL |
| Unicode Release MinDependency | _UNICODE, _ATL_STATIC_REGISTRY |

For both ANSI and Unicode control projects, the MinSize and MinDependency targets offer a choice of whether the control relies on an auxiliary run-time file for ATL services, or incorporates all the code it requires within its own executable file. The choice is between reduced file size and reduced run-time dependency—very similar to an MFC project for which you must choose whether to link statically or dynamically to the MFC library.

The MinSize configuration reduces the size of a control by linking it dynamically to Atl.dll, a 54 KB library file that Visual C++ installs in the

Windows\System folder. When the control executes, it calls into Atl.dll for the service functions that the control requires. This arrangement results in the most efficient use of memory when several ActiveX controls linked to Atl.dll execute together. In this case, the MinSize target can also lead to faster download times when transferring the controls over a network or the Internet, because the combined file size of the controls is reduced—even taking into consideration the addition of Atl.dll, which might also have to be transferred along with the controls.

The MinDependency configuration sets up the control project so that the compiler expands the class templates into full classes instead of stub functions that call into Atl.dll. In this configuration, the control itself contains the interface implementation code it needs, as though the ATL services were statically linked in. (This is only an analogy, because there is no static library LIB file for ATL as there is for MFC.) The resulting ActiveX control does not rely on the Atl.dll file, an independence it purchases at the cost of a larger executable image. The MinDependency target is best for single controls that are not expected to operate together with other ATL controls. Because this description applies to Pulse, select the Release MinDependency configuration in the Build toolbar:

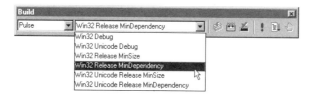

Project files installed from the companion CD-ROM shorten target names to MinSize and MinDep, keeping folder names to less than eight characters. You might prefer short target names for your own ATL projects, if for no other reason than they take up less space in the system Registry. To revise the target names that COM AppWizard sets up, temporarily close the workspace and open the project's DSP file in the text editor. Using the Replace command, replace all occurrences of *Release MinDependency* and *ReleaseMinDependency* with "MinDep." Shorten the MinSize target name through similar steps. Save the DSP file and reopen the project. You should see the new target names listed in the Build toolbar.

We haven't yet talked about compiler optimizations—that's the subject of Chapter 12—but the Visual C++ optimizer can either increase execution speed or reduce code size. The latter is almost always the best choice for ActiveX controls, so the COM AppWizard preselects the small code size optimization setting for you. If this isn't what you want, change the selection in the C++ tab of the Project Settings dialog. Once you have selected the target configuration, click the Build Pulse.dll command on the Build menu to compile and link the Pulse control. If the various compile and link steps complete successfully, Visual C++ helpfully runs RegSvr32.exe to register the control and displays the results in the Output window:

```
Registering ActiveX Control...
RegSvr32: DllRegisterServer in .\MinDep\Pulse.ocx succeeded.
```

 **N OTE** If your ActiveX control requires the C run-time services, first remove the preprocessor definition that prevents linkage to the run-time library. In the C++ tab of the Project Settings dialog, delete the constant _ATL_MIN_ CRT in the box labeled Preprocessor Definitions.

The Tumble2.htm document shown on the next page in Listing 10-3 showcases the new control. If you have created the Pulse control yourself by following the steps outlined here, it has a class identifier different than the one used by the Pulse.ocx control on the companion CD. In this case, you must update the **classid** statement for the Pulse object in the Tumble2.htm document:

```
<OBJECT
    classid="clsid:xxxxxxxx-xxxx-xxxx-xxxx-xxxxxxxxxxxx"
    id=pulse1
>
```

The project's IDL file provides the new class identifier you need. Simply copy into the Clipboard the identifier from the last **uuid** statement in the Pulse.idl file, then paste it into the Tumble2.htm document to update the **classid** value. Although Tumble2 uses a different timer, its animated display duplicates the original Tumble document shown on page 338.

The Test Container utility can also successfully embed our new control, as proved in Figure 10-13 on page 485. Start Test Container, then load the

**Listing 10-3.** *The Tumble2.htm document.*

```
<HTML>
<HEAD>
<TITLE>Tumbling Text Example 2 (Chapter 10)</TITLE>
</HEAD>
<BODY>

<OBJECT
classid="clsid:8C9BABDD-BCE5-11D1-BEC9-D43CA8CB2F51"
id=pulse1
>
</OBJECT>

<OBJECT
classid="clsid:99B42120-6EC7-11CF-A6C7-00AA00A47DD2"
id=label
width=150
height=150
>
<PARAM NAME="Angle"     value="0">
<PARAM NAME="Alignment" value="7">
<PARAM NAME="BackStyle" value="1">
<PARAM NAME="BackColor" value="255">
<PARAM NAME="FontBold"  value="-1">
<PARAM NAME="Caption"   value="Click Here">
<PARAM NAME="FontName"  value="Times New Roman">
<PARAM NAME="FontSize"  value="18">
</OBJECT>

<SCRIPT LANGUAGE="VBSCRIPT">
sub label_Click
    label.Caption       = "Tumbling text!"
    label.FontBold      = "0"
    label.FontUnderline = "-1"
    label.FontItalic    = "-1"
    pulse1.StartPulse( 100 )
end sub

sub pulse1_Pulse
    label.Angle = (label.Angle + 5) mod 360
end sub
</SCRIPT>
</BODY>
</HTML>
```

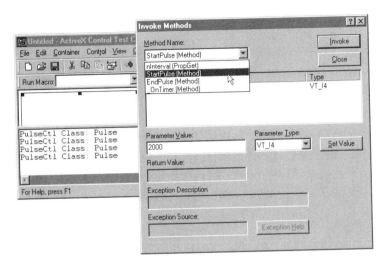

**Figure 10-13.** *Testing the Pulse ActiveX control in the Test Container.*

Pulse control by selecting the New Control tool and double-clicking the PulseCtl Class entry in the list. (The list is sorted alphabetically; pressing P on the keyboard scrolls automatically to the first control that begins with P.) Once the control is loaded in the Test Container, click the Invoke Methods tool, select the *StartPulse* method in the Method Name box as shown in Figure 10-13, set the *nRate* parameter to 2000, and click the Invoke button. This causes the control to fire its *Pulse* event every 2 seconds, which the Test Container notes by adding a new entry to the event log. Invoking the *EndPulse* method ends the firing.

If you would like to see how Pulse.ocx can be embedded in a normal container application, run the Hour2 program provided on the companion CD in the folder Code\Chapter.10\Hour2. Hour2 is a duplicate of the Hour program of Chapter 8, except that it uses the Pulse control for its timing instead of the IETimer control.

# Example 2: The TowerATL ActiveX Control

The Pulse project demonstrates that ATL can help you create ActiveX controls that are smaller than those produced by MFC, but the only accurate means of comparing ATL and MFC is to write the same control using both tools. That's what we'll do in this section. As its name suggests, the TowerATL control duplicates the Tower project of Chapter 9, exporting the same properties, methods, and events. But TowerATL is created entirely through the services of ATL and makes no use of MFC.

TowerATL is a more sophisticated ActiveX control than Pulse, incorporating stock properties, a property sheet, and an About box. The project seems easier to put together, though, because discussions are more compact and less occupied with the range of considerations given our attention in the Pulse project. Now that most of the generalities are out of the way, this project more accurately reflects the time and effort required to create a typical ActiveX control using ATL.

## Step 1: Create the TowerATL Project

Run the ATL COM AppWizard again, this time naming the project *TowerATL*. Click the Finish button to accept the default settings, making the TowerATL control a dynamic link library that does not use MFC. When COM AppWizard finishes, choose New ATL Object from the Insert menu to launch ATL Object Wizard. Select Controls in the dialog's first list and double-click the icon labeled Full Control. TowerATL supports more interfaces than does the Pulse control, and we will need interfaces like *IQuickActivate* and *ISpecifyPropertyPages* that the Full Control option adds to the source code.

Notice in the dialog that ATL treats a control's property page as a separate object. We will return to Object Wizard again to add a property page object before finishing the project. Type *TowerCtl* for the short name in the Names tab of the Properties dialog, accepting the default names in the other boxes. In the Attributes tab, select the Support Connection Points check box as we did for the Pulse project. Accept other default settings in the tab to enable apartment threading, dual interfaces, and aggregation.

The Miscellaneous tab contains switches that set various OLEMISC flags. Selecting the Acts Like Button check box, for example, sets the OLEMISC_ACTSLIKEBUTTON flag, which tells the container that the control responds to mouse clicks and generally behaves as a button. The Acts Like Label check box sets the OLEMISC_ACTSLIKELABEL flag, informing the container that the control serves as a label for the control that follows it in tabbing order—that is, the next control listed in the container's RC script. The Invisible At Runtime check box turns on the OLEMISC_INVISIBLE-

ATRUNTIME flag, appropriate for controls like Pulse that remain invisible even when activated.

Skip the Miscellaneous tab to accept its default settings, and continue to the Stock Properties tab. Like the MFC version of Tower, the TowerATL control contains four stock properties named *BackColor*, *ForeColor*, *Caption*, and *Font*. Add these properties to the Supported box by selecting each in the list and clicking the > button, as shown in Figure 10-14. (The *BackColor* and *ForeColor* properties are labeled Background Color and Foreground Color in the list.) Click the OK button to close the ATL Object Wizard dialog.

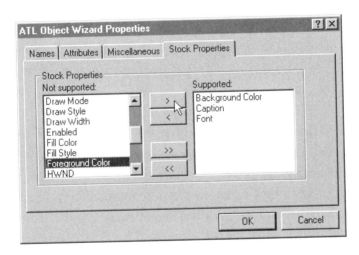

**Figure 10-14.** *Choosing stock properties in ATL Object Wizard.*

## Step 2: Add the *nCurrentBlock* Custom Property

Along with its four stock properties, TowerATL exposes a custom property named *nCurrentBlock* that holds a number identifying the block being dragged. Technically, it's the *ITowerCtl* interface inherited by the object that exposes the property through its *get_nCurrentBlock* method. To add the custom property to the *ITowerCtl* interface, expand the list of Tower-ATL classes in the ClassView window, right-click the *ITowerCtl* entry, and choose the Add Property command to invoke the Add Property To Interface dialog. Select **short** as the property type and type *nCurrentBlock* for the property's name. As we did in Chapter 9, make the *nCurrentBlock* property read-only to prevent a container application from changing its value. Clear the radio button labeled Put Function to tell Object Wizard not to generate a put method for the property, and then close the dialog.

## Step 3: Add the *Reset* Method

TowerATL exports a method function named *Reset*, by which a container application tells the control to start the game over, restacking all the blocks in the left panel. Right-click the *ITowerCtl* interface in ClassView again, choose the Add Method command, then type *Reset* as the function name in the Add Method To Interface dialog. The method takes no parameters, so leave the Parameters box blank.

Click OK to dismiss the Add Method dialog, at which point Visual C++ adds appropriate code for the method to the project's IDL file and also writes a stub *Reset* function in the TowerCtl.cpp file. We will edit the code after adding message handler functions and events to the control.

## Step 4: Add Handler Functions

As you recall from Chapter 9, the control window responds to a WM_LBUTTONDOWN message by initiating a drag operation in which the user moves a colored block from one panel to another. A WM_LBUTTONUP message signals that the block has been dropped into place. This fourth step of the project is very easy, simply adding stub functions to handle the two messages.

In the ClassView pane, right-click the *CTowerCtl* entry and choose Add Window Message Handler from the menu. Double-click WM_MOUSE-MOVE, WM_LBUTTONDOWN, and WM_LBUTTONUP in the list to add them to the righthand box, and then close the dialog:

## Step 5: Add Events

Like the original Tower control, TowerATL fires five events named *Click*, *FromPanel*, *ToPanel*, *Error*, and *Winner*, which collectively keep the container informed about what is happening in the control. Adding the events to the project involves the same steps we followed for the Pulse control:

1. Right-click the *_ITowerCtlEvents* entry in the ClassView pane and choose the Add Methods command from the context menu, then select the **void** return type and enter a function name in the dialog. Repeat for all five event functions. Only *FromPanel* and *ToPanel* take parameters, named *nFromPanel* and *nToPanel* respectively, both of type **short**:

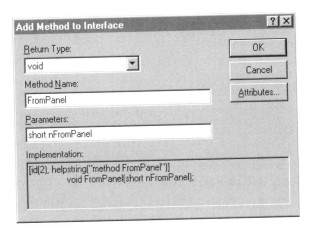

2. Expose the FileView pane in the Workspace window, right-click the entry for TowerATL.idl, and choose the Compile command to create the project's type library file. Ignore the warning messages from the MIDL compiler stating that the "interface does not conform to [oleautomation] attribute." The warnings stem from the compiler's belief that the *pFont* parameter—a pointer to an *IFontDisp* interface—is not a compatible Automation type. But because *IFontDisp* derives from *IDispatch*, a valid Automation interface, the warnings are not correct.

3. In the ClassView pane, right-click *CTowerCtl* and choose the Implement Connection Point command from the menu.

4. Set the check box labeled *_ITowerCtlEvents* and click OK to close the dialog.

It may not seem like it, but the steps we are taking here in adding events to the project are very similar to those we took in the preceding chapter when using MFC to develop the Tower control. Behind the scenes, the ControlWizard of Chapter 9 created an ODL file (similar to IDL) containing these instructions:

```
//{{AFX_ODL_EVENT(CTowerCtrl)
[id(DISPID_CLICK)] void Click();
[id(1)] void FromPanel(short nPanel);
[id(2)] void ToPanel(short nPanel);
[id(DISPID_ERROREVENT)] void Error();
[id(3)] void Winner();
//}}AFX_ODL_EVENT
```

From this information, ClassWizard generated proxy functions such as *FireClick* and *FireWinner*, which call into MFC's *COleControl::FireEvent* function. *FireEvent*, in turn, calls the container's *IDispatch::Invoke* method, exactly the same as the proxy functions that ATL generates.

## Step 6: Add a Property Sheet

The Tower control of Chapter 9 provides a property sheet to allow the user to change the control's caption, font, and colors. Figure 9-13 on page 417 shows what the property sheet looks like. In this section, we'll create a similar property sheet for TowerATL.

ATL sets up each page of a control's property sheet as a separate object, implemented by a class derived from *IPropertyPage*. The system's Msstkprp.dll library provides default class implementations for two property pages labeled Font and Colors, which allow the user to change the *Font*, *BackColor*, and *ForeColor* stock properties. These stock properties in turn determine the font and color of the title displayed at the top of TowerATL's window. To provide access to the *Caption* stock property, which contains the text of the control's title, we must add one more property page, labeling it *Caption* as we did for the original Tower control.

Adding property pages to a control requires the services of ATL's Object Wizard again, running it once for each page that you want to add. To add TowerATL's new *Caption* page, select Controls in Object Wizard's left box and double-click the Property Page icon:

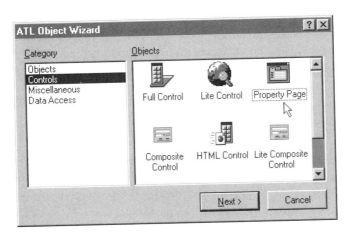

When the ATL Object Wizard Properties dialog appears, type *TowerPPG* for the object's short name:

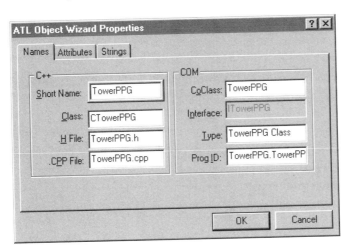

As before, the wizard helpfully fills the other boxes with suggested names. The Interface box is grayed because a property page object has no need for a custom interface. Accept the default settings in the Attributes tab and expose the Strings tab. Type *&Caption* for the page title and *Caption*

*property* in the box labeled Doc String. TowerATL does not provide a help file, so delete the text in the third edit box to leave it blank.

Object Wizard writes the title and document string into the project's RC file where they become part of the control's string resource data. The title specifies the label that appears on the tab of the new property page. The document string is intended to serve as the tab's tooltip text, describing the page's purpose when the mouse cursor pauses over the tab, but the string almost always goes unused and does not appear as a tooltip or anything else. This is because the OLE run-time *OleCreatePropertyFrame* function responsible for creating the property sheet window—known as a property frame in OLE parlance—does not support tooltips.

Click the OK button to dismiss the dialog, at which point Object Wizard makes these additions to the project:

- Adds the TowerPPG.cpp and TowerPPG.h files to implement the new *CTowerPPG* class.

- Writes string resources for the title and tooltip text in TowerATL.rc:

```
IDS_TITLETowerPPG        "&Caption"
IDS_DOCSTRINGTowerPPG    "Caption property"
```

and inserts identifier definitions in the Resource.h file.

- Appends an identifier and **coclass** entry in the TowerATL.idl file for the new property page object:

```
[
    uuid(05D2BAA4-C471-11D1-BEC9-FB1AF66FCC79),
    helpstring("TowerPPG Class")
]
coclass TowerPPG
{
    interface IUnknown;
};
```

- Adds the TowerPPG.rgs file, providing a registry script for the new object.

- Inserts an entry for the page in the control's object map in TowerATL.cpp:

```
BEGIN_OBJECT_MAP(ObjectMap)
    ⋮
    OBJECT_ENTRY(CLSID_TowerPPG, CTowerPPG)
END_OBJECT_MAP()
```

The dialog editor automatically appears when Object Wizard finishes, ready for you to design the new property page. Using the static and edit control tools, edit the dialog so that it appears something like this:

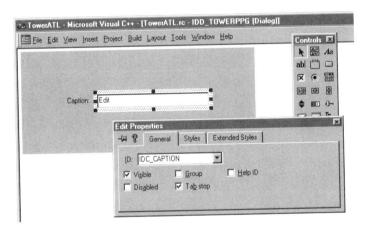

The precise layout of your own property page is not important, but assign the edit box an identifier of IDC_CAPTION as shown in the image. (To invoke the Properties dialog, select the edit box and click Properties on the Edit menu.) Save your work and close the dialog editor.

The TowerATL control is nearly finished at this point. The only significant work remaining involves adding code to the skeleton source files that ATL has generated. That's next.

## Step 7: Edit the TowerPPG.h File

The TowerPPG.h file contains code for the *CTowerPPG* class that handles the control's *Caption* property page object. We need only add instructions to the class that monitor the page's edit box and call the *put_Caption* method whenever the user enters a new *Caption* string. Right-click the *CTowerPPG* class in the ClassView pane and choose the Add Windows Message Handler command. When the New Windows Message dialog appears, select IDC_CAPTION in the small box labeled Class Or Object To

Handle and double-click EN_CHANGE in the list. Accept the suggested function name of *OnChangeCaption* and close the New Windows Message dialog.

The *OnChangeCaption* function executes whenever the user types in the edit box of the property page we added in the preceding step, thus signaling an intent to revise the *Caption* property. The function merely enables the dialog's Apply button by passing a value of TRUE to the *SetDirty* member function. Clicking either the OK or Apply button in the property sheet dialog executes the *Apply* function, which requires additional code. Open the TowerPPG.h file in the text editor and add these lines:

```
#include "resource.h"        // main symbols
#include "TowerAtl.h"
⋮

STDMETHOD(Apply)(void)
{
    USES_CONVERSION;
    char  szCaption[256];

    CComQIPtr<ITowerCtl> pTower( m_ppUnk[0] );
    if (GetDlgItemText( IDC_CAPTION, szCaption, 256 ))
        pTower->put_Caption( A2BSTR( szCaption ) );

    m_bDirty = FALSE;
    return S_OK;
}

LRESULT OnChangeCaption( WORD wNotify, WORD wID,
                         HWND hWnd, BOOL& bHandled )
{
    SetDirty( TRUE );                  // Enable Apply button
    return 0;
}
```

The *Apply* function calls *GetDlgItemText* to copy the new caption string from the edit box to the *szCaption* buffer, and then calls the control's *put_Caption* method to update the *Caption* property with the new string. The *put_Caption* method expects a BSTR parameter, so the code uses the ATL macro A2BSTR to recast the ANSI string in *szCaption* to a BSTR type. As the *Apply* function demonstrates, it's necessary to include the USES_CONVERSION macro before invoking a conversion macro like

A2BSTR. Doing so suppresses a compiler error that otherwise results from the conversion.

The code also demonstrates how an ActiveX control can make use of the *CComQIPtr* smart pointer template class. Because *put_Caption* is a member function of *CTowerCtl*, not *CTowerPPG*, the function must first obtain a pointer to *ITowerCtl* through *QueryInterface*. Casting *pTower* as a smart pointer ensures that *ITowerCtl::Release* is called in the unlikely event that either *GetDlgItemText* or *put_Caption* throws an error.

## Step 8: Edit the TowerCtl.h File

Finishing the TowerATL project involves a little more editing work using the text editor, adding much the same source code as we did for the Tower project of Chapter 9. Open the TowerCtl.h file and begin with **#define** statements for the various colors that TowerATL displays:

```
#include "resource.h"      // main symbols
#include <atlctl.h>
#include "TowerCP.h"

#define    NUM_BLOCKS    7
#define    EMPTY         NUM_BLOCKS
#define    BLACK         RGB(   0,   0,   0 )
#define    BLUE          RGB(   0,   0, 255 )
#define    CYAN          RGB(   0, 255, 255 )
#define    GREEN         RGB(   0, 255,   0 )
#define    MAGENTA       RGB( 255,   0, 255 )
#define    RED           RGB( 255,   0,   0 )
#define    YELLOW        RGB( 255, 255,   0 )
#define    WHITE         RGB( 255, 255, 255 )
#define    GRAY          RGB( 128, 128, 128 )
```

Next, add declarations to the *CTowerCtl* class for the same member variables we used in the original Tower project:

```
class ATL_NO_VTABLE CTowerCtl :
⋮
{
private:
    short       nPanel[3][NUM_BLOCKS];   // Panel contents
    short       nBlockNdx, nFromPanel;   // nPanel index of moved block
    BOOL        bMoving;                 // Flag is set when dragging
    COLORREF    color[NUM_BLOCKS];       // Block colors
```

```
        HCURSOR    hArrow, hCrossHairs;      // Cursor handles
        int        iLeft, iWidth, iHeight;   // Window dimensions
        short      GetPanel( int i );
public:
        HRESULT    FinalConstruct();
        CTowerCtl()
        {
        }
```

An object like *CTowerCtl* that initializes data should override the *CCom-ObjectRootEx::FinalConstruct* member function as shown here. Roughly analogous to MFC's useful *OnInitDialog* function, *FinalConstruct* is called after ATL has finished setting up the object but before the object first becomes active. It's here, rather than in the class constructor, that the control should perform most of its initialization work. The matching *FinalRelease* function demonstrated earlier in the Pulse control allows the control to carry out any necessary clean-up.

Revise the property map to establish the order in which the Caption, Color, and Font pages appear in the control's property sheet:

```
BEGIN_PROP_MAP(CTowerCtl)
    PROP_PAGE( CLSID_TowerPPG )
    PROP_PAGE( CLSID_StockColorPage )
    PROP_ENTRY( "Font", DISPID_FONT, CLSID_StockFontPage )
END_PROP_MAP()
```

The message map contains entries for the control's three message handlers added in Step 4:

```
BEGIN_MSG_MAP(CTowerCtl)
    MESSAGE_HANDLER(WM_MOUSEMOVE, OnMouseMove)
    MESSAGE_HANDLER(WM_LBUTTONDOWN, OnLButtonDown)
    MESSAGE_HANDLER(WM_LBUTTONUP, OnLButtonUp)
    ⋮
END_MSG_MAP()
```

The *OnLButtonDown* and *OnLButtonUp* functions receive control whenever the user presses and releases the left mouse button to drag a colored block between panels. *OnMouseMove* gains control when the mouse moves, and serves only to ensure that the cursor retains its crosshairs shape while the user drags a block.

All functions listed in a message map with a MESSAGE_HANDLER macro must have the same parameter list:

```
LRESULT MessageHandler( UINT uMsg, WPARAM wParam,
                        LPARAM lParam, BOOL &bHandled );
```

The first three parameters are standard for messages. The *OnLButtonDown* handler, for instance, receives the value WM_LBUTTONDOWN in the *uMsg* parameter, current key status in *wParam*, and coordinates of the mouse cursor in *lParam*. The MESSAGE_HANDLER macro gives the *bHandled* flag a value of TRUE before calling the handler function. A handler that does not fully service the message should clear the flag before returning:

```
*bHandled = FALSE;
```

Otherwise, code generated by the MESSAGE_HANDLER macro returns immediately, indicating to the operating system that the message has been completely serviced.

An ATL message map has the same form as in MFC. ATL further matches MFC by providing the COMMAND_HANDLER and NOTIFY_HANDLER macros for WM_COMMAND and WM_NOTIFY messages. To handle a group of different messages with a single function, use one of the RANGE macros instead: MESSAGE_RANGE_HANDLER, COMMAND_RANGE_ HANDLER, or NOTIFY_RANGE_HANDLER. Similar to MFC's ON_COM- MAND_RANGE and ON_NOTIFY_RANGE, these macros route to a single handler function all messages that fall within a specified range of values.

Visual C++ defines the functions *OnDraw*, *OnMouseMove*, *OnLButton- Down*, and *OnLButtonUp* as inline functions inside the *CTowerCtl* class declaration. To keep implementation code in one place and to facilitate comparisons with the original Tower source files, I have moved these four functions to the TowerCtl.cpp file, which is discussed next. The cutting and pasting is entirely optional, of course; if you are creating this project by following the text and prefer to leave the functions in the header file, simply edit their code as described in the next section.

Before leaving the TowerCtl.h file, a final correction may be necessary. At the end of the class declaration, some versions of Visual C++ write a member variable named *m_spFont*. The name must be changed to *m_pFont* to prevent the ATL implementation of the stock Font page from causing an error:

```
CComPtr<IFontDisp> m_pFont;
```

## Step 9: Edit the TowerCtl.cpp File

The source code for TowerCtl.cpp is very similar to the code we added to the same file for the original Tower project—so similar, in fact, that the code description beginning on page 404 of Chapter 9 still applies to this new version of the control. Because the file requires extensive additions, Listing 10-4 shows the entire edited version.

An important difference between the MFC and ATL versions of the control lies in how initializations are handled in TowerCtl.cpp. Where the Tower control used the class constructor and the *PreCreateWindow* virtual function to initialize its data, TowerATL now uses ATL's *FinalConstruct* function. The initialization work remains the same; only the location has changed.

**Listing 10-4.** *The TowerCtl.cpp file.*

```
// TowerCtl.cpp : Implementation of CTowerCtl

#include "stdafx.h"
#include "TowerATL.h"
#include "TowerCtl.h"
#include "TowerBox.h"          // About box dialog

//////////////////////////////////////////////////////////////////
// CTowerCtl

HRESULT CTowerCtl::FinalConstruct()
{
    color[0]        = BLACK;            // Initialize block colors
    color[1]        = BLUE;
    color[2]        = CYAN;
    color[3]        = GREEN;
    color[4]        = MAGENTA;
    color[5]        = RED;
    color[6]        = YELLOW;
```

```
    m_clrBackColor   = GRAY;        // Default background color,
    m_clrForeColor   = WHITE;       //   foreground color,
    m_bstrCaption    = "TowerATL";  //   and caption
    m_bAutoSize      = FALSE;       // Control can be resized
    m_sizeExtent.cx = 7000;         // Init HIMETRIC size for
    m_sizeExtent.cy = 2500;         //   4 x 1.5 width/height ratio
    Reset();                        // Initialize panels

    // Cursors for normal (arrow) and dragging (crosshairs)
    hArrow      = LoadCursor( NULL, IDC_ARROW );
    hCrossHairs = LoadCursor( NULL, IDC_CROSS );
    return S_OK;
}

HRESULT CTowerCtl::OnDraw( ATL_DRAWINFO& di )
{
    RECT&       rc = *(RECT*)di.prcBounds;
    RECT        rect;
    TEXTMETRIC  tm;
    HPEN        hPen, hPenOld;
    HBRUSH      hBrush, hBrushOld;
    HFONT       hFont, hFontOld;
    int         i, j, k, yCaption;
    USES_CONVERSION;

    // Paint control background
    hBrush     = CreateSolidBrush( m_clrBackColor );
    hBrushOld = (HBRUSH) SelectObject( di.hdcDraw, hBrush );
    FillRect( di.hdcDraw, &rc, hBrush );

    // Set caption color and font
    SetBkMode( di.hdcDraw, TRANSPARENT );
    SetTextColor( di.hdcDraw, m_clrForeColor );
    if (m_pFont)
    {
        CComQIPtr<IFont> pFont( m_pFont );
        pFont->get_hFont( &hFont );
        hFontOld = (HFONT) SelectObject( di.hdcDraw, hFont );
    }
    else
    {
        hFont     = (HFONT) GetStockObject( SYSTEM_FONT );
        hFontOld = NULL;
    }

    // Display caption
```

*(continued)*

**Listing 10-4.** *continued*

```
CopyRect( &rect, &rc );
DrawText( di.hdcDraw, OLE2A( m_bstrCaption ), -1,

        &rect, DT_CENTER | DT_TOP );

// Compute height of Caption area
GetTextMetrics( di.hdcDraw, &tm );
yCaption = tm.tmHeight + tm.tmExternalLeading;

// Compute width and height of a panel
iLeft    = rc.left;
iWidth   = (rc.right - rc.left)/3;
iHeight  = rc.bottom - rc.top - yCaption;

// Draw column dividers
hPen     = CreatePen( PS_SOLID, 1, m_clrForeColor );
hPenOld  = (HPEN) SelectObject( di.hdcDraw, &hPen );
MoveToEx( di.hdcDraw, rc.left+iWidth,   rc.top+yCaption, 0 );
LineTo(   di.hdcDraw, rc.left+iWidth,   rc.bottom );
MoveToEx( di.hdcDraw, rc.left+iWidth*2, rc.top+yCaption, 0 );
LineTo(   di.hdcDraw, rc.left+iWidth*2, rc.bottom );

// Outer loop: for each panel...
for (i=0; i < 3; i++)
{
    rect.top    = rc.top + yCaption;
    rect.bottom = rect.top + iHeight/NUM_BLOCKS;

    // Inner loop: for each colored block in panel...
    for (j=0; j < NUM_BLOCKS; j++)
    {
        if (nPanel[i][j] != EMPTY)
        {
            // Determine left and right edges of block
            k = NUM_BLOCKS - 1 - nPanel[i][j];
            rect.left  = rc.left + iWidth*i +
                    (iWidth*k)/(2*NUM_BLOCKS) + 1;
            rect.right = rect.left +
                    iWidth*(nPanel[i][j]+1)/NUM_BLOCKS - 1;

            // Fill rectangle with block's color
            hBrush = CreateSolidBrush( color[nPanel[i][j]] );
            SelectObject( di.hdcDraw, &hBrush );
            FillRect( di.hdcDraw, &rect, hBrush );
        }

        rect.top    = rect.bottom;
```

```
                         rect.bottom += iHeight/NUM_BLOCKS;
            }
        }

        SelectObject( di.hdcDraw, &hPenOld );
        SelectObject( di.hdcDraw, &hBrushOld );
        if (hFontOld)
            SelectObject( di.hdcDraw, &hFontOld );

        DeleteObject( hPen );
        DeleteObject( hBrush );
        return S_OK;
}

STDMETHODIMP CTowerCtl::get_nCurrentBlock( short *pVal )
{
        *pVal = nPanel[nFromPanel][nBlockNdx];
        return S_OK;
}

STDMETHODIMP CTowerCtl::Reset()
{
        int i;

        for (i=0; i < NUM_BLOCKS; i++)  // Initialize panel array
        {
            nPanel[0][i] = i;           // Panel 0 = 0,1,2,3,4,5,6
            nPanel[1][i] = EMPTY;       // Panel 1 = 7,7,7,7,7,7,7
            nPanel[2][i] = EMPTY;       // Panel 2 = 7,7,7,7,7,7,7
        }

        nBlockNdx  = 0;                 // Ndx of block being moved
        nFromPanel = 0;
        FireViewChange();

        return S_OK;
}


//////////////////////////////////////////////////////////////////////
// CTowerCtrl message handlers

LRESULT CTowerCtl::OnLButtonDown( UINT uMsg, WPARAM wParam,
                                  LPARAM lParam, BOOL& bHandled )
{
        short i = 0;
        int   x = LOWORD( lParam );
```

*(continued)*

**Listing 10-4.** *continued*

```
    nFromPanel = GetPanel( x );

    while (nPanel[nFromPanel][i] == EMPTY  && i < NUM_BLOCKS)
        i++;                            // i=ndx of smallest block

    if (i < NUM_BLOCKS)                 // Does panel have a block?
    {
        bMoving   = TRUE;               // If so, block is moving
        nBlockNdx = i;                  // Save ndx of the block
        Fire_FromPanel( nFromPanel ); // Tell container panel #

        // Change cursor to crosshairs while dragging
        SetCursor( hCrossHairs );
    }

    return 0;
}

LRESULT CTowerCtl::OnLButtonUp( UINT uMsg, WPARAM wParam,
                                LPARAM lParam, BOOL& bHandled )
{
    short i = 0, nToPanel;
    int   x = LOWORD( lParam );

    nToPanel = GetPanel( x );   // Panel where block is dropped

    if (bMoving  && nToPanel != nFromPanel)
    {
        while (nPanel[nToPanel][i] == EMPTY && i < NUM_BLOCKS-1)
            i++;                // i = ndx of panel's smallest block

        // Is dragged block smaller than smallest block in panel?
        if (nPanel[nFromPanel][nBlockNdx] < nPanel[nToPanel][i])
        {
            if (nPanel[nToPanel][i] != EMPTY)
                --i;
            nPanel[nToPanel][i] = nPanel[nFromPanel][nBlockNdx];
            nPanel[nFromPanel][nBlockNdx] = EMPTY;
            Fire_ToPanel( nToPanel );        // Tell container

            if (i == 0  && nToPanel == 2)  // If we've filled
            {                              // the third panel,
                Fire_Winner ();            // fire Winner event
                Reset ();                  // and reset game
            }

            FireViewChange();
```

```
        }
        else                                 // If invalid drop,
            Fire_Error ();                   // tell container
    }

    // Restore original arrow cursor
    SetCursor( hArrow );

    bMoving = FALSE;                         // Not moving now
    return 0;
}

short CTowerCtl::GetPanel( int x )
{
    short i = 0;

    x -= iLeft;                              // Convert x to window coords
    if (x > iWidth)                          // Hit test:
        i = 1;                               // i = 0 for first panel
    if (x > iWidth*2)                        //   = 1 for second panel
        i = 2;                               //   = 2 for third panel

    return i;                                // Return panel number
}

LRESULT CTowerCtl::OnMouseMove( UINT uMsg, WPARAM wParam,
                                LPARAM lParam, BOOL& bHandled )
{
    if (bMoving)                             // While dragging, keep
        SetCursor( hCrossHairs );            // crosshairs cursor
    return 0;
}
```

## Step 10: Add an About Box

Besides property pages, ATL Object Wizard can also add to a control project a dialog resource as an individual object. This section explains how to incorporate a dialog object in an ActiveX control, demonstrating by creating an About box for the TowerATL project. Many developers are understandably uncomfortable with the idea of About boxes in ActiveX controls, because even a simple dialog adds at least 2 KB of resource data to the OCX file. But an About box serves as a good illustration for any type of dialog your own controls may need. Moreover, project design compels us to duplicate as closely as possible the original Tower control, which contains its own About box supplied by the MFC ControlWizard.

This section is purposely self-contained, remaining independent of the other parts of the exercise. It illustrates in one place all the steps necessary to include a dialog resource, so you can ignore the section if you wish without affecting the rest of the project. To add TowerATL's About box, run ATL Object Wizard again, this time selecting Miscellaneous in the left box and double-clicking the Dialog icon. Name the object *TowerBox* as shown in Figure 10-15 and click OK to dismiss the dialog.

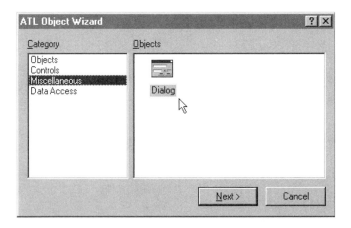

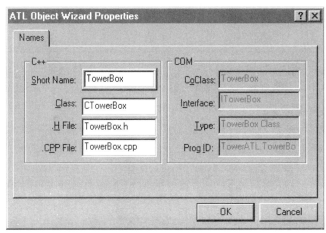

**Figure 10-15.**    *Adding a dialog resource to an ATL ActiveX control project.*

Object Wizard generates source code for the class *CTowerBox*, contained in the files TowerBox.cpp and TowerBox.h. If you already have an About box resource in another project that you want to use, just incorporate the dialog script into TowerATL.rc, adding any necessary **#define** statements to the Resource.h file. Otherwise, design the About box in the dialog editor, which starts automatically when you close Object Wizard. Here's an idea of how the dialog might look:

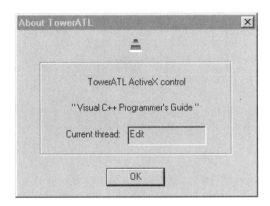

The dialog borrows the project's bitmap, so the decoration does not represent an extravagant waste of resource space. First copy to your project the TowerCtl.bmp file from the Code\Chapter.10\TowerATL folder, overwriting the generic BMP file of the same name supplied by ATL Object Wizard. Use the Picture tool to place the image in the dialog editor, then bring up the Properties dialog and select Bitmap in the Type box and the identifier in the Image box. The edit box on the last line is optional, merely serving as a convenient place to display the identifier of the thread on which the control is running. This will allow us to later confirm the behavior of an apartment-threaded control like TowerATL when running in separate apartments. Assign the edit box an identifier of IDC_THREAD_ID and set the Read Only check box in its Properties dialog.

Save the dialog resource when finished designing the About box, then right-click *ITowerCtl* in the ClassView pane and choose the Add Method command. Enter *AboutBox* for the name of the new method as shown on the next page. Like the *Reset* method, *AboutBox* takes no parameters.

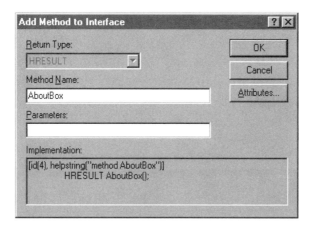

Open the TowerBox.h file in the text editor and add the instruction shown here in gray to the *OnInitDialog* function. Before the About dialog appears, the code retrieves the thread identifier from the system and writes it into the IDC_THREAD_ID edit box:

```
LRESULT OnInitDialog( UINT uMsg, WPARAM wParam,
                      LPARAM lParam, BOOL& bHandled )
{
    SetDlgItemInt( IDC_THREAD_ID,
                   (UINT) ::GetCurrentThreadId(), FALSE );
    return 1;  // Let the system set the focus
}
```

Next, reopen the TowerCtl.cpp file and add these lines to the new *AboutBox* function:

```
STDMETHODIMP CTowerCtl::AboutBox()
{
    CTowerBox dlgAbout;
    dlgAbout.DoModal();
    return S_OK;
}
```

When a container application calls the control's *AboutBox* method, the function creates a *CTowerBox* object and invokes the dialog. The Game2 program described in the next section demonstrates how an application signals TowerATL to display its About box.

## Step 11: Build and Test the TowerATL ActiveX Control

Select the Release MinDependency (or MinDep) configuration and build the TowerATL control. After Visual C++ successfully compiles, links, and registers the control, you can test the finished product in any ActiveX-aware container application. Figure 10-16 shows what TowerATL looks like in the Test Container utility with its property sheet displayed. After adding TowerATL to the Test Container window, click the Properties tool to expose the control's property sheet.

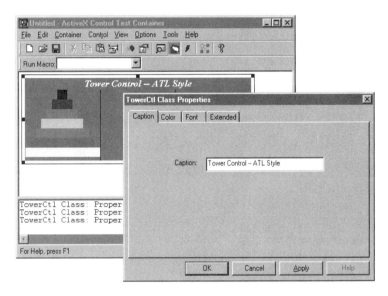

**Figure 10-16.** *TowerATL's property sheet displayed in the Test Container.*

It's illustrative to load another instance of the TowerATL control in the Test Container and invoke the About box for each instance using the Invoke Methods tool. You will find that the thread identifiers displayed in the About boxes are the same for both instances, demonstrating that the Test Container creates all control instances on a single thread. Internet Explorer, on the other hand, executes each window on a separate thread, which we can prove using the simple TowerCtl.htm document shown in Listing 10-5. Locate the document in the Code\Chapter.10\TowerAtl folder on the companion CD. If you created your own version of TowerATL, first revise the document's **classid** entry with your control's class identifier, copying the string from the project's IDL file as we did

**Listing 10-5.**   *The TowerCtl.htm file.*

```
<HTML>
<HEAD>
<TITLE>ATL 3.0 test page for object TowerCtl</TITLE>
</HEAD>
<BODY>
<OBJECT
    classid="clsid:3B365FBA-C3AE-11D1-BEC9-E0F4E352507A"
    id=tower
>
</OBJECT>

<SCRIPT LANGUAGE="VBSCRIPT">
sub tower_Error
    tower.AboutBox()
end sub
</SCRIPT>
</BODY>
</HTML>
```

earlier for the Tumble2.htm document. Then follow these steps to perform the experiment:

- Run Internet Explorer, choose the Open command from the File menu, then browse for TowerCtl.htm. Opening the document displays the TowerATL window if the control is properly registered on your system.

- Choose New from the same menu to open a duplicate window displaying the control.

- In each of the two windows, drag a colored block onto a smaller block to fire the control's *Error* event. The document script is written to invoke the control's About box whenever the event fires.

Comparing the thread identifiers displayed in each About box (Figure 10-17) shows that Internet Explorer runs each control instance in separate STA apartments. Interthreaded marshaling is not required for either instance because TowerATL adopts the apartment threading model, which is perfect for STA clients like Internet Explorer. But had we instead selected the single nonthreaded model for TowerATL, the second instance

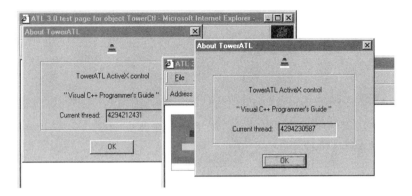

**Figure 10-17.** *Running the TowerATL control in separate STA apartments.*

of the control would run more slowly than the first because COM would be forced to marshal all interactions with it.

The companion CD provides a program named Game2 designed specifically to showcase the new TowerATL control. The Game2.rc file, located in the folder Code\Chapter.10\Game2, references the class identifier value of the TowerATL.ocx control supplied on the CD. If you prefer to run Game2 using a version of TowerATL that you have created yourself, again copy the correct class identifier from your TowerCtl.idl file to replace the identifier string in Game2.rc. Paste the new class identifier string in the dialog script's IDC_TOWERATL statement before rebuilding the Game2 program:

```
IDD_GAME2_DIALOG DIALOGEX 0, 0, 295, 125
⋮
CONTROL        "",IDC_TOWERATL,"{xxxxxxxx-xxxx-xxxx-xxxx-xxxxxxxxxxxx}",
               WS_TABSTOP,5,20,225,100
END
```

Compared to the Tower project of Chapter 9, TowerATL has involved a little more effort and attention to details that MFC shields from us. So it's worthwhile at this point to sum up our losses and gains in writing the control using ATL instead of MFC. The losses are easy to identify: more work. In compensation, however, we gain a much smaller executable image, though you might not think so at first glance. At 70 KB the new TowerATL.ocx is three times the size of the Tower.ocx file we created in

Chapter 9. But when you take into consideration the run-time libraries that Tower.ocx requires, the effective memory footprint of the control's ATL version is more than a megabyte *smaller* than the original MFC version. TowerATL.ocx can travel over the World Wide Web and execute in a user's browser without having to drag other files along with it.

Even over a fast modem, though, we can expect a download time for TowerATL.ocx of more than 20 seconds. That's a significant investment of time for the user, whose patience may have already been eroded by other large components and images dotting the page. ActiveX controls for the Internet face a unique obstacle in that the user generally has no idea of what to expect beforehand, and so may be less inclined to invest much time in finding out. Understandably, impatience often wins out over curiosity. The trick to writing a successful ActiveX control for the Internet is to make it small enough that it appears on the Web page, ready to execute, before curiosity loses the battle.

Today ATL offers the best approach to writing small ActiveX controls, short of straight COM programming. The library represents a compromise between size and labor, between what is possible and what is practical. But the compromise succeeds because ATL rewards a reasonable development effort with excellent results.

## Comparing Component Models

In closing this part of the book that deals with ActiveX controls, let's stand back a moment and consider the subject from a safe distance. When embarking on a component project, a developer must not only weigh the pros and cons of a support technology like ATL, but should first consider whether to use ActiveX at all. Like any other software technology, ActiveX controls are appropriate in some situations but not in others. If the component is intended solely as an extension of an embedding application and will never see service on a Web page, then ActiveX exacts a high cost. By dragging in the COM and ActiveX service libraries, even a simple control like Pulse installs many kilobytes of code in memory and may significantly degrade the loading process of the calling application.

There is another solution. Casting Pulse as a normal dynamic link library instead of an ActiveX control keeps the software in the form of a thread-safe, reusable component without incurring the expense of ActiveX and COM. Instead of setting up a handler function to receive events, the client application passes a pointer to a callback function that the library calls at each lapse of the requested interval. Since an event handler is only a call-back in new clothes, the effect is the same. If you are interested in seeing what a DLL version of Pulse might look like, you can find source files for such a project in the Chapter.10\PulseDLL folder on the companion CD. The most interesting characteristic of the dynamic link library version of Pulse is its size: 3 KB, compared to 37 KB for the ActiveX control version. And PulseDLL has no need of COM.

This brief comparison is intended only to shed light on all sides of the issue, serving as a reminder that at least in some cases the lowly dynamic link library still has a place in the world of component software. This is not to suggest that all non-Internet components should be cast as dynamic link libraries. Far from it. ActiveX offers distinct advantages over dynamic link libraries, particularly in coping with the well-known problem of "versioning." The attractiveness of a dynamic link library often tends to fade with its second release, a problem that does not affect ActiveX controls nearly as much. For example, suppose we decided that Pulse would be a more accurate timer if it called the *timeSetEvent* and *timeKillEvent* API functions instead of relying on the vagaries of the system's *Sleep* timer. The revised version might offer new objects and capabilities to new clients, while old client applications like Hour2 would embed the new Pulse as before, none the wiser that anything had changed. Even over-writing the old Pulse.ocx file with the new version does not affect client applications, whether or not they are written to make use of the extended features. This sort of stability is difficult to achieve with progressive versions of a dynamic link library.

# Advanced Topics

# The Debugger

After designing and coding comes debugging, the third step of software development. Your 3,000-line program may compile without so much as a warning, yet crash regularly or—and this is much worse—crash only occasionally. When your program does not work correctly and you aren't sure why, it's time to turn to the debugger to get an inside view of the program as it runs.

The Visual C++ debugger is one of the best features of the entire product. Intelligent and easy to use, the debugger can help you find nearly any bug you are likely to encounter in Windows software development. But debugging is often as much art as science, requiring clarity of mind and flashes of insight. The debugger is like a microscope in that it can expand your view, but only if you know where to look.

Dynamic link libraries, including ActiveX controls, are not special cases for the Visual C++ debugger. The debugger effortlessly crosses the boundary between projects, which means you can begin debugging a program in one project, and then continue debugging when the program calls into an exported function of a dynamic link library, even if the library and its source files exist as another project or subproject. The reverse also holds. You can start a debugging session in the dynamic link library's project, in which case the debugger automatically executes the calling application and returns control to you when the execution stream reaches one of the library's functions.

The debugger handles multithreaded and ActiveX applications and has the ability to run on one computer while the program you are debugging runs on a separate computer. We'll look at these special cases later in the chapter. First, let's get acquainted with the debugger.

# Debug vs. Release

A project in Visual C++ can produce two types of executable code, called the debug and release versions, or "targets." The debug version is what you work on during development and testing to make the program error-free; the release version is the final result, distributed to your customers. The debug version is larger and usually slower than the release version, filled with symbol information that the compiler places in the object file. The symbol information is a record of everything the compiler knows about the names of functions and variables in the program and the memory addresses they identify. By reading both the original source files and the symbol information contained in the executable file, the debugger can associate each line of the source code with the corresponding binary instructions in the executable image. The debugger runs the executable but uses the source code to show the program's progress.

The release version contains only executable instructions optimized by the compiler, without the symbol information. You can execute a release version inside the debugger but if you do, the debugger informs you that the file has no symbol data. Likewise, you can execute the debug version of a program without the debugger. This has practical consequences because of a Visual C++ feature known as Just-in-time debugging, which is demonstrated later in the chapter. When you run a program's debug version without the debugger, the Windows loader ignores the extra symbol information in the file, allowing the program to run normally. If the program commits an error, however, the system's exception handling causes control to wind its way back to Visual C++, which then executes the debugger. The debugger shows the instruction that caused the fault and displays data values as they existed when the program stopped. This superb feature is especially useful for tracking bugs during program testing and for finding those seemingly random errors that are difficult to reproduce, always the bane of programming.

By the way, if preserving your intellectual property is important to you, you should treat the debug version of your program as you do source code. A program file with symbol information is much easier to reverse engineer, since the file contains the names of all the program variables and functions. Instead of anonymous disassembled statements like these:

```
004017ae    push    ebp
004017af    mov     ebp, esp
```

the debugger helpfully includes function names taken from the symbol data:

```
MyClass::InitInstance:
004017ae    push    ebp
004017af    mov     ebp, esp
```

Although the source code remains unavailable, anyone can now recognize the prologue code of a function named *InitInstance*.

# Using the Debugger

When you debug an ailing program, sometimes called the debuggee, the debugger begins running first, and then executes (or spawns, in UNIX-speak) the program you want to debug. The debugger allows you to regain control when the running program reaches a selected instruction or alters a particular variable. This gives you the opportunity to check current data values while the program is suspended and to ensure that the flow of control proceeds along an expected path.

The debugger can throw a lot of information at you, making it seem more complicated than it is. If you are new to programming, don't be intimidated by the debugger. You will soon find out what every programmer learns, that the debugger is a friend indeed. A typical debug operation consists of several steps. You identify a section of your failing program where you suspect the problem arises, then mark the first instruction of the section. Start the debugger, which executes the program until control reaches the mark you set at the start of the questionable section. When the debugger stops the program's execution, you can then single-step through each instruction, checking the effect of each step.

So how does the debugger know when to interrupt the program? Well, it doesn't exactly. The program interrupts itself when it hits that marker you set. The marker is called a breakpoint.

# Breakpoints

The relationship between the debugger and the program it runs is unique in Windows—no other two programs operate so intimately linked together. The debugger and the program do not run simultaneously in the same sense that other normal applications run simultaneously in a multitasking environment. While the program runs, the debugger sleeps, having nothing to do. It regains control when the executing program triggers a breakpoint.

The debugger lets you set two different types of breakpoints, one based on location in the code and the other based on program data. A location breakpoint is a marker attached to a particular instruction in your source code, similar to a bookmark in the text editor. You set a location breakpoint at the start of any section of suspect code that you want to investigate in detail to see how the error arises. When the executing program tries to execute the marked instruction, it stops or "breaks." (We'll see how in the next section.)

A data breakpoint depends on data rather than code. Use a data breakpoint when you suspect a variable is being incorrectly altered somewhere in your program but you aren't sure where. The data breakpoint tells the debugger to break execution when the variable changes or becomes a certain value as, for example, when a pointer is reassigned or when the variable $x$ exceeds a value of 500.

When a location or data breakpoint is triggered, control returns to the debugger. The debugger updates its windows showing the current values of variables and the section of the source code where the break occurred. You can now walk your way through the code, one instruction at a time, to see how variables change and how the program behaves.

# How a Breakpoint Returns Control to the Debugger

To give you an idea of how breakpoints work, this section examines the steps in which the debugger sets a breakpoint to interrupt a program and regains control when the breakpoint is triggered. The discussion concentrates on Intel and compatible processors, but the procedure outlined here is similar on other processors. In the following discussion, the word "program" refers only to your application, never to the debugger itself. This avoids the phrase "the program being debugged," which is unwieldy, and the word "debuggee," which sounds too much like debugger.

When you set a location breakpoint or single-step from one C/C++ instruction to the next, the debugger overwrites a single byte in the executing program's code segment at the break location. It saves the original value of the byte, and then writes the value 0xCC in its place. The processor interprets 0xCC as an INT 3 instruction, which tells the processor to execute the system handler routine that corresponds to interrupt 3. It's no coincidence that Intel calls interrupt 3 the breakpoint interrupt.

After writing the INT 3 instruction, the debugger goes to sleep by calling the *WaitForDebugEvent* API function. The system turns control over to the program, which executes normally until it reaches the INT 3 instruction. In executing the instruction, the processor writes the current values of the CS and EIP registers on the stack and calls the system's interrupt 3 handler routine. This is how control reverts back to the debugger. The kernel returns from *WaitForDebugEvent*, waking up the debugger, which then updates its windows and waits for your instructions. (See the sidebar on the following page for a description of the CS and EIP registers.)

At this point, your program is frozen. It receives no CPU time and so cannot continue executing past the breakpoint while you interact with the debugger. Normally, the debugger directly controls only one thread in your program, so other threads may continue to receive CPU time. We'll see later in the chapter how to suspend threads other than the one being debugged.

When you resume executing the program, the debugger replaces the byte overwritten by the 0xCC value to restore the original instruction at which

## The CS and EIP Registers

A processor contains a small number of on-chip storage areas called registers that temporarily hold all the information required to process an instruction. An Intel processor has two registers named CS and EIP that continually point to the next instruction in line for processing. Here's a brief account of how the pointers in these registers guide the processor back to a program after an interrupt has occurred.

CS stands for code segment—or, in 32-bit processing, code selector—because the register holds a value called a selector assigned by the operating system that references the base address of the program's code. The EIP (extended instruction pointer) register holds a 32-bit offset that points into the code area at the next instruction that the processor plans to execute. When it responds to an interrupt (such as an INT 3 instruction), an Intel processor first writes the contents of the CS and EIP registers to the stack before jumping to the handler function that services the interrupt. When the handler routine finishes, the original CS and EIP values are popped from the stack, informing the processor where to go next—that is, back to the program instruction it was about to execute when pulled away to service the interrupt. Along with CS and EIP, another register containing current processor flags is also restored from the stack, so that the original program resumes executing unaware of (and unaffected by) the interruption.

Interrupts occur continuously at a furious rate, originating both from INT instructions in an executing program and from hardware events. Pressing a key on the keyboard, for example, triggers an interrupt; another interrupt occurs when you release the key. The system timer regularly interrupts the processor 18 times a second, handing control back to the operating system so that it can redirect the processor to the next thread in line for a time slice. Interrupts are usually serviced quickly, but the breakpoint interrupt is an exception. The operating system and the debugger retain control until you resume debugging, at which time the system exits its interrupt 3 handler and allows the processor to continue running the program being debugged.

you set the breakpoint. Because the EIP value on the stack now points to the byte after the temporary INT 3 instruction, the debugger decrements the value so that it again points to the original instruction. The debugger then goes back to sleep by calling the *ContinueDebugEvent* API function. The operating system restores registers to their original values and executes an IRET (interrupt return) instruction from its interrupt 3 handler to return control to the program. The processor pops the CS and altered EIP values from the stack and resumes executing the program at the interrupted instruction as though nothing had happened.

There's a complication that arises from the fact that all instances of a running Windows program normally share the same section of memory that contains the program code. Since the debugger writes an INT 3 instruction into the program's code, you might expect an instance of the program running outside the debugger to also trigger the interrupt and land in the debugger. But that doesn't happen. Windows provides a mechanism known as copy-on-write that neatly handles these situations. When the debugger calls the system's *WriteProcessMemory* function to write the INT 3 instruction into a page of the program's code, Windows allocates a block of writeable memory, copies the code page to the new block, remaps the page's virtual memory address, and completes the debugger's write operation using the copied page. Any other instances of the program running outside the debugger continue to run from the original code and so do not encounter the INT 3 instruction.

The debugger employs a different method for catching a data breakpoint attached to a variable in your program's data. It isn't practical to set an INT code at every instruction that may alter the variable, so the debugger must step through each instruction in the program, checking the variable each time. If the variable does not change, the debugger executes the next instruction, continuing until an instruction changes the variable. As you can imagine, this continual cycle of interrupting and checking can dramatically slow execution of the program being debugged. Your program may even appear to hang when you debug with data breakpoints because of the many thousands of interruptions that can occur.

Some processors provide special debug registers right on the chip to help the debugger out with this tedious chore. An Intel processor has eight debug registers, though it can monitor a maximum of four data breakpoints because only the first four debug registers, DR0 through DR3, hold memory addresses. When you set a data breakpoint for a variable, the debugger writes the address of the variable into one of the processor's debug registers. It then programs the debug control register DR7 with a bit flag that instructs the processor to monitor memory write instructions. As the processor executes your program, it continually checks each instruction to see whether it writes to the memory that the debug register points to. If so, the processor generates an interrupt 1, called the trace or debugger interrupt, handing control back to the operating system through its interrupt handler routine. When the system returns from *WaitForDebugEvent*, the debugger reads the DR6 status register to determine which of the four breakpoints has triggered the interrupt. The debugger then updates its windows and informs you that the variable has been altered.

It's interesting to note that an Intel processor can also be programmed to break whenever the program accesses a variable—that is, either writes to or reads from the variable. However, the Visual C++ debugger does not take advantage of this option because program instructions that read a variable are usually of much less interest when you are debugging than instructions that write the variable. It's also possible to program the processor's debug registers to monitor location breakpoints as well as data breakpoints, saving the extra work of overwriting code with an INT 3 instruction. But debug registers are a scarce resource, so the Visual C++ debugger compromises by using interrupt 3 to monitor location breakpoints and reserves the debug registers for data breakpoints.

By using debug registers, the debugger places the burden of checking data breakpoints on the processor, effectively eliminating the performance drag that would otherwise result from stepping through each instruction to monitor data changes. However, a data breakpoint can affect program speed despite the use of debug registers when the breakpoint includes a condition, such as whether the variable $x$ exceeds a certain value. A variable assigned a breakpoint may change many thousands of times in the course of a single loop. Each time the variable changes, the processor interrupts and control winds its way back to the debugger, which must then evaluate the condition. A conditional expression that never (or rarely) becomes true can thus degrade program speed by siphoning processor time away from the program. And as we'll see later in the chapter, in some circumstances the debugger does not use debug registers to monitor data breakpoints, relying instead on the much slower method of single-stepping through the program.

# Building a Debug Version

To create a debug executable version of a program, first ensure the active configuration is Win32 Debug. By default, Visual C++ sets the configuration as Win32 Debug when you create a new project, displaying the current configuration in the Build toolbar:

You can also click the Set Active Configuration command on the Build menu to see the current configuration and if necessary change it to the debug version. The Win32 Debug configuration automatically alters program settings, displayed in the Project Settings dialog. Open the Project Settings dialog by clicking the Settings command on the Project menu and exposing the C/C++ and Link tabs. Settings in the dialog should appear similar to those shown in Figure 11-1 on the next page, in which:

- The Optimizations combo box in the C/C++ tab displays the Disable (Debug) option.

- A checkmark appears in the Generate Debug Info check box in the Link tab.

With these settings in place, you can build the project normally. The result is a debug version of your program that contains symbol information for the debugger.

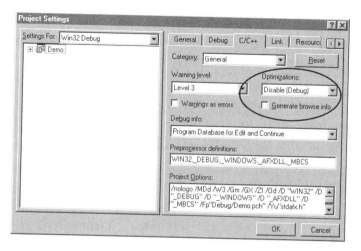

Settings in the C/C++ tab.

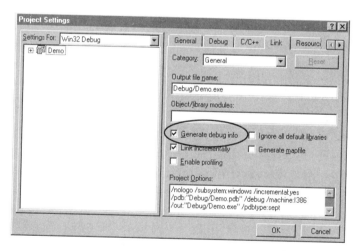

Settings in the Link tab.

**Figure 11-1.** *Setting up a debug build in the Project Settings dialog.*

# The Debugger Interface

Like the Visual C++ editors, the debugger is available only from inside the Developer Studio environment. Debugging a program requires that the project is open and that you have created a debug executable version of the program.

The text editor provides a good place to begin debugging. Open one or more of the program's source files and find the line where you want to interrupt execution when the program runs. Click anywhere on a line to place the caret there, then press F9 to set a location breakpoint. The editor marks the line by placing a small red octagon suggesting a traffic stop sign in the selection margin to the left of the line. If you have the selection margin disabled as described in Chapter 3, the editor instead highlights the entire line in red. To remove a location breakpoint, set the caret anywhere on the line and press F9 again to toggle the breakpoint off.

If you prefer the mouse to the keyboard, you can set or remove a location breakpoint by clicking the right mouse button on the line. A context menu appears as shown in Figure 11-2, from which you can choose the Insert/Remove Breakpoint command to clear or set a breakpoint. The menu also provides a Disable Breakpoint command that allows you to turn a breakpoint off without removing it.

Though less convenient, you can also set a location breakpoint through the Breakpoints dialog. This dialog provides the only means for setting data breakpoints and two other variations, called conditional breakpoints and message breakpoints.

**Figure 11-2.**    *Choosing the Insert/Remove Breakpoint command from the context menu.*

## The Breakpoints Dialog

To display the Breakpoints dialog shown in Figure 11-3, press Ctrl+B or click the Breakpoints command on the Edit menu. The three tabs in the dialog let you set location, data, conditional, and message breakpoints. The following paragraphs describe these four breakpoint types.

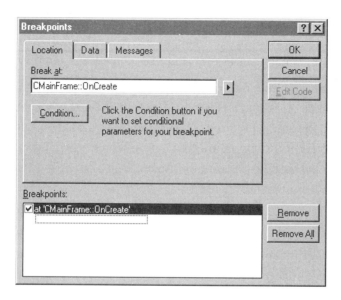

**Figure 11-3.**  *The Breakpoints dialog.*

### Location breakpoints

Setting a location breakpoint in the Breakpoints dialog is less convenient than pressing the F9 key or choosing a command from the editor's context menu, but the dialog provides several enhancements for location breakpoints that often prove useful. For instance, you can type the name of a function in the Break At control to set a location breakpoint at the first line of the function; typing the name of a label sets a breakpoint at the labeled line. (There is little difference between the two since a function name is, after all, merely a label.) Letter case in the Break At control must match the function name or label, and a C++ function name must include the class name and scope resolution operator. Thus, the entry *OnCreate* does not specify a valid breakpoint location, but *CMainFrame:: OnCreate* does.

Typing a function name or label in the Breakpoints dialog sets a valid breakpoint in the source, but does not provide the text editor with a line number. Because the text editor requires a line number to display the breakpoint symbol, it does not mark the line in the document window or give any other visual indication that the labeled line now has a location breakpoint. A list of current breakpoints at the bottom of the Breakpoints dialog provides your only means of confirming the existence of the new breakpoint. The stop sign breakpoint symbol appears in the source listing only when the debugger is active.

To set a location breakpoint at a particular line, type a period followed by the line number in the Break At control. For the current line—that is, the line in the text editor that contains the caret—click the small arrow button to the right of the control and select the given line number. This button also leads to the Advanced Breakpoint dialog in which you can specify a function or label in a source file other than the one displayed in the text editor.

Location breakpoints have characteristics similar to text editor bookmarks, and Visual C++ implements breakpoints and bookmarks using the same logic. Besides marking a specific line, a location breakpoint like a named bookmark remains a permanent fixture of your document until you remove it. If you edit a document outside the Developer Studio environment, both breakpoints and bookmarks can be displaced to another line. Editing a document within the environment while the debugger is active can also jar a location breakpoint out of position, because the breakpoint attaches to a line number. As the document grows or shrinks in size with editing, a new source statement can slip into the line number assigned to a breakpoint. If the new line does not contain a valid program instruction, Visual C++ warns you of what has happened when you next start the debugger:

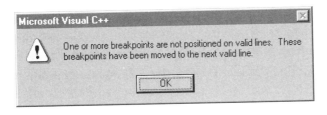

At the appearance of this message you should scan the source code using the text editor, remove the dislocated breakpoints, and reset new ones at their original locations. If you regularly edit your source code outside the Visual C++ environment or make changes while the debugger is active, expect to see the message frequently. It's difficult to see a practical solution to the problem of displaced breakpoints, particularly when you make changes in another editor. Like bookmarks, breakpoints are pointers rather than characters embedded in the source code document (which would only trip up the compiler), so altering text outside the environment inevitably runs the risk of repositioning the pointer targets.

However, the problem of displacement does not affect location breakpoints attached to labels or function names using the Breakpoints dialog. These location breakpoints remain anchored to their labels no matter how the document content changes, because each time it runs, the debugger first scans the source code for the labels, tagging each labeled line with a breakpoint. This is often a compelling reason to set location breakpoints using the Breakpoints dialog rather than the more convenient method of pressing the F9 key. We'll use the dialog method later in the chapter to set location breakpoints in a sample debugging problem.

### Data breakpoints

The Breakpoints dialog provides the only means for setting a data breakpoint. A data breakpoint is triggered either when a specified variable changes in value or when a conditional expression becomes true. If you have used Microsoft's old CodeView debugger, you probably recognize a data breakpoint as a new name for what CodeView called a tracepoint. Click the Data tab in the Breakpoints dialog and type the name of the variable or the expression you want the debugger to monitor (see Figure 11-4). Enter an expression in the form of a standard C/C++ conditional expression, such as $i==100$ or $nCount > 25$.

While the debugger is active, you can set a data breakpoint for a variable not in scope by first typing the expression in the Breakpoints dialog, then clicking the arrow button to the right of the text box labeled Enter The Expression To Be Evaluated. Click the Advanced command that pops up

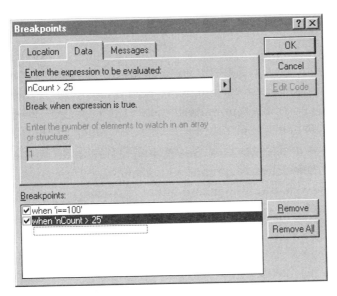

**Figure 11-4.** *Entering a data breakpoint in the Breakpoints dialog.*

and enter the requested context information to enable the debugger to track the variable when it comes into scope.

The debugger can monitor a range of variables identified by a pointer, such as an array or structure name, provided you dereference the pointer in the expression. For instance, typing an array name such as *iArray* in the Enter The Expression text box does not set a data breakpoint for the first element of the array as you might expect. You must dereference the array pointer by typing *iArray[0]*. To monitor more than just the first element of the array, set the number of elements in the smaller control labeled Enter The Number Of Elements To Watch. Notice that this is the number of elements, not the number of bytes. If *iArray* contains integers, for example, typing *iArray[0]* in the first control and the number *10* in the second control causes the program to break if any change occurs in the first 40 bytes of the array (integers *iArray[0]* through *iArray[9]*).

Similarly, to monitor a string of character bytes that the variable *pString* points to, type *\*pString* in the Enter The Expression control. In the smaller control, type the number of bytes that you want the debugger to monitor. Typing *pString* without the asterisk dereference operator means that the breakpoint is triggered only if *pString* is changed to point somewhere else.

In this case the debugger monitors *pString* itself, not the contents of the string it points to.

As mentioned earlier, your program's execution speed can slow significantly when you are debugging with data breakpoints. Program speed degrades when you set more breakpoints than the processor can accommodate in its debug registers, or if you set a data breakpoint for a variable with automatic storage class. Automatic data include function arguments and variables defined in a function without the **static** keyword. Such data live on the stack, blinking in and out of existence as the program executes. Although you can set a data breakpoint for an automatic variable, the debugger does not use the processor's debug registers to monitor the breakpoint, so execution may slow while the variable is in scope. The debugger uses debug registers only to monitor data breakpoints for static variables that exist in the program's data section, not for automatic local data on the stack.

The drag on execution speed imposed by data breakpoints can be so dramatic you may think your program has hung. Be patient when using data breakpoints. If you believe your program has truly stopped responding for some reason, click the Break command on Visual C++'s Debug menu. This interrupts the program and returns control to the debugger.

### Conditional breakpoints

A conditional breakpoint is an extended version of a location breakpoint. Set the breakpoint at a source code instruction the same way as a location breakpoint, but the debugger responds to a conditional breakpoint only if a specified condition is true when control reaches the marked instruction. Conditional breakpoints are invaluable in loops where the same instruction may execute many hundreds of times. A location breakpoint placed in the loop halts execution at each iteration, which may not be what you want. A conditional breakpoint lets you break at the instruction only when some condition occurs—say, when the loop counter reaches a value of 100.

Set a conditional breakpoint in the Location tab of the Breakpoints dialog. After specifying the source code instruction you want to mark with the breakpoint, click the Condition button shown in Figure 11-3 on page 526 to display the Breakpoint Condition dialog box:

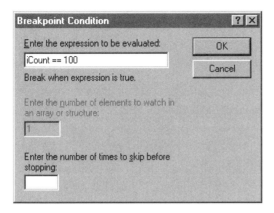

In the top control of the dialog, type the breakpoint condition in the form of a C/C++ conditional expression. Each time the marked instruction executes, the debugger evaluates the expression and breaks program flow only if the expression is TRUE or non-zero. The text box at the bottom of the Breakpoint Condition dialog lets you specify the number of times the condition must become true before the debugger interrupts the program.

### Message breakpoints

A message breakpoint attaches to a window procedure. Execution breaks when the window procedure receives a specified message, such as WM_SIZE or WM_COMMAND. Message breakpoints aren't of much use in C++ programs that use MFC, because window procedures usually lie buried inside the MFC framework rather than in the program source code. To interrupt a specific message in an MFC program, set a location breakpoint for the function that handles the message, which is identified in the class's message map.

Figure 11-5 on the next page illustrates how to set a message breakpoint for a hypothetical window procedure named *ButtonProc*, prototyped like this:

```
int CALLBACK ButtonProc( HWND hwnd, UINT msg,
                         WPARAM wParam, LPARAM lParam );
```

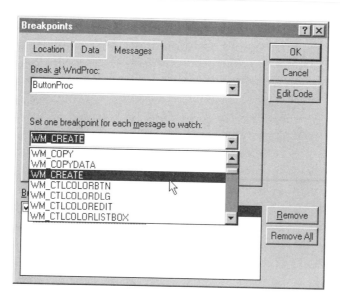

**Figure 11-5.** *Setting a message breakpoint in the Breakpoints dialog.*

When the operating system calls the *ButtonProc* procedure, it passes a message value such as WM_COMMAND or WM_CREATE in the *msg* parameter that informs the procedure why it is being called. To break execution when *ButtonProc* receives a specific message, click the Messages tab in the Breakpoints dialog and type *ButtonProc* in the Break At WndProc control. Click the arrow on the second combo box to expose a drop-down list of message identifiers and select a message, such as the WM_CREATE message shown in Figure 11-5. When you run the program in the debugger, execution breaks at the first line of *ButtonProc* when Windows calls the procedure with the WM_CREATE message.

As you see, a message breakpoint is a specialized form of conditional breakpoint. You can get the same results in the Location tab by setting a location breakpoint at the *ButtonProc* label along with this condition:

```
msg == WM_CREATE
```

## Running the Debugger

Once you have established where and under what conditions you want your program to stop, you are ready to execute it. At this point the text editor, not the debugger, is active. Executing the debug version of your program is a matter of starting the debugger, which in turn runs the program.

Choose the Start Debug command from the Build menu, which presents you with four choices named Go, Step Into, Run To Cursor, and Attach To Process, shown in Figure 11-6. Use the Go command when you have set at least one breakpoint in the source code. The debugger runs the program normally, halting when (and if) the flow of execution in your program reaches a location breakpoint or triggers a data breakpoint. The Step Into command does just what its name suggests: it steps into the program and stops at the first command. The first instruction of a Windows program is the start of the *WinMain* function or, for an MFC program, the *_tWinMain* function. In either case, the debugger opens the source module—which for *_tWinMain* is the Appmodul.cpp file located in the MFC folder—and displays it in the source window.

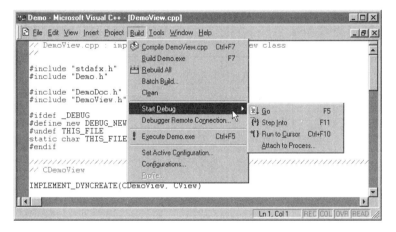

**Figure 11-6.**   *Starting the debugger from the Build menu.*

The Run To Cursor command halts execution at the source line on which the caret rests. If no source file is open in the text editor, the Run To Cursor command is disabled. Otherwise, it gives you a convenient means of quickly jumping into a program without setting a breakpoint. If the program flow triggers a breakpoint before reaching the caret, execution stops at the breakpoint, not at the line with the caret. To continue execution, reset the caret to the target line and click Run To Cursor again. The Attach

To Process command allows you to launch the debugger and attach it to a program that is currently executing. The debugger accomplishes this feat through the services of the *DebugActiveProcess* API function, described in online help.

The debugger provides shortcut keys for the first three subcommands of Start Debug, so you don't have to pull down the Build menu to begin debugging. The shortcut keys are F5 for Go, F11 for Step Into, and Ctrl+F10 for Run To Cursor.

## The Debugger Windows

When the program you are debugging stops at a breakpoint, the debugger updates its windows with information about the program's current state. Perhaps the most important of the debugger windows is the source window, which shows the source code where the program stopped. A small yellow arrow called the instruction pointer appears in the selection margin to the left of the interrupted instruction. (If the selection margin is disabled, the entire line appears highlighted in yellow.) The mark identifies the instruction that has not yet executed but is next in line to do so when the program resumes running.

The Debug toolbar, shown in Figure 11-7, appears on the screen when the debugger regains control. The six buttons in the figure labeled Debugger Windows act as toggles that expose or hide dockable windows containing information about the current state of the program. Table 11-1 describes the type of information displayed in each window. The Debug toolbar does not contain a similar button for the source window, because the debugger only borrows the window from the text editor. Open or close the source window as you would any normal document view.

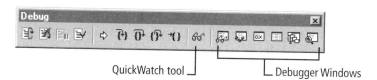

Figure 11-7.    *Tool buttons that toggle debugger windows on and off.*

| Window | Button | Displays |
|---|---|---|
| Watch | | Current values of variables and expressions tracked by the debugger. Specify in the Watch window those variables you always want to know the current value of whenever the program is suspended. |
| Variables | | Current values of variables accessed at or near the break location. The Variables window has three tabs: |
| | | ❐ **Auto**—Displays variables and function return values. |
| | | ❐ **Locals**—Shows variables local to the current function. |
| | | ❐ **this**—In a C++ program, identifies the object that the this pointer currently points to. |
| Registers | | Current contents of the CPU registers. |
| Memory | | Memory dump of a specified address. |
| Call Stack | | List of called functions that have not yet returned. The call stack shows the path of execution leading down through nested function calls to the breakpoint location. |
| Disassembly | | Assembly language translation of the compiled code that supplements the source window on the screen. "Disassembly" means converting the machine code in the program to equivalent assembly instructions. |

**Table 11-1.**   *Information contained in the six debugger windows activated by buttons on the Debug toolbar.*

The Watch window provides a view of specified variables, showing current values as they exist while the program remains suspended. Variables in the Watch window have nothing to do with interrupting program flow, so don't confuse a watch variable with a variable on which you have set a data breakpoint. To add a variable to the Watch window, double-click the dotted new-entry box in the window and type the variable name. The

QuickWatch tool, shown in Figure 11-7 on page 534, provides a way to query for a current value without adding the variable to the Watch window. For the ultimate in convenience, you can query the debugger for a current value simply by pausing the mouse cursor over the variable name in the source window. This displays a pop-up tooltip window containing the current value:

```
if (bCreateFlag && iID > 1)
{
         bCreateFlag = 1
```

For some variables such as structure elements and class members, the name alone may not provide enough resolution for the debugger to unambiguously identify the variable. In these cases, you must first select both object and variable names along with the connecting dot operator (as in *MyClass.Member*), then pause the mouse cursor over the selection in the source window.

Whereas the Watch window provides a view of in-scope variables no matter where they are accessed in the program, the Variables window focuses on the frozen point of execution. Any variables referenced by the instruction that last executed before the program was suspended, and perhaps one or two previous instructions, appear in the Variables window. You can change the value of a variable by double-clicking it in the Variables window and typing a new value.

The Registers window, generally used only when the Disassembly window is active, shows the state of processor registers as they existed when the program was suspended. The Intel processor flags described in Table 11-2 are bit flags, the values of which you can toggle by double-clicking the flag in the Registers window. The Symbol column in the table shows the flag symbols as they appear in the Registers window.

The debugger windows can pack a lot of information, but usually you do not need to see them all at the same time. The windows compete for screen space with the source code displayed in the source window, which should always be visible so that you know where you are in the program.

| Flag name | Symbol | Description |
|---|---|---|
| Overflow | OV | Set when an integer instruction produces a result that is too small or too large to fit in the destination register or memory address. |
| Direction | UP | Determines the direction of repeated string and compare instructions, such as MOVS (Move String) and CMPS (Compare String). |
| Enable interrupt | EI | When clear, the processor ignores hardware interrupts such as keyboard activity. |
| Sign | PL | Contains the high-order bit value of an arithmetic instruction. (It's unclear why the Visual C++ designers chose the letters PL to represent the sign flag. Don't confuse it with the processor's I/O Privilege Level flag.) |
| Zero | ZR | Set when the result of an arithmetic instruction is zero. |
| Auxiliary carry | AC | Contains the carry out of the AL register's four low-order bits (known as a nibble) after an arithmetic instruction. |
| Parity | PE | Set when the binary value of an arithmetic instruction result has an even number of 1-bits. |
| Carry | CY | Similar to the Overflow flag, but indicates an unsigned overflow. Can be explicitly manipulated with the STC (Set Carry) and CLC (Clear Carry) instructions. |

**Table 11-2.** *Intel processor flags.*

As mentioned in Chapter 1, the debugger uses the environment's Output window to display data from the *OutputDebugString* function or the *afxDump* class. The Output window also shows thread termination codes, first-chance exception notifications, and loading information. There is no button on the Debug toolbar to control display of the Output window because the window belongs to the Developer Studio environment, not the debugger. Toggle the visibility of the Output window by clicking the Output button on the Standard toolbar.

It's a little difficult to get a feel for the debugger windows until you actually use them. An example program later in the chapter demonstrates how the debugger windows assist in the debugging process.

## Stepping Through a Program

When tracking down a program error with the debugger, identify the section of code where you believe the problem arises and set a location breakpoint at or just before that section. When the debugger suspends the program at the breakpoint, you can then single-step through the problem area one instruction at a time, checking variables as they change.

The Debug toolbar has a group of four buttons shown in Figure 11-8 that let you step through a suspended program. You can recognize the Step tools by the arrows and curly braces on them; as we'll see, the images convey very well what the buttons do. In the order shown, the buttons activate the Step Into, Step Over, Step Out, and Run To Cursor commands. We've already discussed the Run To Cursor command. The other three need a little more explanation.

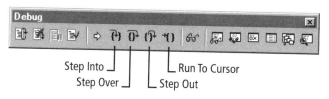

**Figure 11-8.**    *The four Step tools on the Debug toolbar.*

The Step Into and Step Over commands (or their equivalent shortcut keys F11 and F10) let you single-step through the program. When you choose Step Into or Step Over, the debugger allows the program to resume execution, but only for one instruction. After the instruction finishes, the debugger again suspends execution. You might wonder what constitutes an instruction because a single command in a high-level language like C++ may translate into a dozen machine instructions at the processor level. It depends on whether the Disassembly view is enabled. If it is, the single-step commands execute only the current machine instruction, moving the arrow pointer to the next instruction in the disassembled listing. If the Disassembly view is disabled, Step Into or Step Over executes the current C/C++ instruction in the source window, processing as a group whatever machine code makes up the instruction.

The names of Step Into and Step Over make more sense when the commands are used on an instruction that calls a function. Consider what happens when the debugger halts execution at the **if** statement shown here:

```
if (Function1( hdc, Function2( msg ) ))
    x = 3;
else
    y = 100;
```

The Step Over command does as its name implies, processing the entire **if** statement including the calls to *Function1* and *Function2*. The program halts again at either the *x=3* or *y=100* statement, depending on the outcome of the **if** expression. The Step Into command handles the situation differently. When you click the Step Into button at the **if** statement, the debugger steps into *Function2* and stops at the first instruction. If you check the Call Stack window at this point, you will see *Function2* at the top of the list and below that the name of the function you just left.

Here's where the Step Out command becomes useful. This command executes the rest of the current function, and then stops at the next statement after the function call. In other words, when applied to a function call the Step Into and Step Out commands together have the same effect as Step Over. However, if the instruction contains more than one function call as in our example, things get more complicated. When you click the Step Into button at the **if** statement to pause at the first instruction of *Function2* and then click Step Out, the instruction pointer arrow remains pointing to the **if** statement. This is because *Function2* has finished executing, but *Function1* has not yet been called. Activating Step Into again advances to the first instruction of *Function1*. If you click Step Out to return from *Function1*, the instruction arrow still points to the **if** statement because the **if** test itself has not yet been processed.

A disassembled view of the code shows more clearly what is happening. The shaded lines indicate the C source statements, which are followed by the equivalent disassembled instructions. (The disassembled lines serve only to illustrate the internal chain of events within the **if** statement, and are not meant to suggest that the Disassembly window is visible.) At the beginning of the code sequence, the yellow instruction pointer arrow points to the **if** statement.

```
if (Function1( hdc, Function2( msg )))      Instruction pointer arrow is here.
mov     eax, dword ptr [msg]
push    eax
mov     ecx, dword ptr [this]
call    @ILT+30(CMyClass::Function2) (0040101e)
push    eax                                 First Step-Into-Step-Out processes
mov     eax, dword ptr [hdc]                Function2 and ends here. Arrow
push    eax                                 still points to the if statement.
mov     ecx, dword ptr [this]
call    @ILT+85(CMyClass::Function1) (00401055)
test    eax, eax                            Next Step-Into-Step-Out processes
je      CMyClass::Caller+00000071           Function1 and ends here. Arrow
                                            still points to the if statement.

x = 3;                                      Next Step-Into ends here...
mov     dword ptr [x], 00000003
else
jmp     CMyClass::Caller+00000078
y = 100;                                    ...or here, depending on
                                            Function1's return value.
mov     dword ptr [y], 00000064
```

Windows 95 does not allow stepping into system API functions such as those shown here:

```
::SelectObject( hdc, ::GetStockObject( BLACK_PEN ) );
```

If you select Step Into at this instruction, both *GetStockObject* and *SelectObject* execute before the debugger stops execution at the next statement. In this case, Step Into and Step Over have the same effect.

## Stopping and Restarting the Debugger

The Restart button shown in Figure 11-9 lets you abort execution and restart the program from the beginning, throwing away any current allocations such as system resources or memory. The result is a clean slate without your having to exit and restart the debugger. Click the Stop Debugging button to exit the debugger immediately, killing both debugger and program in one step. The Break Execution button has the same effect as the Break command on the Debug menu, halting the program's

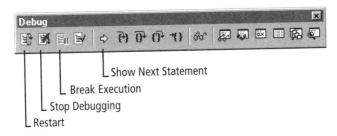

└ Show Next Statement

└ Break Execution

└ Stop Debugging

└ Restart

**Figure 11-9.** *Debugger tools that control the point of execution.*

execution and returning control to the debugger. Use the Break Execution button to stop a program caught in an infinite loop.

The small yellow arrow tool labeled Show Next Statement neatly solves an old problem. Tracking down a bug while the program is suspended often requires investigating other parts of the document and may even lead you into other source files. Clicking the Show Next Statement arrow on the Debug toolbar brings you immediately back to the halted instruction in the source window. The tool icon suggests the instruction pointer arrow that appears in the selection margin adjacent to the halted instruction.

## Corrections on the Fly

When you find an error while debugging your program, Visual C++ in many cases allows you to incorporate corrections without stopping the debugger. The discovery that a variable contains a wrong value, for instance, is often easily solved by typing the correct value in the Variables window before continuing the program's execution. If you prefer to resume running the program from a new instruction, right-click the desired line in the source window and choose the Set Next Statement command from the context menu:

This resets the instruction pointer to the clicked line, allowing you to redo or skip over instructions in the program. The burden is on you, however, to ensure that moving the instruction pointer results in no adverse consequences. Assignment instructions are usually safe to repeat, as are many calls to API functions, but be cautious about re-executing a **new** instruction or other code that allocates a resource.

Typing a new value during a debugging session is at best a temporary solution. It presumes that eventually you will exit the debugger, fix the faulty source code using the text editor, and recompile to permanently establish the correction. But Visual C++ now offers a more convenient alternative to these well-worn steps, letting you permanently fix many problems right in the debugger's source window. When you resume running the program after editing the source, Visual C++ first compiles the revised code and replaces the affected machine instructions with the corrected version. The fix is permanent, exactly as though you had closed the debugger, recompiled the corrected source code, and restarted the debugger again.

Known as Edit and Continue, this feature is always available during debugging, though you have the option of applying it either automatically or manually. By default, the feature is activated automatically when you choose Go or one of the Step commands to resume executing an interrupted program after revising its source. If you prefer more control over whether altered code is recompiled during a debugging session, expose the Debug tab of the Options dialog and clear the check box labeled Debug Commands Invoke Edit And Continue. This does not disable the Edit and Continue feature, but only ensures that the debugger does not invoke it without your permission. You can recompile revised code in the debugger whenever you want by clicking the Apply Code Changes button on the Debug toolbar (Figure 11-10) or by choosing the corresponding command from the Debug menu or the source window's context menu. The Apply Code Changes command is enabled only when you have made changes to

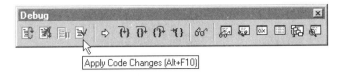

**Figure 11-10.** *Invoking the debugger's Edit and Continue feature.*

the code, either in the debugger's source window or in another text editor outside the Visual C++ environment.

The point of execution sometimes changes after you've recompiled edited code, in which case the debugger notifies you with a message. If the instruction pointer is not where it should be, reset it using the Set Next Statement command.

There are certain limitations to Edit and Continue that you should bear in mind. The feature does not recognize source changes that are impossible, impractical, or unsafe to compile while debugging, such as:

- Alterations to exception handler blocks
- Wholesale deletions of functions
- Changes to class and function definitions
- Changes to static functions
- Changes to resource data in the project's RC file

Attempting to resume execution through Edit and Continue after making any of these changes causes the debugger to display an error message in the status bar that explains the problem. You have the option of continuing to debug using the original code or closing the debugger and recompiling the revised code normally. For safety's sake, Edit and Continue defers applying changes to a function until the call stack completely "unwinds." If you edit the function in which execution is currently frozen, and if (as is usually the case) that function has been called by yet another function, the debugger displays the message shown on the next page when you attempt to resume execution.

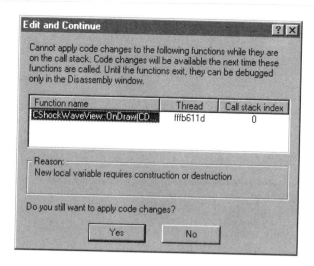

The dialog is not an error message. It serves only to remind you that the function will finish executing using its original code, and your revisions will not take effect until the next time the function executes through the same chain of calls. Click the Yes button to continue execution; click No to cancel Edit and Continue and return to the debugger.

## Programming Breakpoints

Sometimes it's more convenient to sprinkle small confirmation tests throughout your program instead of trying to plant breakpoints at many different locations. The ASSERT macro is commonly used for this purpose, arresting execution only if an error occurs. It's instructive to program our own breakpoints by creating a simple test macro named CHECK that displays a message and halts if a test fails. The breakpoint is easy to program in the macro, simply encoded as an INT 3 instruction using inline assembly. As we saw earlier in the chapter, this instruction turns control over to the debugger when the processor executes it.

The CHECK macro triggers the INT 3 breakpoint only if a condition fails. The macro takes two parameters—an expression that tests the condition, and a pointer to a string that explains the error:

```
#ifdef _DEBUG
  #define CHECK( b, s ) \
    if (b) \
    { \
      ::MessageBox( NULL, s, "CHECK Error", MB_ICONINFORMATION ); \
      _asm int 3 \
    }
#else
  #define CHECK( b, s )
#endif
```

With the macro in place, you can test the logic of your program like this:

```
iRet = Function1();
CHECK( iRet != 1, "Bad return value from Function1" );
```

If the test fails, the macro displays the error message and halts execution at the breakpoint. You can then correct the problem in the debugger, reset the instruction pointer, and try the instruction again through Edit and Continue.

# Example: Developing and Debugging the ShockWave Program

The ShockWave program introduced in this section provides an opportunity to apply some of this knowledge. ShockWave does no more than display concentric rings in a wave pattern of random colors—at least, that's what it's supposed to do. Though it compiles cleanly, ShockWave does not run correctly. The program has two bugs, one obvious, the other a little less so. Some detective work with the debugger is all that's needed to get the program working.

ShockWave shows how to achieve a three-dimensional look through color gradations. You will need a video adapter capable of 24-bit color and at least 1 MB of video memory to see the 3-D look, but because the purpose of the program is to demonstrate the debugger, don't worry about how it appears on your screen. Figure 11-11 on the following page shows what the program looks like when running correctly after having been successfully debugged.

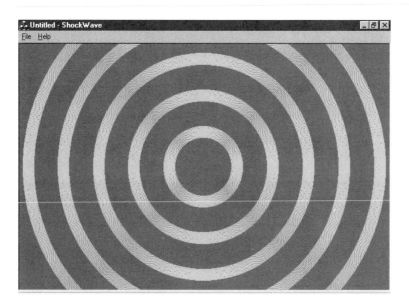

**Figure 11-11.** *The ShockWave example program.*

## Developing ShockWave

ShockWave is an MFC application created with the help of AppWizard. You can set up the project from the build files in the Code\Chapter.11\ ShockWav subfolder copied from the companion CD. The files in this subfolder contain the flawed source code; the corrected version of the program is in the Shock_OK folder. You can also develop ShockWave yourself by following these six steps. The program is simple enough that only its view class requires editing, so developing the project from the ground up is an interesting exercise that does not require an unreasonable amount of typing.

### Step 1: Run AppWizard to create the ShockWave project

Click New on Visual C++'s File menu, select the MFC AppWizard (exe) icon in the Projects tab, and type *ShockWave* as the project name. Click OK to run AppWizard and create the new ShockWave project. When specifying the project options, select the Single Document radio button in

AppWizard's Step 1 and disable the docking toolbar, initial status bar, and print support in Step 4.

The names of the source files that AppWizard creates differ slightly from those on the CD, which are restricted to eight letters or fewer to accommodate older text editors that do not recognize long filenames. Although the filenames differ, the source code in the files matches exactly the code described in these six steps.

### Step 2: Revise ShockWave's menus

ShockWave requires only a menu command to exit the program and so does not need the other commands that AppWizard adds to the menu resource. Using the Visual C++ menu editor, revise ShockWave's menus so that it has only a File menu and a Help menu that look like this:

### Step 3: Add message-handler functions using ClassWizard

ShockWave sizes the wave pattern to fill the client window, accommodating changes in the window size. It also centers new wave patterns on mouse clicks within the client area. To respond to these events, Shock-Wave traps WM_SIZE and WM_LBUTTONDOWN messages with handler functions named *OnSize* and *OnLButtonDown*.

Add these handler functions to the *CShockWaveView* class by clicking the ClassWizard command on the View menu. In the Message Maps tab, set *CShockWaveView* as the class name and select WM_SIZE in the Messages box. Click the Add Function button to automatically create the *OnSize* function, which handles the WM_SIZE message. Do the same for the WM_LBUTTONDOWN message to add the *OnLButtonDown* function, as shown in Figure 11-12 on the next page. We'll add code to the handler functions shortly. Close the ClassWizard dialog before proceeding to the next step.

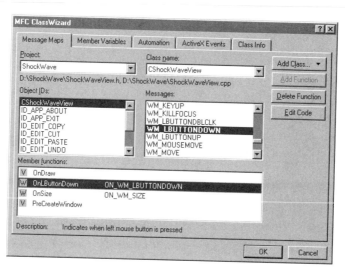

**Figure 11-12.** *Creating the* OnSize *and* OnLButtonDown *handler functions in ClassWizard.*

### Step 4: Edit the ShockWaveView.h file

Open the ShockWaveView.h file in the text editor and locate the *CShock-WaveView* class declaration. (On the companion CD, the file is named ShockVw.h.) Add the shaded lines of code shown here:

```
// ShockWaveView.h : interface of the CShockWaveView class
//
//////////////////////////////////////////////////////////////////////

#define     NUM_COLORS  6
#define     RED         0
#define     GREEN       1
#define     BLUE        2
#define     CYAN        3
#define     MAGENTA     4
#define     GRAY        5

class CShockWaveView : public CView
{
private:
    CPoint      center;
    CRect       rectClient;
    COLORREF    rgb[NUM_COLORS];
    int         iColor;

protected:                      // create from serialization only
    CShockWaveView();
```

```
DECLARE_DYNCREATE(CShockWaveView)
    ⋮
```

### Step 5: Edit the ShockWaveView.cpp file

The ShockWaveView.cpp file (or ShockVw.cpp on the CD) contains all the implementation details for the *CShockWaveView* class. It requires some additions as well, shown here in shaded lines. The WizardBar provides a convenient way to open the file in the text editor. Because the text editor currently displays the class's header file, clicking the wand icon on the WizardBar opens the implementation CPP file. You can immediately return to the header file by clicking the same tool.

The following listing shows source code for the entire ShockWaveView.cpp file. I've interspersed commentary after each important function to explain what is happening.

```
// ShockWaveView.cpp : implementation of the CShockWaveView class
//

#include "stdafx.h"
#include "ShockWave.h"

#include "ShockWaveDoc.h"
#include "ShockWaveView.h"
#include <math.h>

#ifdef _DEBUG
#define new DEBUG_NEW
#undef THIS_FILE
static char THIS_FILE[] = __FILE__;
#endif

/////////////////////////////////////////////////////////////////////
// CShockWaveView

IMPLEMENT_DYNCREATE(CShockWaveView, CView)

BEGIN_MESSAGE_MAP(CShockWaveView, CView)
    //{{AFX_MSG_MAP(CShockWaveView)
    ON_WM_SIZE()
    ON_WM_LBUTTONDOWN()
    //}}AFX_MSG_MAP
END_MESSAGE_MAP()
```

```
/////////////////////////////////////////////////////////////////////
// CShockWaveView construction/destruction

CShockWaveView::CShockWaveView()
{
    SYSTEMTIME st;
    ::GetSystemTime( &st );
    srand( (int) st.wMilliseconds );        // Seed the random number

    rgb[0] = RGB( 128,   0,   0 );          // Red
    rgb[1] = RGB(   0, 128,   0 );          // Green
    rgb[2] = RGB(   0,   0, 128 );          // Blue
    rgb[3] = RGB(   0, 128, 128 );          // Cyan
    rgb[4] = RGB( 128,   0, 128 );          // Magenta
    rgb[5] = RGB( 128, 128, 128 );          // Gray

    iColor = 1;                             // Start with Green
}

CShockWaveView::~CShockWaveView()
{
}
```

The *CShockWaveView* constructor initializes the *rgb* array with COLOR-REF values for six colors. ShockWave randomly selects one of these colors when displaying a shock wave pattern. The variable *iColor* holds an index value for *rgb* that determines which of the colors the program uses to paint the shock waves.

The constructor calls the Windows API function *GetSystemTime* to retrieve the millisecond component of the current system time. This value, which ranges from 0 through 999, provides a convenient seed value for the *srand* function, the C run-time random number generator.

```
BOOL CShockWaveView::PreCreateWindow(CREATESTRUCT& cs)
{
    HCURSOR hCur = ::LoadCursor( NULL, IDC_CROSS );

    cs.lpszClass = AfxRegisterWndClass( CS_HREDRAW | CS_VREDRAW,
                                        hCur, NULL );
    ::DeleteObject( hCur );

    return TRUE;
}
```

ShockWave displays the mouse cursor as crosshairs rather than the normal arrow shape. This slight refinement conveys more clearly to the user the idea of targeting some point in the client area with the mouse cursor and then clicking it. ShockWave uses the click coordinates as the center for the next wave pattern. To change the window cursor shape, *CShockWaveView* overrides the virtual function *PreCreateWindow*. The MFC framework calls *PreCreateWindow* just before it creates the program's main window, passing the function a pointer to a CREATESTRUCT structure. The structure contains the settings that MFC plans to use for the window. Overriding *PreCreateWindow* gives a program the opportunity to modify any of the window's characteristics, such as its cursor shape, before MFC creates the window.

In *CShockWaveView*'s implementation, *PreCreateWindow* first loads the standard Windows crosshairs cursor shape, which has an identification value of IDC_CROSS. The function then registers a new window class, assigning it the crosshairs cursor and a background brush with a value of NULL. A NULL background color signals the operating system that it should not repaint the window background when it resizes the window. Because the window's color changes randomly with each new shock wave, ShockWave itself takes on the responsibility of painting the background.

You might recall that the Color example program presented in Chapter 5 also paints its own background. The Color program does not adjust the window creation flags as does ShockWave, but instead traps the WM_ ERASEBKGND message to prevent the operating system from painting the window. The two programs demonstrate different techniques that achieve the same result.

```
///////////////////////////////////////////////////////////////////////
// CShockWaveView drawing

#define PI          3.1415926
#define NUM_RINGS 5

void CShockWaveView::OnDraw(CDC* pDC)
{
    CPen        pen;
    CRect       rect;
```

```
COLORREF   color;
int        i, j, iPeriod;
double     Angle;

// Set up coordinate system for largest wave

i = min( rectClient.right, rectClient.bottom );    // i = diameter
pDC->SetMapMode( MM_ISOTROPIC );
pDC->SetWindowExt( i, i );
pDC->SetViewportExt( rectClient.right, -rectClient.bottom );
pDC->SetViewportOrg( center.x, center.y );

i = max( rectClient.right, rectClient.bottom )/2; // i = radius
rect.SetRect( -i, -i, i, i );
iPeriod = i/(2*NUM_RINGS);

// Two loops: loop 1 displays one wave per iteration
//            loop 2 draws one color gradation per iteration

for (j=0; j < NUM_RINGS; j++)
{
    for (Angle=0.0, i=1; i < iPeriod; i++)
    {
        Angle += PI/iPeriod;
        color  = 128 + (DWORD)(128.0 * sin( Angle ));
        if (color > 255)
            color = 255;

        switch (iColor)
        {
            case GREEN:
                color <<= 8;
                break;

            case BLUE:
                color <<= 16;
                break;

            case CYAN:
                color = RGB( 0, (int) color, (int) color );
                break;

            case MAGENTA:
                color = RGB( (int) color, 0, (int) color );
                break;

            case GRAY:
                color = RGB( (int) color, (int) color,
```

```
                                       (int) color );
                 break;
        }

        rect.InflateRect( -1, -1 );
        pen.CreatePen( PS_SOLID, 1, color );
        pDC->SelectObject( &pen );
        pDC->Ellipse( rect );
        pDC->SelectStockObject( BLACK_PEN );
        pen.DeleteObject();
    }

    rect.InflateRect( -iPeriod, -iPeriod );
  }
}
```

The *OnDraw* function takes on the entire task of displaying a wave pattern. It draws each wave in a series of thin concentric circles, each circle one pixel wide, beginning at the outer edge of a wave and working toward the center. (For this reason, the wave pattern seems to implode rather than explode as it appears on the screen.) For each pixel-wide circle, the code slightly increases or decreases the intensity (brightness) of the current color. The resulting gradations of intensity give the waves their distinctive three-dimensional appearance.

The function draws the wave pattern in two loops, one nested inside the other. The outer loop repeats five times, drawing a complete wave at each iteration. The inner loop draws a pixel-wide circle at each iteration, continuing until it has drawn enough circles to form an entire wave. For each circle, the inner loop creates a new device context pen that adopts the current color indexed by *iColor*, slightly adjusting the color's intensity. A single line of code varies the intensity at each iteration from a medium brightness value of 128 through a maximum value of 255:

```
color = 128 + (DWORD)(128.0 * sin( Angle ));
```

Since the window background color has an intensity value of 128, each wave seems to rise up out of the background as a sinusoidal curve.

```
//////////////////////////////////////////////////////////////////
// CShockWaveView message handlers

void CShockWaveView::OnSize(UINT nType, int cx, int cy)
```

```
    {
        CView::OnSize(nType, cx, cy);

        rectClient.SetRect( 0, 0, cx, cy );
        center.x = cx/2;                              // Center of shock wave
        center.y = cy/2;
    }

void CShockWaveView::OnLButtonDown(UINT nFlags, CPoint point)
    {
        CView::OnLButtonDown(nFlags, point);

        center = point;
        iColor = rand();
        Invalidate( FALSE );
    }
```

Step 3 of this exercise used ClassWizard to add handler functions for the WM_SIZE and WM_LBUTTONDOWN messages. Here we add code to the stub functions that ClassWizard created.

When the window size changes, the *OnSize* handler centers the wave pattern in the client window and records the new window dimensions in *rectClient*. The *OnDraw* function later uses these dimensions to ensure the wave pattern fills the window. The *OnLButtonDown* function records the coordinates of a mouse click within the client area, which determines the center of the next wave pattern. The function also randomly selects a new color from the six available in the *rgb* array and calls *Invalidate* so that the window repaints itself with the new wave pattern.

### Step 6: Build and run the ShockWave.exe program

Make sure that the Build toolbar shows Win32 Debug as the current program configuration:

Click the Build button on the toolbar (or choose the command from the Build menu) to create a debug version of ShockWave, and then click the Execute command to run the program.

## Debugging ShockWave

The first bug is obvious (though not fatal) when you first run ShockWave. The client window seems to be transparent, allowing toolbars and text in Visual C++ to appear inside ShockWave's window. You probably already see what's wrong, but let's step through the program with the debugger anyway to clearly identify the cause of the problem. Close the ailing ShockWave program using its Exit command.

To begin debugging, use the text editor to look at the ShockWaveView.cpp (or ShockVw.cpp) document. The bug most likely arises somewhere in the view class because it contains the only part of the source code that required extensive alterations. Since something is wrong with ShockWave's window, we should suspect at the outset both the *PreCreateWindow* and *OnDraw* functions, the two functions revised earlier in Step 5 of this exercise. The first function sets the window characteristics; the second function draws the window contents.

Click the Breakpoints command on the Edit menu and type *CShockWave-View::PreCreateWindow* in the Location tab of the Breakpoints dialog. Press Enter and type *CShockWaveView::OnDraw* in the same place. This sets a location breakpoint at the start of each suspect function. Click the OK button to return to the editor.

Now press F5 to start the debugger. Disk activity indicates that Visual C++ is launching the debugger, which in turn runs ShockWave.exe. The debugger source window then appears with the instruction arrow pointing at the first line of the *CShockWaveView::PreCreateWindow* function. The ShockWave program has halted at the first of the two location breakpoints we set. The Visual C++ window now looks something like Figure 11-13 on the next page.

### Inside the *PreCreateWindow* function

Click the Variables tool on the Debug toolbar shown in Figure 11-13 to expose the Variables window. The Variables window lists the variables referenced by the last executed line, which in this case means the single argument *cs* accessed by the function prologue. The *cs* argument points to the CREATESTRUCT structure that MFC will use to create the ShockWave window. Clicking the small plus (+) button adjacent to the *cs* name in the

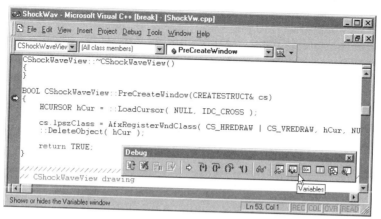

**Figure 11-13.** *The ShockWave program stopped at a breakpoint in the Visual C++ debugger.*

Variables window expands the list to show member variables of the structure.

You can make the Name column wider in the Variables window if some of the names are too long to fit in the column. Place the mouse cursor on the divider between the two column labels, just to the left of the Value label, and drag the divider right or left to resize the columns. Double-clicking the divider adjusts the column width automatically to accommodate the longest name in the column:

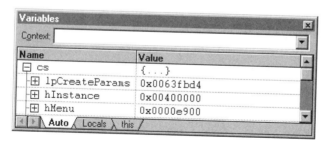

Press the F10 key or click the Step Over tool button to execute the function prolog code. The pointer stops at the next line in the *PreCreate-Window* function:

```
HCURSOR hCur = ::LoadCursor( NULL, IDC_CROSS );
```

The Variables window now includes the current value of *hCur*, but because the instruction has not yet executed, the value shown in the window is meaningless. Execute the instruction by stepping over it, giving *hCur* the value returned by the *LoadCursor* API function. The new value appears in red to indicate the last instruction has changed the value of *hCur*. The color coding is a nice feature of some debugger windows, letting you quickly see which of the listed variable values the instruction has changed.

Press F10 again to execute the call to *AfxRegisterWndClass*:

```
cs.lpszClass = AfxRegisterWndClass( CS_HREDRAW | CS_VREDRAW, hCur, NULL );
```

The Variables window shows that *cs.lpszClass* now points to a valid class name—something like *Afx:400000:3:13ce:0:0*—assigned by the MFC framework. The new value for *cs.lpszClass* affirms that *AfxRegisterWndClass* has executed correctly. This is no surprise; because the operating system creates ShockWave's window correctly, the class must be properly registered. Window drawing, not window creation, is the problem, so the error must occur in the *OnDraw* function. Let's move on to the next breakpoint by pressing the F5 key or by choosing Go from the Debug menu. As you do so, watch the screen carefully.

### Inside the *OnDraw* function

Execution continues briefly until the program flow reaches the next breakpoint, which we set earlier at the *OnDraw* function. In getting to this point of the program, you probably saw ShockWave's window flicker into existence and then disappear. The ShockWave window still exists, but in regaining control the debugger windows have overwritten it. You can expose ShockWave's window by minimizing Visual C++. Notice that ShockWave is completely inactive; it doesn't even have a menu bar yet. Control at this point belongs to the debugger.

Return to the debugger and press F10 repeatedly to single-step over the data declarations down to this section of code:

```
pDC->SetMapMode( MM_ISOTROPIC );
pDC->SetWindowExt( i, i );
pDC->SetViewportExt( rectClient.right, -rectClient.bottom );
pDC->SetViewportOrg( center.x, center.y );
```

The first line sets the mapping mode to MM_ISOTROPIC, ensuring the waves appear on the screen as circles, not as ellipses. The next two lines of the fragment set the window extent and viewport extent to cover Shock-Wave's entire client area. The last line sets the viewport origin at the center of the window. Like many MFC functions, these *CDC* member functions return a positive value when successful, or return NULL to indicate a problem. It would be amazing if these functions failed, so they do not warrant cluttering up the program with additional code to check return values. Even though ShockWave does not store the function return values, you can view the values in the Variables window to make sure the functions execute correctly. As you step over each function, the window displays a return value like this:

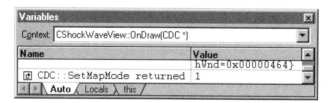

If a function returns an error code when you step over it, the debugger can translate the return value for you into a meaningful message. In the Watch window, double-click the dotted entry box in the Name column and type *err,hr*. In determining the value for this entry, the debugger calls the *GetLastError* API function and converts the results into helpful text such as "The handle is invalid."

The Registers window provides yet another way to check function return values. On Intel-based processors, a Win32 function that returns a value places it in the EAX register just before exiting. (64-bit return values occupy the EDX:EAX register pair.) To check a function's return value, just glance at EAX in the Registers window immediately after stepping over the function call. Like the Variables window, the Registers window displays new values in red, indicating which registers the last instruction has changed. Since none of the above functions returns a zero value, we know that this section of the code executes correctly. At this point, ShockWave is poised at the start of the two loops that draw the wave pattern.

But something is missing. The program should not draw the circular waves yet because the background of ShockWave's client area still remains unpainted.

Recall that the *PreCreateWindow* function revised in Step 5 on page 549 instructs Windows not to repaint ShockWave's background. That was the purpose of the NULL brush value given to *AfxRegisterWndClass* when registering the window class. So as requested, Windows correctly creates the window without filling in the client area. The trouble is, ShockWave does not keep its side of the bargain. Someone has to repaint the window background—if not the system, then ShockWave itself must do it. There's the solution for the first bug: ShockWave needs to paint the window background before drawing the wave pattern.

We have the choice here of correcting the source code and resuming execution through Edit and Continue, but exposing the Call Stack window shows that the *OnDraw* function is the last in line of several nested function calls that wind through both the kernel and the MFC framework. This means that any corrections won't take effect immediately but only when the function next executes. For our purposes, it's just as easy to stop the debugger and return to the editor.

This brings to light an interesting situation. You might assume that continuing with ShockWave's execution would be a prudent way to stop debugging. We could exit ShockWave normally using its Exit command and the debugger would stop, returning us to the text editor. Well, try it. Press F5 to continue running ShockWave.

You can never reach ShockWave's menu this way because each time you press the F5 key, ShockWave's window appears only briefly before you are dropped right back at the breakpoint in the *CShockWaveView::OnDraw* function. It's not difficult to see what is happening. When Shock-Wave regains focus, it must appear on top of Visual C++ and any other windows on the screen. Windows sends ShockWave a WM_PAINT message telling it to repaint itself. But in repainting, the framework calls ShockWave's *OnDraw* function, triggering the breakpoint. The debugger then gets the focus and Visual C++ displays itself right over ShockWave's window. Every time you press F5 to continue executing ShockWave, the process repeats in a never-ending cycle. You can break the cycle by removing or disabling the breakpoint before pressing the F5 key, but the Stop Debugging button on the Debug toolbar (or its equivalent command on the Debug menu) provides a better way to terminate the debugger:

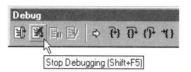

The command returns you to the editor, leaving all breakpoints in place.

### Revising and rebuilding ShockWave

Painting the window background does not require much code. In the text editor, add the lines shown in gray so that the *OnDraw* function looks like this:

```
void CShockWaveView::OnDraw(CDC* pDC)
{
    CPen     pen;
    CRect    rect;
    COLORREF color;
    int      i, j, iPeriod;
    double   Angle;
    CBrush   brush;

    // Paint client area with current color

    brush.CreateSolidBrush( rgb[iColor] );
    pDC->FillRect( rectClient, &brush );
    pDC->SelectStockObject( NULL_BRUSH );
    brush.DeleteObject();
    ⋮
```

The grayed lines allocate a brush with the current color indexed by *iColor*, paint the client area with it, and then destroy the brush. With the new code in place, build a debug version of ShockWave again and run it using the Execute command on the Build menu. It should appear correctly this time, its background painted with a medium intensity of green.

### The second bug

ShockWave still has another bug in it. This bug is more interesting than the first one because it demonstrates how Visual C++ lets you find program errors even when the debugger is not active. To see the second bug, click the mouse anywhere in the ShockWave window. According to the program design, this action should clear the window, repaint it with one of the six available colors, and redraw the wave pattern centered on the coordinates of the mouse click. You may have to click several times, but eventually Windows displays this message:

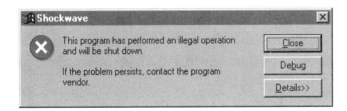

Somewhere ShockWave has tried to access memory that doesn't belong to it. When this happens to a release version of a program, you have no choice but to click the Close button to terminate the program, build an equivalent debug version, launch the debugger again, and hope you can recreate the error. But the above message gives you another option. If you click the Debug button, Windows automatically starts the debugger for you, even if Visual C++ is not currently running. Better yet, you find yourself looking at the ShockWave program as it exists immediately after the error. No need to guess which line caused the protection fault—the yellow instruction pointer arrow is pointing to it. Microsoft calls this feature Just-in-time debugging.

According to the source window, the program crashed at the first instruction of the *CShockWaveView::OnDraw* function:

```
brush.CreateSolidBrush( rgb[iColor] );
```

This is one of the lines we just added; it creates a brush that *OnDraw* uses to paint the background of ShockWave's client window. The variable *iColor* holds an index for the *rgb* array, which is declared in ShockWave-View.h as shown on the next page.

```
#define      NUM_COLORS   6
 ⋮
COLORREF     rgb[NUM_COLORS];
```

The current value of *iColor* thus determines the color used for the background brush. Take a look at *iColor* in the Variables window. It should have a value of 6 or more, which means the current color for the brush is the *iColor*<sup>th</sup> element of the *rgb* array, which is....

There's the problem. Giving *iColor* a value greater than 5 means that the program attempts to access an element of the *rgb* array that does not exist, a sure recipe for a protection fault. We've found the error, but what's the cause? The *iColor* variable receives a value only in the *CShockWaveView:: OnLButtonDown* function, which executes when the system detects a mouse click in the client area:

```
void CShockWaveView::OnLButtonDown(UINT nFlags, CPoint point)
{
    CView::OnLButtonDown(nFlags, point);

    center = point;
    iColor = rand();
    Invalidate( FALSE );
}
```

The line

```
iColor = rand();
```

assigns *iColor* a random number retrieved from the *rand* function. This C run-time function returns a value from 0 through RAND_MAX, which the Stdlib.h header file defines as 0x7FFF, or 32,767. Whoops. No wonder *iColor* ends up with so high a value. We need to ensure that the value of *iColor* never exceeds the number of elements in the *rgb* array so that the *OnDraw* function accesses only valid color elements. You can limit the *iColor* value by replacing the faulty line with this one:

```
iColor = rand() % NUM_COLORS;
```

This cures the second bug by restricting *iColor* to a value from 0 through 5. If you rebuild ShockWave and execute it again through the Execute command, you will see the program run the way it was intended.

# Special Debugging Cases

Win32 programs cover a wide spectrum of tasks, and the simple examples described in this chapter almost certainly do not apply directly to your own programs. That's why I've tried to concentrate on technique rather than specifics. Have confidence that no matter how unusual or sophisticated your own Win32 application may be, the Visual C++ debugger can help you peer inside it.

Here are some tips on how to debug a program that employs advanced Win32 features. The Visual C++ debugger can intercept exceptions, handle applications with multiple threads, and debug ActiveX client and server applications, all before breakfast. The debugger can also run on one computer while controlling the program being debugged as it runs on a second computer.

## Debugging Exceptions

The C++ exception-handling facility allows programs to retain control when unexpected errors occur. When a function detects an error, it notifies the exception handler by invoking the **throw** keyword. The exception handler receives the notification using **catch**. If no catch handler exists for an exception, the debugger notifies you that the exception was not caught. C programs can also perform structured exception handling with the __**try** and __**except** statements rather than **throw** and **catch**.

The Exceptions dialog box shown in Figure 11-14 on the following page lets you specify how the debugger should handle each type of exception. Invoke the dialog by clicking the Exceptions command on the Debug menu. You can set one of two options, Stop Always or Stop If Not Handled, for each exception type that can occur in your program.

If you specify Stop If Not Handled for an exception, the debugger writes a message to the Output window when the exception occurs but does not halt the program or notify you with a dialog box unless the exception

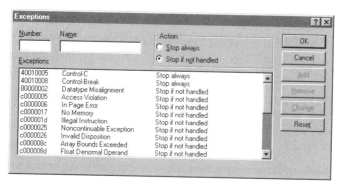

**Figure 11-14.** *The Exceptions dialog.*

handler fails to solve the exception. At that point, it is too late to fix the problem or examine the source code to see where the exception occurred, because the program has already thrown the exception and is executing the exception handler.

Specifying Stop Always for an exception gives you more control over the exception process. When the exception occurs, the debugger immediately stops the program, updates the source window to show the faulty instruction, and notifies you before the exception handler function gains control. In some cases, you can handle the exception yourself by modifying any erroneous variables in the Variables window. If you then press F5 to continue running the program, a dialog box appears asking if you want to pass the exception back to the program's exception handler function. If you fixed the problem, click the No button. Otherwise, click the Yes button to pass control to the exception handler. If the exception handler cannot fix the problem, the debugger halts the program and notifies you again as though you had selected Stop If Not Handled. Because the Stop Always option uses the processor's debug registers, the option is not available for debugging a program on processors that do not have debug registers.

The Exceptions list box shown in Figure 11-14 contains a default list of system exceptions. You can add or remove exceptions from the list, in which case Visual C++ saves the new list in the project's OPT file. The debugger treats any exception not in the list as a Stop If Not Handled exception. Each exception has a unique number. System exceptions are defined in the Winbase.h header file with the EXCEPTION prefix, such as EXCEPTION_ACCESS_VIOLATION.

To add a new exception to the Exceptions list box, invoke the Exceptions dialog and type the exception number in the Number control and the exception name in the Name control. Click either the Stop Always or Stop If Not Handled radio button and then click the Add button. To remove an exception, select it from the Exceptions list and click the Remove button. If you change your mind and want to restore all the deleted system exceptions, click Reset. If you change an option for an exception, such as its name, click the Change button to make the change permanent.

## Debugging Threads

A thread is a path of execution within a running application. Every application runs at least one thread, known as the main or root thread, which may in turn spawn other secondary threads. When debugging a program with multiple threads, you simply select which thread you want to debug and follow its flow of execution.

You can select a thread to debug only after the debugger has begun execution. First set a breakpoint at the desired location. When execution stops at the breakpoint, all threads that pass through the point are suspended. Click Threads on the Debug menu to invoke the Threads dialog, select the thread you want to follow from the list of threads, and click the Set Focus button. As you continue to single-step through the program, the debugger follows the thread that has focus. To prevent other threads from executing the same code, suspend them in the Threads dialog. You can later resume a suspended thread by selecting it in the same dialog and clicking the Resume button.

## Debugging Dynamic Link Libraries

Debugging a dynamic link library in Visual C++ is no different than debugging a normal application, except that the debugger launches the library's calling program and does not load the DLL file itself. The operating system takes care of loading the library when the calling application requires it; when control reaches a breakpoint in the library's code, execution of both caller and DLL is suspended. The only extra step in debugging a dynamic link library is identifying the calling application so that the debugger can execute it. Expose the Debug tab of the Project Settings dialog, invoked through the Settings command on the Project menu, and then type or browse for the path and filename of the calling application:

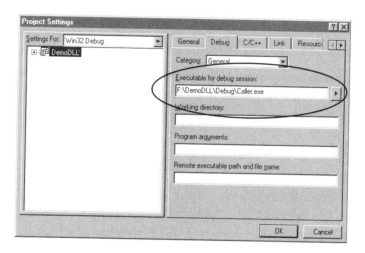

If you leave the Executable For Debug Session box clear, the debugger prompts for the filename when you begin debugging the dynamic link library. Online help recommends that you also select Additional DLLs in the Category box, double-click the blue entry box in the Local Name column, and browse for the DLL file you intend to debug. However, depending on path settings, the operating system may nevertheless fail to locate the DLL file when you begin debugging. You can avoid such problems simply by ignoring the Additional DLLs setting and placing a copy of the calling program's executable file in your project's Debug folder. Placing both caller and DLL in the same folder ensures that Windows can always load the DLL.

After setting breakpoints in the library source code, choose the Go command or press F5 to start the debugger. It makes no difference if the calling program is in debug or release form, but in the latter case Visual C++ displays a message informing you that the program has no symbol information. Because the DLL file is being debugged, not the calling program, this message is only a formality, reminding you that you will not be able to follow the flow of execution back into the calling program. Click the OK button to begin the debugging process.

## Debugging OLE/ActiveX Applications

Except for in-process servers such as ActiveX controls, COM works as a mechanism of remote procedure calls (RPCs) from one application to another. In general terms, the calling application is the client and the called application is the server. If you develop only a server or a client—one without the other—you usually care about only what happens on your side of the remote procedure call. In this case, there is nothing special about debugging an OLE/ActiveX application. For a client, just set a breakpoint at the call that accesses the server, run the debugger, and when the breakpoint activates, ensure that parameters are properly initialized. Then step over the call and check any return values. When debugging a server, set a breakpoint at the handler function that receives the remote procedure call and run the debugger to launch the server. Then switch to the calling application and initiate the call to the server. When you switch back to the debugger, the program should be interrupted at the breakpoint.

If you are developing both a client and server that work together, the Visual C++ debugger lets you debug on both sides of the remote procedure calls. Even if you develop the applications as separate projects, the debugger requires only one extra step. In both projects, choose Options from the Tools menu, then click the Debug tab and enable the OLE RPC Debugging check box. That's all there is to it, except that in Windows NT you must have administrator privileges to enable the check box.

As described in Part 4 of this book, an ActiveX control acts as a server dynamic link library that executes within the same address space as the container process using the control. Debugging an ActiveX control is no different than debugging a normal dynamic link library. An OLE/ActiveX server that executes as an application rather than as a DLL, however, runs in a different address space than the client, communicating across process boundaries through RPC. Visual C++ handles this situation by running two instances of the debugger, one for the client and the other for the server. There are two requirements when debugging on both sides of a remote procedure call, neither of them restrictive. First, you must enable the OLE RPC Debugging check box as explained above. And second, the server application must be local—that is, it must run on the same machine as the client. The Visual C++ debugger cannot launch a remote server that runs on a different machine, interfacing with the client through a network.

To debug the client application, follow its path of execution to the point where it calls the server. If you then step into the call, Visual C++ starts a second instance of the debugger, which loads the server source code if it's available. You can then step through the server as it responds to the remote call. When the server returns from the RPC, control is restored to the first debugger instance and you find yourself back in the client at the next instruction after the call. The second instance of the debugger does not terminate until you stop the server, so stepping again from the client into the server crosses the RPC bridge immediately, without your having to wait for a new debugger instance to launch.

You can also begin debugging from the server side, though you must manually start the client application yourself. Set a breakpoint at the location where you want to interrupt the server, then press F5 to start the debugger and launch the server. Switch to the client application and invoke the call, then switch back to the debugger to continue debugging the server. If you step out of the RPC handler function to enter the client application, Visual C++ launches a second instance of the debugger and attaches it to the executing client. Again, the new debugger instance does not terminate until you exit the client application, allowing you to continue debugging both client and server on opposite sides of a remote procedure call, regardless of which application you started debugging in.

## Debugging with Two Computers

A problem with debugging has always been that the debugger must compete for screen space with the program being debugged. As the program being debugged executes, it displays its output normally on the screen. But the debugger must also use the screen to interact with the user. DOS-based debuggers like CodeView had an effective solution to this problem. Because the debugger ran only in text mode, the programmer could attach to the system a separate monochrome monitor to display the debugger's source window, registers, and watch variables. Meanwhile, the program being debugged displayed normally on the EGA or VGA main system monitor. Two monitors often made the desktop a little crowded, but debugging was much simpler and more efficient.

This solution isn't possible under Windows because the debugger no longer runs in text mode. Both the debugger and the program it runs use the same video memory and, like any other Windows program, both must show their output in one or more windows. This means that when the running program is interrupted and the debugger gets control, the debugger's windows are apt to overlay any windows belonging to the program being debugged. We saw this happen when we were debugging the ShockWave program earlier in the chapter.

Like its CodeView ancestor, the Visual C++ debugger offers a solution that separates the competing displays, directing each to its own monitor. But instead of just a spare monochrome monitor, you need an entire extra computer capable of running your program and its host environment, either Windows 95 or Windows NT. (Power Macintosh is no longer supported.) The two computers must be linked through a network, because Visual C++ no longer supports debugging over a serial null modem connection. One computer serves as a host that displays the debugger's windows while the other computer, designated the remote or target computer, displays output from the program being debugged. Visual C++ calls this arrangement remote debugging.

Remote debugging is a three-step process:

1. Copy files to the remote computer.

2. Configure the host computer.

3. Configure the remote computer.

### Step 1: Copy files to the remote computer

Copy the files Msvcmon.exe, Msvcrt.dll, Tln0t.dll, Dm.dll, Msvcp60.dll, and Msdis110.dll to the Windows folder on the remote computer. If the program being debugged runs under Windows NT, also copy the PsAPI.dll file. These files operate the debugger's remote monitor program. The files are in the Common\MSDev98\Bin and VC98\Redist subfolders of your Visual C++ folder.

### Step 2: Configure the host computer

Configuring the host computer is a matter of telling Visual C++ where to find the program you wish to debug, the kind of remote machine it runs on, and the type of connection between the two machines. First, click Settings on the Project menu. In the Debug tab of the Project Settings dialog box, specify the full path to the program in the text box labeled Remote Executable Path And File Name. This is the path as viewed from the host computer on which the debugger is running. In the box labeled Remote Executable Path And File Name, enter the path to the program as the Msvcmon.exe program sees it from its position on the remote computer.

Next, choose Debugger Remote Connection from the Build menu to display the Remote Connection dialog. Select TCP/IP as the remote computer's connection type, then click the Settings button in the Remote Connection dialog. This displays another dialog that queries for communication settings, including the password of the remote computer.

### Step 3: Configure the remote computer

Run the Msvcmon.exe debugging monitor program on the remote computer. When the Visual C++ Debug Monitor dialog appears, click the Settings button and enter the same password as in the preceding step. Click OK to exit the dialog, then begin the debugger normally on the host machine.

# 12

# Compiler Optimization

The Microsoft Visual C++ compiler translates C and C++ source code into machine code. For a debug version of a program the translation is literal, producing a series of low-level machine instructions in the finished executable program that exactly represent the high-level instructions of the source. A release build gives the compiler much more latitude in which to work, because a literal translation of the source is not necessary nor even always desirable. The compiler has a different mission when creating a release build: to generate the smallest or the fastest object code it can without introducing new and unintended behavior into the program.

This chapter has two goals. The first is to acquaint you with the ways that Visual C++ optimizes code and handles various situations that can affect optimizations. Knowing some of the internal details about the process can help you work with rather than against the optimizer as you program, avoiding source code that is difficult or impossible for the compiler to improve through optimization. The second goal is to explain the many switches and options in Visual C++ that govern the optimization process so that you understand precisely how the compiler will behave when you turn a switch on or off.

To achieve these two goals, the chapter divides roughly into two parts. The first half presents an overview of compiler optimizations, explaining techniques and discussing their advantages and disadvantages. The second half connects the generalities of the first section with specific compiler switches in the Project Settings dialog. A final section puts optimization under the microscope, examining a sample of optimized code at the assembly level.

# An Optimization Primer

Discussions throughout this chapter are careful to distinguish between the qualities of speed and size, and some readers may wonder why there is a distinction at all. Isn't smaller code inherently faster? Intuition says so. So do advertisements, which promise products that are "lean and fast!" or "small and agile!" But in fact no strict correspondence exists between the size and speed of executable code, and an optimization that improves one quality may adversely affect the other.

There exist three levels of code optimization over which programmer and compiler share jurisdiction. The highest level, known as the algorithmic level, belongs to the programmer. A quick-sort algorithm, for example, easily outperforms a simple insertion-sort, and using a binary tree method to search a lookup table is much faster than simply scanning the table from top to bottom. Unfortunately, faster algorithms almost always require more code than simpler, more straightforward methods.

The lowest optimization level, called peephole optimization, belongs to the compiler. At this level the compiler takes advantage of machine-specific tricks to save a byte or clock cycle here and there, savings that become more significant when accumulated over an entire program. Peephole optimizations usually result in code that is both smaller and faster, though not always. For example, the Intel instruction

```
and     dword ptr [iVar], 0
```

is 3 bytes smaller but 3 times slower than

```
mov     dword ptr [iVar], 0
```

Yet both instructions write zero to the integer *iVar* equally well. On 80486 and Pentium processors, the instructions

```
push    1
pop     eax
```

take 3 bytes and 2 clock cycles—nearly half the size but only half the
speed of the equivalent instruction

```
mov     eax, 1
```

The middle level of optimization lies between the algorithmic and peephole levels. It covers traditional optimization techniques that have names
like subexpression elimination, copy propagation, and loop hoisting, all of
which are described in the next section. This middle level is often left to
the compiler, though the programmer is free to put a hand in. For example, the programmer may notice that two separate loops can function as a
single loop (a technique known as loop jamming) and rewrite the code
accordingly. Consider typical loops like these:

```
for (i=0; i < 10; i++)
    nArray1[i] = i;
for (j=0; j < 10; j++)
    nArray2[j] = j;
```

Jamming combines the loops into a single loop that does the same work,
saving the overhead of the second loop:

```
for (i=0; i < 10; i++)
{
    nArray1[i] = i;
    nArray2[i] = i;
}
```

Visual C++ does not recognize a chance to jam loops like this, so without
human intervention the opportunity to optimize would be passed over.

When deciding whether to optimize for speed or size, you should bear in
mind that while savings in speed are almost always measurable, they are
not always discernible. A wide gulf exists between what the computer
clock can measure and what the human mind can discern. Increased program speed that the end user cannot detect represents wasted effort.

Generally, only algorithmic optimizations result in noticeable improvements in execution speed. Lower levels of optimization usually don't save

the millions of clock cycles required for human detection unless applied to specific loops or functions that execute many hundreds of times. For this reason, a school of programming practice has evolved that dictates writing efficient algorithms at the source level and setting the compiler to optimize for size rather than for speed. Multitasking operating systems such as Windows especially encourage this practice. A program with a smaller memory image runs less risk of incurring page faults in conditions of crowded memory. Page faults, in which the operating system must reload memory from disk, are expensive operations. Put enough of them together and a program, no matter how highly optimized for speed, seems unresponsive and slow.

## Optimization Techniques

Visual C++ draws from a collection of optimization techniques, many of which have been used by compilers for decades. Table 12-1 lists the most important optimization techniques that Visual C++ employs and indicates whether the purpose of each is to reduce code size, increase code speed, or both. Because there are so many variables involved, it's sometimes difficult to accurately predict in advance the overall effect of an optimization technique. The table therefore reflects only the compiler's intentions, not necessarily the result. The best optimization settings for a particular program can often be determined only by trial and error.

Here we begin a series of short subsections that examine the 14 optimization methods listed in Table 12-1. Each subsection describes how an optimization works, when it is used, and what its advantages and disadvantages are.

### Use of processor registers

In the old days of C programming, good practice dictated using the **register** keyword to "enregister" one or two of a function's local variables. The register storage class represented a request from the programmer to the compiler to keep a local variable in a processor register, if one were available, rather than in memory allocated on the stack frame. Besides saving a small amount of stack space, keeping a variable in a register assures the fastest possible access to it because the processor reads and writes its own registers much faster than it reads and writes memory. Managing a

| Optimization | Reduce size | Increase speed |
|---|:---:|:---:|
| Use of processor registers | ✓ | ✓ |
| Constant propagation and copy propagation | ✓ | ✓ |
| Elimination of dead code and dead store | ✓ | ✓ |
| Common subexpression elimination | ✓ | ✓ |
| Loop optimizations | ✓ | ✓ |
| Instruction scheduling | | ✓ |
| Strength reduction | ✓ | ✓ |
| Inline expansion | ✓ | ✓ |
| String pooling | ✓ | |
| Frame pointer omission | ✓ | ✓ |
| Disable stack checking | ✓ | ✓ |
| Stack overlays | ✓ | ✓ |
| Assume no aliasing | ✓ | ✓ |
| Function-level linking | ✓ | |

**Table 12-1.** *Optimization techniques of the Visual C++ compiler.*

variable in a register instead of memory can also result in a slight decrease in code size.

Today one rarely sees **register** used anymore because an optimizing compiler like Visual C++ handles the task automatically. (In fact, Visual C++ ignores the **register** keyword.) Nearly any data object is a candidate for enregistering, such as global and local variables, constant values, structure elements, and function arguments, including pointers to arguments passed by reference. The compiler scans a function to determine how it uses its data, assigning each variable a score that represents the benefit derived from storing the variable in a register. When writing the function's object code, the compiler places the highest-scoring variables in registers whenever it can. The result is increased execution speed that under the right circumstances can be significant.

Registers are a very scarce commodity, and the compiler must make intelligent decisions in determining when to use a register to store a variable.

Optimized code spends part of its time juggling data between registers and memory. The code can free a register by writing its contents to the variable's home memory address, but the optimizing compiler must first decide whether the memory access is worthwhile. Freeing a register only to later reload it again with the same value might not pay for itself if it makes the register available only for a short section of code.

## Constant propagation and copy propagation

A guiding principle in code optimization is that registers are faster than constants and constants are faster than memory. If not enough registers are available to contain all the variables in a section of code, replacing an expression with a constant serves as the next best alternative. The compiler has an opportunity to use constants when it encounters constant propagation, in which an assigned constant value is forwarded or propagated through the code. The compiler can optimize the code by replacing expressions that evaluate to a constant value with the value itself. For example, the lines

```
x = 255;
y = x;
```

are better expressed as

```
x = 255;
y = 255;
```

By rewriting the second line with a constant value, the compiler saves an unnecessary memory access. Though the optimization technique itself is often referred to as "propagation," the term more correctly describes the condition that the optimization is meant to fix.

Copy propagation is similar to constant propagation. Copy propagation occurs when a single value is forwarded from one variable to another in a series of assignments in which the intermediate assignees do not use the value except to pass it on to the next variable. It's more efficient to simply assign the value directly to the last variable in the series and skip the others. Here's an example in which removing the copy propagation renders a statement unnecessary. The compiler makes a simple substitution, turning this code sequence:

```
i = nParam;
Function( i );
i = j;
```

into this:

```
i = nParam;
Function( nParam );
i = j;
```

In this fragment, the value *nParam* propagates through *i* to become the parameter of *Function*. But since *i* never uses the value *nParam*, the copy propagation is not necessary. The compiler can safely substitute *nParam* as the function parameter. Because of this optimization, the first assignment statement now becomes useless "dead store," which is discussed next.

### Elimination of dead store and dead code

As we saw in the preceding example, copy propagation often leaves an intermediate assignment statement as dead store, a condition in which a program writes data to a variable without ever reading from it. When it recognizes a dead store assignment, the optimizing compiler simply skips over the instruction so that it does not become part of the object image. The original three instructions in the fragment, for example, are reduced to two instructions after the compiler eliminates the dead store:

```
Function( nParam );
i = j;
```

Opportunities to remove copy propagation and dead store often show up after the compiler has expanded a complicated macro.

Related to dead store is a condition known as dead code. Dead code is an instruction or a block of instructions that the processor cannot possibly reach when the program executes. Such inaccessible code is usually the by-product of a previous optimization. Since the compiler generates no object instructions for dead code or dead store, eliminating these conditions represents the perfect optimization.

### Common subexpression elimination

When the compiler recognizes that a series of subexpressions all reflect the same value, it computes the subexpression once and substitutes the result for all subexpressions in the series. For example, consider a fragment in which the subexpression y * z occurs twice:

```
x = y * z;
w = y * z;
```

By adding an assignment and replacing the two subexpressions with a variable, the compiler eliminates one of the two multiplication operations:

```
temp = y * z;
x = temp;
w = temp;
```

Depending on circumstances and whether the subexpression occurs often enough, the substitution may reduce the code size of the fragment; however, elimination of a common subexpression almost always results in greater speed.

## Loop optimizations

Optimizing inside a loop is particularly advantageous because any gain in speed is multiplied by the number of loop iterations. The optimizations described in the preceding paragraphs only get better when applied to code inside a loop, but there are other optimization techniques available to the compiler that are specific to loops. Perhaps the most common loop optimization technique is known as invariant code motion or hoisting— "hoisting" meaning to move code from inside a loop to the outside, and "invariant" referring to an expression that remains constant through all iterations of the loop. Here's a typical example of an invariant expression inside a loop:

```
for (i=0; i < 10; i++)
    nArray[i] = x + y;
```

By moving the invariant expression out of the loop, the compiler produces code that computes the expression only once instead of 10 times with no significant (if any) increase in code size:

```
temp = x + y;
for (i=0; i < 10; i++)
    nArray[i] = temp;
```

## Instruction scheduling

Superscalar processors like the Pentium series can execute two instructions simultaneously in twin pipelines, provided one instruction does not depend on the outcome of the other. A dependency leads to a condition called pipeline stall. By using instruction scheduling, also known as instruction ordering, the compiler prevents such dependencies by rearranging the order of machine instructions where possible. For example, consider three instructions labeled A, B, and C:

```
add    ax, iShort        ;Instruction A
movsx  ebx, ax           ;Instruction B
xor    ecx, ecx          ;Instruction C
```

Instructions A and B cannot execute simultaneously because B depends on the result of A—that is, before it can execute instruction B, the processor must know the value in register AX and the state of its sign bit. However, instruction C depends on neither A nor B. By reversing the order of instructions B and C, the compiler avoids the potential stall, allowing instructions A and C to execute simultaneously:

```
add    ax, iShort        ;Instruction A
xor    ecx, ecx          ;Instruction C
movsx  ebx, ax           ;Instruction B
```

Instruction scheduling has no effect on code size and benefits only programs that run on a superscalar processor. A discussion in the final section of the chapter has more to say about instruction scheduling.

## Strength reduction

Processors are fast at adding and subtracting but relatively slow at multiplication and division. The Pentium processor, for instance, can add two 32-bit registers in a single clock cycle, yet it needs 10 cycles to multiply and over 40 cycles to divide. When optimizing, the Visual C++ compiler looks for opportunities to reduce the arithmetic complexity or "strength" of an instruction without affecting the outcome of the calculation.

For example, the strength of an instruction that multiplies or divides by a power of 2 can be reduced by substituting an equivalent shift operation.

Assuming that $y$ is an unsigned integer, the compiler can better express the instruction

```
y = y/16;
```

like this:

```
y = y >> 4;
```

The replacement produces the same result as the original instruction because dividing a variable by 16 ($2^4$) has the same effect as shifting its bits four positions to the right. Shifting works in the other direction as well, so that multiplying an integer variable by $2^n$ is equivalent to shifting its bits left by $n$ positions.

The optimization is more impressive when viewed at the assembly level. Here's what the original instruction might look like when disassembled, with timings for each machine instruction listed as comments:

```
// Instructions for y = y/16;
mov     ecx, 16                  ; 1 cycle on a Pentium
mov     eax, dword ptr [y]       ; 1 cycle
cdq                              ; 3 cycles
idiv    ecx                      ;46 cycles
mov     dword ptr [y], eax       ; 1 cycle
                                 ;52 cycles total
```

Strength reduction replaces the lines with a single instruction:

```
// Instruction for y = y >> 4;
sar     dword ptr [y], 4         ; 3 cycles total
```

This example is purely academic in the case of the Visual C++ compiler. Replacing a multiply or a divide operation with an equivalent shift instruction is so obvious an improvement that Visual C++ makes the substitution even when optimizations are turned off.

## Inline expansion

There are several reasons why the act of calling a function slows the progress of a program's execution flow. Because the processor jumps to a new location in code, the list of upcoming instructions stored in the processor's instruction queue may no longer be valid. If the processor does not perform branch prediction (as does the Pentium), it must stall while the queue is flushed and the function's first instruction is retrieved from memory. Worse, the call may generate a series of memory writes as the function's parameters are pushed on the stack along with the processor's EIP register. (For a description of the EIP register, see the sidebar on page 520 in Chapter 11, The Debugger.) After the function finishes, the processor again stalls while the return address is popped from the stack back into the EIP register, the prefetch queue is flushed if necessary, and the next instruction that EIP points to is read from memory. In short, functions are expensive to get to and expensive to leave.

Inline expansion solves these problems but sometimes at a cost of increased code size. In this optimization technique, the compiler inserts the function code into the body of the program, replacing the function call with a copy of the function itself. A CALL machine instruction is never generated, allowing the processor to follow a sequential path of instructions without being deflected elsewhere. By following a sequential logic path, the processor can more accurately prefetch instructions, a savings that is more significant when the expansion occurs inside a loop.

It may seem surprising, but inline expansion often reduces a program's size. Inline expansion (also known as inlining) is most effective when applied to small functions, especially those with parameters that are constants or passed by reference rather than value. In such cases the compiler can dispense with whole sections of code that write parameter values to the stack. Inlining a function saves the expense of a prologue and epilogue section and the creation of a separate stack frame. Inlining also exposes a function's side effects—changes to a global variable, for instance—that otherwise would be invisible to the compiler. This permits more aggressive optimization than might be possible without inlining.

### String pooling
The compiler can determine when a program creates the same string more than once. String pooling is an optimization technique in which the compiler allocates data space only for the first string, and then repoints references to any duplicate strings to the first one.

### Frame pointer omission

Frame pointer omission is an optimization for Intel systems that saves the expense of prologue and epilogue code—a considerable savings for programs that have many functions. Without frame pointer omission, the compiler generates prologue code for each function that requires a stack frame, pointing the processor's EBP register to the top of the frame like this:

```
push    ebp                     ;Save EBP register
mov     ebp, esp                ;Point to top of frame
sub     esp, local_space        ;Allocate stack frame
```

When the function finishes, epilogue code destroys the frame:

```
mov     esp, ebp                ;Restore stack pointer
pop     ebp                     ;Restore EBP register
```

Used this way, the EBP register is called the frame pointer. Variables with automatic storage class are referenced in the stack frame through offsets relative to EBP. Using EBP as the frame pointer is an unnecessary legacy of older versions of Windows designed to run on the Intel 80286 processor. When frame pointer omission is in effect, the compiler references stack data relative to the ESP register instead of the EBP register. A function's prologue becomes a single instruction that adjusts the ESP stack pointer to create the stack frame:

```
sub     esp, local_space        ;Allocate stack frame
```

The epilogue dismantles the frame merely by adding *local_space* back to ESP. Better yet, frame pointer omission frees the EBP register for use in other optimizations. The disadvantage of frame pointer omission is that encoding a memory reference relative to ESP takes one byte more than the same reference relative to EBP.

### Disable stack checking

Stack checking in Win32 is not the same as in 16-bit environments. In 16-bit Windows, stack checking involves a call to a C run-time function known as a stack probe. Called at the beginning of every function in a program, the stack probe confirms that the stack has enough room to accommodate the function's automatic storage requirements. If sufficient stack space exists, the probe returns and the function continues. Otherwise, the probe alerts the developer that the function cannot execute because it would overrun the stack.

Win32 applications do not require this sort of stack testing because of a system service that prevents stack overflow. When a program (or thread) accesses memory near the bottom of its stack, the operating system assumes that stack space has become inadequate and responds by increasing the stack size. This puts more distance between the program's deepest access and the bottom of the stack. Although automatic stack resizing makes the old-style 16-bit stack probes obsolete, stack checking still serves a purpose in Win32 applications. To understand that purpose, it's necessary to examine how the system adds memory to the stack.

Stack space for an application or individual thread is committed in pages. The size of a page depends on the target system; for Intel, MIPS, and PowerPC systems, a page spans 4 KB. The operating system recognizes stack overruns only when an access "falls off the end" of the stack into an area called the guard page. The guard page is the last committed page of the stack. (Windows NT sets up a guard page slightly differently than Windows 95, but the effect is the same.) When the program accesses stack memory in the guard page, the system commits another page to increase the size of the stack, a process referred to as "growing" the stack. Figure 12-1 on the next page shows how the stack grows through pages committed by the operating system.

As Figure 12-1 illustrates, it's possible for an application to overreach the stack's guard page and attempt to dip into reserved memory. This can happen when a function allocates more than a page of stack for its local variables:

```
void BigLocal ( )
{
    char   chArray[3*4096];     // Allocate 3 pages (12 Kb) of stack
    chArray[12000] = -1;        // This assignment may fail

    ⋮

}
```

In this simple illustration, *chArray* consumes three pages (12 KB) of stack. The function allocates space for the automatic data by decrementing the

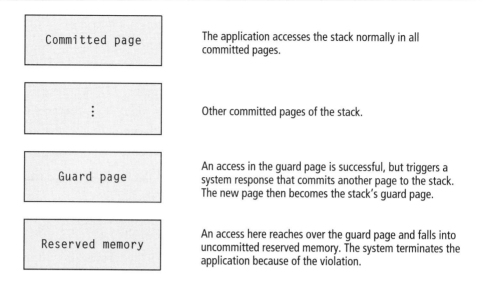

The application accesses the stack normally in all committed pages.

Other committed pages of the stack.

An access in the guard page is successful, but triggers a system response that commits another page to the stack. The new page then becomes the stack's guard page.

An access here reaches over the guard page and falls into uncommitted reserved memory. The system terminates the application because of the violation.

**Figure 12-1.**   *Growing an application's stack.*

processor's stack pointer ESP by the requested 12 KB, but this alone does not commit more stack. If the space allocated for *chArray* begins near the bottom of the stack, accessing a high element of *chArray* may reach over the stack's guard page into reserved memory. This triggers an access violation that the system solves by terminating the application.

Stack checking in Win32 prevents this type of scenario. When stack checking is enabled, the compiler computes the total size of each function's local data. Functions with local variables that consume less than a page of stack cannot overreach the guard page and so do not require stack checking. Each function with more than a page of automatic data, however, is preceded by a call to the stack check routine in the C run-time library. The stack check routine simply touches sequential pages of the stack—that is, it enters a loop that reads a byte on the stack at 4,096-byte increments. The cycle begins at the top of the stack and continues downward until the stack check routine has touched enough pages to fulfill the function's stack requirements.

A glance at Figure 12-1 shows how stack checking solves the problem of the *BigLocal* function. Before *BigLocal* gets control, the stack check routine touches the stack at pages 1, 2, and 3 below the top of the stack.

Assuming the allocation for *chArray* begins in the last committed page of the stack, the first touch accesses the guard page. The system responds by committing another page, making it the new guard page. The second iteration of the loop in the stack check routine touches the new guard page, causing the system to commit another page. The process repeats a third time, adding three pages to the stack before the stack check routine returns and *BigLocal* gets control. Now when *BigLocal* accesses an element near the end of *chArray*, the access falls into a committed page of the stack and does not trigger a fault.

So could *BigLocal* solve its own problem without the stack check? Absolutely. Simply by accessing elements such as *chArray[4000]* and *chArray[8000]* before *chArray[12000]*, the function takes care of committing the required memory and ensures that the stack is not overrun. Stack checking adds overhead to a program, and disabling it saves code and enhances speed for applications with large automatic storage demands. Such applications do not require stack checking as long as they access stack data in sequential pages working from the top of the stack toward the bottom.

### Stack overlays

The stack overlay optimization may or may not have a benefit. It depends on the extent of stack usage. By using stack overlays, the compiler reuses stack space to store local variables whose lives do not overlap. This means that if the last access of *x* occurs in a function before the first access of *y*, both *x* and *y* can safely occupy the same position of the stack frame.

By minimizing the depth of occupied stack, the compiler reduces the chance of a stack overrun when the program executes. Although the system response of growing the stack remains transparent to the user, the operation can take a lot of time. Stack overlays can also reduce a function's executable size by minimizing the distance between a local variable on the stack and the top of the stack frame. Recall that the function's frame pointer points to the top of the frame. If a local variable occupies a position on the stack less than 128 bytes from the frame pointer, encoding each reference to the variable uses three fewer bytes than if the offset is greater than 128 bytes.

```
mov   eax, [EBP + 4]        ;This instruction is 3 bytes smaller
mov   eax, [EBP + 256]      ;than this instruction
```

Any benefits derived from overlaying variables on the stack depend on circumstances—but then, stack overlays have no cost, either.

### Assume no aliasing

Aliasing means using more than one name to refer to a single memory object. Pointers and unions offer the programmer endless opportunities to alias, as shown in this typical example in which *c* and *\*cptr* refer to the same byte in memory:

```
char  c;
char  *cptr = &c;
```

Aliasing inhibits the compiler's ability to perform certain optimizations, such as enregistering variables. In this code fragment, for example, the compiler cannot safely store the variable *c* in a register if the possibility exists that the program will later write a new value to memory using *cptr* instead of *c*. If that happened, the value in the register would no longer be valid. The compiler can often successfully track the usage of *c* and *cptr*, however, and it may still enregister *c* when safe to do so despite the aliasing. (The *cptr* variable can be enregistered in any case.)

Aliasing can assume subtle forms that a compiler cannot identify. The following code illustrates a case in which two variables, *ptr1* and *ptr2*, both point to the same array. Yet the compiler does not recognize the alias because *ptr2* gets its value from another function outside the scope of *main*.

```
char  chArray[5];                    // Global scope

main ()
{
    char *ptr1 = chArray;            // ptr1 points to chArray
    char *ptr2 = GetPointer();       // So does ptr2
    ⋮
}
char * GetPointer (void)
{
    return chArray;
}
```

When conservatively optimized, the above example works correctly. Because the compiler cannot know the value of *ptr2* in advance, it allows for the possibility that both *ptr1* and *ptr2* might alias the same memory object, and so it performs no optimizations that involve either pointer. This assumption is certainly safe but may cause the compiler to pass up opportunities for legitimate optimization.

The Visual C++ compiler offers an Assume No Aliasing optimization switch that deals with situations like this. By using this switch, the programmer promises the compiler that variables have no hidden aliases, as in the case of *chArray* in the example. The switch gives the compiler permission to aggressively optimize code that involves pointers, unfettered by concerns of unseen aliasing.

Visual C++ also offers a less aggressive form of the Assume No Aliasing option, named Assume Aliasing Across Function Calls. This optimization switch tells the compiler to assume aliasing does not exist in the code except across a function call. The switch gives the compiler only qualified permission to optimize code involving pointers, but is better than no permission at all. A section later in the chapter discusses how the two optimization switches are often applied on a trial-and-error basis.

### Function-level linking

It's possible for a function to be optimized out of existence, either through inlining or because the compiler has figured out how to compile the program in such a way that the function is never called. The function must still be compiled and included in the object image, however, because the compiler has no way of determining whether other source modules access the function. Only the linker can recognize when a function remains unreferenced in a program. If the compiler writes an unreferenced function in "packaged" form, the linker omits it from the finished executable.

Function-level linking ensures that all functions in a source module are packaged—that is, identified in the object code by a COMDAT record. COMDAT records are in Common Object File Format (COFF) and contain information that allows the linker to recognize unreferenced functions and remove them from the executable image, a procedure called transitive

COMDAT elimination. Without a COMDAT record, an unreferenced function remains in the image after linking, taking up space.

# Optimization Switches

Now let's turn from generalities to specifics. This section connects what we've learned so far about compiler optimizations with the switches in Visual C++ that control the optimization process. The switches are contained in the Project Settings dialog shown in Figure 12-2, which is invoked using the Settings command on the Project menu. The Project Settings dialog is a rabbit warren of switches and options that affect the build process and the efficiency of the finished executable. This section concentrates on the dialog's C/C++ tab, which contains all of the switches that govern how (or if) the compiler optimizes a project's source files.

Default optimization settings depend on the build target. Visual C++ switches off optimizations when building a debug version, ensuring that the executable program is a literal translation of the source. For a release version, the compiler by default optimizes for speed, even at the expense of increasing code size. For many projects the default optimization settings are acceptable, and as example programs have demonstrated throughout this book, you can easily create and develop a project without ever entering the Project Settings dialog. But as we will see, there are good reasons why you may want to manually fine-tune a project's optimization settings.

Figure 12-2 shows that the left half of the Project Settings dialog contains a list of the project's source files, similar to the FileView pane of the Workspace window. Before setting an optimization switch, select either the project name at the top of the list or an individual file. To select a group of files, click the desired filenames while pressing the Ctrl key. The selection in the file list indicates to which file or group of files you want an optimization switch to apply. Selecting the project name makes an optimization setting universal for all source files; selecting individual modules allows you to optimize some for maximum speed, some for minimum size, and others with a mix of optimization criteria of your choice. The initial build target shown in the upper-left corner of the dialog

1. Select the entire project or individual source files.

2. Make sure the target is Win32 Release.

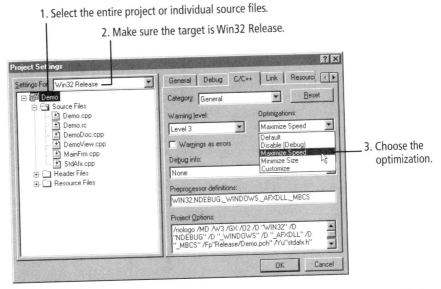

3. Choose the optimization.

**Figure 12-2.** *The quick way to choose an optimization goal in the Project Settings dialog.*

depends on the current active configuration for the project. The target should be Win32 Release when setting compiler optimizations. Selecting the target in the Project Settings dialog does not change the project's active configuration.

For even finer control over optimizations, insert the **optimize** pragma at key locations in your source code. This pragma sets compiler optimization switches for individual functions, overriding the current project settings. You can optimize the speed of a specific function, for example, while optimizing the rest of the source module for size. Refer to online help for more information about the **optimize** pragma.

The appearance of the C/C++ tab in the Project Settings dialog depends on the current selection in the Category box at the top of the dialog. Of the eight categories of compiler settings listed in the box, four categories contain all the switches that pertain to compiler optimizations:

■ **General category**—Convenient selections for a general optimization goal, but without fine control over individual optimization methods

- **Code Generation category**—Processor-specific optimizations and the project's default calling convention
- **Customize category**—String pooling and function-level linking
- **Optimizations category**—Fine-tuning for a project's optimizations

The Reset button appears in the C/C++ tab for all categories, and provides a convenient way to return to the compiler's default settings. When all switches are set to their defaults, the Reset button is disabled, becoming active only when you make a change in any category. Clicking the Reset button restores the defaults of all categories, not just the category that is visible.

## General Category

The General category lets you quickly choose from among several coarse-grained optimization settings named Default, Disable, Maximize Speed, Minimize Size, and Customize (Figure 12-2). Because the Disable setting represents the only way to completely suppress all compiler optimizations, it is used for debug builds. The Default setting clears all optimization switches including the Disable switch, which means that the compiler still performs some optimizations that favor faster code. (In a moment we'll see what favoring faster code entails.) The Default setting is therefore not very useful. Select the Customize setting only if you want manual control over switches for the string pooling and function-level linking optimizations. These switches appear in the Customize category, which is described shortly.

The most important optimization settings in the General category are Minimum Size and Maximize Speed. These switches serve as shortcuts that turn on most (but not all) of the available optimization techniques, letting you select an optimization goal without getting involved in details. Table 12-2 shows the specific optimizations enabled by the Maximize Speed and Minimize Size settings.

The Maximize Speed and Minimize Size settings are convenient but somewhat conservative. As Table 12-2 indicates, neither setting enables aliasing optimizations. (The Assume No Aliasing optimization is part of the Optimizations category.) Although the Maximize Speed setting

| Optimization | Minimize Size | Maximize Speed |
|---|:---:|:---:|
| Global optimizations | ✓ | ✓ |
| Generate intrinsic functions inline | | ✓ |
| Favor small code | ✓ | |
| Favor fast code | | ✓ |
| Frame pointer omission | ✓ | ✓ |
| Disable stack checking | ✓ | ✓ |
| String pooling | ✓ | ✓ |
| Function-level linking | ✓ | ✓ |

**Table 12-2.** *Optimizations enabled by the Maximize Speed and Minimize Size settings.*

includes optimizations for string pooling and function-level linking, these optimization techniques generally improve only code size, not speed.

We haven't yet encountered the first four entries in Table 12-2, so they may require a little explanation. "Global optimizations" is a catch-all term for certain compiler optimizations described in the first half of the chapter, such as peephole optimizations, use of processor registers, loop optimizations, strength reduction, and elimination of unneeded elements like dead store and dead code. The first eight compiler optimizations listed in Table 12-1 on page 575 fall under the umbrella of global optimizations.

Normally provided by the run-time libraries, the functions listed in Table 12-3 have special forms dubbed intrinsics. The compiler writes intrinsic

| | | | | | |
|---|---|---|---|---|---|
| *_disable* | *_lrotr* | *_strset* | *exp* | *memcp* | *strcat* |
| *_enable* | *_outp* | *abs* | *fabs* | *memcpy* | *strlen* |
| *_inp* | *_outpw* | *atan* | *labs* | *memset* | *strcmp* |
| *_inpw* | *_rotl* | *atan2* | *log* | *sin* | *strcpy* |
| *_lrotl* | *_rotr* | *cos* | *log10* | *sqrt* | *tan* |

**Table 12-3.** *Intrinsic run-time functions in Visual C++.*

functions inline—that is, without a function call—when you select the Maximize Speed option. Placing intrinsic functions inline can help increase program speed but can also result in a larger program size, depending on how heavily the program uses intrinsic functions. For example, the intrinsic form of the *strcpy* function occupies 41 bytes of code in an application running on an Intel processor. Calling the normal run-time version of the function takes at most 18 bytes, including the instructions to pass the two string pointers on the stack and the subsequent stack cleanup, which is handled by the caller. Using the run-time version of *strcpy* instead of its intrinsic form can result in a substantial reduction of code size for an application that makes heavy use of the function. The savings may seem less important when applied to only one or two calls.

In addition to inlining calls to the functions listed in Table 12-3, turning on the intrinsics optimization also speeds up calls to the *acos*, *asin*, *cosh*, *fmod*, *pow*, *sinh*, and *tanh* math library functions. Although these functions are not true intrinsics, the compiler optimizes their performance by writing code that places the function arguments directly in the floating-point chip instead of pushing them onto the stack. The result is less time spent inside the function but at the cost of slightly more code.

The Favor Small Code and Favor Fast Code optimizations influence the compiler's decision when it encounters certain code sequences that can be optimized to improve either speed or size, but not both. For example, consider an instruction that multiplies the variable $x$ by 71. Because the compiler cannot accomplish the multiplication through simple shifting, it has two valid choices when deciding how to translate the operation into machine code. Shown here with timings for a Pentium processor, the first choice is slower but requires less code:

```
// Instructions for x *= 71;
mov     eax, dword ptr [x]          ;          1 cycle      4 bytes
imul    eax, eax, 71                ;         10 cycles     3 bytes
mov     dword ptr [x], eax          ;          1 cycle      4 bytes
                                    ;Total: 12 cycles      11 bytes
```

The second choice uses an Intel-specific trick to avoid the expensive IMUL instruction, resulting in a faster but longer code sequence:

```
// Instructions for x *= 71;
mov    ecx, dword ptr [x]          ;           1 cycle    4 bytes
lea    eax, dword ptr [ecx+ecx*8]  ;           1 cycle    3 bytes
shl    eax, 3                      ;           1 cycle    3 bytes
sub    eax, ecx                    ;           1 cycle    2 bytes
mov    dword ptr [x], eax          ;           1 cycle    4 bytes
                                   ;Total:    5 cycles   16 bytes
```

Comparing the true speeds of two code fragments is often difficult because clock cycles rarely tell the whole story. Cycles measure only the time the processor spends executing an instruction, not the time required to read the instruction and any necessary data from memory into the processor. Although the second code sequence is clearly much faster than the first in terms of processing time, the net increase in speed may be less than that indicated strictly by the numbers. Because the second sequence is longer, the processor must spend more time accessing and decoding the extra bytes of code. This is less of an issue, however, if the sequence appears inside a loop, because after the loop's first iteration the processor thereafter pulls the code from its instruction cache instead of from memory.

When trying to decide which of the two sequences represents the faster code, consider another factor that further clouds the issue. The second sequence uses one more register than the first—a register that might otherwise be available to help optimize another part of the code. Trying to guess the overall effects of alternative optimizations is often a prickly path. Generally you're on safer ground when making assumptions about size rather than speed.

## Code Generation Category

Select Code Generation in the Category box to choose the options shown on the following page in Figure 12-3, which include:

- The type of processor to optimize for

- The default calling convention that the compiler should assume

- The type of run-time library the application uses

- The alignment of structure members

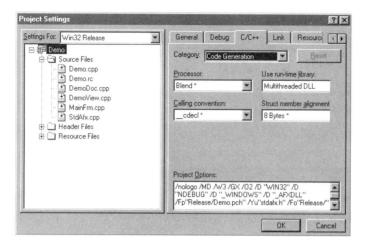

**Figure 12-3.** *Options in the Code Generation category.*

### Processor

The Processor box lets you select the level of Intel processor to optimize for. The default setting, named Blend, represents a compromise that is something of a moving target these days. In Visual C++ version 4, the Blend setting caused the compiler to optimize mainly for the Intel 80486, adding optimizations for the 80386 and Pentium processors that do not impede performance on the 80486. In versions 5 and 6 the Blend setting targets the Pentium, adding selected optimizations for the lower-level 80486 processor.

Regardless of the processor setting, the compiler generates only machine instructions recognizable to the 80386. This ensures that an optimized program can run on a lower-level processor even if compiled with the Pentium or Pentium Pro setting. In fact, the Pentium and Blend settings have the same effect.

### Calling convention

The selection in the Calling Convention box determines the default calling convention for the project or selected source files. The setting specifies only the default calling convention; any convention explicitly included in a function prototype overrides the default setting. The calling convention lays out the rules for both the caller and the function being called, specifying in what order parameters are pushed onto the stack, how external names are decorated, and who cleans up the stack when the function returns.

Visual C++ recognizes the **_cdecl**, **_fastcall**, and **_stdcall** calling conventions, which are named for the C keywords that specify a convention in a function declaration. The conventions are summarized here:

| Calling convention | Parameter order | Stack cleanup | Name decoration |
|---|---|---|---|
| **_cdecl** | Right to left | Caller | _function |
| **_fastcall** | Right to left | Called function | @function@nnn |
| **_stdcall** | Right to left | Called function | _function@nnn |

The rightmost column of the table describes how the function name appears in the object listing, where *function* represents the function name as it appears in the source and *nnn* represents the size of the parameter list in bytes. The name decoration schemes summarized in the table apply only to C programs and C++ functions declared with the **extern "C"** keywords. Without the keywords, C++ uses a different system of decoration (also known as name mangling).

The **_cdecl** setting specifies the C calling convention. This convention allows variable parameter lists because the caller takes on the responsibility of cleaning the stack after the function returns. Cleaning the stack after a function call requires only a single machine instruction to reset the stack pointer. This isn't much code, especially if the function takes a single parameter, in which case a 1-byte POP instruction serves to reset the pointer. But when multiplied by many function calls, instructions that clean the stack can nevertheless add a slight amount of overhead to a program.

The **_fastcall** convention improves the speed of calls to C functions that take at least one parameter. In this convention, the first two suitable values of a function's parameters are passed in processor registers. All other parameters are passed to the function by pushing them onto the stack in right to left order. Visual C++ uses the ECX and EDX registers to pass parameters for **_fastcall** functions on Intel systems. Although the ECX and EDX registers have been used for **_fastcall** since the days of C 7, Microsoft does not guarantee that future releases of Visual C++ will continue to use the same registers. (This caveat concerns only **_fastcall** functions that contain inline assembly code.) Besides enhancing execution speed, the **_fastcall** convention typically results in a small decrease in code size. The convention's only disadvantage is that it does not allow variable parameter lists.

The **_stdcall** convention is the calling convention used by the Windows API. When applied to functions that have a fixed parameter list, **_stdcall** is similar to **_fastcall** except that it does not pass parameters in registers. The convention helps reduce a program's code size because the responsibility of stack cleanup belongs to the called function instead of to the caller. Functions under both **_stdcall** and **_fastcall** efficiently clean the stack through a RET (return) instruction without having to explicitly adjust the ESP stack pointer register. The **_stdcall** convention also allows variable parameter lists for functions, in which case the call is implemented in the same way as **_cdecl**, forcing the caller to clean the stack.

### Run-time library

Selecting a proper run-time library can help reduce an application's code size, though usually there is no need to adjust the default setting. Don't misunderstand the meaning of the Multithreaded DLL and Debug Multi-threaded DLL settings. The "DLL" in the setting refers to the run-time library, not the project, and does not mean that the run time applies only to projects that create a dynamic link library. The Multithreaded DLL setting links the project to an import library for Msvcrt.dll, which is a redistributable dynamic link library that contains a thread-aware version of the C run-time library. Linking statically or dynamically with a run-time library involves the same considerations as linking statically or dynamically to the MFC library. Static linking makes the size of the executable file larger; dynamic linking makes code smaller but may require distribution of Msvcrt.dll with the finished application.

Table 12-4 summarizes the settings in the Use Run-Time Library box of the Code Generation category that specify a project's run-time library.

| Setting | Run-time library | Description |
|---|---|---|
| Single-Threaded | Libc.lib | Static link to library, single thread |
| Multithreaded | Libcmt.lib | Static link to library, multiple threads |
| Multithreaded DLL | Msvcrt.lib | Import library for Msvcrt.dll |
| Debug Single-Threaded | Libcd.lib | Static link, single thread (debug version) |
| Debug Multithreaded | Libcmtd.lib | Static link, multiple threads (debug version) |
| Debug Multithreaded DLL | Msvcrtd.lib | Import library for Msvcrtd.dll |

**Table 12-4.** *Settings in the Use Run-Time Library box that determine how a program attaches to the C run-time library.*

### Structure alignment

The final setting in the Code Generation category specifies the boundary on which structure and union members are aligned. After the first member of a structure, each following member falls on a memory boundary determined either by the size of the member or by the alignment setting, whichever is smallest. Setting a structure alignment value of 1 ensures that no memory is wasted in gaps between structure members, a technique known as packing the structure.

Packing can reduce stack usage for structures with automatic storage class, or reduce program size when applied to structures with static storage class. For packing to have any effect, however, a structure must contain at least one element that spans only 1 or 2 bytes placed before a larger multibyte element such as an integer. For example, consider the effect of packing on this simple structure:

```
struct s
{
    char ch;        // One-byte element
    int  i;         // Four-byte element
};
```

An alignment value of 4 or more wastes 3 bytes of memory between the two elements because the compiler places the element $i$ on a double-word boundary. An alignment value of 1, however, packs $i$ adjacent in memory to $ch$:

| Alignment = 4 | Alignment = 2 | Alignment = 1 |
|---|---|---|
| s.ch | s.ch | s.ch |
| | | s.i (byte 1) |
| | s.i (byte 1) | (byte 2) |
| | (byte 2) | (byte 3) |
| | | |
| s.i (byte 1) | (byte 3) | (byte 4) |
| (byte 2) | (byte 4) | |
| (byte 3) | | |
| (byte 4) | | |

While packing can reduce the size of a structure, the savings may not translate to an overall reduction in the size of a program's data area. It depends on the mix of elements in the structure and the data object that follows the structure in memory. If an integer appears in memory after the structure $s$, for example, the compiler aligns the integer on the next double-word boundary after $s.i$, thus wasting the bytes saved by packing the structure.

Structure packing can exact a cost in execution speed because the processor stalls when reading misaligned data from memory. Both the Intel 80486 and Pentium processors can fetch a 4-byte integer in a single memory reference cycle, provided the integer is aligned on a double-word boundary. If the integer lies offset from its optimum boundary, the processor must wait three additional cycles for the fetch. As shown in the preceding illustration, alignment settings of 1 or 2 may save space when storing the integer $s.i$, but the cost is a fourfold increase in access time when reading or writing the integer.

Structure packing can also lead to subtle problems for dynamic link libraries and component software such as ActiveX controls. If the library exports a function that either takes a structure as an argument or returns a pointer to a structure, both the calling application and the exported function must agree on the structure's alignment. A glance at the preceding diagram will convince you of the problems that can result when a calling application compiled with an alignment setting of 4 or higher attempts to pass structure *s* to a dynamic link library that has been compiled with an alignment setting of 1 or 2. When this happens, the caller and the library do not look to the same memory position for the integer *s.i.*

If your library passes a structure or a pointer to a structure, give some thought to the ramifications of packing. Visual Basic assumes structures align on WORD boundaries, so an alignment setting of 2 is necessary for a library and its Visual Basic callers to successfully share a structure. You should also consider using the **pack** pragma when declaring the structure in a header file, and then make the header file available to developers writing C/C++ applications that call your library. Compiling both library and calling application with the same header file ensures agreement on the structure's alignment, regardless of the selection in the Project Settings dialog:

```
#pragma pack( push, PACK_S )     // Save current alignment setting
#pragma pack( 2 )                // Word-align the structure
struct s
{
    char ch;
    int  i;
};
#pragma pack( pop, PACK_S )      // Restore original alignment
```

## Customize Category

The Customize category (Figure 12-4 on the next page) controls optimizations that enable function-level linking and the elimination of duplicate strings (string pooling). Both optimizations are an integral part of the Maximize Speed option. If you set Maximize Speed in the General category, the check boxes labeled Enable Function-Level Linking and Eliminate Duplicate Strings are disabled in the Customize category. This might seem to indicate that the optimizations are disabled as well, but that's not the case—selecting Maximize Speed turns on both optimizations. To enable

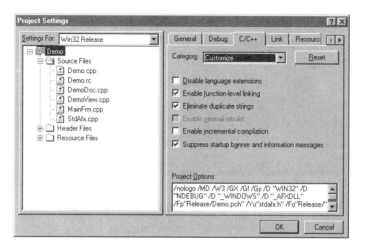

**Figure 12-4.**    *Options in the Customize category.*

the check boxes, first select Minimize Size or Customize in the General category, as described earlier.

Function-level linking applies only to packaged functions—that is, functions identified to the linker through a COMDAT record in the object listing. Inline member functions defined inside a C++ class declaration are automatically packaged, though other member functions are not. To compile all functions in packaged form, the Enable Function-Level Linking check box must be turned on (or left disabled if the Maximize Speed setting is selected).

## Optimizations Category

The Optimizations category offers finer control over the types of optimizations applied to a project, and also lets you specify whether the compiler should expand functions inline. The category displays the same optimization setting selected in the General category. The setting must be Customize to enable the check boxes shown in Figure 12-5, which allow you to choose from among a list of compiler optimizations. The Customize setting provides the only way to turn on the Assume No Aliasing optimization.

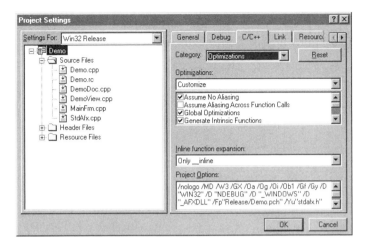

**Figure 12-5.** *Options in the Optimizations category.*

The last check box switch in the list, labeled Full Optimization, turns on a series of optimizations including inline expansion, intrinsic functions, favor fast code, no stack checking, and global optimizations. The list's only other check box that might need some explanation is labeled Improve Float Consistency. This switch is actually an optimization when turned off. At a cost of more code and slower floating-point operations, turning the switch on causes the compiler to take the following steps to reduce the chance of floating-point round-off errors:

■ Add instructions that copy data from memory to the floating-point registers before each floating-point operation. Although this slows the operation considerably, the result of the calculation is guaranteed to have no more precision than the data type can accommodate.

■ Disable the inline intrinsic form of run-time functions that perform floating-point calculations, which are listed in Table 12-3 on page 591. The program uses the standard run-time functions instead.

■ Disable other optimizations that may allow a calculation result to persist in the 80-bit precision of the floating-point processor.

These steps maintain the results of floating-point calculations in 32-bit or 64-bit precision and help ensure that two floating-point numbers can be tested for exact equality. However, even if you turn on the Improve Float

Consistency switch, it's still a good idea to allow a small tolerance when comparing numbers of **float** or **double** type, like this:

```
#define  TOLERANCE  0.00001

double  x = 2.0, y = sqrt( 4.0 );
if (x + TOLERANCE > y  &&  x - TOLERANCE < y)
{
    // x and y are equal
}
```

A combo box in the Optimizations category gives you a certain amount of control over how the compiler replaces function calls with equivalent inline code. The three choices are:

- **Only __inline**—Replaces only calls that target functions marked with the **__inline**, **inline**, or **__forceinline** keyword or, for class member functions, defined within the class declaration. When optimizing for speed, the compiler replaces all such function calls with inline code. The same is not necessarily true when Visual C++ is optimizing for size. If the Favor Small Code option is in effect, the compiler does not expand functions marked **__inline** or **inline** that are too large. This assures proper optimization results even when inlining is used excessively. The new **__forceinline** keyword overrides the compiler's discretionary powers, though not in every case. It is not possible, for instance, to force inlining for functions that take a variable argument list or for recursive functions not identified by the **inline recursion** pragma.

- **Any Suitable**—Besides functions covered by the Only __inline setting, this selection also replaces calls to functions that the compiler deems small enough to warrant inlining. Microsoft does not document the compiler's criteria for choosing such functions.

- **Disable**—No inlining is done, even for calls to functions marked **__inline** or **__forceinline**.

# From Debug to Release

Building a release version of an application usually occurs relatively infrequently during the product cycle. The first release build may come only after weeks or months spent developing the debug version. Normally, creating the release target involves no more than a new build, but occasionally there can be problems. This section discusses some of the potential pitfalls that can occur when moving from debug to release targets and explains how to avoid them.

To build a release version of a program, either click the Set Active Configuration command on the Build menu and select Win32 Release, or select the target on the Build toolbar:

Set the desired optimization switches in the Project Settings dialog, then click the Build command. You may notice that compiling a release version of the program takes longer than compiling a debug version. This is because the compiler performs more work when optimizing.

It's not unusual for an application that works correctly in its debug form to break when recompiled as a release target, casting immediate suspicion on the optimizer. Rarely is the suspicion warranted, and then only in the case of aliasing. Hidden aliasing may exist in the code unbeknownst to the programmer. If a debugged application fails when the Assume No Aliasing option is turned on, the problem may stem from the presence of hidden aliasing. The condition is easily tested by rebuilding the release version with Assume No Aliasing turned off. If the application still fails, you should give up blaming the optimizer. There exist other far more likely reasons why an application might break when moving from debug to release versions.

ASSERTs, for example. In release mode, the compiler ignores code in ASSERT macros. This leads to problems if the asserted code calls a function or performs some other task required by code outside the ASSERT. Consider the following example:

```
ASSERT ((ptr = GetPointer()) != NULL);
x = *ptr;
```

In debug form, this code works correctly. In release form, the code may cause a fault because *ptr* is never initialized. The solution is to either call the *GetPointer* function before the ASSERT or to use the VERIFY macro instead of ASSERT. A similar problem can occur with conditional code prefixed by **#ifdef** _DEBUG. Because the compiler does not predefine _DEBUG in release mode, code in the conditional block must not perform any actions that affect code outside the block. Although it seems an obvious point, many a programmer has made this simple mistake.

Disabling stack checking can also cause problems for a function that requires more than a page of stack space for its local variables. Although the function may run successfully in the program's debug version by first calling a stack check routine, the function may fail when stack checking is disabled as an optimization. The solution is either to rewrite the function to touch stack memory in sequential pages, or to insert a **check_stack** pragma to selectively enable the stack check for the function.

Compiler behavior can change in other more subtle ways between debug and release modes. For example, in a debug version, the **new** operator adds extra guard bytes to memory allocations. A program that inadvertently relies on the presence of these extra bytes may fail in its release version.

Function parameters can be evaluated in any order, and you have no guarantee that the order will be the same in a program's debug and release versions. Thus the following example may work correctly in one version but not in the other:

```
Function1( ptr = GetPointer(), *ptr );
```

Hidden thread problems sometimes surface only in a program's release build. Consider the common mistake of two threads simultaneously accessing a function that writes a static variable. In a debug version the variable always remains in memory, so the potential conflict between threads may never arise due to slight differences in timing. In a release build, however, the window of opportunity for error is wider, because the variable may well be enregistered for the duration of the function's execution. This makes it more likely that one thread will overwrite the results of the other.

An optimized program can fail because of many other types of source code problems, some of which are listed in Table 12-5. To track down a problem, try turning on these optimizations individually to determine under what circumstances the error arises. The table's second column offers suggestions of what to look for when examining your code.

| Optimization | Possible cause of problem |
| --- | --- |
| Inline expansion | Uninitialized local variable |
| Global optimizations | Uninitialized local variable |
| Generate intrinsic functions inline | Uninitialized local variable |
| Improve floating-point consistency | Relying on exact precision in comparisons |
| Frame pointer omission | Stack corruption due to incorrect function prototype |

**Table 12-5.** *Typical source code problems that can arise from code optimization.*

It's perhaps human nature to suspect the optimizer when the release version breaks. After all, the compiler is rewriting our code in unknown ways. But the art of code optimization has attained a very high degree of reliability in the Visual C++ compiler. Microsoft places enough trust in its own product that Microsoft developers optimize release versions of major products written in C/C++ such as Windows 95, Windows NT, and Microsoft Office. This fact alone should allay any lingering concerns that optimization is somehow unsafe.

# Benchmarking Visual C++

When Visual C++ version 4.0 was in beta testing, Microsoft asked me to conduct a benchmark test of the new product and produce a white paper discoursing on methods and results of the benchmark. The test compared

Visual C++ against three competing products to see which compiler, given the same source code, produced the fastest or smallest executable. The differences would be a reliable measure of each compiler's ability to discover how to best optimize the source code.

Visual C++ did very well in the benchmark test—extremely well, in fact, though that's not the point of this section. It is illuminating, however, to review a single function of the benchmark code that involved the calculation of complex numbers. This particular function, which represented the widest divergence of results found during the benchmark test, vividly demonstrates some of the potential gains of clever compiler optimizations. Although all four compilers were set to optimize the function for maximum speed, the executable that Visual C++ produced for this part of the test ran more than three times faster than the code that took second place. The disassembled code shows the reasons why:

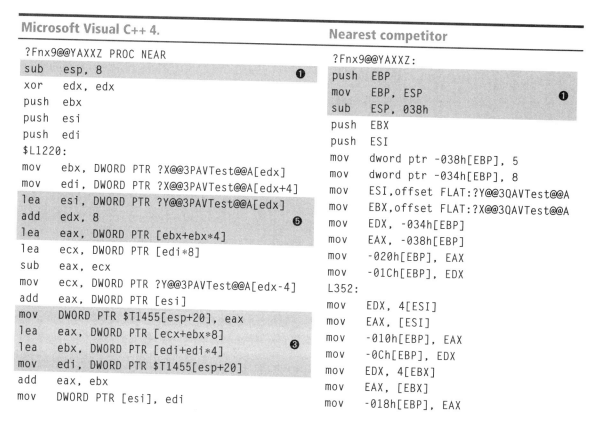

| Microsoft Visual C++ 4. | Nearest competitor |
|---|---|
| `?Fnx9@@YAXXZ PROC NEAR` | `?Fnx9@@YAXXZ:` |
| `sub     esp, 8`                              ❶ | `push    EBP` |
| `xor     edx, edx` | `mov     EBP, ESP`                         ❶ |
| `push    ebx` | `sub     ESP, 038h` |
| `push    esi` | `push    EBX` |
| `push    edi` | `push    ESI` |
| `$L1220:` | `mov     dword ptr -038h[EBP], 5` |
| `mov     ebx, DWORD PTR ?X@@3PAVTest@@A[edx]` | `mov     dword ptr -034h[EBP], 8` |
| `mov     edi, DWORD PTR ?X@@3PAVTest@@A[edx+4]` | `mov     ESI,offset FLAT:?Y@@3QAVTest@@A` |
| `lea     esi, DWORD PTR ?Y@@3PAVTest@@A[edx]` | `mov     EBX,offset FLAT:?X@@3QAVTest@@A` |
| `add     edx, 8`                              ❺ | `mov     EDX, -034h[EBP]` |
| `lea     eax, DWORD PTR [ebx+ebx*4]` | `mov     EAX, -038h[EBP]` |
| `lea     ecx, DWORD PTR [edi*8]` | `mov     -020h[EBP], EAX` |
| `sub     eax, ecx` | `mov     -01Ch[EBP], EDX` |
| `mov     ecx, DWORD PTR ?Y@@3PAVTest@@A[edx-4]` | `L352:` |
| `add     eax, DWORD PTR [esi]` | `mov     EDX, 4[ESI]` |
| `mov     DWORD PTR $T1455[esp+20], eax` | `mov     EAX, [ESI]` |
| `lea     eax, DWORD PTR [ecx+ebx*8]` | `mov     -010h[EBP], EAX` |
| `lea     ebx, DWORD PTR [edi+edi*4]`          ❸ | `mov     -0Ch[EBP], EDX` |
| `mov     edi, DWORD PTR $T1455[esp+20]` | `mov     EDX, 4[EBX]` |
| `add     eax, ebx` | `mov     EAX, [EBX]` |
| `mov     DWORD PTR [esi], edi` | `mov     -018h[EBP], EAX` |

| Microsoft Visual C++ 4. | | Nearest competitor | |
|---|---|---|---|
| mov | DWORD PTR [esi], edi | mov | -018h[EBP], EAX |
| mov | DWORD PTR [esi+4], eax | mov | -014h[EBP], EDX |
| cmp | edx, 8000 | mov | ECX, -020h[EBP] |
| jl | SHORT $L1220 | imul | ECX, -018h[EBP] |
| pop | edi | mov | EDX, -01Ch[EBP] |
| pop | esi | imul | EDX, -014h[EBP] |
| pop | ebx | sub | ECX, EDX |
| add | esp, 8 ❷ | mov | -030h[EBP], ECX |
| ret | 0 | mov | ECX, -020h[EBP] |
| | | imul | ECX, -014h[EBP] |
| | | mov | EDX, -01Ch[EBP] |
| | | imul | EDX, -018h[EBP] |
| | | add | ECX, EDX |
| | | mov | -02Ch[EBP], ECX ❹ |
| | | mov | EDX, -02Ch[EBP] |
| | | mov | EAX, -030h[EBP] |
| | | mov | -8[EBP], EAX |
| | | mov | -4[EBP], EDX |
| | | mov | ECX, -010h[EBP] |
| | | add | ECX, -8[EBP] |
| | | mov | -028h[EBP], ECX |
| | | mov | ECX, -0Ch[EBP] |
| | | add | ECX, -4[EBP] |
| | | mov | -024h[EBP], ECX |
| | | mov | EDX, -024h[EBP] |
| | | mov | EAX, -028h[EBP] |
| | | mov | [ESI], EAX |
| | | mov | 4[ESI],EDX |
| | | mov | ECX, 8 |
| | | add | ESI, ECX |
| | | add | EBX, ECX |
| | | cmp | EBX,offset FLAT:?Y@@3QAVTest@@A |
| | | jb | L352 |
| | | pop | ESI |
| | | pop | EBX |
| | | mov | ESP, EBP ❷ |
| | | pop | EBP |
| | | ret | |

Besides the obvious disparity in size, an immediate difference between the two listings appears in their prologue and epilogue sections, marked ❶ and ❷. Optimized through frame pointer omission, the code produced by Visual C++ merely allocates 8 bytes of stack and accesses the function's stack frame by using an offset from the ESP register. The other compiler, which did not offer frame pointer omission as an optimization, must push and pop the EBP register to make it available as the frame pointer. Closer inspection, however, reveals that a stack frame is not even necessary for the function, and Visual C++ misses an opportunity to further optimize the code marked ❸ in the listing. Although the EBP register is now free because of the frame pointer omission, the code still uses the stack to temporarily hold an intermediate calculation. This wastes what is often the main benefit of frame pointer omission: freeing the EBP register for use in other optimizations. The sequence at marker ❸ would be slightly faster and smaller if written like this:

```
mov    ebp, eax                         ;Store intermediate calculation
lea    eax, DWORD PTR [ecx+ebx*8]       ;With value temporarily saved,
lea    ebx, DWORD PTR [edi+edi*4]       ;  we can use EAX
mov    edi, ebp                         ;Recover calculation in EDI
```

Using EBP to store the intermediate calculation would save two memory accesses at each loop iteration.

The Visual C++ version saves code space and gains speed by combining address modes where possible into a single instruction. This allows it to use the LEA (load effective address) instruction for simple arithmetic, a well-known feature of Intel processors. By using left-shifting and addition, the LEA instruction can manipulate base and index registers to perform certain multiplication operations faster than the processor's multiply instructions MUL and IMUL. For instance, here's how a single LEA instruction can multiply the value stored in the EAX register:

| Instruction | Description |
| --- | --- |
| lea  eax, [eax*2] | Multiply EAX by 2 |
| lea  eax, [eax + eax*2] | Multiply EAX by 3 |
| lea  eax, [eax*4] | Multiply EAX by 4 |

| Instruction | Description |
| --- | --- |
| `lea  eax, [eax + eax*4]` | Multiply EAX by 5 |
| `lea  eax, [eax*8]` | Multiply EAX by 8 |
| `lea  eax, [eax + eax*8]` | Multiply EAX by 9 |

Although using LEA in this manner is well documented by Intel, the other compiler resorted to four IMUL instructions which, since they occur in a loop that iterates a thousand times, are particularly expensive. The length of the loop produced by the other compiler is also telling, spanning 39 machine instructions. The Visual C++ version of the loop requires only 18 instructions and has no IMUL instructions at all.

The other compiler was surprisingly careless in its use of registers. Consider this sequence taken from the code at marker ❹, in which a value is written to the stack and then immediately accessed again:

```
mov   -02Ch[EBP], ECX
mov   EDX, -02Ch[EBP]
```

Because the ECX register is already charged, reading the value again from memory is not necessary. The sequence would be smaller if compiled like this:

```
mov   -02Ch[EBP], ECX          ;Store the ECX value
mov   EDX, ECX                 ;Also copy it to EDX
```

Both compilers seemed to make reasonable attempts to avoid pipeline stalls through proper instruction ordering. One should not expect perfect ordering from a compiler because it would require too many passes through the code, resulting in unacceptably long build times. In searching for the optimum instruction ordering, the Visual C++ compiler slipped only once, producing this sequence of three instructions at marker ❺:

```
lea   esi, DWORD PTR ?Y@@3PAVTest@@A[edx]
add   edx, 8
lea   eax, DWORD PTR [ebx+ebx*4]
```

The second instruction cannot alter the EDX register until the first instruction has finished reading it. Changing the order of the second and third instructions avoids the potential stall, assuring that adjacent instructions in the sequence can execute simultaneously:

```
lea    esi, DWORD PTR ?Y@@3PAVTest@@A[edx]
lea    eax, DWORD PTR [ebx+ebx*4]
add    edx, 8
```

So much for version 4. Version 5 incorporated significant advances to the optimizer, firmly establishing Visual C++ as a state of the art optimizing compiler for personal computers. The current release introduces even further improvements, but concentrates less on new technology and more on tuning the compiler's ability to find opportunities for making code smaller and faster. Microsoft estimates that Visual C++ 6 reduces executable size by more than 10 percent over version 4, and recompiling the code discussed in this section shows that there is indeed a significant improvement. The size of the code shrinks by 16 percent and the compiler now figures out how to do away with the stack frame entirely, dispensing with prologue and epilogue code:

```
?Fnx9@@YAXXZ PROC NEAR
        push    esi
        push    edi
        xor     eax, eax
$L1621:
        mov     edx, DWORD PTR ?X@@3PAVTest@@A[eax+4]
        mov     ecx, DWORD PTR ?X@@3PAVTest@@A[eax]
        add     eax, 8
        lea     edi, DWORD PTR [edx*8]
        lea     edx, DWORD PTR [edx+edx*4]
        lea     esi, DWORD PTR [ecx+ecx*4]
        lea     ecx, DWORD PTR [edx+ecx*8]
        mov     edx, DWORD PTR ?Y@@3PAVTest@@A[eax-8]
        sub     esi, edi
        mov     edi, DWORD PTR ?Y@@3PAVTest@@A[eax-4]
        add     edx, esi
        add     ecx, edi
        mov     DWORD PTR ?Y@@3PAVTest@@A[eax-8], edx
        mov     DWORD PTR ?Y@@3PAVTest@@A[eax-4], ecx
        cmp     eax, 8000
        jl      SHORT $L1621
        pop     edi
        pop     esi
        ret     0
```

❻

The section of code marked ❻ offers further insight into the workings of the optimizing compiler. The optimizer writes this section as three steps, in which the code reads two integers from memory, adds them to values in registers, and then writes the sums back to memory. An alternative is to simply add the registers directly to the integers in memory, replacing all the code at marker ❻ with these three lines:

```
sub     esi, edi
add     DWORD PTR ?Y@@3PAVTest@@A[eax-8], esi
add     DWORD PTR ?Y@@3PAVTest@@A[eax-4], ecx
```

The revision renders the read operations unnecessary and further reduces the size of the function by 21 percent, though it does not improve execution speed. Adding a register value to memory is slower than copying the value, but the reduced number of instructions compensates because the processor has less code to read. The revised function, though smaller, would thus execute at the same speed as the original produced by the Visual C++ compiler.

If you are interested in studying the effects of compiler optimizations in your own programs, Visual C++ can produce assembly-language listings like the ones shown in this section. In the C/C++ tab of the Project Settings dialog, select the Listing Files category, then choose the type of assembly listing you desire in the Listing File Type box.

# 13

# Customizing Visual C++

As you become more familiar with Visual C++, you may find yourself wanting to change some of its characteristics to better mesh with your working style. Many aspects of the environment can be altered to conform to your preferences, from details of the text editor window to the appearance of a custom toolbar. And by using its sophisticated macro language and add-in libraries, you can expand the environment's large repertoire of commands, programming new capabilities into Visual C++ that the designers never thought of. This chapter explains some of the many ways you can customize Visual C++ to make it a more efficient environment in which to work.

Most behavioral aspects of the environment have "memory," meaning that you need only adjust a setting once. The adjustment thereafter becomes the default behavior the next time Visual C++ starts. So, for example, if document windows are full-size in the text editor when you quit Visual C++, they automatically appear full-size again the next time you start the program. Some customization settings are less obvious, and a few can even be difficult to find if you don't know where to look.

The Options and Customize commands, both of which are located on the Tools menu, offer direct access to the switches and options that govern the behavior of the Developer Studio environment. Although these commands do not provide access to all customization settings, they are a good place to start.

# The Options Dialog

The Options command displays the tabbed dialog shown in Table 13-1. The Options dialog contains a wide-ranging collection of settings that cover the behavior and appearance of Visual C++ editors and the debugger, tab spacing and indentations in the text editor, directory locations of include files and libraries used during compiling and linking, and fonts and text colors for various windows. Table 13-1 lists only some of the dialog's options.

**Table 13-1.**  *Settings in the Options dialog, invoked by clicking Options on the Tools menu.*

| Tab in Options dialog | Description |
| --- | --- |
| 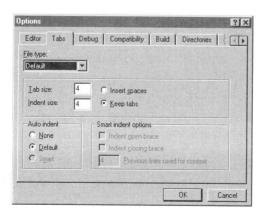 | **Text editor**—Enable scroll bars and selection margin in the text editor. Select settings that affect how the editor saves a document and whether the statement completion feature appears automatically in a document window. |
| | **Tab spacing in text documents**—Set tab width in text documents and automatic indentation for source code. Determine whether the editor should accept tabs as ASCII #9 characters or convert them to an equivalent number of spaces as you type. |

| Tab in Options dialog | Description |
|---|---|
| 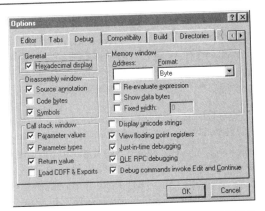 | **Debugger settings**—Select hexa-decimal or decimal display and appearance of various windows in the debugger. Specify the default address displayed in the Memory window. Enable Just-in-time debugging and choose between automatic or manual application of the Edit and Continue feature. |
| | **Text editor options**—Select text editor emulation (Developer Studio, BRIEF, Epsilon). Enable other options, such as virtual space and behavior of double-clicking in the dialog editor. |
| 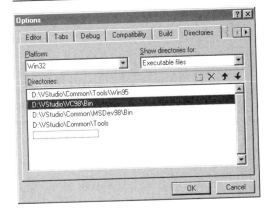 | **Directories for locating files**—Select either Executable files, Include files, Library files, or Source files, then add or delete paths to files. Visual C++ searches for files by scanning each path in the order listed. |

*(continued)*

615

**Table 13-1.** *continued*

| Tab in Options dialog | Description |
|---|---|
| 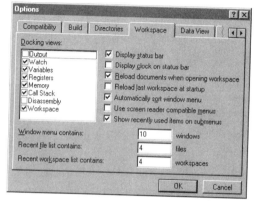 | **Workspace options**—Enable or disable docking for windows. Set up automatic loading of most recent project when Visual C++ starts. Determine whether the Window menu sorts its list of documents in alphabetical order. Set the extent of the lists displayed by the Recent Files and Recent Workspaces commands on the File menu. |
| 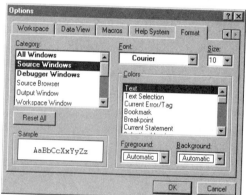 | **Fonts and colors in text windows**—Set the font type and size for a selected window. Set colors of various text elements such as comments, keywords, and HTML tags. |

The Editor, Tabs, and Compatibility tabs of the Options dialog apply only to the text editor. Most settings in these tabs simultaneously affect the editor's normal and full-screen views, as well the debugger's source text window. Other settings depend on the current viewing mode and whether the debugger is active. This makes it possible to create three different screen layouts in the environment: one for editing in normal view, another for full-screen view, and a third layout for debugging.

# The Customize Dialog

The Customize command displays the dialog shown in Table 13-2, which provides the means to:

- Add or delete menu commands

- Add icons to menu commands

- Turn toolbars on or off

- Add or delete toolbar buttons

- Create named keystroke commands

**Table 13-2.** *Settings in the Customize dialog, invoked by clicking Customize on the Tools menu.*

| Tab in Customize dialog | Description |
| --- | --- |
| 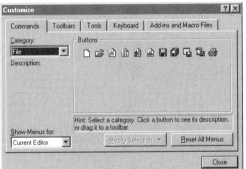 | **Adding commands to menus—** Modify a menu command or restore default menus. |
| 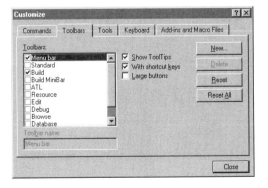 | **Toolbars**—Make toolbars visible or invisible, enable tooltip messages for toolbar buttons, display accelerator keystrokes in tooltip messages, and select normal or large toolbar buttons. |

*(continued)*

**Table 13-2.** *continued*

| Tab in Customize dialog | Description |
|---|---|
| 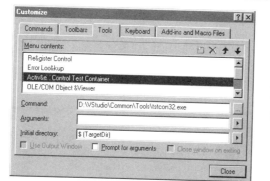 | **Tools menu commands**—Add or delete commands for utility programs, specifying the path, filename, and command-line arguments for each program. Specify the initial directory that the utility uses. |
| 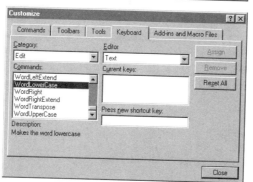 | **Unbound keyboard commands**—Assign new keystrokes to Visual C++ commands. |
| 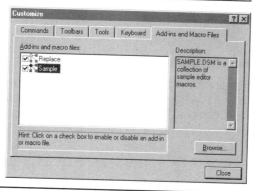 | **Macro files**—Enable or disable a macro file or add-in utility. |

We have already briefly encountered some of these commands in other chapters. For example, Chapter 3, The Text Editor, demonstrated how to assign keystrokes for two unbound commands named WordUpperCase and WordLowerCase.

The Commands tab of the Customize dialog gives you control over the contents of the environment's menus. While the Customize dialog is visible on the screen, you can display the menus, but individual commands in the menus are not active. Instead, the environment acts as a menu editor in which you can add or delete menu commands, change the order of commands, and add icons to existing commands.

For example, here's how to add an icon image to the Page Setup command on the File menu, which normally has no icon. The first step is to borrow a suitable image and store it on the Clipboard. A screen capture program serves well for this purpose, or you can design your own 16-by-16 image in the Visual C++ graphics editor. You can also capture an icon image to the Clipboard from any of the environment's toolbars. With the Commands tab visible in the Customize dialog, right-click a toolbar button to display the context menu shown in Figure 13-1. The menu's Copy Button Image command copies the button's icon image to the Clipboard.

The Customize dialog itself serves as a convenient source of button images. All the icon images in the Visual C++ toolbars can be displayed within (and borrowed from) the Customize dialog. First click the Category combo box in the Commands tab to display a drop-down list of menus. Selecting a menu in the list displays a collection of small icons for commands on the menu. For our example, select File from the Category drop-down list and right-click one of the icon images in the list that roughly conveys the idea of "page setup." This displays the same context menu

**Figure 13-1.** *When the Customize dialog is visible, right-clicking a menu command or toolbar button exposes this context menu.*

shown in Figure 13-1, from which you can choose the Copy Button Image command to copy the image to the Clipboard.

Once you have a 16-by-16 image stored on the Clipboard, transfer the image to the Page Setup command on the File menu. With the Commands tab still visible, click File on the menu bar to expose the menu, then right-click the Page Setup command to display the context menu shown in Figure 13-1. Choose the Paste Button Image command to place the new icon image to the left of the Page Setup command on the File menu:

If you change your mind about the result, you can undo your work in two ways. The first is to click the Reset All Menus button in the Customize dialog, which restores all menu commands to their original state. If you want only to remove an icon image from a particular menu command, right-click the command and choose Text Only from the context menu. Again, the Customize dialog must be visible on the screen for this to work.

You can also add icon images to the menu bar itself. Right-click a menu caption to display its context menu, then choose Paste Button Image as before. Here's a possibility for a customized menu bar, created with icon images borrowed from various locations in the Visual C++ environment:

Adding a new command to one of the environment's menus takes only two steps:

1.  Pull down the menu while the Commands tab of the Customize dialog appears on the screen.

2. Select the desired group of tools from the Category drop-down list and drag the tool icon or command name from the dialog onto the menu. A horizontal placement bar indicates the menu position.

To delete the new command from the menu, right-click the command and choose Delete from the pop-up menu. You can add menu entries for macros and unbound commands as well. Choose All Commands from the Category drop-down list, locate the command name in the list, then drag the command name from the list to the desired position on the menu. Figure 13-2 shows the procedure for adding the WordUpperCase command to the Edit menu.

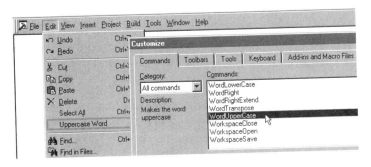

**Figure 13-2.** *Placing a new command on a menu.*

# Toolbars

The appearance of toolbars on the screen depends on the active editor and on whether the editor is in full-screen mode. By default, toolbars remain invisible in full-screen viewing; to make a toolbar visible, turn on full-screen viewing and press Alt+T to pull down the Tools menu. Click the Customize command and the Toolbars tab, then turn on the check box adjacent to the desired toolbar in the list. You can also make the menu bar visible in full-screen mode this way. Because the change occurs in full-screen mode, the appearance of the toolbar and its position on the screen apply only to full-screen viewing. When you press Esc to return to normal viewing, the toolbar returns to its original position and may not even be visible.

If you prefer a toolbar to float rather than dock against another window or the edge of the screen, double-click any blank area on the toolbar. To return a floating toolbar to its previous docked position, double-click the toolbar's title bar. As mentioned in Chapter 1, The Environment, holding down the Ctrl key while dragging a floating toolbar prevents it from docking to another window. Pressing the Shift key while dragging the toolbar into a docked position switches the toolbar window between horizontal and vertical orientations.

Visual C++ lets you easily alter the appearance and contents of toolbars, so you can copy buttons from one toolbar to another, storing in a single toolbar the tools you use most often. First, display the Customize dialog either by using the Tools menu or by right-clicking the toolbar and choosing Customize from its context menu. If the toolbar that you want to modify does not appear on the screen, click the Toolbars tab and expose the toolbar. In the dialog's Commands tab, select a menu name from the Category box to display tool buttons belonging to commands on the selected menu. Clicking a tool button in the dialog displays a brief description of the tool, so you can always identify the purpose of a button. Make sure the target toolbar and the Customize dialog do not overlap on the screen, and then drag the tools you want from the dialog onto the toolbar. You can even place tool buttons on the environment's menu bar if you prefer.

Like menu commands, toolbar buttons are not active when the Customize dialog appears on the screen. This allows you to drag a toolbar button and place it in a different position on the same toolbar, or to drag the button to a different toolbar. You can insert a space between buttons by moving a button left or right about half the width of a button. Click the dialog's Close button when you're finished. Actually, you don't even need the Customize dialog to move tools from one toolbar to another. Expose the toolbars and drag the tool button you want from one toolbar to the other while pressing the Alt key. Pressing the Alt and Ctrl keys simultaneously lets you copy a button instead of moving it.

## Custom Toolbars

If some of the large toolbars occupy too much of the screen for your taste, you might wish Visual C++ offered one or two small toolbars that you could discreetly tuck away in the corner, providing access to only a few tools you really need. The answer is a custom toolbar, which takes only a few steps to create. Chapter 3 introduced the subject of custom toolbars, demonstrating with the WordUpperCase and WordLowerCase commands. Here's an expanded review of the procedure.

First, set the screen mode to normal or full-screen, depending on where you want to use the new toolbar, then click the Customize command on the Tools menu and expose the dialog's Commands tab. For an unbound command like WordUpperCase, choose All Commands from the Category box to display a list of command names. Locate the desired command in the list, then drag the entry from the list and drop it onto a toolbar. To copy one of the environment's predefined buttons, select a menu from the Category list and drag a button from the Customize dialog onto a toolbar.

You don't have to use a predefined toolbar to receive the new tool button, because the environment offers two methods for creating a custom toolbar. The first method is to click the New button on the Toolbars tab of the Customize dialog, and then give the new toolbar a name:

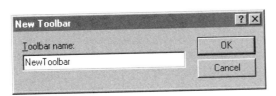

When you click OK, Visual C++ creates a blank toolbar on which you can place buttons as just described.

The second method for creating a new toolbar is even easier—just drag a command out of the Customize dialog and drop it onto any area of the screen not covered by a toolbar. For a new command like WordUpper-Case, select All Commands from the Category list and drag the desired entry out of the Commands list. The procedure is similar to the way we placed WordUpperCase on a menu earlier. Select a button icon in the Button Appearance dialog, add appropriate text to label the button, and click OK. Visual C++ automatically creates a new toolbar to hold the button:

To copy one of the environment's predefined commands, select a menu name from the Category list and drag an icon out of the Customize dialog onto a blank area of the screen as shown in Figure 13-3. This method has the advantage of copying both an icon image and button text in one step. To display both image and text in the new toolbar button, right-click the button on the toolbar and choose Image And Text from the context menu.

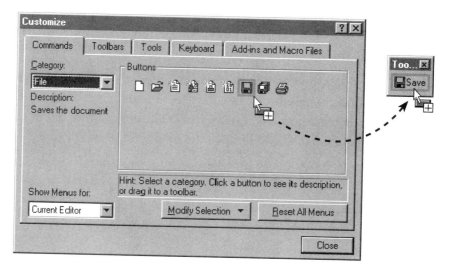

**Figure 13-3.**  *Creating a new custom toolbar.*

It's easy to remove a button from any toolbar, whether custom or predefined. While the Customize dialog is visible, drag a button off the toolbar and release it in a blank area of the screen. At the same time, you can rename a toolbar or any of the button captions. To revise a button caption, right-click the button on its toolbar, choose the Button Appearance command from the pop-up menu, then retype the button caption in the edit box at the bottom of the Button Appearance dialog. You can change a button icon at any time by cutting and pasting from the Clipboard.

Changing the name of a custom toolbar requires a visit to the Toolbars tab of the Customize dialog. (You can rename only custom toolbars that you have created, not the predefined Developer Studio toolbars.) Select the custom toolbar from the list and type a new title in the Toolbar Name box. The new name appears in the toolbar's title area and in the Toolbars list in the Customize dialog, so you can turn the new toolbar on and off the same way as any other toolbar. If the new toolbar has only a few buttons, keep the name brief or there might not be room for it in the title bar. Figure 13-4 shows how to change the name of the toolbar created in Chapter 3 from Toolbar1 to Word Case.

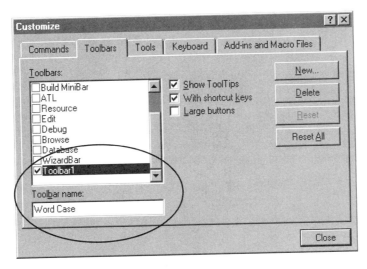

**Figure 13-4.** *Renaming a toolbar in the Customize dialog.*

Selecting a custom toolbar from the list enables the Delete button. This button provides the only means of permanently removing a custom toolbar.

# Adding a Command to the Tools Menu

The last section of Chapter 3 showed how to add a command to the Tools menu for launching a third-party text editor while you are in the Developer Studio environment. You can do the same for any program, not just a text editor. This section takes a closer look at the process of adding a command, describing available options that let you integrate another application into the environment.

First let's review the process by adding a simple utility to the Tools menu that requires no arguments or special handling. The MfcTree3 application lists a hierarchy of MFC classes and is a more complete version of the dialog-based MfcTree2 program developed in Chapter 5, Dialog Boxes and Controls. Source code for MfcTree3 hasn't changed much from its previous incarnations, except that the program now stores class names as string resources instead of hard-coding them in a long list of calls to *CTree-Ctrl::InsertItem* in the dialog's *OnInitDialog* function. You can find all source files in the Chapter.13\ MfcTree3 folder on the companion CD, but for the following demonstration you need only the MfcTree3.exe program file copied from the CD to any location on your hard disk.

Add the MfcTree3 tool to the environment by invoking the Customize dialog. In the Tools tab, double-click the new-item box, which appears as a dotted rectangle after the last tool in the list (Figure 13-5). Type the menu item text *&MFC Tree List* to specify the menu entry with the letter "M" serving as the command mnemonic.

Press the Enter key and in the Command box type the full path and filename for MfcTree3 including the EXE extension. When you close the Customize dialog, Visual C++ adds the command to the bottom of the Tools menu. Clicking the new MFC Tree List command launches the MfcTree3 application, which displays the list of MFC classes shown in Figure 13-6.

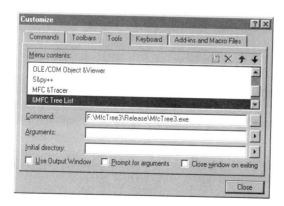

**Figure 13-5.** *Adding the new MFC Tree List command to the Tools menu.*

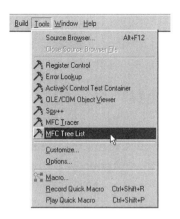 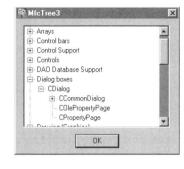

**Figure 13-6.** *The new MFC Tree List command on the Tools menu and the MfcTree3 application.*

MfcTree3 is easy to add to the Tools menu because the program takes no command-line arguments and displays its output in a single window. Other utility programs are not so simple, as we'll see in the next section.

## Command-Line Arguments

Some applications, especially console-based programs, use command-line arguments specified by the user when running the program. There are two methods for supplying command-line arguments to a program launched from the Tools menu. The first method configures Visual C++ to query for arguments every time you run the utility. Set the configuration in the Customize dialog by selecting the Prompt For Arguments check box shown in Figure 13-5. When turned on, the check box causes Visual C++ to prompt for arguments when you run the utility from the Tools menu, and then pass the arguments to the program via the command line.

As an illustration, let's look at what happens when the Windows Notepad utility is added to the environment's Tools menu with the Prompt For Arguments check box turned on. Running Notepad from the Tools menu first displays a prompt in which you can type a filename, as shown in Figure 13-7 on the following page. When you click OK, Notepad starts up and automatically loads the specified file.

If you want a utility program to receive the same command-line arguments every time it runs, the second method for supplying arguments proves much more convenient. Clear the Prompt For Arguments check box and

**Figure 13-7.** *Prompting for command-line arguments when running a program from the Tools menu.*

type the command-line arguments in the Arguments box shown in Figure 13-5. Thereafter, Visual C++ passes the arguments to the program without prompting.

## Argument Macros

Visual C++ provides a nice feature known as argument macros, which can greatly facilitate argument specifications for Tools programs. As described in Table 13-3, each macro expands into a string that describes a characteristic of the current project or file.

A simple example illustrates the flexibility of argument macros. Say you want the Notepad tool to always open the document that is currently active in the text editor. Instead of prompting each time for the filename, it's much easier to use the $(FilePath) macro. This macro expands into the full file specification of the document that currently has input focus. If no document has focus, the macro generates an empty string. To use the macro with the Notepad tool, clear the Prompt For Arguments check box in the Customize dialog and type *$(FilePath)* in the Arguments box like this:

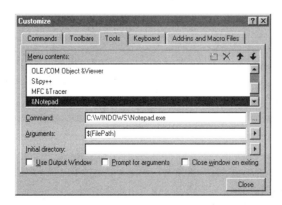

| Macro | Name | Description |
|---|---|---|
| $(CurCol) | Current Column | Column number of the caret position in the text window |
| $(CurDir) | Current Directory | Current working directory, expressed as *d:path\* |
| $(CurLine) | Current Line | Row number of the caret position in the text window |
| $(CurText) | Current Text | Current text, which is either the word on which the caret rests, or a single line of selected text |
| $(FileDir) | File Directory | Directory of the source file in the active window, expressed as *d:path\* |
| $(FileExt) | File Extension | Filename extension of the source file in the active window |
| $(FileName) | File Name | Filename of the source file in the active window |
| $(FilePath) | File Path | Complete specification of the source file in the active window, expressed as *d:\path\filename* |
| $(TargetArgs) | Target Arguments | Command-line arguments passed to the project application |
| $(TargetDir) | Target Directory | Path to the project executable contained in the Debug or Release subdirectory, expressed as *d:\path\* |
| $(TargetExt) | Target Extension | Filename extension of the project executable, such as EXE or DLL |
| $(TargetName) | Target Name | Filename of the project executable (usually the project name) |
| $(TargetPath) | Target Path | Complete specification of the project executable, expressed as *d:\path\filename* |
| $(WkspDir) | Workspace Directory | Directory containing the project files, expressed as *d:\path\* |
| $(WkspName) | Workspace Name | Project name |

**Table 13-3.**   *Argument macros available in the Tools tab.*

When you launch the tool while editing a document in the text editor, Notepad automatically opens the same document. Table 13-3 provides a complete list of the 15 different argument macros available in the Tools tab.

You can use argument macros when Visual C++ queries for command-line arguments as shown in Figure 13-7, but the macros are most useful in the Arguments and Initial Directory text boxes pictured on page 628. You don't need to memorize the macros, because clicking the arrow buttons adjacent to the text boxes displays a menu with a complete list of the macro names. Click a macro name in the list and it appears in the adjacent text box. The macro names are not case sensitive so, for instance, $(FileDir) and $(filedir) expand to the same string. Path strings produced by macros such as $(FileDir) and $(TargetDir) end in a backslash.

## Example: The Struct Utility Tool

Argument macros provide a way to more closely integrate a utility program into the Developer Studio environment. By automating command-line arguments that are appropriate for the current project or document, argument macros let you create add-on utilities for the Tools menu specifically designed for use in Visual C++.

Here's an example of how a tool program can respond to the current caret position in the text editor and even display output inside the Developer Studio environment. The Struct utility described here receives a command-line argument that contains a word taken from the current text document. If the argument holds the name of one of the Win32 API structures represented in the program's small database, Struct displays the structure's declaration in Developer Studio's Output window. The command-line argument, which is generated by the $(CurText) macro, can be either selected text in the document or, if no text is selected, the word on which the caret rests. If Struct does not recognize the supplied structure name, it displays a message saying the structure is unknown.

Figure 13-8 shows how to set up the Struct program in the Customize dialog as a tool on the Tools menu. Struct has access to the Output window because the Use Output Window check box is turned on. This check box is enabled only for console-based programs. Setting the check box causes

Developer Studio to intercept all standard output from the utility and display it in a separate tab of the Output window. The name of the tool appears on the tab to identify the source of the output.

Struct is a very simple program that recognizes only a few Win32 API structures such as RECT and POINT. Written in C as a console-based program, Struct is hardly more than a program shell, but it can easily be expanded to include additional structures and other information such as function prototypes and message parameters. In spite of its limitations, the program clearly demonstrates some of the possibilities for integrating tools into Visual C++. You can install and test the Struct utility by following these steps:

1. If you did not run the Setup program to copy projects from the companion CD, copy the Struct.exe program file to a convenient location on your hard disk. The program file is located in the Code\Chapter.13\Struct\Release subfolder on the CD.

2. In the Tools tab of the Customize dialog, add a command for Struct to the Tools menu, as illustrated in Figure 13-8. In the Command box, type the path and filename of Struct.exe, including the EXE extension, specifying the folder on your hard disk to which you copied the program. Type *$(CurText)* in the Arguments box or click the adjacent arrow button and select Current Text from the list. Be sure to turn on the Use Output Window check box at the lower-left corner of the dialog.

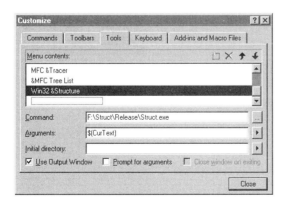

**Figure 13-8.**   *Setting up a menu command for the Struct utility program.*

3. Either open the Struct.c source file (Listing 13-1) in the text editor or use the New command on the File menu to create a new text document. Type a single line in the new document that contains some of the names of API structures that Struct recognizes, like this:

```
RECT  RECTL  POINT  POINTL  SIZE  POINTS  FILETIME  SYSTEMTIME
```

4. Position the caret anywhere on one of the function names in the document and click the Win32 Structure command on the Tools menu. Figure 13-9 shows what the utility's message looks like in the Win32 Structure tab of the Output window.

**Figure 13-9.**    *Output from the Struct utility appears in its own tab in the Output window.*

**Listing 13-1.**    *The Struct.c source file.*

```c
// Struct.c      Displays Win32 structure in Output window
//               Copyright (c) 1998, Beck Zaratian

#include <stdio.h>
#include <string.h>

char *pszStruct[] =
{
    "FILETIME\n{\n  DWORD  dwLowDateTime;\n  DWORD  " \
    "dwHighDateTime;\n}",

    "OVERLAPPED\n{\n  DWORD   Internal;\n  DWORD   " \
    "InternalHigh;\n  DWORD   Offset;\n  DWORD   " \
    "OffsetHigh;\n  HANDLE  hEvent;\n};",

    "POINT\n{\n  LONG  x;\n  LONG  y;\n};",

    "POINTL\n{\n  LONG  x;\n  LONG  y;\n};",

    "POINTS\n{\n  SHORT  x;\n  SHORT  y;\n};",

    "PROCESS_INFORMATION\n{\n  HANDLE  hProcess;\n  HANDLE  " \
```

```
    "hThread;\n  DWORD   dwProcessId;\n  DWORD  dwThreadId;\n};",

    "RECT\n{\n  LONG  left;\n  LONG  top;\n  LONG  right;" \
    "\n  LONG  bottom;\n};",

    "RECTL\n{\n  LONG  left;\n  LONG  top;\n  LONG  right;" \
    "\n  LONG  bottom;\n};",

    "SECURITY_ATTRIBUTES\n{\n  DWORD   nLength;\n  LPVOID  " \
    "lpSecurityDescriptor;\n  BOOL    bInheritHandle;\n}",

    "SIZE\n{\n  LONG  cx;\n  LONG  cy;\n};",

    "SYSTEMTIME\n{\n  WORD  wYear;\n  WORD  wMonth;\n  WORD  " \
    "wDayOfWeek;\n  WORD  wDay;\n  WORD  wHour;\n  WORD  " \
    "wMinute;\n  WORD  wSecond;\n  WORD  wMilliseconds;\n};"
};

main( int argc, char *argv[], char *envp[] )
{
    char    *sz;
    size_t  iLen;
    int     i, iCount = sizeof(pszStruct)/sizeof(char*);

    if (argc > 1)
    {
        for (i=0; i < iCount; i++)
        {
            // Determine length of structure name
            sz   = pszStruct[i];
            iLen = (size_t) (strchr( sz, '\n' ) - sz);

            // If structure is in database, display declaration
            if (strlen( argv[1] ) == iLen &&
                !strncmp( sz, argv[1], iLen ))
            {
                printf( "Structure declaration:\n\n" );
                printf( "struct %s\n\n", pszStruct[i] );
                break;
            }
        }

        if (i == iCount)
            printf( "Structure not recognized\n\n" );
    }

    return 0;
}
```

# Macros

Visual C++ incorporates an excellent macro language in the form of Visual Basic Scripting Edition, better known as VBScript. By storing macro scripts in files, the environment enables you to make a permanent collection of useful macros that can be shared with others. You can create a macro by recording a sequence of tasks or by writing a programmed script. And as we'll see in this section, VBScript provides a library of functions that allow a running macro to query for user input, display message boxes, perform mathematical calculations, manipulate strings, and carry out many other tasks that are beyond the abilities of the user interface.

VBScript is a scaled-down subset of Microsoft Visual Basic for Applications (VBA), the programming language for Microsoft programs such as Access. Designed as a scripting language for Web documents written in Hypertext Markup Language (HTML), VBScript provides a way for HTML pages to embed ActiveX controls and other objects. But VBScript also functions as a general scripting language that can interpret a list of commands specific to an application and execute the commands through Automation. In other words, VBScript can serve as a macro language. It's in this context that Visual C++ uses VBScript.

A macro represents a set of instructions bundled into a single command. Macros written in VBScript are in a real sense simple programs for which the macro script serves as the source code. Executing a macro executes all of the instructions contained in the script. We saw in Chapter 3 how to create a VBScript macro by recording keystrokes and mouse clicks. Recording gives you a macro that plays back a sequence of recorded commands. You need only manually go through the commands once to record a macro. Thereafter, Developer Studio duplicates the same steps automatically whenever you run the recorded macro.

The untabify macro of Chapter 3 was created using the Record Quick Macro command. Although convenient, the Record Quick Macro command creates only a temporary macro that is lost forever the next time you invoke the command and record another macro. In contrast, the Macro command on the Tools menu lets you record permanent macros, storing several related macros in a single file. To demonstrate, here's how to create a permanent version of the untabify macro and enhance it with a corresponding tabify macro. The macros extend the TabifySelection and UntabifySelection commands to tabify and untabify an entire document, not just selected text. The first step is to create a macro file, then add scripts for the new tabify and untabify macros. With a document open in the text editor, choose the Macro command from the Tools menu to open the Macro dialog, click the Options button, and then click the New File button. Enter a filename and description for the macro file, as shown here:

Click OK, and then type *UntabifyAll* for the name of the first macro. Click the Record button and type an optional description in the Add Macro dialog such as *Expands tabs into spaces*. When you click the OK button, the main Macro dialog closes and returns you to the document in the text editor. The Record toolbar is now visible and the mouse cursor includes the image of a cassette tape, indicating that Visual C++ is now recording every keystroke and mouse click. Follow the same three steps as in Chapter 3 to create the macro:

1. On the Edit menu, click the Select All command to select the entire document.

2. Choose Advanced from the Edit menu and click the Untabify Selection command.

3. Press Ctrl+Home to return the caret to the top of the document.

Click the Stop Recording button on the Record toolbar to end the recording, at which point the text editor automatically opens the new VBScript macro file, named Tabs.dsm, in case you want to edit the macro. (The file extension stands for Developer Studio macro.) To return to the original text document, click the filename on the Window menu.

When you display the Macro dialog again, the Tabs filename appears in the Macro File combo box. To add a new tabify macro follow the same steps as before, except this time do not click the Options and New File buttons because you are adding to the macro file, not creating a new one. Just type *TabifyAll* to name the second macro, click the Record button, and enter a description for the new macro such as *Converts spaces into tabs*. Then follow the steps above to create the second macro, this time using the Tabify Selection command. The Tabs macro file now contains two macros, listed in the Macro dialog as UntabifyAll and TabifyAll. To run a macro, select it from the list in the dialog and click the Run button. The effect is the same as retyping the recorded keystrokes manually.

During recording, Visual C++ compiles a list of every command you execute and writes them in VBScript code to the DSM file. You can work in any editor while recording, and even switch back and forth between editors. Clicking the second button on the Record toolbar pauses the recording, allowing you to carry out operations that are not included in the finished macro. To resume recording, click the same button again. Normally, before running a macro, you should first move the caret to the document location where you want the recorded keystrokes to play back, though this step is not required for the TabifyAll and UntabifyAll macros.

Most of your macro needs can be fulfilled by recording a sequence of commands this way. But there may be times when you want a macro to perform tasks that cannot be recorded. To create such a macro, you must write a script and save it as a DSM file. The next section shows how.

## Example: A Macro for Columnar Search and Replace

VBScript comprises both a compiler and a run-time library. The VBScript compiler interprets commands listed in a macro, and the library provides functions that the macro can call. Appendix C contains a brief tutorial on VBScript, describing language elements and the VBScript library functions. VBScript is simple enough to learn very quickly, and fortunately many of its programming characteristics are similar to the C language.

A simple example demonstrates some of the capabilities of a VBScript macro. Chapter 3 mentioned that although it is possible to select a columnar block of text in a document, the text editor provides no means of restricting a search-and-replace operation to the selected column. If you mark a column of text and choose Replace from the Edit menu, the Replace dialog disables the Selection radio button. Replacing text only inside a marked column is a very desirable feature for an editor. With a macro, we can program the Developer Studio text editor to do just that.

It's often convenient to begin a macro by recording as much as possible, then use the text editor to add to the macro script file other commands that cannot be recorded. For this example, we won't record anything because the macro file Replace.dsm has been coded from scratch. To try out the macro, copy Replace.dsm from the Chapter.13 folder on the companion CD to the Visual C++ Macros folder on your hard disk. The default path to the folder is Common\MsDev98\Macros.

Choose the Macro command from the Tools menu, click the Options button, and then click the Loaded Files button. This exposes the familiar Customize dialog in which the new Replace.dsm file appears in a list of macro files stored in the Macros folder. Turn on the Replace check box in the list, close the dialog, and again invoke the Macro command. The Replace macro file now appears in the drop-down list of the Macro dialog. Selecting the file as shown in Figure 13-10 adds the single macro ColumnarReplace to the list.

If you prefer to type the macro yourself, begin with the New command and double-click the Macro File icon in the Files tab. Type the script as

**Figure 13-10.** *Invoking the ColumnarReplace macro.*

shown in Listing 13-2 on page 640, then save the file as Replace.dsm in the Common\MsDev98\Macros folder. Developer Studio still does not recognize the new macro file, so you must turn on its check box in the Customize dialog as explained in the preceding paragraph.

The Chapter.13 folder on the companion CD contains a text file named Column.txt that provides a simple testing ground for demonstrating the ColumnarReplace macro. (You can use any text document you wish for experimentation.) To change a column of words in the text, select a columnar block by dragging the mouse cursor as shown in Figure 13-11 while pressing the Alt key. Normally, you can mark a block by dragging in the opposite direction from the lower-right corner toward the upper-left corner, but the ColumnarReplace macro assumes that the mouse cursor moves from upper left to lower right.

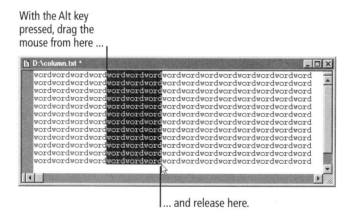

With the Alt key pressed, drag the mouse from here ...

... and release here.

**Figure 13-11.**   *Marking a columnar block of text.*

Next, click the Macro command on the Tools menu, select Replace from the Macro File drop-down list if necessary, and double-click Columnar-Replace in the box shown in Figure 13-10. As the macro runs, it queries for both the search string and the replacement string. Type *word* at the first query:

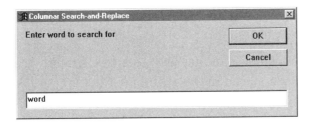

Type replacement text such as *NEW* at the second query:

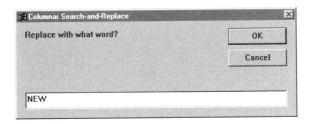

When you press the Enter key or click OK at the second query, the macro replaces every occurrence of "word" in the selected block, leaving the other "word" strings intact:

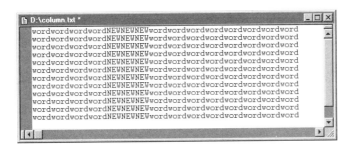

Assigning a keystroke combination to the macro gives you instant access to it. In the Keyboard tab of the Customize dialog, select Macros from the Category box and ColumnarReplace from the Commands list. Click the box labeled Press New Shortcut Key and type a keystroke combination such as Alt+R (for "replace") that best reminds you of the macro's purpose. You can also add a macro command to a toolbar or menu the same way you add any other Visual C++ command. In the Commands tab of the Customize dialog, select Macros from the Category list, and then drag the macro name from the displayed list onto a toolbar or menu as described earlier in this chapter.

Listing 13-2 shows the ColumnarReplace macro script. For an explanation of VBScript elements used in the script, refer to the tutorial in Appendix C. A brief discussion follows the listing that walks through the important sections and describes how the macro works.

**Listing 13-2.**   *The ColumnarReplace macro script.*

```
'-----------------------------------
'Macro:  Columnar search-and-replace
'-----------------------------------

Sub ColReplace ()

  'If no text selected, exit
  If ActiveDocument.Selection = "" Then Exit Sub

  strTitle = "Columnar Search-and-Replace"
  'Get column coordinates: (x1,y1) = upper-left corner
  '                        (x2,y2) = lower-right corner
  y2 = ActiveDocument.Selection.CurrentLine
  x2 = ActiveDocument.Selection.CurrentColumn
  y1 = ActiveDocument.Selection.TopLine
  x1 = Int( x2 - InStrB(ActiveDocument.Selection, vbCR)/2 + .5)

  'Prompt for search/replace strings
  strFind    = InputBox( "Enter word to search for", strTitle )
  If strFind = "" Then Exit Sub
  strReplace = InputBox( "Replace with what word?", strTitle )

  'Temporarily add a copy of the search string to the end of
  'the line. This prevents ReplaceText from cycling to the
  'top of the document after the final replacement.
  ActiveDocument.Selection.EndOfLine
  ActiveDocument.Selection = ActiveDocument.Selection + strFind

  'Start from top line of selection and work down
  Do While y1 <= y2
    ActiveDocument.Selection.GoToLine y1
    ActiveDocument.Selection.StartOfLine

    Do While ActiveDocument.Selection.CurrentColumn < x1
      ActiveDocument.Selection.CharRight dsMove, 1
    Loop
```

```
     Do While ActiveDocument.Selection.CurrentColumn < x2
       ActiveDocument.Selection.CharRight dsExtend, 1
     Loop

     ActiveDocument.Selection.ReplaceText strFind, strReplace
     y1 = y1 + 1
   Loop

   'Remove temporary string at end of line
   ActiveDocument.Selection.EndOfLine
   For i = 1 To Len( strFind )
     ActiveDocument.Selection.BackSpace
   Next

 End Sub
```

*ActiveDocument.Selection* is a VBScript property that contains all text selected in the current document. (The word "property" is a Visual Basic term that refers to a value of an object, used here in the same sense as in Chapter 8, Using ActiveX Controls. This makes sense when you remember that ActiveX controls trace their lineage to Visual Basic custom controls.) If no text is selected in the document, *ActiveDocument.Selection* contains an empty string. The ColumnarReplace macro first ensures that text has been selected in the document by checking the contents of *ActiveDocument.Selection*. If the string is empty, the macro terminates without taking any action.

The macro next determines the coordinates of the selected columnar block. Coordinates are the row and column positions of the upper-left and lower-right corners of the block. The properties *ActiveDocument.Selection.CurrentLine* and *ActiveDocument.Selection.CurrentColumn* give the row and column of the caret position at coordinates (*x2, y2*) at the lower-right corner of the block. This explains why the macro requires you to drag the mouse cursor downward instead of upward to select the columnar block—the caret must rest at the lower-right corner of the block when the macro begins. *ActiveDocument.Selection.TopLine* provides the top row of the block, stored in coordinate *y1*. No corresponding property exists for the column at which the block starts, so the macro relies on the fact that Developer Studio inserts a return character to mark the end of each line of a columnar selection contained in *ActiveDocument.Selection*. By locating the string's first return character (represented by the vbCR constant), the macro determines the width of the block in screen columns. It then computes the block's first column *x1* by subtracting the width of the block from the *x2* coordinate.

Separate calls to the *InputBox* library function query the user for the search string and its replacement string. If the user presses the Cancel button or does not specify a search string, the macro terminates. There is no similar test for the replacement string because the macro allows an empty replacement string as a valid entry. If the replacement string is empty, the macro merely replaces the search string with nothing—that is, it deletes the string from the text. The *InputBox* function provides no means of distinguishing between clicking OK with an empty replacement string and clicking Cancel, so the macro treats both actions the same way.

Developer Studio provides its own means for canceling a running macro. When a macro is active, the Developer Studio macro icon appears in the tray at the right side of the Windows taskbar:

Double-clicking the icon displays a confirmation message for terminating the macro. Since the macro continues to run while the confirmation message is displayed, you must respond to the message quickly.

Each iteration of the main loop in ColumnarReplace replaces text in one line of the selected block. The loop begins at the top line (*y1*) of the block, and then works down through the document one line at a time until it reaches the bottom line (*y2*) of the block:

```
Do While y1 <= y2
    ⋮
    ActiveDocument.Selection.ReplaceText strFind, strReplace
    y1 = y1 + 1
Loop
```

The first nested loop moves the caret from the start of the line to the first column of the block:

```
'Find left edge of selected column
Do While ActiveDocument.Selection.CurrentColumn < x1
    ActiveDocument.Selection.CharRight dsMove, 1
Loop
```

The second nested loop then moves the caret across the block one character at a time, selecting text as it goes:

```
'Select text across width of column
Do While ActiveDocument.Selection.CurrentColumn < x2
    ActiveDocument.Selection.CharRight dsExtend, 1
Loop
```

The result is a band of selected text that spans the original block, as shown here:

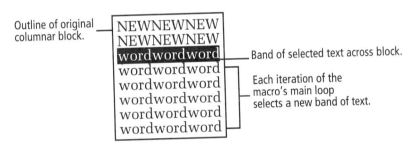

Outline of original columnar block.

Band of selected text across block.

Each iteration of the macro's main loop selects a new band of text.

Once it has selected a band on a line, the macro calls *ReplaceText*. This Developer Studio method replaces every occurrence of the search string *strFind* with the replacement string *strReplace*. The search is not sensitive to differences in letter case, although ColumnarReplace could easily be revised to accommodate case-sensitive searches. The key to the entire macro is that *ReplaceText* acts only on the selected band of text, not on the entire line. When the main loop iterates, the process repeats for the next line down through the last row of the columnar block.

# Developer Studio Add-Ins

You can further enhance the Developer Studio environment by creating add-ins, which are ActiveX dynamic link libraries that Visual C++ loads at startup and interacts with in response to user commands. Add-ins can provide integrated features for the environment in ways not possible with macros. Because they have access to the entire Windows API, add-ins can perform tasks such as file input/output, communications, printing, Internet support—anything you want to program. While a macro can interface with the user only through dialogs displayed by the *InputBox* and *MsgBox* functions, add-ins contain their own resource data and can thus display dialogs and property sheets of your own design. The disadvantage of add-ins is that they take more work to create than macros.

This section takes only a general look at Developer Studio add-ins. It describes how add-ins work and how to get started writing one, but the subject of add-ins runs fairly deep because of the many objects, properties, methods, and events that must be documented. A full discussion of the topic is beyond the scope of this introductory review. For more detailed information, consult Visual C++ online help or study the source code for the Api2Help sample project provided with Visual C++. To copy the Api2Help project to your hard disk, follow the steps outlined in the online article titled "Copying the Sample Add-ins," located under the index entry *sample add-ins.*

Begin an add-in project by choosing the New command from the File menu and clicking the Projects tab. Enter a project name and double-click the DevStudio Add-in Wizard icon to launch a single-step wizard that creates the project:

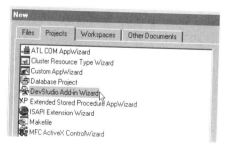

The Add-in Wizard automatically sets up the project and generates source code that relies on both MFC and ATL for most of the mundane work of writing an add-in. For an add-in project that does not require MFC, begin the project using ATL COM AppWizard instead of DevStudio Add-in Wizard, choose the New ATL Object command from the Insert menu, and double-click the Add-in Object icon in the ATL Object Wizard dialog. You can also write an add-in using C or Visual Basic, but you must consequently forego the advantages and convenience of the wizards.

After coding and building your add-in dynamic link library, the next step is to inform Developer Studio about the DLL file so that it loads the library and calls into it. Invoke the Customize dialog and click the tab labeled Add-Ins And Macro Files, then browse for the DLL file and double-click the file in the list. You can also copy the file to the Common\MsDev98\ Addins folder, which makes browsing unnecessary. To load the add-in library in the current Developer Studio session, turn on the check box for the add-in file in the Customize dialog. Leaving the check box on causes Visual C++ to automatically load the dynamic link library file at startup.

The diagram in Figure 13-12 illustrates how an add-in and Developer Studio interact. An add-in exposes two objects to Developer Studio, named *Commands* and *DSAddIn*, for which the Add-in Wizard creates class source code in the Commands.cpp and DSAddIn.cpp files. The *Commands* object contains all the methods that implement whatever commands the add-in provides. The *DSAddIn* object contains two methods named *OnConnection* and *OnDisconnection*. Developer Studio calls the

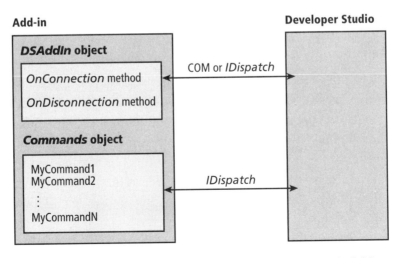

**Figure 13-12.** *How Developer Studio interacts with an add-in dynamic link library.*

first method when it loads (or "connects") the add-in, and calls the second method when the add-in is unloaded. When the add-in begins executing, the *OnConnection* method gains control and calls Developer Studio's *AddCommand* function. The call to *AddCommand* adds a new command to the environment and provides all the information about the command that Developer Studio needs to present it to the user. The new command is serviced by the add-in dynamic link library, but to the user it looks like any other command in Developer Studio's set of internal commands. Parameters for *AddCommand* specify information such as the name of the command, text that appears in Developer Studio's status bar when the command is selected in a menu, text for tooltips and the command's toolbar button, and the name of the method exported by the add-in dynamic link library that Developer Studio should call when the user invokes the command.

Developer Studio exports two other methods that allow the add-in to make the command more immediately accessible to the user. *AddCommand-BarButton* instructs Developer Studio to create a toolbar button for a command exported by the add-in. *AddKeyBinding* assigns a keystroke combination to a command. While hard-wiring a keystroke saves the user the trouble of assigning a key, calling *AddKeyBinding* is not recommended because it runs the risk of overriding an existing keystroke, potentially causing confusion for the user. It's generally better to leave an add-in command unbound and let the user assign a keystroke in the Customize dialog after the add-in first begins. An add-in has no way to query Developer Studio for a list of current keystroke combinations.

Developer Studio provides a set of objects that represent aspects of the environment, such as build and configuration information, open documents, the debugger, windows, and much more. (Appendix C explains how Visual C++ macros can use these same objects.) Through an object's properties and methods, an add-in can get or set detailed information pertaining to the environment. For example, the main Developer Studio object (named *Application*) contains the extensive collection of properties and methods listed in Table 13-4 on the facing page and Table 13-5 on page 649. You can gain familiarity with property strings and other values by displaying them in a simple macro script. For instance, executing this line in a macro:

```
MsgBox( Application.Name + " version " + Application.Version )
```

produces this message:

*Application* and *Debugger* are the only Developer Studio objects that fire events. *Debugger* fires only the *BreakPointHit* event, which notifies the add-in that a breakpoint has been triggered in the debugger. (See the section titled "Breakpoints" on page 518 of Chapter 11 for a description of debugger breakpoints.) The *Application* object fires the 12 events listed in Table 13-6 on page 650. The *CCommands* class generated by Add-in Wizard contains shell handler functions for all fired events. If you want your add-in to be notified of Developer Studio's current status, add implementation code to selected event handler functions in the Commands.cpp file.

**Table 13-4.** *Properties of the Application object.*

| Property | Description |
| --- | --- |
| *Active* | Boolean value that indicates whether Developer Studio is active. |
| *ActiveConfiguration* | String containing the current project configuration, usually either *Win32 Release* or *Win32 Debug*. |
| *ActiveDocument* | Name of the active document window. |
| *ActiveProject* | Name of the current project. |
| *ActiveWindow* | Title of the currently active Developer Studio window. |
| *CurrentDirectory* | Current directory used by the Open command. |
| *Debugger* | Object that represents the Visual C++ debugger. |
| *Documents* | Object that represents the collection of open documents. |

*continued*

**Table 13-4.** *continued*

| Property | Description |
| --- | --- |
| *FullName* | Path and filename of the Developer Studio executable. Usually this is C:\Program Files\Microsoft Visual Studio\Common\MsDev98\Bin\MsDev.exe. |
| *Height* | Value of type **long** containing the height in pixels of the main Developer Studio window. |
| *Left* | Value of type **long** containing the x-coordinate of the main window's left side. |
| *Name* | String that contains the text *Microsoft Developer Studio.* |
| *Parent* | Parent object of *Application.* |
| *Path* | Path to the Developer Studio executable. Usually this is C:\Program Files\Microsoft Visual Studio\Common\MsDev98\Bin. |
| *Projects* | Collection object representing all projects in the current workspace. |
| *TextEditor* | Object representing the Visual C++ text editor. |
| *Top* | Value of type **long** containing the y-coordinate of the main window's top border. |
| *Version* | String containing the current Developer Studio version, such as *6.0.* |
| *Visible* | Boolean value that determines whether the Developer Studio main window is visible. |
| *Width* | Value of type **long** containing the width in pixels of the Developer Studio main window. |
| *Windows* | Collection object representing all open windows. |
| *WindowState* | A **long** value that represents the state of the main wndow. Possible values include the constants dsWindowStateMaximized and dsWindowStateMinimized, which indicate whether Developer Studio is maximized or minimized. |

**Table 13-5.**    *Methods of the Application object.*

| Method | Description |
|---|---|
| *AddCommand* | Adds to Visual C++ a command defined by an add-in. |
| *AddCommand-BarButton* | Creates a toolbar for an add-in. |
| *AddKeybinding* | Assigns a key combination to an add-in command. |
| *Build* | Builds a project by processing only the files that have changed. |
| *EnableModeless* | Enables or disables modeless windows in Developer Studio. |
| *ExecuteCommand* | Executes a specified command or VBScript macro. |
| *ExecuteConfiguration* | Runs the program created by the project. |
| *GetPackageExtension* | Provides access to other objects outside of Developer Studio. |
| *PrintToOutputWindow* | Writes a string to the Macro tab of the Output window. (For an example, see page 679 in Appendix C.) |
| *Quit* | Prompts the user to save documents if necessary, closes any document windows, and shuts down Developer Studio. |
| *RebuildAll* | Executes the Developer Studio Rebuild All command. |
| *SetAddInInfo* | Provides information about an add-in. |

**Table 13-6.** *Events of the Application object.*

| Application event | When fired |
|---|---|
| *BeforeApplicationShutDown* | Just before Developer Studio shuts down. |
| *BeforeBuildStart* | Just after the user selects the Developer Studio Build command but before compilation begins. |
| *BeforeDocumentClose* | Just before a document is closed. The document is still open when the event fires. |
| *BuildFinish* | When a build successfully or unsuccessfully completes. |
| *DocumentOpen* | Just after a document is opened. |
| *DocumentSave* | Just after a document is saved. The old document file is already overwritten when the event fires. |
| *NewDocument* | When a new document is created. The document is open when the event fires. |
| *NewWorkspace* | When a new workspace is created. |
| *WindowActivate* | When a window becomes active. This event applies to both document windows in the editors and Developer Studio application windows, such as the debugger windows. |
| *WindowDeactivate* | Just after a window is deactivated or closed. |
| *WorkspaceClose* | Just after the workspace is closed. |
| *WorkspaceOpen* | Just after the workspace is opened. |

PART

# 6

Appendixes

# ASCII and ANSI File Formats

The Visual C++ text editor saves files in ANSI format, which is the preferred format of Windows-based text editors such as the Notepad utility that comes with Windows 95. DOS text editors generally use the similar ASCII format. Both the ANSI and ASCII formats assign a number from 0 through 255 to each of 256 characters.

Text editors almost always save files in either ASCII or ANSI format rather than in a proprietary format like a word processor. Originally, the acronym ASCII referred to a convention that assigned a number 32–127 to each of 96 characters, including numerals, punctuation marks, and lowercase and uppercase letters. This number fit comfortably into the range of values possible with seven bits (because $2^7$ equals 128). The ASCII convention sets aside values 0–31 as printer control codes and reserves the eighth bit of each byte for parity checking. Because memory today does not require parity checking, the eighth bit of every byte is free for data, doubling to 256 the number of characters that a single byte can represent. Today, what we think of as the ASCII character set combines characters for values 0–31, the original 96 ASCII characters, plus an additional 128 characters added by the original PC designers at IBM to utilize the extra eighth bit. These 128 extra characters, referred to as upper ASCII or the IBM character set, are shown in Table A-1 on page 655.

Some of the characters in the upper ASCII set, particularly the box-drawing characters, do not serve well in a graphical environment like Windows, which prefers the ANSI standard. ASCII and ANSI agree on most of the first 128 characters, but assign different characters to the higher numbers. That's why if you use a DOS-based text editor to create a document that contains upper ASCII characters, the characters appear as something else in the Visual C++ text editor.

Technically, any file consists of ASCII (or ANSI) characters. But in ASCII and ANSI formats, each character is taken at face value. Z, é, and ¼ mean "Z," "é," and "¼." Characters represent only themselves, not codes, instructions, or anything else. The only exceptions to this rule are the tab and return characters. A tab is a single character (ASCII value 9) that represents a variable number of spaces. The form of the return character, which marks the end of a line of text, depends on the editor and the operating system. In the world of DOS and Windows, a return consists of a pair of characters with ASCII values 13 and 10. ASCII 13, called a carriage return, signals a cursor move to the beginning of the line, whereas ASCII 10, called a linefeed, indicates a move down to the next row. The order of the characters is important; ASCII 13 must precede ASCII 10 or the return is usually not recognized. In the UNIX operating system, the linefeed alone serves as the end-of-line marker, implying a new line as well as a carriage return. The Visual C++ text editor recognizes both styles of returns, either ASCII 13-10 pairs or a single ASCII 10.

| Dec | Hex | Char | Dec | Hex | Char | Dec | Hex | Char | Dec | Hex | Char |
|-----|-----|------|-----|-----|------|-----|-----|------|-----|-----|------|
| 128 | 80 | Ç | 160 | A0 | á | 192 | C0 | └ | 224 | E0 | α |
| 129 | 81 | ü | 161 | A1 | í | 193 | C1 | ┴ | 225 | E1 | ß |
| 130 | 82 | é | 162 | A2 | ó | 194 | C2 | ┬ | 226 | E2 | Γ |
| 131 | 83 | â | 163 | A3 | ú | 195 | C3 | ├ | 227 | E3 | π |
| 132 | 84 | ä | 164 | A4 | ñ | 196 | C4 | ─ | 228 | E4 | Σ |
| 133 | 85 | à | 165 | A5 | Ñ | 197 | C5 | ┼ | 229 | E5 | σ |
| 134 | 86 | å | 166 | A6 | ª | 198 | C6 | ╞ | 230 | E6 | μ |
| 135 | 87 | ç | 167 | A7 | º | 199 | C7 | ╟ | 231 | E7 | τ |
| 136 | 88 | ê | 168 | A8 | ¿ | 200 | C8 | ╚ | 232 | E8 | Φ |
| 137 | 89 | ë | 169 | A9 | ⌐ | 201 | C9 | ╔ | 233 | E9 | Θ |
| 138 | 8A | è | 170 | AA | ¬ | 202 | CA | ╩ | 234 | EA | Ω |
| 139 | 8B | ï | 171 | AB | ½ | 203 | CB | ╦ | 235 | EB | δ |
| 140 | 8C | î | 172 | AC | ¼ | 204 | CC | ╠ | 236 | EC | ∞ |
| 141 | 8D | ì | 173 | AD | ¡ | 205 | CD | = | 237 | ED | ø |
| 142 | 8E | Ä | 174 | AE | « | 206 | CE | ╬ | 238 | EE | ε |
| 143 | 8F | Å | 175 | AF | » | 207 | CF | ╧ | 239 | EF | ∩ |
| 144 | 90 | É | 176 | B0 | ░ | 208 | D0 | ╨ | 240 | F0 | ≡ |
| 145 | 91 | æ | 177 | B1 | ▓ | 209 | D1 | ╤ | 241 | F1 | ± |
| 146 | 92 | ff | 178 | B2 | ▓ | 210 | D2 | ╥ | 242 | F2 | ≥ |
| 147 | 93 | ô | 179 | B3 | │ | 211 | D3 | ╙ | 243 | F3 | ≤ |
| 148 | 94 | ö | 180 | B4 | ┤ | 212 | D4 | ╘ | 244 | F4 | ⌠ |
| 149 | 95 | ò | 181 | B5 | ╡ | 213 | D5 | ╒ | 245 | F5 | ⌡ |
| 150 | 96 | û | 182 | B6 | ╢ | 214 | D6 | ╓ | 246 | F6 | ÷ |
| 151 | 97 | ù | 183 | B7 | ╖ | 215 | D7 | ╫ | 247 | F7 | ≈ |
| 152 | 98 | ÿ | 184 | B8 | ╕ | 216 | D8 | ╪ | 248 | F8 | ° |
| 153 | 99 | Ö | 185 | B9 | ╣ | 217 | D9 | ┘ | 249 | F9 | · |
| 154 | 9A | Ü | 186 | BA | ║ | 218 | DA | ┌ | 250 | FA | · |
| 155 | 9B | ¢ | 187 | BB | ╗ | 219 | DB | █ | 251 | FB | √ |
| 156 | 9C | £ | 188 | BC | ╝ | 220 | DC | ▄ | 252 | FC | ⁿ |
| 157 | 9D | ¥ | 189 | BD | ╜ | 221 | DD | ▌ | 253 | FD | ² |
| 158 | 9E | ₧ | 190 | BE | ╛ | 222 | DE | ▐ | 254 | FE | ■ |
| 159 | 9F | ƒ | 191 | BF | ┐ | 223 | DF | ▀ | 255 | FF | |

**Table A-1.**     *Upper ASCII character set, values 128–255.*

Table A-2 lists all 256 characters of the US ANSI set, some of which Windows does not display. These undisplayable ANSI characters, normally rendered on the screen as a box or blank space, appear in Table A-2 as a generic box like this □. The table lists octal rather than hexadecimal values for each character. Knowing a character's value in octal base allows you to include the character in a resource string or a static text box by typing a backslash followed by the character's octal value. To include the ANSI character ½ in a string, for example, type \275. Notice that Windows can render some characters, such as the trademark symbol ™, only in TrueType fonts.

**Table A-2.** *ANSI character set, values 0–255.*

| Dec | Octal | Char | Dec | Octal | Char | Dec | Octal | Char | Dec | Octal | Char |
|-----|-------|------|-----|-------|------|-----|-------|------|-----|-------|------|
| 0 | 000 | □ | 20 | 024 | □ | 40 | 050 | ( | 60 | 074 | < |
| 1 | 001 | □ | 21 | 025 | □ | 41 | 051 | ) | 61 | 075 | = |
| 2 | 002 | □ | 22 | 026 | □ | 42 | 052 | * | 62 | 076 | > |
| 3 | 003 | □ | 23 | 027 | □ | 43 | 053 | + | 63 | 077 | ? |
| 4 | 004 | □ | 24 | 030 | □ | 44 | 054 | , | 64 | 100 | @ |
| 5 | 005 | □ | 25 | 031 | □ | 45 | 055 | - | 65 | 101 | A |
| 6 | 006 | □ | 26 | 032 | □ | 46 | 056 | . | 66 | 102 | B |
| 7 | 007 | □ | 27 | 033 | □ | 47 | 057 | / | 67 | 103 | C |
| 8 | 010 | □ | 28 | 034 | □ | 48 | 060 | 0 | 68 | 104 | D |
| 9 | 011 | □ | 29 | 035 | □ | 49 | 061 | 1 | 69 | 105 | E |
| 10 | 012 | □ | 30 | 036 | □ | 50 | 062 | 2 | 70 | 106 | F |
| 11 | 013 | □ | 31 | 037 | □ | 51 | 063 | 3 | 71 | 107 | G |
| 12 | 014 | □ | 32 | 040 | □ | 52 | 064 | 4 | 72 | 110 | H |
| 13 | 015 | □ | 33 | 041 | ! | 53 | 065 | 5 | 73 | 111 | I |
| 14 | 016 | □ | 34 | 042 | " | 54 | 066 | 6 | 74 | 112 | J |
| 15 | 017 | □ | 35 | 043 | # | 55 | 067 | 7 | 75 | 113 | K |
| 16 | 020 | □ | 36 | 044 | $ | 56 | 070 | 8 | 76 | 114 | L |
| 17 | 021 | □ | 37 | 045 | % | 57 | 071 | 9 | 77 | 115 | M |
| 18 | 022 | □ | 38 | 046 | & | 58 | 072 | : | 78 | 116 | N |
| 19 | 023 | □ | 39 | 047 | ' | 59 | 073 | ; | 79 | 117 | O |

| Dec | Octal | Char | Dec | Octal | Char | Dec | Octal | Char | Dec | Octal | Char |
|---|---|---|---|---|---|---|---|---|---|---|---|
| 80 | 120 | P | 110 | 156 | n | 140[TT] | 214 | Œ | 170 | 252 | ª |
| 81 | 121 | Q | 111 | 157 | o | 141 | 215 | □ | 171 | 253 | « |
| 82 | 122 | R | 112 | 160 | p | 142 | 216 | □ | 172 | 254 | ¬ |
| 83 | 123 | S | 113 | 161 | q | 143 | 217 | □ | 173 | 255 | |
| 84 | 124 | T | 114 | 162 | r | 144 | 220 | □ | 174 | 256 | ® |
| 85 | 125 | U | 115 | 163 | s | 145 | 221 | ' | 175 | 257 | ¯ |
| 86 | 126 | V | 116 | 164 | t | 146 | 222 | ' | 176 | 260 | ° |
| 87 | 127 | W | 117 | 165 | u | 147[TT] | 223 | " | 177 | 261 | ± |
| 88 | 130 | X | 118 | 166 | v | 148[TT] | 224 | " | 178 | 262 | ² |
| 89 | 131 | Y | 119 | 167 | w | 149[TT] | 225 | □ | 179 | 263 | ³ |
| 90 | 132 | Z | 120 | 170 | x | 150[TT] | 226 | – | 180 | 264 | ´ |
| 91 | 133 | [ | 121 | 171 | y | 151[TT] | 227 | — | 181 | 265 | µ |
| 92 | 134 | \ | 122 | 172 | z | 152[TT] | 230 | ~ | 182 | 266 | ¶ |
| 93 | 135 | ] | 123 | 173 | { | 153[TT] | 231 | ™ | 183 | 267 | · |
| 94 | 136 | ^ | 124 | 174 | \| | 154[TT] | 232 | š | 184 | 270 | ¸ |
| 95 | 137 | _ | 125 | 175 | } | 155[TT] | 233 | › | 185 | 271 | ¹ |
| 96 | 140 | ` | 126 | 176 | ~ | 156[TT] | 234 | œ | 186 | 272 | º |
| 97 | 141 | a | 127 | 177 | □ | 157 | 235 | □ | 187 | 273 | » |
| 98 | 142 | b | 128 | 200 | □ | 158 | 236 | □ | 188 | 274 | ¼ |
| 99 | 143 | c | 129 | 201 | □ | 159[TT] | 237 | Ÿ | 189 | 275 | ½ |
| 100 | 144 | d | 130[TT] | 202 | ‚ | 160 | 240 | □ | 190 | 276 | ¾ |
| 101 | 145 | e | 131[TT] | 203 | ƒ | 161 | 241 | ¡ | 191 | 277 | ¿ |
| 102 | 146 | f | 132[TT] | 204 | „ | 162 | 242 | ¢ | 192 | 300 | À |
| 103 | 147 | g | 133[TT] | 205 | … | 163 | 243 | £ | 193 | 301 | Á |
| 104 | 150 | h | 134[TT] | 206 | † | 164 | 244 | ¤ | 194 | 302 | Â |
| 105 | 151 | i | 135[TT] | 207 | ‡ | 165 | 245 | ¥ | 195 | 303 | Ã |
| 106 | 152 | j | 136[TT] | 210 | ^ | 166 | 246 | ¦ | 196 | 304 | Ä |
| 107 | 153 | k | 137[TT] | 211 | ‰ | 167 | 247 | § | 197 | 305 | Å |
| 108 | 154 | l | 138[TT] | 212 | Š | 168 | 250 | ¨ | 198 | 306 | Æ |
| 109 | 155 | m | 139[TT] | 213 | ‹ | 169 | 251 | © | 199 | 307 | Ç |

*(continued)*

**Table A-2.** *continued*

| Dec | Octal | Char | Dec | Octal | Char | Dec | Octal | Char | Dec | Octal | Char |
|-----|-------|------|-----|-------|------|-----|-------|------|-----|-------|------|
| 200 | 310 | È | 214 | 326 | Ö | 228 | 344 | ä | 242 | 362 | ò |
| 201 | 311 | É | 215 | 327 | × | 229 | 345 | å | 243 | 363 | ó |
| 202 | 312 | Ê | 216 | 330 | Ø | 230 | 346 | æ | 244 | 364 | ô |
| 203 | 313 | Ë | 217 | 331 | Ù | 231 | 347 | ç | 245 | 365 | õ |
| 204 | 314 | Ì | 218 | 332 | Ú | 232 | 350 | è | 246 | 366 | ö |
| 205 | 315 | Í | 219 | 333 | Û | 233 | 351 | é | 247 | 367 | ÷ |
| 206 | 316 | Î | 220 | 334 | Ü | 234 | 352 | ê | 248 | 370 | ø |
| 207 | 317 | Ï | 221 | 335 | Ý | 235 | 353 | ë | 249 | 371 | ù |
| 208 | 330 | Đ | 222 | 336 | Þ | 236 | 354 | ì | 250 | 372 | ú |
| 209 | 321 | Ñ | 223 | 337 | ß | 237 | 355 | í | 251 | 373 | û |
| 210 | 322 | Ò | 224 | 340 | à | 238 | 356 | î | 252 | 374 | ü |
| 211 | 323 | Ó | 225 | 341 | á | 239 | 357 | ï | 253 | 375 | ý |
| 212 | 324 | Ô | 226 | 342 | â | 240 | 360 | ð | 254 | 376 | þ |
| 213 | 325 | Õ | 227 | 343 | ã | 241 | 361 | ñ | 255 | 377 | ÿ |

□ Indicates Windows does not display this character
π Indicates TrueType font only

# MFC Classes Supported by ClassWizard

As described in Chapter 6, ClassWizard is a tool designed to help you create classes derived from MFC. This appendix lists and briefly describes the MFC classes from which ClassWizard can generate starter code for derived classes. The list includes five classes new for this release of MFC: *CComboBoxEx*, *CDateTimeCtrl*, *CHtmlView*, *CIPAddressCtr*, and *CMonthCalCtrl*.

ClassWizard displays the New Class dialog to prompt for the name and base of a new class, as illustrated in Figure 6-4 on page 278. The radio buttons in the dialog's Automation group box determine whether the new class should support Automation or provide a type identifier:

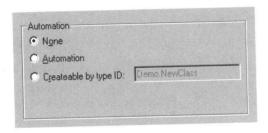

The identifier is a name, more correctly known as a programmatic identifier or ProgID, by which client applications can create an object of the class using Automation. The MFC macro IMPLEMENT_OLECREATE records the programmatic identifier in the system Registry as an alias of the class's unique class identifier number.

Not all MFC classes support Automation options, in which case the radio buttons are disabled in the New Class dialog. The Support column in Table B-1 includes an A or I code to indicate which classes support Automation or type identification. The D code in the Support column flags dialog-based classes, such as *CDialog*, which require a dialog resource.

**Table B-1.**     *MFC classes recognized by ClassWizard.*

| MFC class | Support* | Description |
| --- | --- | --- |
| *CAnimateCtrl* | A, I | Animation common control. |
| *CAsyncMonikerFile* | | Provides support for asynchronous monikers in an ActiveX control. |
| *CAsyncSocket* | | Encapsulates the Windows Sockets API. See also *CSocket*. |
| *CButton* | A, I | Button control object. |
| *CCachedData-PathProperty* | | Allows an ActiveX control to asynchronously transfer property data and cache the data in memory. See also *CDataPathProperty*. |
| *CCmdTarget* | A, I | Base class for objects that can receive and respond to messages. |
| *CColorDialog* | | Common dialog for color selection, providing a list of colors that are defined for the display system. |
| *CComboBox* | A, I | Combo box object. |
| *CComboBoxEx* | A, I | Derivation of *CComboBox* class that supports image lists in the combo box control. |
| *CDaoRecordset* | | Represents a set of records selected from a data source. *CDaoRecordset* objects are available in three forms: table-type recordsets, dynaset-type recordsets, and snapshot-type recordsets. |

| MFC class | Support* | Description |
|---|---|---|
| *CDaoRecordView* | D, A | Provides a form view to display database records in a control. The form view is part of a *CDaoRecordset* object. See also *CFormView* and *CRecordView*. |
| *CDataPathProperty* | | Implements an ActiveX control property capable of loading its data asynchronously. This class allows an ActiveX control to become active while downloading property data in the background. |
| *CDateTimeCtrl* | A, I | Encapsulates the new date/time picker control (demonstrated in the DirList2 example program of Chapter 7, The Gallery). |
| *CDialog* | D, A | Dialog box object for containment of control windows. |
| *CDocument* | A | Class for managing program data. |
| *CDragListBox* | A, I | Windows list box that allows the user to drag items into different positions. |
| *CEdit* | A, I | Child window control for text entry. |
| *CEditView* | A | Provides the functionality of a Windows edit control. Because *CEditView* is derived from *CView*, objects can be used with documents and document templates. |
| *CFileDialog* | | Common file dialog, providing implementation for Open and Save As dialogs. |
| *CFontDialog* | | Common font dialog, which displays a list of fonts currently installed on the system. |
| *CFormView* | D, A | Window that can contain dialog box controls. |
| *CFrameWnd* | A | Single document interface (SDI) frame window. |
| *CHeaderCtrl* | A, I | Header common control. |
| *CHotKeyCtrl* | A, I | Hot key common control. |

*(continued)*

**Table B-1.** *continued*

| MFC class | Support* | Description |
| --- | --- | --- |
| *CHtmlView* | A | A view class that implements the Web Browser control, able to access HTML documents locally or over the Web. See also Microsoft Web Browser ActiveX control in the Gallery. |
| *CHttpFilter* | | Creates and handles a Hypertext Transfer Protocol filter object, which filters server notifications for HTTP requests. |
| *CHttpServer* | | Wrapper class for the Internet Server API (ISAPI). |
| *CIPAddressCtrl* | A, I | IP Address control. Similar to an edit box, the control accepts an address in Internet Protocol format. |
| *CListBox* | A, I | List box object. |
| *CListCtrl* | A, I | List view common control. For an example, see the MfcTree project in Chapter 5, Dialog Boxes and Controls. |
| *CListView* | | Simplifies use of *CListCtrl*, adding support for documents and view. |
| *CMDIChildWnd* | A | Multiple document interface (MDI) child frame window. |
| *CMiniFrameWnd* | A | A half-height frame window, typically used for floating toolbars. A miniframe window does not have minimize and maximize buttons but otherwise is similar to a normal frame window. |
| *CMonthCalCtrl* | A, I | Month calendar control, which displays a calendar from which the user can select a date. |
| *COleDocument* | A | Treats a document as a collection of *CDocItem* objects. Both containers and servers require this architecture because their documents must be able to contain OLE items. |

| MFC class | Support* | Description |
| --- | --- | --- |
| *COleLinkingDoc* | A | Base class for OLE container documents that support linking to the embedded items they contain. |
| *COleServerDoc* | A | Base class for OLE server documents. |
| *COleServerItem* | A | Provides a server interface to OLE items. |
| *CPrintDialog* | | Common dialog box for printing, providing implementation for the Print and Print Setup dialog boxes. |
| *CProgressCtrl* | A, I | Common progress indicator control. |
| *CPropertyPage* | D, A | Represents an individual page of a property sheet. See the DirList1 example project in Chapter 5. |
| *CPropertySheet* | A | Property sheet, otherwise known as a tabbed dialog box. A property sheet consists of a *CPropertySheet* object and one or more *CPropertyPage* objects. |
| *CRecordset* | | Class for accessing a database table or query. |
| *CRecordView* | D, A | Window containing dialog box controls mapped to recordset fields. |
| *CRichEditCtrl* | A, I | Window in which the user can enter and edit text, providing character and paragraph formatting and support for embedded OLE objects. |
| *CScrollBar* | A, I | Scroll bar object. |
| *CScrollView* | A | Scrolling window, derived from *CView*. |
| *CSliderCtrl* | A, I | Provides a window containing a slider and optional tick marks. For an example showing how to use *CSliderCtrl*, see the Color project in Chapter 5. |
| *CSocket* | | Wrapper class for the Windows Socket API. |
| *CSpinButtonCtrl* | A, I | Provides arrow buttons that the user can click to increment or decrement a value in a control. See the DirList2 example project in Chapter 7. |

*(continued)*

**Table B-1.** *continued*

| MFC class | Support* | Description |
|---|---|---|
| *CStatic* | A, I | A simple text box that labels another control or provides other information to the user. |
| *CStatusBarCtrl* | A, I | Provides a horizontal window, usually placed at the bottom of a parent window, for displaying status information about an application. |
| *CTabCtrl* | A, I | Allows an application to display multiple pages in the same area of a window or dialog box. |
| *CToolBarCtrl* | A, I | Toolbar common control. |
| *CToolTipCtrl* | A, I | Provides the functionality of a tooltip control, which appears as a small pop-up window containing a single line of text describing the purpose of a tool. |
| *CTreeCtrl* | A, I | Displays a hierarchical list of items. |
| *CTreeView* | | Simplifies use of *CTreeCtrl*. |
| *CView* | A | Class for displaying program data. |
| *CWinThread* | | Represents a thread of execution within an application. |
| generic *CWnd* | A, I | Custom window. |
| splitter | A | An MDI child window that contains a *CSplitterWnd* class. The user can split the resulting window into multiple panes. |

*Support codes: D = Dialog   A = Automation   I = Programmatic identifier

# A VBScript Primer

Visual Basic Scripting Edition, better known as VBScript, is a subset of Visual Basic for Applications (VBA), which in turn is a dialect of Visual Basic. Incorporated in Visual C++ as its macro language, VBScript has at last brought serious macro capabilities to Visual C++. VBScript comes packaged as a compiler (more accurately an interpreter) and a run-time library. A macro script written in the VBScript language can recreate a series of Developer Studio commands, automating nearly any task that you can do by hand. And by drawing on the VBScript run-time library, a macro can perform many other tasks not otherwise possible in Visual C++, such as displaying information in a standard Windows message box and querying for user input.

Visual C++ provides two techniques for creating a macro: recording and programming. Most macros can be created simply by recording a sequence of actions, a technique that does not require an understanding of VBScript. Behind the scenes, the environment automatically creates a VBScript macro file that replicates the recorded commands. But as demonstrated in Chapter 13, Customizing Visual C++, recording a macro has limitations. A recorded macro is "hard-wired," well suited for duplicating a specific set of actions but not general enough to react to different circumstances when the macro runs. Flexibility in a macro requires programming, and that requires knowledge of VBScript. Fortunately, VBScript is very easy to learn, and C/C++ programmers will immediately recognize many of its characteristics. You already know much of VBScript, even if you've never seen the language before. This appendix fills in some of the gaps, providing an introductory tutorial on macro programming geared toward the C/C++ programmer. To learn more about VBScript—particularly its use in documents—consult one of the many books available or visit Microsoft's Web site at

*http://www.microsoft.com/vbscript*

The first half of this appendix describes various language elements of VBScript, such as variables, program flow statements, and procedures. Each discussion illustrates by using commented code fragments. Comments in VBScript begin with a single quote character and continue to the end of the line. VBScript also recognizes the old-style **Rem** statement of the BASIC language, but **Rem** is seldom used anymore:

```
'        This is a comment
Rem      So is this
```

The second half of the appendix concentrates on functions in the VBScript library, offering a brief description of each function and often demonstrating with example code.

# Variables

VBScript recognizes one data type, named **Variant**, which contains either numeric or text information, depending on context. If you assign numeric data to a variable in VBScript, the variable takes on a numeric data type suitable for the data. Assigning text data to a **Variant** variable turns it into a string. VBScript provides several functions to convert one internal data type into another. Table C-1 lists some of the data types that **Variant** can mimic.

A variable's name should give an indication of its internal subtype. Use Hungarian notation or a similar convention when naming a variable to indicate the type of data the variable contains. Names like *bFlag*, *iNumber*, and *strString* are self-documenting, making it easy to recognize variables that contain BOOL, **int**, and text data.

| Data type | Description |
|-----------|-------------|
| BOOL | Either TRUE (non-zero) or FALSE (zero). |
| BYTE | 8-bit unsigned integer value from 0 through 255. |
| **int** | 16-bit signed integer value from -32,768 through 32,767. |
| **long** | 32-bit signed integer value from -2,147,483,648 through 2,147,483,647. |
| **float** | Single-precision floating-point value with negative values ranging from -3.402823E38 through -1.401298E-45 and positive values from 1.401298E-45 through 3.402823E38. |
| **double** | Double-precision floating-point value with negative values ranging from -1.79769313486232E308 through -4.94065645841247E-324 and positive values from 4.94065645841247E-324 through 1.79769313486232E308. |
| Date | Represents date and time from January 1, 100 through December 31, 9999. |
| String | String of BSTR type, up to approximately 2 billion characters in length. |

**Table C-1.**   *Data types that **Variant** simulates.*

A variable name must comply with these rules:

- Begin with an alphabetic character

- Cannot contain an embedded period

- Have a maximum length of 255 characters

- Be unique in the scope in which it is declared

Except for arrays, it isn't necessary to declare a variable before using it. If you prefer to declare variables at the beginning of a procedure, use the **Dim** statement (short for "dimension") like this:

```
Dim    x

x = 3
y = x    'This statement is legal, even though y was not declared
```

To help catch typographical errors, you can force mandatory variable declarations in a macro by including the Option Explicit statement. With this statement in effect, using a variable is legal only if the script has previously declared the variable with a **Dim** statement. Place the Option Explicit statement at the top of the macro file as shown here:

```
Option Explicit
⋮

Dim     x

x = 3     'Legal
y = x     'Not legal, because y has not been previously declared
```

The **Const** keyword has the same effect in VBScript as in the C language. For a variable intended to contain only unchanging data, use **Const** at the variable's initial assignment. Thereafter, the VBScript interpreter allows no other assignment for the variable:

```
Const x = 3
x = 5                       'This statement causes an error
```

## Arrays

A macro must specifically declare an array by using the **Dim** statement:

```
Dim iArray(10)             'A one-dimensional array
```

As in the C language, arrays in VBScript are zero-based. But unlike declarations in C, the array subscript of a **Dim** statement specifies the highest element index, not the number of elements. The above declaration therefore actually allocates 11 elements, accessed as *iArray(0)* through *iArray(10)*. An array can have up to 60 dimensions, indicated in the **Dim** statement using a list of subscripts separated by commas:

```
Dim iArray(5, 10)          'A two-dimensional array
Dim iArray(5, 10, 15)      'A three-dimensional array
```

An array allocated without a subscript list is dynamic, meaning that the macro can resize the array at run time. Use the **ReDim** statement to resize a dynamic array, like this:

```
Dim iArray()                    'Define but don't allocate an array
  ⋮
ReDim iArray(100)               'Allocate space for 101 elements
  ⋮
ReDim Preserve iArray(50)  'Resize the array for 51 elements
```

**ReDim** can resize an array to make it either smaller or larger. The array *iArray* in the fragment initially holds 101 integer elements, but is subsequently reduced in size to hold only 51 elements. The **Preserve** keyword ensures that reducing the array maintains the values of the first 51 elements, though elements *iArray(51)* through *iArray(100)* are lost when the array is resized. Without the **Preserve** keyword, resizing an array to make it larger or smaller erases its original contents. VBScript does not impose a limit to the number of times a macro can resize an array. However, if the code declares an array with a subscript in the **Dim** statement, the array cannot be resized with a **ReDim** statement. Attempting to do so causes an error.

### Strings

Assign values to string variables as you would in C by enclosing the text in double quotes:

```
strName = "John Q. Public"
```

Use pound signs to enclose strings containing dates:

```
dateBirth = #07-04-76#
```

# Operators

All VBScript operators except one fall neatly into three categories named arithmetic, comparison, and logical. When operators of different categories appear in the same expression, arithmetic operators have the highest precedence—that is, VBScript evaluates arithmetic operators such as addition and multiplication before operators of other categories. Comparison operators come next, followed by logical operators. As in the C language, operators inside parentheses are evaluated before operators outside parentheses, regardless of category. These two lines demonstrate how parentheses can change the order in which VBScript evaluates the operators of an expression:

```
x + y And z     'AND the variable z with the sum of x + y
x + (y And z)   'Add to the variable x the result of y AND z
```

Precedence order also exists within the arithmetic and logical categories. Comparison operators all have equal precedence and are evaluated left to right in the order they appear in an expression. Table C-2 lists the VBScript operators, arranging arithmetic and logical operators in descending order of precedence. The general order of precedence in the table thus decreases in the right and downward directions.

| Arithmetic operators | | Comparison operators | | Logical operators | |
|---|---|---|---|---|---|
| Description | Symbol | Description | Symbol | Description | Symbol |
| Exponentiation | ^ | Equality | = | Negation | Not |
| Unary negation | - | Inequality | <> | Logical AND | And |
| Multiplication | * | Less than | < | Logical OR | Or |
| Division | / | Greater than | > | Exclusive OR | Xor |
| Integer division | \ | Less than or equal to | <= | Equivalence | Eqv |
| Modulo arithmetic | Mod | Greater than or equal to | >= | | |
| Addition | + | | | | |
| Subtraction | - | | | | |

**Table C-2.** *VBScript operators listed in descending order of precedence.*

As in the C programming language, multiplication and division operators have equal precedence. So do addition and subtraction operators. VBScript provides a string concatenation operator (&) that does not fall into any of the three categories listed in Table C-2. In its order of precedence, the concatenation operator lies between arithmetic and comparison operators.

# Controlling Program Flow

A macro controls program flow by using conditional branching and loops, and by calling procedures. VBScript does not recognize labels and does not have the equivalent of a **goto** statement, which means a macro cannot jump unconditionally from one location in the script to another. A method named *GoToLine* exists, but *GoToLine* serves only to move the caret in a document and has nothing to do with controlling program flow in an executing macro.

## Conditional Branching

The **If...Then...Else** group of statements is functionally equivalent to C's **if...else** statements, except that VBScript does not use brackets { } to enclose blocks of code:

```
If ActiveDocument.Selection = "" Then str = "No selection"
Else str = ActiveDocument.Selection
```

A condition that spans two or more lines must end with an **End If** statement:

```
If x < y Then
    iLine = ActiveDocument.Selection.CurrentLine
    iCol  = ActiveDocument.Selection.CurrentColumn
End If
```

When a condition becomes too complex for the simple yes-or-no test of **If...Then...Else**, VBScript's **Select Case** command offers a better alternative. The command provides a clean method of conditional branching based on the value of a variable, very much like the **switch** statement of C. As in C, branch targets are each marked by a **Case** statement and a unique value. Control reaches a **Case** statement when its value matches that given to the **Select Case** command:

```
Select Case i
    Case 1
    'Come here when i = 1

    Case 2
    'Come here when i = 2
```

```
        'And so forth
End Select
```

VBScript does not provide a **break** keyword, so each **Case** statement implies the end of the preceding **Case** block. After a block finishes, program flow continues to the next statement following the **End Select** statement that terminates the **Select Case** section. The **Case Else** statement performs the same function as C's **default** keyword, marking a block of code that executes if control does not branch to any other **Case** statement:

```
Select Case strColor
    Case "red"      strHiLite = "magenta"
    Case "blue"     strHiLite = "cyan"
    Case "brown"    strHiLite = "yellow"
    Case Else       strHiLite = "undefined"
End Select
```

## Loops

VBScript recognizes several loop constructions that offer no surprises to a C/C++ programmer:

- **Do While...Loop** or **Do...Loop While**—Iterates while a condition is true

- **Do Until...Loop** or **Do...Loop Until**—Iterates until a condition is true

- **For...Next**—Iterates as governed by a loop counter variable

The **Do** keyword begins a repeating block of code that ends with a **Loop** statement. The **While** and **Until** keywords can appear either on the **Do** line at the top of the block or on the **Loop** line at the bottom of the block, depending on whether you want the VBScript interpreter to examine the condition before or after executing the loop. A few code fragments illustrate the proper formats for loops in VBScript:

```
Do While x < y
    'Loop is not entered unless x is less than y
Loop

Do
    'Loop executes at least once and repeats only if i is less than j
Loop While i < j
Do Until x = 10
```

```
        'Loop is not entered if x is equal to 10
        'When x attains a value of 10, the loop exits
Loop

Do
        'Loop executes at least once and repeats only
        'until i is not equal to j
Loop Until i <> j
```

By default the loop counter in a **For...Next** loop increments by 1:

```
For i = 1 To 10
        'This loop iterates 10 times, incrementing i from 1 to 10
Next
```

Use the **Step** keyword in a **For...Next** loop to specify a different increment value for the loop counter:

```
For i = 1 To 10 Step 2
        'This loop iterates 5 times
Next

For i = 10 To 2 Step -2
        'This loop also iterates 5 times
Next
```

The first **For...Next** loop in the fragment iterates five times. It initializes the loop counter *i* with a value of 1, then increments it at successive iterations to values of 3, 5, 7, and 9. During the final pass of the loop, *i* has a value of 9; the loop exits when *i* attains a value of 11. The second **For...Next** loop also iterates five times, but *i* decreases rather than increases as the loop repeats because the **Step** value is negative. Initialized with a value of 10, *i* decrements at each loop iteration to values of 8, 6, 4, and 2. When the loop exits, *i* has a value of 0.

## Procedures

Besides its own library of built-in functions, VBScript recognizes two types of procedures in a macro script, labeled **Sub** and **Function**. Both types accept arguments, but only **Function** can return a value. Otherwise there is little difference between the two types.

Every macro script has a main **Sub** procedure, the name of which determines the name of the macro that appears in Visual C++'s Macro dialog.

The main **Sub** procedure appears first in the macro script and does not take arguments. The script's callable subprocedures follow the main procedure in arbitrary order. As shown here, every **Sub** procedure (including the first) ends with an **End Sub** statement:

```
Sub MacroName ()                'Main procedure
    ⋮
End Sub

Sub Subroutine1( arg1, arg2 )
    'Code for first callable procedure goes here
End Sub

Sub Subroutine2( arg1, arg2 )
    'Code for second callable procedure goes here
End Sub
```

A callable **Sub** procedure—that is, any **Sub** procedure but the first—can be invoked either through a **Call** statement or through the procedure name as a stand-alone program statement. This mimics the way functions are invoked in C/C++. The format differs slightly for the two methods. The **Call** statement requires that the **Sub** procedure's arguments are enclosed in parentheses after the procedure name. Without the **Call** statement, arguments follow the procedure name separated by commas without parentheses. These two lines thus have the same effect:

```
Call AnySub( param1, param2 )
AnySub param1, param2
```

Because a **Function** procedure returns data, it can serve as a righthand value the same way as a C function. To return a value, a **Function** procedure must contain a variable that has the same name as the procedure itself. The interpreter returns the value of this variable to the caller when the procedure exits. Because all values are of **Variant** type, the interpreter performs no type-checking for return values. Unlike **Sub** procedures, the argument list of a **Function** procedure always appears enclosed in parentheses. If a **Function** procedure has no arguments, it must include an empty set of parentheses. Here's a simple example that computes the area of a circle from its radius:

```
Sub Main ()
    iRadius = InputBox( "Enter radius of circle:" )
    MsgBox( "Area is " & Area( iRadius ) & " square units" )
End Sub

Function Area( iRadius )
    Area = iRadius * iRadius * 3.1415926
End Function
```

The VBScript interpreter determines the precision of the *Area* variable by the maximum precision of the values from which *Area* is computed. If *iRadius* has a value of 2, for example, the value of pi carried out to seven decimal places in the above example implies the same precision for *Area*:

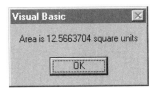

Arguments are passed by value in VBScript, not by reference. Neither a **Sub** nor a **Function** procedure can alter external data except for variables with global scope. VBScript refers to scope as level, so that local variables are said to be "procedure level." A procedure-level variable lives only from the time it is declared until the procedure exits. Since a procedure-level variable has local scope, it does not retain its value the next time the procedure is entered. Variables with global scope are "script level" and exist throughout the life of the executing macro. VBScript follows the same rules as C for establishing scope: declaring a variable inside a procedure gives it procedure-level scope. Any variables declared outside a procedure have script-level scope, as illustrated here:

```
Dim  iGlobal          'This variable has script-level scope
Sub Main ()
    Dim  iLocal       'This variable has procedure-level scope
    ⋮
End Sub
```

A procedure cannot hold more than 127 variables; an array counts as a single variable.

# Objects

Various aspects of Developer Studio can appear to a running macro as a collection of 17 different objects. For example, the debugger can be represented as an object, as can the Visual C++ editors, windows, and so forth. Each object supports properties and methods through which a macro learns about or adjusts the object's current status. The main Developer Studio object is named *Application*, whose properties, methods, and events are listed in Tables 12-4, 12-5, and 12-6 beginning on page 597. *Application* is the default object in a macro script, so you can use elements of *Application* without specifically naming the object. For example, this command displays the active configuration of the current project—either Win32 Release or Win32 Debug—without referring to the *Application* object:

```
MsgBox( "The configuration is " & ActiveConfiguration )
```

To give you a feel for objects, this section discusses the *TextSelection* object, which represents text selected in a document window opened in the text editor. A macro determines the selected text in the active document by using the *ActiveDocument.Selection* property. We met this property in the ColumnarReplace macro of Chapter 13 (see Listing 13-2 on page 640). Tables C-3 and C-4 list *TextSelection* properties and methods, which a macro can use to manipulate selected text, move the caret, scroll, and perform many other tasks. Each property and method must appear in the macro script attached to the *ActiveDocument.Selection* property with a period operator. For example, this line uses the *Copy* method to copy the selected text to the Clipboard:

```
ActiveDocument.Selection.Copy
```

**Table C-3.** TextSelection *properties.*

| Property | Description |
|----------|-------------|
| *BottomLine* | The line number of the bottom line of the selection. |
| *CurrentColumn* | The column number at which the caret is currently positioned. |
| *CurrentLine* | The line number at which the caret is currently positioned. |
| *Text* | A string containing the selected text. If the selection spans two or more lines, the string includes a newline character at the end of each selected line except the last. Because the *Text* property is the default, specifying the property is not required. Thus these two lines have the same result:<br><br>`str = ActiveDocument.Selection`<br>`str = ActiveDocument.Selection.Text` |
| *TopLine* | The line number of the top line of the selection. |

**Table C-4.** TextSelection *methods.*

| Method | Description |
|--------|-------------|
| *Backspace* | Same effect as pressing the Backspace key. |
| *Cancel* | Same effect as pressing the Esc key. |
| *ChangeCase* | Changes the case of the selected text to either lower-case, uppercase, or capitalization of the first letter of each word. |
| *CharLeft* | Moves the caret left a specified number of positions. |
| *CharRight* | Moves the caret right a specified number of positions. |
| *ClearBookmark* | Removes an unnamed bookmark from the current line. |
| *ClearBookmarks* | Removes all unnamed bookmarks from the document. |
| *Copy* | Copies the selected text to the Clipboard. |
| *Cut* | Copies the selected text to the Clipboard, and then deletes the selected text from the document. |
| *Delete* | Deletes the selected text from the document. |

*(continued)*

**Table C-4.** *continued*

| Method | Description |
| --- | --- |
| *DeleteWhitespace* | Deletes all spaces and tabs (white space) adjacent to the caret. Text need not be selected. |
| *DestructiveInsert* | Replaces the selected text with new text. |
| *EndOfLine* | Moves the caret to the end of the current line. See also *StartOfLine*. |
| *EndOfDocument* | Moves the caret to the end of the document. See also *StartOfDocument*. |
| *FindText* | Searches for a specified string in the document and, if found, positions the caret at the beginning of the located string. |
| *GoToLine* | Moves the caret to the beginning of a specified line. |
| *Indent* | Adds one indentation level to the current line. This has the same effect as placing the caret at the beginning of the line and pressing the Tab key. Be careful when using *Indent* because the function deletes selected text. |
| *LineDown* | Moves the caret down a specified number of lines. |
| *LineUp* | Moves the caret up a specified number of lines. |
| *MoveTo* | Moves the caret to a specified line and column. |
| *NewLine* | Same effect as pressing the Enter key. |
| *NextBookmark* | Moves the caret forward to the next named or unnamed bookmark. See also *PreviousBookmark*. |
| *PageDown* | Same effect as pressing the PgDn key. |
| *PageUp* | Same effect as pressing the PgUp key. |
| *Paste* | Pastes the current contents of the Clipboard into the document at the caret position. |
| *PreviousBookmark* | Moves the caret backward to the preceding named or unnamed bookmark. See also *NextBookmark*. |
| *ReplaceText* | Finds and replaces text within the selection. For an example of how *ReplaceText* is used, see the ColumnarReplace macro described in Chapter 13. |
| *SelectAll* | Selects the entire document. |

| Method | Description |
|---|---|
| *SelectLine* | Selects the line that contains the caret. |
| *SetBookmark* | Sets an unnamed bookmark for the line that contains the caret. |
| *SmartFormat* | Formats the selected text according to the current smart formatting settings. |
| *StartOfDocument* | Moves the caret to the start of the document. See also *EndOfDocument.* |
| *StartOfLine* | Moves the caret to the start of the current line. See also *EndOfLine.* |
| *Tabify* | Tabifies the selection. For more information on Developer Studio's Tabify command, see page 94 in Chapter 3, The Text Editor. |
| *Unindent* | Removes one indentation level from all lines in a selection. This has the same effect as pressing Shift+Tab. |
| *Untabify* | Untabifies the selection. |
| *WordLeft* | Moves the caret left a specified number of words. |
| *WordRight* | Moves the caret right a specified number of words. |

# Debugging a VBScript Macro

Usually you can effectively debug a macro by displaying current values of variables at key points as the macro runs. Display debug strings using either the *MsgBox* function or the *PrintToOutputWindow* method, which writes a message in the Macro tab of Visual C++'s Output window, described in Chapter 1, The Environment. While the *MsgBox* function halts the running macro and demands user input, the *PrintToOutput-Window* method does not interrupt the macro.

This code fragment produces the debug strings shown in Figure C-1 on the next page:

```
x = 3
MsgBox( "x = " & x )                'Displays a message box
PrintToOutputWindow("x = " & x )  'Writes to Output window
```

**Figure C-1.**   *Displaying a debug string with* MsgBox *and* PrintToOutputWindow.

When you need more debugging firepower, you can sometimes recreate parts of a macro in Visual Basic, which allows you to single-step through a macro, set breakpoints, inspect variables, and so forth. These same advantages are also available from the Microsoft Script Debugger. Although designed for VBScript code embedded in HTML pages open in Microsoft Internet Explorer, the Script Debugger can handle some VBScript code found in Visual C++ macros.

For more information about the Script Debugger, refer to the online help article indexed under *script debugging.* You can also download a copy from Microsoft's VBScript Web page cited at the beginning of this appendix. The Script Debugger package includes documentation.

# Library Functions

The rest of this appendix is devoted to descriptions of the VBScript library functions available to a Visual C++ macro script. Table C-5 categorizes the library functions into several groups, allowing you to determine which functions pertain to a particular programming need. Table C-6 on page 682 lists the functions in alphabetical order and provides brief descriptions and example code fragments. Find the function you need in Table C-5, and then consult Table C-6 or Visual C++ online help for a description of the function. The library functions are contained in the VBScript.dll file, which is usually located in the Windows System or System32 folder.

By convention, function names appear in a macro script as a combination of uppercase and lowercase letters. The VBScript interpreter does not consider case, however, and properly recognizes function names regardless of case. A "C" prefix identifies conversion functions, such as the *CByte* and *CDate* functions. These functions coerce values from one data type to another, providing a mechanism similar to typecasting in C/C++.

## Array, arithmetic, and trigonometric

| | | | | | |
|---|---|---|---|---|---|
| Abs | Cos | Hex | Log | Round | Sqr |
| Array | Exp | Int | Oct | Sgn | Tan |
| Atn | Fix | LBound | Rnd | Sin | UBound |

## Conversion and variable type

| | | | | | |
|---|---|---|---|---|---|
| CBool | CDate | CInt | CStr | IsEmpty | TypeName |
| CByte | CDbl | CLng | IsArray | IsNull | VarType |
| CCur | Chr | CSng | IsDate | IsNumeric | |

## Date and time

| | | | |
|---|---|---|---|
| Date | DateValue | MonthName | TimeValue |
| DateAdd | Day | Now | WeekDay |
| DateDiff | Hour | Second | WeekDayName |
| DatePart | Minute | Time | Year |
| DateSerial | Month | TimeSerial | |

## Formatting

| | | | |
|---|---|---|---|
| FormatCurrency | FormatNumber | FormatPercent | FormatDateTime |

## Strings and text

| | | | | |
|---|---|---|---|---|
| Asc | Join | Mid | ScriptEngine | StrComp |
| Filter | LCase | MsgBox | ScriptEngine-BuildVersion | String |
| InputBox | Left | Replace | ScriptEngine-MajorVersion | StrReverse |
| InStr | Len | Right | Space | Trim |
| InstrRev | LTrim | RTrim | Split | UCase |

**Table C-5.**  *VBScript library functions arranged by category.*

**Table C-6.** *VBScript library functions.*

| Function | Description |
|----------|-------------|
| *Abs* | Returns the absolute value (unsigned magnitude) of a number. For example, *Abs(-2)* and *Abs(2)* both return the value 2. |
| *Array* | Returns a **Variant** containing an array. In the following example, the first statement creates a variable named *x*. The second statement assigns an array to variable *x* and initializes the array elements. The remaining statements demonstrate how the given values are arranged in the new *x* array: |

```
Dim x
x = Array(10,20,30)
a = x(0)              'a = 10
b = x(1)              'b = 20
c = x(2)              'c = 30
```

| Function | Description |
|----------|-------------|
| *Asc* | Returns the ANSI character code of the first letter in a string. A similar function named *AscB* returns the first byte of a string. The related *AscW* function returns the byte and Unicode (wide) character code of a string's first character, thereby avoiding the conversion from Unicode to ANSI. |
| *Atn* | Returns the arctangent (in radians) of a value. The range of the result is -pi/2 to pi/2 radians. To convert degrees to radians, multiply the number of degrees by pi/180. *Atn* is the inverse trigonometric function of *Tan*, which takes an angle as its argument and returns the ratio of two sides of a right triangle. |
| *CBool* | Returns the Boolean value of an expression. |
| *CByte* | Returns the byte value of an expression. |
| *CCur* | Converts an expression to the Currency subtype. The *CCur* function provides correct conversions based on international settings current for the host system. Use this function to ensure that your macro correctly displays currency values for any locale. |
| *CDate* | Converts an expression to the Date subtype: |

```
str = mm & "-" & dd & "-" & yy
date = CDate( str )
```

| Function | Description |
|----------|-------------|
| *CDbl* | Returns the double-precision value of an expression. |

| Function | Description |
|----------|-------------|
| *Chr* | Returns the ANSI character corresponding to a character code. Character codes 0 through 127 are the same as standard ASCII codes. For example, *Chr(10)* returns a linefeed character. For a discussion of ASCII and ANSI character codes, refer to Appendix A. |
| | A similar function named *ChrB* should be used with byte data contained in a string. Instead of returning a character, which may be one or two bytes, *ChrB* always returns a single byte. The *ChrW* function is provided for 32-bit platforms that use Unicode characters. |
| *CInt* | Converts an expression to the Integer subtype. *CInt* differs from the *Fix* and *Int* functions, which truncate rather than round the fractional part of a number. When the fractional part is exactly 0.5, the *CInt* function always rounds the result to the nearest even number. For example, 0.5 rounds to 0, and 1.5 rounds to 2. |
| *CLng* | Converts an expression to the Long subtype. *CLng* rounds the fractional part of a number. When the fractional part is exactly 0.5, the *CLng* function always rounds the result to the nearest even number. |
| *Cos* | Returns the cosine of an angle: |
| | `cosx = Cos( x )      'Where x is in radians` |
| | See also descriptions for the *Sin* and *Tan* functions. |
| *CSng* | Converts an expression to the Single (single-precision) subtype. |
| *CStr* | Converts an expression to the String subtype: |
| | `x   = 111`<br>`str = "The numeric value is " + CStr(x)`<br>`MsgBox( str )`<br><br>`str = "The Boolean value is " + CStr( CBool(x) )`<br>`MsgBox( str )` |
| *Date* | Returns the current system date: |
| | `MsgBox( "The current date is " & Date )` |

*(continued)*

**Table C-6.** *(continued)*

| Function | Description |
|---|---|
| *DateAdd* | Returns a date to which a specified time interval has been added. The *DateAdd* function does not return an invalid date, such as February 31. It accounts for leap years and recognizes the number of days in each month. It does not allow dates before January 1, 100 or after December 31, 9999. Specify the interval using one of the special strings listed here: |

| String | Meaning | String | Meaning |
|---|---|---|---|
| "d" | day | "q" | quarter |
| "ww" | week of the year | "yyyy" | year |
| "m" | month | "h" | hour |
| "w" | day of the week | "m" | minute |
| "y" | day of the year | "s" | second |

Here are a few examples of the *DateAdd* function:

```
str = DateAdd( "d", -1, Date )
MsgBox( "Yesterday was " & str )

str = DateAdd( "ww", -1, Date )
MsgBox( "Last week was " & str )

str = DateAdd( "m", 1, Date )
MsgBox( "Next month will be " & str )

str = DateAdd( "q", 1, Date )
MsgBox( "Three months from now will be " & str )
```

| Function | Description |
|---|---|
| *DateDiff* | Returns the number of intervals between two dates. See the description of the *DateAdd* function for a list of special strings used to indicate the interval: |

```
str = DateDiff( "d", Date, #12-25# )
MsgBox( "Only " & str & "days till Christmas" )
```

| Function | Description |
|----------|-------------|
| *DatePart* | Returns a specified part of a given date: |

```
str = DatePart( "ww", Date )
MsgBox( "This week is number " & str & " of the year" )
day1 = DatePart( "d", Date )
day2 = day1
Do While day2 > 9
    day2 = day2 - 10
Loop
suffix = "th"
If (day1 = 1) Then suffix = "st"
If (day1 = 2) Then suffix = "nd"
If (day1 = 3) Then suffix = "rd"
MsgBox( "Today is the " & day1 & suffix )
```

| Function | Description |
|----------|-------------|
| *DateSerial* | Returns a string containing a specified year, month, and day. *DateSerial* allows a macro to compute an absolute date from a serial span of time. For example, the following call to *DateSerial* returns the date 100 days from the present date: |

```
iYear  = DatePart( "yyyy", Date )
iMonth = DatePart( "m", Date )
iDay   = DatePart( "d", Date )
str    = DateSerial( iYear, iMonth, iDay + 100 )
MsgBox( "100 days from now will be " & str )
```

When the year parameter contains a value from 0 through 99, *DateSerial* assumes the value represents a year 1900 through 1999. For all other year arguments, use a complete four-digit year such as 2010.

| Function | Description |
|----------|-------------|
| *DateValue* | Returns a string containing a formatted date. The *DateValue* function is adept at recognizing dates in various formats, depending on regional settings. Under United States settings, for example, these lines all return the string "12/31/99": |

```
DateValue( "December 31, 1999" )
DateValue( "Dec 31, 1999" )
DateValue( "12-31-99" )
DateValue( "12 31 1999" )
```

*(continued)*

**Table C-6.** *(continued)*

| Function | Description |
| --- | --- |
| *Day* | Reads a date string and extracts the day of the month as a whole number from 1 through 31. |
| *Exp* | Returns e (the base of natural logarithms) raised to a power. The constant e is approximately 2.718282. |
| *Filter* | Extracts from an array of strings either the strings that contain a specified substring or the strings that do not contain the substring. The array that *Filter* returns contains only the strings that meet the match criteria. In this example, the *x* array contains the string "string2" because that is the only string in the *str* array that contains the substring "2": |

```
Dim str(3)

str(0) = "string0"
str(1) = "string1"
str(2) = "string2"
str(3) = "string3"
x = Filter( str, "2" )
MsgBox( x(0) )
```

In this case, attempting to access another element such as *x(1)* results in an error.

| Function | Description |
| --- | --- |
| *Fix* | Returns the integer portion of a floating-point number. Both the *Int* and *Fix* functions truncate the fractional portion of a number and return the integer portion. Consider the variable *x* as an example. If *x* is positive, both functions have the same effect. If *x* is negative, *Int* returns the first negative integer less than or equal to *x*, whereas *Fix* returns the first negative integer greater than or equal to *x*. If *x* is -5.6, for example, *Int* returns -6 and *Fix* returns -5. |
| *FormatCurrency* | Returns an expression with proper currency formatting using regional settings established in the system Control Panel. |
| *FormatDateTime* | Returns an expression formatted as a date or time that conforms to current regional settings. |
| *FormatNumber* | Returns a number expressed as a string. The string is formatted according to system regional settings so that, for example, values over 1,000 are formatted with commas in the United States and periods in Europe. |

| Function | Description |
|----------|-------------|
| *FormatPercent* | Returns an expression formatted as a percentage (multiplied by 100) with a trailing % character. |
| *Hex* | Returns a string representing a number in hexadecimal form. A macro can express a hexadecimal number by prefixing the number with &H. See also the description for *Oct*. |
| *Hour* | Returns a whole number from 0 through 23 representing the hour of the given time. Between 6:00 and 7:00 in the evening, for example, the following fragment returns the number 18:<br><br>`hr = Hour( Time )`<br>`MsgBox( "The current hour is " & hr )`<br><br>See also descriptions for the *Minute* and *Second* functions. |
| *InputBox* | Displays a dialog with a specified prompt message and returns the string typed in the dialog by the user. For an example of the *InputBox* function, see the ColumnarReplace macro described in Chapter 13. |
| *InStr* | Returns the position of the first occurrence of one string within another. |
| *InstrRev* | Similar to the *InStr* function, *InstrRev* returns the position of one string within another, working in reverse from the end of the string. |
| *Int* | See the description of the *Fix* function. |
| *IsArray* | Returns a Boolean value indicating whether a given variable is an array. |
| *IsDate* | Returns a Boolean value indicating whether a given expression can be converted to a date. |
| *IsEmpty* | Returns a Boolean value indicating whether a given variable has been initialized. *IsEmpty* returns True when the variable is uninitialized or explicitly set to Empty; otherwise, the function returns False. See the description for *IsNull*. |

*(continued)*

**Table C-6.**  *(continued)*

| Function | Description |
|---|---|
| *IsNull* | Returns a Boolean value indicating whether a given variable contains valid data. *IsNull* returns True when the variable is Null (contains no valid data); otherwise, the function returns False. VBScript recognizes a difference between Null and Empty variables. Empty means that a variable has not yet been initialized. A zero-length string, sometimes referred to as a null string, is not a Null variable. |
| *IsNumeric* | Returns a Boolean value indicating whether a given expression is a number. |
| *Join* | Forms a new string by concatenating strings in an array. |
| *LBound* | Returns the smallest available subscript for an array dimension. The default lower bound for an array dimension is 0. |
| *LCase* | Converts all letters in a string to lowercase. See also the description for the *UCase* function. |
| *Left* | Returns a string formed by the leftmost characters of a string. A macro can determine the length of a string by calling the *Len* function. See also the description for the *Right* function. |
| *Len* | Returns the number of characters in a string. |
| *Log* | Returns the natural (base e) logarithm of a number. The base *n* logarithms for a number *x* is the ratio of the natural logarithm of *x* and the natural logarithm of *n*: `lognx = Log(x) / Log(n)` |
| *LTrim* | Trims leading spaces from a string. See descriptions for *RTrim* and *Trim*. |
| *Mid* | Extracts a substring from a given string. |
| *Minute* | Returns a whole number from 0 through 59 for the minute of the given time. At 6:47:53, for example, the following fragment returns the number 47: `min = Minute( Time )` `MsgBox( "The current minute is " & min )` See also descriptions for the *Hour* and *Second* functions. |

| Function | Description |
|----------|-------------|
| *Month* | Returns a whole number from 1 through 12 for the month of the given year:<br><br>```Dim mnth(11)\nmnth(0)  = "January"\nmnth(1)  = "February"\n    ⋮\nmnth(11) = "December"\nm = Month( Date )\nMsgBox( "The current month is " & mnth(m-1) )``` |
| *MonthName* | Returns a string containing the month specified by a number 1 through 12. By using the *MonthName* function, the preceding example fragment can be rewritten like this:<br><br>```m = Month( Date )\nMsgBox( "The current month is " & MonthName(m) )``` |
| *MsgBox* | Displays a standard Windows message box with optional OK, Cancel, Abort, Retry, Ignore, Yes, and No buttons. *MsgBox* returns one of the following values to indicate which button the user clicked to close the message box: |

| Constant | Value | Button |
|----------|-------|--------|
| vbOK | 1 | OK |
| vbCancel | 2 | Cancel |
| vbAbort | 3 | Abort |
| vbRetry | 4 | Retry |
| vbIgnore | 5 | Ignore |
| vbYes | 6 | Yes |
| vbNo | 7 | No |

*MsgBox* can display an optional Help button in the message box which, when clicked, shows context-sensitive help drawn from a specified help file. The user can also press the F1 key to view the Help topic corresponding to the context.

*(continued)*

**Table C-6.** *(continued)*

| Function | Description |
|---|---|
| *Now* | Returns a string containing the current date and time in a format appropriate for the current regional settings. For United States settings, for example, the returned string has the format "12/31/99 3:33:57 PM." See also descriptions for the *Time* and *Date* functions. |
| *Oct* | Returns a string representing a number in octal (base 8) form. An octal number can be expressed in a macro by prefixing the number with &O. See also the description for *Hex*. |
| *Replace* | Takes a string as input, and then returns a new version of the string in which a specified substring has been replaced with another. See also the *ReplaceText* function listed in Table C-4 on page 677. |
| *Right* | Returns a string formed by the rightmost characters of a string. A macro can determine the length of a string by calling the *Len* function. See also the description for the *Left* function. |
| *Rnd* | Returns a random number that is less than 1 but greater than or equal to 0. To generate a random integer between a lower and upper bound, use this formula:<br><br>`iRange = iUpperBound - iLowerBound + 1`<br>`Int( iRange * Rnd + iLowerBound )`<br><br>Use the *Randomize* statement to seed the VBScript random number generator with a value from the system timer<br><br>`Randomize`<br>`iRandom = Rnd` |
| *Round* | Rounds a floating-point number to a specified precision. |
| *RTrim* | Trims trailing spaces from a string. See also descriptions for *LTrim* and *Trim*. |
| *ScriptEngine* | Returns a string identifying the scripting language in use. For Visual Basic Scripting Edition, the function returns "VBScript." |
| *ScriptEngine-BuildVersion* | Returns the build version number of the script engine in use. |
| *ScriptEngine-MajorVersion* | Returns the major version number of the script engine in use. |

| Function | Description |
|----------|-------------|
| *Second* | Returns a whole number from 0 through 59 representing the seconds component of the given time. At 6:47:53, for example, the following fragment returns the number 53:<br><br>```\nsec = Second( Time )\nMsgBox( "The current second is " & sec )\n```<br><br>See also descriptions for the *Hour* and *Minute* functions. |
| *Sgn* | Determines the sign of a given number. *Sgn* returns an integer containing a value of -1, 0, or 1, indicating that the given number is less than zero, equal to zero, or greater than zero:<br><br>```\nDim str(2)\nstr(0) = "less than zero"\nstr(1) = "equal to zero"\nstr(2) = "greater than zero"\ni      = InputBox( "Enter a number" )\nMsgBox( "The number is " & str(Sgn( i )+1) )\n``` |
| *Sin* | Returns the sine of an angle.<br><br>```\nsinx = Sin( x )        'Where x is in radians\n```<br><br>See also descriptions for the *Cos* and *Tan* functions. |
| *Space* | Returns a string consisting of a specified number of spaces. |
| *Split* | Creates an array of strings from a single string in which substrings are delimited by any specified character. The following example splits a string into three separate strings separated by the plus sign (+):<br><br>```\nx = Split( "string1+string2+string3", "+" )\nMsgBox( x(0) )        'Display "string1"\nMsgBox( x(1) )        'Display "string2"\nMsgBox( x(2) )        'Display "string3"\n``` |
| *Sqr* | Returns the square root of a number. |

*(continued)*

**Table C-6.** *(continued)*

| Function | Description |
|---|---|
| *StrComp* | Compares two strings and returns a value indicating whether the strings differ. The usage and syntax of *StrComp* are similar to the *strcmp* function of the C run-time library: |

```
If StrComp( string1, string2 ) = 0 Then
    MsgBox( "Strings are equal" )
End If
```

*StrComp* returns one of the following values:

| Return Value | Meaning |
|---|---|
| -1 | *string1* is less than *string2* |
| 0 | *string1* and *string2* are the same |
| 1 | *string1* is greater than *string2* |

| Function | Description |
|---|---|
| *StrReverse* | Reverses the order of characters in a given string. |
| *String* | Creates a string of a given length composed of a single repeating character. |

```
str = String( 10, "a" )    'str = "aaaaaaaaaa"
```

| Function | Description |
|---|---|
| *Tan* | Returns the tangent of an angle. |

```
tanx = Tan( x )            'Where x is in radians
```

See also descriptions for the *Sin* and *Cos* functions.

| Function | Description |
|---|---|
| *Time* | Returns a string containing the current system time, formatted appropriately for the current regional settings. In the United States, for example, the returned string has the format "3:33:57 PM." With European settings in effect, the same time is represented as "15:33:57." See also the description for the *Now* function. |
| *TimeSerial* | Returns a string containing the time for a given hour, minute, and second, formatted appropriately for the current regional settings. For United States settings, the following line assigns the string "6:47:53 PM" to the variable *x*: |

```
x = TimeSerial( 18, 47, 53 )
```

| Function | Description |
|----------|-------------|
| *TimeValue* | Returns a string containing a formatted time. Like the *DateValue* function, *TimeValue* recognizes various formats, depending on regional settings. For United States settings, for example, these lines all return the string "6:47:53 PM": |

```
TimeValue( "6:47:53PM" )
TimeValue( "18:47:53" )
TimeValue( "6:47:53 pm" )
```

| Function | Description |
|----------|-------------|
| *Trim* | Trims leading and trailing spaces from a string. See also *RTrim* and *LTrim*. |
| *TypeName* | Takes a variable as a parameter and returns one of the following strings indicating the variable's subtype: |

| Return string | Variable subtype |
|---------------|------------------|
| "Byte" | Byte value |
| "Integer" | Integer value |
| "Long" | Long integer |
| "Single" | Single-precision floating-point |
| "Double" | Double-precision floating-point |
| "Currency" | Currency string |
| "Decimal" | Decimal value |
| "Date" | Date or time string |
| "String" | Character string |
| "Boolean" | Boolean value |
| "Empty" | Uninitialized |
| "Null" | No valid data |

This fragment demonstrates the *TypeName* function:

```
x = 3
MsgBox( TypeName( x ) )      'Displays "Integer"
y = "string"
MsgBox( TypeName( y ) )      'Displays "String"
z = #12-31-99#
MsgBox( TypeName( z ) )      'Displays "Date"
MsgBox( TypeName( w ) )      'Displays "Empty"
```

*(continued)*

693

**Table C-6.**  *(continued)*

| Function | Description |
|----------|-------------|
| *UBound* | Returns the largest available subscript for the indicated dimension of an array. For example:<br><br>```\nDim A(100,3,4)\nx = UBound(A, 1)    'x = 99\ny = UBound(A, 2)    'y = 2\nz = UBound(A, 3)    'z = 3\n``` |
| *UCase* | Converts all letters in a string to uppercase. See also the description for the *LCase* function. |
| *VarType* | Takes a variable as a parameter and returns one of the following integer values indicating the variable's subtype. Notice this function's similarity to the *TypeName* function. |

| Constant | Value | Variable subtype |
|----------|-------|------------------|
| vbEmpty | 0 | Uninitialized |
| vbNull | 1 | No valid data |
| vbInteger | 2 | Integer |
| vbLong | 3 | Long integer |
| vbSingle | 4 | Single-precision floating-point |
| vbDouble | 5 | Double-precision floating-point |
| vbCurrency | 6 | Currency string |
| vbDate | 7 | Date or time string |
| vbString | 8 | Character string |
| vbBoolean | 11 | Boolean value |
| vbVariant | 12 | An array of **Variant** type |
| vbByte | 17 | Byte value |
| vbArray | 8192 | Array. The *VarType* function returns the sum of the array value (8192) plus the value for the variable subtype that populates the array. |

| Function | Description |
|----------|-------------|
| *Weekday* | Returns an integer 1 through 7 representing the day of the week, beginning with 1 for Sunday. See the example fragment for the *WeekDayName* function. |
| *WeekDayName* | Returns a string indicating the specified day of the week:<br><br>`d = Weekday( Date )`<br>`MsgBox( "Today is " & WeekdayName(d) )` |
| *Year* | Extracts the year from a given date and returns it as an integer value:<br><br>`MsgBox( "The year is " & Year( Date ) )` |

# T

## About the Author

**Beck Zaratian** has been programming computers for 25 years. A degree in civil engineering led him to different parts of the country, where he applied languages as diverse as FORTRAN, PL/1, APL, and C to problems such as arch dam design and earthquake analysis. Along the way, he was a ski instructor in Colorado and worked construction in Alaska before settling permanently in Seattle, where his expertise in assembly language caught the attention of Microsoft. Since then he has contributed to several Microsoft books, including *Macro Assembler Programmer's Guide*, *C for Yourself*, *Programmer's Guide for Pen Windows*, and Charles Petzold's *Programming Windows 95*.

Beck is the owner of Witzend Software, a provider of custom programming services in the Seattle area. He can be reached at *beckz@witzendsoft.com*.

The manuscript for this book was prepared and submitted to Microsoft Press in electronic form. Text files were prepared using Microsoft Word 97 for Windows. Pages were composed by Labrecque Publishing using Corel Ventura 8, with text in Melior and display type in Frutiger Condensed. Composed pages were delivered to the printer as electronic prepress files.

*Cover Designer*
**Tim Girvin**

*Interior Graphic Designer*
**Kim Eggleston**

*Production Manager*
**Lisa Labrecque**

*Copy Editor*
**Chrisa Hotchkiss**

*Interior Graphic Artist*
**Lisa Bravo**

*Page Compositor*
**Curtis Philips**

*Proofreader*
**Andrea Fox**

*Indexer*
**Katherine Stimson**

# MICROSOFT LICENSE AGREEMENT

### (Book Companion CD)

**IMPORTANT—READ CAREFULLY:** This Microsoft End-User License Agreement ("EULA") is a legal agreement between you (either an individual or an entity) and Microsoft Corporation for the Microsoft product identified above, which includes computer software and may include associated media, printed materials, and "online" or electronic documentation ("SOFTWARE PRODUCT"). Any component included within the SOFTWARE PRODUCT that is accompanied by a separate End-User License Agreement shall be governed by such agreement and not the terms set forth below. By installing, copying or otherwise using the SOFTWARE PRODUCT, you agree to be bound by the terms of this EULA. If you do not agree to the terms of this EULA, you are not authorized to install, copy or otherwise use the SOFTWARE PRODUCT; you may, however, return the SOFTWARE PRODUCT, along with all printed materials and other items that form a part of the Microsoft product that includes the SOFTWARE PRODUCT, to the place you obtained them for a full refund.

## SOFTWARE PRODUCT LICENSE

The SOFTWARE PRODUCT is protected by United States copyright laws and international copyright treaties, as well as other intellectual property laws and treaties. The SOFTWARE PRODUCT is licensed, not sold.

1. **GRANT OF LICENSE.** This EULA grants you the following rights:

    a. **Software Product.** You may install and use one copy of the SOFTWARE PRODUCT on a single computer. The primary user of the computer on which the SOFTWARE PRODUCT is installed may make a second copy for his or her exclusive use on a portable computer.

    b. **Storage/Network Use.** You may also store or install a copy of the SOFTWARE PRODUCT on a storage device, such as a network server, used only to install or run the SOFTWARE PRODUCT on your other computers over an internal network; however, you must acquire and dedicate a license for each separate computer on which the SOFTWARE PRODUCT is installed or run from the storage device. A license for the SOFTWARE PRODUCT may not be shared or used concurrently on different computers.

    c. **License Pak.** If you have acquired this EULA in a Microsoft License Pak, you may make the number of additional copies of the computer software portion of the SOFTWARE PRODUCT authorized on the printed copy of this EULA, and you may use each copy in the manner specified above. You are also entitled to make a corresponding number of secondary copies for portable computer use as specified above.

    d. **Sample Code.** Solely with respect to portions, if any, of the SOFTWARE PRODUCT that are identified within the SOFTWARE PRODUCT as sample code (the "SAMPLE CODE"):

    i. **Use and Modification.** Microsoft grants you the right to use and modify the source code version of the SAMPLE CODE, *provided* you comply with subsection (d)(iii) below. You may not distribute the SAMPLE CODE, or any modified version of the SAMPLE CODE, in source code form.

    ii. **Redistributable Files.** Provided you comply with subsection (d)(iii) below, Microsoft grants you a nonexclusive, royalty-free right to reproduce and distribute the object code version of the SAMPLE CODE and of any modified SAMPLE CODE, other than SAMPLE CODE, or any modified version thereof, designated as not redistributable in the Readme file that forms a part of the SOFTWARE PRODUCT (the "Non-Redistributable Sample Code"). All SAMPLE CODE other than the Non-Redistributable Sample Code is collectively referred to as the "REDISTRIBUTABLES."

    iii. **Redistribution Requirements.** If you redistribute the REDISTRIBUTABLES, you agree to: (i) distribute the REDISTRIBUTABLES in object code form only in conjunction with and as a part of your software application product; (ii) not use Microsoft's name, logo, or trademarks to market your software application product; (iii) include a valid copyright notice on your software application product; (iv) indemnify, hold harmless, and defend Microsoft from and against any claims or lawsuits, including attorney's fees, that arise or result from the use or distribution of your software application product; and (v) not permit further distribution of the REDISTRIBUTABLES by your end user. Contact Microsoft for the applicable royalties due and other licensing terms for all other uses and/or distribution of the REDISTRIBUTABLES.

2. **DESCRIPTION OF OTHER RIGHTS AND LIMITATIONS.**

    - **Limitations on Reverse Engineering, Decompilation, and Disassembly.** You may not reverse engineer, decompile, or disassemble the SOFTWARE PRODUCT, except and only to the extent that such activity is expressly permitted by applicable law notwithstanding this limitation.

    - **Separation of Components.** The SOFTWARE PRODUCT is licensed as a single product. Its component parts may not be separated for use on more than one computer.

    - **Rental.** You may not rent, lease or lend the SOFTWARE PRODUCT.

- **Support Services.** Microsoft may, but is not obligated to, provide you with support services related to the SOFTWARE PRODUCT ("Support Services"). Use of Support Services is governed by the Microsoft policies and programs described in the user manual, in "online" documentation and/or other Microsoft-provided materials. Any supplemental software code provided to you as part of the Support Services shall be considered part of the SOFTWARE PRODUCT and subject to the terms and conditions of this EULA. With respect to technical information you provide to Microsoft as part of the Support Services, Microsoft may use such information for its business purposes, including for product support and development. Microsoft will not utilize such technical information in a form that personally identifies you.

- **Software Transfer.** You may permanently transfer all of your rights under this EULA, provided you retain no copies, you transfer all of the SOFTWARE PRODUCT (including all component parts, the media and printed materials, any upgrades, this EULA, and, if applicable, the Certificate of Authenticity), **and** the recipient agrees to the terms of this EULA.

- **Termination.** Without prejudice to any other rights, Microsoft may terminate this EULA if you fail to comply with the terms and conditions of this EULA. In such event, you must destroy all copies of the SOFTWARE PRODUCT and all of its component parts.

3. **COPYRIGHT.** All title and copyrights in and to the SOFTWARE PRODUCT (including but not limited to any images, photographs, animations, video, audio, music, text, SAMPLE CODE, REDISTRIBUTABLES, and "applets" incorporated into the SOFTWARE PRODUCT), and any copies of the SOFTWARE PRODUCT are owned by Microsoft or its suppliers. The SOFTWARE PRODUCT is protected by copyright laws and international treaty provisions. Therefore, you must treat the SOFTWARE PRODUCT like any other copyrighted material **except** that you may install the SOFTWARE PRODUCT on a single computer provided you keep the original solely for backup or archival purposes. You may not copy the printed materials accompanying the SOFTWARE PRODUCT.

4. **U.S. GOVERNMENT RESTRICTED RIGHTS.** The SOFTWARE PRODUCT and documentation are provided with RESTRICTED RIGHTS. Use, duplication, or disclosure by the Government is subject to restrictions as set forth in subparagraph (c)(1)(ii) of the Rights in Technical Data and Computer Software clause at DFARS 252.227-7013 or subparagraphs (c)(1) and (2) of the Commercial Computer Software—Restricted Rights at 48 CFR 52.227-19, as applicable. Manufacturer is Microsoft Corporation/One Microsoft Way/Redmond, WA 98052-6399.

5. **EXPORT RESTRICTIONS.** You agree that you will not export or re-export the SOFTWARE PRODUCT, any part thereof, or any process or service that is the direct product of the SOFTWARE PRODUCT (the foregoing collectively referred to as the "Restricted Components"), to any country, person, entity or end user subject to U.S. export restrictions. You specifically agree not to export or re-export any of the Restricted Components (i) to any country to which the U.S. has embargoed or restricted the export of goods or services, which currently include, but are not necessarily limited to Cuba, Iran, Iraq, Libya, North Korea, Sudan and Syria, or to any national of any such country, wherever located, who intends to transmit or transport the Restricted Components back to such country; (ii) to any end-user who you know or have reason to know will utilize the Restricted Components in the design, development or production of nuclear, chemical or biological weapons; or (iii) to any end-user who has been prohibited from participating in U.S. export transactions by any federal agency of the U.S. government. You warrant and represent that neither the BXA nor any other U.S. federal agency has suspended, revoked or denied your export privileges.

## DISCLAIMER OF WARRANTY

**NO WARRANTIES OR CONDITIONS.** MICROSOFT EXPRESSLY DISCLAIMS ANY WARRANTY OR CONDITION FOR THE SOFTWARE PRODUCT. THE SOFTWARE PRODUCT AND ANY RELATED DOCUMENTATION IS PROVIDED "AS IS" WITHOUT WARRANTY OR CONDITION OF ANY KIND, EITHER EXPRESS OR IMPLIED, INCLUDING, WITHOUT LIMITATION, THE IMPLIED WARRANTIES OF MERCHANTABILITY, FITNESS FOR A PARTICULAR PURPOSE, OR NONINFRINGEMENT. THE ENTIRE RISK ARISING OUT OF USE OR PERFORMANCE OF THE SOFTWARE PRODUCT REMAINS WITH YOU.

**LIMITATION OF LIABILITY.** TO THE MAXIMUM EXTENT PERMITTED BY APPLICABLE LAW, IN NO EVENT SHALL MICROSOFT OR ITS SUPPLIERS BE LIABLE FOR ANY SPECIAL, INCIDENTAL, INDIRECT, OR CONSEQUENTIAL DAMAGES WHATSOEVER (INCLUDING, WITHOUT LIMITATION, DAMAGES FOR LOSS OF BUSINESS PROFITS, BUSINESS INTERRUPTION, LOSS OF BUSINESS INFORMATION, OR ANY OTHER PECUNIARY LOSS) ARISING OUT OF THE USE OF OR INABILITY TO USE THE SOFTWARE PRODUCT OR THE PROVISION OF OR FAILURE TO PROVIDE SUPPORT SERVICES, EVEN IF MICROSOFT HAS BEEN ADVISED OF THE POSSIBILITY OF SUCH DAMAGES. IN ANY CASE, MICROSOFT'S ENTIRE LIABILITY UNDER ANY PROVISION OF THIS EULA SHALL BE LIMITED TO THE GREATER OF THE AMOUNT ACTUALLY PAID BY YOU FOR THE SOFTWARE PRODUCT OR US$5.00; PROVIDED HOWEVER, IF YOU HAVE ENTERED INTO A MICROSOFT SUPPORT SERVICES AGREEMENT, MICROSOFT'S ENTIRE LIABILITY REGARDING SUPPORT SERVICES SHALL BE GOVERNED BY THE TERMS OF THAT AGREEMENT. BECAUSE SOME STATES AND JURISDICTIONS DO NOT ALLOW THE EXCLUSION OR LIMITATION OF LIABILITY, THE ABOVE LIMITATION MAY NOT APPLY TO YOU.

## MISCELLANEOUS

This EULA is governed by the laws of the State of Washington USA, except and only to the extent that applicable law mandates governing law of a different jurisdiction.

Should you have any questions concerning this EULA, or if you desire to contact Microsoft for any reason, please contact the Microsoft subsidiary serving your country, or write: Microsoft Sales Information Center/One Microsoft Way/Redmond, WA 98052-6399.

# Register Today!

## Return this
## *Microsoft® Visual C++® 6.0*
## *Programmer's Guide*
## registration card for
## a Microsoft Press® catalog

U.S. and Canada addresses only. Fill in information below and mail postage-free. Please mail only the bottom half of this page.

---

**1-57231-866-X**      *MICROSOFT® VISUAL C++® 6.0*      *Owner Registration Card*
                              *PROGRAMMER'S GUIDE*

NAME

INSTITUTION OR COMPANY NAME

ADDRESS

CITY                              STATE        ZIP

# *Microsoft*®*Press*
## *Quality Computer Books*

**For a free catalog of
Microsoft Press® products, call
1-800-MSPRESS**

## BUSINESS REPLY MAIL
FIRST-CLASS MAIL     PERMIT NO. 53     BOTHELL, WA

POSTAGE WILL BE PAID BY ADDRESSEE

NO POSTAGE
NECESSARY
IF MAILED
IN THE
UNITED STATES

**MICROSOFT PRESS REGISTRATION**
MICROSOFT® VISUAL C++® 6.0
PROGRAMMER'S GUIDE
PO BOX 3019
BOTHELL  WA    98041-9946